D1582122

DISCARDED

Standard Catalogue of British Coins

COINS OF ENGLAND

AND
THE UNITED KINGDOM

41st Edition

SPINK
LONDON

A Catalogue of the Coins of Great Britain
and Ireland
first published 1929

Standard Catalogue of British Coins
Coins of England and the United Kingdom
41st edition, 2006

© Spink & Son Ltd, 2005
69 Southampton Row, Bloomsbury
London WC1B 4ET

Typeset by Design to Print UK Ltd,
The Studio, Forge House, Lower Road, Forest Row, East Sussex RH18 5HE
Printed in Great Britain by
Cromwell Press
Trowbridge
Wiltshire

ISBN 1-902040-68-6

CONTENTS

CONTENTS

APPENDICES:

Welcome to this 41st edition of Coins of England, released to coincide once again with Coinex in London.

Coinex, now the 27th such show, is the annual trade event organised by the British Numismatic Trade Association (B.N.T.A.). It is traditionally held over the first weekend in October and is attended by dealers from all over the world. It presents an opportunity for collectors to meet with dealers to buy and sell coins or just to look around at what is undoubtedly the finest offering of coins in one room at any time during the year in the UK.

The B.N.T.A. is the recognised body for standards in the numismatic trade in the UK so collectors can confidently deal with its members and be assured a high level of professionalism.

Spink have been ever-present at this event and our specialists look forward each year to meeting with our many clients from around the World who make the trip. Whilst we cannot display our entire stock we attempt to carry a varied selection of material from Ancient coins up to modern items with a wide price range. You can also find a good range of publications and reference books covering many aspects of coin collecting whether beginner or expert.

The centrally located premises of Spink in the Holborn area of London are in addition open the year round for business from Monday to Friday and collectors are always welcome to visit without appointment to buy and sell or discuss your collection with a view to selling through one of our many auctions which take place throughout the year.

Spink have been instrumental in securing many world record prices for British coins at auction and we pride ourselves in producing high-quality catalogues which are works of reference in their own right.

Spink also publish many other books about coins for collectors and a free mail order catalogue is available on request or you can visit our website www.spink.com to view the selection on-line. You will also find coins, medals and banknotes for sale.

Many collectors continue to offer suggestions and specialised information which go towards improving this catalogue and we appreciate your time and effort. Coin collecting is an ancient hobby and transcends many languages, in fact it has a language all of its own. It is this sharing of information between collectors and the relationships between collectors and dealers which make this such a rewarding and interesting pursuit.

In addition to the usual review of prices across the board, this edition carries all the up to date information about new issues from the Royal Mint and sees a thorough revision of the Tower Mint coins of Charles I. We have also improved the quality of the photographs in the grading sections which now better illustrate the differences between grades. The overview of the British coin market in our annual 'Market Trends' again provides a fascinating review of the year which has seen a number of highlights and makes for interesting reading as we see continued growth in the market.

Thank you once again to our in-house specialists who have contributed their expertise and in-depth knowledge of the market to ensure that this publication is still regarded as the most comprehensive and accurate guide to British coins.

Philip Skingley
Editor, Coins of England

Arrangement

The arrangement of this catalogue is not completely uniform, but generally it is divided into metals (gold, silver, copper, etc) under each reign, then into coinages, denominations and varieties. In the Celtic section the uninscribed coins are listed before the dynastic coins; under Charles II all the hammered coins precede the milled coinage; the reign of George III is divided into coins issued up to 1816 and the new coinage from 1816 to the end of the reign; and under Elizabeth II the decimal issues are separated from the pre-decimal (*£.s.d.*) coinages.

Every major coin type is listed though not every variety. We have endeavoured to give rather more coverage to the varieties of relatively common coins, such as the pennies of Edward I, II and III, than to the very much rarer coins of, for instance, King Offa of Mercia.

Values

The values given represent the range of retail prices at which coins are being offered for sale at the time of going to press and **not** the price which a dealer will pay for those coins. These prices are based on our knowledge of the numismatic market, the current demand for particular coins, recent auction sale prices and, in those cases where certain coins have not appeared for sale for some years, our estimation of what they would be likely to sell at today, bearing in mind their rarity and appeal in relation to somewhat similar coins where a current value is known. Values are given for two grades of preservation from the Celtic period onwards and three to four grades of preservation for coins of the 17th to the 20th century.

Collectors normally require coins in the best condition they can afford and, except in the case of a really rare coin, a piece that is considerably worn is not wanted and has little value. The values given in the catalogue are for the exact state of preservation stated at the head of each column and bearing in mind that a score of identical coins in varying states of wear could be lined up in descending order from mint condition (FDC, *fleur de coin*), through very fine (VF) to *poor* state. It will be realized that only in certain instances will the values given apply to particular coins. A 'fine' (F) coin may be worth anything between one quarter and a half of the price quoted for a 'very fine' (VF); on the other hand, a piece in really mint condition will be valued substantially higher than the price quoted for 'extremely fine' (EF). The designation BV has been adopted for coins whose value on the market has yet to exceed its bullion value. Purchasing sovereigns, catalogued as BV, will attract a dealers' premium.

We emphasize again that the purpose of this catalogue is to give a general value for a particular class of coin in a specified state of preservation, and also to give the collector an idea of the range and value of coins in the English series. The value of any particular piece depends on three things:

Its exact design, legend, mintmark or date.

Its exact state of preservation; this is of prime importance.

The demand for it in the market at any given time.

Some minor varieties are much scarcer than others and, as the number of coins issued varies considerably from year to year, coins of certain dates and mintmarks are rarer and of more value than other pieces of similar type. The prices given for any type are for the commonest variety, mintmark or date of that type.

The Scope

Coin collecting, numismatics, is a fascinating hobby. It requires very little physical exertion and only as much mental effort as one wishes or is able to put into it at any time. There is vast scope and boundless ramifications and byways encompassing not only things historical and geographical, but also touching on economics, metallurgy, heraldry, literature, the fine arts, politics, military history and many other disciplines. This catalogue is solely concerned with British coinage from its earliest times right up to date. From the start the beginner should appreciate that the coinage of our own nation may be seen as a small but very important part of the whole story of world currency.

The first coins, made of electrum, a natural alloy of gold and silver, were issued in western Asia Minor (Lydia) in the later seventh century B.C. Over the next century or so coinage of gold and silver spread across the Aegean to mainland Greece, southwards to the eastern Mediterranean lands and eventually westward to the Greek colonies in southern Italy, Sicily (Magna Graecia) and beyond. The coins of the Greeks are noted for their beautiful, sometimes exquisite craftsmanship, with many of the coin types depicting the patron deities of their cities. Coins of Philip II of Macedon (359-336 B.C.), father of Alexander the Great, circulated amongst the Celtic peoples of the Danubian Basin and were widely copied through central Europe and by the Gauls in France. Gold Gaulish staters were reaching Britain around the beginning of the first century B.C. and the earliest gold to be struck in the island must have been produced shortly afterwards. Although their types and designs copy the Apollo head and racing charioteer of Philip II's gold coins, they are stylistically much removed from the original representation and very individually Celtic in concept.

The coins of the Romans cover some seven centuries and include an enormous number of different types that were current throughout a major part of the civilized world from Spain to Syria and from the Rhine in the north to the Sudan in the south. The Roman province of Britain was part of this vast empire for four hundred years from AD 43 until the early fifth century. Innumerable Roman coins have been recovered from sites in this country, most being made of brass or bronze. Many of these are quite inexpensive and very collectable. In recent years many hoards of gold and silver coins have been found, usually by use of metal detectors.

Following the revival of commerce after the Dark Ages, coinage in Western Europe was virtually restricted to silver until the thirteenth century, though gold was still being minted in Byzantium and in the Islamic world. In the Middle Ages many European cities had their own distinctive coinage and money was issued not only by the kings but also by nobles, bishops and abbots. From the time of the later Crusades gold returned to the West, and the artistic developments of the Renaissance in the fifteenth century brought improved portraiture and new minting techniques.

Large silver crown-size thalers were first minted at Joachimsthal in Bohemia early in the sixteenth century. The substantial shipments of silver coming to Europe from the mines of Spanish America over the next couple of centuries led to a fine series of larger coins being issued by the European states and cities. The larger size allowed greater artistic freedom in the designs and the portraits on the coins.

Both Germany and Italy became unified nation states during the later nineteenth century, thereby substantially reducing the number of mints and coin types. Balancing the reduction in European minting authorities were the new coins that were issued by the independent states of South and Central America. Since the 1950s many new nations have established their independence and their coinage provides a large field for the collector of modern coins.

It can be seen that the scope for the collector is truly vast, but besides the general run of official coinage there is also the large series of token coins—small change unofficially produced to supplement the inadequate supply of authorized currency. These tokens were issued by merchants, innkeepers and manufacturers in many towns and villages in the seventeenth, eighteenth and nineteenth centuries and many collectors specialize in their local issues.

Some coins have designs of a commemorative nature; an example being the Royal Wedding crown of 1981, but there are also large numbers of commemorative medals which, though never intended for use as coinage, are sometimes confused with coins because they are metal objects of a similar shape and sometimes a similar size to coins. This is another interesting field for collectors as these medals often have excellent portraits of famous men or women, or they may commemorate important events or scientific discoveries. Other metallic objects of coin-like appearance that can be confusing for the beginner are reckoning counters, advertising tickets, various other tickets and passes, and items such as brass coin weights.

Minting processes
From the time of the earliest Greek coins in the late seventh century BC to about the middle of the sixteenth century AD, coins were made by hand. The method of manufacture was simple. The obverse and reverse designs were engraved or punched into the prepared ends of two bars of bronze or iron, shaped or tapered to the diameter of the required coin. The obverse die, known as the *pile,* was usually spiked so that it could be anchored firmly into a block of wood or metal. The reverse die, the *trussel,* was held by hand or grasped by tongs.

The coin was struck by placing a metal blank between the two dies and striking the trussel with a hammer. Thus, all coinage struck by this method is known as 'hammered'. Some dies are known to have been hinged so there would be an exact register between the upper and lower die. Usually a 'pair of dies' consisted of one obverse die (normally the more difficult to make because it had the finer detail, such as the ruler's portrait) and two reverse dies. This was because the shaft of iron bearing the reverse design eventually split under the constant hammering; two reverse dies were usually needed to last out the life of the obverse die.

Some time toward the middle of the sixteenth century, experiments, first in Germany and later in France, resulted in the manufacture of coins by machinery.

The term 'milled', which is applied to all machine-made coins, comes from the type of machinery used – the mill and screw press. With this machinery the obverse die was fixed as the lower die and the reverse die brought down into contact with the blank by heavy vertical pressure applied by a screw or worm-drive connected to a cross bar with heavy weights at each end. These weights usually had long leather thongs attached which allowed a more powerful force to be applied by the operators who revolved the arms of the press. New blanks were placed on the lower die and the struck coins were removed by hand. The screw press brought more pressure to bear on the blanks and this pressure was evenly applied, producing a far better and sharper coin.

Various attempts were made during the reigns of Elizabeth I and Charles I to introduce this type of machinery with its vastly superior products. Unfortunately problems associated with the manufacture of blanks to a uniform weight greatly reduced the rate of striking and the hand manufacture of coins continued until the Restoration in 1660, when Charles II brought to London from Holland the Roettiers brothers and their improved screw press.

The first English coins made for circulation by this new method were the silver crowns of 1662, which bore an inscription on the edge, DECVS ET TVTAMEN, 'an ornament and a safeguard', a reference to the fact that the new coins could not be clipped, a crime made easy by the thin and often badly struck hammered coins.

The mill and screw press was used until new steam-powered machinery made by Boulton and Watt was installed in the new mint on Tower Hill in London. This machinery had been used most successfully by Boulton to strike the large 'cartwheel' two- and one-penny pieces of 1797 and other coins, including 'overstriking' Spanish *eight-reale* pieces into Bank of England 'dollars' since the old Mint presses were not able to exert sufficient power to do this. This new machinery was first used at the Mint to strike the 'new coinage' halfcrowns of 1816, and it operated at a far greater speed than the old type of mill and screw presses and achieved a greater sharpness of design.

The very latest coining presses now operating at the Royal Mint at Llantrisant in South Wales, are capable of striking at a rate of up to 800 coins a minute.

Condition

One of the more difficult problems for the beginner is to assess accurately the condition of a coin. A common fault among collectors is to overgrade and, consequently, to overvalue their coins.

Most dealers will gladly spare a few minutes to help new collectors. Many dealers issue price lists with illustrations, enabling collectors to see exactly what the coins look like and how they have been graded.

Coins cannot always be graded according to precise rules. Hammered coins often look weak or worn on the high parts of the portrait and the tops of the letters; this can be due to weak striking or worn dies and is not always attributable to wear through long use in circulation. Milled coins usually leave the Mint sharply struck so that genuine wear is easier to detect. However a x5 or x10 magnifying glass is essential, especially when grading coins of Edward VII and George V where the relief is very low on the portraits and some skill is required to distinguish between an uncirculated coin and one in EF condition.

The condition or grade of preservation of a coin is usually of greater importance than its rarity. By this we mean that a common coin in superb condition is often more desirable and more highly priced than a rarity in poor condition. Coins that have been pierced or mounted as a piece of jewellery generally have little interest to collectors.

One must also be on the lookout for coins that have been 'plugged', i.e. that have been pierced at some time and have had the hole filled in, sometimes with the missing design or letters re-engraved.

Badly cleaned coins will often display a complexity of fine interlaced lines and such coins have a greatly reduced value. It is also known for coins to be tooled or re-engraved on the high parts of the hair, in order to 'increase' the grade of coin and its value. In general it is better to have a slightly more worn coin than a better example with such damage.

Cleaning coins

Speaking generally, *do not* clean coins. More coins are ruined by injudicious cleaning than through any other cause, and a badly cleaned coin loses much of its value. A nicely toned piece is usually considered desirable. Really dirty gold and silver can, however, be carefully washed in soap and water. Copper coins should never be cleaned or washed, they may be lightly brushed with a brush that is not too harsh.

Buying and selling coins

Exchanging coins with other collectors, searching around the antique shops, telling your relatives and friends that you are interested in coins, or even trying to find your own with a metal detector, are all ways of adding to your collection. However, the time will come when the serious collector needs to acquire specific coins or requires advice on the authenticity or value of a coin.

At this point an expert is needed, and the services of a reputable coin dealer are necessary. There are now a large number of coin dealers in the UK, many of whom belong to the B.N.T.A. (The British Numismatic Trade Association) or the I.A.P.N. (The International Association of Professional Numismatists) and a glance through the 'yellow pages' under 'coin dealer' or 'numismatist' will often provide local information. Many dealers publish their own lists of coins. Studying these lists is a good way for a collector to learn about coins and to classify and catalogue their own collections.

The Standard Catalogue of Coins of England and the UK has been published since 1929. It serves as a price guide for all coin collectors. Spink also publish books on many aspects of English, Greek, Roman and Byzantine coins and on British tokens which serve as a valuable source of information for coin collectors. Our books are available directly from Spink or through reputable booksellers. Many branches of W. H. Smith, and other High Street booksellers, stock copies of *The Standard Catalogue.*

Numismatic Clubs and Societies

There are well over one hundred numismatic societies and clubs in the British Isles. For details of how to contact them see page 531. Joining one is the best way to meet fellow enthusiasts, learn about your coins and other series and acquire coins in a friendly and informative way.

Useful suggestions

Security and insurance. The careful collector should not keep valuable coins at home unless they are insured and have adequate protection. Local police and insurance companies will give advice on what precautions may be necessary.

Most insurance companies will accept a valuation based on *The Standard Catalogue.* It is usually possible to have the amount added to a householder's contents policy but particularly valuable individual coins may have to be separately listed. A 'Fire, Burglary and Theft' policy will cover loss only from the insured's address, but an 'All Risks' policy will usually cover accidental damage and loss anywhere within the U.K.

For coins deposited with a bank or placed in a safe-deposit box a lower insurance premium is usually payable.

Keeping a record. All collectors are advised to have an up-to-date record of their collection and, if possible, photographs of the more important and more easily identifiable coins. This should be kept in a separate place from the collection so that a list and photographs can be given to the police should loss occur. Note the price paid, from whom purchased, the date of acquisition and the condition of the coin.

Storage and handling. New collectors should get into the habit of handling coins by the edge. This is especially important as far as highly polished proof coins are concerned.

Collectors may initially keep their coins in paper or plastic envelopes housed in boxes, albums or special containers. Many collectors will eventually wish to own a hardwood coin cabinet in which the collection can be properly arranged and displayed. If a home-made cabinet is being constructed avoid using oak and cedar wood; mahogany, walnut and rosewood are ideal. It is important that coins are not kept in a humid atmosphere; especial care must be taken with copper and bronze coins which are very susceptible to damp or condensation which may result in a green verdigris forming on them.

From beginner to numismatist

The new collector can best advance to becoming an experienced numismatist by examining as many coins as possible, noting their distinctive features and by learning to use the many books of reference that are available. It will be an advantage to join a local numismatic society, as this will provide an opportunity for meeting other enthusiasts and obtaining advice from more experienced collectors. Most societies have a varied programme of lectures, exhibitions and occasional auctions of members' duplicates.

Those who become members of one or both of the national societies, the Royal Numismatic Society and the British Numismatic Society, receive an annual journal containing authoritative papers and have access to the societies' library and programme of lectures.

Many museums have coin collections available for study, although they may not always be displayed, and a number of museum curators are qualified numismatists.

ABBREVIATIONS

Archb.	Archbishop	laur.	laureate
Æ	bronze	*mm.*	*mintmark*
AR	silver	mon.	monogram
AV	gold	*O., obv.*	obverse
Bp.	Bishop	p.	new penny, pence
BV	bullion value	pl	plume
cuir.	cuirassed	quat.	quatrefoil
d.	penny, pence	qtr.	quarter
diad.	diademed	rad.	radiate
dr.	draped	R., *rev.*	reverse
ex.	exergue	r.	right
grs.	grains	s.	shillings
hd.	head	stg.	standing
i.c.	inner circle	trun.	truncation
illus.	illustration	var.	variety
l.	left	wt.	weight

The British coin market remains, as it has been for several years, a very strong one with unsatisfied demand continuing to drive up prices for the more sought after material. More recently, however, the trend for collectors to eschew average material in favour of pieces of more exceptional interest or condition has become increasingly evident. Prices for routine middle grade coins are now rising relatively modestly, particularly in the milled series. There has been a sharp surge in value for material at the top end of the market.

Overall in the year 2004/5 prices have performed well compared to many other forms of asset, hammered coins have risen, on average, by 11.5% in very fine condition and by 6.5% in fine condition. Milled coins, which remain largely unchanged in fine and very fine, have also risen by 10% in the highest grades. These figures, however, hide a noticeable discontinuity based on value. Hammered coins worth over £5,000 have appreciated, on average, by 17.5% in very fine condition and by 10% in fine condition, but for hammered coins worth less than £5,000 the comparable figures are 10% in very fine condition and only 2.5% in fine condition. While overall 50% of hammered coin prices have risen, nearly 40% are unchanged, and just over 10% have fallen, though usually by a fairly small amount.

These figures can be taken as a sign that the market is becoming more mature. A leading London dealer recently quoted the adage that "there will always be more coins than there is money". Like all truisms, this needs to be qualified. Most of the turnover in any market consists, by definition, of items that are relatively common and the coin market is no exception. A Henry VI anulet Noble, a Cromwell silver Crown or a George III Northumberland shilling are attractive and desirable items but they are not rare. Examples in average condition flow onto the market, come sunshine or rain, in a steady stream. In the early phases of a boom the availability of such coins does not keep up with demand and prices rise very rapidly, however the supply keeps coming and, sooner or later when the surge of demand abates, the status quo is re-established, these coins become relatively commonplace again, most professional dealers have examples in stock, and the price stabilises. This is realistically the current market position.

In contrast, the top of the market consists of a select layer of material which is intrinsically desirable and rare, sometimes extremely so. Even with the aid of price guides and informed auction catalogues, it requires experience to differentiate between attractive but common items which have been driven up in price by temporary demand, and those coins which really are significant and difficult to obtain. In the early stages of a boom the latter even tend to be neglected because they do not appear on the market with sufficient frequency to plot a chart of conveniently rising prices. It is when the market has been strong for some time that the rarest and best material comes to the fore and then it can outperform the market in a quite dramatic fashion. This is now beginning to happen.

A remarkable feature of the 2004/5 season has been the quantity of top material which has become available. In 2003/4 the highest price at auction was £34,500 for the magnificent Henry VIII testoon in the Marshall collection. In 2004/5 no less than eighteen coins sold for sums in excess of this figure, and the £200,000 barrier was breached for the first time. The extent of this change can be measured by the number of items which have sold for over £20,000. In 2003/4 there were 16 such coins, amounting to a modest aggregate of £460,000. In 2004/5 45 coins sold for over £20,000 each, totalling more than £2,000,000. While the world market for British coins remains a small one in absolute terms, with annual sales amounting to around £15 million, this surge in values at the top end has boosted turnover by 30% in the last year. If quality material continues to become available in this way, this figure can be expected to rise.

The year kicked off in fine style with the sale of the unique Coenwulf gold penny of London, cover coin on last year's Spink Standard Catalogue, which realized £230,000 in Spink's 2004 COINEX auction. By far and away the most important coin ever found by a British metal detectorist, of great historical importance, unique in many different ways and in magnificent condition. It fetched a new world record price for a British coin at auction. The previous auction record, also held by Spink, was £170,500 for a George III 'Three Graces' pattern crown in gold of 1817, sold in the Herman Selig collection, Spink Auction 131, 2 March 1999. This in turn had superceded the £159,500 for the superb Henry III gold penny, once in the famous Montagu collection, sold in Spink Auction 114, 9 July 1996. The Coenwulf gold penny was the first British coin to breach £200,000, not a significant figure in world terms, but a considerable psychological price barrier in the British market. Now, a year on, such a coin might well be expected to fetch appreciably more.

The 2004 Spink COINEX sale also featured the late Saxon and Norman series, these have been a strong market recently. They start at attractively modest prices and combine portraits of some historically important rulers with the added feature of being struck at a range of interesting and collectable local mints, some of considerable rarity. For many years the price premium, for instance an Edward the Confessor penny in extremely fine condition over one in very fine grade, was not very great. The COINEX auction showed that the value for a good looking piece, bearing a strong portrait, and preferably in sound metal with an attractive old tone, may be several times that of a routine 'found' example.

The 100 pennies of Henry I and Stephen from the PIMPREZ hoard, also in this sale, formed an exceptional offering. Found north of Paris and officially exported from France, this picked selection representing the cream of the hoard included an unrivalled run of the popular 'double inscription' type of Henry I, no less than six of the mints for the type being previously unrecorded. The sale generated enormous interest and commensurate prices, the highest being £5,520 for a penny of the Watchet (Somerset) mint, only the second known example of this very rare mint for the entire reign of Henry I.

In contrast the earlier British series – Celtic, early Saxon sceattas and broad flan pennies of the Heptarchy have proved quite a quiet market, prices in very fine condition having stabilized with a barely perceptible advance, on average, of 1-2%. Celtic continues to be a series in transition from a "British" series in which rare small denominations are sought after, to an "Ancient" series in which large denominations, of fine style and in high grade, reign supreme. Celtic also remains one of the few series in which the activities of metal-detectorists remain an important influence on prices, restricting the prices achieved at the top end due to the possibility of further discoveries. Sceattas, and particularly early Anglo-Saxon gold thrymsas are also effected by this consideration. The quietness in the Anglo-Saxon middle period, in contrast, is due to the lack of good material coming onto the market. There was an expectation that the collection of Saxon coins formed by Dr Jacob Terner, small but of superb quality, would be sold at auction in conjunction with the Long Beach show, California in June 2005, but the coins were sold en-bloc privately. Many of the leading collectors in the field have mature collections and, in the absence of an event to draw attention to this major series, the occasional important coin offered has not attracted undue attention.

The second part of the definitive collection of short cross pennies formed by the late Professor Jeffrey Mass was sold by auction in March 2005. When a collection is too large for a single auction to be feasible and is disposed of in sections, it is very difficult to avoid weighting the first portion with a disproportionate number of the better coins and so it has proved in this case. The second part contained far fewer of the good solid collectable coins of John and Richard I which had been a feature of the first portion. An exception was the inclusion of the only short cross round halfpenny in the collection. These, with the allied round farthings, have always been a tricky denomination to price for they are very small coins, a negative feature, of great rarity and historical interest, a positive feature, but forming part of the generally inexpensive short cross series, a negative feature. Professor Mass himself was very reluctant to expend the £2,250 that this coin cost to purchase in 1997 and only did so on the prospect of publishing his collection in Sylloge, SCBI 56, form. In the event short cross pennies have enjoyed a resurgence of interest and his estate was rewarded when the halfpenny attracted feverish bidding, the Fitzwilliam Museum, Cambridge, emerging successful at £8,650.

On 5 May 2005 Spink held the auction of the year, the Samuel King collection of highly important English gold coins, with a hammer price total of £1,417,500 for 217 lots. Only the sale of C18th and C19th gold coins salvaged from the Douro cargo, Spink Auction 118, 20 November 1996, has realized a higher total for a Spink coin sale held in London since the firm entered the auction business in 1978. The collection had been formed relatively recently, mainly over the last ten years, with an emphasis on the large gold denominations, both hammered and milled, and the vendor was fortunate that these are precisely the denominations which have risen most strongly in price. In 2004/5 hammered gold once again outperformed all other series, rising by 17.5% on average, in very fine condition, while coins valued at over £5,000 have performed best of all, appreciating by 20% in the last year. This favourable atmosphere offset fears that the Samuel King collection contained too much material to offer at one time, particularly the 60 Five Guinea pieces, and many new records were set.

One of the most enduringly popular coins of the English series is the fine gold Sovereign of Henry VII showing the king holding an orb and sceptre and splendidly enthroned. Twice the weight of any of the denominations which preceded it, and a very rare piece, the Sovereign was designed to impress the late C15th world as it still does today. The Samuel King collection contained two examples, the finer having last appeared in a Christie's auction on 26 February 1991 when it sold for £10,450. It now realized £40,250. Another famous piece is the gold George Noble of Henry VIII, depicting St. George on horseback spearing the dragon, the only English medieval coin to do so. The example in the Samuel King collection was first recorded in the famous J D Cuff collection, sold in 1854, and boasted a particularly fine provenance. In Spink Auction 97, 13 May 1993, this piece could have been purchased for £5,940, it now sold for £26,450. The highest pre-sale estimate was £40,000-50,000 for the desirable 1703 VIGO Five Guinea piece of Queen Anne, struck under the personal supervision of Sir Isaac Newton from bullion captured from the Spanish during the battle of Vigo Bay in 1702. Only four other examples have been offered at auction in London in the last 45 years, and this combination of rarity, historical interest and a strong underlying market drove the price up to a remarkable £149,500.

The hammered silver series remains one of the most 'numismatic' of British coinages. It can be collected at the entry level of one coin or denomination of each reign, but on closer study it dissolves like a fractal into ever deeper layers of complexity. The study of the silver coins of a reign such as Henry VII can be the work of a lifetime. Over the last decade the trend has led very much away from amassing large numbers of near identical specimens towards putting together a balanced collection of attractive and complimentary examples of different reigns, types and denominations. This has changed the price structure of the market and put more price pressure on 'type' coins in high grade rather than on varieties, however rare. The adjustment has not yet fully worked through, and the true relative value of a Henry VI York groat as against a Charles I Pontefract shilling, in various conditions of preservation has not yet stabilized. This is the background to some quite erratic prices for pieces in the "upper middle end" range at auction, prices which the knowledgeable collector or dealer can profitably exploit. Thus a pleasing, but sketchily catalogued, Charles I Oxford silver crown of 1642 sold at a well attended London auction in September 2004 for £1,870. Six months later the same coin realized £6,300 when resold in Davissons Ltd Auction 22 with a fuller description and, crucially, the discovery that it had once formed part of the celebrated R C Lockett collection. It is easy to quote that a coin is worth what it last realized at auction but this is very rarely true.

Hammered silver has now been a strong market for a number of years, indeed hammered groats were one of the few series to be competitively collected in the early 1990's and they remain a popular denomination with both specialist and general collectors today. Prices in the medieval silver series are now rising more gradually, up by 5% in the last year, but continue to be firm. Tudor silver, however, particularly portrait coins have risen very sharply in the last five years and there is now some resistance to some of the high prices being asked unless the material is truly of top quality. This is reflected by a 7.5% unsold rate for Tudor silver coins at auction, not enormous, but higher than for most other series. In contrast demand for the coins of Charles I, and particularly the provincial coinage, remains robust and very fine prices have risen, on average, by 12.5%. The civil war coinage has enduring appeal both to the collector and to the general public and the fascination is not hard to understand.

The 2004/5 season saw one particularly interesting sale, that of the "Cheshire" collection, part of the Pre-Long Beach auction, held in Los Angeles on 1 June 2005. This was a substantial collection of British hammered and milled coins in gold, silver and copper, with over 1200 lots valued at nearly £1 million, which had been put together even more recently than the Samuel King collection. Many of the coins had been purchased in England over the last two or three years, but all had been slabbed and re-graded according to the American numerical system with the intention of presenting them to a different type of buyer. The catalogue provided very few of the original provenances, so this sale provided a realistic test of this form of presentation. The result was mixed. As with the Samuel King collection, the vendor benefited from the strong market for large denominations, particularly gold, in high grade. An extremely fine James I gold Rose-ryal purchased from the Ure collection in 2002 for £8,000 now sold for £22,500, and an almost extremely fine Edward VI silver crown of 1551 purchased in a London auction in November 2004 for £4,600 was re-rated to £12,500. Determined competition between two bidders drove the price of a Victoria 1839 proof "Una & Lion" gold £5, of the normal variety, to almost £35,000. The downside was a rather patchy and erratic saleroom with a high unsold percentage, over 25% by value, and whole runs of material, particularly milled copper coins in which this collection was very strong, were unwanted in the room.

The problem lay in the grading. There is a complete mismatch between the American numerical system of grading (VF-30+; EF-40+; AU-50+; and MS (mint state)-60+) and the British descriptive system (F, VF, EF and UNC). The American system was mainly developed to deal with high quality machine made C19th and C20th coins and its more recent extension to the earlier milled series and particularly the hammered coinage, has not been a happy one. Being numerical rather than descriptive it has no real capacity to deal with the many production flaws - double-striking, striking cracks, uneven flans with areas of weak strike, ghosting etc, which are an intrinsic aspect of these earlier coinages. The Cheshire collection, for instance, contained a number of medieval coins, almost all graded MS-62 to MS-64, a remarkable grade for a medieval coin. A noble of Richard II with a strong portrait was rated MS-64 with no mention of the fact that it was so badly double struck that the most of the obverse legend and the whole of the reverse was illegible. A few lots later a Henry VI annulet issue gold half-noble had also been slabbed MS-64. This coin was recently sold in London, Spink Auction 161, 14 November 2002, where it was graded as 'a pleasing full round coin, very fine'. Even allowing for some conservatism by the Spink cataloguer and rating the coin as good very fine, this is an enormous gap. In reality a British EF is a very good coin, equating to a true American MS-63 or so, and far better than an American AU, let alone an American EF. To this it must be added that flaws on a MS-63, particularly scratches and striking cracks, are not always mentioned whereas under the British system they are noted as supplementary information and the danger of taking the 'slabbed' grade on a British coin at face value is thus evident.

The high unsold percentage in sales such as the Cheshire collection is a reflection of this situation. In some cases the 'slabbed' grade is taken at face value and reflected in the price paid. In most cases, however, dealers and collectors of British coins are sufficiently sophisticated to take the true grade into account, and items which are unrealistically estimated are left in the hands of the auctioneer. Grade inflation, though virtually inevitable in periods of a strong market when items may sell despite flaws which would mark them down in quieter times, is a curious imperative for it has never been the route to sustained higher prices, let alone a confident market. In the days when Mr Bill French ran Glendining & Co with a rod of iron, and Glendining's were *the* London coin auction house, he was a great advocate of conservative grading and everybody, whether buyer or seller, was satisfied. Even in the Cheshire collection this principle applied, for the Edward VI 1551 crown, mentioned above, on which the vendor realised a near threefold profit in six months was not graded MS-61, or even AU-55, but a lowly EF-45. It has been suggested that where British coins in slabs are catalogued for the world market they should be graded according to both systems, a form of American/British bilingualism, and this is possibly the best solution.

Two days after the sale of the Cheshire collection, and also associated with the Long Beach show, Heritage World Coin Auctions offered a magnificent Charles I Oxford mint triple unite of 1643, one of two known specimens struck from the 'pattern' obverse die. This coin had sold in the Beresford-Jones sale in 1983 for £33,600 and again in the Selig collection, Spink Auction 70, in 1989 for £48,400. In the latter sale it was one of the few coins to appreciate in value in a falling market and the price paid was regarded as a full one. It now sold for £235,000, another new world record for a British coin at auction.

The outlook for the British coin market remains excellent. Although prices have risen several fold in the last few years, they remain modest in historical terms, and levels at the top end are now only just beginning to approach those which have long been the rule in other world coin markets. It does, however, depend on the continued application of professional numismatic skill and expertise. Internet sales have made considerable advances over the last two or three years but they remain the 'wild west' of numismatics and are largely restricted to coins under £1,000. The pleasure of acquisition for most collectors, aside from the 'bargain hunting' impulse, lies in examining and assessing a piece before it is purchased. Auctions, similarly, do not provide the solid base for a successful industry, particularly if the unsold percentage is allowed to rise to much over 20%. The British coin market is fortunate that it continues to be served by a strong dealer network with long experience of all cycles of the business and it is on this that its prosperity continues to depend.

Obverse	That side of the coin which normally shows the monarch's head or name.
Reverse	The side opposite to the obverse, the 'Tails'.
Blank	The coin as a blank piece of metal, i.e. before it is struck.
Flan	The whole piece of metal after striking.
Type	The main, central design.
Legend	The inscription. Coins lacking a legend are called 'mute' or anepigraphic.
Field	That flat part of the coin between the main design and the inscription or edge.
Exergue	That part of the coin below the main design, usually separated by a horizontal line, and normally occupied by the date.
Die	The block of metal, with design cut into it, which actually impresses the coin blank with the design.
Die variety	Coin showing slight variation of design.
Mule	A coin with the current type on one side and the previous (and usually obsolete) type on the other side, or a piece struck from two dies that are not normally used together.
Graining or reeding	The crenellations around the edge of the coin, commonly known as 'milling'.
Proof	Carefully struck coin from special dies with a mirror-like or matt surface. (In this country 'Proof' is *not* a term used to describe the state of preservation, but the method of striking.)
Hammered	Refers to the old craft method of striking a coin between dies hammered by hand.
Milled	Coins struck by dies worked in a coining press. The presses were hand powered from 1560-1800, powered by steam from 1790 and by electricity from 1895.

CELTIC COINAGE

The Celtic or Ancient British issues are amongst the most interesting and varied of all British coins. They are our earliest coins and are the product of a society that left no historical sources of its own. It is therefore often difficult to be specific about for whom, when or where they were produced. Despite only being used for approximately a hundred and fifty years they do provide a rich variety of designs and types in gold, silver and bronze. Collectors looking for a theme to concentrate on may find the coins of one tribe, an individual ruler or a particular phase in the coinage interesting.

Grading Celtic Coins

The majority of Celtic coins were struck by hand, sometimes resulting in a loss of definition through weak striking. In addition, the design on the dies was often bigger than the blank flan employed, resulting in the loss of some of the design. Coins with full legends are generally more valuable than examples with incomplete legends. Bronze coins in good condition (VF or better) and especially toned examples attract a premium. Factors that detract from a coin's value are chips, scratches and verdigris on bronze coins. It is important to take into account these factors as well as the amount of wear on a coin when assessing its grade.

| Cunobelin Bronze Unit | Epaticcus Silver Unit | Cunobelin Gold Stater |

Fine

Very Fine

Plated Coins

Plated gold staters, quarter staters and silver units are recorded for many known types. They vary considerably in the quality of their production and are usually priced at around a quarter of the substantive types value. Their exact purpose or relation to the type they copy is not fully understood.

References and Select Bibliography.

M   Mack, R.P. (1975) 3rd edition, The Coinage of Ancient Britain.
V   Van Arsdell, R.D. (1989), Celtic Coinage of Britain.
BMC   Hobbs, R. (1996), British Iron Age Coins in the British Museum.

de Jersey, P. (1996), Celtic Coinage in Britain. *A good general introduction to the series.*
Nash, D. (1987), Coinage in the Celtic World. *Sets the coinage in its social context.*

The layout of the following list is derived from the standard works by Mack, Van Arsdell and the British Museum Catalogue by Richard Hobbs. References are made to these works where possible, in the case of the last work it should be noted that the British Museum collection is not exhaustive, and therefore should not be used to assess the rarity of a coin. More detailed information than that given here can be gained from these works.

IMPORTED COINAGE

The earliest coins to circulate in Britain were made in northern Gaul (Belgica) and imported into the south-east of England from around 150 B.C. onwards. They were principally the product of two tribal groups in this region, the Ambiani and Suessiones. In Britain these types are known as Gallo-Belgic A to F. The first type Gallo-Belgic A is ultimately derived from the Macedonian gold staters (M) of Philip II (359-336 B.C.)

The reasons why they were imported are not fully understood. However, the context for their importation is one of close social, political and economic ties between Britain and Gaul. Within this cross-channel relationship they undoubtedly had various functions, such as payment for military service or mercenaries, in exchanges between the elite of each society: in cementing alliances for example, or as gifts in a system of exchange.

Numbers in brackets following each entry refer to numbers employed in previous editions of this catalogue.

GALLO-BELGIC ISSUES

GOLD

M	2	3	5	7

		F	VF
		£	£

From c.150 B.C. – c.50 B.C.

		F £	VF £
1	**Stater.** Gallo-Belgic A. (Ambiani). Good copy of Macedonian stater, large flan. Laureate head of Apollo r. R. Horse r. *M. 1; V. 10. (1)*	575	2750
2	Similar, but head and horse l. *M. 3; V. 12. (1)*	500	1450
3	B. (Ambiani). Somewhat similar to 1, but small flan and 'defaced' *obv.* die. R. Horse r. *M. 5; V. 30. (3)*	325	950
4	— Similar, but with lyre between horse's legs. *M. 7; V. 33. (3)*	400	1350
5	C. (Ambiani), *Stater.* Disintegrated Apollo head. R. horse. *M. 26; V. 44. (5)*	225	650
6	**Quarter Stater.** Gallo-Belgic A. Similar to 1. *M. 2; V .15. (2)*	250	675
7	— Similar to 2. *M. 4; V. 20. (2)*	225	600
8	B. Similar to 3. *M. 6; V. 35. (4)*	175	450
9	— Similar. R. Two horses l. with lyre between legs. *M. 8; V. 37. (4)*	135	325
10	D. Portions of Apollo head R. A mixture of stars, crescents, pellets, zig-zag lines; often referred to as 'Geometric' types,(See also British 'O', S. 46.). *M. 37, 39, 41, 41a, 42; V. 65/7/9/146. (6)*	65	125

From *c*.50 B.C.

11

		F £	VF £
11	**Stater.** Gallo-Belgic E. (Ambiani). Blank obv. R̵. Disjointed curved horse r., pellet below, zig-zag in exergue. *M. 27; V. 52, 54. (7)*	150	275
12	F. (Suessiones). Devolved Apollo head r. R̵. Disjointed horse r. With triple-tail. *M. 34a; V. 85. (8)*	275	850
13	Xc. Blank except for VE monogram at edge of coin, R̵. S below horse r. *M. 82; V. 87-1. (9)*	225	650

BILLON

Armorican (Channel Islands and N.W. Gaul, *c*.75-50 B.C.)

14   15

14	**Stater.** Class I. Head r. R̵. Horse, boar below, remains of driver with Victory above, lash ends in or two loops, or 'gate'. *(12)*	35	120
15	— Class II. Head r. R̵. Horse, boar below, remains of Victory only, lash ends in small cross of four pellets. *(13)*	30	110
16	— Class III. Head r., anchor-shaped nose. R̵. Somewhat similar to Class I. *(14)*	30	110
17	— Class IV. Head r. R̵. Horse with reins, lyre shape below, driver holds vertical pole, lash ends in three prongs. *(15)*	35	120
18	— Class V. Head r. R̵. Similar to last, lash ends in long cross with four pellets. *(16)*	40	135
19	— Class VI. Head r. R̵. Horse, boar below, lash ends in 'ladder' *(17)*	45	160
20	**Quarter Stater.** Similar types to above. *(18)*	45	150

20

CELTIC COINS STRUCK IN BRITAIN

Coin production in Britain began at the very end of the second century B.C. with the cast potin coinage of Kent (Nos 62-64). Inspired by Gaulish issues and ultimately derived from the potin coins of Massalia (Marseilles) in southern Gaul, the precise function and period of use of this coinage is not fully understood. The domestic production of gold coins started around 70 B.C., these issues are traditionally known as British A-P and are derived from imported Gallo-Belgic issues. Broadly contemporary with these issues are quarter staters, silver units, and bronze units. Recent work by John Sills has further enhanced our understanding of this crucial early period with the identification of two new British staters (Insular Belgic C or Kentish A and the Ingoldisthorpe type) and their related quarters and a Westerham quarter stater. The Insular Belgic C or Kentish A type derived from Gallo-Belgic C now becomes the first British stater.

EARLY UNINSCRIBED COINAGE

GOLD

20A   20B

		F £	VF £
20A	**Stater.** Insuler Belgic C/Kentish A type. Devolved Apollo head r. R. Disjointed horse r, a rosette behind or in front, or both. *M.* —; *V.* —; *BMC* —	450	1400
20B	Ingoldisthorpe type. Similar to last, as illustration. *M.*—; *V.*—; *BMC*—..	425	1300

21   22   23   24

21	British A. Westerham type. Devolved Apollo head r. R. Disjointed horse l. large pellet below. *M. 28, 29; V. 200, 202; BMC 1-32 (19)*	175	400
22	B. Chute type. Similar to 9 but crab-like object below horse. *M. 32; V. 1205; BMC 35-76. (20)*	150	275
23	C. Yarmouth type. Similar to 9 but star-like object in front of horse. *M. 31; V. 1220; BMC 78-85. (21)*	425	1350
24	D. Cheriton type. Similar to Chute type but with large crescent face. *M. 33; V. 1215; BMC 86-128. (22)*	225	675
25	E. Waldingfield type. Annulet and pellet below horse. *M. 48; V. 1462; BMC — —. (23)*	675	2250

26 27

	F	VF
	£	£

26 F. Clacton type 1. Similar to Westerham type but rosette below horse.
M. 47; V. 1458; BMC 137-44. (24).. 300 875

27 G. Clacton type 2. Similar but horse r., with pellet, or pellet with two
curved lines below. M. 46, 46a; V. 30, 1455; BMC 145-79. (25)............. 300 875

28 30

28 H. North-East Coast type. Variety of 9, pellet or rosette below horse
to r. M. 50, 50a, 51, 51a; V. 800; BMC 182-191. (26) 200 425

29 I. — Similar, horse l., pellet, rosette or star with curved rays below.
M. 52-57; V. 804, 805, 807; BMC 193-211. (27) 175 400

30 J. Norfolk Wolf type. R. Crude wolf to r. M. 49; V. 610-1; BMC 212-16. (28) 225 575

31 — Similar but wolf to l. Usually base gold. M. 49a/b; V. 610-2/3,
BMC 217-78. (28A).. 150 400

32 L. Whaddon Chase type. R. Spirited horse r. of new style, various
symbols below. M. 133-138a, 139a; V. 1470-6; 1485/7/9/93;
BMC 279-343. (31) 175 475

33 — Plain. R. Horse r. With ring ornament below or behind.
M. 140-143; V. 1498-1505; BMC 344-46. (32) 200 575

33A — Climping type. Similar to Whaddon Chase type but horse left, bird-like
object above, pellet in ring and crescent below. M.-;V.-; BMC-. 475 1350

34 Lx. NorthThames group. Blank apart from reversed SS. R. Similar to
last. M. 146; V. 1509; BMC 350. (33)... 800 2500

35 Lz. Weald group. Blank with some traces of Apollo head. R. Horse r.,
large wheel ornament below. M. 144-145; V. 1507; BMC 347-49. (36).. 475 1350

33A 36

36 Ma. Wonersh type. Crossed wreath design with crescents back to back
in centre. R. Spiral above horse, wheel below. M. 148; V. 1520;
BMC 351-56. (37) 350 900

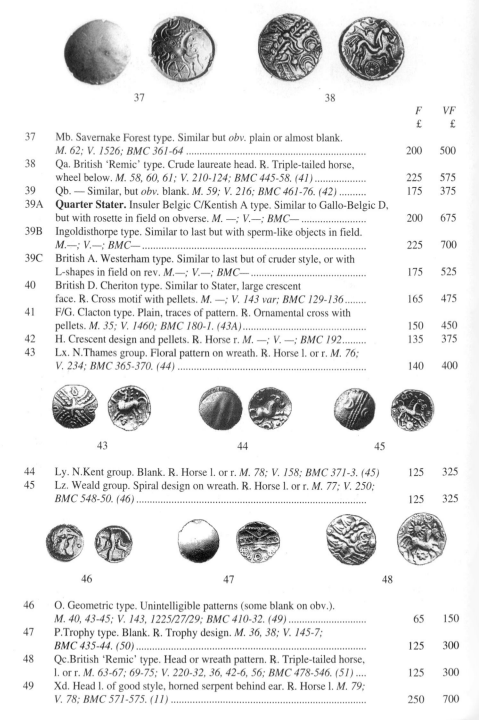

37   38

		F £	VF £
37	Mb. Savernake Forest type. Similar but *obv.* plain or almost blank. *M. 62; V. 1526; BMC 361-64*	200	500
38	Qa. British 'Remic' type. Crude laureate head. R. Triple-tailed horse, wheel below. *M. 58, 60, 61; V. 210-124; BMC 445-58. (41)*	225	575
39	Qb. — Similar, but *obv.* blank. *M. 59; V. 216; BMC 461-76. (42)*	175	375
39A	**Quarter Stater.** Insuler Belgic C/Kentish A type. Similar to Gallo-Belgic D, but with rosette in field on obverse. *M. —; V.—; BMC—*	200	675
39B	Ingoldisthorpe type. Similar to last but with sperm-like objects in field. *M.—; V.—; BMC—*	225	700
39C	British A. Westerham type. Similar to last but of cruder style, or with L-shapes in field on rev. *M.—; V.—; BMC—*	175	525
40	British D. Cheriton type. Similar to Stater, large crescent face. R. Cross motif with pellets. *M. —; V. 143 var; BMC 129-136*	165	475
41	F/G. Clacton type. Plain, traces of pattern. R. Ornamental cross with pellets. *M. 35; V. 1460; BMC 180-1. (43A)*	150	450
42	H. Crescent design and pellets. R. Horse r. *M. —; V. —; BMC 192*	135	375
43	Lx. N.Thames group. Floral pattern on wreath. R. Horse l. or r. *M. 76; V. 234; BMC 365-370. (44)*	140	400

43   44   45

44	Ly. N.Kent group. Blank. R. Horse l. or r. *M. 78; V. 158; BMC 371-3. (45)*	125	325
45	Lz. Weald group. Spiral design on wreath. R. Horse l. or r. *M. 77; V. 250; BMC 548-50. (46)*	125	325

46   47   48

46	O. Geometric type. Unintelligible patterns (some blank on obv.). *M. 40, 43-45; V. 143, 1225/27/29; BMC 410-32. (49)*	65	150
47	P.Trophy type. Blank. R. Trophy design. *M. 36, 38; V. 145-7; BMC 435-44. (50)*	125	300
48	Qc.British 'Remic' type. Head or wreath pattern. R. Triple-tailed horse, l. or r. *M. 63-67; 69-75; V. 220-32, 36, 42-6, 56; BMC 478-546. (51)*	125	300
49	Xd. Head l. of good style, horned serpent behind ear. R. Horse l. *M. 79; V. 78; BMC 571-575. (11)*	250	700

SILVER

Units (unless otherwise stated)

50   52

		F £	VF £
50	Lx. Head l.or r. Ŗ. Horse l. or r. *M. 280, 435, 436, 438, 441; V. 80, 1546, 1549, 1555; BMC 376-382. (53)*	70	225
51	— Head l. Ŗ. Stag r. with long horns. *M. 437; V. 1552; BMC 383-7. (54)*	100	375
52	— **Half Unit.** Two horses or two beasts. *M. 272, 442, 443, 445; V. 474, 1626, 1643, 1948; BMC 389-400. (55)*	95	350
53	Lz. Danebury group. Head r. with hair of long curves. Ŗ. Horse l., flower above. *M. 88; V. 262; BMC 580-82*	85	300

54   54A

54	— Helmeted head r. Ŗ. Horse r. wheel below. *M. 89; V. 264; BMC 583 -592. (58)*	95	350
54A	Cruciform pattern with ornaments in angles. Ŗ. Horse l., ear of corn between legs, crescents and pellets above, *M.—; V.—; BMC—*	85	300
55	— **Quarter Unit.** As last. *M. 90; V. 268; BMC 642-43. (59)*	45	150
56	— Head r. Ŗ. Horse r. star above, wheel below. *M. –; V. 280; BMC 595-601*	75	250
57	— Head l., pellet in ring in front. Ŗ. Horse l. or r. *M. –; V. 284; BMC 610-630*	60	175
58	— Serpent looking back. Ŗ. Horse l. *M. –; V. 286; BMC 631-33*	85	250
59	— **Quarter Unit.** Cross pattern. Ŗ. Two-tailed horse. *M. 119; V. 482; BMC 654-56. (56C). (Formerly attributed to Verica)*	40	135

BRONZE

60	**Unit.** Lx. Winged horse l. Ŗ. Winged horse l. *M. 446; V. 1629; BMC 401 (78)*	80	350
61	Chichester Cock type. Head r. Ŗ. Head r. surmounted by cock. *M. –; V. — BMC 657-59*	75	300

POTIN
(Cast Copper/Tin alloy)

62

		F £	VF £

62   **Unit.** Thurrock type.Head l. R. Bull butting l. or r. *M. —; V. 1402-42; BMC 660-666. (84A)*..   35   120

63   64

63   Class I type. Crude head. R. Lines representing bull *(Allen types A-L.)*
      M. 9-22a; V. 104, 106, 108, 112, 114, 115, 117, 119, 120, 122, 123, 125,
      127, 129, 131, 133; BMC 667-714. (83)...   25   75
64   Class II type. Smaller flan, large central pellet. *(Allen types M-P.)*
      M. 23-25; V. 135-39; BMC 715-23. (84)...   25   70

CELTIC DYNASTIC AND LATER UNINSCRIBED COINAGE

From Julius Caesar's expeditions to Britain in 55/54 B.C. and his conquest of Gaul in 52 B.C. to the Claudian invasion in 43 A.D., southern Britain was increasingly drawn into the orbit of the Roman world. This process is reflected not only in the coins but also in what we know about their issuers and the tribes they ruled. Latin legends begin to appear for the first time and increasingly accompany objects and designs drawn from the classical world. A lot of what we know about the Celtic tribes and their rulers, beyond just their names on coins, is drawn from contemporary and slightly later Roman historical sources. A great deal however is still uncertain and almost all attributions to either tribes or historically attested individuals have to be seen as tentative.

The coin producing tribes of Britain can be divided into two groups, those of the core and those of the periphery. The tribes of the core, the Atrebates/Regni, Trinovantes/Catuvellauni and Cantii, by virtue of their geographical location controlled contact with the Roman world. Unlike the tribes of the periphery they widely employed Latin legends, classical designs and used bronze coinage in addition to gold and silver.

Following the Roman invasion of 43 A.D. it is likely that some coinage continued to be produced for a short time. However in 61 A.D. with the death of King Prasutagus and the suppression of the Boudiccan revolt that followed, it is likely that Celtic coinage came to an end.

TRIBAL/MINT MAP

Known Mints
1 – Camulodunum (Colchester)
2 – Verulamium (St. Albans)
3 – Calleva (Silchester)

CORIELTAUVI

ICENI

DOBUNNI

TRINOVANTES
1 ●

CATUVELLAUNI
● 2

ATREBATES
● 3

CANTII

DUROTRIGES

REGNI

G
A
U
L

ATREBATES AND REGNI

The joint tribal area of these two groups corresponds roughly with Berkshire and Sussex and parts of northern and eastern Hampshire. The Atrebatic portion being in the north of this region with its main centre at Calleva (Silchester). The Regni occupying the southern part of the region centred around Chichester.

COMMIUS
(Mid to Late 1st Century B.C.)

The first inscribed staters to appear in Britain, closely resemble British Q staters (no.38) and are inscribed 'COMMIOS'. Staters and silver units with an inscribed 'E' are also thought to be related. Traditionally this Commius was thought to be the Gaulish chieftain who Caesar refers to in De Bello Gallico, as firstly serving him in his expeditions to Britain and finally fleeing to Britain c.50 B.C. This attribution does however present chronological problems, and the appearance of a few early staters reading 'COM COMMIOS' suggests that the Commius who issued coins is more likely to have been the son of Caesar's Commius.

GOLD

65

		F £	VF £
65	**Stater.** Devolved Apollo head r. Ɍ. COMMIOS around triple tailed horse r., wheel below. *M. 92; V. 350; BMC 724-29. (85)*	325	900

66   67

66	Similar, but 'E' symbol above horse instead of legend. *M. —; V. 352.* *BMC 730*	350	950
67	**Quarter Stater.** Blank except for digamma. Ɍ. Horse l. *M. 83; V. 353-5; BMC —. (10)*	125	300

SILVER

69

69	**Unit.** Head l. Ɍ. Horse l. Mostly with 'E' symbol above. *M. —;V. 355; BMC 731-58. (57)*	45	175

70

| | F £ | VF £ |
70 **Minim.** Similar to Unit. *M. —; V. 358-5; BMC 759-60* .... | 45 | 140 |

TINCOMARUS or TINCOMMIUS
(Late 1st Century B.C. – Early 1st Century A.D.)

Successor to Commius and on his coins styled as 'COM.F' (son of Commius). Early coins of the reign like his predecessors are very obiviously Celtic in their style. However later coins exhibit an increasing tendancy towards Roman designs. Indeed Tincommius is recorded as a supliant king of the Roman emperor Augustus (Res Gestae, xxxii), finally fleeing to Rome in the early 1st century A.D. The discovery of the Alton Hoard in 1996 brought to light gold staters with the new legend TINCOMARVS.

GOLD

71   73

71	**Stater.** *Celtic style.* Devolved Apollo head r. R. TINC COMM. F. around horse. *M. 93; V. 362; BMC —. (86)*	425	1350
72	Similar but legend reads TINCOMARVS. *M. 94; V. 363; BMC 761-765. (86)*	325	850
73	**Quarter Stater.** Spiral with pellet centre. R. Horse r. T above. *M. 81; V. 366; BMC 781-797. (46)*	100	225

74   75

| 74 | TINCOM, zig-zag ornament below. R. Horse l. *M. 95; V. 365; BMC 798-810. (87)* .... | 125 | 350 |
| 75 | **Stater.** *Classical style.* TINC(O) on a sunk tablet. R. Horseman with javelin r. often with CF in field. *M. 96-98; V. 375-76; BMC 765-769. (88)* | 300 | 775 |

76   77

		F £	VF £
76	COM.(F). on a sunk tablet. Ŗ. Horseman with javelin r. TIN in field *M. 100; V. 385; BMC 770-774. (88)*	250	650
77	**Quarter Stater.** TINC on a tablet, C above, A or B below. Ŗ. Winged head (Medusa?) facing. *M. 97; V. 378; BMC 811-826. (89)*	175	450
78	TIN on tablet. Ŗ. Boar l. *M. 99; V. 379; BMC 827-837. (90)*	100	250

79   83

79	COMF on tablet. Ŗ. Horse r. TIN around. *M. 101; V. 387; BMC 838-841. (90)*	120	275
80	— Ŗ. Horse l. TIC around. *M. 102; V. 388; BMC 842-851. (90)*	120	275
81	COM on tablet. Ŗ. Horse l. T above. *M. 103; V. 389; BMC 852-3. (90)* .	110	275
82	COMF on tablet. Ŗ. Horse r. TINC around. *M. 104; V. 390; BMC 854-879. (90)*	100	250

SILVER

83	**Unit.** Laureate head r. TINCOM in front, V behind. Ŗ. Eagle stg. on snake. *M. 105; V. 397; BMC 880-905. (91)*	50	175
84	Laureate head l. Ŗ. Bull l. TINC around. *M. 106; V. 396; BMC 906-910. (91A)*	50	185
85	Laureate head r. Ŗ. Bull r. TIN(C) around. *M. —; V. 381; BMC 911-925. (92B)*	40	140
86	Facing head. Ŗ. Bull l. TINC around. *M. —; V. 370; BMC 926-29 (92)*..	50	185

87   91

87	TINC in angles of cross, Ŗ. Lion l. *M. —; V. 372; BMC 930-45. (93B)* ..	45	150
88	Star. Ŗ. Boy riding dolphin r. TINC in field. *M. —; V. 371; BMC 946-977. (93C)*	35	130
89	TINC around pellet. Ŗ. Lion l. *M. 106a; V. 382; BMC 978-80. (93)*	50	170
90	Head l. TINCOMMIVS in front. Ŗ. Horse l. lyre above. *M. 131b; V. 473; BMC —. (92C) (Formerly attributed to Verica)*...............................	50	175
91	**Minim.** CF within two interlinked squares. Ŗ. Boar? r. TINC. *M. 118; V. 383-1; BMC 981-82. (94)*	35	110
92	As above but CO. Ŗ. Bull r. TI. *M. —; V. 383-5; BMC —*....................	35	125

	F	VF
	£	£

93   C inside box, box above and below. R. Bull r. TIN. *M. —; V. 383-7;*
BMC 983 40   135
94   Cross, T? in angles. R. uncertain object. *M. 120; V. 483; BMC 984-85.*
(Formerly attributed to Verica) 35   120

EPPILLUS
(Later 1st Century B.C. – Early 1st Century A.D.)

His reign is likely to have coincided with that of Tincommius's, who also claimed to be a son of Commius. Two coinages appear in his name, one for Kent and one minted at Calleva (Silchester, Hants.) in the northern part of the territory of the Atrebates and Regni. The coins of Calleva conform to the southern denominational structure of gold and silver with fractions of each, whilst the Kentish series is distinctly tri-metallic, replacing the silver minim with bronze. A joint coinage was issued by Eppillus and Verica. It is not understood if Eppillus held both territories simultaneously.

COINAGE STRUCK AT CALLEVA
GOLD

95   **Stater.** Devolved Apollo head r. R. EPPI COMMI F around horse.
M. —; V. 405; BMC — 975   3500

96

96   **Quarter Stater.** CALLEV, star above and below. R. Hound r. EPPI.
M. 107; V. 407-08; BMC 986-1005. (95) 100   250

97   98

97   COMM F EPPILV, around crescent. R. Horse r. *M. —; V. 409;*
BMC 1006-1009. (95A) 110   285
98   EPPI COMF in two lines. R. Winged horse r. *M. 302; V. 435;*
BMC 1010-15. (129) 100   250

SILVER

99   100

99   **Unit.** Crescent REX CALLE above and below. R. Eagle r. EPP. *M. 108;*
V.415. BMC 1016-1060. (96) 40   140
100   Bearded hd. r. in wreath. R. Boar r. EPPI(L) F CO(M). *M. —; V. 416;*
BMC 1061-87. (96A) 40   150

		F £	VF £
101	Bearded hd. in pellet border. R̶. Lion r. EPP COMF. *M. 305; V. 417;* *BMC 1088-1115. (131)*	50	140
102	**Minim.** Floral cross. R̶. Eagle r. EPPI. *M. —; V. 420; BMC 1116-17*	40	140
103	Spiral and pellets. R̶. Ram r. EPP. *M. —; V. 421; BMC 1118-20. (96C)* .	40	150
104	Bulls head facing. R̶. Ram r. EPP. *M. —; V. 422; BMC 1121-24. (96D)*.	45	165
105	Wreath pattern. R̶. Boar r. EPP. *M. —; V. 423; BMC —*	50	175
106	Crescent cross. R̶. Hand holding trident. *M. —; V. 487; BMC —. (111C)*	50	175

KENTISH TYPES
GOLD

107	**Stater.** COMF within wreath. R̶. Horseman l. EPPILLVS above. *M. 300; V. 430; BMC 1125-26. (127)*	1000	3500

108   107

108	Victory holding wreath l., within wreath. R̶. Horseman r. holding carnyx, F EPPI COM below. *M. 301; V. 431; BMC 1127-28. (128)*	1350	4500
109	**Quarter Stater.** Crossed wreaths, EPPI in angles. R̶. Horse l. *M. 303;* *V. 436; BMC 1129. (130)*	300	850
110	COMF in pellet border. R̶. Horse r. EPPI. *M. 304; V. 437;* *BMC 1130-31. (130)*	275	700

SILVER

111	**Unit.** Head l. EPPIL in field. R̶. Horseman holding carnyx, EPPILL. *M. 306; V. 441; BMC 1132. (131)*	175	550

BRONZE

112	**Unit.** Bow cross, EPPI COMF around. R̶. Eagle facing. *M. 309; V. 450;* *BMC 1137-38. (134)*	60	275
113	Bull r., EPPI COF around. R̶. eagle facing. *M. 310; V. 451;* *BMC 1139-41. (134)*	60	275
114	Head l., EPPI in front. R̶. Victory l. holding wreath and standard. *M. 311; V. 452; BMC 1142. (133)*	70	325
115	Bearded hd. r., EPPI CF. R̶. Biga r. CF. *M. 312; V. 453; BMC —*	75	375

JOINT TYPES OF EPPILUS AND VERICA
SILVER

	F £	VF £

116   **Unit.** Head l. CO VIR in front. R. Victory, EP. *M. 307; V. 442;*
BMC 1133-34. (132)..   250   750

117

117   Head r. VIR CO in front. R. Capricorn l. EPPI COMF. *M. 308/a; V. 443;*
BMC 1135-36. (132)   150   475

VERICA
(*c.*10.-*c.*40 A.D.)

The exact details of Verica's succession and relationship to Eppillus and Tincommius are not fully understood. However by c.10 A.D. it seems likely that Verica was the sole ruler of the southern region. His close contact with Rome, both political and economic, seen in the increasing use of classical designs on his coins, culminated in his flight to Rome in c.42 A.D. to seek assistance from Claudius.

GOLD

118   **Stater.** COM:F on tablet. R. Horseman r. holding spear, VIR below.
M. 109; V. 460; BMC 1143-44. (97)......................................   275   700
119   COM.F. on tablet, pellet in ring ornament above and below. R.
Similar to last. *M.121; 461; BMC 1146-53. (97)*...................................   275   700

120   121

120   COM.F on tablet. R. Horseman r. holding spear, VIR above, REX below.
M. 121 var; V. 500; BMC 1155-58. (98)   200   500
121   Vine-leaf dividing VI RI. R. Horseman r. with shield and spear. COF in
field. *M. 125; V. 520-1; BMC 1159-73. (99)*...   250   625
122   Similar, reads VE RI. *M. 125; V. 520-5/7; BMC 1174-76. (99)*..............   250   650
123   **Quarter Stater.** COMF on tablet. R. Horse l. VIR. *M. 111; V. 465;*
BMC 1177-78. (100)   110   300

124

124   COMF on tablet, pellet in ring ornament above and below R. Horse
r. VI. *M. 112; V. 466; BMC 1179-1206. (100)*......................................   120   240

		F £	VF £
125	COMF on tablet, pellet border. Ŗ. Horse r. VI above. *M. 113; V. 467;* *BMC 1207-16. (100)*	120	250

126   128

126	COM FILI. in two lines, scroll in between. Ŗ. Horse r. VIR(I) above. *M. 114; V. 468; BMC 1217-22. (100)*	110	275
127	VERI COMF, crescent above, star below. Ŗ. Horse r. REX below. *M. 122; V. 501; BMC 1223-36. (101)*	110	275
128	VERI beneath vine-leaf. Ŗ. Horseman r. with sword and shield, FRX in field. *M. 124; V. 525; BMC 1237-38. (102)*	185	650
129	COM, horseman r. Ŗ. Seated figure, VERICA around. *M. 126; V. 526;* *BMC 1239. (103)*	275	900
130	Similar to last. Ŗ. Laureate bust r., VIRI in front. *M. 127; V. 527;* *BMC 1240. (103)*	265	850

SILVER

| 131 | **Unit.** COMF, crescent and or pellet in ring above and below. Ŗ. Boar r.
VI(RI) below. *M. 115; V. 470/72; BMC 1241-1331. (104)* .... | 35 | 135 |

132   133

| 132 | VERICA COMMI F around pellet in ring. R. Lion r. REX below.
M. 123; V. 505; BMC 1332-1359. (105) .... | 50 | 175 |
| 133 | COMMI F, horseman with shield r. Ŗ. VERI CA, mounted warrior with
spear r. *M. 128; V. 530; BMC 1360-92. (106)* .... | 50 | 180 |

134   137

134	Two cornucopiae, COMMI F. Ŗ. Figure seated r. VERICA. *M. 129;* *V. 531; BMC 1393-1419. (107)*	40	140
135	Bust r. VIRI. R. Figure seated l. *M. 130; V. 532; BMC 1420. (108)*	85	300
136	Naked figure l. Ŗ. Laureate bust r., COMMI F. *M. 131; V. 533;* *BMC 1421-49. (108)*	40	150
137	VERICA REX, bull r. Ŗ. Figure stg. l., COMMI F. *M. —; V. 506;* *BMC 1450-84. (108B)*	40	160
138	COMF, in tablet and scroll. Ŗ. Eagle facing, VI RI. *M. —; V. 471;* *BMC 1485-1505. (104A)*	40	150

		F £	VF £

139 VIRIC across field,ornaments above and below. R. Pegasus r., star design below. *M. —; V. —; BMC —. (104B)*........... 75 275
140 Head r. Verica. R. COMMI F., eagle l. *M. 131A; V. 534; BMC —. (108A)* 85 350
141 **Minim.** COF in tablet, R. Facing head (Medusa?), VE below. *M. —; V. 384; BMC 1506.(94A). (Formerly attributed to Tincommius)*........... 40 150
142 Head r. R. Horse r., VIRICO. *M. 116; V. 480; BMC —. (109)*......... 40 150
143 Pellet and ring pattern. R. Lion r. VIR. *M. 120a/c; V. 484; BMC 1514-17. (109)*......... 35 120
144 VIRIC reversed. R. Boar r. *M. —; V. 485; BMC 1518*......... 35 120
145 Cross. R. Trident. *M. —; V. 486-1; BMC —*......... 45 160
146 Uncertain. R. Boar r. *M. 120b; V. 510-1; BMC —. (109)*......... 30 110
147 Crescent cross. R. Boar r. *M. —; V. 510-5; BMC 1521-23. (109)*......... 40 135
148 VIR VAR in tablets. R. Winged horse r. CO. *M. 120d; V. 511; BMC 1507-12. (109)*......... 35 135

149 150

149 Vine-leaf, CFO. R. Horse r. VERI CA. *M. —; V. 550; BMC 1524-25*..... 35 135
150 CF in torc. R. Head r. VERIC. *M. 132; V. 551; BMC 1526-33. (111A)*... 30 125
151 Altar, CF, R. Bulls head facing, VERICA. *M. 120e; V. 552; BMC 1534-37. (109)*......... 45 165
152 Temple, CF. R. Bull r, VER REX. *M. —; V. 553; BMC 1538-41*......... 30 110

153 154

153 Cornucopia, VER COM. R. Lion r. *M. —; V. 554; BMC 1542*......... 35 135
154 Two cornucopiae. R. Eagle l. *M. —; V. 555; BMC 1543-58*......... 30 100
155 Floral pattern, CF. R. Lion r. *M.—; V. 556; BMC 1559-63. (111E)*......... 35 135
156 Sphinx r., CF, R. dog curled up, VERI. *M. —; V. 557; BMC 1564-68. (109B)*......... 30 120
157 VERI. R. Urn, COMMI F. *M. —; V. 559; BMC —*......... 40 150
158 A in star. R. Bird r. *M. 316; V. 561; BMC 1569-71*......... 45 160
159 Urn, Rex. R. Eagle r., VERRICA COMMI F. *M. —; V. 563; BMC 1572-78. (109C)*......... 30 110
160 VIR inside tablet. R. Boars head r. *M. 117; V. 564; BMC 1579-81. (109A)* 30 120
161 Cross. R. bull l. *M. —; V. —; BMC 1582*......... 35 140
162 Boars head r., CF, R. Eagle, VE. *M. —; V. —; BMC 1583-86*......... 30 110

163

163 Head r, COMM IF., R. Sphinx, R VE. *M. —; V. —; BMC 1587-89*........ 35 140

	F	VF
	£	£

164 A in tablet. Ṛ. Boar r. VI CO. *M.* —; *V.* —; *BMC 1590* 45 160
The two following coins are possibly issues of Epatticus.
165 Bull r. Ṛ. Eagle with snake l. *M.* —; *V. 512; BMC 2366-70* 35 140
166 Bust r. Ṛ. dog r. *M.* —; *V. 558; BMC 2371-74* 40 150

CANTII

The Cantii, who gave their name to Kent, occupied a similar area to that of the modern county. Caesar considered this the most civilised part of Britain and the early production of potin units in Kent can be seen as indicative of this. A number of Kentish rulers for whom we have coins, appear to be dynasts from the two neighbouring kingdoms, who were involved in struggles to acquire territory. Eppillus (see Atrebates and Regni) produced coins specifically for circulation in Kent and like those of Cunobelin they circulated widely.

EARLY UNINSCRIBED
GOLD

167 **Stater.** Ly. Blank. Ṛ. Horse l. numerous ring ornaments in field.
M. 293; V. 142; BMC 2472. (34) 350 1200
168 Blank. Ṛ. Horse r. numerous ornaments in field. *M. 294; V. 157;*
BMC— (34) 350 1200

169

169 Lz. Blank. Ṛ. Horse l., box with cross hatching below. *M. 84, 292;*
V. 150, 144; BMC 2466-68. (35) 425 1350

170 171

170 **Quarter Stater.** Ly. Blank. Ṛ. Horse r., pentagram below. *M. 285;*
V. 163; BMC 2473-74. (45) 120 250
171 Blank. Ṛ. Horse r., 'V' shape above. *M. 284; V. 170; BMC 2475-77. (45)* 120 240
172 Lz. Blank. Ṛ. Horse l., 'V' shape above. *M. 85; V. 151; BMC 2469-70. (47)* 120 250

SILVER

173 **Unit.** Curved star. Ṛ. Horse r. Pentagram below. *M. 272a; V. 164;*
BMC—. (56) 135 425
174 Serpent torc. Ṛ. Horse r., box with cross hatching below. *cf Mossop 8;*
BMC 2478 .... 165 600
175 **Half Unit.** Spiral of three arms. Ṛ. Horse l. *M.* —; *V.* —; *BMC 2479*...... 65 275

BRONZE

		F £	VF £
176	**Unit.** Various animal types, R. Various animal types. *M. 295-96, 316a-d; V. 154/167; BMC 2480-91. (80/141-44)*	50	225

DUBNOVELLAUNUS

(Late 1st Century B.C.)

Likely to be the same Dubnovellaunus recorded on coins in Essex (see Trinovantes / Catuvellauni). The two coinages share the same denominational structure and have some stylistic similarities. It has been suggested that Dubnovellaunus is the British king of that name mentioned along with Tincommius as a client king in the Res Gestae of the Roman emperor Augustus.

GOLD

177

177	**Stater.** Blank. R. Horse r., bucranium above, serpent like object below, DUBNOV[ELLAUNUS] or similar around. *M. 282; V. 169; BMC 2492-96. (118)*	250	600
178	— R. Horse r., but without bucranium and with wheel below. *M. 283; V. 176; BMC 2497-98. (118)*	300	875

SILVER

179	**Unit.** Winged animal r. R. Horse l., DVBNO. *M. 286; V. 171; BMC 2499-2501. (119)*	125	350

180

180	Winged animal l. R. Seated fig. l., holding hammer, DVBNO. *M. 287; V. 178; BMC 2502-03. (119)*	135	450

BRONZE

181	**Unit.** Horse r. R. Lion l., DVBN. *M. 290; V. 166; BMC 2504-06. (122).*	75	300
182	Boar l., DVBNO. R. Horseman r. *M. 291; V. 181; BMC 2507-08. (121).*	75	300
183	Boar r., DVBNO. R. Eagle facing. *M. 289; V. 180; BMC 2509-10. (121)*	70	275

VOSENOS
(Late 1st Century B.C./ Early 1st Century A.D.)
Little is known of this ruler who issued coins in a characteristically Kentish style similar to those of Dubnovellaunus.

GOLD

	F £	VF £
184 **Stater.** Blank. R. Horse l., bucranium above, serpent like object below., [VOSE]NOS. *M. 297; V. 184; BMC 2511-12. (123)*	1350	3750

185

185 **Quarter Stater.** Blank. R. Horse r., VOSI below. *M. 298; V. 185; BMC 2514-15. (124)*	425	1250

SILVER

186 **Unit.** Horse and griffin. R. Horse r., retrograde legend. *M. 299a; V. 186; BMC —. (125)*	175	600

"SA" or "SAM"
(Late 1st Century B.C./ Early 1st Century A.D.)
An historically unattested individual whose coins are stylistically associated with those of Dubnovellaunus and Vosenos. His coins have been predominantly found in north Kent

SILVER

187 **Unit.** Head l., R. Horse l., SA below. *M. —; V. —; BMC —*	200	700

BRONZE

187A **Unit.** Boar l., R. Horse l., SA below. *M. 299; V. 187; BMC 2516-19. (126)*	110	400

187B

187B Horse l., SAM below. R. Horse l., SAM below. *M. —; V. —; BMC —* ...	125	425

AMMINUS
(Early 1st Century A.D.)
Issued a coinage stylistically distinct from other Kentish types and with strong affinities to those of Cunobelin. Indeed it has been suggested that he is the Adminius recorded by Suetonius, as a son of Cunobelin. The enigmatic legend DVN or DVNO may be an unknown mint site.

SILVER

188

	F £	VF £
188 Unit. Plant, AMMINUS around. R. Winged horse r., DVN. *M. 313; V. 192; BMC 2522-23. (136)*	100	375

189

| 189 (Last year 190). A in wreath. R. Capricorn r., S AM. *M. 314; V. 194; BMC 2520-21. (137)* | 85 | 350 |

BRONZE

190

| 190 (Last year 189). AM in wreath. R. Horse r., DVNO. *M. —; V. 193; BMC* —— | 100 | 375 |
| 191 **Unit.** Head r. R. Hippocamp r., AM. *M. 315; V. 195; BMC 2524. (139).* | 85 | 375 |

TRINOVANTES AND CATUVELLAUNI

Occupying the broad area of Essex, southern Suffolk, Bedfordshire, Buckinghamshire, Hertfordshire, parts of Oxfordshire, Cambridgeshire and Northamptonshire, they are likely to have been two separate tribes for most of their history. The Trinovantes were originally located in the eastern half of this area, with their main centre at Camulodunum (Colchester). The original Catuvellauni heartland was further west, with their main centre at Verulamium (St.Albans). The whole area eventually came under the control of Cunobelin at the end of the period.

TRINOVANTES

ADDEDOMAROS
(Late 1st Century B.C.)

Unknown to history, he appears to have been a contemporary of Tasciovanus. The design of his staters is based on the Whaddon Chase type (No.32) which circulated widely in this region.

GOLD

200

		F £	VF £

200   **Stater.** Crossed wreath. R. Horse r., wheel below, AθθDIIDOM above. *M. 266; V. 1605; BMC 2390-94. (148)* 275   625

201   202

201   Six armed spiral. R. Horse r., cornucopia below, AθθDIIDOM above. *M. 267; V. 1620; BMC 2396-2404. (148)* 225   500

202   Two opposed crescents. R. Horse r., branch below, spiral or wheel above, AθθDIIDOM. *M. 268; V. 1635; BMC 2405-2415. (149)* 275   675

203   **Quarter Stater.** Circular flower pattern. R. Horse r. *M. 271; V. 1608; BMC 2416. (44)* 135   350

204   Cross shaped flower pattern. R. Horse r. *M. 270; V. 1623; BMC 2417-21. (44)* 125   275

205   Two opposed crescents. R. Horse r., AθθDIIDOM around. *M. 269; V. 1638; BMC 2422-24. (150)* 165   475

BRONZE

206   **Unit.** Head l. R. Horse l. *M. 274; V. 1615/46 BMC 2450-60. (77)* 35   120

DUBNOVELLAUNUS

(Late 1st Century B.C./ Early 1st Century A.D.)

Dubnovellaunus is likely to have been the successor to Addedomaros, with whom his coins are stylistically related. It is not clear if he was the same Dubnovellaunus who also issued coins in Kent (see Cantii) or if he is the same Dumnobeallaunos mentioned in the Res Gestae of the emperor Augustus c.AD14.

GOLD

207   208

		F	VF
		£	£
207	**Stater.** Two crescents on wreath. R. Horse l., leaf below, pellet in ring, DVBNOVAIIAVNOS above. *M. 275; V. 1650; BMC 2425-40. (152)*....	300	825
208	**Quarter Stater.** Similar. *M. 276; V. 1660; BMC 2442. (153)*................	135	325

SILVER

209	Unit. Head l., DVBNO. R. Winged horse r., lattice box below. *M. 288; V. 165; BMC 2443-44. (120)*......................................	135	425
210	Head l., legend ?, R. Horse l. DVB[NOV]. *M. 278; V. 1667; BMC 2445. (154)*..	110	325

BRONZE

211	**Unit.** Head l., R. Horse l., DVBNO above. *M. 281; V. 1669; BMC 2446-48. (154)*..	60	200
212	Head r., R. Horse l. *M. 277; V. 1665; BMC 2461-65. (154)*..................	50	175

DIRAS

(Late 1st Century B.C./ Early 1st Century A.D.)

An historically unattested ruler, responsible for a gold stater related stylistically to Dubnovellaunus's.

GOLD

213	**Stater.** Blank. R. Horse r., DIRAS? above, yoke like object above. *M. 279; V. 162; BMC 2449. (151)*...	1350	3750

CATUVELLAUNI

TASCIOVANUS
(Late 1st Century B.C./ Early 1st Century A.D.)

The early gold coins of Tasciovanus, like those of his contemporary Addedomaros, are based on the Whaddon Chase stater. Verulamium (St.Albans) appears to have been his principal mint, appearing as VER or VERL on the coinage. Staters and quarter staters inscribed CAM (Camulodunum/Colchester) are known and perhaps suggest brief or weak control of the territory to the east. The later coins of Tasciovanus use increasingly Romanised designs. The adoption of the title RICON, perhaps a Celtic equivalent to the Latin REX (King), can be seen as a parallel move to that of his contemporary Tincommius to the south.

GOLD

214   217

		F	VF
		£	£
214	**Stater.** Crescents in wreath. R. TASCIAV and bucranium over horse r. M. 149; V. 1680; BMC 1591-1603. (157)	350	1000
215	— R. Similar reads TAXCIAV. M. 150; V. 1682; BMC 1604-05. (157).	375	1100
216	— R. Similar reads TASCIOVAN above, CAM below. M. 186/a; V. 1684; BMC 1606-07. (160)	625	1750
217	— R. Horseman r. helmeted and with carnyx, TASC in field. M. 154-55/57; V. 1730-32; BMC 1608-1613. (158)	300	850
218	Crescents in wreath, with V or VER in design. R. Similar to last. M. 156-57; V. 1734-35; BMC 1623-24. (158)	350	1000

219   221

219	TASCIO(V) RICON in panel. R. Horseman l., wearing armour and holding sword and shield. M. 184; V. 1780; BMC 1628-36. (161)	550	1400
220	**Quarter Stater.** Floral design. R. Horse r. M. —; V. —; BMC 1638-39.	175	475
221	Crossed Wreath. R. Horse l. M. 151; V. 1688; BMC 1651-53. (44)	110	250
222	— R. Horse r., CAM. M. 187; V. 1694; BMC 1640. (164)	135	375
223	Similar, TASCI in wreath. R. Horse r., TASC. M. 153; V. 1692; BMC 1641. (163)	110	250

224 226

		F £	VF £
224	Similar, VERO in wreath. R. Horse l., TAS. *M. 152; V. 1690; BMC 1642-43. (163)*	100	250
225	TASCIO on tablet. R. Horse l. *M. 195; V. 1848; BMC 1646. (166)*	150	450
226	TASC on tablet. R. Horse l. *M. 185; V. 1786; BMC 1647-50. (165)*	100	235

SILVER

		F £	VF £
227	**Unit.** Head l. R. Horse r. *M. —; V. 1698; BMC 1654*	65	200
228	Cross and box. R. Horse r., VER in front. *M. —; V. —; BMC 1655*	65	225
229	Cross and crescent. R. Horse l., TASCI. *M. —; V. —; BMC 1665-57*	65	200
230	Bearded head l. R. Horseman r., TASCIO. *M. 158; V. 1745; BMC 1667-68. (167)*	75	300
231	Winged horse l., TAS. R. Griffin r., within circle of pellets. *M. 159; V. 1790; BMC 1660. (168)*	70	250
232	Eagle stg. l., TASCIΛ. R. Griffin r. *M. 160; V. 1792; BMC 1658-59. (169)*	75	300
233	VER in beaded circle. R. Horse r., TASCIA. *M. 161; V. 1699; BMC 1670-73. (170)*	70	275
234	— R. Naked horseman. *M. 162; V. 1747; BMC 1674-76. (171)*	70	275

235 238 242

		F £	VF £
235	Laureate hd. r., TASCIA. R. Bull l. *M. 163; V. 1794; BMC 1681-82. (172)*	70	250
236	Cross and box, VERL. R. Boar r. TAS. *M. 164; V. 1796; BMC 1661-62. (173)*	75	275
237	TASC in panel. R. Winged horse l. *M. 165; V. 1798; BMC 1664-65. (174)*	65	200
238	— R. Horseman l., carrying long shield. *M. 166; V. 1800; BMC 1677-79. (174)*	60	185
239	Two crescents. R. Winged griffin, VIR. *M. —; V. —; BMC 1666*	90	325
240	Head r., TAS?. R. Horseman r. *M. —; V. —; BMC 1669*	80	300

BRONZE

241

		F £	VF £
241	**Double Unit.** Head r., TASCIA, VA. R. Horseman r. *M. 178; V. 1818; BMC 1685-87. (190)*	175	575

		F	VF
		£	£
242	**Unit.** Two heads in profile, one bearded. R. Ram l., TASC. *M. 167; V. 1705; BMC 1711-13. (178)*	50	200
243	Bearded head r. VER(L). R. Horse l., VIIR or VER. *M. 168; V. 1707; BMC 1714-21. (179)*	45	185
244	Bearded head r. R. Horse l., TAS. *M. 169; V. 1709; BMC 1722-23. (179)*	50	200
245	Head r., TASC. R. Winged horse l., VER. *M. 170; V. 1711; BMC 1688-89. (180)*	45	185
246	— R. Horseman r., holding carnyx, VIR. *M. 171; V. 1750; BMC 1724-27. (182)*	45	185

247

247	VERLAMIO between rays of star. R. Bull l. *M. 172; V. 1808; BMC 1745-51. (183)*	40	175
248	Similar without legend. R. Bull r. *M. 174; V. 1810; BMC 1752-55. (185)*	50	200
249	Similar. R. Horse l., TASCI. *M. 175; V. 1812; BMC 1709-10. (186)*	50	200
250	Head r., TASCIO. R. Lion r., TA SCI. *M. 176; V. 1814; BMC 1736-38. (188)*	40	175
251	Head r. R. Figure std. l., VER below. *M. 177; V. 1816; BMC 1739-44. (189)*	50	200
252	Cross and Crescents. R. Boar r., VER. *M. 179; V. 1713; BMC 1702-05. (191)*	45	185
253	Laureate head r. R. Horse l., VIR. *M. 180; V. 1820; BMC 1706-08. (192)*	45	185
254	Raised band across centre, VER or VERL below. R. Horse grazing r. *M. 183a; V. 1717; BMC —. (193)*	75	275
255	**Fractional Unit.** Animal r. R. Sphinx l. *M. 181; V. 1824; BMC 1760-61. (198)*	40	175
256	Head l., VER. R. Goat r. *M. 182; V. 1715; BMC 1765-68. (199)*	30	135
257	Head r. R. Boar r, *M. 183; V. 1826; BMC 1762-64. (199)*	30	135
258	Head l. R. Animal with curved tail. *M. 183b, c; V. 1822; BMC 1759. (200)*	35	150

ASSOCIATES OF TASCIOVANUS
(Early 1st Century A.D.)

Towards the end of his reign, a number of joint issues bearing his name and the name of either Sego or Dias appear. In addition coins similar in style to those of Tasciovanus appear with either the name Andoco or Rues. It has been suggested that these issues belong to a period of struggle following the death of Tasciovanus and are all rival contestants for the throne. Another theory is that they are associates or sub-kings of Tasciovanus responsible for areas within the wider territory.

SEGO

GOLD

259

		F £	VF £
259	**Stater.** TASCIO in tablet, annulets above. R. Horseman with carnyx r., SEGO. *M. 194; V. 1845; BMC 1625-27. (162)*	1350	3500

SILVER

260

260	**Unit.** SEGO on panel. R. Horseman r. *M. 196; V. 1851; BMC 1684. (176)*	325	875

BRONZE

261	**Unit.** Star shaped pattern. R. Winged sphinx l., SEGO. *M. 173; V. 1855; BMC 1690. (184)*...	150	475

ANDOCO

GOLD

262

262	**Stater.** Crescents in wreath. R. Bucranium over horse r., AND below. *M. 197; V. 1860; BMC 2011-14. (202)*.......................................	450	1250

		F £	VF £

263 **Quarter Stater.** Crossed wreaths, ANDO in angles. R. Horse l. *M. 198; V. 1863; BMC 2015-17. (203)* 125 350

SILVER

264

264 **Unit.** Bearded head l. R. Winged horse l., ANDOC. *M. 199; V. 1868; BMC 2018. (204)* 125 375

BRONZE

265

265 **Unit.** Head r., ANDOCO. R. Horse r., ANDOCO. *M. 200; V. 1871; BMC 2019-20. (205)* 65 235

266 Head r., TAS ANDO. R. Horse r. *M. 175a; V. 1873; BMC —. (187)* 85 325

DIAS
SILVER

267   268

267 **Unit.** Saltire over cross within square. R. Boar r., TASC DIAS. *M. —; V. —; BMC 1663. (173A)* 125 350

268 DIAS CO, in star. R. Horse l., VIR. *M. 188; V. 1877; BMC 1683. (177)*. 125 375

BRONZE

269

269 **Unit.** Bearded head r., DIAS TASC. R. Centaur r., playing pan pipes. *M. 192; V. 1882; BMC 1728-35. (197)* 100 400

RUES
BRONZE

		F	VF
		£	£
270	**Unit.** Lion r., RVII. ℞. Eagle. *M. 189; V. 1890; BMC 1691. (194)*.........	75	325
271	— ℞. Similar reads RVE. *M. 189; V. 1890-3; BMC 1692. (194)*............	70	300

272   273

272	Bearded head r., RVIIS. ℞. Horseman r., VIR. *M. 190; V. 1892;* *BMC 1698-1701. (195)*...............	75	325
273	RVIIS on tablet. ℞. Winged sphinx l. *M. 191; V. 1895;* *BMC 1693-97. (196)*...............	75	325
274	**Fractional Unit.** Annulet within square with curved sides. ℞. Eagle l., RVII. *M. 193; V. 1903; BMC 1756-58. (201)*...............	65	275

CUNOBELIN
(Early 1st Century A.D. to *c.*40 A.D.)

Styled as son of Tasciovanus on some of his coins, Cunobelin appears to have ruled over the unified territories of the Trinovantes and Catuvellauni, with additional territory in Kent. His aggressive policy of expansion that involved members of family eventually lead to Roman concern over the extent of his power. Following his death just prior to 43 AD, the emperor Claudius took the decision to invade Britain.

During his long reign an extensive issue of gold, silver and bronze coins used ever increasingly Romanised designs. It has been estimated from a study of known dies that around one million of his gold corn ear staters were produced. His main centre and mint was at Camulodunum (Colchester) appearing as the mint signature CAMV. The names SOLIDV and AGR appear on a few coins associated with Cunobelin and are likely to represent personal names.

GOLD

280   281

280	**Stater.** Biga type. CAMVL on panel. ℞. Two horses l., wheel below, CVNOBELIN. *M. 201; V. 1910; BMC 1769-71. (207)*...............	650	1800
281	Linear type. Corn ear dividing CA MV. ℞. Horse r., branch above, CVN. *M. 210; V. 1925; BMC 1772-76. (208)*	240	550
282	— Similar, privy mark 'x' above a letter in *obv.* legend. *M. 210a;* *VA 1925-3/5; BMC 1777-81. (208)*...............	300	850

283   285

		F £	VF £
283	Wild type. Corn ear dividing CA MV. R. Horse r., branch above., CVN(O). *M. 211/2; V. 1931/33; BMC 1784-92/1804-08. (208)*	275	500
284	— Similar, heart shaped object between horses forelegs. *M. 211 var; V. 1931-3; BMC 1793. (208)*	325	900
285	— Similar, privy mark pellet or pellet triangle above a letter(s) in *obv.* legend. *M. —; V. 1931-5/7/9; BMC 1797-1803. (208)*	275	650

286   288

286	Plastic type. Corn ear dividing CA MV. R. Horse r., branch above., CVNO. *M. 203/13; V. 2010-1/3/5; BMC 1809-11/15-23. (208)*	250	550
287	— Similar, 'B' in front of horse. *M. —; V. 2010-7; BMC 1813. (208)*	325	875

289   290

288	Classic type. Corn ear dividing CA MV. R. Horse r., branch above., CVNO. *M. 206-07; V. 2025/27; BMC 1827-31/33. (208)*	275	675
289	— Similar, horse l., lis like object above. *M. 208; V. 2029; BMC 1834-35. (209)*	475	1250
290	**Quarter Stater.** Biga type. Similar to 280. *M. 202; V. 1913; BMC 1836/A. (210)*	200	475

292   296

292	Linear type. Similar to 281. *M. 209; V. 1927; BMC 1837-42. (211)*	125	300
293	Wild type. Similar to 283. *M. —; V. 1935; BMC 1843-44. (211)*	125	275
294	Plastic type. Similar to 286. *M. 204; V. 2015; BMC 1846-48. (211)*	110	250
295	— Similar but corn ear dividing CAM CVN. *M. 205; V. 2017; BMC 1845. (212)*	125	300
296	Classic type. Similar to 288. *M. —; V. 2038; BMC —. (211)*	175	450

SILVER

299

		F	VF
		£	f
299	**Unit.** Two bull headed serpents, inter twined. R̟. Horse l., CVNO. *M. 214; V. 1947; BMC 1856. (213)*	125	450
300	Curled serpent inside wheel. R̟. Winged horse l., CVN. *M. —; V. —; BMC 1857*	125	450
301	CVN on panel R̟. Horse l., (C)M. *M. 255; V. 1949; BMC 1858-59. (228)*	75	250
302	CVNO BELI on two panels. R̟. CVN below horseman r. *M. 216/7; V. 1951/53; BMC 1862. (215)*	85	275
303	Head l., CAMVL. R̟. CVNO beneath Victory std. r. *M. 215; V. 2045; BMV 1863-65. (214)*	85	300

304   305

304	Two leaves dividing CVN. R̟. Horseman r., CAM. *M. 218; V. 2047; BMC 1866-67. (216)*	100	350
305	Flower dividing CAMV. R̟. CVNO below horse r. *M. 219; V. 2049; BMC1867A. (217)*	100	375
306	CVNO on panel. R̟. CAMV on panel below griffin. *M. 234; V. 2051; BMC 1868-69. (218)*	95	350
307	CAMVL on panel. R̟. CVNO below centaur l. carrying palm. *M. 234a; V. 1918; BMC —. (219)*	110	400
308	CAMVL on panel. R̟. Figure seated l. holding wine amphora, CVNOBE. *M. —; V. —; BMC —. (219A)*	75	250
309	Plant, CVNOBELINVS. R̟. Figure stg. r. holding club and thunderbolt dividing CA MV. *M. —; V .—; BMC 1897. (219B)*	110	425
310	Laur. hd. r., CVNOBELINVS. R̟. Winged horse springing l., CAMV below. *M. —; V. —; BMC —. (219C)*	100	375
311	CVNO on panel, wreath around. R̟. Winged horse r., TASC F. *M. 235; V. 2053; BMC 1870. (220)*	100	375

312   313

312	Head r., CVNOBELINI. R̟. Horse r., TASCIO. *M. 236; V. 2055; BMC 1871-73. (221)*	75	250
313	Winged bust r., CVNO. R̟. Sphinx std. l., TASCIO. *M. 237; V. 2057; BMC 1874-78. (222)*	55	180

314 316

	F £	VF £
314 Draped female fig. r., TASCIIOVAN. R. Figure std. r. playing lyre, tree behind. *M. 238; V. 2059; BMC 1879-82. (223)*	80	275
315 Figure stg. l., holding club and lionskin., CVNO. R. Female rider r., TASCIOVA. *M. 239; V. 2061; BMC 1884-85. (224)*	80	275
316 Female head r., CVNOBELINVS. R. Victory r., TASCIO(VAN). *M. —; V. —; BMC 1883. (224A)*	80	275
317 Fig. r. carrying dead animal, CVNOBELINVS. R. Fig. stg. holding bow, dog at side, TASCIIOVANI. *M. 240; V. 2063; BMC 1886-88. (225)*	80	275
318 CVNO on panel, horn above, dolphin below. R. Fig. stg. r. altar behind. *M. 241/41a; V. 2065; BMC 1889-90. (226)*	95	350

319

319 CVN on panel. R. Fig. holding club walking r., CVN. *M. 254; V. 2067; BMC 1891-92. (227)*	90	325
320 CVN in wreath. R. CAM, dog? trampling on serpent r. *M. 256; V. 2069; BMC 1893. (229)*	120	425
321 Winged horse l., CVN. R. Std. fig. r. *M. 258; V. 2071; BMC 1896. (230)*	95	350
322 CVNO in angles of cross. R. Capricorn r., CVNO. *M. —; V. —; BMC 1898*	95	350

BRONZE

323 Head l., CVNO. R. Boar l., branch above. *M. 220; V. 1969; BMC—. (232)*	60	225
324 CVNOB ELINI in two panels. R. Victory std. l., TASC. *M. 221; V. 1971; BMC 1921-27. (233)*	45	165
325 Winged horse l., CAM. R. Winged Victory stg l., CVN. *M. 222; V. 1973; BMC 1938-43. (234)*	45	175

326

326 Bearded head facing R. Boar l., CVN. *M.223; V.1963; BMC 1904-05. (235)*	45	185
327 Ram-headed animal coiled up in double ornamental circle. R. Animal l., CAM. *M. 224; V. 1965; BMC —. (236)*	50	200
328 Griffin r., CAMV. R. Horse r., CVN. *M. 225; V. 2081; BMC 1909-12. (237)*	45	175

		F	VF
		£	£
329	Bearded head l., CAMV. R. CVN or CVNO below horse l. *M. 226, 229; V. 2085/2131; BMC 1900-01. (238)*	40	165
330	Laureate head r., CVNO. R. CVN below bull butting l. *M. 227; V. 2083; BMC 1902-03. (239)*	50	200
331	Crude head r., CVN R. Figure stg. l., CVN. *M. 228; V. 2135; BMC —. (240)*	55	225

332

332	CAMVL / ODVNO in two panels. R. CVNO beneath sphinx crouching l. *M. 230; V. 1977; BMC 1928-30. (241)*	45	175
333	Winged horse l., CAMV. R. Victory stg. r. divides CV NO. *M. 231; V. 1979; BMC 1931-34. (242)*	45	175
334	Victory walking r. R. CVN below, horseman r. *M. 232; V. 1981; BMC 1935. (243)*	55	225
335	Head l., CAM. R. CVNO below eagle. *M. 233; V. 2087; BMC —. (244)*	55	225

336   337

336	Head l., CVNOBELINI. R. Centaur r., TASCIOVANI.F. *M. 242; V. 2089; BMC 1968-71. (245)*	40	150
337	Helmeted bust r. R. TASCIIOVANII above, sow stg. r., F below. *M. 243; V. 2091; BMC 1956-60. (246)*	40	150
338	Horseman galloping r. holding dart and shield, CVNOB. R. Warrior stg. l., TASCIIOVANTIS. *M. 244; V. 2093; BMC 1961-67. (247)*	40	140

339

339	Helmeted bust l., CVOBELINVS REX. R. TASC FIL below boar l., std. on haunches. *M. 245; V. 1983; BMC 1952-55. (248)*	50	200
340	Bare head r., CVNOBELINVS REX. R. TASC below bull butting r. *M. 246; V. 2095; BMC 1944-51. (249)*	40	160
341	Bare head l., CVNO. R. TASC below bull stg. r. *M. 247; V. 1985; BMC —. (250)*	50	200

342 343

	F £	VF £

342 Head l., CVNOBELIN. R̸. Metal worker std. r. holding hammer, working
on a vase, TASCIO. *M. 248; V. 2097; BMC 1972-83. (251)* 45 185

343 Winged horse r., CVNO. R̸. Victory r. sacrificing bull, TASCI. *M. 249;
V. 2099; BMC 1913-19. (252)* 35 125

344 CVNO on panel within wreath. R̸. CAMV below horse, prancing r.
M. 250; V. 2101; BMC 1987-90. (253).. 45 175

345 346

345 Bearded head of Jupiter Ammon l., CVNOBELIN. R̸. CAM below
horseman galloping r. *M. 251; V. 2103; BMC 1984-86. (254)*................. 45 175

346 Janus head, CVNO below. R̸. CAMV on panel below, sow std. r.
beneath a tree. *M. 252; V. 2105; BMC 1998-2003. (255)*......................... 45 175

347

347 Bearded head of Jupiter Ammon r., CVNOB. R̸. CAM on panel below
lion crouched r. *M. 253; V. 2107; BMC 1991-97. (256)*........................... 40 165

348 Sphinx r., CVNO. R̸. Fig stg. l. divides CA M. *M. 260; V. 2109;
BMC 2004-09. (257)* 45 175

349 Horse r. R̸. CVN below horseman r. *M. 261; V. 1987; BMC 1936-47. (258)* 50 200

350 Animal l. looking back. R̸. CVN below horse l. *M. 233a; V. 1967;
BMC— . (259)*.. 50 200

350A Ship, CVN below. R̸. Fig. r. dividing S E. *M. —; V. 1989; BMC 2010.* .. 135 650

"SOLIDV"

SILVER

351

	F	VF
	£	£

351   **Unit.** SOLIDV in centre of looped circle. R, Stg. fig. l., CVNO.
M. 259; V. 2073; BMC 1894-95. (231).. | 325 | 1000

"AGR"

GOLD

352   Quarter Stater. Corn ear dividing CAM CVN. R. Horse r., branch
above., AGR below M. —; V. —; BMC 1854... | 350 | 975

353

353   — R. Horse r., branch above., cross and A below. M. —; V. —;
BMC 1855 .... | 350 | 950

SILVER

354   **Unit.** AGR inside wreath. R. Female dog r., AGR below. M. —; V. —;
BMC 1899 .... | 300 | 875

EPATICCUS
(1st Half 1st Century A.D.)

Epaticcus, styled as a son of Tasciovanus on his coins, was most probably a brother of Cunobelin. The corn ear employed on his staters is similar to that of his brother's produced at Colchester. His coins appear in northern Atrebatic territory and conform to the area's denominational structure. It seems likely that Epaticcus's coinage reflects an incursion into Atrebatic territory by the Trinovantian/Catuvellaunian dynasty.

GOLD

355

355   **Stater.** Corn ear dividing TAS CIF. R. Horseman r., with spear and
shield. EPATI. M. 262; V. 575; BMC 2021-23. (112).............................. | 675 | 1900

SILVER

356   357

	F £	VF £
356 **Unit.** Head of Hercules r., EPAT(I). Ŗ. Eagle stg. on snake. M. 263/a; V. 580; BMC 2024-2268/2270-76. (113)	30	90
357 Victory seated r. TASCIOV. Ŗ. Boar r., EPAT. M. 263; V. 581; BMC 2294-2328. (114)	35	135

358

358 Bearded head l., TASCIO. Ŗ. EPATI below lion r. M. —; V. 582; BMC 2329	125	375
359 EPATI inside panel. Ŗ. Lion r. M. —; V. 583; BMC 2330. (114A)	110	350

360   361

360 **Minim.** EPATI. Ŗ. Boars head r., TA. M. 264; V. 585; BMC 2331-46. (115)	35	110
361 TA inside star. Ŗ. Winged horse r., EPA below. M. —; V. 560; BMC 2351-57. (116)	30	100
362 Helmeted head r. Ŗ. Horse r., E below. M. —; V. —; BMC 2358-63	35	130
363 EPATI. Ŗ. Winged horse r., cross below. M. —; V .—; BMC 2365	45	175

CARATACUS
(1st Half 1st Century A.D.)

Coins inscribed CARA have been traditionally associated with the historically attested son of Cunobelin, Caratacus the leader of British resistance against Rome. His coins appear in the same area as those of Epaticcus and he may have been his successor.

SILVER

364   364A

364 **Unit.** Head of Hercules r., CARA. Ŗ. Eagle stg. on snake. M. 265; V. 593; BMC 2376-84. (117)	90	300
364A **Minim.** CARA around pellet in ring. Ŗ. Winged horse r. M. —; V. 595; BMC 2385-89. (117A)	75	200

DUROTRIGES

(Mid 1st Century B.C. to Mid 1st Century A.D.)

The Durotriges inhabited West Hampshire, Dorset and adjoining parts of Somerset and Wiltshire. Their coinage is one of the most distinctive in Britain due to its rapid debasement. The disappearance of precious metals from the coinage should perhaps be linked to the declining trade between the south-west and western Gaul, following the Roman conquest of the Gaul. Hengistbury Head is the probable mint site of the cast bronzes. Coins inscribed CRAB have been traditionally associated with the tribe.

UNINSCRIBED

SILVER

		F £	VF £
365	**Stater.** White Gold type. Derived from Westerham stater (no. 21). *M. 317; V. 1235, 52, 54, 55; BMC 2525-2731. (60)*	95	300

366   368

366	Silver type. Similar. *M. 317; V. 1235, 52, 54, 55; BMC 2525-2731. (60)*	35	110
367	Billon type. Similar. *M. 317; V. 1235, 52, 54, 55; BMC 2525-2731. (60)*	25	75
368	**Quarter Stater.** Geometric type. Crescent design. ℞. Zig-zag pattern. *M. 319; V. 1242/29; BMC 2734-79. (61). Quality of metal varies, obv. almost blank on later issues*	30	90

369

369	Starfish type. Spiral. ℞. Zig-zag pattern. *M. 320; V. 1270; BMC 2780-81 (61A)*	45	185
	Hampshire Thin Flan type. Crude head of lines and pellets. ℞. Stylised horse l. *M. 321; V. 1280; BMC 2782-87. (62)*	55	200

BRONZE

371	**Stater.** Struck Bronze type. Similar to No.365-67. *M. 318; V. 1290; BMC 2790-2859. (81)*	20	50

372

	F £	VF £
372 Cast Bronze type. Many varities, as illustration. *M. 322-70; V. 1322-70; BMC 2860-2936. (82)*	35	125

"CRAB"

SILVER

373

373 **Unit.** CRAB in angles of cross. Ŗ. Eagle. *M. 371; V. 1285; BMC 2788. (145)*	275	850
373A **Minim.** CRAB on tablet. Ŗ. Star shape. *M. 372; V. 1286; BMC 2789. (146)*	150	500

DOBUNNI
(Mid 1st Century B.C. to Mid 1st Century A.D.)

Dobunnic territory stretched over Gloucestershire, Hereford and Worcester and into parts of Somerset, Wiltshire and Gwent. The earliest Dobunnic coins are developed from the British Q stater, and have the distinctive tree-like motif of the tribe on the obverse. The inscribed coinage is difficult to arrange chronologically and it may be that some of the rulers named held different parts of the territory simultaneously.

UNINSCRIBED
GOLD

374 **Stater.** Plain except for tree-like object. Ŗ. Three tailed horse r., wheel below. *M. 374; V. 1005; BMC 2937-40. (43)*	275	825
375 **Quarter Stater.** Plain with traces of wreath pattern. Ŗ. Horse r. *M. 68; V. 1010-3; BMC 2942-46. (52)*	150	325
376 Wreath pattern. Ŗ. Horse l., pellet in ring motifs in field. *M. 74; V. 1015; BMC 2949. (51)*	100	350

SILVER

377 378

		F £	VF £
377	**Unit.** Allen types A-F/I-J. Regular series. Head r. R. Triple-tailed horse l. or r. *M. 374a, b/75/76, 378a-384; V. 1020/45/49/74/78/95/1135/1137; BMC 2950-3011. (63-64). Style becomes progressively more abstract, from-*	25	90
378	Allen types L-O. Irregular series. Similar to last. *M. 377-384d; V. 1170-85; BMC 3012-22. (63-64)*	35	135

INSCRIBED
The following types are not arranged chronologically.

ANTED
GOLD

379	**Stater.** Dobunnic emblem, R. ANTED or ANTEDRIG over triple tailed horse r., wheel below. *M. 385-86; V. 1062-69; BMC 3023-3031. (260)*	425	1100

SILVER

380	**Unit.** Crude head r. R. ANTED over horse. *M. 387; V. 1082; BMC 3032-38. (261)*	50	150

EISV
GOLD

381

381	**Stater.** Dobunnic emblem. R. EISV or EISVRIG over triple tailed horse r., wheel below. *M. 388; V. 1105; BMC 3039-42. (262)*	475	1350

SILVER

382

382	**Unit.** Crude head r. R. Horse l., EISV. *M. 389; V. 1110; BMC 3043-55. (263)*	45	135

INAM or INARA

GOLD

	F £	VF £
383 **Stater.** Dobunnic emblem. R̶. INAM or INARA over triple tailed horse r., wheel below. *M. 390; V. 1140; BMC 3056. (264)*......................	825	2650

CATTI

GOLD

384

384 **Stater.** Dobunnic emblem. R̶. CATTI over triple tailed horse r., wheel
below. *M. 391; V. 1130; BMC 3057-60. (265)* 350 1000

COMUX

GOLD

385 **Stater.** Dobunnic emblem. R̶. COMVX retrograde, over triple tailed
horse r., wheel below. *M. 392; V. 1092; BMC 3061-63. (266)* 750 2350

CORIO

GOLD

386 387

386 **Stater.** Dobunnic emblem. R̶. CORIO over triple tailed horse r., wheel
below. *M. 393; V. 1035; BMC 3064-3133. (267)* 350 1050
387 **Quarter Stater.** COR in centre. R̶. Horse r., without legend. *M. 394;*
V. 1039; BMC 3134. (268) 375 1000

BODVOC

GOLD

388 389

		F	VF
		£	£
388	**Stater.** BODVOC across field. R. Horse r., without legend. *M. 395; V. 1052; BMC 3135-42. (269)*	650	1800

SILVER

| 389 | **Unit.** Head l., BODVOC. R. Horse r., without legend. *M. 396; V. 1057; BMC 3143-45. (270)* .... | 125 | 375 |

CORIELTAUVI

The Corieltauvi, formerly known as the Coritani, occupied Lincolnshire and adjoining parts of Yorkshire, Northamptonshire, Leicestershire and Nottinghamshire. The earliest staters, the South Ferriby type, are developed from Gallo-Belgic C staters, and are associated with the silver Boar/Horse types. The distinctive dish shaped scyphate coinages have no parallels in Britain and stand apart from the main series. The later inscribed issues present a complex system of inscriptions. It has been suggested that some of the later inscriptions refer to pairs of names, possibly joint rulers or moneyers and rulers.

EARLY UNINSCRIBED
(Mid to Late 1st Century B.C.)

GOLD

390 393

390	**Stater.** South Ferriby type. Crude laureate head. R. Disjointed horse l., rosette or star below, anchor shape and pellets above. *M. 449-50; V. 809-815/19; BMC 3146-3179. (30)*	135	325
391	Wheel type. Similar, but wheel below horse. *M. 449c; V. 817; BMC 3180*	325	875
392	Kite type. Similar to 390, but diamond shape containing pellets above, spiral below horse. *M. 447; V. 825; BMC 3181-84. (29)*	200	525
393	Domino type. Similar to last, but with rectangle containing pellets. *M. 448; V. 829; BMC 3185-86. (29)*	185	475

394   395

		F £	VF £
394	Trefoil type. Trefoil with central rosette of seven pellets. R. Similar to 390. *M. 450a; V. 821; BMC —. (30A)*	1350	4500
395	North Lincolnshire Scyphate type. Stylised boar r. or l. R. Large S symbol with pellets and rings in field. *M. —; V. —; BMC 3187-93*	250	650

* *chipped or cracked specimens are often encountered and are worth less*

SILVER

396

		F £	VF £
396	**Unit.** Boar/Horse type I.Boar r., large pellet and ring motif above, reversed S below. R. Horse l. or r., pellet in ring above. *M. 405-06, 451; V. 855-60, 864, 867; BMC 3194-3214. (66)*	50	165
397	Boar Horse type II. Vestiges of boar on obv. R. Horse l. or r. *M. 410, 452-53; V. 875-877; BMC 3214-27. (68)*	35	110

398   399

		F £	VF £
398	Boar Horse type III. Blank. R. Horse l.or r. *M. 453-54; V. 884-77; BMC 3228-35. (69)*	30	90
399	**Fractional Unit.** Similar to 396-97. *M. 406a, 451a; V. 862/66; BMC 3236-3250. (67)*	35	100
400	Similar to 398. *M. —; V. 877-81; BMC 3251-55. (70/71)*	25	75
401	Pattern/Horse. Flower pattern. R. Horse l. *M. —; V. —; BMC 3256-57...*	60	225

INSCRIBED

(Early to Mid 1st Century A.D.)
The following types are not arranged chronologically.

AVN COST

GOLD

	F £	VF £
402 Stater. Crude wreath design. R. Disjointed horse l., AVN COST. *M. 457; V. 910; BMC 3258. (286)*	475	1350

SILVER

403

403 Unit. Remains of wreath or blank. R. AVN COST, horse l. *M. 458; V. 914; BMC 3261-66. (287)*	35	100
404 Fractional Unit. Similar. *M. —; l V. 918; BMC 3267-68. (288)*	35	90

ESVP RASV

GOLD

405 Stater. Crude wreath design. R. Disjointed horse l., IISVP RASV. *M. 456b; V. 920; BMC 3269. (289)*	375	975

SILVER

406 Unit. Similar. *M. 456c; V. 924; BMC 3272-73. (290)*	75	250

VEP

GOLD

407 Stater. Blank or with traces of wreath. R. Disjointed horse l., VEP. *M. —; V. 905; BMC 3274-75. (296)*	375	975

SILVER

408 Unit. Blank or with traces of wreath. R. VEP, horse r. *M. —; V. 963; BMC 3277-82. (297)*	45	150
409 Half Unit. Similar. *M. 464b; V. 967; BMC 3283-3295. (298)*	35	90

VEP CORF

GOLD

410

	F	VF
	£	£

410 **Stater.** Crude wreath design. R. Disjointed horse l., VEP CORF.
M. 459, 460; V. 930/40/60; BMC 3296-3304. (291).................................. 350 850

SILVER

411 **Unit.** Similar. *M. 460b/464; V. 934/50; BMC 3305-14. (292)* 35 120

412

412 Similar but VEPOC (M)ES, pellet in ring below horse. *M. —; V. 955;*
BMC —. (294) 50 175
413 **Half Unit.** Similar. *M. 464a; V. 938/58; BMC 3316-24. (293/95)*........... 35 100

DVMNO TIGIR SENO

GOLD

414

414 **Stater.** DVMN(OC) across wreath. R. Horse l., TIGIR SENO. *M. 461;*
V. 972; BMC 3325-27. (299) 525 1450

SILVER

415

415 **Unit.** DVMNOC in two lines. R. Horse r., TIGIR SENO. *M. 462;*
V. 974; BMC 3328-29. (300) 165 525

VOLISIOS DVMNOCOVEROS

GOLD

416

		F	VF
		£	£
416	**Stater.** VOLISIOS between three lines in wreath. R. Horse r. or l., DVMNOCOVEROS. *M. 463/a; V. 978-80; BMC 3330-3336. (301)*.......	350	950

SILVER

417	**Unit.** Similar. R. Horse r., DVMNOCO. *M. 463a; V. 980; BMC 3339. (302)*..................	175	575
418	**Half Unit.** Similar. *M. 465; V. 984; BMC 3340-41. (303)*......................	70	225

VOLISIOS DVMNOVELLAUNOS

GOLD

419	**Stater.** VOLISIOS between three lines in wreath. R. Horse r. or l., DVMNOVELAVNOS. *M. 466; V .988; BMC 3342-43. (304)*...............	675	2000

SILVER

420	**Half Unit.** As last but DVMNOVE. *M. 467; V. 992; BMC 3344-46. (305).*	135	425

VOLISIOS CARTIVEL

SILVER

421	**Half Unit.** VOLISIOS between three lines in wreath. R. Horse r., CARTILEV. *M. 468; V. 994; BMC 3347-48. (306)*.................................	225	675

IAT ISO E

SILVER

422	**Unit.** IAT ISO (retrograde)on tablet, rosettes above and below. R. Horse r., E above. *M. 416; V. 998; BMC 3349-51. (284)*......................	150	475

CAT

SILVER

422A	**Unit.** Boar r., pellet ring above, CAT above. R. Horse r. *M. —; V. —; BMC 3352*	250	700

LAT ISON

GOLD

423

	F	VF
	£	£

423   **Stater.** LAT ISO(N) in two lines retrograde. R. Horse r., ISO in box
above, N below. *M.* —; *V.* —; *BMC* —. *Only recorded as an AE/AV
plated core, as illustrated.* .... *Extremely rare*

ICENI

The Iceni, centered on Norfolk but also occupying neighbouring parts of Suffolk and
Cambridgeshire, are well attested in the post conquest period as the tribe who under Boudicca
revolted against Roman rule. Their earliest coins are likely to have been the British J staters, Norfolk
Wolf type (no.30/31), replaced around the mid first century B.C. by the Snettisham, Freckenham and
Irstead type gold staters and quarter staters. Contemporary with these are silver Boar/Horse and
Face/Horse units and fractions. The introduction of legends around the beginning of the millennia
led to the adoption of a new obverse design of back to back crescents. The continuation of the
coinage after the Roman invasion is attested by the coins of King Prasutagus. Some of the
Face/Horse units (no.434) have been attributed to Queen Boudicca.

EARLY UNINSCRIBED
(Mid to Late 1st Century B.C.)
GOLD

424   425

424   **Stater.** Snettisham type. Blank or with traces of pellet cross. R. Horse
r., serpent like pellet in ring motif above. *M.* —; *V.*—; *BMC 3353-59....*   300   850
425   Similar. Blank or with 3 short curved lines. R. Horse r., symbol above
more degraded. *M.* —; *V.* —; *BMC 3360-83*   275   700

426 427

		F £	VF £

426 Freckenham type. Two opposed crescents with stars or pellets in field.
R. Horse r., various symbols in field. *M. 397/99; V. 620;*
BMC 3384-89. (38) 250 600

427 Similar. Blank or with traces of pellet cross. R. Horse r., wheel or arch
containing pellets above. *M. 400; V. 624; BMC 3390-95. (40)* 275 675

428

428 Similar. Trefoil on cross design. R. Similar. *M. 401-03; V. 626;*
BMC 3396-3419. (39) 250 600

429 430

429 **Quarter Stater.** Snettisham type. Wreath cross. R. Horse r. *M. —;*
V. —; BMC 3420-35 .... 125 300

430 Irstead type. Hatched box, wreaths at sides. R. Horse r. *M. 404; V. 628;*
BMC 3436-39. (48) 100 190

SILVER

431 432

431 **Unit.** Boar / Horse type. Boar r. R. Horse r. *M. 407-09; V. 655-59;*
BMC 3440-3512. (72) 25 70

432 Bury type. Head l. or r. R. Horse l. or r. *M. —; V. —; BMC 3524-35* 75 220

433   433

		F £	VF £

433 Early Face / Horse type. Celticised head l. or r. R. Horse l. or r.
M. 412/413a-c/e; BMC 3536-3555. (74) 90 325

434   435

434 Face / Horse Regular type. Head r. R. Horse r. M. 413/d; V. 790-94;
BMC 3556-3759. (74). Attributed to Queen Boudicca by
R.D. van Arsdell 50 165

435 Early Pattern / Horse type. Cross of two opposed crescents. R. Horse
l. or r. M. 414-15; V. 675-79; BMC 3763-74. (75) 30 90

436

436 ECEN symbol type. Two opposed crescents. R. Horse r. M. 429;
V. 752; BMC 4297-4325 .... 20 60

437 **Half Unit.** Boar / Horse type. Similar to 431. M. 411; V. 661;
BMC 3513-20. (73) 20 55

438 **Fractional Unit.** Early Pattern / Horse type. Similar to 435. M. 417/a;
V. 681-83; BMC 3775-89. (76/A).. 20 60

INSCRIBED
(Early to Mid 1st Century A.D.)
The following types are not arranged chronologically.

CAN DVRO

SILVER

439

439 **Unit.** Boar. R. Horse r., CAN(S) above, DVRO below. M. 434; V. 663;
BMC 3521-23. (271) 90 275

ANTED

GOLD

440

		F £	VF £
440	**Stater.** Triple crescent design. R. Horse r., ANTED monongram below. *M. 418; V. 705; BMC 3790. (272)*	525	1350

SILVER

441

441	**Unit.** Two opposed crescents. R. Horse r., ANTED. *M. 419-21;* *V. 710-11/15; BMC 3791-4025. (273)*	25	65
442	**Fractional Unit.** Similar to last. *M. 422; V. 720; BMC 4028-31. (274)*..	25	75

ECEN

GOLD

443

443	**Stater.** Triple crescent design. R. Horse r., ECEN below. *M. —; V. 725;* *BMC 4032.*	950	3250

SILVER

443A	**Unit.** Two opposed crescents. R, Horse r., ECEN. *M. 424; V. 730;* *BMC 4033-4215. (275)*	25	65
443B	**Half Unit.** Similar to last. *M. 431; V. 736; BMC 4216-17. (276)*	20	60

EDN

SILVER

		F £	VF £
444	**Unit.** Two opposed crescents. R, Horse r., ED, E, EI or EDN. *M. 423, 425b; V. 734/40; BMC 4219-81. (277)*	20	65

ECE

GOLD

444A	**Stater** Triple crescent design R. Horse r., ECE *M. — ; V. — ;*	950	3500

SILVER

445

445	**Unit.** Two opposed crescents. R, Horse r., ECE. *M. 425-28; V. 761-66; BMC 4348-4538. (278-80)*	25	65

SAENU

SILVER

446	**Unit.** Two opposed crescents. R. Horse r., SAENV. *M. 433; V. 770; BMC 4540-57. (281)*	40	120

AESU

SILVER

447

447	**Unit.** Two opposed crescents. R. Horse r., AESV. *M. 432; V. 775; BMC 4558-72. (282)*	40	120

ALE SCA

SILVER

448	**Unit.** Boar r., ALE. R. Horse r., SCA. *M. 469; V. 996; BMC 4576*	110	350

AEDIC SIA

SILVER

	F	VF
	£	£

449 **Unit.** AEDIC in two lines. ℞. Horse r., SIA? below. *M.—; V.—;*
BMC 4581 .... 225 625

PRASUTAGUS

SILVER

450

450 **Unit.** Romanised head l., SUB RII PRASTO. ℞. Rearing horse r.,
ESICO FECIT. *M. 434a; V. 780; BMC 4577-80. (283)*........................ 525 1650
*This legend translates as "Under King Prasto, Esico made me", giving the name of both
King and moneyer.*

The systematic conquest of Britain by the Romans began in A.D. 43 when the Emperor Claudius (41-54), anxious to enhance his military reputation, authorized an invasion in which he personally participated, albeit in a purely symbolic role. The initial military contact between the two cultures had taken place almost a century before when Julius Caesar, during the course of his conquest of Celtic Gaul, led expeditions to the island in 55 and 54 B.C. Although no actual Roman occupation of Britain resulted from Caesar's reconnoitring campaigns, commercial intercourse was certainly accelerated, as evidenced by the 'Romanization' of the British Celtic coinage in the final decades of its production.

The Claudian conquest, commencing in A.D. 43, brought about a complete change in the nature of the currency circulating in Britain and ushered in a period lasting more than three and a half centuries during which Roman coinage was the only official medium of exchange. Local copies of the money brought with them by the four legions of the invasion army began to appear at a very early stage, the most popular type for imitation being the well-known Claudian copper as with reverse type fighting Minerva. Some of these copies are well-executed and of a style not much inferior to the prototype, suggesting that their local minting may have been officially sanctioned by the Roman government in order to make good a shortage of currency in the newly-conquered territory. Other examples are of much poorer style and execution and are frequently well below the normal weight of a Claudian as (usually between 10 and 11 grams). These copies must have been issued unofficially and provide evidence of the huge demand for this type of currency in a population which had never before experienced the benefits of having base metal coins available for small everyday transactions.

In the decades that followed, the boundaries of the Roman province of Britannia were continually pushed further north and west until, under the celebrated Flavian governor Gnaeus Julius Agricola, the Roman army even penetrated to northern Scotland (A.D. 83/4). A few years later, under Trajan, the northern frontier was established along the Tyne-Solway line, a barrier made permanent by the construction of Hadrian's Wall following the emperor's visit to the province in 122. For a brief period in the mid-2nd century the frontier was temporarily advanced to the Forth-Clyde line with the building of the Antonine Wall, though this seems to have been abandoned early in the reign of Marcus Aurelius (ca. 163) when the Hadrianic barrier was re-commissioned and became the permanent frontier. The security thus provided to the now-peaceful province in the south facilitated urban expansion and the development of commerce. The new prosperity brought a flood of Roman coinage into the island-province and it was no longer necessary for shortages to be made good by large scale local imitation.

Until the mid-3rd century the production of Roman coinage remained the prerogative of the mint in the capital, with only occasional issues from provincial centres to serve short-term local needs. But with the deepening political and economic crisis in the third quarter of the century there was a dramatic decentralization of minting operations, with permanent establishments being set up in many important cities in the western as well as the eastern provinces. Britain, however, still remained without an official mint at this time and in the dark days of the 270s, when the separatist Gallic Empire to which Britain belonged was close to collapse, large scale production of imitative antoniniani (commonly called 'barbarous radiates') occurred in the province. The integrity and prestige of the Empire was, to some extent, restored by a rapid succession of Illyrian 'soldier emperors', until the situation was finally stabilized by Diocletian (A.D. 284-305) who established the tetrarchy system under which governmental responsibility was shared by four rulers. By the end of the 3rd century Britain had been reorganized into a civil diocese of four provinces: it had already been subdivided into Britannia Superior and Britannia Inferior almost a hundred years before, under Septimius Severus or Caracalla.

It was left to the colourful and enigmatic usurper Carausius (A.D. 287-293) to establish mints in Britain. It was, of course, vital for him to do so as his dominion was mostly confined to the island-province. Londinium (London) was his principal mint, with a secondary establishment at a place usually signing itself 'C' (probably Camulodunum, modern Colchester). After the downfall of Carausius' murderer and successor Allectus (293-296) Britain was restored to the central government, an event commemorated by the celebrated gold medallion of Constantius I showing the Caesar riding alongside the Thames approaching the gateway of the city of Londinium. At this point the mysterious 'C' mint disappears from the picture. Londinium, on the other hand, retained its status as an official mint under Diocletian's tetrarchy and its successors down to A.D. 325, when it was closed by Constantine the Great who regarded it as superfluous to his needs. In nearly four decades of existence as a Roman mint Londinium had produced a varied and extensive coinage in the names of almost all the emperors, empresses and Caesars of the period. It was destined never again to be active during Roman times, unless the extremely rare gold and silver issues of the late 4th century usurper Magnus Maximus, signed AVG, AVGOB and AVGPS, are correctly attributed to Londinium under its late Roman name of Augusta.

The termination of Roman rule in the British provinces is traditionally dated to A.D. 410 when the emperor Honorius, in response to an appeal for aid from his British subjects, told them to arrange for their own defence as best they might ('Rescript of Honorius'). In reality, the end probably came quite gradually. As the machinery of government ground to a halt and the soldiers stopped receiving their pay there would have been a steady drift of population away from the semi-ruinous cities and military installations to the countryside, where they could better provide for themselves through farming. Under these conditions the need for coinage would have been drastically reduced, as a primitive economy based on barter would largely have replaced the complex monetary economy of the late Roman period. In any case the supply of coinage from the Continent would now have dried up. The few monetary transactions which still took place were made with worn-out coins from earlier periods augmented by local imitations, production of which in Britain had resumed in the mid-4th century. Such was the pitiful end of the long tradition of Roman coinage in the remote island-province of Britannia. More than two centuries of 'Dark Ages' were to elapse before England's new rulers, the Anglo-Saxons, commenced the issue of gold thrymsas, the designs of many of which were based on late Roman types.

As Rome's Imperial coinage provided the currency needs of this country over a period of almost four centuries no representative collection of British coins is complete without some examples of these important issues. The following listing is divided into four categories: 1. Regular Roman issues, all of which would have been legal tender in Britain after A.D. 43; 2. Issues with types referring specifically to the province of Britannia, usually in commemoration of military campaigns in the north; 3. Official Roman coinage struck in Britain; 4. Imitations of Roman coins produced in Britain, all but possibly some of the earliest being of unofficial origin. The reference 'R.R.C.' is to the listing of the type in Michael Crawford's *Roman Republican Coinage* (Cambridge, 1974); and 'R.I.C.' to *The Roman Imperial Coinage* (London, 1923-1994, in ten volumes).

For more detailed collectors' information on Roman coinage, including a more comprehensive listing of types, the reader is referred to *Roman Coins and their Values Volumes 1, 2 and 3* by David R. Sear. A complete catalogue of silver issues may be found in the 5 volumes of *Roman Silver Coins* (H.A. Seaby and C.E. King) which provides a quick and convenient reference and is especially aimed at the collector. Gilbert Askew's *The Coinage of Roman Britain* (2nd edition) concentrates on those issues which are particularly associated with the Roman province of Britannia, but does not provide valuations. More recent works on this subject include R. Reece's *Coinage in Roman Britain* and *The Coinage of Roman Britain,* and also David R. Sear's *The History and Coinage of the Roman Imperators, 49—27 BC* which is devoted to the vital two decades of transition from Republic to Empire.

The standard works on the coinages of the Roman Republic and the Roman Empire have already been mentioned *(Roman Republican Coinage and Roman Imperial Coinage).* These monumental publications are essential to the advanced collector and student and their importance cannot be overstated. The British Museum Catalogues (3 volumes of Republican, 6 volumes of Imperial recently reprinted by SPINK) are also vital. They contain superb interpretive material in their introductions and are very fully illustrated. A similar work is Anne S. Robertson's *Roman Imperial Coins in the Hunter Coin Cabinet,* in 5 volumes (volume 4 is especially important for the later 3rd century coinage). For more general reading we may recommend J.P.C. Kent and M. & A. Hirmer's *Roman Coins,* undoubtedly the most lavishly illustrated book on the subject; C.H.V. Sutherland's *Roman Coins;* and R.A.G. Carson's *Coins of the Roman Empire.* Finally, for a most useful single-volume work on interpretation and background information, we would suggest A *Dictionary of Ancient Roman Coins* by John Melville Jones.

1. REGULAR ROMAN ISSUES

A token selection of the types of Roman coins which might be found on Romano-British archaeological sites. Many of the rarer emperors and empresses have been omitted and the types listed often represent only one of hundreds of variant forms which might be encountered.

		F	VF
		£	£
451	**THE REPUBLIC: P. Aelius Paetus** (moneyer), 138 B.C. Æ *denarius*. Helmeted hd. of Roma r. Rev. The Dioscuri galloping r. R.R.C. 233/1 ...	20	60

Although dating from long before the Roman conquest many Republican coins circulated well into the Imperial period and found their way to Britain where they are often represented in early hoards.

| 452 | **L. Thorius Balbus** (moneyer), 105 B.C. Æ denarius. Hd. of Juno Sospita r., clad in goat's skin. Rev. Bull charging r. *R.R.C. 316/1.* | 25 | 70 |
| 453 | **Q. Antonius Balbus** (moneyer), 83-82 B.C. Æ *denarius*. Laur. hd. of Jupiter r. Rev. Victory in quadriga r. *R.R.C. 364/1.* | 25 | 70 |

454   456

454	**C. Calpurnius Piso** (moneyer), 67 B.C. Æ *denarius*. Laur. hd. of Apollo r. Rev. Horseman galloping r., holding palm-branch. *R.R.C. 408/1a.*	30	70
455	**Mn. Acilius Glabrio** (moneyer), 49 B.C. Æ *denarius*. Laur. hd. of Salus r. Rev. Valetudo stg. l., holding snake and resting on column. *R.R.C. 442/1.*	20	60
456	**Julius Caesar** (dictator), visited Britain 55 and 54 B.C., died 44 B.C. Æ *denarius*. CAESAR. Elephant r. Rev. Priestly emblems. *R.R.C. 443/1.*	75	175
456A	— Wreathed hd. of Caesar r. Rev. P. SEPVLLIVS MACER. Venus stg. l., holding Victory and sceptre. *R.R.C. 480/9.*	300	800
457	**Mark Antony** (triumvir), died 30 B.C. Æ *denarius*. Galley r. Rev. LEG. II. Legionary eagle between two standards. *R.R.C. 544/14.*	50	125

458   459

| 458 | **Octavian** (triumvir), named Augustus 27 B.C. Æ *denarius*. Bare hd. of Octavian r. Rev. IMP. CAESAR. Trophy set on prow. *R.I.C. 265a.* | 90 | 200 |
| 459 | **THE EMPIRE: Augustus,** 27 B.C.-A.D. 14. Æ *denarius*. Rev. C. L. CAESARES AVGVSTI F COS DESIG PRINC IVVENT. The emperor's grandsons, Gaius and Lucius, stg. facing, with spears and shields. *R.I.C. 207.* | 60 | 140 |

Almost all the coins in the Roman Imperial series have a head or bust of the emperor, empress or prince as their obverse type. Therefore, in most instances only the reverses will be described in the following listings.

		F £	VF £
460	Æ as. ROM. ET AVG. The altar of Lugdunum. *R.I.C. 230.*	50	125
460A	Æ quadrans. Obv. Anvil. Rev. Moneyers' inscription around large S. C. *R.I.C. 443.*	15	35
461	**Augustus and Agrippa,** general and designated heir of Augustus, died 12 B.C. Æ *dupondius.* Obv. Their hds. back to back. Rev. COL. NEM. Crocodile r., chained to palm-branch. *R.I.C. 159.* .... *See also no. 468.*	60	150
462	**Divus Augustus,** deified A.D. 14. Æ as. PROVIDENT S. C. Large altar. *R.I.C. 81.*	60	150
463	**Tiberius,** A.D. 14-37. *N aureus.* PONTIF MAXIM. Livia (?) seated r., holding sceptre and branch. *R.I.C. 29.*	400	1100

464   467

464	*R denarius. Similar. *R.I.C. 30.* .... *This type is commonly referred to as the 'Tribute Penny' of the Bible (Matthew 22, 17-21).*	80	175
464A	Æ *as.* Inscription around large S. C. *R.I.C. 44.*	55	140
465	**Livia,** wife of Augustus, mother of Tiberius. Æ *dupondius.* Obv. Veiled bust of Livia as Pietas r. Rev. Inscription of Drusus Caesar around large S. C. *R.I.C. 43.*	150	375
466	**Drusus,** son of Tiberius. Æ *as.* Inscription around large S. C. *R.I.C. 45.*	65	175
467	**Caligula,** A.D. 37-41. Æ *as.* VESTA S. C. Vesta seated l. *R.I.C. 38.*.......	85	240

468

468	**Agrippa,** grandfather of Caligula, died 12 B.C. Æ *as.* S. C. Neptune stg. l., holding dolphin and trident. *R.I.C. 58.* .... *See also no. 461 and under Category 4.*	60	180
469	**Germanicus,** father of Caligula, brother of Claudius, died A.D. 19. Æ *as.* Inscription of Caligula around large S. C. *R.I.C. 35.*	75	175
470	**Agrippina Senior,** mother of Caligula, died A.D. 33. Æ *sestertius.* S.P.Q.R. MEMORIAE AGRIPPINAE. Carpentum drawn l. by two mules. *R.I.C. 55.*	250	850

471   474

	F £	VF £

471   **Claudius,** A.D. 41-54, initiated the conquest of Britain by his invasion in
A.D. 43. Æ *as.* LIBERTAS AVGVSTA S. C. Libertas stg. r., holding pileus.
R.I.C. 113. .... 65 175

471A Æ *quadrans.* Obv. Hand holding scales. Rev. Inscription around large
S. C. *R.I.C. 85.* 15 35
See also under Categories 2 and 4.

472   **Nero Claudius Drusus,** father of Claudius, died 9 B.C. Æ *sestertius.*
TI. CLAVDIVS CAESAR AVG. P. M. TR .P. IMP. P. P. S. C. Claudius seated
l. on curule chair amidst arms. *R.I.C. 109.* 130 450
See also under Category 4.

473   **Antonia,** mother of Claudius, died A.D. 37. Æ *dupondius.* TI. CLAVDIVS
CAESAR AVG P.M. TR. P. IMP. S. C. Claudius stg. l., holding simpulum.
R.I.C. 92. .... 100 275
See also under Category 4.

474   **Nero,** 54-68, emperor at the time of Queen Boudicca's rebellion in Britain.
N *aureus.* SALVS. Salus seated l. *R.I.C. 66.* 550 1300

475   Æ *denarius.* IVPPITER CVSTOS. Jupiter seated l. *R.I.C. 53.* 85 275

476   Æ *sestertius.* ROMA S. C. Roma seated l., holding Victory and parazonium.
R.I.C. 274. .... 150 475

476A Æ *as.* S. C. Victory hovering l., holding shield inscribed S. P. Q. R. *R.I.C. 312.* 60 160

477   **Galba,** 68-69. Æ *denarius.* S.P.Q.R. / OB / C.S. within oak-wreath. *R.I.C. 167.* 100 275

478   **Otho,** 69. Æ *denarius.* SECVRITAS P. R. Securitas stg. l. *R.I.C. 10.* 200 550

479   **Vitellius,** 69. Æ denarius. CONCORDIA P. R. Concordia seated l. *R.I.C. 90.* 100 250

480   **Vespasian,** 69-79, commanded Legio II in the Claudian invasion of Britain
(43) and appointed Agricola to governorship of the province in 77/8. N *aureus.*
ANNONA AVG. Annona seated l. *R.I.C. 131a* 500 1200

481

481   Æ *denarius.* VICTORIA AVGVSTI. Victory advancing r., crowning standard.
R.I.C. 52. .... 30 80

481A Æ *dupondius.* FELICITAS PVBLICA S. C. Felicitas stg. l. *R.I.C. 554...* 40 110

482   **Titus,** 79-81 (Caesar 69-79). Æ *denarius.* TR. P. IX. IMP. XV. COS. VIII.
P. P. Thunderbolt on throne. *R.I.C. 23a.* 50 140

483 485

| | F | VF |
| | £ | £ |

483 **Domitian,** 81-96 (Caesar 69-81), recalled Agricola in 83/4 and abandoned
the conquest of northern Scotland (ca. 87). *Æ denarius.* IMP. XIX. COS.
XIIII. CENS. P. P. P. Minerva stg. l., resting on spear. *R.I.C. 140.* 25 75

484 *Æ dupondius.* VIRTVTI AVGVSTI S. C. Virtus stg. r. *R.I.C. 393.* 35 85

484A *Æ as.* MONETA AVGVSTI S. C. Moneta stg. l. *R.I.C. 354b.* 35 85

485 **Nerva,** 96-98. *Æ denarius.* AEQVITAS AVGVST. Aequitas stg. l. *R.I.C. 13.* 50 120

485A *Æ as.* LIBERTAS PVBLICA S. C. Libertas stg. l. *R.I.C. 86.* 55 140

486 **Trajan,** 98-117, established the northern frontier in Britain along the
Tyne-Solway line (ca. 100). *N aureus.* P. M. TR. P. COS. VI. P. P. S. P. Q. R.
Genius stg. l., holding patera and corn-ears. *R.I.C. 347.* 450 1100

487 490

487 *Æ denarius.* COS. V. P. P. S. P. Q. R. OPTIMO PRINC. Military trophy.
R.I.C. 147. .... 25 75

488 *Æ sestertius.* S. P. Q. R. OPTIMO PRINCIPI S. C. Spes walking l.,
holding flower. *R.I.C. 519.* 50 175

488A *Æ dupondius.* SENATVS POPVLVSQVE ROMANVS S. C. Emperor
advancing between two trophies. *R.I.C. 676.* 50 100

489 **Hadrian,** 117-138, visited Britain in 122 and initiated the construction of
a fortified frontier line (Hadrian's Wall). *N aureus.* HISPANIA. Hispania
reclining l. *R.I.C. 305.* 500 1200

490 *Æ denarius.* P. M. TR. P. COS. III. Roma stg. l., holding Victory and spear.
R.I.C. 76. .... 30 85

491 *Æ sestertius.* COS. III. S. C. Neptune stg. r., holding dolphin and trident,
foot on prow. *R.I.C. 632.* 50 175

491A *Æ as.* FELICITATI AVG COS. III. P. P. S. C. Galley travelling l. over waves.
R.I.C. 719. .... 40 120

See also under Category 2.

492 **Sabina,** wife of Hadrian. *Æ denarius.* IVNONI REGINAE. Juno stg. l.
R.I.C. 395a. 40 120

493 **Aelius Caesar,** heir of Hadrian, 136-138. *Æ denarius.* CONCORD. TR.
POT. COS. II. Concordia seated l. *R.I.C. 436.* 75 200

493A *Æ as.* TR. POT. COS. II. S. C. Spes walking l., holding flower. *R.I.C. 1067.* 50 130

F	*VF*
£	£

494   **Antoninus Pius,** 138-161, ordered the expansion of the Roman province
to include southern Scotland and constructed the Antonine Wall on the
Forth-Clyde line (beginning ca. 143). An uprising in northern Britain in the
150s results in a permanent withdrawal to the Hadrianic frontier early in
the next reign. *N aureus.* COS. IIII. Togate emperor stg. l., holding globe.
R.I.C. 233b.   400   900

495   *Æ denarius.* PIETATI AVG. COS. IIII. Pietas stg. l. between two children,
holding two more in her arms. *R.I.C. 313c.*   25   70

496

496   *Æ sestertius.* SALVS AVG. S. C. Salus stg. l. at altar, feeding snake.
R.I.C. 635.   40   160

496A *Æ dupondius.* TR. POT. XX. COS. IIII. S. C. Providentia stg. l., pointing
at globe at her feet and holding sceptre. *R.I.C. 2025.*   25   60
See also under Categories 2 and 3.

497   **Antoninus Pius and Marcus Aurelius Caesar.** *Æ denarius.* Obv. Laur.
hd. of Antoninus Pius r. Rev. AVRELIVS CAESAR AVG PII F. COS. Bare
hd. of young Marcus Aurelius r. *R.I.C. 417a.*   50   130

498   501

498   **Divus Antoninus Pius,** deified 161. *Æ denarius.* CONSECRATIO.
Four-storeyed crematorium of Antoninus Pius. *R.I.C. 436.*   25   75

499   **Diva Faustina Senior,** wife of Antoninus Pius, deified 141. *Æ denarius.*
AETERNITAS. Aeternitas stg. l., holding globe and billowing veil. *R.I.C. 351.*   25   75

499A *Æ sestertius.* AVGVSTA S. C. Ceres stg. l., holding two torches. *R.I.C. 1120.*   30   110

500   **Marcus Aurelius,** 161-180 (Caesar 139-161), re-established Hadrian's Wall
as the permanent northern frontier of the province, ca. 163. *N aureus.*
PROV. DEOR. TR. P. XV. COS. III. Providentia stg. l., holding globe and
cornucopiae. *R.I.C. 19.*   450   950

501   *Æ denarius.* PIETAS AVG. Priestly emblems. *R.I.C. 424a.*   25   75

501A — SALVTI AVG. COS. III. Salus stg. l. at altar, feeding snake. *R.I.C. 222.*   20   70

502   *Æ sestertius.* CONCORD. AVGVSTOR. TR. P. XVI. COS. III. S. C. Marcus
Aurelius and Lucius Verus stg. face to face, clasping hands. *R.I.C. 826.*   40   160

502A *Æ as.* HONOS TR. POT. II. COS. II. S. C. Honos stg. r. *R.I.C. 1271a.* ...   30   75

	F	VF
	£	£

503 **Divus Marcus Aurelius,** deified 180. Æ *denarius.* CONSECRATIO.
Eagle stg. r. on altar. *R.I.C. 272.* 25 70

504 506A

504 **Faustina Junior,** daughter of Antoninus Pius, wife of Marcus Aurelius.
Æ *denarius.* FECVNDITAS. Fecunditas stg. r., holding sceptre and child.
R.I.C. 677. .... 25 60
504A Æ *sestertius.* HILARITAS S. C. Hilaritas stg. l. *R.I.C. 1642.* 35 120
505 **Diva Faustina Junior,** deified 175. Æ *as.* S. C. Crescent and seven stars.
R.I.C. 1714. .... 35 80
506 **Lucius Verus,** 161-169. Æ denarius. PAX TR. P. VI. IMP. IIII. COS. II.
Pax stg. l. *R.I.C. 561.* 30 80
506A Æ *dupondius.* TR. P. IIII. IMP. II. COS. II. S. C. Mars stg. r., resting on
spear and shield. *R.I.C. 1387.* 35 95
507 **Lucilla,** daughter of Marcus Aurelius, wife of Lucius Verus. Æ *denarius.*
IVNONI LVCINAE. Juno stg. l., holding child in swaddling clothes.
R.I.C. 771. .... 30 75
507A Æ *sestertius.* PIETAS S. C. Pietas stg. l., altar at feet. *R.I.C. 1756.* 35 120
508 **Commodus,** 177-192 (Caesar 175-177), major warfare on the British
frontier early in the reign; situation restored by Ulpius Marcellus in 184/5,
followed by unrest in the British legions. Æ *denarius.* LIB. AVG. IIII. TR.
P. VI. IMP. IIII. COS. III. P. P. Liberalitas stg. l. *R.I.C. 22.* 30 80

509 511

509 Æ *sestertius.* IOVI VICTORI IMP. III. COS. II. P. P. S. C. Jupiter seated l.
R.I.C. 1612. .... 40 140
509A Æ *as.* ANN. AVG. TR. P. VII. IMP. IIII. COS. III. P. P. S. C. Annona stg. l.,
modius at feet. *R.I.C. 339.* 25 70
See also under Category 2.
510 **Crispina,** wife of Commodus. Æ *denarius.* CONCORDIA. Clasped hands.
R.I.C. 279. .... 30 75
511 **Pertinax,** January-March 193, formerly governor of Britain, ca. 185-7. Æ
denarius. PROVID. DEOR. COS. II. Providentia stg l., reaching up to star.
R.I.C. 11a. 250 600

512   513A

	F	VF
	£	£

512   **Didius Julianus,** March-June 193. Æ *denarius.* CONCORD MILIT.
       Concordia Militum stg. l., holding standards. *R.I.C. 1.* 375   850
513   **Clodius Albinus,** 195-197 (Caesar 193-195), governor of Britain (from
       191/2) at the time of his imperial proclamation by his troops. Æ *denarius.*
       MINER. PACIF. COS. II. Minerva stg. l. *R.I.C. 7.* 60   140
513A   — FIDES LEGION. COS. II. Clasped hands holding legionary eagle.
       R.I.C. 20b. 75   175

514   516

514   **Septimius Severus,** 193-211, restored the frontier forts in northern Britain
       following the downfall of Clodius Albinus; later repaired Hadrian's Wall,
       and spent the years 208-11 in Britain campaigning in Scotland; divided
       Britannia into two provinces, Superior and Inferior; died at York, February
       211. Æ *denarius.* VIRT AVGG. Roma stg. l., holding Victory, spear and
       shield. *R.I.C. 171a.* 20   50
514A   — P.M. TR. P. XVIII. COS. III. P. P. Jupiter stg. l. between two children.
       R.I.C. 240. 20   50
       See also under Category 2.
515   **Julia Domna,** wife of Septimius Severus, mother of Caracalla and Geta,
       accompanied her husband and sons on the British expedition, 208-211, and
       probably resided in London during the northern campaigns. Æ *denarius.*
       VENERI VICTR. Venus stg. r., resting on column. *R.I.C. 536.* 15   45
515A   — VESTA. Vesta stg. l., holding palladium and sceptre. *R.I.C. 390.* 15   45
516   **Caracalla,** 198-217 (Caesar 196-198), accompanied his father and brother
       on the British expedition, 208-211, and led the final campaign in Scotland
       in 210 during Severus' illness; made frontier dispositions before returning
       to Rome and finalized his father's arrangements for the division of Britain
       into two provinces. Æ *antoninianus (double denarius,* introduced in 215).
       VENVS VICTRIX. Venus stg. l., holding Victory and resting on shield.
       R.I.C. 311c. 30   75
517   Æ *denarius.* PART. MAX. PONT. TR. P. IIII. Trophy with two captives at
       base. *R.I.C. 54b.* 15   50
517A   — P. M. TR. P. XV. COS. III. P. P. Hercules stg. l., holding olive-branch
       and club. *R.I.C. 192.* 15   50
       See also under Category 2.

		F £	VF £

518   **Plautilla,** wife of Caracalla. Æ *denarius.* PROPAGO IMPERI. Caracalla
and Plautilla clasping hands. *R.I.C. 362.* 25   75

519   522A

519   **Geta,** 209-212 (Caesar 198-209), accompanied his father and brother on
the British expedition, 208-211, and took charge of the civil administration
in London during the northern campaigns. Æ *denarius.* PRINC. IVVENTVTIS.
Prince stg. l. beside trophy, holding branch and spear. *R.I.C. 18.* 20   50

519A — FORT RED TR. P. III. COS. II. Fortuna seated l. *R.I.C. 75.* 25   65
See also under Category 2.

520   **Macrinus,** 217-218. Æ *denarius.* PROVIDENTIA DEORVM. Providentia
stg. l., globe at feet. *R.I.C. 80.* 35   110

521   **Diadumenian,** 218 (Caesar 217-218). Æ *denarius.* PRINC. IVVENTVTIS.
Prince stg. l., two standards behind. *R.I.C. 109.* 70   175

522   **Elagabalus,** 218-222. Æ *antoninianus.* MARS VICTOR. Mars advancing r.
R.I.C. 122. 22   55

522A Æ *denarius.* P. M. TR. P. III. COS. III. P. P. Jupiter seated l., eagle at feet
R.I.C. 27. 20   40

523   **Julia Paula,** first wife of Elagabalus. Æ *denarius.* CONCORDIA.
Concordia seated l. *R.I.C. 211.* 40   100

524   **Aquilia Severa,** second wife of Elagabalus. Æ *denarius.* CONCORDIA.
Concordia stg. l., altar at feet. *R.I.C. 226.* 60   150

525   **Julia Soaemias,** mother of Elagabalus. Æ *denarius.* VENVS CAELESTIS.
Venus seated l., child at feet. *R.I.C. 243.* 30   75

526   **Julia Maesa,** grandmother of Elagabalus and Severus Alexander. Æ
denarius. SAECVLI FELICITAS. Felicitas stg. l., altar at feet. *R.I.C. 271.* 25   60

527   **Severus Alexander,** 222-235 (Caesar 221-222). Æ *denarius.*
PAX AETERNA AVG. Pax stg. l. *R.I.C. 165.* 15   40

527A — P. M. TR. P. XIII. COS. III. P. P. Sol advancing l., holding whip. *R.I.C. 123.* 15   40

528

528   Æ *sestertius.* MARS VLTOR S. C. Mars advancing r., with spear and shield.
R.I.C. 635. 30   85

F	*VF*
£	£

529 **Orbiana,** wife of Severus Alexander. Æ *denarius*. CONCORDIA AVGG.
Concordia seated l. *R.I.C. 319.* 70   175
530 **Julia Mamaea,** mother of Severus Alexander. Æ *denarius*. VESTA.
Vesta stg. l. *R.I.C. 362.* 20   50
530A Æ *sestertius*. FELICITAS PVBLICA S. C. Felicitas stg. facing, hd. l.,
resting on column. *R.I.C. 676.* 30   85

531

531 **Maximinus I,** 235-238. Æ *denarius*. PAX AVGVSTI. Pax stg. l. *R.I.C. 12.*   20   50
531A Æ *sestertius*. SALVS AVGVSTI S. C. Salus seated l., feeding snake arising
from altar. *R.I.C. 85.* 30   85
532 **Maximus Caesar,** son of Maximinus I. Æ *denarius*. PRINC IVVENTVTIS.
Prince stg. l., two standards behind. *R.I.C. 3.* 50   175
533 **Gordian I Africanus,** March-April 238, governor of Britannia Inferior
late in the reign of Caracalla. Æ *denarius*. P. M. TR. P. COS. P. P. Togate
emperor stg. l. *R.I.C. 1.* 250   650
534 **Gordian II Africanus,** March-April 238. Æ *denarius*. VIRTVS AVGG.
Virtus stg. l., with shield and spear. *R.I.C. 3.* 250   650
535 **Balbinus,** April-July 238. Æ *antoninianus*. FIDES MVTVA AVGG.
Clasped hands. *R.I.C. 11.* 75   175
535A Æ *denarius*. PROVIDENTIA DEORVM. Providentia stg. l., globe at feet.
R.I.C. 7. 50   140
536 **Pupienus,** April-July 238. Æ *antoninianus*. AMOR MVTVVS AVGG.
Clasped hands. *R.I.C. 9a.* 75   175
536A Æ *denarius*. PAX PVBLICA. Pax seated l. *R.I.C. 4.* 50   140
537 **Gordian III,** 238-244 (Caesar 238). Æ *antoninianus*. LAETITIA AVG. N.
Laetitia stg. l. *R.I.C. 86.* 15   30
538 Æ *denarius*. DIANA LVCIFERA. Diana stg. r., holding torch. *R.I.C. 127.*   15   30

538A

538A Æ *sestertius*. AETERNITATI AVG. S.C. Sol stg. l., holding globe. *R.I.C. 297a.*   22   65

539

		F	VF
		£	£
539	**Philip I,** 244-249. Æ *antoninianus.* ROMAE AETERNAE. Roma seated l. *R.I.C. 65.*	12	30
539A	Æ *sestertius.* SECVRIT. ORBIS S. C. Securitas seated l. *R.I.C. 190.*	25	75
540	**Otacilia Severa,** wife of Philip I. Æ *antoninianus.* PIETAS AVGVSTAE. Pietas stg. l. *R.I.C. 125c.*	15	40
540A	Æ *sestertius.* CONCORDIA AVGG. S. C. Concordia seated l. *R.I.C. 203a.*	25	75
541	**Philip II,** 247-249 (Caesar 244-247). Æ *antoninianus.* PRINCIPI IVVENT. Prince stg. l., holding globe and spear. *R.I.C. 218d.*	20	50
541A	Æ *sestertius.* PAX AETERNA S. C. Pax stg. l. *R.I.C. 268c.*	25	80

542   543

542	**Trajan Decius,** 249-251. Æ *antoninianus.* DACIA. Dacia stg. l., holding staff with ass's hd. *R.I.C. 12b.*	15	35
542A	Æ *sestertius.* PANNONIAE S. C. The two Pannoniae stg., each holding standard. *R.I.C. 124a.*	25	75
543	**Herennia Etruscilla,** wife of Trajan Decius. Æ *antoninianus.* PVDICITIA AVG. Pudicitia stg. l. *R.I.C. 58b.*	15	35
544	**Herennius Etruscus,** 251 (Caesar 250-251). Æ *antoninianus.* PIETAS AVGG. Mercury stg. l., holding purse and caduceus. *R.I.C. 142b.*	25	65
545	**Hostilian,** 251 (Caesar 251). Æ *antoninianus.* PRINCIPI IVVENTVTIS. Apollo seated l., holding branch. *R.I.C. 180.*	35	85
546	**Trebonianus Gallus,** 251-253. Æ *antoninianus.* FELICITAS PVBLICA. Felicitas stg. l., resting on column. *R.I.C. 34A.*	12	30
546A	Æ *sestertius.* SALVS AVGG S. C. Salus stg. r., feeding snake held in her arms. *R.I.C. 121a.*	25	75
547	**Volusian,** 251-253 (Caesar 251). Æ *antoninianus.* VIRTVS AVGG. Virtus stg. l. *R.I.C. 186.*	12	30
548	**Aemilian,** 253. Æ *antoninianus.* PACI AVG. Pax stg. l., resting on column. *R.I.C. 8.*	50	120
549	**Valerian,** 253-260. Billon antoninianus. FIDES MILITVM. Fides stg. r., holding two standards. *R.I.C. 241.*	8	20
550	**Diva Mariniana,** wife of Valerian, deified 253. Billon *antoninianus.* CONSECRATIO. Empress seated on peacock flying r. *R.I.C. 6.*	45	110

		F	*VF*
		£	£
551	**Gallienus,** 253-268, during whose reign Rome temporarily lost control over Britain when Postumus rebelled and established the independent Gallic Empire in 260. Billon *antoninianus.* VIRT GALLIENI AVG. Emperor advancing r., captive at feet. *R.I.C. 54.*	10	25

552

552	— DIANAE CONS. AVG. Doe l. *R.I.C. 176.*	8	20
552A	— SOLI INVICTO. Sol stg. l., holding globe. *R.I.C. 658.*	8	18
553	**Salonina,** wife of Gallienus. Billon *antoninianus.* VENVS FELIX. Venus seated l., child at feet. *R.I.C. 7.*	8	20
553A	— IVNONI CONS. AVG. Doe l. *R.I.C. 16.*	8	20
554	**Valerian Junior,** son of Gallienus, Caesar 256-258. Billon *antoninianus.* IOVI CRESCENTI. Infant Jupiter seated on goat r. *R.I.C. 13.*	15	35
555	**Divus Valerian Junior,** deified 258. Billon *antoninianus.* CONSECRATIO. Large altar. *R.I.C. 24.*	12	30
556	**Saloninus,** 260 (Caesar 258-260). Billon *antoninianus.* PIETAS AVG. Priestly emblems. *R.I.C. 9.*	12	30
557	**Macrianus,** usurper in the East, 260-261. Billon *antoninianus.* SOL. INVICTO. Sol stg. l., holding globe. *R.I.C. 12.*	35	85
558	**Quietus,** usurper in the East, 260-261. Billon *antoninianus.* INDVLGENTIAE AVG. Indulgentia seated l. *R.I.C. 5.*	35	85
559	**Postumus,** usurper in the West, 260-268, founder of the 'Gallic Empire' which temporarily detached Britain from the rule of the central government, a state of affairs which continued until Aurelian's defeat of Tetricus in 273. Billon *antoninianus.* HERC. DEVSONIENSI. Hercules stg. r. *R.I.C. 64.*	12	30

560

560	— MONETA AVG. Moneta stg. l. *R.I.C. 75.*	10	25
560A	Æ *sestertius.* FIDES MILITVM. Fides stg. l., holding two standards. *R.I.C. 128.*	50	140
561	**Laelianus,** usurper in the West, 268. Billon *antoninianus.* VICTORIA AVG. Victory advancing r. *R.I.C. 9.*	110	275
562	**Marius,** usurper in the West, 268. Billon *antoninianus.* CONCORDIA MILITVM. Clasped hands. *R.I.C. 7.*	35	85
563	**Victorinus,** usurper in the West, 268-270. Billon *antoninianus.* INVICTVS. Sol advancing l. *R.I.C. 114.*	8	20

	F £	VF £

564 **Tetricus,** usurper in the West, 270-273, defeated by Aurelian, thus ending the 'Gallic Empire' and the isolation of Britain from the authority of Rome. Billon *antoninianus*. LAETITIA AVGG. Laetitia stg. l. *R.I.C. 87.* 8 25
See also under Category 4.

565 **Tetricus Junior,** son of Tetricus, Caesar 270-273. Billon *antoninianus*. SPES PVBLICA. Spes walking l., holding flower *R.I.C. 272.* 8 20
See also under Category 4.

566 **Claudius II Gothicus,** 268-270. Billon *antoninianus*. IOVI STATORI. Jupiter stg. r. *R.I.C. 52.* 8 20

567 **Divus Claudius II,** deified 270. Billon *antoninianus*. CONSECRATIO. Large altar. *R.I.C. 261.* 8 20
See also under Category 4.

568 **Quintillus,** 270. Billon *antoninianus*. DIANA LVCIF. Diana stg. r., holding torch. *R.I.C. 49.* 18 45

569 **Aurelian,** 270-275, restored Britain to the rule of the central government through his defeat of Tetricus in 273; possibly began construction of the chain of 'Saxon Shore' forts on the eastern and southern coastlines. Billon *antoninianus*. ORIENS AVG. Sol stg. l. between two captives. *R.I.C. 63.* 10 25

569A — RESTITVT. ORBIS. Female stg. r., presenting wreath to emperor stg. l. *R.I.C. 399.* 10 25

570 **Aurelian and Vabalathus,** ruler of Palmyra 267-272 and usurper in the East from 271. Billon *antoninianus*. Obv. Laur. bust of Vabalathus r. Rev. Rad. bust of Aurelian r. *R.I.C. 381.* 25 70

571   574A

571 **Severina,** wife of Aurelian. Billon *antoninianus*. PROVIDEN. DEOR. Concordia (or Fides) Militum stg. r., facing Sol stg. l. *R.I.C. 9.* 18 45

572 **Tacitus,** 275-276. Billon *antoninianus*. SECVRIT. PERP. Securitas stg. l., leaning on column. *R.I.C. 163.* 15 35

573 **Florian,** 276. Billon *antoninianus*. LAETITIA FVND. Laetitia stg. l. *R.I.C. 34.* 30 75

574 **Probus,** 276-282, suppressed governor's revolt in Britain and lifted restrictions on viticulture in Britain and Gaul. Billon *antoninianus*. ADVENTVS PROBI AVG. Emperor on horseback l., captive seated before. *R.I.C. 160.* 10 25

574A — VICTORIA GERM. Trophy between two captives. *R.I.C. 222.* 15 40

575 **Carus,** 282-283. Billon *antoninianus*. PAX EXERCITI. Pax stg. l., holding olive-branch and standard. *R.I.C. 75.* 15 40

576 **Divus Carus,** deified 283. Billon *antoninianus*. CONSECRATIO. Eagle facing, hd. l. *R.I.C. 28.* 18 45

577 **Carinus,** 283-285 (Caesar 282-283). Billon *antoninianus*. SAECVLI FELICITAS. Emperor stg. r. *R.I.C. 214.* 12 35

		F	VF
		£	£

578 **Magnia Urbica,** wife of Carinus. Billon *antoninianus.* VENVS VICTRIX.
Venus stg. l., holding helmet, shield at feet. *R.I.C. 343.* 60 150

579 **Numerian,** 283-284 (Caesar 282-283). Billon *antoninianus.* CLEMENTIA
TEMP. Emperor stg. r., receiving globe from Jupiter stg. l. *R.I.C. 463.* .. 15 40

580 **Diocletian,** 284-305. *Æ argenteus.* VIRTVS MILITVM. The four tetrarchs
sacrificing before gateway of military camp. *R.I.C. 27a (Rome).* 100 200

581 Billon *antoninianus.* IOVI CONSERVAT AVGG. Jupiter stg. l. *R.I.C. 162.* 10 25

582 *Æ follis.* GENIO POPVLI ROMANI. Genius stg. l. R.I.C. 14a *(Alexandria).* 10 30

582A — (post-abdication coinage, after 305). PROVIDENTIA DEORVM QVIES
AVGG. Quies and Providentia stg. facing each other. *R.I.C. 676a (Treveri).* 22 65
See also under Category 3.

583 **Maximian,** 286-305 and 306-308, failed in his attempts to suppress the
usurpation of Carausius in Britain. *Æ argenteus.* VICTORIA SARMAT. The
four tetrarchs sacrificing before gateway of military camp. *R.I.C. 37b (Rome).* 100 200

584

584 Billon *antoninianus.* SALVS AVGG. Salus stg. r., feeding snake held in
her arms. *R.I.C. 417.* 8 20

585 *Æ follis.* SAC. MON. VRB. AVGG. ET CAESS. NN. Moneta stg. l.
R.I.C. 105b (Rome). 12 35

585A — (second reign). CONSERVATORES VRB SVAE. Roma seated in
hexastyle temple. *R.I.C. 84b (Ticinum).* 12 35
See also under Category 3.
*[For coins of the usurpers **Carausius** and **Allectus** see under Category 3]*

586 **Constantius I,** 305-306 (Caesar 293-305), invaded Britain 296 and defeated
the usurper Allectus, thus restoring the island to the rule of the central
government; Britain now divided into four provinces and the northern
frontier defences reconstructed; died at York, July 306. *Æ argenteus.*
PROVIDENTIA AVGG. The four tetrarchs sacrificing before gateway
of military camp. *R.I.C. 11a (Rome).* 110 220

587

587 *Æ follis.* GENIO POPVLI ROMANI. Genius stg. l. *R.I.C. 26a (Aquileia).* 12 35

587A — SALVIS AVGG. ET CAESS. FEL. KART. Carthage stg. l., holding
fruits. *R.I.C. 30a (Carthage).* 15 40
See also under Category 3.

588

		F £	VF £
588	**Galerius,** 305-311 (Caesar 293-305). Æ argenteus. VIRTVS MILITVM. The four tetrarchs sacrificing before gateway of military camp. R.I.C. 15b (Ticinum).	100	200
588A	— XC / VI in wreath. R.I.C. 16b (Carthage).	150	350
589	Æ follis. GENIO AVGG ET CAESARVM NN. Genius stg. l. R.I.C. 11b (Cyzicus).	12	35
589A	— GENIO IMPERATORIS. Genius stg. l. R.I.C. 101a (Alexandria). See also under Category 3.	8	25
590	**Galeria Valeria,** wife of Galerius. Æ follis. VENERI VICTRICI. Venus stg. l. R.I.C. 110 (Alexandria).	35	85
591	**Severus II,** 306-307 (Caesar 305-306). Æ follis. FIDES MILITVM. Fides seated l. R.I.C. 73 (Ticinum). See also under Category 3.	35	85
592	**Maximinus II,** 310-313 (Caesar 305-310). Æ follis. GENIO CAESARIS. Genius stg. l. R.I.C. 64 (Alexandria).	8	25
592A	— GENIO POP. ROM. Genius stg. l. R.I.C. 845a (Treveri). See also under Category 3.	8	20

![593 coin]

593

593	**Maxentius,** 306-312 (Caesar 306). Æ follis. CONSERV. VRB. SVAE. Roma seated in hexastyle temple. R.I.C. 210 (Rome).	10	30
594	**Romulus,** son of Maxentius, deified 309. Æ quarter follis. AETERNAE MEMORIAE. Temple with domed roof. R.I.C. 58 (Ostia).	35	85
595	**Licinius,** 308-324. Æ follis. GENIO AVGVSTI. Genius stg. l. R.I.C. 198b (Siscia).	8	20
595A	Æ 3. IOVI CONSERVATORI AVGG. Jupiter stg. l. R.I.C. 24 (Nicomedia). See also under Category 3.	8	20
596	**Licinius Junior,** son of Licinius, Caesar 317-324. Æ 3. CAESARVM NOSTRORVM around wreath containing VOT. / V. R.I.C. 92 (Thessalonica).	8	22
597	**Constantine I, the Great,** 307-337 (Caesar 306-307), campaigned with his father Constantius I against the Picts in northern Britain, summer 306, and proclaimed emperor by the legions at York on Constantius' death in July; closed the London mint early in 325 ending almost four decades of operation. Æ follis. GENIO POP ROM. Genius stg. l. R.I.C. 719b (Treveri).	12	35
598	— SOLI INVICTO COMITI. Sol stg. l. R.I.C. 307 (Lugdunum).	6	18
598A	Æ 3. PROVIDENTIAE AVGG. Gateway of military camp. R.I.C. 153 (Thessalonica).	5	15

599 600

| | | F | VF |
| | | £ | £ |

599 — VIRTVS EXERCIT. Trophy between two captives. *R.I.C. 280 (Treveri)*.   12   30

599A Æ 3/4. GLORIA EXERCITVS. Two soldiers stg. either side of two standards.
R.I.C. 518 (Treveri).   4   12
See also under Category 3.

600 'Urbs Roma', after 330. Æ 3/4. Obv. Helmeted bust of Roma l. Rev.
She-wolf l., suckling twins. *R.I.C. 195 (Nicomedia)*.   5   15

601 604

601 'Constantinopolis', after 330. Æ 3/4. Obv. Helmeted bust of
Constantinopolis l. Rev. Victory stg. l., foot on prow. *R.I.C. 339 (Rome)*.   5   15

602 Fausta, wife of Constantine I. Æ 3. SALVS REIPVBLICAE. Empress
stg. l., holding two children. *R.I.C. 459 (Treveri)*.   18   45
See also under Category 3.

603 Helena, mother of Constantine I. Æ 3. SECVRITAS REIPVBLICE.
Empress stg. l., holding branch. *R.I.C. 38 (Alexandria)*.   18   40

603A Æ 4 (posthumous issue, 337-340). PAX PVBLICA. Pax stg. l. *R.I.C. 78
(Treveri)*.   10   25
See also under Category 3.

604 Theodora, second wife of Constantius I. Æ 4 (posthumous issue, 337-340).
PIETAS ROMANA. Pietas stg. r., holding child. R.I.C. 43 *(Treveri)*.   12   30

605 Crispus, eldest son of Constantine I, Caesar 317-326. Æ 3. CAESARVM
NOSTRORVM around wreath containing VOT. / V. *R.I.C. 68 (Aquileia)*.   8   20
See also under Category 3.

606 Delmatius, nephew of Constantine I, Caesar 335-337. Æ 3/4. GLORIA
EXERCITVS. Two soldiers stg. either side of two standards. *R.I.C. 90
(Antioch)*.   18   45

607 Hanniballianus, nephew of Constantine I, Rex 335-337. Æ 4. SECVRITAS
PVBLICA. River-god Euphrates reclining r. *R.I.C. 147 (Constantinople)*.   100   225

608 Constantine II, 337-340 (Caesar 317-337). Æ 3. BEATA
TRANQVILLITAS. Altar inscribed VOT / IS / XX. *R.I.C. 312 (Treveri)*.   8   20

608A Æ 3/4. GLORIA EXERCITVS. Two soldiers stg. either side of standard.
R.I.C. 392 (Rome).   4   10
See also under Category 3.

609 Constans, 337-350 (Caesar 333-337), visited Britain in 343, the last
reigning emperor to do so. Æ 2. FEL. TEMP. REPARATIO. Soldier r.,
dragging barbarian from hut beneath tree. *R.I.C. 103 (Aquileia)*.   10   30

609A   611B

| | F | VF |
| | £ | £ |

609A — FEL. TEMP. REPARATIO. Emperor stg. l. on galley steered by Victory.
R.I.C. 219 (Treveri). 10 30

609B Æ 4. VICTORIAE DD. AVGG. Q. NN. Two Victories stg. face to face.
R.I.C. 195 (Treveri). 5 10

610 **Constantius II,** 337-361 (Caesar 324-337). Æ 3/4. GLORIA EXERCITVS.
Two soldiers stg. either side of two standards. *R.I.C. 85 (Cyzicus).* 5 12

611 Æ *siliqua.* VOTIS / XXX. / MVLTIS / XXXX. in wreath. *R.I.C. 207 (Arelate).* 25 70

611A Æ 2. FEL. TEMP. REPARATIO. Emperor stg. l. on galley. *R.I.C. 218
(Treveri).* 10 30

611B Æ 3. FEL. TEMP. REPARATIO. Soldier advancing l., spearing fallen
horseman. *R.I.C. 189 (Lugdunum).* 5 15
See also under Categories 3 and 4.

612   616

612 **Magnentius,** usurper in the West, 350-353, temporarily detached Britain
from the rule of the legitimate Constantinian dynasty. Æ 1. SALVS DD.
NN. AVG. ET CAES. *Chi-Rho* Christian monogram between Alpha
and Omega. *R.I.C. 34 (Ambianum).* 75 175

612A Æ 2. FELICITAS REIPVBLICE. Emperor stg. l., holding Victory and
labarum. *R.I.C. 264 (Treveri).* 15 40
See also under Category 4.

613 **Decentius,** brother of Magnentius, Caesar 351-353. Æ 2. VICTORIAE DD.
NN. AVG. ET CAE. Two Victories supporting between them shield
inscribed VOT. / V. / MVLT. / X. *R.I.C. 146 (Lugdunum).* 20 50
See also under Category 4.

614 **Vetranio,** 'usurper' in the Balkans, 350. Æ 2. CONCORDIA MILITVM.
Emperor stg. l., holding two labara. *R.I.C. 281 (Siscia).* 50 125

615 **Constantius Gallus,** Caesar under Constantius II, 351-354. Æ 2. FEL.
TEMP. REPARATIO. Soldier advancing l., spearing fallen horseman.
R.I.C. 94 (Cyzicus). 15 40

616 **Julian II,** 360-363 (Caesar 355-360). Æ *siliqua.* VOT. / X. / MVLT. / XX.
in wreath. *R.I.C. 309 (Arelate).* 25 70

		F	VF
		£	£

617 Æ 1. SECVRITAS REIPVB. Bull stg. r. *R.I.C. 411 (Siscia)*................. 45 140

617A Æ 3. VOT. / X. / MVLT. / XX. in wreath. *R.I.C. 108 (Sirmium)*. 8 25

618 **Jovian,** 363-364. Æ 3. VOT. / V. / MVLT. / X. in wreath. *R.I.C. 426 (Siscia)*. 12 35

619 **Valentinian I,** 364-375 (in the West), during whose reign the Roman province of Britannia was devastated by the simultaneous attack of hordes of invaders on several fronts (the 'Barbarian Conspiracy'); order eventually restored by Count Theodosius, father of the future emperor . *N solidus.* RESTITVTOR REIPVBLICAE. Emperor stg. r., holding standard and Victory. *R.I.C. 2b (Antioch)*. 120 275

619A Æ 3. GLORIA ROMANORVM. Emperor advancing r., dragging barbarian and holding labarum. *R.I.C. 14a (Siscia)*. 5 15

619B

619B — SECVRITAS REIPVBLICAE. Victory advancing l. *R.I.C. 32a (Treveri)*. 5 15

620 **Valens,** 364-378 (in the East). *R siliqua.* VRBS ROMA. Roma seated l. *R.I.C. 27e (Treveri)*. 25 70

620A Æ 3. SECVRITAS REIPVBLICAE. Victory advancing l. *R.I.C. 42b (Constantinople)*.................... 5 15

621 **Procopius,** usurper in the East, 365-366. Æ 3. REPARATIO FEL. TEMP. Emperor stg. r., holding standard and shield. *R.I.C. 17a (Constantinople)*. 50 125

622 **Gratian,** 367-383 (in the West), overthrown by Magnus Maximus who had been proclaimed emperor by the army in Britain. *R siliqua.* VRBS ROMA. Roma seated l. *R.I.C. 27f (Treveri)*. 30 75

623 **Valentinian II,** 375-392 (in the West). Æ 2. REPARATIO REIPVB. Emperor stg. l., raising kneeling female figure. *R.I.C. 20c (Arelate)*. 10 30

623A Æ 4. SALVS REIPVBLICAE. Victory advancing l., dragging barbarian. *R.I.C. 20a (Alexandria)*. 5 12

624 **Theodosius I,** the Great, 379-395 (in the East), son of the Count Theodosius who had cleared Britain of barbarian invaders in the reign of Valentinian I; the Emperor Theodosiua twice restored Britain to the rule of the central government, by his defeat of the usurpers Magnus Maximus (in 388) and Eugenius (in 394). *R siliqua.* CONCORDIA AVGGG. Constantinopolis enthroned facing, foot on prow. *R.I.C. 55a (Treveri)*. 30 75

624A

624A — VIRTVS ROMANORVM. Roma enthroned facing. *R.I.C. (Aquileia) 28d.* 30 75

624B Æ 2. VIRTVS EXERCIT. Emperor stg. r., foot on captive, holding labarum and globe. *R.I.C. 24b (Heraclea)*. 12 35

		F	VF
		£	£

625   **Aelia Flaccilla,** wife of Theodosius I. Æ 2. SALVS REIPVBLICAE.
      Victory seated r., inscribing Christian monogram on shield set on cippus.
      R.I.C. 81 (Constantinople). 25   65

626   627

626   **Magnus Maximus,** usurper in the West, 383-388, proclaimed emperor
      by the army in Britain, invaded Gaul, and overthrew the legitimate western
      emperor Gratian; possibly reopened the London mint for a brief issue of
      precious metal coinage (Rudyard Kipling presented a rather fanciful
      version of his career in "Puck of Pook's Hill"). *Æ siliqua.* VIRTVS
      ROMANORVM. Roma enthroned facing. *R.I.C. 84b (Treveri).* 35   95
      See also under Category 3.
627   **Flavius Victor,** son of Magnus Maximus, co-emperor 387-388. Æ 4.
      SPES ROMANORVM. Gateway of military camp. *RIC 55b (Aquileia).* 40   100
628   **Eugenius,** usurper in the West, 392-394, recognized in Britain until his
      defeat by Theodosius the Great. *Æ siliqua.* VIRTVS ROMANORVM.
      Roma seated l. on cuirass. *R.I.C. 106d (Treveri).* 120   275
629   **Arcadius,** 395-408 (in the East, co-emperor with his father Theodosius I
      from 383). *N solidus.* VICTORIA AVGGG. Emperor stg. r., foot on
      captive, holding standard and Victory. *R.I.C. 1205 (Milan).* 100   250

629A   631

629A Æ 2. GLORIA ROMANORVM. Emperor stg. l., holding standard and
      shield, captive at feet. *R.I.C. 41 (Antioch).* 15   40
630   **Honorius,** 395-423 (in the West, co-emperor with his father Theodosius I
      and brother Arcadius from 393), this reign saw the end of Roman rule in
      Britain following a succession of usurpations in the province, culminating
      in that of Constantine III against whom the Britons rebelled in 409;
      Honorius' celebrated 'Rescript' of the following year instructed the
      provincials to look to their own defence as he was no longer able to assist
      them. *N solidus.* VICTORIA AVGGG. Emperor stg. r., foot on captive,
      holding standard and Victory. *R.I.C. 1287 (Ravenna).* 100   250
630A *Æ siliqua.* VIRTVS ROMANORVM. Roma seated l. on cuirass.
      R.I.C. 1228 (Milan). 35   85
631   **Constantine III,** usurper in the West, 407-411, proclaimed emperor by the
      army in Britain, but his authority rejected by the Romano-Britons two years
      later, thus effectively ending 366 years of Roman rule in Britain. *Æ siliqua.*
      VICTORIA AVGGG. Roma enthroned l. *R.I.C. 1532 (Treveri).* 150   325

F	*VF*
£	£

632   **Valentinian III,** 425-455 (in the West), during whose reign the Saxon
conquest of the former Roman province commenced, following the final
unsuccessful appeal of the Romano-Britons for help addressed to the general
Aetius in 446. *N solidus.* VICTORIA AVGGG. Emperor stg. facing, foot
on human-headed serpent. *R.I.C. 2010 (Ravenna).*   125   300

632A   Æ 4. VOT. PVB. Gateway of military camp. *R.I.C. 2123 (Rome).*   25   75

2. ISSUES WITH TYPES REFERRING SPECIFICALLY TO THE PROVINCE OF BRITANNIA

Struck in Rome, unless otherwise indicated. These usually commemorate military operations in the
northern frontier region of the province or beyond.

633   635

F	*VF*
£	£

633   **Claudius,** A.D. 41-54. AV aureus, celebrating the early stages of the
Roman conquest of Britain which commenced in A.D. 43. DE BRITANN
on architrave of triumphal arch. *R.I.C. 33.*   1000   2500

634   Æ *denarius.* Similar. *R.I.C. 34.*..   300   750

634A   Æ *didrachm* of Caesarea in Cappadocia. DE BRITANNIS. Emperor in
triumphal quadriga r. *R.I.C. 122.*   300   750

635   **Hadrian,** 117-138. Æ as, commemorating the restoration of order in the
province following a serious uprising (or invasion) in the north, probably
early in the governorship of Q. Pompeius Falco (118-122). BRITANNIA
PONT. MAX. TR. POT. COS. III. S. C. Britannia seated facing on rock.
R.I.C. 577a.   175   450

636   Æ *sestertius,* commemorating Hadrian's visit to the province in 122, when
he planned and initiated the construction of the northern frontier system
which bears his name. ADVENTVI AVG. BRITANNIAE S.C. Emperor
and Britannia stg. either side of altar. *R.I.C. 882.* ....   *Extremely rare*

637

637   — BRITANNIA S. C. Britannia seated facing, foot resting on rock.
R.I.C. 845. ....   *Extremely rare*

	F £	VF £

637A Æ *dupondius* or as. *Similar. R.I.C. 846.*... *Extremely rare*

638 Æ *sestertius,* commemorating Hadrian's attention to the legionary garrison
strength of the province, principally his transfer of *VI Victrix* from
Germany in 122. EXERC. BRITANNICVS S. C. Emperor on horseback
r., addressing gathering of troops. *R.I.C. 912.* .... *Extremely rare*

638A — EXERC. BRITANNICVS S.C. Emperor stg. r. on tribunal, addressing
gathering of troops. *R.I.C. 913.*... *Extremely rare*

639 **Antoninus Pius, 138-161.** *N aureus,* commemorating the conquests in
Scotland by the governor Q. Lollius Urbicus (138/9-142/3) at which time
construction of the Antonine Wall was begun. BRITAN. IMPERATOR II.
Victory stg. l. on globe. *R.I.C. 113.*   800   2000

640

640 Æ *sestertius.* BRITANNIA S. C. Britannia seated l. on rock, holding
standard. *R.I.C. 742.*...   550   1400

641 — BRITAN. IMPERATOR II. S. C. Helmeted Britannia seated l., foot on
rock. *R.I.C. 743.*   550   1450

642 — BRITAN. IMPERATOR II. S. C. Britannia seated l. on globe above
waves, holding standard. *R.I.C. 744.*   650   1700

643 — BRITAN. IMPERATOR II. S. C. Victory stg. l. on globe. *R.I.C. 719.*   200   500

643A — BRITANNIA IMPERATOR II. S. C. Britannia seated l. on rock,
holding standard. *R.I.C. 745.*   550   1400

644 Æ *as.* IMPERATOR II. S. C. Victory hovering l., holding shield inscribed
BRI / TAN. *R.I.C. 732.*   90   225

645 Æ *dupondius,* commemorating the quelling of a serious uprising in the
north, ca. 154/5, necessitating the evacuation of the recently constructed
Antonine Wall in Scotland. BRITANNIA COS. IIII. S. C. Britannia seated
l. on rock, shield and vexillum in background. *R.I.C. 930.*   80   200

		F	VF
		£	£

646   Æ *as*. Similar. *R.I.C. 934.*   75   185

*Many specimens of this type are carelessly struck on inadequate flans.
Moreover, they have been found in significant quantities on Romano-British
sites, notably in Coventina's Well at Carrawburgh fort on Hadrian's Wall,
raising the interesting possibility that they may have been issued from a
temporary mint in Britain. The style of the engraving is quite regular,
indicating that even if locally produced these coins would have been struck
from normal Roman dies brought to Britain especially for this purpose.
See under Category 3.*

647   **Commodus,** 177-192. Æ *sestertius*, commemorating the victories in
Scotland of the governor Ulpius Marcellus in 184/5. These were in
retribution for a major barbarian invasion several years earlier resulting
in serious damage to Hadrian's Wall, which had been temporarily overrun,
and the defeat and death of an unknown governor. BRITT. P. M. TR. P.
VIIII. IMP. VII. COS. IIII. P. P. S. C. Britannia stg. l., holding curved
sword and helmet. *R.I.C. 437.* ....   *Extremely rare*

648

648   — VICT. BRIT. P. M. TR. P. VIIII. (or X.) IMP. VII. COS. IIII. P. P. S. C.
Victory seated r., about to inscribe shield. *R.I.C. 440, 452*   120   300

649

649   **Septimius Severus,** 193-211. *N aureus*, commemorating the success of
the punitive Roman campaigns in Scotland during 209 and 210 culminating
in the illness and death of Severus at York in Feb. 211. VICTORIAE BRIT.
Victory advancing l. *R.I.C. 334.*   1200   3000

650   — VICTORIAE BRIT. Victory advancing r., leading child by hand.
R.I.C. 302.   1500   3500

651   Æ *denarius*. VICTORIAE BRIT. Victory advancing r. *R.I.C. 332.*   40   90

651A   — VICTORIAE BRIT. Victory stg. facing beside palm-tree with shield
attached. *R.I.C. 336.*   40   90

651B   — VICTORIAE BRIT. Victory stg. l. *R.I.C. 333.*   40   90

651C   — VICTORIAE BRIT. Victory seated l., holding shield. *R.I.C. 335.*   40   85

652

	F	VF
	£	£

652 Æ *sestertius*. VICTORIAE BRITTANNICAE S. C. Two Victories placing shield on palm-tree with captives at base. *R.I.C. 818.* .... | 300 | 875

653 — P. M. TR. P. XVIII. COS. III. P. P. S. C. Similar. *R.I.C. 796.* .... | 175 | 400

654 Æ *dupondius*. VICT. BRIT. P. M. TR. P. XIX. COS. III. P. P. S. C. Victory stg. r. between two captives, holding vexillum. *R.I.C. 809.* .... | 100 | 275

655 Æ *as*. VICTORIAE BRITTANNICAE S. C. Similar. *R.I.C. 837a.* .... | 100 | 275

656 Billon *tetradrachm* of Alexandria in Egypt. NEIKH KATA BRET. Nike flying l. *Milne 2726.*,.. | *Extremely rare*

657 **Caracalla,** 198-217. *N aureus,* commemorating the victories achieved by the Romans in Scotland during the campaigns led jointly by Severus and Caracalla in 209, and by Caracalla alone the following year during his father's illness. VICTORIAE BRIT. Victory seated l., holding shield. *R.I.C. 174.* .... | 1200 | 3000

658   659A

658 Æ *denarius*. VICTORIAE BRIT. Victory advancing l. *R.I.C. 231.* .... | 40 | 85

658A — VICTORIAE BRIT. Victory advancing r., holding trophy. *R.I.C. 231A.* | 40 | 85

659 Æ *sestertius*. VICTORIAE BRITTANNICAE S. C. Victory stg. r., erecting trophy to r. of which Britannia stands facing, captive at feet. *R.I.C. 464.* | 250 | 675

659A — VICT. BRIT. TR. P. XIIII. COS. III. S.C. Similar. *Cf. R.I.C. 483c.* ... | 225 | 600

660 Æ *dupondius*. VICTORIAE BRITTANNICAE S. C. Victory stg. r., inscribing shield set on palm-tree. *R.I.C. 467.* .... | 100 | 275

661 Æ *as*. VICT. BRIT. TR. P. XIIII. COS. III. S. C. Similar. *R.I.C. 490.* ..... | 100 | 250

662 **Geta,** 209-212. Æ *denarius,* commemorating the victories achieved by his father and brother in Scotland in 209-10 while he and his mother were resident in London. VICTORIAE BRIT. Victory stg. l. *R.I.C. 92.* .... | 40 | 85

662A — VICTORIAE BRIT. Victory advancing r. *R.I.C. 91.*............................ | 40 | 85

663

		F	VF
		£	£
663	Æ *sestertius.* VICTORIAE BRITTANNICAE S. C. Victory seated r., inscribing shield set on knee. *R.I.C. 166.*	300	750
663A	— VICT. BRIT. TR. P. III. COS. II. S. C. Similar. *R.I.C. 172b.*	250	600
664	Æ *as.* VICTORIAE BRITTANNICAE S. C. Victory seated l., balancing shield on knee. *R.I.C. 191a.*	100	275
665	Billon *tetradrachm* of Alexandria in Egypt. NEIKH KATA BRETAN. Nike advancing l. *B.M.C. (Alexandria) 1481.*	*Extremely rare*	

3. OFFICIAL ROMAN COINAGE STRUCK IN BRITAIN

The London mint, and the associated 'C' mint (possibly Colchester), were created by the usurper Carausius soon after his seizure of Britain in 287. Prior to this, in the mid-2nd century, there may have been minting of 'Britannia' asses of Antoninus Pius in the province using dies brought from Rome, though this has not been firmly established. After the downfall of the rebel British regime in 296 the minting establishment in London (though not the subsidiary mint) was retained by the tetrarchal government and the succeeding Constantinian administration. Early in 325, however, Constantine the Great closed the London mint after almost four decades of operation. A possible brief revival under the usurper Magnus Maximus has been postulated for gold and silver coins marked 'AVG', 'AVGOB' and 'AVGPS', though the attribution has not received universal acceptance.

		F	VF
		£	£
666	**Antoninus Pius,** 138-161. Æ *as,* struck in northern Britain (?) in 155. BRITANNIA COS. IIII. S. C. Britannia seated l. on rock, shield and vexillum in background. *R.I.C. 930.*	75	185

Many poorly struck examples of this type have been found on Romano-British sites, notably at Brocolitia (Carrawburgh) fort on Hadrian's Wall in Northumberland, where no fewer than 327 specimens were discovered in the great votive deposit in the well which formed part of the shrine of the water-nymph Coventina. There appears to be a very real possibility that many of these 'Britannia' asses had been issued from a temporary mint in Britain, most likely situated in the north. The dies, however, are quite regular, and would thus have been brought from Rome to the island province for the express purpose of supplementing the money supply at a time of crisis.

| 667 | **Carausius,** usurper in Britain and northwestern Gaul, A.D. 287-293. N *aureus,* London. CONSERVAT. AVG. Jupiter stg. l., eagle at feet, ML in ex. *R.I.C. 1.* | 5000 | 12500 |
| 668 | Æ *denarius,* London. EXPECTATE VENI. Britannia stg. r. and emperor l., clasping hands, RSR in ex. *R.I.C. 555.* | 450 | 1200 |

669 672A

	F	VF
	£	£

669 — RENOVAT. ROMANO. She-wolf r., suckling twins, RSR in ex.
R.I.C. 571. .... 350 900

670 Billon *antoninianus,* London. COMES AVG. Victory stg. 1., S—P in field,
ML in ex. *R.I.C. 14.* 45 110

670A — HILARITAS AVG. Hilaritas stg. 1., B—E in field, MLXXI in ex. *R.I.C. 41.* 30 80

671 — LAETITIA AVG. Laetitia stg. 1., F—O in field, ML in ex. *R.I.C. 50.* 30 80

671A — LEG. II. AVG. Capricorn 1., ML in ex. *R.I.C. 58.* 80 195
Legio II Augusta was stationed at Isca (Caerleon in South Wales).

672 — LEG. XX. V. V. Boar stg. r. *R.I.C. 82.* 80 195
*Legio XX Valeria Victrix was stationed at Deva (Chester in the northwest
Midlands).*

672A — PAX AVG. Pax stg. 1., F O in field, ML in ex. *R.I.C. 101.* 25 70

673 — Similar, but without mint mark. *R.I.C. 880.* 25 65

673A — PROVIDENT. AVG. Providentia stg. 1., B—E in field, MLXXI in ex.
R.I.C. 149. .... 30 80

674 — SALVS AVGGG. Salus stg. r., feeding snake held in her arms, S—P
in field, ML in ex. *R.I.C. 164.* 30 80
*The reverse legends with triple-ending (AVGGG.) presumably are
subsequent to Carausius' recognition by Diocletian and Maximian in 289
following the failure of the latter's attempt to dislodge the usurper from
his island stronghold.*

674A — TEMPORVM FELICITAS. Felicitas stg. 1., B—E in field, ML in ex.
R.I.C. 172. .... 25 70

675 — VIRTVS AVGGG. Mars (or Virtus) stg. r., holding spear and shield,
S—P in field, MLXXI in ex. *R.I.C. 183.* 30 80

676 Billon *antoninianus,* Colchester (?). CONCORDIA MILIT. Emperor stg.
r. and Concordia 1., clasping hands, C in ex. *R.I.C. 205.* 55 130

676A — EXPECTATE VENI. Britannia stg. r. and emperor 1., clasping hands,
MSC in ex. *R.I.C. 216.* 100 250

677 — FELICITAS AVG. Galley with mast and rowers, CXXI in ex. *R.I.C. 221.* 80 200

677A — FORTVNA RAEDVX. Fortuna seated 1., SPC in ex. *R.I.C. 237.* 40 100

678 — LAETITIA AVG. Laetitia stg. 1., globe at feet, S—P in field, C in ex.
R.I.C. 255. .... 30 80

678A — MONETA AVG. Moneta stg. 1., CXXI in ex. *R.I.C. 287.* 30 80

679 — ORIENS AVG. Sol stg. 1., C in ex. *R.I.C. 293.* 35 85

679A — PAX AVGGG. Pax stg. 1., S—P in field, MC in ex. *R.I.C. 335.* 30 70

680

		F	VF
		£	£

680 — PROVID. AVG. Providentia stg. l., S—P in field, C in ex. *R.I.C. 353.*   30   80
680A — SALVS AVG. Salus stg. l. at altar, feeding snake, S—C in field,
       C in ex. *R.I.C. 396.*   30   80
681 — SPES PVBLICA. Spes walking l., holding flower, S—P in field,
       C in ex. *R.I.C. 413.*   30   80
681A — VICTORIA AVG. Victory advancing l., captive at feet, MC in ex.
       R.I.C. 429.   35   85
682 **Carausius, Diocletian and Maximian,** after 289. Billon *antoninianus,*
       Colchester (?). Obv. CARAVSIVS ET FRATRES SVI. Conjoined busts
       of the three emperors l. Rev. PAX AVGGG. Pax stg. l., S—P in field,
       C in ex. *R.I.C. 1.* 800 2000

682A   684A

682A — MONETA AVGGG. Moneta stg. l., S—P in field, C in ex. *R.I.C. —.*   1000   2500
       See also nos. 693-4 and 698-700 as well as regular Carausian types with
       the triple-ending 'AVGGG.' on reverse.
683 **Allectus,** usurper in Britain, 293-296. *Ɲ aureus,* London. ORIENS AVG.
       Sol stg. l. between two captives, ML in ex. *R.I.C. 4.* 7000 17500
684 Æ *antoninianus,* London. LAETITIA AVG. Laetitia stg. l., S—A in field,
       MSL in ex. *R.I.C. 22.*   30   80
684A — PAX AVG. Pax stg. l., S—A in field, ML in ex. *R.I.C. 28.*   35   80
685 — PROVID. AVG. Providentia stg. l., holding globe and cornucopiae,
       S—P in field, ML in ex. *R.I.C. 36.*   35   85
685A — SALVS AVG. Salus stg. r., feeding snake held in her arms, S—A in
       field, MSL in ex. *R.I.C. 42.*   30   80
686 — TEMPOR. FELICITAS. Felicitas stg. l., S—A in field, ML in ex. *R.I.C. 47.*   30   80
686A — VICTORIA AVG. Victory advancing l., S—P in field, ML in ex. *R.I.C. 48.*   30   80
687 Æ *antoninianus,* Colchester (?). AEQVITAS AVG. Aequitas stg. l., S—P
       in field, C in ex. *R.I.C. 63.*   30   80
687A — FIDES MILITVM. Fides stg. l., holding two standards, S—P in field,
       C in ex. *R.I.C. 69.*   30   80

688A

		F	VF
		£	£

688 — LAETITIA AVG. Laetitia stg. l., S—P in field, CL in ex. *R.I.C. 79.*.   40   100
This form of mint mark has given rise to the alternative identification of this mint as Clausentum (Bitterne, Hants.)

688A — MONETA AVG. Moneta stg. l., S—P in field, C in ex. *R.I.C. 82.*   40   95

689 — PAX AVG. Pax stg. l., S—P in field, C in ex. *R.I.C. 86.*   35   80

689A — PROVIDENTIA AVG. Providentia stg. l., globe at feet, S—P in field,
C in ex. *R.I.C. 111.*   30   80

690 — TEMPORVM FELIC. Felicitas stg. l., S—P in field, CL in ex. *R.I.C. 117.*   40   100

690A — VIRTVS AVG. Mars stg. r., holding spear and shield, S—P in field,
C in ex. *R.I.C. 121.*   30   80

691 Æ '*quinarius*', London. VIRTVS AVG. Galley l., QL in ex. *R.I.C. 55.* ..   30   85
An experimental denomination issued only during this reign, the types of the so-called 'quinarius' would seem to indicate that it was in some way associated with the operations of the fleet upon which the survival of the rebel regime in Britain was totally dependent.

692   693

692 Æ '*quinarius*', Colchester (?). LAETITIA AVG. Galley r., QC in ex.
R.I.C. 124.   35   85

692A — VIRTVS AVG. Galley l., QC in ex. *R.I.C. 128.*   35   85

693 **Diocletian,** 284-305. Billon *antoninianus* of London, struck by Carausius
between 289 and 293. PAX AVGGG. Pax stg. l., S—P in field, MLXXI
in ex. *R.I.C. 9.*   35   85

694 Billon *antoninianus* of Colchester (?), same date. PROVID AVGGG.
Providentia stg. l., globe at feet, S—P in field, C in ex. *R.I.C. 22.*   35   85

695

	F	VF
	£	£

695   Æ *follis*, London. GENIO POPVLI ROMANI. Genius stg. l., LON in ex.
      R.I.C. 1a.   125   275
      By the time the central government had recovered control of Britain in 296
      the antoninianus had been replaced by the larger follis under Diocletian's
      sweeping currency reform. London was retained as an official imperial
      mint, but the secondary British establishment (at Colchester?) was now
      abandoned. Except for its initial issue in 297 (marked 'LON') the London
      mint under the tetrarchic government produced only unsigned folles
      throughout its first decade of operation. Perhaps Constantius did not
      wish to draw attention to his employment of a mint which had been the
      creation of a rebel regime.

696

696   — Similar, but without mint mark. *R.I.C. 6a.*   15   35
697   — (post-abdication coinage, after 305). PROVIDENTIA DEORVM
      QVIES AVGG. Quies and Providentia stg. facing each other (no mint mark).
      R.I.C. 77a.   30   65
697A — QVIES AVGG. Quies stg. l., holding branch and sceptre, PLN in ex.
      R.I.C. 98.   20   50
698   **Maximian,** 286-305 and 306-308. *N aureus* of London, struck by
      Carausius between 289 and 293. SALVS AVGGG. Salus stg. r., feeding
      snake held in her arms, ML in ex. *R.I.C. 32.* ....   *Extremely rare*
699   Billon *antoninianus* of London, same date. PROVIDENTIA AVGGG.
      Providentia stg. l., S—P in field, MLXXI in ex. *R.I.C. 37.*   35   85
700   Billon *antoninianus* of Colchester (?), same date. PAX AVGGG. Pax stg.
      l., S—P in field, C in ex. *R.I.C. 42.*   35   85
701   Æ *follis,* London. GENIO POPVLI ROMANI. Genius stg. l., LON in ex.
      R.I.C. 2.   100   250
702   — Similar, but without mint mark. *R.I.C. 23b.*   15   35
703   — (post-abdication coinage, after 305). PROVIDENTIA DEORVM
      QVIES AVGG. Quies and Providentia stg. facing each other (no mint mark).
      R.I.C. 77b.   30   65

704

		F	VF
		£	£
704	— (second reign). GENIO POP. ROM. Genius stg. l., PLN in ex. *R.I.C. 90.*	20	40
704A	— HERCVLI CONSERVATORI. Hercules stg. l., resting on club, PLN in ex. *R.I.C. 91.*	30	75
705	**Constantius I,** 305-306 (Caesar 293-305). *Æ follis,* London (as Caesar). GENIO POPVLI ROMANI. Genius stg. l., LON in ex. *R.I.C. 4a.*	110	275

706

706	— Similar, but without mint mark. *R.I.C. 30*	15	35
707	— (as Augustus). Similar. *R.I.C. 52a.*	20	45
708	**Divus Constantius I,** deified 306. *Æ follis,* London. MEMORIA FELIX. Altar flanked by eagles, PLN in ex. *R.I.C. 110.*	20	50
709	**Galerius,** 305-311 (Caesar 293-305). *Æ follis,* London (as Caesar). GENIO POPVLI ROMANI. Genius stg. l., LON in ex. *R.I.C. 4b.*	110	275
710	— Similar, but without mint mark. *R.I.C. 15.*	10	25
711	— (as Augustus). Similar. *R.I.C. 42.*	12	30
711A	— GENIO POP. ROM. Genius stg. l., PLN in ex. *R.I.C. 86.*	18	45
712	**Severus II,** 306-307 (Caesar 305-306). *Æ follis,* London (as Caesar). GENIO POPVLI ROMANI. Genius stg. l. (no mint mark). *R.I.C. 58a*	35	85
713	— (as Augustus). Similar. *R.I.C. 52c.*	35	85
714	**Maximinus II,** 310-313 (Caesar 305-310). *Æ follis,* London (as Caesar). GENIO POPVLI ROMANI. Genius stg. l. (no mint mark). *R.I.C. 57.*	15	40
715	— GENIO POP. ROM. Genius stg. l., PLN in ex. *R.I.C. 89a.*	15	40
716	— (as Augustus). Similar, but with star in r. field. *R.I.C. 209b.*	12	30
717	**Licinius,** 308-324. *Æ follis,* London. GENIO POP. ROM. Genius stg. l., star in r. field, PLN in ex. *R.I.C. 209c.*	12	30
717A	— Similar, but with S—F in field. *R.I.C. 3.*	8	20
718	— SOLI INVICTO COMITI. Sol stg. l., holding globe, S—P in field, MSL in ex. *R.I.C. 79.*	10	25
719	**Constantine I, the Great,** 307-337 (Caesar 306-307). *Æ follis,* London (as Caesar). GENIO POPVLI ROMANI. Genius stg. l. (no mint mark). *R.I.C. 72.*	25	65
719A	— GENIO POP. ROM. Genius stg. l., PLN in ex. *R.I.C. 88b*	15	35

	F £	VF £
720 — PRINCIPI IVVENTVTIS. Prince stg. l., holding standards, PLN in ex. *R.I.C. 97.*	25	60
721 — (as Augustus). ADVENTVS AVG. Emperor on horseback l., captive on ground before, star in r. field, PLN in ex. *R.I.C. 133.*	22	55

722

	F £	VF £
722 — COMITI AVGG. NN. Sol stg. l., holding globe and whip, same mint mark. *R.I.C. 155.*	18	45
723 — CONCORD. MILIT. Concordia stg. l., holding standards, same mint mark. *R.I.C. 195.*	15	40
724 — MARTI CONSERVATORI. Mars. stg. r., holding spear and shield, star in l. field, PLN in ex. *R.I.C. 254.*	15	35
724A — SOLI INVICTO COMITI. Sol stg. l., holding globe, S—F in field, MLL in ex. *R.I.C. 27.*	10	25
725 Æ 3, London. VICTORIAE LAETAE PRINC. PERP. Two Victories supporting shield, inscribed VOT. / P. R., over altar, PLN in ex. *R.I.C. 159.*	10	25
726 — VIRTVS EXERCIT. Vexillum, inscribed VOT. / XX., between two captives, PLN in ex. R.I.C. 191.	10	25
727 — BEAT. TRANQLITAS. Altar, inscribed VOT / IS / XX., surmounted by globe and three stars, PLON in ex. *R.I.C. 267.*	10	25
727A — SARMATIA DEVICTA. Victory advancing r., trampling captive, PLON and crescent in ex. *R.I.C. 289.*	20	45
728 — PROVIDENTIAE AVGG. Gateway of military camp, PLON in ex. *R.I.C. 293.*	10	25
729 **Fausta,** wife of Constantine I. Æ 3, London. SALVS REIPVBLICAE. Empress stg. l., holding two children, PLON in ex. *R.I.C. 300.*	60	150
730 **Helena,** mother of Constantine I. Æ 3, London. SECVRITAS REIPVBLICE. Empress stg. l., holding branch, PLON in ex. *R.I.C. 299.*	60	150
731 **Crispus,** eldest son of Constantine I, Caesar 317-326. Æ 3, London. SOLI INVICTO COMITI. Sol stg. l., holding globe, crescent in l. field, PLN in ex. *R.I.C. 144.*	12	30
731A — VIRTVS EXERCIT. Vexillum, inscribed VOT. / XX., between two captives, PLN in ex. *R.I.C. 194.*	12	30
732 — BEATA TRANQVILLITAS. Altar, inscribed VOT / IS / XX., surmounted by globe and three stars, P—A in field, PLON in ex. *R.I.C. 211.*	12	30
733 — CAESARVM NOSTRORVM around wreath containing VOT. / X., PLON and crescent in ex. *R.I.C. 291.*	12	30

734   737A

	F	VF
	£	£

734 — PROVIDENTIAE CAESS. Gateway of military camp, PLON in ex.
R.I.C. 295.   10   25

735 **Constantine II,** 337-340 (Caesar 317-337). Æ 3, London (as Caesar).
CLARITAS REIPVBLICAE. Sol stg. l., holding globe, crescent in l. field,
PLN in ex. R.I.C. 131.   12   30

736 — VICTORIAE LAETAE PRINC. PERP. Two Victories supporting shield,
inscribed VOT. / P. R., over altar ornamented with wreath, PLN in ex.
R.I.C. 182.   12   30

737 — VIRTVS EXERCIT. Vexillum, inscribed VOT. / XX., between two
captives, PLON in ex. R.I.C. 190.   12   30

737A — BEATA TRANQVILLITAS. Altar, inscribed VOT / IS / XX.,
surmounted by globe and three stars, PLON in ex. R.I.C. 236.   10   25

738 — CAESARVM NOSTRORVM around wreath containing VOT. / X.,
PLON and crescent in ex. R.I.C. 292.   10   25

738A — PROVIDENTIAE CAESS. Gateway of military camp, PLON in ex.
R.I.C. 296.   10   25

739 **Constantius II,** 337-361 (Caesar 324-337). Æ 3, London (as Caesar).
PROVIDENTIAE CAESS. Gateway of military camp, PLON in ex.
R.I.C. 298.   25   60

740 **Magnus Maximus,** usurper in the West, 383-388. N solidus, London (?).
RESTITVTOR REIPVBLICAE. Emperor stg. r., holding labarum and
Victory, AVG in ex. R.I.C. 1. ....   *Unique*
The attribution to London of this rare series has not been firmly established,
though Maximus was certainly proclaimed emperor in Britain and it is
well attested that the principal city of the British provinces bore the name
'Augusta' in the late Roman period (Ammianus Marcellinus XXVII, 8, 7;
XXVIII, 3, 7).

741

741 — VICTORIA AVGG. Two emperors enthroned facing, Victory hovering
in background between them, AVGOB in ex. R.I.C. 2b.   5000   10000
Maximus appears to have struck a similar type in the name of the eastern
emperor Theodosius I (cf. R.I.C. 2a), though it is presently known only
from a silver-gilt specimen preserved in the British Museum.

		F	VF
		£	£
742	Æ *siliqua*, London (?). VOT. / V. / MVLT. / X. within wreath, AVG below. *R.I.C. 4.*	850	2000
742A	— VICTORIA AVGG. Victory advancing l., AVGPS in ex. *R.I.C. 3.*	750	1750

4. IMITATIONS OF ROMAN COINS PRODUCED IN BRITAIN

At certain periods during the three and a half centuries of its occupation Roman Britain seems to have been the source of much local imitation of the official imported coinage. This began soon after the Claudian invasion in A.D. 43 when significant quantities of sestertii, dupondii and asses (especially the last) were produced in the newly conquered territory, as evidenced by the frequency of their occurrence in archaeological finds. The technical excellence of many of these 'copies', together with the surprising extent of their minting, would seem to indicate that some, at least, of these coins were produced with official sanction in order to make good an unexpected deficiency in the currency supply. Others are much poorer and well below weight, representing the 'unofficial' branch of this operation, some of it probably emanating from territory as yet unconquered. As conditions in the new province settled down rapid Romanization and urbanization of British society brought a general increase in wealth, and with it a much greater volume of currency flowing into the country. Local imitation now virtually ceased, except for the occasional activities of criminal counterfeiters, and this state of affairs lasted down to the great political crisis and financial collapse of the second half of the 3rd century. At this point large scale minting of imitations of the debased antoniniani of the late 260s and early 270s began in Britain and in the other northwestern provinces, all of which had been serioulsy affected by the political dislocation of this turbulent era. This class of imitations is usually referred to as 'barbarous radiates', the emperor's spiky crown being a constant and conspicuous feature of the obverses. Most frequently copied were the antoniniani of the Gallic rulers Tetricus Senior and Tetricus Junior (ca. 270-273) and the posthumous issues of Claudius Gothicus (died 270). The quality of the 'barbarous radiates' is variable in the extreme, some exhibiting what appears to be a revival of Celtic art forms, others so tiny that it is virtually impossible to see anything of the design. Their production appears to have ended abruptly with Aurelian's reconquest of the western provinces in 273. A similar phenomenon, though on a lesser scale, occurred in the middle decades of the following century when normal life in Britain was again disrupted, not only by usurpation but additionally by foreign invasion. With supplies of currency from the Continent temporarily disrupted local imitation, particularly of the 'Æ 2' and 'Æ 3' issues of Constantius II and the usurper Magnentius, began in earnest. How long this continued is difficult to determine as life in the island province was now subject to increasingly frequent episodes of dislocation. By now urban life in Britain was in serious decline and when Roman rule ended early in the 5th century, bringing a total cessation of currency supplies, the catastrophic decline in monetary commerce in the former provinces rendered it no longer necessary for the deficiency to be made good.

		F	VF
		£	£
743	**Agrippa,** died 12 B.C. Æ as, of irregular British mintage, imitating the Roman issue made under Agrippa's grandson Caligula, A.D. 37-41. S. C. Neptune stg. l., holding dolphin and trident.....................................	40	100
	The large official issue of Agrippa asses was made shortly before the Claudian invasion of Britain in A.D. 43 and would thus have comprised a significant proportion of the 'aes' in circulation at this time. In consequence, it would soon have become familiar to the new provincials providing an ideal prototype for imitation.		
744	**Claudius,** 41-54. Æ *sestertius,* of irregular British mintage. SPES AVGVSTA S. C. Spes walking l., holding flower.	75	250
745	Æ *dupondius,* of irregular British mintage. CERES AVGVSTA S. C. Ceres enthroned l., holding corn- ears and torch.	35	100

746

		F	VF
		£	£

746   Æ *as,* of irregular British mintage. S. C. Minerva advancing r., brandishing
spear and holding shield..   30   85
This is by far the commonest of the Claudian imitations and the prototypes
must have represented the bulk of the aes coinage carried by the legions at
the time of the invasion. The martial type may well have been specially
selected as a suitable theme for the initial import of coinage into the newly
conquered territory.

747   **Nero Claudius Drusus,** father of Claudius, died 9 B.C. Æ *sestertius,* of
irregular British mintage. TI. CLAVDIVS CAESAR AVG. P. M. TR .P.
IMP. S. C. Claudius seated l. on curule chair amidst arms......................   85   300
This type was issued by Claudius half a century after his father's death and
would thus have been prominently represented in the initial wave of coinage
imported into the new province.

748   **Antonia,** mother of Claudius, died A.D. 37. Æ *dupondius,* of irregular British
mintage. TI. CLAVDIVS CAESAR AVG P.M. TR. P. IMP. P. P. S. C. Claudius
stg. l., holding simpulum..   60   175
Another Claudian issue for a deceased parent, this represents one of only
two dupondius types struck during this reign and would have entered
Britain in significant quantities at the time of the invasion in A.D. 43.

749A   749B

749C

749   **'Barbarous radiates',** ca. 270-273. British and Continental imitations of
billon *antoniniani,* principally of Divus Claudius II (A), Tetricus Senior
(B) and Tetricus Junior (C). The inscriptions are usually blundered and
the types sometimes unrecognizable. British mintage can only be
established by provenance.   5   10

F	*VF*
£	£

750 **Barbarous 4th century,** mostly of the second half of the century, and
principally imitated from 'Æ 2' and 'Æ 3' issues of the later Constantinian
period, notably those of Constantius II ('soldier spearing fallen horseman'
type), and the usurpers Magnentius and Decentius ('two Victories' type).
The copies, especially those of Magnentius and Decentius, are often of
excellent style and execution, though the legends frequently contain small
errors. Those of Constantius II are sometimes very barbarous and poorly
struck, occasionally over regular issues of the earlier Constantinian period.
Again, the likelihood of British mintage can only be established by
provenance. 5-8   10-15

Grading of Hammered Coins

As the name suggests, hammered coins were struck by hand with a hammer. This can lead to the coin being struck off centre, double struck, weak in the design, suffer cracks or flan defects. It is important to take these factors into account when assessing the grade of this series. Value is considerably reduced if the coin is holed, pierced, plugged or mounted.

Extremely Fine
Design and legends
sharp and clear.

Very Fine
Design and legends
still clear but with
slight evidence of wear
and/or minor damage.

Fine
Showing quite a lot of
wear but still with
design and legends
distinguishable.

William I PAXS type penny

Henry VIII 1st coinage gold Angel

Edward VI silver shilling

EARLY & MIDDLE ANGLO-SAXON KINGDOMS & MINTS (C.650-973)

Approximate extent of Danelaw

Approximate extent of Hiberno-Norse Kingdom of York

NORTHUMBRIA

York

Lincoln

Chester

Newark (?)

Derby

Nottingham

Stafford

Shrewsbury

Leicester

Stamford (?)

Norwich

Tamworth

EAST ANGLIA

MERCIA

Thetford

Northampton

Huntingdon

Warwick

Newport

Bedford

Hereford

Buckingham

Hertford

Maldon

Gloucester

Oxford

Malmesbury

Wallingford

London

Bath

Rochester

Canterbury

Wilton

Winchester

KENT

Dover

Barnstaple

Langport

Lympne

Shaftesbury

Southampton

Lewes

WESSEX

Exeter

Bridport

Wareham

Chichester

Totnes

EARLY ANGLO-SAXON PERIOD, *c.* 600-*c.* 775

The withdrawal of Roman forces from Britain early in the 5th century A.D. and the gradual decline of central administration resulted in a rapid deterioration of the money supply. The arrival of Teutonic raiders and settlers hastened the decay of urban commercial life and it was probably not until late in the 6th century that renewed political, cultural and commercial links with the kingdom of the Merovingian Franks led to the appearance of small quantities of Merovingian gold *tremisses* (one-third solidus) in England. A purse containing such pieces was found in the Sutton Hoo ship-burial. Native Anglo-Saxon gold *thrymsas* were minted from about the 630s, initially in the style of their continental prototypes or copied from obsolete Roman coinage and later being made in pure Anglo-Saxon style. By the middle of the 7th century the gold coinage was being increasingly debased with silver, and gold had been superseded entirely by about 675.

These silver coins, contemporary with the *deniers or denarii* of the Merovingian Franks, are the first English pennies, though they are commonly known today as *sceattas* (a term more correctly translated as 'treasure' or 'wealth'). They provide important material for the student of Anglo-Saxon art.

Though the earliest sceattas are a transition from the gold thrymsa coinage, coins of new style were soon developed which were also copied by the Frisians of the Low Countries. Early coins appear to have a standard weight of 20 grains (1.29 gms) and are of good silver content, though the quality deteriorates early in the 8th century. These coins exist in a large number of varied types, and as well as the official issues there are mules and other varieties which are probably contemporary imitations. Many of the sceattas were issued during the reign of Aethelbald of Mercia, but as few bear inscriptions it is only in recent years that research has permitted their correct dating and the attribution of certain types to specific areas. Some silver sceattas of groups II and III and most types of groups IV to X were issued during the period (A.D. 716-757) when Aethelbald, King of Mercia, was overlord of the southern English. Though a definitive classification has not yet been developed, the arrangement given below follows the latest work on the series: this list is not exhaustive.

This section has been catalogued in line with research published by Dr D. M. Metcalf. Wherever possible the catalogue number previously in use has been retained. Where it has been necessary to allocate a new and different number, the 'old' S. number is listed, in brackets, at the end of the entry. New entries are given a new number. The primary sceattas are followed by the secondary sceattas and, finally, the continental sceattas. This is not chronologically correct but has been adopted for ease of reference and identification. The reference 'B.M.C.' is to the type given in *British Museum Catalogue: Anglo-Saxon Coins.* Other works of reference include:

North, J. J. *English Hammered Coinage*, Vol. 1, *c.* 650-1272 (1994).
Metcalf, D.M. *Thrymsas and Sceattas in the Ashmolean Museum,* Vols I-III.
Rigold, S. E. 'The two primary series of sceattas', *B.N.J.,* xxx (1960).
Sutherland, C. H. V. *Anglo-Saxon Gold Coinage in the light of the Crondall Hoard* (1948).

ᚠᚪᚦᛖᚱᚴ·ᚷᚹᚻᚾ�ᛁ·ᚩᛋᚳᛁᛠᛏᛒᛗᚪᚾᚷᛉᚻᛟᚠᚫᛟ·ᛁ

f   u   th o r k . z w h   n   i   j   ih   p   x   s   t b e   m   l ng   d   oe a Æ ea   y

Early Anglo-Saxon Runes

GOLD

	F	VF
	£	£

A.   Early pieces, of uncertain monetary status

751   Thrymsa. Name and portrait of Bishop Leudard (chaplain to Queen Bertha
of Kent). ℞. Cross. ....   *Extremely rare*

752   Solidus. Imitating solidi of Roman rulers. Blundered legends, some
with runes. ....   *Extremely rare*

753   754   755

	F	VF
	£	£

B.   Crondall types, *c.*620 – *c.*645

Twelve different types, which are almost certainly English, were found in the Crondall hoard of 1828. All are thrysmas, containing 70-40% gold.

753   'Witmen' type. Bust r. with trident. R. Cross. Legend normally blundered.
M. 1-21 700   1650

754   London-derived type. Head r. with pseudo-legend. R. Cross. Pseudo-legend.
M. 22-32 825   2250

755   'Licius' type. Elegant imitation of Roman triens. Bust l. R. VOT XX.
M. 33-41 950   2750

756   757   758

756   'LEMC' type. Head l. R. Maltese cross with letters L, E, M, C in angles,
or cross on steps. *M. 42-9* 750   2000

757   'LONDINIV' type. Facing bust, crosslets l. and r. R. Tall cross,
LONDVNIV and pseudo-legend around. *M. 51-7* 1100   3250

758   — similar, but bust r. AVDVARLD REGES. R. Tall cross, LONDENV.
Usually garbled. *M. 50* 1000   3000

759   762

759   Other crude types, usually with head or bust, R. Cross. *M. 58-72* 600   1450

C.   Ultra-Crondall types, *c.*620 – 655?

Thrymsas not represented in the Crondall hoard, but probably of the same date range.

760   'Benutigo' type. Bust r., blundered legend. R. Cross on steps, runic
legend (Benutigoii?) 900   2500

761   'Wuneetton' type. Bust r., cross before. R. Cross. Blundered legend
(WVNEETON or similar). *M. 77* 750   2000

762   'York' type. Kite-shaped shield enclosing cross, crosslets to l. and r.,
squared pattern beneath. R. Cross. Blundered (runic?) legend. *M. 76* 1100   3250

D.   Post-Crondall types, *c.*655 – *c.*675

Pale gold types, visibly debased and sometimes almost silvery, containing 35-10% gold.

764   'Crispus' type. Helmeted bust, r. CRISPUS NOB CAES. R. Cross and XX
in wreath, runic legend De Lundonia (?). *N.7* 1100   3250

765   'Concordia' type. Radiate bust r. R. Clasped hands. *N.5* 1100   3250

766   'Oath-taking' type. Bust r. or l. with hand placed against cross. R.
Lyre-shaped object, or eight-rayed symbol. *N.6* 850   2350

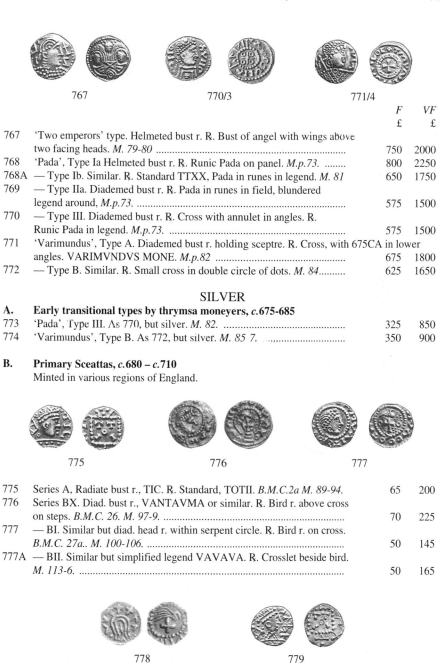

767   770/3   771/4

		F	VF
		£	£
767	'Two emperors' type. Helmeted bust r. R. Bust of angel with wings above two facing heads. *M. 79-80*	750	2000
768	'Pada', Type Ia Helmeted bust r. R. Runic Pada on panel. *M.p.73.*	800	2250
768A	— Type Ib. Similar. R. Standard TTXX, Pada in runes in legend. *M. 81*	650	1750
769	— Type IIa. Diademed bust r. R. Pada in runes in field, blundered legend around, *M.p.73.*	575	1500
770	— Type III. Diademed bust r. R. Cross with annulet in angles. R. Runic Pada in legend. *M.p.73.*	575	1500
771	'Varimundus', Type A. Diademed bust r. holding sceptre. R. Cross, with 675CA in lower angles. VARIMVNDVS MONE. *M.p.82*	675	1800
772	— Type B. Similar. R. Small cross in double circle of dots. *M. 84*	625	1650

SILVER

A.   **Early transitional types by thrymsa moneyers, *c.675-685***

773	'Pada', Type III. As 770, but silver. *M. 82.*	325	850
774	'Varimundus', Type B. As 772, but silver. *M. 85 7.*	350	900

B.   **Primary Sceattas, *c.680 – c.710***

Minted in various regions of England.

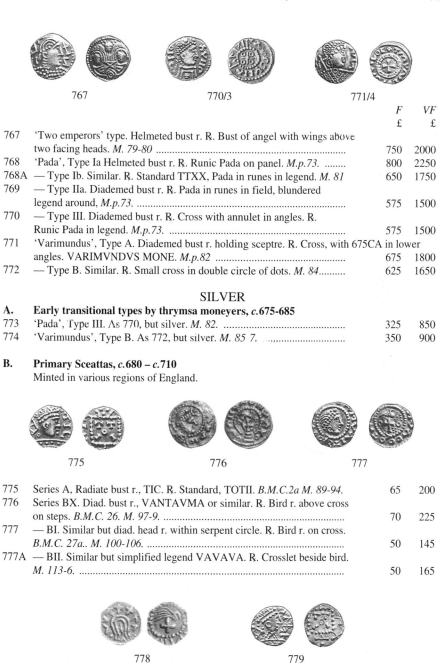

775   776   777

775	Series A, Radiate bust r., TIC. R. Standard, TOTII. *B.M.C.2a M. 89-94.*	65	200
776	Series BX. Diad. bust r., VANTAVMA or similar. R. Bird r. above cross on steps. *B.M.C. 26. M. 97-9.*	70	225
777	— BI. Similar but diad. head r. within serpent circle. R. Bird r. on cross. *B.M.C. 27a.. M. 100-106.*	50	145
777A	— BII. Similar but simplified legend VAVAVA. R. Crosslet beside bird. *M. 113-6.*	50	165

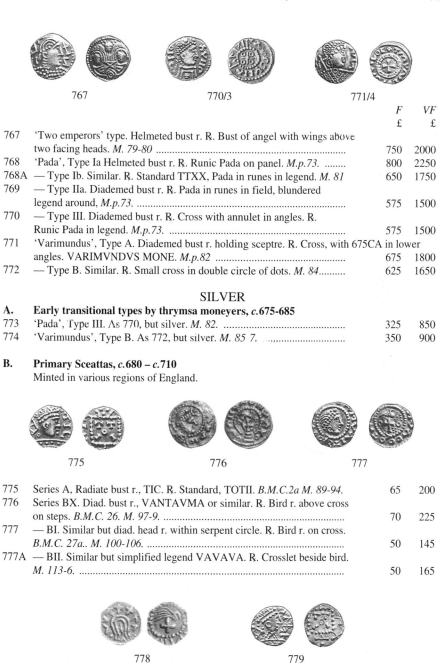

778   779

778	— BZ. Crude facing head. R. Crude bird on cross (imitation of 776). *M. 138-9.*	70	200
779	Series C. Radiate bust r., similar to 775 but runic aepa replaces TIC. R. Standard, TOTII. *B.M.C. 2b. M. 117-125.*	40	100

780   782

	F £	VF £
780 King Aethelred of Mercia? (674-704). 'Porcupine'. R̶. Aethiliraed on runes in two lines. *M. 134-5.*	125	375
781 Series F. Bust r., with broad-rimmed hat, blundered legend. R̶. Small cross on steps, annulets around. *M. 136-7.*	60	135
782 Series Z. Facing head with moustaches. R̶. Long-legged dog r. with head lowered. *M. 140-2.*	175	475
782A Series Z-related. Crude animal r., perhaps copy of 782. R̶. Crude cross-crosslet design *M. 143-4.*	135	400

782A   784   791

783 'Vernus' type. Porcupine-related head r., VER before. R̶. Standard. *M. 146-8.*	65	165
784 'Saroaldo' type. Unusual bust r. R̶. Saltire and pellets in square, SAROALDO legend around. *M. 151-3.*	90	250
785 Series W. Half or full-length facing figure holding two crosses. R̶. Cross crosslet on saltire. *M. 155.*	125	400

C.   Secondary Sceattas, c.710-760

Minted in all the main regions of southern and eastern England, but especially in the south-east and the Thames basin.

791 Series J, Type 85. Large head r. R̶. Bird on cross. *M. 293-5.*	50	150
791A — Type 36. Bust r., cross in front. R̶. One large and one small bird r. *M. 301-2.*	80	250

792   793   797

792 — Type 37. Two heads face-to-face. R̶. Four birds clockwise round cross. *M. 296-300.*	65	180
792A — Type 72. Similar. R̶. Bird r., looking back. *M. 303.*	75	200
793 Series U, Type 23b. Standing figure r. holds two crosses. R̶. Pecking bird. *M. 445-51*	85	250
794 Series K, Type 42. Bust r. with bird, cross or flower. R̶. Hound 1., plant behind. *M. 311-3*	95	300
795 — Type 20. Bust r. with chalice. R̶. Standing figure holds cross and hawk. *M. 314-18.*	75	225
796 — Type 32a. Bust r. with cross. R̶. Wolf curled head to tail. *M. 309*	110	350
797 — — Similar. R̶. Wolf-headed serpent. *M. 310*	80	250
798 — Type 32b. Similar. but R̶. Wolf-serpent within torque. *M. 307-8.*	100	325

		F £	VF £
799	— Type 33. Bust r., cross in front. ℞. Wolf's head with long tongue, l. or r. *M. 306.*	120	375

800   801   802   803

800	'Archer' type. Kneeling archer r. ℞. Bird on branch r., head turned back. *M. 349.*	325	1000
801	'Carip' group. Bust r., CARIP. ℞. Pecking bird, wolf-serpent, or standing figure. *M. 336-40.*	150	450
802	Series O, Type 38. Bust r. in cable border. ℞. Bird r. in torque. *M. 373-5.*	85	250
803	— Type 21. Similar, but bust l. ℞. Standing figure with two crosses. *M. 376*	135	475

804   805   806

804	'Triquetras' eclectic group. Facing bust, man and crosses, winged figure, or bird and branch. ℞. Interlace pattern. *M.p.425.*	125	375
805	Series H, Type 39. Pecking bird. ℞. Round shield with bosses. *M. 283-4.*	85	225
806	— Type 49. 'Wodan' head, annulets around. ℞. Pecking bird. *M. 285-8.*	90	250
807	— Type 48. Whorl of 3 wolf heads. ℞. Round shield with bosses. *M. 289-92.*	80	225

808   809A   810

808	Series G. Bust r., cross before. ℞. Standard with 3 or 4 X's. *(Minted in Northern France?)* *M. 267-70.*	60	175
809	— crude copies, some with bird or bird on cross. *M. 271-4.*	35	95
809A	Series M. Prancing dog l. or r. ℞. Spiral branch. *M. 363-6.*	90	275
810	Series N. Two standing figures. ℞. Monster looking back r. or l. *M. 368-72.*	75	225

811   813   815

811	Series O, Type 40. Standing figure holds two crosses. ℞. As last. *M. 379-81.*	80	235
812	— Type 43. Interlace shield. ℞. As last. *M.p.482.*	120	375
813	— Type 57. Bust r. in cable border. ℞. Monster looking back l. *M. 377.*	120	375
814	'Animal mask' group. Facing animal (lion?) mask. ℞. Bird, figure, monster or cross. *M. 354-6.*	250	800
815	Series V. Wolf and twins. ℞. Bird in vine. *M. 453.*	150	475

816   818   822

		F	VF
		£	£
816	Series T. Diad. bust r., +LEL. Ŗ. 'Porcupine' l. *M. 442-4.*	110	325
818	Series L, Type 12. Bust r., LVNDONIA. Ŗ. Standing figure holds two crosses. *M. 319-22.*	135	400
820	— Type 13. Similar. Ŗ. Seated figure holds hawk and cross. *M.p.409.* ...	225	675
821	— Type 14. Similar, but bust l. Ŗ. Celtic cross. *M.p.427.*	125	400
822	— Type 15. Bust r. with cross, no legend. Ŗ. Standing figure holds two crosses. *M. 323-6.*	85	275
825	— Type 16. Bust r. with floral scroll. Ŗ. Standing figure holds branch and cross, or two branches. *M. 329-30.*	90	300
827	— Type 18. Bust r. with cross. Ŗ. Standing figure holds cross and bird. *M. 331-3.*	80	250
828	— Type 19. Similar, but bust l. *M. 335.*	90	275
828A	— Type 34. Bust r. with cross or sceptre. Ŗ. Celtic cross. *M. 345-6.*	100	325
828B	Series L-related. Bust r. rosettes in field. Ŗ. Standing figure holds two crosses. *M. 347.*	150	475

829   831   832

829	Type 22. Victory standing with wreath. Ŗ. Winged figure, or standing figure holding two crosses. *M. 350-1.*	165	500
830	Type 23e. Standing figure holds two crosses. Ŗ. Whorl of 3 wolf heads. *M. 359-62.*	85	275
831	Series S. Female centaur. Ŗ. Whorl of 4 wolf heads. *M. 438-41.*	85	275
832	Series R. Bust r. or l. Epa, Wigraed, Spi, etc in runes. Ŗ. Standard. *M. 391-428.*	45	110

833   834A   836

832B	Series Q(R), Type 73. Crude radiate bust r. or l. Ŗ. Quadruped r. *M. 388.*	85	250
833	'Saltire Standard' types. Bust l. or r. with cross, two standing figures, or double croix ancree. Ŗ. Saltire and pellets in square. *M. 432-5.*	70	225
834	'Monita Scorum' type. Small bird looking back, MONITA SCORUM. Ŗ. Standard with saltire of annulets. *M.p.436.*	275	800
834A	— Bust r., MONITA SCORUM. Ŗ. 'porcupine' l., figure with two crosses, or triquetra. *M. 348.*	300	825
835	Type 70. Saltire-standard. Ŗ. Standard. *M. 436-7.*	40	110
836	Series Q, Types QII-IVd Bird l. or r. Ŗ. Quadruped l. or r. *M. 386-7.*	110	300
836A	— Type QIVe Quadruped both sides. *M.p.501*	110	350
836B	— Type QIe Bust r. with cross. Ŗ. Walking bird l. *M. 383.*	125	375

	F £	VF £
836C — Type QIf Standing figure with two crosses. R. Walking bird l. *M. 384.*	150	525
836D — Type QIg Facing head. R. Long-legged quadruped looking back. *M.p.492.*	200	625

844   844A

| 844   Type 30. Facing 'Wodan' head. R. Two standing figures, or standard. *M. 429-31.* | 135 | 450 |
| 844A — Type 53. 'Porcupine', similar to 787. R. Stepped cross, annulet at centre. *Mint? M. 258-62.* | 70 | 175 |

C. Continental Sceattas, c.695-c.740
Most are from the Rhine area, or Frisia

786

| 786   Series E. Porcupine-like figure, body with annulet at one end, triangle at other. R. 'Standard' with four pellets around central annulet. *Dorestad. M. 209-11.* | 30 | 80 |

787   789   790

787 — Similar, with triangular fore-leg. R. 'Standard' with four lines and central annulet. *M. 200-5.*	35	75
788 — Similar, with parallel lines in curve of body. R. 'Standard' with VICO. *M. 194-8.*	35	75
789 — Figure developed into plumed bird. R. Standard. *M. 190-3.*	35	100
790 Later issues. R. 'Standard' 'Porcupine'. Innumerable varieties. *M. 214-53.*	30	65
832A Type 10. Bust r., AEPA or APA. R. Porcupine modified into profile face. *Mint? M.p.248.*	175	350
838 'Porcupine' R. Small cross, S E D E in angles. *Mint? M. 263.*	225	700

839   840   843

839 Series D, Type 2c. Bust r., pseudo-runes. R. Plain cross with pellets in angles. *Domburg? M. 158-80.*	40	90
840 — Type 8. Standard. R. As 839. *M. 183-6.*	30	70
841 'Maastricht' Type. Crude head l. R. Quatrefoil interlace. *M. 265-6.*	150	450
843 Series X. Facing 'Wodan' head. R. Monster l. *Ribe, Jutland, M. 275-81.*	100	275
843A — cruder copies. *English, M. 282.*	120	375

KINGS OF NORTHUMBRIA AND BISHOPS OF YORK

The issues associated with pre-Viking Northumbria encompass a late seventh-century emission of gold, the following series of silver sceattas and the subsequent styca coinage. On the fringe of the later are two special issues, Eanred's penny and Wigmund's *solidus,* for neither of which is there yet evidence of use within the kingdom.

The Stycas developed in two phases, becoming a robust currency of small-denomination coins which seem to have been of great practical use. Production must have ceased early in Osberht's reign, although the old money may have continued in circulation until the Viking capture of York in 867. The official styca coinage, however, does appear to have been overwhelmed by irregular issues, which may reflect a period of civil war during the years *c.* 843 to *c.* 855.

The separation of kings and archbishops is no longer regarded as appropriate and the classification is chronological. In the spelling of names *U* for *W* would be appropriate in the Northumbrian context. *W* is based on West Saxon practice, but is used here on grounds of familiarity.

		F	VF
		£	£
762	AV thrymsa, *temp.* Kite-shaped shield enclosing cross, crosslets to l. and r., squared pattern beneath. R. Cross. Blundered (runic?) legend. *M. 76 (see also under Early Anglo-Saxon Period, Ultra-Crondall types)*	1100	3250

Æ sceattas (a). Regal issues

846	Aldfrith (685-705). Pellet in annulet. R. Canine, lying l., stylized tree ..	225	575
847	Eadberht (737-758). Small cross (mainly). R. Stylized stag, to l. or r.	80	225
848	Aethelwald Moll (759-765). (A possible, though disputed, issue is known)	*Extremely rare*	

849   852

849	Alchred (765-774). Small cross. R. Stylized stag to l. or r.	175	475
850	Aethelred I (first reign, 774-779/80). R. Stylized stag to l. or r.	250	800
851	Aelfwald I (779/80-788). R. Stylized stag to l. or r.	200	575

Æ sceattas (b). Joint issues, by kings and archbishops

852	Eadberht with Abp. Ecgberht (737-758). Small cross. R. Mitred figure holding two crosses	165	400
853	Aethelwald Moll with Abp. Ecgberht (759-765). Cross each side	450	1250
854	Alchred with Abp. Ecgberht (765-766). Cross each side	275	800
855	Aethelred I, with Abp. Eanbald I (*c.* 779-780). Various motifs.	175	525

Stycas Phase Ia. Issues in base silver, for kings and archbishop separately, c. 790-830, with moneyers named

856	Aethelred I (second reign, 789-796). R. CUDHEARD, or others	95	225
857	– R. 'Shrine', CUDCILS	250	675

858

		F £	VF £
858	**Eardwulf** (first reign, 796-806). R. Small cross, CUDHEARD	575	1500
859	**Aelfwald II** (806-808). R. Small cross, CUDHEARD	200	575
860	**Eanred** (810-841 (total reign)). R. CUDHEARD, or others	35	120

860   865

861	**Abp. Eanbald II** (796-835 (total tenure)). R. EADWULF or EDILWEARD	70	200
861A	**Eanred,** *c.* 830. *R penny.* Bust right. R. Cross, part moline part crosslet....	2250	7500

861   863A   870

Stycas Phase Ib. Early issues in copper alloy, *c.* 830-835, with moneyers named

862	**Eanred.** R DAEGBERCT, EADUINI, HEARDWULF or HERRED	25	60
863	**Abp. Eanbald II** R EADWULF, or EDILWEARD	65	175
863A	**Abp. Wigmund** (837-849/50). *N solidus.* Facing bust. R. Cross in wreath	18500	67500

Stycas Phase II. Later issues in copper alloy, *c.* 837-*c.*855, with moneyers named

864	**Eanred.** R MONNE or others	15	45
865	**Aethelred II** (first reign, 841-843/4). R. MONNE or others	15	45
866	– R. Hound 1., LEOFDEGN	150	450
867	**Redwulf** (843/4). R. MONNE or others	25	75
868	**Aethelred II** (second reign, 843/4-849/50). R. EARDWULF or others	15	50
869	**Osberht** (849/50-867). R. WINIBERHT or others	25	85
870	**Abp. Wigmund** (837-849/50). R. EDILVEARD or others	15	45
871	**Abp. Wulfhere** (849/50-900). R. WULFRED	60	160
872	**Irregular Issues** (*c.*843/4-*c.*855). Various types; legends often mere nonsense.	15	45

Pirie E.J.E. Coins of the Kingdom of Northumbria c.700-867. 1996

In the kingdom of the Franks a reformed coinage of good quality *deniers* struck on broad flans had been introduced by Pepin in 755 and continued by his son Charlemagne and his descendants. A new coinage of *pennies* of similar size and weighing about 20 grains (1.3 gms) was introduced into England, probably by Offa, the powerful king of Mercia, about 755/780, though early pennies also exist of two little known kings of Kent, Heaberht and Ecgberht, of about the same period.

The silver penny (*Lat*. 'denarius', hence the *d*. of our £ *s. d*.) remained virtually the sole denomination of English coinage for almost five centuries, with the rare exception of occasional gold coins and somewhat less rare silver halfpence. The penny reached a weight of 24 grains, i.e., a 'pennyweight' during the reign of Alfred the Great. Silver pennies of this period normally bear the ruler's name, though not always his portrait, and the name of the moneyer responsible for their manufacture.

Pennies were issued by various rulers of the Heptarchy for the kingdoms of Kent, Mercia, East Anglia and Wessex by the Danish settlers in the Danelaw and the Hiberno-Norse kings of York, and also by the Archbishops of Canterbury and a Bishop of London. Under Eadgar, who became the sole ruler of England, a uniform coinage was instituted throughout the country, and it was he who set the pattern for the 'reformed' coinage of the later Anglo-Saxon and Norman period.

Halfpence were issued by most rulers from Alfred to Eadgar between 871-973 for S. England, and although all are rare today, it is probable that reasonable quantities were made.

Nos. 873-1387 are all silver pennies except where stated.

NB. Many pennies of the early part of this period have chipped flans and prices should be reduced accordingly.

KINGS OF KENT

		F	VF
		£	£
873	**Heaberht** (*c*. 765). Monogram for REX. R. Five annulets, each containing a pellet, joined to form a cross	3000	8500
874	**Ecgberht** (*c*. 780). Similar. R. Varied	850	2500

875   877

875	**Eadberht Praen.** Type 1. (796-798). As illustration. R. Varied	950	3000
875A	— Type 2. (*c*. 798). His name around Ⓜ, in centre, R. Moneyer's name in angles of a tribrach	925	3000
876	**Cuthred** (798-807). *Canterbury*. Various types without portrait	625	1650
877	— — Portrait. R. Cross and wedges or A	575	1500

878   881

878	**Anonymous** (*c*. 822-823). *Canterbury*. As illustration or 'Baldred' style head	675	2350
879	**Baldred** (*c*. 823-825). *Canterbury*. diademed head r. R. DRUR CITS within inner circle	900	3000

		F	VF
		£	£
880	— Cross each side..	675	1850
881	*Rochester.* Bust r. R. Cross moline or wheel design..............................	825	2750

ARCHBISHOPS OF CANTERBURY

882

881A	**Jaenberht** (765-792). New type (early). Under Ecgberht II of Kent (?). (before *c.* 780 ?) His name around small cross of pellets in centre. R. PONTIFEX in three lines..	975	3250
882	Under Offa of Mercia (*c.* 780-792) His name around central ornament or cross and wedges. R. OFFA REX in two lines	800	2350
883	— His name in three lines. R. OFFA or OFFA REX between the limbs of Celtic cross...	875	2650
884	**Aethelheard** (cl. 792, cons. 793, d. 805). With Offa as overlord. First issue (792-?), with title *Pontifex*..	800	2250

885   887

885	— Second issue (?-796), with title *Archiepiscopus*	700	2000
885A	— Third issue (*c.* 796-798), with title *Archiepiscopus*. His name and AR around EP in centre. R. Moneyer's name, EADGAR or CIOLHARD.....	850	2650
886	— With Coenwulf as overlord. (798-800 ?) Fourth Issue. As last. R. King's name in the angles of a tribrach	800	2350
886A	— Fifth issue (*c.* 798-805?). As last R. Coenwulf's name around Ⓜ in centre	675	1850
887	**Wulfred** (805-832). group I (805-*c.* 810). As illustration. R. Crosslet, alpha-omega..	675	2250
888	— Group II (*c.* 810). As last. R. DOROVERNIA C monogram	600	1850
889	— Group III (pre- 823). Bust extends to edge of coin. R. As last	575	1750
890	— Groups IV and V (*c.* 822-823). Anonymous under Ecgberht. Moneyer's name in place of the Archbishop's. R. DOROBERNIA CIVITAS in three or five lines..	625	2000
891	— Group VI (*c.* 823-825). Baldred type. Crude portrait. R. DRVR CITS in two lines	875	3000
892	— Group VII (*c.* 832). Second monogram (Ecgberht) type. Crude portrait r., PLFRED. R. DORIB C. Monogram as 1035......................................	800	2750

893   894

		F	VF
		£	£
893	**Ceolnoth** (833-870). Group I with name CIALNOD. Tonsured bust facing. ℞. Varied	425	1100
894	— Group II. Similar but CEOLNOD. ℞. Types of Aethelwulf of Wessex	425	1100
895	— Group III. Diad. bust r. ℞. Moneyer's name in and between lunettes .	600	1750

896   898

896	**Aethelred** (870-889). Bust r. ℞. As illustration or with long cross with lozenge panel	1250	5250
897	— Cross pattee. ℞. ELF / STAN	875	3250
898	**Plegmund** (890-914). DORO in circle. ℞. As illustration above, various moneyers	525	1600
899	— Similar, but title EPISC, and XDF in centre	550	1750
900	— Small cross pattee. ℞. Somewhat as last	475	1250
901	— Crosses moline and pommee on *obv.*	600	2000
901A	— Halfpenny. As 900	875	3250

KINGS OF MERCIA

Until 825 Canterbury was the principal mint of the Kings of Mercia and some moneyers also struck coins for the Kings of Kent and Archbishops of Canterbury.

GOLD

902   903

902	**Offa** (757-796). Gold *dinar*. Copy of Arabic dinar of Caliph Al Mansur, dated 157 A.H. (A.D. 774), with OFFA REX added on *rev.*	67500	250000
903	Gold *penny*. Bust r., moneyer's name. ℞. Standing figure, moneyer's name	15000	45000

A copy of a solidus with a diademed bust appears to read CIOLHEARD and is probably Mercian of this or the following reign.

SILVER

904 905 906

		F	VF
		£	£
904	Light Coinage. (*c.* 780?-792) *London and Canterbury.* Various types without portraits. Small flans	450	1100
905	— (*c.* 780?-792) *London and Canterbury.* Various types with portraits. Small flans.	800	2250
906	— East Anglia. Various types with portraits. R. Some with runic letters, small flans	850	2500

908 909

907	— — Various types without portraits. R. often with runic letters, small flans	600	1500
908	Heavy Coinage. (*c.* 792-796) *London, Canterbury and East Anglia.* Various types without portraits, large flans.	525	1250
909	**Cynethryth** (wife of Offa). Coins as light coinage of Offa. As illustration	1650	5250
910	— *O. As rev.* of last. R. EOBA on leaves of quatrefoil	825	2750
911	**Eadberht** (Bishop of London, died 787/789). EADBERHT EP in three lines or aDBERHT in two lines within a beaded rectangle, EP below. R. Name of Offa	900	3000

912

912	**Coenwulf, King of Mercia** (796-821). Gold *penny* or *Mancus* of 30 pence. London, diademed bust of Coenwulf right, finely drawn with four horizontal lines on the shoulders	35000	135000
912A	Penny. Group I (796-805). *London.* Without portrait. His name in three lines. R. Varied	525	1500
913	— *Canterbury.* Name around Ⓜ as illus. below. R. Moneyer's name in two lines	625	1750

914   915

		F £	VF £
914	— *Both mints.* Tribrach type	325	750
915	— Group II (*c.* 805-810). *Canterbury.* With portrait. Small flans. R̸. Varied but usually cross and wedges	525	1450
916	— Groups III and IV (*c.* 810-820). *Canterbury.* Similar but larger flans. R̸. Varied	475	1250
917	— *Rochester.* Large diad. bust of coarse style. R̸. Varied. (Moneyers: Dun, Ealhstan)	625	1750
918	— *London.* With portrait generally of Roman style. R̸. Crosslet	575	1750
919	— *E. Anglia.* Crude diad. bust r. R̸. Moneyer's name LVL on leaves in arms of cross	425	975
920	— — *O.* as last. R̸. Various types	425	975

921   929

		F £	VF £
921	**Ceolwulf I** (821-823). *Canterbury.* Group I. Bust r. R̸. Varied. (Moneyers: Oba, Sigestef)	850	2750
922	— — Group II. Crosslet. R̸. Varied	675	2000
923	— — Group III. Tall cross with MERCIORŪ. R̸. Crosslet. SIGESTEF DOROBERNIA	800	2500
924	— *Rochester.* Group I. Bust r. R̸. Varied	775	2350
925	— — Group IIA. As last but head r.	850	2650
926	— — Group IIB. Ecclesiastical issue by Bp. of Rochester. With mint name, DOROBREBIA, but no moneyer	900	3000
927	— *East Anglia.* Crude style and lettering with barbarous portrait. R̸. Varied 1250	525	1500
928	**Beornwulf** (823-825). Bust r. R̸. Moneyer's name in three lines	725	2200
929	— R̸. Cross crosslet in centre	700	2000
930	Crude copy of 928 but moneyer's name in two lines with crosses between	850	2500
931	**Ludica** (825-827). Bust r. R̸. Moneyer's name in three lines as 928	2250	7500

932 933

| | *F* | *VF* |
| | £ | £ |

932 — Similar. Ꝛ. Moneyer's name around cross crosslet in centre, as 929 .. 2500 8000
933 **Wiglaf,** first reign (827-829). Crude head r. Ꝛ. Crosslet 2000 6500

934 935

934 Second reign (830-840). Cross and pellets, or ⚏ Ꝛ. Moneyer's name in
three lines or between lunettes of pellets 1500 5000
935 **Berhtwulf** (840-852). Various types with bust 700 2250
936 — without bust.. 750 2350
937 As before. Ꝛ. IAETHELWLF REX. cross pommee over cross pattée
(crude die copying on obverse of Aethelwulf of Wessex)........................ 725 2250

938 939 940 941

938 **Burgred** (852-874). *B.M.C. type A.* Bust r. Ꝛ. Moneyer's name in and
between lunettes.. 145 375
939 — — B. Similar but lunettes broken in centre of curve 225 700
940 — — C. Similar but lunettes broken in angles 150 385
941 — — D. Similar but legend divided by two lines with a crook at each end 145 375
942 — — E. As last, but m above and below.. 425 1350
943 **Ceolwulf II** (874-*c.* 880). Bust r. Ꝛ. Two emperors seated. Victory above 2750 10000

944 945

944 — R. Moneyer's name in angles of long cross with lozenge centre........ 1250 3500

KINGS OF EAST ANGLIA

			F	*VF*
			£	£
945	**Beonna,** King of East Anglia, *c.* 758. Æ sceat. Pellet in centre, Runic inscription. ℞. EFE in Roman characters around saltire cross		400	1000
945A	— Similar. ℞. WILRED in runic around pellet or cross		450	1250
945B	— Similar. ℞. Interlace pattern (large flans)		825	2500
945C	**Alberht** (749-?). Pellet in centre, AETHELBERT (runic) around ℞. Rosette in circle, TIAELRED (runic) around.		1250	4000

946

946	**Aethelberht** (d. 794). As illustration	3500	13500
947	**Eadwald** (*c.* 798). King's name in three lines. ℞. Moneyer's name in quatrefoil or around cross	725	2100
947A	— King's name around cross or Ϻ in centre. ℞. Moneyer's name in quatrefoil	750	2250

948   951

948	**Aethelstan I** (*c.* 825-840). Bust r. or l. ℞. Crosslet or star	725	2350
949	Bust r. ℞. Moneyer's name in three or four lines	750	2500
950	Alpha or A. ℞. Varied	300	800
951	*O.* and *rev.* Cross with or without wedges or pellets in angles	325	850
952	— Similar, with king's name both sides	400	950
952A	Name around ship in centre. ℞. Moneyer Eadgar, around cross of pellets or in two lines (Possibly the earliest of his coins.)	1650	6500

953   954

953	**Aethelweard** (*c.* 840-*c.* 855), A. Omega or cross and crescents. ℞. Cross with pellets or wedges	425	1050
954	**Edmund** (855-870). Alpha or A. ℞. Cross with pellets or wedges	225	600
955	— *O.* Varied. ℞. Similar	225	600

For the St. Edmund coins and the Danish issues struck in East Anglia bearing the name of Aethelred I, see Danish East Anglia.

Danish East Anglia, c. 885-915

957

		F £	VF £
956	**Aethelstan II** (878-890), originally named Guthrum? Cross pattee. R. Moneyer's name in two lines..	850	2750
957	**Oswald** (unknown except from his coins). Alpha or A. R. Cross pattee..	1250	4000
958	— Copy of Carolinigian 'temple' type. R Cross and pellets	1250	4250
959	**Aethelred I.** (c.870) As last, with name of Aethelred I. R. As last, or cross-crosslet..	1000	3250
959A	— As 954	825	2500
960	**St. Edmund,** memorial coinage, Æ *penny,* type as illus. below, various legends of good style..	100	275

961   962

961	— Similar, but barbarous or semi-barbarous legends.............................	95	250
962	*Halfpenny.* Similar	350	975

963   966

963	**St. Martin of Lincoln.** As illustration...	1500	5500
964	**Alfred.** (Viking imitations, usually of very barbarous workmanship.) Bust r. R. *Londonia* monogram..	700	2000
965	— Similar, but *Lincolla* monogram	825	2500
966	— Small cross, as Alfred group II *(Br. 6),* various legends, some read REX DORO	250	625
967	— Similar. R. 'St. Edmund type' A in centre	425	950
968	— Two emperors seated. R. As 964. (Previously attributed to Halfdene.)	1500	5500
969	*Halfpenny.* As 964 and 965...	350	850

970

	F £	VF £
970 — As 966	300	650

DANELAW, c. 898-915

971   975

971	**Alfred** (Imitations). ELFRED between ORSNA and FORDA. R. Moneyer's name in two lines (occasionally divided by horizontal long cross)	400	850
972	— *Halfpenny.* Similar, of very crude appearance	425	1100
973	**Alfred/Plegmund.** *Obv.* ELFRED REX PLEGN	550	1500
974	**Plegmund.** Danish copy of 900	375	950
975	**Earl Sihtric.** Type as 971. SCELDFOR between GVNDI BERTVS. R SITRIC COMES in two lines	1750	5750

Viking Coinage of York?
References are to 'The Classification of Northumbrian Viking Coins in the Cuerdale hoard', by C. S. S. Lyon and B. H. I. H. Stewart, in Numismatic Chronicle, 1964, p. 281 ff.

975A	**Guthfrith.** GU DE F. RE Small cross. R. Moneyer's name in two lines.	1350	5000
976	**Siefred.** C. SIEFRE DIIS REX in two lines. R. EBRAICE CIVITAS (or contractions), small cross. *L. & S. Ia, Ie, Ii*	225	625
977	— Cross on steps between. R. As last. *L. & S. If, Ij*	300	800
978	— Long cross. R. As last. *L. & S. Ik*	275	750
979	SIEFREDVS REX, cross crosslet within legend. R. As last. *L. & S. Ih*...	150	350

980   984

980	SIEVERT REX, cross crosslet to edge of coin. R. As last. *L. & S. Ic, Ig, Im*	175	450
981	— Cross on steps between. R. As last. *L. & S. Il*	275	800
982	— Patriarchal cross. R. DNS DS REX, small cross. *L. & S. Va*	250	650
983	— — R. MIRABILIA FECIT, small cross. *L. & S. VIb*	275	750
984	REX, at ends of cross crosslet. R. SIEFREDVS, small cross. *L. & S. IIIa, b*	175	475

		F	VF
		£	£
985	— Long cross. ℞. As last. *L. & S. IIIc*	165	450
986	*Halfpenny.* Types as 977, *L. & S. Ib; 980, Ic; and 983, VIb*	475	1200
987	**Cnut.** CNVT REX, cross crosslet to edge of coin. ℞. EBRAICE CIVITAS, small cross. *L. & S. Io, Iq*	175	475
988	— — ℞. CVNNETTI, small cross. *L. & S. IIc*	165	450
989	— Long cross. ℞. EBRAICE CIVITAS, small cross. *L. & S. Id, In, Ir*	125	285
990	— — ℞. CVNNETTI, small cross. *L. & S. IIa, IId*	115	250
991	— Patriarchal cross. ℞. EBRAICE CIVITAS, small cross. *L. & S. Ip, Is*	100	235
992	— — ℞.— *Karolus* monogram in centre. *L. & S . It*	600	1750

993   995

993	— — ℞. CVNNETTI, small cross. *L. & S. IIb, IIe*	95	225
994	*Halfpenny.* Types as 987, *L. & S. Iq; 989, Id; 991, Is; 992, Iu; 993, IIb and e*	350	825
995	As 992, but CVNNETTI around *Karolus* monogram. *L. & S. IIf*	325	800
996	**Cnut and/or Siefred.** CNVT REX, patriarchal cross. ℞. SIEFREDVS, small cross. *L. & S. IIId*	140	375
997	— — ℞. DNS DS REX, small cross. *L. & S. Vc.*	275	750

998

998	— — ℞. MIRABILIA FECIT. *L. & S. VId*	150	350
999	EBRAICE C, patriarchal cross. ℞. DNS DS REX, small cross. *L. & S. Vb*	250	650

1000   1002

1000	— — ℞. MIRABILIA FECIT. *L. & S. VIc*	150	350
1001	DNS DS REX in two lines. ℞. ALVALDVS, small cross. *L. & S. IVa*	650	2000
1002	DNS DS O REX, similar. ℞. MIRABILIA FECIT. *L. & S. VIa*	300	750
1003	*Halfpenny.* As last. *L. & S. VIa*	475	1350
1004	**'Cnut'.** Name blundered around cross pattée with extended limbs. ℞. QVENTOVICI around small cross. *L. & S. VII*	325	950

F	*VF*
£	£

1005 *Halfpenny. Similar. L. & S. VII*   475   1350
       Possibly not Northumbrian; the reverse copied from the Carolingian coins
       of Quentovic, N. France.

York, early tenth century issues

1006   1009

1006	**St. Peter coinage.** Early issues. SCI PETRI MO in two lines. R. Cross		
	pattee	210	550
1007	— similar. R. 'Karolus' monogram	750	2500
1008	*Halfpenny.* Similar. R. Cross pattee	600	1350
1009	**Regnald** (blundered types). RAIENALT, head to l. or r. R. EARICE CT,		
	'Karolus' monogram	1500	5500

1010

1010	— Open hand. R. Similar	1350	4000
1011	— Hammer. R. Bow and arrow	1500	5500
1012	Anonymous R. Sword	1350	4250

ENGLISH COINS OF THE HIBERNO-NORSE VIKINGS

Early period, *c.* **919-925**

1013	**Sihtric** (921-927). SITRIC REX, sword. R. Cross, hammer or T	1450	5000
1014	**St. Peter coinage.** Late issues SCI PETRI MO, sword and hammer. R.		
	EBORACEI, cross and pellets	600	1600

1015   1016

1015	— Similar. R. Voided hammer	525	1350
1016	— Similar. R. Solid hammer	625	1650
	St. Peter coins with blundered legends are rather cheaper.		

	F £	VF £

Later period, 939-954 (after the battle of Brunanburh). Mostly struck at York.

1017 **Anlaf Guthfrithsson,** 939-941. Flower type. Small cross, ANLAF REX TO D. R. Flower above moneyer's name 1650 6500

1018 — Circumscription type, with small cross each side, ANLAF CVNVNC, M in field on reverse *(Derby)* 1500 4750

1018A— Two line type. ONLAF REX. Large letter both sides *(Lincoln?)*........ 1500 4750

1019   1020

1019 — Raven type. As illustration, ANLAF CVNVNC................................ 1350 4500

1020 **Olaf Sihtricsson,** first reign, 941-944. Triquetra type. As illus., CVNVNC. R. Danish standard 1500 5250

1021 — Circumscription type (a). Small cross each side, CVNVNC 1250 4500

1022 — Cross moline type, CVNVN C. R. Small cross 1350 4750

1023 — Two line type. Small cross. R. ONLAF REX. R. Name in two lines .. 1250 4500

1024 **Regnald Guthfrithsson,** 943-944. Triquetra type. As 1020. REGNALD CVNVNC.. 1500 5250

1025   1030

1025 — Cross moline type. As 1022, but REGNALD CVNVNC.................... 1500 5250

1026 **Sihtric Sihtricsson,** *c.* 942. Triquetra type. As 1020, SITRIC CVNVNC 1500 5250

1027 — Circumscription type. Small cross each side 1350 4750

1027A**Anonymous?** Two line type. Small cross ELTANGERHT. R. RERNART in two lines 1100 3250

1028 **Eric Blood-axe,** first reign, 948. Two line type. Small cross, ERICVC REX A; ERIC REX AL; or ERIC REX EFOR. R. Name in two lines............. 2000 6500

1029 **Olaf Sihtricsson,** second reign, 948-952. Circumscription type (b). Small cross each side. ONLAF REX 1350 4500

1029A— Flower type. small cross ANLAF REX R. Flower above moneyer's name.. 1500 5500

1029B— Two line type. Small cross, ONLAF REX. R. Moneyer's name in two lines 1250 4500

1030 **Eric Blood-axe,** second reign, 952-954. Sword type. ERIC REX in two lines, sword between. R. Small cross.. 2250 7500

Later, KINGS OF ALL ENGLAND FROM 959
All are silver pennies unless otherwise stated

BEORHTRIC, 786-802

Beorhtric was dependent on Offa of Mercia and married a daughter of Offa.

1031

	F £	VF £
1031 As illustration	2750	9000
1032 Alpha and omega in centre. ℞. Omega in centre	2500	8500

ECGBERHT, 802-839

King of Wessex only, 802-825; then also of Kent, Sussex, Surrey, Essex and East Anglia, 825-839, and of Mercia also, 829-830.

1033 *Canterbury.* Group I. Diad. hd. r. within inner circle. ℞. Various	800	2400
1034 — II. Non-portrait types. ℞. Various	650	1850

1035

1035 — III. Bust r. breaking inner circle. ℞. DORIB C	800	2500
1036 *London.* Cross potent. ℞. LVN / DONIA / CIVIT	1200	4000
1037 — — ℞. REDMVND MONE around TA	800	2500
1038 *Rochester,* royal mint. Non-portrait types with king's name ECGBEO RHT	675	2000
1039 — — Portrait types, ECGBEORHT	850	2650
1040 *Rochester,* bishop's mint. Bust r. ℞. SCS ANDREAS (APOSTOLVS)...	900	3500
1041 *Winchester.* SAXON monogram or SAXONIORVM in three lines. ℞. Cross	700	2000

Son of Ecgberht; sub-King of Essex, Kent, Surrey and Sussex, 825-839; King of all southern England, 839-855; King of Essex, Kent and Sussex only, 855-858. No coins are known of his son Aethelbald who ruled over Wessex proper, 855-860.

1043   1045

		F	VF
		£	£
1042	*Canterbury.* Phase I (839-c. 843). Head within inner circle. R. Various. *Br. 3*	350	1000
1043	— — Larger bust breaking inner circle. R. A. *Br. 1 and 2*	375	1100
1044	— — Cross and wedges. R. SAXONIORVM in three lines in centre. *Br. 10*	275	850
1045	— — Similar, but OCCINDENTALIVM in place of moneyer. *Br. 11*	300	900
1046	— Phase II (*c.* 843-848?). Cross and wedges. R. Various, but chiefly a form of cross or a large A. *Br. 4*	275	850
1047	— — New portrait, somewhat as 1043. R. As last. *Br. 7*	375	1000
1048	— — Smaller portrait. R. As last, with *Chi/Rho* monogram. *Br. 7*	400	1250

1049   1051

		F	VF
1049	— Phase III (*c.* 848/851-*c.* 855). DORIB in centre. R. CANT mon. *Br. 5*	275	850
1050	— — CANT mon. R. CAN M in angles of cross. *Br. 6*	400	1200
1051	— Phase IV (*c.* 855-859). Type as Aethelberht. New neat style bust R. Large voided long cross. *Br. 8*	350	950
1052	*Winchester.* SAXON mon. R. Cross and wedges. *Br. 9*	400	1200

Son of Aethelwulf; sub-King of Kent, Essex and Sussex, 858-860; King of all southern England, 860-865/6.

1053

		F	*VF*
		£	£
1053	As illustration above	325	900
1054	*O*. Similar, R. Cross fleury over quatrefoil	575	1750

AETHELRED I, 865/866-871

Son of Aethelwulf; succeeded his brother Aethelberht.

1055

1055	As illustration	350	925
1056	Similar, but moneyer's name in four lines	625	2000

For another coin with the name Aethelred see 959 under Viking coinages.

Brother and successor to Aethelred, Alfred had to contend with invading Danish armies for much of his reign. In 878 he and Guthrum the Dane divided the country, with Alfred holding all England south and west of Watling Street. Alfred occupied London in 886.

Types with portraits

1057   1058

	F	VF
	£	£
1057 Bust r. R̂. As Aethelred I. *Br. 1 (name often* AELBRED)	425	1050
1058 — R̂. Long cross with lozenge centre, as 944, *Br. 5*	1000	3750
1059 — R̂. Two seated figures, as 943. *Br. 2*	4250	15000
1060 — R̂. As Archbp. Aethered; cross within large quatrefoil. *Br. 3*	1350	5000

1061   1062

1061 *London.* Bust. r. R̂. LONDONIA monogram	875	2650
Copies made of tin at the Wembley Exhibition are common		
1062 — R̂. Similar, but with moneyer's name added	975	3000
1063 — *Halfpenny.* Bust r. or rarely l. R̂. LONDONIA monogram as 1061	350	900
1064 *Gloucester.* R̂. Æ GLEAPA in angles of three limbed cross	2500	8500

Types without portraits

1065 King's name on limbs of cross, trefoils in angles. R̂. Moneyer's name in quatrefoil. *Br. 4.*	2000	6500

1066   1069

1066 Cross pattée. R̂. Moneyer's name in two lines. *Br. 6*	350	725
1067 — As last, but neater style, as Edw, the Elder	350	750
1068 — *Halfpenny.* As 1066	300	675
1069 *Canterbury.* As last but DORO added on *obv. Br. 6a*	375	850
1070 *Exeter?* King name in four lines. R̂. EXA vertical	2250	7500
1071 *Winchester?* Similar to last, but PIN	2250	7500
1071A *Oxford.* Elfred between OHSNA and FORDA. R̂. Moneyer's name in two lines (much commoner as a Viking Imitation see 971)	675	2000
1072 'Offering penny'. Very large and heavy. AELFRED REX SAXORVM in four lines. R̂. ELIMO in two lines i.e. (*Elimosia,* alms)	6500	27500

For other pieces bearing the name of Alfred see under the Viking coinages.

Edward, the son of Alfred, aided by his sister Aethelflaed 'Lady of the Mericians', annexed all England south of the Humber and built many new fortified boroughs to protect the kingdom.

1074   1078

	F £	VF £
Rare types		
1073 *Br. 1. Bath?* R. BA	1250	4000
1074 — *2. Canterbury.* Cross moline in pommee. R. Moneyer's name	900	3000
1075 — *3. Chester?* Small cross. R. Minster	1200	3750
1076 — *4.* — Small cross. R. Moneyer's name in single line	725	2000
1077 — *5.* — R. Two stars	850	2750

1081   1082

1078 — *6.* — R. Flower above central line, name below	1000	3500
1079 — *7.* — R. Floral design with name across field	1200	3750
1080 — *8.* — R. Bird holding twig	1750	6500
1081 — *9.* — R. Hand of Providence, several varieties	1350	4500
1082 — *10.* — R. City gate of Roman style	1250	4000
1083 — *11.* — R. Anglo-Saxon burg	1000	3500

Ordinary types

1084   1087

1084 *Br. 12.* Bust l. R. Moneyer's name in two lines	625	1850
1086 — *12a.* Similar, but bust r. of crude style	700	2000
1087 — *13.* Small cross. R. Similar (to 1084)	175	475
1087A — — As last, but in *gold*	17500	60000
1088 *Halfpenny.* Similar to last	650	1750
1088A— — R. Hand of Providence	900	3250

Aethelstan, the eldest son of Eadward, decreed that money should be coined only in a borough, that every borough should have one moneyer and that some of the more important boroughs should have more than one moneyer.

1089

		F £	VF £
1089	**Main issues.** Small cross. Ṛ. Moneyer's name in two lines	200	575
1090	Diad. bust r. Ṛ. As last	725	2250
1091	— Ṛ. Small cross	650	1750
1092	Small cross both sides	275	700

1093   1094

1093	— Similar, but mint name added	275	675
1094	Crowned bust r. As illustration. Ṛ. Small cross	500	1450
1095	— Similar, but mint name added	525	1500
1096	**Local Issues.** *N. Mercian mints.* Star between two pellets. Ṛ. As 1089...	825	2250
1097	— Small cross. Ṛ. Floral ornaments above and below moneyer's name..	900	2750
1098	— Rosette of pellets each side	325	875
1099	— Small cross one side, rosette on the other side	350	900

1100   1104

1100	*N.E. mints.* Small cross. Ṛ. Tower over moneyer's name	975	3500
1101	Similar, but mint name added	1000	3750
1102	— Bust in high relief r. or l. Ṛ. Small cross	725	2250
1103	— Bust r. in high relief. Ṛ. Cross-crosslet	725	2250
1104	'Helmeted' bust or head r. Ṛ. As last or small cross	750	2400
1104A	Halfpenny, small cross. Ṛ. Moneyer's name in two lines	675	1750

Eadmund, the brother of Aethelstan, extended his realm over the Norse kingdom of York.

1105   1107

	F £	VF £
1105 Small cross, rosette or annulet. R̥. Moneyer's name in two lines with crosses or rosettes between	200	575
1106 Crowned bust r. R̥. Small cross	475	1400
1107 Similar, but with mint name	525	1500
1108 Small cross either side, or rosette on one side	300	850
1109 Cross of five pellets. R̥. Moneyer's name in two lines	275	750
1110 Small cross. R̥. Flower above name	1000	3500
1111 'Helmeted' bust r. R̥. Cross-crosslet	725	2250

1111   1112

1112 *Halfpenny.* small cross, R̥. Moneyer's name in two lines or one line between rosettes	625	1650
1112A— Flower. R̥. As 1105	800	2250

EADRED, 946-955

Eadred was another of the sons of Eadward. He lost the kingdom of York to Eric Bloodaxe.

1113   1115

1113 As illustration. R̥. Moneyer's name in two lines	185	475
1114 — Similar, but mint name after REX	475	1250
1115 Crowned bust r. As illustration	475	1350
1116 — R̥. Similar, with mint name added	525	1450

	F	VF
	£	£
1117 Rosette. ℞. As 1113...	300	750
1118 Small cross. ℞. Rosette	300	750
1119 — ℞. Flower enclosing moneyer's name. *B.M.C. II*...............................	1000	3250
1120 *Halfpenny*. Similar to 1113 ....,......................................	575	1350

HOWEL DDA, d. 949/950

Grandson of Rhodri Mawr, Howel succeeded to the kingdom of Dyfed *c.* 904, to Seisyllog *c.* 920 and became King of Gwynedd and all Wales, 942.

1121

1121 HOPÆL REX, small cross or rosette. ℞. Moneyer's name in two lines .	7500	26500

EADWIG, 955-959

Elder son of Eadmund, Eadwig lost Mercia and Northumbria to his brother Eadgar in 957.

1122	1123

1122 *Br. 1*. Type as illustration..	325	825
1123 — — Similar, but mint name in place of crosses	575	1500
1124 — 2. As 1122, but moneyer's name in one line...............................	825	2500
1125 — 3. Similar. ℞. Floral design	1250	3750
1126 — 4. Similar. ℞. Rosette or small cross..	500	1350
1127 — 5. Bust r. ℞. Small cross	2250	8000

1128

1128 *Halfpenny*. Small cross. ℞. Flower above moneyer's name	875	2500
1128A— Similar. ℞. PIN (Winchester) across field..	975	3500
1128B— Star. ℞. Moneyer's name in two lines...	800	2000

King in Mercia and Northumbria from 957; King of all England 959-975.

It is now possible on the basis of the lettering to divide up the majority of Eadgar's coins into issues from the following regions: N.E. England, N.W. England, York, East Anglia, Midlands, S.E. England, Southern England, and S.W. England. (See 'Anglo-Saxon Coins', ed. R. H. M. Dolley.)

1129   1135

		F	VF
		£	£
1129	*Br I.* Small cross. R. Moneyer's name in two lines, crosses between, trefoils top and bottom	150	350
1130	— — R. Similar, but rosettes top and bottom (a N.W. variety)	165	400
1131	— — R. Similar, but annulets between	175	425
1132	— — R. Similar, but mint name between (a late N.W. type)	225	650
1133	— *2.* — R. Floral design	950	3000
1134	— *4.* Small cross either side	150	350
1135	— — Similar, with mint name	225	625
1136	— — Rosette either side	200	550
1137	— — Similar, with mint name	275	800
1138	— *5.* Large bust to r. R. Small cross	650	1750
1139	— — Similar, with mint name	675	1850
1140	*Halfpenny.* (8.5 grains.) *Br. 3.* Small cross. R. Flower above name	825	2500
1140A	— — R. Mint name around cross (Chichester)	975	3000
1140B	— Bust r. R. 'Londonia' monogram	675	2000

For Eadgar 'reform' issues see next page.

In 973 Eadgar introduced a new coinage. A royal portrait now became a regular feature and the reverses normally have a cruciform pattern with the name of the mint in addition to that of the moneyer. Most fortified towns of burghal status were allowed a mint, the number of moneyers varying according to their size and importance: some royal manors also had a mint and some moneyers were allowed to certain ecclesiastical authorities. In all some seventy mints were active about the middle of the 11th century (see list of mints pp. 128-9).

The control of the currency was retained firmly in the hands of the central government, unlike the situation in France and the Empire where feudal barons and bishops controlled their own coinage. Coinage types were changed at intervals to enable the Exchequer to raise revenue from new dies and periodic demonetization of old coin types helped to maintain the currency in a good state. No halfpence were minted during this period. During the latter part of this era, full pennies were sheared into 'halfpennies' and 'farthings'. They are far rarer than later 'cut' coins.

Eadgar, 959-975 *continued*

1141

	F	VF
	£	£
1141 **Penny.** Type 6. Small bust l. R. Small cross, name of moneyer and mint.	675	1850

EDWARD THE MARTYR, 975-978
Son of Eadgar and Aethelflaed, Eadward was murdered at Corfe Castle, reputedly on the orders of his stepmother Aelfthryth.

1142

1142 Type as illustration above	750	2000

1. Gothabyrig*	16. Cadbury	31. Cricklade	46. Canterbury	61. Ipswich	76. Tamworth
2. Launceston	17. Bruton	32. Oxford	47. Rochester	62. Norwich	77. Derby
3. Lydford	18. Dorchester	33. Wallingford	48. Horndon	63. Thetford	78. Leicester
4. Barnstaple	19. Wareham	34. Reading	49. Southwark	64. Huntingdon	79. Nottingham
5. Totnes	20. Shaftesbury	35. Guildford	50. London	65. Northampton	80. Melton Mowbray
6. Exeter	21. Warminster	36. Chichester	51. Hertford	66. Warwick	81. Stamford
7. Watchet	22. Bath	37. Cissbury	52. Aylesbury	67. Worcester	82. Newark
8. Taunton	23. Bristol	38. Steyning	53. Buckingham	68. Pershore	83. Torksey
9. Langport	24. Berkeley	39. Lewes	54. Newport Pagnell	69. Winchcombe	84. Lincoln
10. Petherton	25. Malmesbury	40. Hastings	55. Bedford	70. Gloucester	85. Horncastle
11. Crewkerne	26. Wilton	41. Romney	56. Cambridge	71. Hereford	86. Caistor
12. Bridport	27. Salisbury	42. Lympne	57. Bury St Edmunds	72. Grantham*	87. York
13. Axbridge	28. Southampton	43. Hythe	58. Sudbury	73. Shrewsbury	88. Wilton. Norfolk*
14. Ilchester	29. Winchester	44. Dover	59. Maldon	74. Chester	89. Frome
15. Miborne Port	30. Bedwyn	45. Sandwich	60. Colchester	75. Stafford	90. Droitwich

Possible location of uncertain mint

He was the son of Eadgar and Aelfthryth. His reign was greatly disturbed by incursions of Danish fleets and armies which massive payments of money failed to curb. He was known as 'The Unready', from UNREDE, meaning 'without counsel', ie. he was without good advice.

1143   1144

	F £	VF £
1143 First small cross type. Style of 1142, usually backless dress, 3 pellets in front, *Br. 1; B.M.C. I*	475	1350
1144 First Hand type. Bust r., no sceptre. R. Hand of Providence. *Br. 2; B.M.C. IIa*	110	250
1145 — Similar, but bust to l. *B.M.C. IIb*	475	1350

1146   1147

1146 Second Hand type, with sceptre. *B.M.C. IId*	110	275
1147 Benediction type. *O.* As last. R. Hand giving Benediction. *B.M.C. IIf*	675	2000

1148   1150

1148 CRVX type. *Br. 3; B.M.C. IIIa*	85	200
1149 — Lightweight issue. Small flan, sceptre slants into drapery	85	210
1150 Intermediate small cross type. Somewhat as 1143, no pellets, similar bust to CRVX type (1148) but no sceptre	675	2000

1151   1152

		F	VF
		£	£
1151	Long cross type. *Br. 5; B.M.C. IVa*	90	225
1152	Helmet type. *Br. 4; B.M.C. VIII*	100	250
1153	— — Similar, but struck in **gold**	22500	75000

1154   1156

1154	Last small cross type. As 1143, but different style	85	180
1154A	Similar, but bust r.	225	675
1155	— Similar, but bust to edge of coin. *B.M.C. Id*	350	1000
1156	Agnus Dei type. *c. 1009. Br. 6; B.M.C. X*	3000	10500

Son of Swegn Forkbeard, King of Denmark, Cnut was acclaimed King by the Danish fleet in England in 1014 but was forced to leave. He returned in 1015 and in 1016 agreed on a division of the country with Eadmund Ironsides, the son of Aethelred. No coins of Eadmund are known and on his death in November 1016 Cnut secured all England, marrying Emma of Normandy, widow of Aethelred.

Main types

| | 1157 | 1158 | 1159 | 1160 |

		F	VF
		£	£
1157	Quatrefoil type. *Br. 2; B.M.C. VIII*	85	175
1158	Helmet type. *Br. 3; B.M.C. XIV*	75	145
1159	Short cross type. *Br. 4; B.M.C. XVI*	70	140
1159A	— Similar, but with banner in place of sceptre	575	1500
1160	Jewel cross type. *Br. 6; B.M.C. XX*. Type as 1163	375	1000

This type is now considered to be a posthumous issue struck under the auspices of his widow, Aelgifu Emma.

HAROLD I, 1035-1040

Harold, the son of Cnut and Aelgifu of Northampton, initially acted as regent for his half-brother Harthacnut on Cnut's death, was then recognised as King in Mercia and the north, and King throughout England in 1037.

| | 1163 | | 1165 | |

1163	Jewel cross type, as illustration. *Br. 1; B.M.C. 1*	200	550
1164	Long cross and trefoils type. *Br. 2; B.M.C. V*	225	575
1165	— Similar, but fleur de lis in place of trefoils. *B.M.C. Vc*	200	550

He was the son of Cnut but lost the throne to his half-brother Harold owing to his absence in Denmark. On Harold's death he recovered his English realm.

	F	VF
	£	£
1166　**Early period, 1036.** Jewel cross type, as 1163; bust l. *Br. 1; B.M.C. I* ...	850	2500

1167　　　　　　　　　　　　　　　1168

| 1167　— Similar, but bust r. *B.M.C. Ia* .... | 750 | 2250 |
| 1168　**Restoration, 1040-1042.** Arm and sceptre type, with name Harthacnut. *Br. 2; B.M.C. II* .... | 675 | 1750 |

1169　　　　　　　　　　　　　　1170

| 1169　— Similar, but with name 'Cnut'.. | 325 | 850 |
| 1170　**Danish types,** of various designs, some of English type mostly struck at Lund, Denmark (now Sweden) .... | 200 | 525 |

EDWARD THE CONFESSOR, 1042-1066

Edward was the son of Aethelred II and Emma of Normandy. A number of new mints were opened during his reign.

1171　　　　　　　　　　　　　　1173

1170A Arm and Sceptre type. *B.M.C. IIIc*	800	2250
1171　PACX type, cross extends to edge of coin. *Br. 4; B.M.C. IV*	165	475
1172　— Similar, but cross ends at legend. *B.M.C. IVa*	165	475
1173　Radiate type. *Br. 2; B.M.C. I*	85	190

1174 1175

		F	VF
		£	£
1174	Trefoil quadrilateral type. *Br. 1; B.M.C. III*	90	220
1175	Short cross type, small flans. *Br. 3; B.M.C. II*	80	180

1176 1179

1176	Expanding cross type; light issue (18 grs.). *Br. 5; B.M.C. V*	95	240
1177	— — Heavy issue (27 grs.)	100	240
1178	— — Similar, but struck in **gold**	22500	75000
1179	Helmet type. *Br. 6; B.M.C. VII*	100	250
1180	— — Similar but bust l.	475	1350

1181 1182

1181	Sovereign type. *Br. 7; B.M.C. IX*	110	250
1182	Hammer cross type. *Br. 8; B.M.C. XI*	95	225

1183 1184

1183	Facing bust type. *Br. 9; B.M.C. XIII*	90	200
1184	Pyramids type. *Br. 10; B.M.C. XV*	95	225

1185

		F	*VF*
		£	£
1185	Transitional Pyramids type. *B.M.C. XIV*..	975	3000

Most York coins of this reign have an annulet in one quarter of the reverse.

HAROLD II, 1066

Harold was the son of Godwin Earl of Wessex. He was the brother-in-law of Edward the Confessor and was recognised as King on Edward's death. He defeated and killed Harald of Norway who invaded the north, but was himself defeated and killed at the Battle of Hastings by William of Normandy.

1186   1187

1186	Bust l. with sceptre. R. PAX across centre of *rev. B.M.C. I*....................	525	1100
1187	Similar, but without sceptre. *B.M.C. Ia*	575	1350
1188	Bust r. with sceptre *B.M.C. 1b*..	1000	3500

In late Anglo-Saxon and Norman times coins were struck in the King's name at a large number of mints distributed in centres of population, and in times of emergency in places of refuge, across England and Wales. During the 10th century the use of a mint signature was sporadic but from the Reform type of Edgar the mint name is almost invariably given, usually in conjunction with that of the moneyer responsible, e.g. EDGAR ON BERCLE. At the peak, 71 mints struck the quatrefoil type of Cnut and 65 the PAXS type of William I and they provide a valuable insight into the economic and social structures of the period.

The output of the mints varied enormously and a dozen are exceptionally rare. Approximately 100,000 pennies survive, half of which emanate from the great centres of London, Canterbury, Lincoln, Winchester and York. At the other end of the scale a mint such as Rochester is known from about 500 coins, Derby from around 250, Guildford 100, Bedwyn 25, Horncastle 4 and Pershore 1. Many of these coins, particularly those from the great Scandinavian hoards, are in museum collections and are published in the Sylloge of Coins of the British Isles (SCBI) series.

There are too many type for mint combinations, over 1500 Saxon and 1000 Norman, to price each individually and our aim is to give an indication of value for the commonest Saxon and Norman type, in VF condition, for each of the 102 attested mints (excluding Baronial of Stephen's reign), and for a further 10 mints whose location or attribution is uncertain. The threshold VF price for a Norman coin (W1 PAXS type £375) exceeds that for a Saxon coin (Cnut short cross £125) accounting for the difference in starting level. Prices for coins in lower grade would be less and there is a premium for the rarer types for each mint, but for many types, e.g. in the reigns of Harthacnut or Henry I, the value of the type itself far exceeds that of many of the constituent mints and a scarce mint is only worth a modest premium over a common one.

We also give the most characteristic mint signatures (often found abbreviated) and the reigns for which the mint is known. There are many pitfalls in identifying mints, not least that Saxon and Norman spelling is no more reliable than that of other ages and that late Saxon coins were widely imitated in Scandinavia. There is extensive literature and the specialist in this fascinating series can, for further details, consult J J North, English Hammered Coinage Vol.1.

Alf	—	Alfred the Great	Hd1	—	Harold I
EdE	—	Edward the Elder	HCn	—	Harthacnut
A'stn	—	Aethelstan	EdC	—	Edward the Confessor
Edm	—	Edmund	Hd2	—	Harold II
Edw	—	Edwig	W1	—	William I
Edg	—	Edgar	W2	—	William II
EdM	—	Edward the Martyr	H1	—	Henry I
Ae2	—	Aethelred	St	—	Stephen
Cn	—	Cnut			

Berkeley   Hastings

	SAXON VF £	NORMAN VF £
Axbridge (AXAN, ACXEPO) Edg, Ae2, Cn, HCn	2000	—
Aylesbury (AEGEL, AEEL), Ae2, Cn, EdC	1750	—
Barnstable (BARD, BEARDA) Edw, Edg, Ae2-Hd1, EdC, W1, H1	700	1000
Bath (BADAN) EdE-A'stn, Edw-EdC, W1-St	300	500
Bedford (BEDAN, BEDEFOR) Edw-St	275	500
Bedwyn (BEDEPIN) EdC, W1	1000	2500
Berkeley (BEORC, BERCLE) EdC	6000	—
Bramber (BRAN) St	—	2750
Bridport (BRYDI, BRIPVT) A'stn, Ae2, Cn, HCn, EdC-W1	700	750
Bristol (BRICSTO, BRVCSTO) Ae2-St	300	450
Bruton (BRIVT) Ae2, Cn, HCn, EdC	1500	—
Buckingham (BVCIN) Edg, EdM-Hd1, HCn, EdC	1500	—
Bury St.Edmunds (EDMVN, S.EDM) EdC, W1, H1, St	600	525
Cadbury (CADANBY) Ae2, Cn	3500	—
Caistor (CASTR, CESTR) EdM, Ae2, Cn	3500	—
Cambridge (GRANTE) Edg-St	200	575
Canterbury (DORO, CAENTPA, CNTL) Alf, A'stn, Edr, Edg-St	140	375
Cardiff (CIVRDI, CAIERDI) W1, H1, St, Mat	—	900
Carlisle (CARD, EDEN) H1, St	—	1500
Castle Rising (RISINGE) St (type II-VII)	—	1250
Chester (LEIGE, LEGECE, CESTRE) A'stn, Edm, Edg-St	275	450
Chichester (CISSAN, CICEST) A'stn, Edg, Ae2-St	225	400
Christchurch (orig. Twynham) (TVEHAM, TPIN) W1, H1	—	1750
Cissbury (SIDESTEB, SIDMES) Ae2, Cn	1500	—
Colchester (COLN, COLECES) Ae2-St	200	425
Crewkerne (CRVCERN) Ae2, Cn, Hd1	2500	—
Cricklade (CROCGL, CRECCELAD, CRIC) Ae2-W2	750	750
Derby (DEORBY, DERBI) A'stn, Edm, Edg-St	500	650
Dorchester (DORCE, DORECES) Ae2-H1	600	650
Dover (DOFERA, DOFRN) A'stn, Edg, Ae2-St	175	400
Droitwich (PICC, PICNEH) EdC, Hd2	3000	—
Dunwich (DVNE) St	—	1250
Durham (DVNE, DVRHAM, DVNHO) W1-St	—	1750
Exeter (EAXA, EAXCESTRE, IEXECE) Alf, A'stn, Edw-St	200	450
Frome (FRO) Cn, HCn, EdC	3000	—
Gloucester (GLEAP, GLEPECE, GLOPEC) Alf, A'stn, Edg-St	300	450
Grantham (GRANTHA, GRE) Ae2	3500	—
Guildford (GYLD, GILDEFRI) EdM-W2	800	1750
Hastings (HAESTINGPOR, AESTI) Ae2-St	225	500
Hedon (HEDVN) St	—	5000
Hereford (HEREFOR, HRFRD) A'stn, Edg, Ae2-St	350	500
Hertford (HEORTF, HRTFI, RET) A'stn, Edw-EdC, W1-H1	275	1000
Horncastle (HORN) EdM, Ae2	5000	—
Horndon (HORNIDVNE) EdC	5000	—
Huntingdon (HVNTEN, HVTD) Edg, Ae2-St	225	750
Hythe (HIÐEN, HIDI) EdC, W1, W2	2500	900
Ilchester (GIFELCST, GIVELC, IVELCS) Edg, Ae2-St	450	900
Ipswich (GIPESWIC, GYPES) Edg-St	225	400
Langport (LANCPORT, LAGEPOR) A'stn, Cn-EdC	1500	—
Launceston (LANSTF, LANSA, SANCTI STEFANI) Ae2, W1-H1	3000	1500
Leicester (LIHER, LEHRE, LEREC) A'stn, Edg, Ae2-St	300	500
Lewes (LAEPES, LEPEEI, LAPA) A'stn, Edg-St	225	500
Lincoln (LINCOLN, NICOLE) Edr, Edg-St	140	375
London (LVNDO, LVNDENE) Alf, A'stn, Edw-St	140	375
Lydford (LYDANFOR) Edg-EdC	275	—
Lympne (LIMENE, LIMNA) A'stn, Edg-Cn	700	—
Maldon (MAELDVN, MIEL) A'stn, Edg, Ae2-Hd1, EdC-W2	275	800
Malmesbury (MALD, MEALDMES, MELME) Edg, Ae2-W2	750	1250
Marlborough (MAERLEBI) W1, W2	—	3000
Melton Mowbray (MEDELTV) Ae2, Cn	5000	—
Milborne Port (MYLE) Ae2, Cn	5000	—
Newark (NEWIR, NIWOR) Edg-Cn	3000	—
Newcastle (CAST) St	—	1500

	SAXON VF £	NORMAN VF £
Newport (NIPANPO, NIPEPORT) Edw, Edg, EdC	3000	—
Northampton (HAMTVN, HMTI, NORHAM) Edw, Edg-St	275	450
Norwich (NORDPIC) A'stn-Edr, Edg-St	150	375
Nottingham (SNOTING) A'stn, Ae2-St	500	900
Oxford (OXNA, OCXEN, OXENFO) Alf, A'stn, Edr-St	250	400
Pembroke (PEI, PAN, PAIN) H1, St	—	1750
Pershore (PERESC) EdC	6000	—
Petherton (PEDR, PEDI) Cn, EdC	5000	—
Pevensey (PEFNESE, PEVEN) W1-St	—	1750
Reading (READIN, REDN) EdC	4000	—
Rhuddlan (RVDILI) W1	—	3000
Rochester (ROFEC, ROFSC) A'stn, Edg-H1	275	1000
Romney (RVMED, RVMNE) Ae2-H1	300	500
Rye (RIE) St	—	2500
Salisbury (SEREB, SEARB, SALEB) Ae2-EdC, W1-St	250	400
Sandwich (SANDPI) EdC, W1-St	275	450
Shaftesbury (SCEFTESB, CEFT, SAFTE) A'stn, Edg-St	350	500
Shrewsbury (SCROB, SCRVBS, SALOP) A'stn, Edg, Ae2-St	300	500
Southampton (HAMPIC, HAMTVN) A'stn, Edw-Cn	400	—
Southwark (SVDBY, SVDGE, SVDPERC) Ae2-St	140	375
Stafford (STAFFO, STAEF) A'stn, Edg, Ae2-Hd1, EdC, W1-St	350	600
Stamford (STANFORD) Edg-St	140	400
Steyning (STAENIG, STENIC) Cn-W2, St	225	450
Sudbury (SVDBI, SVBR) Ae2, Cn, EdC, W1-St	350	450
Swansea (SVENSEI) St	—	2500
Tamworth (TOMPEARÐ, TAMPRÐ) A'stn, Edg-Hd1, EdC, W1-St	900	700
Taunton (TANTVNE) Ae2-St	500	600
Thetford (ÐEOTFOR, DTF, TETFOR) Edg-St	140	375
Torksey (TVRC, TORC) EdM-Cn	2500	—
Totnes (DARENT, TOTANES, TOTNES) A'stn, Edw-HCn, W2, H1	275	1250
Wallingford (PELINGA, PALLIG) A'stn, Edm, Edg, Ae2-H1	275	500
Wareham (PERHAM, PERI) A'stn, Edg-St	350	500
Warminster (PORIME) Ae2-Hd1, EdC	2000	—
Warwick (PAERINC, PERPIC, PAR) A'stn (?), Edg-St	450	650
Watchet (PECED, PICEDI, WACET) Ae2-EdC, W1-St	900	1250
Wilton (PILTVNE) Edg-St	200	450
Winchcombe (WENCLES, PINCEL, PINCL) Edg, Ae2, Cn, HCn-W1	900	1000
Winchester (PINTONIA, PINCEST) Alf, A'stn, Edw-St	140	375
Worcester (PIGER, PIHREC, PIREC) EdM, Ae2-St	400	500
York (EBORACI, EFORPIC, EVERWIC) A'stn, Edm, Edg-St	140	450

Mints of uncertain identification or location

"Brygin" (BRYGIN) Ae2	2500	—
"Dyr/Dernt" (DYR, DERNE, DERNT) EdC	1000	—
"Weardburh" (PEARDBV) A'stn, Edg	2500	—
Abergavenny (?) (FVNI) W1	—	1750
Gothabyrig (GEODA, GODABYRI, IODA) Ae2-HCn	2500	—
Eye (?) (EI, EIE) St	—	1250
Peterborough (?) (BVRI) W1, St	—	3000
Richmond, Yorks (?) (R1), St (type 1)	—	1750
St Davids (?) (DEVITVN) W1	—	1750
Wilton, Norfolk (?) (PILTV) Ae2 (LSC)	2000	—
Bamborough (BCI, CIB, OBCI) Henry of Northumberland	—	5000
Corbridge (COREB) Henry of Northumberland	—	5000

Aylesbury

Barnstaple

Cricklade

Dunwich

Exeter

Frome

Guildford

Horncastle

Ilchester

London

Milborne Port

Newark

Oxford

Pevensey

Rochester

Stafford

Torksey

Winchcombe

York

NORMAN MINTS (WILLIAM I TO HENRY I)

1. Launceston	13. Bath	25. Chichester	37. London	49. Huntingdon	61. Rhuddlan
2. Barnstaple	14. Marlborough	26. Steyning	38. Hertford	50. Bedford	62. Chester
3. Totnes	15. Wilton	27. Lewes	39. Maldon	51. Northampton	63. Shrewsbury
4. Exeter	16. Salisbury	28. Pevensey	40. Colchester	52. Warwick	64. Stafford
5. Watchet	17. Christchurch	29. Hastings	41. Ipswich	53. Worcester	65. Tamworth
6. Taunton	18. Abergavenny*	30. Romney	42. Sudbury	54. Winchcombe	66. Leicester
7. Bridport	19. Winchester	31. Hythe	43. Cambridge	55. Oxford	67. Derby
8. Dorchester	20. Bedwyn	32. Dover	44. Bury	56. Gloucester	68. Nottingham
9. Wareham	21. Malmesbury	33. Sandwich	45. Thetford	57. Hereford	69. Lincoln
10. Shaftesbury	22. Cricklade	34. Canterbury	46. Norwich	58. Cardiff	70. York
11. Ilchester	23. Wallingford	35. Rochester	47. Stamford	59. Pembroke	71. Durham
12. Bristol	24. Guildford	36. Southwark	48. Peterborough	60. St Davids*	72. Carlisle

Possible location of uncertain mint

There were no major changes in the coinages following the Norman conquest. The controls and periodic changes of the type made in the previous reigns were continued. Nearly seventy mints were operating during the reign of William I; these had been reduced to about fifty-five by the middle of the 12th century and, under Henry II, first to thirty and later to eleven. By the second half of the 13th century the issue of coinage had been centralized at London and Canterbury, with the exception of two ecclesiastical mints. Of the thirteen types with the name PILLEMVS, PILLELM, etc. (William), the first eight have been attributed to the Conqueror and the remaining five to his son William Rufus. Cut 'halfpennies' and 'farthings' were still made in this period and are scarce until the later issues of Henry I and Stephen.

From William I to Edward II inclusive all are silver pennies unless otherwise stated.

WILLIAM I, 1066-1087

William Duke of Normandy was the cousin of Edward the Confessor. After securing the throne of England he had to suppress several rebellions.

	1250		1251

		F	VF
		£	£
1250	*Penny.* Profile left type. *Br. I*	250	675

	1252		1253

| 1251 | Bonnet type. *Br. II* | 185 | 450 |
| 1252 | Canopy type. *Br. III* | 275 | 800 |

	1254		1255

1253	Two sceptres type. *Br. IV*	235	600
1254	Two stars type. *Br. V*	200	475
1255	Sword type. *Br. VI*	275	750

1256 1257

		F	VF
		£	£
1256	Profile right type. *Br VII*	325	850
1257	PAXS type. *Br. VIII*	175	375

WILLIAM II, 1087-1100

William Rufus was the second son of William I, his elder brother Robert succeeded to the Dukedom of Normandy. He was killed while hunting in the New Forest.

1258 1259

1258	Penny. Profile type. *Br. 1*	550	1250
1259	Cross in quatrefoil type. *Br. 2*	475	1100

1260 1261

1260	Cross voided type. *Br. 3*	475	1100
1261	Cross pattée and fleury type. *Br. 4*	525	1250

1262

1262	Cross fleury and piles type. *Br. 5*	575	1350

Fifteen types were minted during this reign. In 1106-7 provision was made for minting round halfpence again, none having been struck since the time of Eadgar, but relatively few can have been made. The standard of coinage manufacture was now beginning to deteriorate badly. Many genuine coins were being cut to see if they were plated counterfeits and there was a reluctance by the public to accept such damaged pieces. About 1107-8 an extraordinary decision was taken to order the official mutilation of all new coins by snicking the edges, thus ensuring that cut coins had to be accepted. Pennies of types VII to XII (Nos. 1268-1273) usually have a cut in the flan that sometimes penetrated over a third of the way across the coin.

At Christmas 1124 the famous 'Assize of the Moneyers' was held at Winchester when all the moneyers in England were called to account for their activities and a number are said to have been mutilated for issuing coins of inferior quality.

The dates and the order of Henry's issues have been modified several times since Brooke. The main changes are as follows: BMC 11 preceded 10 and BMC 9 follows 6. The order of BMC 7 and 8 remains uncertain. The issues were not made for equal periods of time, as BMC 15 began in early 1125. The contemporary chronicles mention the round halfpenny (and farthings) and the order to snick whole coins under 1107 or 1108. The halfpennies are now dated to agree with these references when BMC 6 and 9 pennies were current. A few pennies of BMC 6 are snicked as are most of the halfpennies. Snicks continue to be used on coins of BMC 13 and 14, though the cut is smaller and only a quarter to a half of the coins are snicked. [Brooke 1916; Archibald and Conté SNC 1990; Blackburn RNS 1990.]

	1263	1263A

		F £	VF £
1263	**Penny.** *Br.* I. Annulets type	425	1100
1263A	— II. Profile l. ℞. Cross fleury	300	825

	1264	1265

1264	— III. PAX type	250	675
1265	— IV. Facing bust. ℞. Five annulets and four piles	350	850

	1266	1267

1266	— V. — ℞. Voided cross with fleur in each angle	625	1650
1267	— VI. Pointing bust and stars type	900	3000

1268

		F	VF
		£	£
1268	*Br.* VII. Facing bust. R. Quatrefoil with piles	300	750

1269   1270

| 1269 | — VIII. Large bust l. R. Cross with annulet in each angle | 1250 | 4000 |
| 1270 | — IX. Facing bust. R. Cross in quatrefoil | 550 | 1350 |

1271   1272

| 1271 | — X. Small facing bust in circle. R. Cross fleury | 185 | 575 |
| 1272 | — XI. Very large bust l. R. 'Double inscription' around small cross pattee | 525 | 1250 |

1273   1274

| 1273 | — XII. Small bust l. R. Cross with annulet in each angle | 400 | 975 |
| 1274 | — XIII. Star in lozenge fleury type | 375 | 950 |

1275   1276

		F	*VF*
		£	£
1275	Br. XIV. Pellets in quatrefoil type	200	525
1276	— XV. Quadrilateral on cross fleury type	145	350

1277

| 1277 | *Halfpenny.* Facing head. R. Cross potent with pellets in angles | 1250 | 3000 |
| 1277A | — As above R. Struck from a penny die of type IX | 1750 | 5500 |

STEPHEN, 1135-1154
and the Civil War and Anarchy, 1138-1153

Stephen of Blois, Count of Boulogne and a nephew of Henry I, hastily crossed the Channel on his uncle's death and secured the throne for himself, despite Henry's wishes that his daughter Matilda should succeed him. She was the widow of the German emperor Henry V, and was then married to Geoffrey, Count of Anjou. Two years later Matilda arrived in England to claim the throne, supported by her half-brother Robert of Gloucester.

During the protracted civil war that ensued Matilda and later her son, Henry of Anjou, set up an alternative court at Bristol and held much of the west of England, striking coins at mints under their control. Many irregular coins were struck during this troubled period, some by barons in their own name. Particularly curious are the coins from the Midlands and E. Anglia which have Stephen's head defaced, now believed to have been issued during the Interdict of 1148. In 1153, following the death of Stephen's son, Eustace, a treaty between the two factions allowed for the succession of Matilda's son Henry and a uniform coinage was once more established throughout the kingdom.

B.M.C. Norman Kings, 2 vols. (1916). *M.—* Mack, R. P., 'Stephen and the Anarchy 1135-54', *BNJ, XXXV* (1966), pp. 38-112.

Regular regal issuess

1278   1280

	F	VF
	£	£
1278 **Penny.** Cross moline (Watford) type. Bust r., with sceptre. R. Cross moline with lis in angles. *B.M.C. I; M. 3-42*	200	525
1279 — Similar, but obv. reads PERERIC or PERERICM. *M. 43-50*	500	1350
1280 Voided cross type. Facing bust with sceptre. R. Voided cross pattée with mullets in angles. *East and South-east mints only. B.M.C. II; M. 53-66*	225	575

1281   1282

1281 Cross fleury type. Bust l. with sceptre. R. Cross fleury with trefoils in angles. *East and South-east mints only. B.M.C. VI; M. 77-99*	375	900
1282 Cross pommee (Awbridge) type. Bust half-left with sceptre. R. Voided cross pommee with lis in angles. *B.M.C. VII; M. 99z-135b*	250	675
For B.M.C. types III, IV & V, see 1300-1302.		

LOCAL AND IRREGULAR ISSUES OF THE CIVIL WAR

A. Coins struck from erased or defaced dies (interdict of 1148)

1283

		F £	VF £
1283	As 1278, with king's bust defaced with long cross. *East Anglian Mints.* M. 137-147	675	1750
1284	— Similar, but king's bust defaced with small cross. *Nottingham. M. 149*	575	1450
1285	— Similar, but sceptre defaced with bar or cross. *Nottingham, Lincoln and Stamford. M. 148 and 150-154*	475	1250
1286	— Similar, but king's name erased. *Nottingham. M. 157*	425	975
1286A	— Other defacements	450	1000

B. South-Eastern variant

1287	As 1278, but king holds mace instead of sceptre. *Canterbury. M. 158*	750	2500

C. Eastern variants

1288

1288	As 1278, but roundels in centre or on limbs of cross or in angles. *Suffolk mints. M. 159-168*	575	1350
1288A	As 1278, but star before sceptre and annulets at tips of *fleurs on reverse. Suffolk mints. M. 188*	650	1650
1289	As 1278, but thick plain cross with pellet at end of limbs, lis in angles. *Lincoln. M. 169-173*	675	1750
1290	— Similar, but thick plain cross superimposed on cross moline. *M. 174.*	650	1650
1290A	As 1278. R. Quadrilateral over voided cross. *M. 176*	850	2500
1290B	As 1278. R. Long cross to edge of coin, fleurs outwards in angles. *Lincoln. M. 186-187*	850	2500

	F £	VF £

D. Southern variants

1291   As 1278, but with large rosette of pellets at end of obverse legend.
M. 184-185.. 600 1350

1292   — Similar, but star at end of obverse legend. *M. 187y*........................... 475 1000

1293   Crowned bust r. or l. with rosette of pellets before face in place of sceptre.
R. As 1280, but plain instead of voided cross. *M. 181-183*..................... 725 2000

1291   1295

1295   As 1278, but usually collar of annulets. R. Voided cross moline with
annulet at centre. *Southampton. M. 207-212* 250 600

E. Midland variants

1296

1296   As 1278, but cross moline on reverse has fleured extensions into legend.
Leicester. M. 177-178 .... 675 1750

1297   As 1278 but crude work. R. Voided cross with lis outwards in angles.
Tutbury. M. 179.. 725 2000

1298   1300

1298   Somewhat similar. R. Voided cross with martlets in angles. *Derby. M. 175* 1350 4250

1299   As 1278. R. Plain cross with T-cross in each angle. *M. 180*..................... 850 2500

1300   Facing bust with three annulets on crown. R. Cross pattée, fleurs inwards
in angles. *Northampton or Huntingdon (?). B.M.C. III; M. 67-71* 950 3000

1301   1302

		F	VF
		£	£

1301   Facing bust with three fleurs on crown. R. Lozenge fleury, annulets in
       angles. *Lincoln or Nottingham. B.M.C. IV; M. 72-75*.............................. 575   1350
1302   Bust half-right with sceptre. R. Lozenge with pellet centre, fleurs inwards
       in angles. *Leicester. B.M.C. V; M. 76*...................................... 900   2750
1303   **Robert,** Earl of Leicester(?). As 1280, but reading ROBERTVS. *M. 269*   1750   6500

F. North-east and Scottish border variants
1304   As 1278, but star before sceptre and annulets at tips of fleurs on reverse.
       M. 188 650   1650
1305   As 1278, but a voided cross extending to outer circle of reverse.
       M. 189-192 650   1650
1306   As 1278, but crude style, with Stephen's name. *M. 276-279 and 281-282*   575   1350
1307   — Similar. R. Cross crosslet with cross-pattée and crescent in angles.
       M. 288 1350   3750
1308   **David I** (K. of Scotland). As 1305, but with name DAVID REX. *M. 280*   1650   4500
1309   **Henry** (Earl of Northumberland, son of K. David). hENRIC ERL.
       As 1278. *M. 283-285*.. 1750   5250
1310   — Similar. R. Cross fleury. *M. 286-287*.. 1750   5250
1311   — As 1307, but with name NENCI : COM on obverse. *M. 289*.............. 1850   5500

G. 'Ornamented' series. *So-called 'York Group' but probably minted in Northern France*
1312   As 1278, with obverse inscription NSEPEFETI, STEFINEI or RODBDS.
       R. WISÐ. GNETA, etc., with ornament(s) in legend (sometimes retro-
       grade). *M. 215-216 and 227*... 1350   4250

1313   1315

1313   Flag type. As 1278, but king holds lance with pennant, star to r. R. As
        1278, mostly with four ornaments in legend. *M. 217* 925   2500
1313A— Similar, but with eight ornaments in reverse inscription. *M. 217*........ 950   2650
1314   As 1278, but STIEN and ornaments, sceptre is topped by pellet in lozenge.
        R. Cross fleury over plain cross, ornaments in place of inscription. *M. 218*   1200   3250
1314A King stg. facing, holding sceptre and long standard with triple-tailed
        pennon. R. Cross pattee, crescents and quatrefoils in angles, pellets around,
        ornaments in legend 1750   5250
1315   **Stephen and Queen Matilda.** Two standing figures holding sceptre, as
        illustration. R. Ornaments in place of inscription. *M. 220*...................... 1850   6000

1316   1320

	F	VF
	£	£

1316 **Eustace.** EVSTACIVS, knight stg. r. holding sword. ℞. Cross in quatrefoil,
EBORACI EDTS (or EBORACI TDEFL). *M. 221-222* 1350 4500
1317 — Similar, but ThOMHS FILIuS VIF. *M. 223* 1350 4500
1318 — Similar, but mixed letters and ornaments in *rev.* legend. *M. 224* 1300 4250
1319 [EVSTA] CII . FII . IOANIS, lion passant r, collonnade (or key?) below.
℞. Cross moline with cross-headed sceptres in angles, mixed letters and
ornaments in legend. *M. 225* 1450 4750
1320 Lion rampant r., looped object below, EISTAOhIVS. ℞. Cross fleury with
lis in angles, mostly, ornaments in legend. *M. 226* 1400 4500
1320A**William.** Knight stg. r. holding sword. ℞. Cross in quatrefoil. As 1316 .. 2750 8500

1321   1322

1321 **Rodbert.** Knight on horse r., RODBERTVS IESTV (?). ℞. As 1314.
M. 228 .... 2350 8000
1322 **Bishop Henry.** Crowned bust r., crozier and star to r., HENRICVS EPC.
℞. Somewhat as last, STEPhANVS REX. M. 229 .... 2250 7250

H. Uncertain issues
1323 Crowned bust r. with sceptre, -NE Γ:. ℞. Cross pattée with annulets in
angles (as Hen. I type XIII). *M. 272* 650 1350
1324 Crowned facing bust with sceptre, star to r. (as Hen. I type XIV). ℞.
As last. *M. 274 Extr* 850 2500
1325 Other types 650 1350

1326

1326 **Matilda,** Dowager Empress, Countess of Anjou (in England 1139-1148).
As 1278, but cruder style, MATILDI IMP. etc. *M. 230-240* 975 3000
1326A Obv. similar. ℞. Cross pattée over cross fleury (Cardiff hoard) 975 3000
1326B Similar, but triple pellets or plumes at end of cross (Cardiff hoard) 1100 3500

	F	VF
	£	£
1326C **Henry of Neubourg,** Bust r., R. As 1276A or 1278	1500	4500
1327 **Duke Henry,** son of Matilda and Geoffrey of Anjou, Duke of Normandy from 1150 (in England 1147-1149-1150 and 1153-1154). As 1278 but hENRICVS, etc. *M. 241-245*	1350	4250
1327A As 1295 but hENRIC. *M. 246*	1350	4250
1327B As 1326B, but hENNENNVS R, etc...	1500	4500
1328 Obverse as 1278. R. Cross crosslet in quatrefoil. *M. 254*	1650	5000
1329 Crowned bust r. with sceptre. R. Cross fleury over quadrilateral fleury. *M. 248-253*	1500	4500

1330   1331

1330 Crowned facing bust, star each side. R. Cross botonnée over a quadrilateral pommée. *M. 255-258*	1750	5500
1331 Obverse as 1330. R. Voided cross botonnée over a quadrilateral pommée. *M. 259-261*	1750	5500
1331A **Robert,** Earl of Gloucester, 1143-7, Lion. r. R. Cross fleury	1350	3750
1332 **William,** Earl of Gloucester (succeeded his father, Earl Robert, in 1147). Type as Henry of Anjou, no. 1329. *M. 262*	1600	4750
1333 Type as Henry of Anjou, no. 1330. *M. 263*	1750	5500
1334 Type as Henry of Anjou, no. 1331. *M. 264-268*	1750	5500
1334A — Lion. R. Cross fleury	1250	3500
1335 **Brian Fitzcount,** Lord of Wallingford (?). Type as Henry of Anjou, no. 1330. *M. 270*	2500	8000
1336 **Patrick,** Earl of Salisbury (?). Helmeted bust r. holding sword, star behind. R. As Henry of Anjou, no. 1329. *M. 271*	2650	8500

Tealby (1158-80)

Short Cross (1180-1247)

Voided Long Cross (1247-79)

New coinage (1279-1327).

Moneyer table for the Cross and Crosslets (Tealby) coinage

	From F £
London: Accard (CD), Alwin (ABCDF), Edmund (ACDE), Geffrei (ACE), Godefrei (ACDEF), Godwin (BDE), Hunfrei (AC), Iohan (ACDEF), Lefwine (BCEF), Martin (ABC), Pieres (ACEF), Pieres Mer. (ABD), Pieres Sal. (AEF), Ricard (ABCD), Rodbert (AC), Swetman (ABC), Wid (A),	90
Canterbury: Alferg (A), Goldhavoc (ABCDEF), Goldeep (C), Lambrin (F), Raul (CDEF), Ricard (ABCDEF), Ricard Mr. (ABCDE), Rogier (ABCDEF), Rogier F. (A), Willem (C), Wiulf (ABCDEF),	90
Bedford: Arfin (A),	Extremely Rare
Bristol: Elaf (ACF), Rogier (ADEF), Tancard (ABD),	200
Bury St Edmunds: Henri (BDE), Raul (F), Willem (A),	120
Carlisle: Willem (ACDEF),	120
Chester: Andreu (A), Willem (AD),	185
Colchester: Alwin (AC), Pieres (CE),	200
Durham: Cristien (C), Iohan (B), Walter (A),	150
Exeter: Edwid (AC), Guncelin (AC), Rainir (BC), Ricard (A), Rogier (AD),	185
Gloucester: Godwin (A), Nicol (A), Rodbert (A), Sawulf (A),	230
Hereford: Driu (AC), Osburn (A), Stefne (A), [—]ward (A),	200
Ilchester: Adam (CDF), Reinard (A), Ricard (A), Rocelin (A),	185
Ipswich: Nicole (BCDEF), Robert (CEF), Turstain (CF),	90
Launceston: Willem (A),	Extremely Rare
Leicester: Ricard (A), Robert (A),	200
Lewes: uncertain (F),	Extremely Rare
Lincoln: Andreu (ABCDE), Godric (ABCD), Lanfram (ABCDF), Raulf (ABCDEF), Raven (ACF), Swein (ACD),	120
Newcastle: Willem (ACDEF),	130
Northampton: Ingeram (AC), Iosep (A), Pieres (A), Reimund (AC), Stefne (A), Waltier (AC), Warnier (AC),	150

HENRY II, 1154-1189

Cross-and-crosslets ('Tealby') Coinage, 1158-1180

Coins of Stephen's last type continued to be minted until 1158. Then a new coinage bearing Henry's name replaced the currency of the previous reign which contained a high proportion of irregular and sub-standard pennies. The new Cross and Crosslets issue is more commonly referred to as the 'Tealby' coinage, as over 5000 of these pennies were discovered at Tealby, Lincolnshire, in 1807. Thirty mints were employed in this re-coinage, but once the re-minting had been completed not more than a dozen mints were kept open. The issue remained virtually unchanged for twenty-two years apart from minor variations in the king's portrait. The coins tend to be poorly struck on irregular flans.

Cut coins occur with varying degrees of frequency during this issue, according to the type and local area. Further reading: *A Catalogue of English Coins in the British Museum. The Cross-and-Crosslet ("Tealby") Type of Henry II.* (London: 1951) by D.F. Allen.

		F	VF
	1337A B C	£	£
1337	Class A (1158-c.1163). No hair, no collar. Mantle falls from chin as two parallel lines between which is a line of pellets.	90	250
1338	Class B (c.1162-c.1163). Similar, but mantle of two folds which meet at chin (various compositions)	100	275
1339	Class C (c.1163-c.1167). Curl of hair at temple. Jewelled collar, mantle of many folds, field between sometimes jewelled, as is cuff.	95	260

	D E F		
1340	Class D (c.1167-c.1170). Jewelled collar continues down shoulder unbroken. Single curl of hair at temple, folds of mantle horizontal	90	250
1341	Class E (c.1170-c.1174). Similar to 1340. Jewelled collar only. Folds of mantle rise from hand to top of shoulder.	100	275
1342	Class F (c.1174-c.1180). Similar to 1341, but hair falls in long ringlets from temple.	90	250

Moneyer table for the Cross and Crosslets (Tealby) coinage (cont.)

	From F £
Norwich: Gilebert (ABF), Herbert (ACD), Herbert R (A)., Hugo (ACF), Nicol (AC), Picot (ABC), Reiner (AD), Ricard (A),	*150*
Oxford: Adam (ADE), Aschetil (A), Rogier (A),	*185*
Pembroke: Walter (A),	*Extremely Rare*
Salisbury: Daniel (A), Levric (A),	*185*
Shrewsbury: Warin (A),	*Extremely Rare*
Stafford: Colbrand (AC), Willem (C),	*230*
Thetford: Siwate (ACD), Turstain (ACD), Willem (ACDF), Willem Ma (A), Willem De (A),	*120*
Wallingford: Fulke (A),	*Extremely Rare*
Wilton: Anschetil (A), Lantier (A), Willem (A),	*185*
Winchester: Herbert (AC), Hosbert (ACD), Ricard (AE), Willem (AC),	*120*
York: Cudbert (A), Gerrard (A), Godwin (AD), Griffin (AD), Herbert (ACD), Hervi (A), Iordan (A), Norman (A), Willem (A), Wulfsi (A),	*120*

Letters in brackets after mint name indicate Class known to exist for the mint and moneyer combination

The publishers would like to thank the late Prof. Jeffrey Mass for re-organising and updating the short cross series. All illustrations were kindly supplied by Prof. Mass.

'Short Cross' coinage of Henry II (1180-1189)

In 1180 a coinage of new type, known as the Short Cross coinage, replaced the Tealby issue. The new coinage is remarkable in that it covers not only the latter part of the reign of Henry II, but also the reigns of his sons Richard and John and on into the reign of his grandson Henry III, and the entire issue bears the name 'hENRICVS'. There are no English coins with the names of Richard or John. The Short Cross coins can be divided chronologically into various classes: ten mints were operating under Henry II and tables of mints, moneyers and classes are given for each reign.

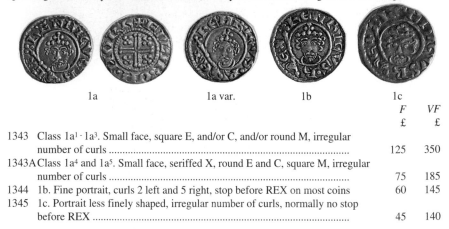

| 1a | 1a var. | 1b | 1c |

	F	VF
	£	£
1343 Class 1a¹ - 1a³. Small face, square E, and/or C, and/or round M, irregular number of curls	125	350
1343A Class 1a⁴ and 1a⁵. Small face, seriffed X, round E and C, square M, irregular number of curls	75	185
1344 1b. Fine portrait, curls 2 left and 5 right, stop before REX on most coins	60	145
1345 1c. Portrait less finely shaped, irregular number of curls, normally no stop before REX	45	140

RICHARD I, 1189-1199

Pennies of Short Cross type continued to be issued throughout the reign, all bearing the name hENRICVS. The coins of class 4, which have very crude portraits, continued to be issued in the early years of the next reign. The only coins bearing Richard's name are from his territories of Aquitaine and Poitou in western France.

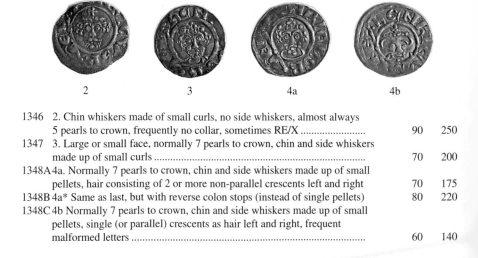

| | 2 | 3 | 4a | 4b |

1346 2. Chin whiskers made of small curls, no side whiskers, almost always 5 pearls to crown, frequently no collar, sometimes RE/X	90	250
1347 3. Large or small face, normally 7 pearls to crown, chin and side whiskers made up of small curls	70	200
1348A 4a. Normally 7 pearls to crown, chin and side whiskers made up of small pellets, hair consisting of 2 or more non-parallel crescents left and right	70	175
1348B 4a* Same as last, but with reverse colon stops (instead of single pellets)	80	220
1348C 4b Normally 7 pearls to crown, chin and side whiskers made up of small pellets, single (or parallel) crescents as hair left and right, frequent malformed letters	60	140

'Short Cross' coinage *continued.* All with name hЄNRICVS

The Short Cross coins of class 4 continued during the early years of John's reign, but in 1205 a re-coinage was initiated and new Short Cross coins of better style replaced the older issues. Coins of classes 5a and 5b were issued in the re-coinage in which sixteen mints were employed. Only ten of these mints were still working by the end of class 5. The only coins to bear John's name are the pennies, halfpence and farthings issues for Ireland.

| | 4c | | 5a1 | | | 5a2 | |

| | 5b | | 5c | | 6a | |

	F	VF
	£	£
1349 4c. Reversed S, square face at bottom, 5 pearls to crown, normally single crescents as hair left and right..	80	225
1350A 5a1 Reversed or regular S, irregular curved lines as hair (or circular curls containing no pellets), cross pattee as initial mark on reverse, *London and Canterbury* only	150	450
1350B 5a2 Reversed S, circular curls left and right (2 or 3 each side) containing single pellets, cross pomme as initial mark on reverse.............................	70	175
1350C 5a/5b or 5b/5a...	60	150
1351 5b. Regular S, circular pelleted curls, cross pattee as initial mark on reverse	50	140
1352 5c. Slightly rounder portrait, letter X in the form of a St. Andrew's cross	45	125
1353 6a. Smaller portrait, with smaller letter X composed of thin strokes or, later, short wedges..	50	135

For further reading and an extensive listing of the English Short Cross Coinage see:
Sylloge of Coins of the British Isles. *The J. P. Mass Collection of English Short Cross Coins 1180-1247*

'Short Cross' coinage *continued* (1216-47)

The Short Cross coinage continued for a further thirty years during which time the style of portraiture and workmanship deteriorated. By the 1220s minting had been concentrated at London and Canterbury, one exception being the mint of the Abbot of Bury St. Edmunds.

Halfpenny and farthing dies are recorded early in this issue; a few halfpennies and now farthings have been discovered. See nos 1357 D-E.

| 6b | 6c | 6c orn. | 6x | 6d |

	F	VF
	£	£
1354 6b. Very tall lettering and long rectangular face	30	75
1355 6c. Lettering now shorter, face narrow and triangular	35	80
1355A 6c. orn. Various letters now ornamental in design, curls 3/3 left and right	75	225
1355B 6x. Canterbury mint only, RE/X, curls 2/2, nostril pellets outside nose...	350	850
1355C 6d. Face less distinct in shape, N's containing a pellet along the crossbar	50	175

| 7a | 7b | 7c |

1356A 7a. Small compact face, letter A with top coming to a point under crossbar	25	60
1356B 7b. Letter A with square top, M appears as H	25	60
1356C 7c. Degraded portrait, letter A and M as in 7b, large lettering	25	65

| 8a | 8b | 8c |

1357A 8a. New portrait; letter X in shape of curule; cross pattee as initial mark on reverse (early style), or cross pommee (late style)	75	225
1357B 8b. Degraded portrait, wedge-shaped X, cross pomme as initial mark	30	85
1357C 8c. Degraded portrait, cross pomme X, cross pomme as initial mark	30	85
1357D Round halfpenny in style of class 7, initial mark in shape of up-turned crescent, London mint only	1350	4500
1357E Round farthing in style of class 7, initial mark in shape of up-turned crescent, London mint only	1000	3250

| 1357D | 1357E |

Moneyer tables for the short cross coinage

Fine

Henry II:
London: Aimer (1a-b), Alain (1a-b), Alain V (1a-b), Alward (1b), Davi (1b-c),
Fil Almer (1a-b), Gefrei (1c), Gilebert (1c), Godard (1b), Henri (1a-b),
Henri Pi (1a), Iefrei (1a-b), Iohan (1a-b), Osber (1b), Pieres (1a-c),
Pieres M (1a-b), Randvl (1a-b), Ravl (1b-c), Reinald (1a-b), Willelm (1a-b)   45
Carlisle: Alain (1b-c)   85
Exeter: Asketil (1a-b), Iordan (1a-b), Osber (1a-b), Ravl (1b), Ricard (1b-c),
Roger (1a-c)   75
Lincoln: Edmvnd (1b-c), Girard (1b), Hvgo (1b), Lefwine (1b-c), Rodbert (1b),
Walter (1b), Will. D.F. (1b), Willelm (1b-c)   65
Northampton: Filip (1a-b), Hvgo (1a-b), Ravl (1a-c), Reinald (1a-c), Simvn (1b),
Walter (1a-c), Willelm (1a-b)   50
Oxford: Asketil (1b), Iefrei (1b), Owein (1b-c), Ricard (1b-c), Rodbert (1b),
Rodbt. F. B. (1b), Sagar (1b)   70
Wilton: Osber (1a-b), Rodbert (1a-b)   75
Winchester: Adam (1a-c), Clement (1a-b), Gocelm (1a-c), Henri (1a),
Osber (1a-b), Reinier (1b), Rodbert (1a-b)   45
Worcester: Edrich (1b), Godwine (1b-c), Osber (1b-c), Oslac (1b)   75
York: Alain (1a-b), Efrard (1a-c), Gerard (1a-b), Hvgo (1a-c), Hunfrei (1a-b),
Isac (1a-b), Tvrkil (1a-c), Willelm (1a-b)   45

Richard I
London: Aimer (2-4a), Fvlke (4a-b), Henri (4a-b), Ravl (2), Ricard (2-4b),
Stivene (2-4b), Willelm (2-4b)   50
Canterbury: Goldwine (3-4b), Hernavd (4b), Hve (4b), Ioan (4b), Meinir (2-4b),
Reinald/Reinavd (2-4b), Roberd (2-4b), Samvel (4b), Simon (4b), Vlard (2-4b)   50
Carlisle: Alein (3-4b)   125
Durham: Adam (4a), Alein (4a-b), Pires (4b)   150
Exeter: Ricard (3)   135
Lichfield: Ioan (2)   2500
Lincoln: Edmvnd (2), Lefwine (2), Willelm (2)   100
Northampton: Giferei (4a), Roberd (3), Waltir (3)   110
Northampton or Norwich: Randvl (4a-b), Willelm (4a-b)   100
Shrewsbury: Ive (4a-b), Reinald/Reinavd (4a-b), Willem (4a)   175
Winchester: Adam (3), Gocelm (3), Osbern (3-4a), Pires (4a), Willelm (3-4a)   65
Worcester: Osbern (2)   250
York: Davi (4a-b), Efrard/Everard (2-4b), Hvgo/Hve (2-4a), Nicole (4a-b),
Tvrkil (2-4a)   60

John
London: Abel (5c-6a), Adam (5b-c), Beneit (5b-c), Fvlke (4c-5b), Henri (4c-5b/5a),
Ilger (5b-6a), Ravf (5c-6a), Rener (5a/b-5c), Ricard (4c-5b), Ricard B (5b-c),
Ricard T (5a/b-5b), Walter (5c-6a), Willelm (4c-5b), Willelm B (5a/b-5c),
Willelm L (5b-c), Willelm T (5b-c)   40
Canterbury: Goldwine (4c-5c), Hernavd/Arnavd (4c-5c), Hve (4c-5c), Iohan (4c-5c),
Iohan B (5b-c), Iohan M (5b-c), Roberd (4c-5c), Samvel (4c-5c), Simon (4c-5c)   40
Bury St Edmunds: Fvlke (5b-c)   90
Carlisle: Tomas (5b)   110
Chichester: Pieres (5b/a-5b), Ravf (5b/a-5b), Simon (5b/a-5b), Willelm (5b)   80
Durham: Pieres (5a-6a)   90
Exeter: Gileberd (5a-b), Iohan (5a-b), Ricard (5a-b)   75

Ipswich: Alisandre (5b-c), Iohan (5b-c)   60
Kings Lynn: Iohan (5b), Nicole (5b), Willelm (5b)   125
Lincoln: Alain (5a), Andrev (5a-5c), Hve (5a/b-5c), Iohan (5a), Ravf (5a/b-5b),
Ricard (5a-5b/a), Tomas (5a/b-5b)   40
Northampton: Adam (5b-c), Roberd (5b), Roberd T (5b)   60
Northampton or Norwich: Randvl (4c)   80
Norwich: Gifrei (5a/b-5c), Iohan (5a-c), Renald/Renavd (5a-c)   60
Oxford: Ailwine (5b), Henri (5b), Miles (5b)   70
Rochester: Alisandre (5b), Hvnfrei (5b)   90
Winchester: Adam (5a-c), Andrev (5b-c), Bartelme (5b-c), Henri (5a), Iohan (5a-c),
Lvkas (5b-c), Miles (5a-c), Ravf (5b-c), Ricard (5a-b)   40
York: Davi (4c-5b), Nicole (4c-5c), Renavd (5b), Tomas (5a/b-5b)   45

Henry III

London: Abel (6b-7a), Adam (7b-c), Elis (7a-b), Giffrei (7b-c), Ilger (6b-7b),
Ledvlf (7b-c), Nichole (7c-8c), Ravf (6b-7b), Ricard (7b), Terri (7a-b),
Walter (6b-c)   20
Canterbury: Arnold (6c/6x, 6x), Henri (6b-6c/d, 7a-c), Hivn/Ivn (6b-7b),
Iohan (6b-7c, 8b-c), Ioan Chic (7b-c), Ioan F. R. (7b-c), Nichole (7c, 8b-c),
Osmvnd (7b-c), Robert (6b, 7b-c), Robert Vi (7c), Roger (6b-7b),
Roger of R (7a-b), Salemvn (6x, 7a-b), Samvel (6b-d, 7a), Simon (6b-d, 7a-b),
Tomas (6d, 7a-b), Walter (6b-7a), Willem (7b-c, 8b-c), Willem Ta (7b-c)   20
Bury St Edmunds: Iohan (7c-8c), Norman (7a-b), Ravf (6c-d, 7a), Simvnd (7b-c),
Willelm (7a)   35
Durham: Pieres (7a)   80
Winchester: Henri (6c)   125
York: Iohan (6c), Peres (6c), Tomas (6c), Wilam (6c)   125

Irregular Local Issue
Rhuddlan (in chronological order)   95
Group I (c. 1180 – pre 1205) Halli, Tomas, Simond
Group II (c.1205 – 1215) Simond, Henricus

Rhuddlan

'Long Cross' coinage (1247-72)

By the middle of Henry's reign the coinage in circulation was in a poor state, being worn and clipped. In 1247 a fresh coinage was ordered, the new pennies having the reverse cross extended to the edge of the coin to help safeguard the coins against clipping. The earliest of these coins have no mint or moneyers' names. A number of provincial mints were opened for producing sufficient of the Long Cross coins, but these were closed again in 1250, only the royal mints of London and Canterbury and the ecclesiastical mints of Durham and Bury St. Edmunds remained open.

In 1257, following the introduction of new gold coinages by the Italian cities of Brindisi (1232), Florence (1252) and Genoa (1253), Henry III issued a gold coinage in England. This was a gold 'Penny' valued at 20 silver pence and twice the weight of the silver penny. The coinage was not a success, being undervalued, and it ceased to be minted after a few years; few coins have survived.

Cut halfpennies and farthings are common for this period, with a greater concentration in the early part. They are up to 100 times commoner than in late Anglo-Saxon times.

Without sceptre

Ia   Ib

		F	VF
		£	£
1358	Class Ia. hENRICVS: REX. R. ANGLIE TERCI..................................	300	900
1359	Ib. hENRICVS REX. ANG. R. LIE TERCI LON *(London)*, CAN		
	(Canterbury) (rare) or AED *(Bury St. Edmunds)* (very rare)...................*from*	40	100
1360	—— I/II mule...	40	100

II   IIIb   IIIc

1361	Class II. hENRICVS REX TERCI. R. Moneyer and mint......................	25	65
1362	— IIIa. hENRICVS REX ·. III, thin face as class II................................	20	50
1363	— IIIb. Smaller, rounder face	20	50
1364	— IIIc. Face with pointed chin, neck indicated by two lines, often a		
	pellet between curls, usually REX: III...	20	50

With sceptre

IVa   IVb   Va   Vb

	F £	VF £
1365 Class IVa. Similar to last, but with sceptre	50	150
1366 — IVb. Similar, but new crown with half-fleurs and large central fleur ..	70	200
1367 — Va. With class IV bust, crown as IVa or IVb, round eyes, from now on legend begins at 10 o'clock. Ball-tailed R̶.	20	50
1368 — Vb. Narrower face, wedge-tailed R̶, round eyes	20	50
1369 — Vc. Shorter, broader face with almond-shaped eyes	20	50

Vd   Ve   Vf   Vg   Vh

1370 — Vd. Portrait of quite different style; new crown with true-shaped fleur	50	135
1371 — Ve. Similar, with jewelled or beaded crown	100	300
1372 — Vf. New style larger face, double-banded crown	20	50
1373 — Vg. Single band to crown, low central fleur, curule chair shaped X ...	20	55
1374 — Vh. Crude copy of Vg, with pellets in lieu of fleur	40	125
1375 — Vi. Similar to last, but triple line of pellets for beard	150	425

Vi   1376

1376 **Gold penny** of 20d. As illustration	27500 110000

Mints, Moneyers, and classes for Henry III 'Long Cross' coinage

London: Davi or David (IIIc-Vf), Henri (IIIa-Vd, f, g), Ion, Ioh, Iohs or Iohan (Vc-g), Nicole (Ib/II mule, II-Vc), Renaud (Vg-i), Ricard (IIIc-Vg), Robert (Vg), Thomas (Vg), Walter (Vc-g), Willem (Vc-g and gold penny)..............................

Bristol: Elis (IIIa, b, c), Henri (IIIb) , Iacob (IIIa, b, c), Roger (IIIa, b, c), Walter (IIIb, c) ....

Bury St. Edmunds: Ion or Iohs (II-Va, Vg, h, i), Randulf (Va-f), Renaud (Vg), Stephane (Vg)..

Fine

20

25

25

Fine

Canterbury: Alein (Vg, h), Ambroci (Vg), Gilbert (II-Vd/c mule, Vf, g), Ion, Ioh,
Iohs, or Iohanes (IIIe-Vd, f, g), Nicole or Nichole (Ib/II mule, II-Vh), Ricard
(Vg, h), Robert (Vc-h), Roger (Vh), Walter (Vc-h), Willem or Willeme
(Ib/II mule, II-Vd, f, g).. 20
Carlisle: Adam (IIIa, h), Ion (IIIa, b), Robert (IIIa, b), Willem (IIIa, b)............. 50
Durham: Philip (IIIb), Ricard (V, b, c), Roger (Vg), Willem (Vg) 70
Exeter: Ion (II-IIIc), Philip (II-IIIc), Robert (II-IIIc), Walter (II-IIIb)........ ,,,.. 30
Gloucester: Ion (II-IIIc), Lucas (II-IIIc), Ricard (II-IIIc), Roger (II-IIIc)........... 35
Hereford: Henri (IIIa, b), Ricard (IIIa, b, c), Roger (IIIa, b, c), Walter (IIIa, b, c) 40
Ilchester: Huge (IIIa, b, c), Ierveis (IIIa, b, c), Randulf (IIIa, b, c), Stephe
(IIIa, b, c)... 70
Lincoln: Ion (II-IIIc), Ricard (II-IIIc), Walter (II-IIIc), Willem (II-IIIc)............. 25
Newcastle: Adam (IIIa, b), Henri (IIIa, b, c), Ion (IIIa, b, c), Roger (IIIa, b, c).. 25
Northampton: Lucas (II-IIIb), Philip (II-IIIc), Tomas (II-IIIc), Willem (II-IIIc) 25
Norwich: Huge (II-IIIc), Iacob (II-IIIc), Ion (II-IIIc), Willem (II-IIIc) 30
Oxford: Adam (II-IIIc), Gefrei (II-IIIc), Henri (II-IIIc), Willem (II-IIIc) 35
Shrewsbury: Lorens (IIIa, b, c), Nicole (IIIa, b, c), Peris (IIIa, b, c), Ricard (IIIa,
b, c) 45
Wallingford: Alisandre (IIIa, b), Clement (IIIa, b), Ricard (IIIa, b), Robert (IIIa,
b) 60
Wilton: Huge (IIIb, c), Ion (IIIa, b, c), Willem (IIIa, b, c)................................... 35
Winchester: Huge (II-IIIc), Iordan (II-IIIc), Nicole (II-IIIc), Willem (II-IIIc) 25
York: Alain (II-IIIb), Ieremie (II-IIIb), Ion (II-IIIc), Rener (II-IIIc), Tomas (IIIb, c) 25

EDWARD I, 1272-1307

'Long Cross' coinage (1272-79). With name hENRICVS

The earliest group of Edward's Long Cross coins are of very crude style and known only of Durham
and Bury St. Edmunds. Then, for the last class of the type, pennies of much improved style were
issued at London, Durham and Bury, but in 1279 the Long Cross coinage was abandoned and a
completely new coinage substituted.

Cut halfpennies and farthings also occur for this issue, and within this context are not especially rare.

VI   VII

		F	VF
		£	£
1377	Class VI. Crude face with new realistic curls, ℰ and N ligate..................	25	65
1378	— VII. Similar, but of improved style, usually with Lombardic U..........	45	135

Mints, moneyers, and classes for Edward I 'Long Cross' coinage

London: Phelip (VII), Renaud (VII) ....*from*	40
Bury St. Edmunds: Ioce (VII), Ion or Ioh (VI, VII) ....*from*	25
Durham: Roberd (VI), Robert (VII) ....*from*	250

New Coinage (from 1279).

A major re-coinage was embarked upon in 1279 which introduced new denominations. In addition to the penny, halfpence and farthings were also minted and, for the first time, a fourpenny piece called a 'Groat', wt. 89 grs., (from the French *Gros*).

The groats, though ultimately unsuccessful, were struck from more than thirty obverse dies and form an extensive series with affinities to the pence of classes 1c to 3g. The precise chronology is still uncertain and they are arranged in accordance with the classification set out in SCBI 39.

As mint administration was now very much centralized, the practice of including the moneyer's name in the coinage was abandoned (except for a few years at Bury St. Edmunds). Several provincial mints assisted with the re-coinage during 1279-81, then minting was again restricted to London, Canterbury, Durham and Bury.

The provincial mints were again employed for a subsidiary re-coinage in 1299-1302 in order to remint lightweight coins and the many illegal *esterlings* (foreign copies of the English pennies, mainly from the Low Countries), which were usually of poorer quality than the English coins.

		F	VF
		£	£
1379A	**Groat.** *London.* Variety a. (Fox 5). Small crowned bust within a quatrefoil of three lines, flowers in spandrels. Flat crown with pellet ornaments, drapery of two wedges with rosette below	1450	5250
1379B	— b. (Fox 6). Larger face with flat hair. Unusual crescent crown carrying pearl ornaments, drapery with rosette in centre	1350	5250
1379C	— c. (Fox 3). Similar face with bushy hair. Crown with plain band and pearl ornaments, drapery is foreshortened circle with rosette in centre....	1450	5500
1379D	— d. (Fox 7). New portrait with smaller pointed face, trefoils in spandrels. Crown with spearhead ornaments, drapery is segment of a circle with rosette in centre	1450	5500

1379E

1379E	— e. (Fox 4). Larger oval face with bushy hair, flowers in spandrels. Crown with spearhead ornaments, thick curved drapery without rosette	1350	5250
1379F	— f. (Fox 1). Broader face and shorter hair. Crown with spread side fleurs, drapery of two wedges, trefoil of pellets below	1750	6500
1379G	—— (Fox 2). Quatrefoil of two lines. Drapery of two wedges, trefoil of pellets below	1450	5500

1379H

1379H	— g. (Fox -). Quatrefoil of two lines. Crown with bifoliate side fleurs, drapery of two wedges with annulet (?) on breast, two annulets after ANG	1750	6500

Edward I groats were often mounted as brooches and gilt. Such specimens are worth considerably less

1a   1b   1c

		F	VF
		£	£

1380 **Penny.** *London.* Class 1a. Crown with plain band, ЄDW RЄX; Lombardic
Ո on *obv;* pellet 'barred' S on rev. A with sloping top 165 525
1381 — 1b. — ЄD RЄX; no drapery on bust, Roman N 675 2500
1382 — 1c. — ЄDW RЄX; Roman N, normal or reversed; small lettering 25 75
1383 — 1d. — ЄDW R;—; large lettering and face 25 70

1d(1384)   2a   2b

1384 — — — Annulet below bust 80 250
1385 — 2a. Crown with band shaped to ornaments; usually broken left petal
to central fleur portrait as ld. N usually reversed 20 50
1386 — 2b. — tall bust; long neck; N reversed 20 50

3a   3b   3c

1387 — 3a. Crescent-shaped contraction marks; pearls in crown, drapery is
foreshortened circle with hook ends 25 70
1388 — 3b. — — drapery is segment of a circle, pearls in crown 20 60
1389 — 3c. — normal crown; drapery in one piece, hollowed in centre 20 45

3e   3f   3g   4a

1390 — 3d. — — drapery in two pieces, broad face 20 50
1391 — 3e. — long narrow face (Northern mints) 20 50
1392 — 3f. — broad face, large nose, rougher work, late S first used 25 80
1393 — 3g. — Spread crown small neat bust, narrow face 20 45

4b   4c   4d   4e

		F £	VF £
1394	— 4a. Comma-shaped contraction mark, late S always used, C and Є open	20	50
1395	— 4b. Similar, but face and hair shorter	20	45
1396	— 4c. Larger face with more copious hair; nick to band of crown	25	60
1397	— 4d. Pellet at beginning of *obv.* and *rev.* legend	20	45
1398	— 4e. Three pellets on breast, ropy hair, pellet in *rev.* legend (no pellets on Bury or Durham)	20	50

5a   5b

1399	— 5a. Well spread coins, pellet on breast, face as 1398, A normally unbarred	25	80
1400	— 5b. Coins more spread, tall lettering, long narrow face, pellet on breast	25	80

6a   6b   7a   7b

1401	— 6a. Smaller coins, smaller lettering with closed E (from now on) initial cross almost plain, crown with wide fleurs, crude appearance	65	200
1402	— 6b. Initial cross pattée	35	110
1403	— 7a. Rose on breast (except Bury), short hair; almond-shaped eyes, double barred N	30	85

8b   8c

1404	— 7b. Rose on breast (London only) longer hair, new crown	40	110
1405	— 8a. Crown resembling 7b with central fleur usually broken	25	55
1406	— 8b. Similar to 1405 with wider drapery, top-tilted S	25	60
1406A	— 8c — — Crown with very arched band	30	85

9a 9b

		F	*VF*
		£	£

1407 — 9a. Drapery of two wedges, pellet eyes, crown of 8a-b or new flatter
one; often star on breast 20 45

1408 — 9b. Small coins; Roman N, normal, un-barred, or usually of pot-hook
form; often star or (very rarely) pellet on breast. Some Durham coins are
from locally made dies 20 45

1408A– 9c. Larger crude lettering with barred A and abbreviation marks.
(only found in combination with dies of 9b or 10ab, except Bury). 30 90

10ab

1409 — 10ab. ЄDWARD. Bifoliate crown (converted 9b or new taller one).
Narrow incurved lettering. 20 45

1409A— 10ab. Similar with annulet on breast or a pellet each side of head
and on breast 65 175

1409B — 10ab. ЄDWAR (rarely ЄDWR). Similar to 1409. A few early coins
have the trifoliate crown of 9b. 20 45

10cf1 10cf2

Crown 1 Crown 2 Crown 3 Crown 4 Crown 5

1410 — 10cf1. Crown 1 (Axe-shaped central fleur, wedge-shaped petals).
ЄDWA from now on. Stub-tailed. R...................................... 20 45

1411 — 10cf2. Crown 2 (Well-shaped central lis, no spearheads). Spreading hair. 20 45

	10cf3	10cf4	10cf5	F	VF
				£	£

1412 — 10cf3. Crown 3 (Left-hand arrowhead inclines to right). Early coins
have the broken lettering of 10cf2; later have new lettering with ....
round-backed Є.   20   45
1413 — 10cf4. Crown 4 (Neat with hooked petal to right-hand side fleur).   25   75
1414 — 10cf5. Crown 5 (taller and more spread, right-hand ornament inclines
to left). Later coins are on smaller flans.   20   50

For a more detailed classification of Class 10, see 'Sylloge of British Coins, 39, The J. J. North Collection, Edwardian English Silver Coins 1279-1351', The Classification of Class 10, c. 1301-10, by C. Wood.

Prices are for full flan, well struck coins.
The prices for the above types are for London. For coins of the other mints see following pages; types are in brackets, prices are for the commonest type of each mint.

Berwick Type 1   Type II   Type III   Type IV

1415 *Berwick-on-Tweed.* (Blunt types I-IV) Local dies   20   60
1416 *Bristol.* (2; 3b; c, d; 3f, g; 9b).   20   50
1417 *Bury St. Edmunds.* Robert de Hadelie (3c, d, g; 4a, b, c).   40   110
1418 — Villa Sci Edmundi (4e; 5b; 6b; 7a; 8ab, 9a – 10 cf 5).   20   50
1419 *Canterbury.* (2; 3b-g; 4; 5; 7a; 7b; 9;10).   20   45
1420 *Chester.* (3g; 9b)   35   90
1421 *Durham.* Plain cross mm (9b; 10ab; 10cf 2-3; 10cf 5)   20   50
1422 — Bishop de Insula (2; 3b, c, e, g; 4a).   20   50
1423 — Bishop Bec (4b-e; 5b; 6b; 7b; 9a, 9b, 10) with *mm.* cross moline   20   50
1424 — — (4b) cross moline in one angle of *rev.*   110   375
1425 *Exeter.* (9b).   30   80
1426 *Kingston-upon-Hull.* (9b).   35   90
1427 *Lincoln.* (3c, d, f, g).   20   45
1428 *Newcastle-upon-Tyne.* (3e; 9b; 10ab)   20   45
1429 *York.* Royal mint (2; 3b, c, d, e, f; 9b)   20   45
1430 — Archbishop's mint (3e, f; 9b). R. Quatrefoil in centre   20   45
1431 **Halfpenny,** *London.* Class 3b. ЄDWR ANGL DNS hYB, drapery
composed of curved line with wedges above.   40   120
1432 — 3c Drapery composed of two wedges   20   60

1434A   1433

1433 — 3g. New wide crown, thick-waisted S, drapery as 3b   25   65
1433A— — 4c. Narrower crown, drapery of two unequal wedges   30   90
1433B— — Similar, pellet before LON.   35   110

	F	VF
	£	£

1434	— 4e. Single-piece collar with (usually) three pellets on breast	40	135
1434A	— 6. Small face with short hair, large coarse crown, closed Є	45	140
1435	— 7. Larger face with square jaw, open Є, usually double-barred N.......	40	125
1436	— 8. Similar, new crown with straight sides	40	125
1437	— 10. ЄDWAR R ANGL DNS hYB, bifoliate or trifoliate crown, new waisted letters...................... ....,,,,,,...,,,,...	30	90

The above prices are for London; halfpence of the mints given below were also struck.

1438	*Berwick-on-Tweed.* (Blunt types I, II and III)...	50	135
1439	*Bristol.* Class 3c, 3g, 4c..	30	100
1440	*Lincoln.* Class 3c	35	110
1441	*Newcastle.* Class 3e, single pellet in each angle of *rev.*	50	135
1442	*York.* Class 3c-e...	35	110

1443A   1445

1443	**Farthing,** *London.* Class 1a. Base silver issue (6.65 grains), ЄDWARDVS RЄX. bifoliate crown with no intermediate jewels, inner circle. R. LONDONIЄNSIS, (rarely LONDRIЄNSIS), ...	40	135
1443A	— 1c. Similar trifoliate crown	30	110
1444	— 2. Smaller face, trifoliate crown with intermediate jewels	25	70
1445	— 3c. New tapering face, wide at top, crown with curved band.	25	70
1445A	— 3de. Sterling silver issue (5.51 grains.) Є R ANGLIЄ bust (usually) to bottom of coin, no inner circle. R. LONDONIЄNSIS.........................	30	90
1446	— 3g. Similar, new wide crown with curving side fleurs........................	20	75
1446A	— 4de. Similar to 3de. R. CIVITAS LONDON	35	135
1446B	— 5. Similar, crude wide crown.	35	125
1447	— 6-7. New large face with wide cheeks, pellet or almond eyes	35	125
1448	— 8. Similar, small rounded face, tall crude crown	30	100
1449	— 9a. Є R ANGL DN, small tapering face, (a variety has the face of class 6-7)	30	110
1449A	— 9b. Small ugly face, usually wide crown with outwards-sloping sides. .	35	120
1450	— 10 ЄDWARDVS REX (-, A, AN or ANG,) large bust within inner circle	20	55

      Type 1450 often appears on oval flans.

It is now thought that the order of London Farthings is class 4de, 6-7, 5, 9a, 8, 9b

1446   1452

1451	*Berwick-on-Tweed.* (Blunt type I, IIIb)...	100	325
1452	*Bristol.* Class 2, 3c, 3de...	30	90
1453	*Lincoln.* Class 3de	35	100
1453A	*Newcastle.* Class 3de, R NOVI CASTRI..	175	600
1454	*York.* Class 2, 3c, 3de...	40	125

For further information see Farthings and Halfpennies, Edward I and II, Paul and Bente R Withers, 2001

The coinage of this reign differs only in minor details from that of Edward I. No groats were issued in the years *c.* 1282-1351.

			F	VF
			£	£

1455 **Penny,** *London.* Class 11a. Broken spear-head or pearl on l. side of crown; long narrow face, straight-sided N; round back to C and Є...................... 20 | 50

1456 — 11b. — Є with angular back (till 15b), N with well-marked serifs (late) 20 | 50

1457 — 11c. — — A of special form... 40 | 110

1458 — 12a. Central fleur of crown formed of three wedges; thick cross mm. 25 | 70

1458A— 12b — Crown with diamond-shaped petals and cruciform central fleur; cross of four wedges mm .... 45 | 150

1458B— 12c — Crown with heart-shaped petals; cross patte mm.................... 65 | 200

1459 — 13. Central fleur of crown as Greek double axe .... 25 | 60

1460 — 14. Crown with tall central fleur; large smiling face with leering eyes 20 | 50

1461 — 15a. Small flat crown with both spear-heads usually bent to l.; face of 14 25 | 65

1462 — 15b. — very similar, but smaller face.. 20 | 60

1463 — 15c. — large face, large Є... 25 | 60

Berwick Type V   Type VI   Type VII

1464 *Berwick-on-Tweed.* (Blunt types V, VI and VII) Local dies except V ..... 25 | 70

1465 *Bury St. Edmunds.* (11; 12; 13; 14; 15)... 20 | 50

1466 *Canterbury.* (11; 12a; 13; 14; 15) .... 20 | 50

1467 *Durham.* King's Receiver (11a), *mm.* plain cross.................................... 20 | 55

1468 — Bishop Bec. (11a), *mm.* cross moline... 20 | 55

1469 — Bishop Kellawe (11; 12a; 13), crozier on *rev.* .... 20 | 55

1470 — Bishop Beaumont (13; 14; 15), *mm.* lion with lis .... 25 | 85

1471 *mm.* plain cross (11a, 14, 15c) .... 55 | 150

1472 **Halfpenny,** *London.* Class 10-11, ЄDWARDVS REX (-, A, AN, ANG, ANGL or ANGLI,) bifoliate or trifoliate crown .... 45 | 135

1473 — *Berwick-on-Tweed.* (Blunt type V).. 85 | 250

1474 **Farthing,** *London.* Class 11, 13, ЄDWARDVS REX (-, A, AN, or AG), face with pellet eyes... 25 | 80

1475 — *Berwick-on-Tweed.* (Blunt type V)... 100 | 350

During Edward's early years small quantities of silver coin were minted following the standard of the previous two reigns, but in 1335 halfpence and farthings were produced which were well below the .925 Sterling silver standard. In 1344 an impressive gold coinage was introduced comprising the Florin or Double Leopard valued at six shillings, and its half and quarter, the Leopard and the Helm. The design of the Florin was based on the contemporary gold of Philip de Valois of France.

The first gold coinage was not successful and it was replaced later the same year by a heavier coinage, the Noble, valued at 6s. 8d, i.e., 80 pence, half a mark or one third of a pound, together with its fractions. The Noble was lowered in weight in two stages over the next few years, being stabilized at 120 grains in 1351. With the signing of the Treaty of Bretigni In 1360 Edward's title to the Kingdom of France was omitted from the coinage, but it was resumed again in 1369.

In 1344 the silver coinage had been re-established at the old sterling standard, but the penny was reduced in weight to just over 20 grains and in 1351 to 18 grains. Groats were minted again in 1351 and were issued regularly henceforth until the reign of Elizabeth.

Subsequent to the treaty with France which gave England a cross-channel trading base at Calais, a mint was opened there in 1363 for minting gold and silver coins of English type. In addition to coins of the regular English mints, the Abbot of Reading also minted silver pence, halfpence and farthings with a scallop shell in one quarter of the reverse while coins from Berwick display one or two boar's or bear's heads.

There is evidence of re-use of dies at later periods, e.g. 3rd coinage halfpennies.

For further study of the English Hammered Gold Coinage see: Sylloge of Coins of the British Isles, 47, the Herbert Schneider Collection Volume One, by Peter Woodhead. 1996.

Mintmarks

| 6 | 1 | 2 | 3 | 74 | 4 | 5 | 7a |

1334-51	Cross pattée (6)	1356	Crown (74)
1351-2	Cross 1 (1)	1356-61	Cross 3 (4)
1351-7	Crozier on cross end (76a, *Durham*)	1361-9	Cross potent (5)
1352-3	Cross 1 broken (2)	1369-77	Cross pattée (6)
1354-5	Cross 2 (3)		Plain cross (7a)

The figures in brackets refer to the plate of mintmarks in Appendix III.

GOLD

Third coinage, 1344-51
First period, 1344

1476	1477	1478

	F	*VF*
	£	£
1476 **Double-florin.** (=6s.; wt. 108 grs.). King enthroned beneath canopy; crowned leopard's head each side. ℞. Cross in quatrefoil	25000	100000
1477 **Florin.** Leopard sejant with banner l. ℞. Somewhat as last......................	9750	30000
1478 **Half-florin .** Helmet on fleured field. ℞. Floriate cross	6000	17500

Second period, 1344-46

1479

1479 **Noble** (=6s. 8d., wt. 138.46 grs.). King stg. facing in ship with sword and shield. ℞. L in centre of royal cross in tressure...	4500	17500
1479A **Half-noble.** Similar...	2250	8000
1480 **Quarter-noble.** Shield in tressure. ℞. As last..	975	2750

Third period, 1346-51

1481 **Noble** (wt. 128.59 grs.). As 1479, but Є in centre; large letters	1000	2850
1482 **Half-noble.** Similar...	975	3250
1483 **Quarter-noble.** As 1480, but Є in centre..	300	800

Fourth coinage, 1351-77
Reference: L. A. Lawrence, *The Coinage of Edward III from 1351.*
Pre-treaty period, 1351-61. With French title.

1484 **Noble** (wt. 120 grs.), series B (1351). Open Є and C, Roman M; *mm.* cross 1 (1)...	675	1750
1485 — — *rev.* of series A (1351). Round lettering, Lombardic M and N; closed inverted Є in centre..	725	2000

		F	VF
		£	£
1486	C (1351-1352). Closed Є and C, Lombardic M; *mm.* cross 1 (1).........	575	1350
1487	D (1352-1353). *O.* of series C. R. *Mm.* cross 1 broken (2).........	1250	3750

1488   1498

1488	E (1354-1355). Broken letters, V often has a nick in r. limb; *mm.*		
	cross 2 (3)..	575	1350
1489	F (1356). *Mm.* crown (74)...	725	2000
1490	G (1356-1361). *Mm.* cross 3 (4). Many varieties...................	550	1200
1491	**Half-noble,** B. As noble with *rev.* of series A, but closed Є in centre not		
	inverted...	475	1250
1492	C. *O.* as noble. *Rev.* as last...................................	525	1350
1493	E. As noble...	675	2000
1494	G. As noble. Many varieties..	375	975
1495	**Quarter-noble,** B. Pellet below shield. R. Closed Є in centre.....	265	675
1496	C. *O.* of series B. *Rev.* details as noble......................	300	850
1497	E. *O.* as last. *Rev.* details as noble, pellet in centre.........	275	750
1498	G. *Mm.* cross 3 (4). Many varieties..............................	225	525

Transitional treaty period, 1361. French title omitted, replaced by that of Aquitaine on the noble and (rarely) on the half-noble, but not on the quarter-noble; irregular sized letters; *mm.* cross potent (5).

1499

| 1499 | **Noble.** R. Pellets or annulets at corners of central panel......... | 575 | 1450 |

1500   1503

		F	VF
		£	£
1500	**Half-noble.** Similar...	275	725
1501	**Quarter-noble.** Similar. Many varieties. Pellet and rarely Є in centre....	190	385

Treaty period, 1361-69. Omits FRANC, new letters, usually curule-shaped X; *mm.* cross potent(5).

1502	**Noble.** *London.* Saltire or nothing before ЄDWARD	585	1275
1503	— Annulet before ЄDWARD (with, rarely, crescent on forecastle)........	575	1250
1504	*Calais.* C in centre of *rev.,* flag at stern of ship	625	1350
1505	— — without flag	625	1350

1506   1508

1506	**Half-noble.** *London.* Saltire before ЄDWARD	350	900
1507	— Annulet before ЄDWARD...	375	950
1508	*Calais.* C in centre of *rev.,* flag at stern of ship	625	1450
1509	— — without flag	750	2000
1510	**Quarter-noble.** *London.* As 1498. R. Lis in centre	200	425
1511	— — annulet before ЄDWARD...	200	425
1512	*Calais.* R. Annulet in centre..	215	475
1513	— — cross in circle over shield...	235	575
1514	— R. Quatrefoil in centre; cross over shield..............................	275	675
1515	— — crescent over shield..	325	750

Post-treaty period, 1369-1377. French title resumed.

1516	**Noble.** *London.* Annulet before ЄD. R. Treaty period die......................	750	2250
1517	— — — crescent on forecastle...	625	1450
1518	— — post-treaty letters. R. Є and pellet in centre...................................	575	1350
1519	— — — R. Є and saltire in centre..	675	1650
1520	*Calais.* Flag at stern. R. Є in centre	650	1500

1521

		F	VF
		£	£
1521	— — *Rev.* as 1518, with Є and pellet in centre	600	1375
1522	— As 1520, but without flag. R̥. Є in centre	650	1500
1523	**Half-noble.** *London. O.* Treaty die. *Rev.* as 1518	900	2750
1524	*Calais.* Without AQT, flag at stern. R̥. Є in centre	800	2250
1525	— — R̥. Treaty die with C in centre	875	2500

SILVER

First coinage, 1327-35 (0.925 fineness)

1526   1530

1526	**Penny.** *London.* As Edw. II; class XVd with Lombardic n's	300	850
1527	*Bury St. Edmunds.* Similar	375	1000
1528	*Canterbury; mm.* cross pattée with pellet centre	200	550
1529	— — three extra pellets in one quarter	185	500
1530	*Durham.* R̥. Small crown in centre	575	1500
1530A	*Reading.* R̥. Escallop in 2nd quarter	650	1750
1531	*York.* As 1526, but quatrefoil in centre of *rev;* three extra pellets in TAS quarter	175	475
1532	— — — pellet in each quarter of *mm.*	175	475
1534	— — — Roman N's on *obv.*	175	475
1535	*Berwick* (1333-1342, Blunt type VIII). Bear's head in one quarter of *rev.*	475	1350
1536	**Halfpenny.** *London.* Indistinguishable from EDWARD II (cf. 1472)	45	135
1537	*Berwick* (Bl. VIII). Bear's head in one or two quarters	60	175
1538	**Farthing.** *London.* Indistinguishable from those of EDWARD II (cf. 1474)	25	80
1539	*Berwick* (Bl. VIII). As 1537	50	150

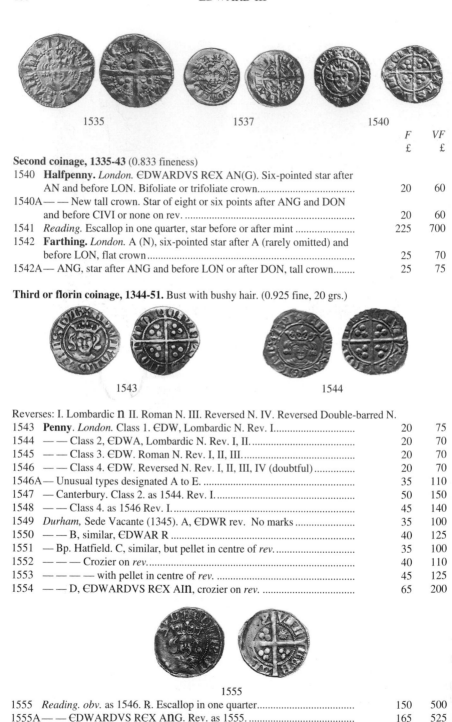

1535   1537   1540

	F	VF
	£	£

Second coinage, 1335-43 (0.833 fineness)

1540 **Halfpenny.** *London.* ЄDWARDVS RЄX AN(G). Six-pointed star after
AN and before LON. Bifoliate or trifoliate crown.................................... 20 60

1540A— — New tall crown. Star of eight or six points after ANG and DON
and before CIVI or none on rev. 20 60

1541 *Reading.* Escallop in one quarter, star before or after mint 225 700

1542 **Farthing.** *London.* A (N), six-pointed star after A (rarely omitted) and
before LON, flat crown.. 25 70

1542A— ANG, star after ANG and before LON or after DON, tall crown........ 25 75

Third or florin coinage, 1344-51. Bust with bushy hair. (0.925 fine, 20 grs.)

1543   1544

Reverses: I. Lombardic П II. Roman N. III. Reversed N. IV. Reversed Double-barred N.

1543 **Penny.** *London.* Class 1. ЄDW, Lombardic N. Rev. I............................... 20 75

1544 — — Class 2, ЄDWA, Lombardic N. Rev. I, II.. 20 70

1545 — — Class 3. ЄDW. Roman N. Rev. I, II, III... 20 70

1546 — — Class 4. ЄDW. Reversed N. Rev. I, II, III, IV (doubtful) 20 70

1546A— Unusual types designated A to E. 35 110

1547 — Canterbury. Class 2. as 1544. Rev. I.. 50 150

1548 — — Class 4. as 1546 Rev. I.. 45 140

1549 *Durham,* Sede Vacante (1345). A, ЄDWR rev. No marks 35 100

1550 — — B, similar, ЄDWAR R 40 125

1551 — Bp. Hatfield. C, similar, but pellet in centre of *rev.* 35 100

1552 — — — Crozier on *rev.*.. 40 110

1553 — — — — with pellet in centre of *rev.* 45 125

1554 — — D, ЄDWARDVS RЄX AІП, crozier on *rev.* 65 200

1555

1555 *Reading. obv.* as 1546. Ŗ. Escallop in one quarter.................................. 150 500

1555A— — ЄDWARDVS RЄX AПG. Rev. as 1555. .... 165 525

1556 *York. obv.* as 1546. Ŗ. Quatrefoil in centre 20 60

	F	VF
	£	£
1557 **Halfpenny.** *London.* EDWARDVS REX	15	40
1558 — — EDWARDVS REX An...	15	45
1559 — — as 1558 with pellet or small saltire each side of crown and/or in one reverse quarter..	25	75
1560 — *Reading.* as 1557. Rev. Escallop in one quarter...............................	185	525
1561 — — as 1558. Rev. as 1560......................... ,,,,,,,,,,,, ...	200	550
1562 **Farthing.** *London.* EDWARDVS REX	25	75
1562A *Reading.* As S.1562. Rev. as 1560.	225	725
1562B — — EDWARDVS REX An. Rev. as 1560	250	750

Fourth coinage, 1351-77
Reference: L. A. Lawrence, *The Coinage of Edward III from 1351.*
A large variety of mules exist between styles and issue.
Pre-treaty period, 1351-61. With French title.

1563   1567

		F	VF
1563 **Groat** (=4d., 72 grs.). *London,* series B (1351). Roman M, open C and E; *mm.* cross 1..		175	575
1564 — — — crown in each quarter...		1500	6000
1565 — C (1351-2). Lombardic m, closed C and E, R with wedge-shaped tail; *mm.* cross 1..		45	175
1566 — D (1352-3). R with normal tail; *mm.* cross 1 or cross 1 broken (2).....		60	225
1567 — E (1354-5). Broken letters, V often with nick in r. limb; *mm.* cross 2 (3)		45	175
1568 — — — lis on breast		50	200
1569 — F (1356). *Mm.* crown (74)...		60	200

1570   1572

		F	VF
1570 — G (1356-61). Usually with annulet in one quarter and sometimes under bust, *mm.* cross 3 (4). Many varieties		45	165
1571 *York,* series D. As London		150	475
1572 — E. As London		65	200

1573   1574

	F £	VF £
1573 **Halfgroat.** *London,* series B. As groat	85	275
1574 — C. As groat	35	110
1575 — D. As groat	35	120
1576 — E. As groat	35	120
1577 — F. As groat	40	125
1578 — G. As groat	35	110
1579 — — — annulet below bust	35	120
1580 *York,* series D. As groat	70	225
1581 — E. As groat	45	150
1582 — — — lis on breast	60	200
1583 **Penny.** *London.* Series A (1351). Round letters, Lombardic m and n, annulet in each quarter; *mm.* cross pattee	65	250

1584   1587   1591

	F	VF
1584 — C. Details as groat, but annulet in each quarter	20	70
1585 — D. Details as groat, but annulet in each quarter	25	80
1586 — E. Sometimes annulet in each quarter	20	70
1587 — F. Details as groat	25	85
1588 — G. Details as groat	20	70
1589 — — — annulet below bust	20	75
1590 — — — saltire in one quarter	35	125
1591 *Durham,* Bp. Hatfield. Series A. As 1583, but extra pellet in each quarter, VIL LA crozier DVRRЄM	75	250
1592 — C. Details as groat. R. Crozier, CIVITAS DVNЄLMIЄ	20	75
1593 — D — — —	25	85
1594 — E — — —	30	90
1595 — F — R. Crozier, CIVITAS DVRЄMЄ	25	85
1596 — G — — —	25	80
1597 — — — — — annulet below bust	25	85
1598 — — — — — saltire in one quarter	35	115
1599 — — — — — annulet on each shoulder	30	100
1600 — — — — — trefoil of pellets on breast	30	100
1601 — — — R. Crozier, CIVITAS DVRЄLMIЄ	40	135

		F	VF
		£	£
1602	*York,* Royal Mint. Series D	25	80
1603	— — E	20	70
1604	— Archb. Thoresby. Series D. R. Quatrefoil in centre	25	90
1605	— — G —	20	70
1606	— — — annulet or saltire on breast	25	85
1607	**Halfpenny.** *London.* Series E. ЄDWARDVS RЄX AN	70	225
1608	— G, but with *obv.* of F (*mm.* crown). Annulet in one quarter................	100	350
1609	**Farthing.** *London.* Series E. ЄDWARDVS RЄX	75	250
1609A	— — Series G. Annulet in one quarter.....................................	80	275

Transitional treaty period, 1361. French title omitted, irregular sized letters; *mm.* cross potent (5).

| 1610 | **Groat.** *London.* Annulet each side of crown .... | 325 | 1000 |

1611   1612

1611	**Halfgroat.** Similar, but only seven arches to tressure	110	325
1612	**Penny,** *London.* Omits RЄX, annulet in two upper qtrs. of *mm*..............	75	225
1613	*York,* Archb. Thoresby. Similar, but quatrefoil enclosing pellet in centre of *rev.*	50	150
1614	*Durham.* Bp. Hatfield. Similar. R. Crozier, CIVITAS DORЄLMЄ........	60	175
1615	**Halfpenny.** Two pellets over *mm.,* ЄDWARDVS RЄX AN	75	250

Treaty period, 1361-69. French title omitted, new letters, usually 'Treaty' X, rarely curule chair X *mm.* cross potent (5).

1616	**Groat,** *London.* Many varieties	75	220
1617	— Annulet before ЄDWARD...	75	225
1618	— Annulet on breast	110	350

1617   1619

| 1619 | *Calais.* As last .... | 125 | 400 |

1621   1635

		F £	VF £
1620	**Halfgroat,** *London.* As groat	35	120
1621	— — Annulet before ЄDWARDVS	35	125
1622	— — Annulet on breast	40	150
1623	*Calais.* As last	75	250
1624	**Penny,** *London.* ЄDWARD AПGL R, etc	30	100
1625	— — — pellet before ЄDWARD	35	120
1626	*Calais.* R. VILLA CALЄSIE	100	300
1627	*Durham.* R. CIVITAS DVПЄLMIS	45	150
1628	— R. Crozier, CIVITAS DVRЄMЄ	35	125
1629	*York,* Archb. Thoresby. Quatrefoil in centre of *rev.,* ЄDWARDVS DЄI G RЄX AП	35	125
1630	— — — — ЄDWARDVS RЄX AПGLI	25	90
1631	— — — — quatrefoil before ЄD and on breast	30	95
1632	— — — — annulet before ЄD	30	100
1633	— — — ЄDWARD AПGL R DПS HYB	35	125
1634	**Halfpenny.** ЄDWARDVS RЄX AП, pellet stops	20	85
1635	— Pellet before ЄD, annulet stops	25	90
1636	**Farthing.** ЄDWARDVS RЄX, pellet stops	80	275

Post-treaty period, 1369-77. French title resumed, X like St. Andrew's cross; *mm.* 5, 6, 7a.

1637   1639

1637	**Groat.** Various readings, *mm.* cross pattee	90	325
1638	— — row of pellets across breast (chain mail)	350	1200
1639	— row of annulets below bust (chain mail); *mm.* cross potent with four pellets	375	1250
1640	**Halfgroat.** Various readings	110	325

1640A

		F	VF
		£	£
1640A—	Thin portrait of Richard II	125	475
1641	— row of pellets one side of breast (chain mail)	150	575
1642	**Penny,** *London.* No marks on breast	35	125
1643	— Pellet or annulet on breast	40	125
1644	— Cross or quatrefoil on breast	30	100
1645	*Durham,* Bp. Hatfield. *Mm.* 7a, CIVITAS DVnOLM, crozier	35	120
1646	— — — — annulet on breast	40	125
1647	— — — — lis on breast	35	120
1648	*York.* Archb. Thoresby or Neville. R. Quatrefoil in centre	25	90
1649	— — — lis on breast	30	100
1650	— — — annulet on breast	30	100
1651	— — — cross on breast	35	110

1652

1652	**Farthing.** ЄDWARD RЄX ANGL, large head without neck	100	350

For further reading see:
Halfpennies and Farthings of Edward III and Richard II. *Paul and Bente R. Withers, 2002.*

There was no change in the weight standard of the coinage during this reign and the coins evolve from early issues resembling those of Edward III to late issues similar to those of Henry IV.

There is no overall, systematic classification of the coins of Richard II but a coherent scheme for the gold coinage has been worked out and is published in the Schneider Sylloge (SCBI 47). This classification has been adopted here.

Reference: *Silver coinages of Richard II, Henry IV and V.* (B.N.J. 1959-60 and 1963).

Mintmark: cross pattée (6)

	F £	VF £

GOLD

1653	**Noble,** *London.* Style of Edw. III. IA. Lis over sail	825	1850

1654   1658

1654	— IB. Annulet over sail	700	1500
1655	French title omitted. IIA. Crude style, saltire over sail. IIB. Fine style, trefoil over sail. IIC. Porcine style, no mark over sail	725	1650
1656	French title resumed. IIIA. Fine style, no marks	725	1650
1657	— IIIB. Lis on rudder. IIIC. Trefoil by shield	825	2000
1658	Henry IV style. IVA. Escallop on rudder. IVB. Crescent on rudder	875	2500
1659	*Calais.* Style of Edw. III, IA, Edw. III lettering	975	3000
1660	Style of Edw. III. IB. New lettering. Voided quatrefoil over sail	750	1750

1661   1662

1661	French title omitted. IIA. Crude style, no marks. IIB. Fine style, trefoil over sail. IIC. Porcine style, no marks	700	1600
1662	French title resumed. IIIA. Fine style, no marks	750	1750
1663	— IIIB. Lion on rudder. IIIC. Two pellets by shield	875	2350
1664	**Half-noble,** *London.* With altered *obv.* of Edw. III. Usually muled with *rev.* or altered *rev.* of Edw. III	825	2250

1665

1673

		F	VF
		£	£
1665	Style of Edw. III. IB. No marks or saltire over sail	725	2000
1666	French title omitted. IIA. New style, no marks	800	2250
1667	French title resumed. IIIA. No marks. IIIB. Lion on rudder	850	2400
1668	Henry IV style. IVB. Crescent on rudder	925	2750
1669	*Calais*. Mule with *obv.* or *rev.* of Edw. III	1250	3500
1670	Style of Edw. III. IB. Quatrefoil over sail	1200	3250
1671	Late style. French title. IIIA. No marks. IIIB. Saltire by rudder	1000	3000
1672	**Quarter-noble,** *London.* IA. R in centre of *rev.*	425	950
1673	IB Lis in centre of *rev.*	375	825
1674	— lis or cross over shield	400	900

1675

1677

		F	VF
1675	IIIA. Pellet in centre of *rev.*	375	825
1676	IIIB. Trefoil of annulets over shield or trefoils in spandrels	450	1000
1677	IVA. Escallop over shield	400	925

SILVER

1679

1682

		F	VF
1678	**Groat.** I. Style of Edw. III, F *(i.e. et)* before FRANC, etc.	375	1250
1679	II. New lettering, retrograde Z before FRANC, etc.	325	1050
1680	III. Bust with bushy hair, 'fishtail' serifs to letters	375	1250
1681	IV. New style bust and crown, crescent on breast	975	4000
1682	**Halfgroat.** II. New lettering; with or without French title	185	625
1683	III. As 1680	225	750
1684	— — with *obv.* die of Edw. III (1640A)	300	1000

		F	*VF*
		£	£
1685	IV. As 1681, but no crescent...	525	2000
1686	**Penny,** *London.* I Lettering as 1678, RICARDVS RЄX AПGLIЄ	150	475
1688	— II. As 1679, Z FRAПC lis on breast	165	500

1689

1692

1689	— III. As 1680, RICARD RЄX AnGLIЄ, fish-tail letters	175	575
1690	*York.* I. Early style, usually with cross or lis on breast, quatrefoil in centre of *rev*	45	185
1691	— II. New bust and letters, no marks on breast...	45	185
1692	— Local dies. Pellet above each shoulder, cross on breast, REX AПGLIE or AПGILIE	45	200
1693	— — — RЄX DNS ЄB	85	325
1694	— — — RЄX AПG FRAПC...	80	300
1695	— III. As 1680, RЄX AПGL Z FRAПC (scallop after TAS)	65	250
1696	— IV. Very bushy hair, new letters, R. R in centre of quatrefoil	135	500
1697	*Durham.* Cross or lis on breast, DVПOLM	110	375

1698   1699   1701   1704

1698	**Halfpenny.** Early style. LONDON, saltire or annulet (rare) on breast	45	150
1699	Intermediate style. LOПDOП, no marks on breast...................................	30	95
1700	Type III. Late style. Similar, but fishtail letters	30	100
1700A	Type IV. Short, stubby lettering..	35	120
1701	**Farthing.** Small bust and letters	90	300
1703	Similar but no neck	85	275
1704	Rose in each angle of *rev.* instead of pellets	125	400
1704A	Large head with broad face as Henry IV	135	425

For further reading see:
Halfpennies and Farthings of Edward III and Richard II. *Paul and Bente R. Withers, 2002.*

HENRY IV, 1399-1413

In 1412 the standard weights of the coinage were reduced, the noble by 12 grains and the penny by 3 grains, partly because there was a scarcity of bullion and partly to provide revenue for the king, as Parliament had not renewed the royal subsidies. As in France, the royal arms were altered, three fleur-de-lis taking the place of the four or more lis previously displayed.

Mintmark: cross pattée (6)

GOLD

Heavy coinage, 1399-1412

	1707		1705

	F	VF
	£	£
1705 **Noble** (120 grs.), *London.* Old arms with four lis in French quarters; crescent or annulet on rudder	4000	13000
1706 — New arms with three lis; crescent, pellet or no marks on rudder	4000	12500
1707 *Calais.* Flag at stern, old arms; crown on or to l. of rudder	4750	15000

	1708		1710

1708 — — new arms; crown or saltire on rudder	4500	14000
1709 **Half-noble,** *London.* Old arms	3250	10000
1710 — new arms	3000	9500
1711 *Calais.* New arms	4250	12500
1712 **Quarter-noble,** *London.* Crescent over old arms	975	3000
1713 — — — new arms	925	2750
1714 *Calais.* New arms. R. *Mm.* crown	1000	3500

1715

	F £	VF £

Light coinage, 1412-13

1715 **Noble** (108 grs.). Trefoil, or trefoil and annulet, on side of ship. R. Trefoil
in one quarter 1350 3500

1716 **Half-noble.** Similar, but always with annulet.. 1850 5250

1717

1717 **Quarter-noble.** Trefoils, or trefoils and annulets beside shield, lis above. R.
Lis in centre.. 525 1250

SILVER

Heavy coinage, 1399-1412

1718	1722	1723

	F £	VF £
1718 **Halfgroat** (36 grs.). Star on breast	975	3000
1718A— Muled with Edw. III (1640A) *obv.*	675	2000
1719 **Penny,** *London.* Similar, early bust with long neck.................................	550	1650
1720 — later bust with shorter neck, no star	550	1650
1722 *York* Bust with broad face, round chin..	350	950
1723 **Halfpenny.** Early small bust..	125	475
1724 — later large bust, with rounded shoulders, ...	125	475
1725 **Farthing.** Face without neck	525	1500

Light coinage, 1412-13

	1728		1731		1737		

		F	*VF*
		£	£
1726	**Groat** (60 grs.). I. Pellet to l., annulet to r. of crown; altered die of Richard II	1650	5250
1727	New dies; II. Annulet to l., pellet to r. of crown, 8 or 10 arches to tressure	1500	5000
1728	— III. Similar but 9 arches to tressure	1350	4750
1729	**Halfgroat.** Pellet to l., annulet to r. of crown	575	1500
1730	Annulet to l., pellet to r. of crown	400	1250
1731	**Penny,** *London.* Annulet and pellet by crown; trefoil on breast and before CIVI	375	1200
1732	— — annulet or slipped trefoil before LON	400	1250
1733	— Pellet and annulet by crown	375	1100
1734	*York.* Annulet on breast. R. Quatrefoil in centre	225	675
1735	*Durham.* Trefoil on breast, DVnOLM	200	625
1737	**Halfpenny.** New dies; annulets by crown or neck, or no marks	145	550
1738	**Farthing.** Face, no bust; trefoil after REX	525	1500

For further information see:
Halfpennies and Farthings of Henry IV, V and VI. *Paul and Bente R. Withers, 2003.*

There was no change of importance in the coinage of this reign. There was, however, a considerable development in the use of privy marks which distinguished various issues, except for the last issue of the reign when most marks were removed. The Calais mint, which had closed in 1411, did not re-open until just before the end of the reign.

Mintmarks

Cross pattee (4)   Pierced cross with   Pierced cross (18).
                       pellet centre (20)

GOLD

		F	*VF*
		£	£
1739	**Noble.** A. Quatrefoil over sail and in second quarter of *rev.* Short broad letters, no other marks	1350	4000
1740	— B. Ordinary letters; similar, or with annulet on rudder	825	2000
1741	— C. Mullet by sword arm, annulet on rudder	725	1650

1742

1742	— — — broken annulet on side of ship	675	1500
1743	—D. Mullet and annulet by sword arm, trefoil by shield, broken annulet on ship	750	1750

1744

1744	— E. Mullet, or mullet and annulet by sword arm, trefoil by shield, pellet by sword point and in one quarter, annulet on side of ship	725	1650
1745	— — Similar, but trefoil on ship instead of by shield	750	1750
1746	— F. Similar, but no pellet at sword point, trefoil in one quarter	800	1850
1747	— G. No marks; annulet stops, except for mullet after first word	925	2250
1748	**Half-noble.** B. As noble; Hen. IV *rev.* die	1350	4250
1749	— C. Broken annulet on ship, quatrefoil below sail	700	1650

		F £	VF £
1750	—— Mullet over shield, broken annulet on *rev.*	625	1350
1751	— F. Similar, but no annulet on ship, usually trefoil by shield	825	2500

1752   1756

1752	— F/E. As last, but pellet in 1st and annulet in 2nd quarter	800	2350
1753	— G. As noble, but quatrefoil over sail, mullet sometimes omitted after first word of *rev.*..	675	1750
1754	**Quarter-noble.** A. Lis over shield and in centre of *rev.* Short broad letters; quatrefoil and annulet beside shield, stars at corners of centre on *rev.*......	625	1650
1755	— C. Ordinary letters; quatrefoil to l., quat. and mullet to r. of shield.....	350	825
1756	——— annulet to l., mullet to r. of shield...	275	600
1757	— F. Ordinary letters; trefoil to l., mullet to r. of shield...........................	300	700
1758	– G. — no marks, except mullet after first word	325	750

SILVER

1759	**Groat.** A. Short broad letters; 'emaciated' bust..	950	3250

1759

1760	—— muled with Hen. IV *obv*...	975	3750
1761	—— muled with Hen. IV *rev*...	950	3250

1762   1765

1762	B. Ordinary letters; 'scowling' bust	325	1000
1762A	—— mullet in centre of breast..	350	1100
1762B	—— mullet to r. of breast...	375	1250
1763	—— muled with Hen. IV...	525	1500
1764	C. Normal bust..	225	750
1765	—— mullet on r. shoulder	125	375

		F	VF
		£	£
1766	— — R muled with Hen. IV	475	1500
1767	G. Normal bust; no marks	275	850
1768	**Halfgroat.** A. As groat, but usually with annulet and pellet by crown	450	1250
1769	B. Ordinary letters; no marks	300	850
1770	— — muled with Hen. IV *obv.*	475	1500
1771	C. Tall neck, broken annulet to l. of crown	100	350
1772	— — — mullet on r. shoulder	110	375

1773   1774

1773	— — — mullet in centre of breast	100	325
1774	F. Annulet and trefoil by crown, mullet on breast	110	350
1775	G. New neat bust: no marks.	110	350
1776	**Penny.** *London.* A. Letters, bust and marks as 1768	225	650
1777	— Altered Hen. IV *obv.* with mullet added to l. of crown	375	1200

1778   1791

1778	— C. Tall neck, mullet and broken annulet by crown	25	110
1779	— D. Similar, but whole annulet	30	120
1780	— F. Mullet and trefoil by crown	35	125
1781	— G. New neat bust, no marks, DI GRA	35	135
1782	*Durham.* C. As 1778 but quatrefoil at end of legend	35	125
1783	— D. As 1779	35	125
1784	— G. Similar, but new bust. R. Annulet in one qtr.	40	140
1785	*York.* C. As 1778, but quatrefoil in centre of *rev.*	20	85
1786	— D. Similar, but whole annulet by crown	25	90
1787	— E. As last, but pellet above mullet	40	140
1788	— F. Mullet and trefoil by crown	20	85
1789	— — Trefoil over mullet to l., annulet to r. of crown	35	110
1790	— G. Mullet and trefoil by crown (London dies)	30	110
1791	— — Mullet and lis by crown, annulet in one qtr. (usually local dies)....	30	110
1792	**Halfpenny.** A. Emaciated bust, annulets by crown	110	375
1793	— altered dies of Hen. IV	135	475
1794	C. Ordinary bust, broken annulets by crown	20	80
1795	D. Annulets, sometimes broken, by hair	20	80

1796   1798

	F	VF
	£	£
1796 F. Annulet and trefoil by crown	20	80
1797 G. New bust; no marks, (usually muled with Henry VI annulet *rev.*)	35	135
1797A **Farthing.** *London.* B. Very large head	275	800
1798 — G. Small face with neck	140	475
1798A *Calais.* G. as 1798, VILLA CALIS	325	1000

For further information see:
Halfpennies and Farthings of Henry IV, V and VI. *Paul and Bente R. Withers, 2003.*

The supply of gold began to dwindle early in the reign, which accounts for the rarity of gold after 1426. The Calais mint had reopened just before the death of Henry V and for some years a large amount of coin was struck there. It soon stopped minting gold; the mint was finally closed in 1440. A royal mint at York was opened for a short time in 1423/4.

Marks used to denote various issues become more prominent in this reign and can be used to date coins to within a year or so.

Reference: C. A. Whitton Heavy Coinage of Henry VI. (B.N.J. 1938-41).

Mintmarks

136	7a	105	18	133	8	9	15

1422-7	Incurved pierced cross (136)	1422-34	Cross pommée (133)
1422-3	Lis (105, York)	1427-34	Cross patonce (8)
1422-60	Plain cross (7a, intermittently		Cross fleury (9)
	Lis (105, on gold)	1434-35	Voided cross (15)
1422-27	Pierced cross (18)	1435-60	Cross fleury (9)
1460	Lis (105, on rev. of some groats)		

For Restoration mintmarks see page 198.

GOLD

1799

	F	VF
	£	£
Annulet issue, 1422-7		
1799 **Noble.** *London.* Annulet by sword arm, and in one spandrel on *rev.;* trefoil stops on *obv.* with lis after hℭnRIC, annulets on *rev.,* with mullet after IhC	525	1250
1800 — Similar, but *obv.* from Henry V die	975	3000
1801 — As 1799, but Flemish imitative coinage	350	900
1802 *Calais.* As 1799, but flag at stern and C in centre of *rev*	725	2250

1803

		F	VF
		£	£
1803	— — with h in centre of *rev.*	600	1500
1804	*York.* As London, but with lis over stern	700	2000

1805

1805	**Half-noble.** *London.* As 1799	375	1000
1806	— Similar, but *obv.* from Henry V die	750	2250
1807	*Calais.* As noble, with C in centre of *rev.*	750	2250
1808	— — with h in centre of *rev.*	700	2000
1809	*York.* As noble	800	2500
1810	**Quarter-noble.** *London.* Lis over shield; *mm.* large lis	210	500
1811	— — — trefoil below shield	225	550
1812	— — — pellet below shield	235	575
1813	*Calais.* Three lis over shield; *mm.* large lis	325	750

1814   1819

1814	— Similar but three lis around shield	275	650
1815	— As 1810, but much smaller *mm.*	235	575
1816	*York.* Two lis over shield	275	650

	F £	VF £

Rosette-mascle issue, 1427-30

1817 **Noble.** *London.* Lis by sword arm and in *rev.* field; stops, rosettes, or
rosettes and mascles 875 2500
1818 *Calais.* Similar, with flag at stern 1250 3500
1819 **Half-noble.** *London.* Lis in *rev.* field; stops, rosettes and mascles........... 1350 4000
1820 *Calais.* Similar, flag at stern; stops, rosettes 1450 4500
1821 **Quarter-noble.** *London.* As 1810; stops, as noble 625 1350
1822 — without lis over shield 675 1500
1823 *Calais.* Lis over shield, rosettes r. and l., and rosette stops 725 1750

Pinecone-mascle issue, 1430-4

1824

1824 **Noble.** Stops, pinecones and mascles 800 2250
1825 **Half-noble.** *O.* Rosette-mascle die. R. As last.. 1750 5750
1826 **Quarter-noble.** As 1810, but pinecone and mascle stops 750 1850

Leaf-mascle issue, 1434-5

1827 **Noble.** Leaf in waves; stops, saltires with two mascles and one leaf 1850 6250
1828 **Half-noble.** (Fishpool hoard and Reigate hoard)...................................... 1650 5500
1829 **Quarter-noble.** As 1810; stops, saltire and mascle; leaf on inner circle of *rev.* 750 1850

Leaf-trefoil issue, 1435-8

1830 **Noble.** Stops, leaves and trefoils.. 1750 5500
1830A **Half-noble.** 1850 6250
1831 **Quarter-noble.** Similar 750 2000

Trefoil issue, 1438-43

1832 **Noble.** Trefoil to left of shield and in *rev.* legend..................................... 1750 5500

Leaf-pellet issue, 1445-54

1833 **Noble.** Annulet, lis and leaf below shield... 1900 6500

Cross-pellet issue, 1454-60

1834 **Noble.** Mascle at end of *obv.* legend.. 2250 7500

Muling exists in Henry VI coins spanning two or three issues. Full flan coins in the smaller denominations are difficult to find.

SILVER

Annulet issue, 1422-7

	1836	1838		
			F	VF
			£	£

1835	**Groat.** *London.* Annulet in two quarters of *rev.*	50	120
1836	*Calais.* Annulets at neck. R. Similar	45	110
1837	— — no annulets on *rev.*	55	175
1838	*York.* Lis either side of neck. R. As 1835	750	2750
1839	**Halfgroat.** *London.* As groat	35	100

	1840	1843

1840	*Calais.* As 1836	30	85
1841	— — no annulets on *rev.*	40	125

	1845	1849	1852

1843	*York.* As groat	575	1750
1844	**Penny.** *London.* Annulets in two qtrs.	30	90
1845	*Calais.* Annulets at neck. R. As above	25	80
1846	— — only one annulet on *rev.*	30	110
1847	*York.* As London, but lis at neck	525	1500
1848	**Halfpenny.** *London.* As penny	15	50
1849	*Calais.* Similar, but annulets at neck	15	50
1850	*York.* Similar, but lis at neck	250	750
1851	**Farthing.** *London.* As penny, but *mm.* cross pommée	85	200
1852	*Calais.* Similar, but annulets at neck	100	300
1852A	*York.* Similar, but lis at neck	425	1250

	F £	VF £
Annulet-trefoil sub-issue		
1854 **Groat.** *Calais,* as 1836 but trefoil to l. of crown.	60	175
1855 **Halfgroat.** *Calais,* similar, only known as a mule with annulet issue		
(both ways) or with rosette mascle rev.	60	200
1856 **Penny.** *Calais.* Similar, only one annulet on *rev*	60	200

Rosette-mascle issue, 1427-30. All with rosettes (early) or rosettes and mascles somewhere in the legends.

| 1858 **Groat.** *London.* .... | 55 | 165 |

1859   1861

1859 *Calais*	45	120
1860 — mascle in two spandrels (as illus. 1863)	55	150
1861 **Halfgroat.** *London.*	70	275
1862 *Calais*	35	100

1863   1872

1863 — mascle in two spandrels, as illustrated..............................	40	110
1864 **Penny.** *London.*..	85	325
1865 *Calais*	35	100
1866 *York.* Archb. Kemp. Crosses by hair, no rosette	25	90
1867 — — Saltires by hair, no rosette..	30	100
1868 — — Mullets by crown	25	90
1869 *Durham,* Bp. Langley. Large star to l. of crown, no rosette, DVnOLMI	40	135
1870 **Halfpenny,** *London*	15	50
1871 *Calais*	15	50
1872 **Farthing,** *London*	110	350
1873 *Calais. Mm.* cross pommée..	125	400

Pinecone-mascle issue, 1430-4. All with pinecones and mascles in legends.

1874   18/6/7   1879

		F	VF
		£	£
1874	**Groat,** London	50	125
1875	*Calais*	40	110
1876	**Halfgroat,** *London*	45	150
1877	*Calais*	40	115
1878	**Penny,** *London*	35	110
1879	*Calais*	30	95
1880	*York,* Archb. Kemp. Mullet by crown, quatrefoil in centre of *rev.*	30	100
1881	— — rosette on breast, no quatrefoil	30	100
1882	— — mullet on breast, no quatrefoil	30	110
1883	*Durham,* Bp. Langley. DVnOLMI	40	125

1884   1888

1884	**Halfpenny,** *London*	15	55
1885	*Calais*	20	60
1886	**Farthing,** *London*	110	300
1887	*Calais. Mm.* cross pommée	125	400

Leaf-mascle issue, 1434-5. Usually with a mascle in the legend and a leaf somewhere in the design.

1888	**Groat.** *London.* Leaf below bust, all appear to read DOnDOn	150	550
1889	— — *rev.* of last or next coinage	125	375
1890	*Calais.* Leaf below bust, and usually below MЄVM	100	275
1891	**Halfgroat.** *London.* Leaf under bust, pellet under TAS and DON	110	325

1892   1897

		F	VF
		£	£
1892	*Calais.* Leaf below bust, and sometimes on *rev.*	110	325
1893	**Penny.** *London.* Leaf on breast, no stops on *rev.*......	50	125
1894	*Calais.* Leaf on breast and below SIЄ................	60	150
1895	**Halfpenny.** *London.* Leaf on breast and on *rev.*......	30	75
1896	*Calais.* Leaf on breast and below SIЄ................	65	175

Leaf-trefoil issue, 1435-8. Mostly with leaves and trefoil of pellets in the legends.

		F	VF
1897	**Groat.** *London.* Leaf on breast	70	185
1898	— without leaf on breast................................	65	175
1899	*Calais.* Leaf on breast	475	1350
1900	**Halfgroat.** *London.* Leaf on breast; *mm.* plain cross........	60	175
1901	— *O. mm.* cross fleury; leaf on breast................	55	160
1902	— — without leaf on breast..........................	60	175
1902A	*Calais.* leaf on breast, mule with leaf mascle *rev.*	125	425
1903	**Penny.** *London.* Leaf on breast..................	45	125
1903A	*Calais.* Similar	250	700
1904	*Durham,* Bp. Neville. Leaf on breast. R. Rings in centre, no stops, DVПOLM	100	275
1905	**Halfpenny.** *London.* Leaf on breast................	20	55
1906	— without leaf on breast..............................	20	60
1906A	*Calais.* leaf on breast, mule with leaf mascle rev.	90	275
1907	**Farthing.** *London.* Leaf on breast; stops, trefoil and saltire on *obv.*	95	275

Trefoil issue, 1438-43. Trefoil of pellets either side of neck and in legend, leaf on breast.

1909   1911A

		F	VF
1908	**Groat.** *London.* Sometimes a leaf before LON.	75	235
1909	— Fleurs in spandrels, sometimes extra pellet in two qtrs.	100	300
1910	— Trefoils in place of fleurs at shoulders, none by neck, sometimes extra pellets	85	250
1911	*Calais*	200	700
1911A	**Halfgroat,** *London* Similar, but trefoil after DEUM and sometimes after POSUI Mule only with leaf trefoil *obv.*	110	375
1911B	— *Calais Obv.* Similar to 1911, mule with leaf mascle *rev.*	275	800
1912	**Halfpenny,** *London*	20	70
1912A	**Farthing,** *London*	125	350

Trefoil pellet issue, 1443-5

1912   1913   1915   1917

	F	VF
	£	£
1913 **Groat.** Trefoils by neck, pellets by crown, small leaf on breast; sometimes extra pellet in two quarters	125	350

Leaf-pellet issue, 1445-54. Leaf on breast, pellet each side of crown, except where stated.

		F	VF
1914	**Groat.** ANGL; extra pellet in two quarters	65	200
1915	*Similar,* but ANGLI	60	185
1916	— — trefoil in *obv.* legend	75	225
1917	Leaf on neck, fleur on breast, often extra pellet in two quarters	60	185
1918	As last, but two extra pellets by hair	150	525
1919	**Halfgroat.** As 1914 *mm.*Cross patonce	65	180
1920	Similar, but *mm.* plain cross, some times no leaf on breast, no stops	60	170
1921	**Penny.** *London.* Usually extra pellets in two quarters	40	100
1922	— — pellets by crown omitted	40	110
1923	— — trefoil in legend	45	125
1924	*York,* Archb. Booth. R. Quatrefoil and pellet in centre	30	95
1925	— — two extra pellets by hair (local dies)	30	95
1926	*Durham,* Bp. Neville. Trefoil in *obv.* legend. R. Two rings in centre of cross	50	135

1927   1932

1927	— — Similar, but without trefoil	50	140
1928	**Halfpenny.** Usually extra pellet in two quarters	15	55
1929	— *mm.* plain cross	15	55
1930	**Farthing.** As last	110	325

Unmarked issue, 1453-4

1931	**Groat.** No marks on *obv.;* two extra pellets on *rev.*	400	1250
1932	— four extra pellets on *rev.*	450	1350
1933	**Halfgroat.** As 1931	225	675

	F £	VF £

Cross-pellet issue, 1454-60

1934 **Groat.** Saltire either side of neck, pellets by crown, leaf and fleur on breast, extra pellets on *rev.* .... 300 | 850

1935 Saltire on neck, no leaf, pellets by crown, usually mullets in legend; extra pellets on *rev.* .... 90 | 275

1935   1940

1936 — Similar, but mascles in place of mullets on *obv.*................................... 100 | 325
1937 — — pellets by hair instead of by crown .... 135 | 475
1938 **Halfgroat.** Saltire on neck, pellets by crown and on *rev.,* mullets in legend 200 | 625
1939 **Penny.** *London.* Saltire on neck, pellets by crown and on *rev.,* mascle(s), or mullet and mascle in legend .... 135 | 450
1940 *York,* Archb. Wm. Booth. Saltires by neck, usually leaf on breast, pellets by crown. ℞. Cross in quatrefoil in centre. .... 30 | 110
1941 *Durham,* Bp. Laurence Booth. Saltire and B or B only at neck, pellets by crown. ℞. Rings in centre.. 45 | 135
1942 **Halfpenny.** Saltires by neck, usually two extra pellets on *rev.* .... 35 | 125
1943 Similar, but saltire on neck, sometimes mullet after hЄnRIC................. 25 | 75
1944 **Farthing**. Saltire on neck, usually pellets by crown and on *rev.,* but known without either. .... 135 | 375

Lis-pellet issue, 1456-60

1945

1945 **Groat.** Lis on neck; pellets by crown. ℞. Extra pellets .... 200 | 675

For further information see:
Halfpennies and Farthings of Henry IV, V and VI. *Paul and Bente R. Withers, 2003.*

EDWARD IV, First Reign, 1461-70

In order to increase the supply of bullion to the mint the weight of the penny was reduced to 12 grains in 1464, and the current value of the noble was raised to 8s. 4d. Later, in 1465, a new gold coin was issued, the Ryal or 'Rose Noble', weighing 120 grains and having a value of 10s. However, as 6s. 8d. had become the standard professional fee the old noble was missed, and a new coin was issued to take its place, the Angel of 80 grains.

Royal mints were opened at Canterbury and York to help with the re-coinage, and other mints were set up at Bristol, Coventry and Norwich, though they were not open for long.

Reference: C. E. Blunt and C. A Whitton, *The Coinage of Edward IV and Henry VI (Restored),* B.N.J. 1945-7.

Mintmarks

✤	✚	✛	✿	Y	✳	♛	✝
105	9	7a	33	99	28	74	11

1461-4	Lis (105)	1467-70	Lis (105, *York*)	
	Cross fleury (9)	1467-8	Crown (74)	(often
	Plain cross (7a)		Sun (28)	combined)
1464-5	Rose (33 and 34)	1468-9	Crown (74)	(sometimes
1464-7	Pall (99, *Canterbury*)		Rose (33)	combined)
1465-6	Sun (28)	1469-70	Long cross	
1466 7	Crown (74)		fitchee (l.c.f) (11)	(often
			Sun (28)	combined)

GOLD

Heavy coinage, 1461-4

		F	VF
		£	£
1946	**Noble** (=6s. 8d., wt. 108 grs.). Normal type, but *obv.* legend commences at top left, lis below shield; *mm.*-/lis (Spink's sale May 1993)	2250	6750
1947	— Quatrefoil below sword arm; *mm.* rose/lis	2500	8250
1948	— R. Roses in two spandrels; *mm.* rose	2650	9500
1949	**Quarter-noble**	1500	4250

1946   1950

	F £	VF £

Light coinage, 1464-70

1950 **Ryal** or rose-noble (=10s., wt. 120 grs.), *London*. As illustration. Large
       fleurs in spandrels; *mm.* 33-74 .... 575 1300
1951 — — Small trefoils in spandrels; *mm.* 74-11 .... 575 1300

1952

1952 — Flemish imitative coinage (mostly 16th cent. on a large flan)	400	850
1953 *Bristol.* B in waves, large fleurs; *mm.* sun, crown	675	1750
1954 — — small fleurs in spandrels; *mm.* sun, crown	700	1800
1955 *Coventry.* C in waves; *mm.* sun	1350	3250
1956 *Norwich.* n in waves; *mm.* sun, rose	1375	3500
1957 *York.* Є in waves, large fleurs in spandrels, *mm.* sun, lis	650	1650
1958 — — small fleurs, *mm.* sun. lis	675	1700
1959 **Half-ryal.** *London.* As 1950	525	1250
1960 *Bristol.* B in waves; *mm.* sun, sun/crown	700	1800
1961 *Coventry.* C in waves; *mm.* sun	2500	8500
1962 *Norwich.* n in waves; *mm.* rose	2250	7500

1963   1965

1963 *York.* Є in waves; *mm.* 28, 105, 33/105	550	1300
1963A Similar but lis instead of Є in waves (probably York)	625	1500
1964 **Quarter-ryal.** Shield in tressure of eight arcs, rose above. R. Somewhat as half ryal; *mm.* sun/rose...	750	2000
1965 Shield in quatrefoil, R. Є above, rose on l., sun on r.; *mm.* 33/28-74/33..	275	700
1966 — — sun on l., rose on r.; *mm.* 74-11...	300	750

1967

	F	VF
	£	£

1967 **Angel** (=6s. 8d., wt. 80 grs.). St. Michael spearing dragon. R. Ship, rays of
sun at masthead, large rose and sun beside mast; *mm.*-/33 .... 3500 12500
1968 — — small rose and sun at mast; *mm.*-/74 .... 3750 13500

SILVER

Heavy coinage, 1461-4
1969 **Groat** (60 grs.). Group I, lis on neck, pellets by crown; *mm.* 9, 7a, 105,
9/105 .... 125 375
1970 — Lis on breast, no pellets; *mm.* plain cross, 7a/105.............................. 135 450
1971 — — with pellets at crown; *mm.* plain cross 135 450

1972

1972 II, quatrefoils by neck, crescent on breast; *mm.* rose 125 375
1973 III, similar but trefoil on breast; *mm.* rose... 110 325
1974 — — — eye in *rev.* inner legend, *mm.* rose... 110 310
1975 — Similar, but no quatrefoils by bust... 175 575
1976 — — Similar, but no trefoil on breast 150 475
1977 IV, annulets by neck, eye after TAS; *mm.* rose....................................... 225 750

1974   1978

1978 **Halfgroat.** I, lis on breast, pellets by crown and extra pellets in two qtrs.;
mm. 9, 7a 325 1000

	F	VF
	£	£
1979 II, quatrefoils at neck, crescent on breast; *mm.* rose	275	675
1980 III, similar, but trefoil on breast, eye on rev.; *mm.* rose	200	525
1981 — Similar, but no mark on breast	200	525
1982 IV, annulets by neck, sometimes eye on *rev.; mm.* rose	225	675
1983 **Penny** (15 grs.), *London.* I, marks as 1978, but mascle after RЄX; *mm.* plain cross	225	650
1984 II, quatrefoils by neck; *mm.* rose	175	475

1985

	F	VF
1985 III, similar, but eye after TAS; *mm.* rose	150	425
1986 IV, annulets by neck; *mm.* rose	175	475
1987 *York,* Archb. Booth. Quatrefoils by bust, voided quatrefoil in centre of *rev.; mm.* rose	100	250
1988 *Durham. O.* of Hen. VI. R. DVПOLIП	110	275
Some of the Durham pennies from local dies may belong to the heavy coinage period, but if so they are indistinguishable from the light coins.		
1989 **Halfpenny.** I, as 1983, but no mascle	60	175
1990 II, quatrefoils by bust; *mm.* rose	40	100
1991 — saltires by bust; *mm.* rose	35	90
1992 III, no marks by bust; *mm.* rose	35	90
1992A—saltires by bust, eye after TAS, *mm.* rose	75	225
1993 IV, annulets by bust; *mm.* rose	40	100
1994 **Farthing.** I, pellets by crown, extra pellets on rev., with or without lis on breast	175	500
1994A II. saltires by bust; *mm.* rose	185	525
1994B III, no marks by bust; *mm.* rose	150	475

Light coinage, 1464-70. There is a great variety of groats and we give only a selection. Some have pellets in one quarter of the reverse, or trefoils over the crown; early coins have fleurs on the cusps of the tressure, then trefoils or no marks on the cusps, while the late coins have only trefoils.

	F	VF
1995 **Groat** (48 grs.), *London.* Annulets at neck, eye after TAS; *mm.* 33 (struck from heavy dies, IV)	110	350
1996 — — — Similar, but new dies, eye after TAS or DOП	120	375
1997 — Quatrefoils at neck, eye; rose (heavy dies, III)	85	240
1998 — — — Similar, but new dies, eye in *rev.* legend	85	240
1999 — No marks at neck, eye; *mm* rose	135	425

2000 2002

Light coinage, silver, *continued.*

		F	VF
		£	£
2000	— Quatrefoils at neck, no eye; *mm.* 33, 74, 28, 74/28, 74/33, 11/28	45	135
2001	— — — rose or quatrefoil on breast; *mm.* 33, 74/28..............................	50	165
2002	— No marks at neck; *mm.* 28, 74, 11/28, 11...	55	185
2003	— Trefoils or crosses at neck; *mm.* 11/33, 11/28, 11...............................	50	165
2004	*Bristol.* B on breast, quatrefoils at neck; *mm.* 28/33, 28, 28/74, 74, 74/28	60	200
2005	— — trefoils at neck; *mm.* sun	80	275
2006	— — no marks at neck; *mm.* sun...	135	475
2007	— Without B, quatrefoils at neck; *mm.* sun...	135	450
Bristol is variously rendered as BRESTOLL, BRISTOLL, BRESTOW, BRISTOW.			
2008	*Coventry.* C on breast, quatrefoils at neck, COVETRE; *mm.* 28/33, 28...	110	325
2009	— — Local dies, similar; *mm.* rose	125	375
2010	— — — as last, but no C or quatrefoils..	125	375
2011	Norwich. Π on breast, quatrefoils at neck, ΠORWIC or ΠORVIC, *mm.* 28/33, 28..	95	275
2012	*York.* Є on breast, quatrefoils at neck, ЄBORACI; *mm.* 28, 105/74, 105, 105/28...	55	170
2013	— Similar, but without Є on breast, *mm.* lis..	70	225
2014	— Є on breast, trefoils at neck; *mm.* 105/28, 105.................................	65	200
2015	**Halfgroat.** *London.* Annulets by neck (heavy dies); *mm.* 33	185	575
2016	— Quatrefoils by neck; *mm.* 33/-, 28/-, 74, 74/28	45	145
2017	— Saltires by neck; *mm.* 74, 74/28	60	180
2018	— Trefoils by neck; *mm.* 74, 74/28, 11/28	60	180
2019	— No marks by neck; *mm.* 11/28	90	275
2020	*Bristol.* Saltires or crosses by neck; *mm.* 33/28, 28, 74, 74/-..................	125	375
2021	— Quatrefoils by neck; *mm.* 28/-, 74, 74/-	110	325
2022	— Trefoils by neck; *mm.* crown..	135	375
2023	— No marks by neck; *mm.* 74/28	150	425
2024	*Canterbury,* Archb. Bourchier (1464-7). Knot below bust; quatrefoils by neck; *mm.* 99/-, 99, 99/33, 99/28..	35	120
2025	— — — quatrefoils omitted *mm.* 99...	35	120
2026	— — — saltires by neck; *mm.* 99/-, 99/28	40	125
2026A	— — — trefoils by neck; *mm.* 99...	40	135

2027   2030

		F £	VF £
2027	— — — wedges by hair and/or neck; *mm.* 99, 99/–, 99/33, 99/28	35	125
2028	— — As 2024 or 2025, but no knot	40	125
2029	— Royal mint (1467-9). Quatrefoils by neck; *mm.* 74, 74/-	35	120
2030	— — Saltires by neck; *mm.* 74/-, 74	35	120
2031	— — Trefoils by neck; *mm.* 74, 74/-, 74/28, 33	35	110
2032	— No marks by neck; *mm.* sun	60	175
2033	*Coventry.* Crosses by neck; *mm.* sun	450	1250
2034	*Norwich.* Quatrefoils or saltires by neck; *mm.* sun	425	1200
2035	*York.* Quatrefoils by neck; *mm.* sun, lis, lis/-	60	175
2036	— Saltires by neck; *mm.* lis	60	170
2037	— Trefoils by neck; *mm.* lis, lis/-	65	185
2038	— Є on breast, quatrefoils by neck; *mm.* lis/-	65	185
2039	**Penny** (12 grs.), *London.* Annulets by neck (heavy dies); *mm.* rose	135	400
2040	— Quatrefoils by neck; *mm.* 74, sun. crown	40	110
2041	— Trefoil and quatrefoil by neck; *mm.* crown	40	115
2042	— Saltires by neck; *mm.* crown	40	120
2043	— Trefoils by neck; *mm.* crown, long cross fitchée	40	120
2044	— No marks by neck; *mm.* long cross fitchée	100	325
2045	*Bristol.* Crosses, quatrefoils or saltires by neck, BRISTOW; *mm.* crown	110	325
2046	— Quatrefoils by neck; BRI(trefoil)STOLL	110	350
2047	— Trefoil to r. of neck BRISTOLL	125	375
2048	*Canterbury,* Archb. Bourchier. Quatrefoils or saltires by neck, knot on breast; *mm.* pall	60	160
2049	— — Similar, but no marks by neck	60	160
2050	— — As 2048, but no knot	65	175
2051	— — Crosses by neck, no knot	65	175
2052	— Royal mint. Quatrefoils by neck; *mm.* crown	125	375
2053	— *Durham,* King's Receiver (1462-4). Local dies, mostly with rose in centre of *rev.*; *mm.* 7a, 33	25	75
2054	— Bp. Lawrence Booth (1465-70). B and D by neck, B on *rev.*; *mm.* 33	30	125
2055	— — Quatrefoil and B by neck; *mm.* sun	25	110
2056	— — B and quatrefoil by neck; *mm.* crown	30	125
2057	— — D and quatrefoil by neck; *mm.* crown	30	125
2058	— — Quatrefoils by neck; *mm.* crown	25	110
2059	— — Trefoils by neck; *mm.* crown	25	110
2060	— Lis by neck; *mm.* crown	25	110
2061	*York,* Sede Vacante (1464-5). Quatrefoils at neck, no quatrefoil in centre of *rev.*; *mm.* sun, rose	35	135
2062	— Archb. Neville (1465-70). Local dies, G and key by neck, quatrefoil on *rev.*; *mm.* sun, plain cross	25	100

2063   2068

		F £	VF £
2063	— — London-made dies, similar; *mm.* 28, 105, 11	30	125
2064	— — Similar, but no marks by neck; *mm.* large lis.................................	30	125
2065	— — — Quatrefoils by neck; *mm.* large lis	30	125
2066	— — — Trefoils by neck; *mm.* large lis...	25	110
2067	**Halfpenny,** *London.* Saltires by neck; *mm.* 34, 28, 74	20	80
2068	— Trefoils by neck; *mm.* 28, 74, 11..	20	80
2069	— No marks by neck; *mm.* 11...	30	115
2070	*Bristol.* Crosses by neck; *mm.* crown...	75	225
2071	— Trefoils by neck; *mm.* crown..	70	200
2072	*Canterbury.* Archb. Bourchier. No marks; *mm.* pall....................	60	150
2072A	— — Trefoils by neck, *mm.* pall..	60	150
2073	— Royal mint. Saltires by neck; *mm.* crown	55	135
2074	— — Trefoils by neck; *mm.* crown...	50	130
2074A	*Norwich.* Quatrefoils by neck., *mm.* Sun	200	600
2075	*York.* Royal mint. Saltires by neck; *mm.* lis/-, sun/-................................	45	125
2076	— — Trefoils by neck; *mm.* lis/-	40	110
2077	**Farthing,** *London.* ЄDWARD DI GRA RЄX, trefoils by neck, *mm.* crown	225	675

Full flan coins are difficult to find in the smaller denominations.

For further information see:
Halfpennies and Farthings of Edward IV to Henry VII. *Paul and Bente R. Withers, 2004.*

The coinage of this short restoration follows closely that of the previous reign. Only angel gold was issued, the ryal being discontinued. Many of the coins have the king's name reading hɛnRICV—another distinguishing feature is an R that looks like a B.

Mintmarks

Cross pattée (6)   Rose (33, Bristol)
Restoration cross (13)   Lis (105)
Trefoil (44 and 45)   Short cross fitchée (12)

GOLD

2078

		F £	*VF* £
2078	**Angel,** *London.* As illus. but no B; *mm.* -/6, 13, -/105, none	1100	2850
2079	*Bristol.* B in waves; *mm.* -/13, none	1450	4500
2080	**Half-angel,** *London.* As 2078; *mm.* -/6, -/13, -/105	1350	4250
2081	*Bristol.* B in waves; *mm.* -/13	2250	6500

SILVER

2082   2084

2082	**Groat,** *London.* Usual type; *mm.* 6, 6/13, 6/105, 13, 13/6, 13/105, 13 /12	135	425
2083	*Bristol.* B on breast; *mm.* 13, 13/33, 13/44, 44, 44/13, 44/33, 44/12	200	625
2084	*York.* Є on breast; *mm.* lis, lis/sun	150	475
2085	**Halfgroat,** *London.* As 2082; *mm.* 13, 13/-	165	575
2086	*York.* Є on breast; *mm.* lis	275	750
2087	**Penny,** *London.* Usual type; *mm.* 6, 13, 12	175	525

	F	VF
	£	£
2087A *Bristol.* Similar; *mm.* 12	325	900
2088 *York.* G and key by neck; *mm.* lis	175	525
2089 **Halfpenny,** *London.* As 2087; *mm.* 12, 13,	75	225
2090 *Bristol.* Similar; *mm.* cross	175	525

EDWARD IV, Second Reign, 1471-83

The Angel and its half were the only gold denominations issued during this reign. The main types and weight standards remained the same as those of the light coinage of Edward's first reign. The use of the 'initial mark' as a mintmark to denote the date of issue was now firmly established.

Mintmarks

33	105	12	55	44	55	28	56	17

30	37	6	18	19	20	31	11	38

1471-83	Rose (33, *York & Durham*)	1473-7	Cross pattée (6)
	Lis (105, *York*)		Pierced cross 1 (18)
1471	Short cross fitchee (12)	1477-80	Pierced cross and
1471-2	Annulet (large, 55)		pellet (19)
	Trefoil (44)		Pierced cross 2 (18)
	Rose (33, *Bristol*)		Pierced cross, central
1471-3	Pansy (30, *Durham*)		pellet (20)
1472-3	Annulet (small, 55)		Rose (33, *Canterbury*)
	Sun (28, *Bristol*)	1480-3	Heraldic cinquefoil (31)
1473-7	Pellet in annulet (56)		Long cross fitchee
	Cross and four pellets (17)		(11, *Canterbury*)
	Cross in circle (37)	1483	Halved sun and rose (38)
			(Listed under Ed. IV/V.)

GOLD

2091   2093

	F	VF
	£	£
2091 **Angel.** *London.* Type as illus.; *mm.* 12, 55, 56, 17, 18, 19, 31	475	1100
2092 *Bristol.* B in waves; *mm.* small annulet	1750	4500
2093 **Half-angel.** As illus.; *mm.* 55, cross in circle, 19, 20/19, 31	450	1050

	F	VF
	£	£
2094 King's name and title on rev.; *mm.* 12/-...	475	1250
2095 King's name and the title both sides; *mm.* 55/-...	525	1350

SILVER

2096   2101

2096	**Groat,** *London.* Trefoils on cusps, no marks by bust; *mm.* 12-37	55	165
2097	— — roses by bust; *mm.* pellet in annulet	80	275
2098	— Fleurs on cusps; no marks by bust; *mm.* 18-20	55	165
2099	— — pellets by bust; *mm.* pierced cross..	75	250
2100	— — rose on breast; *mm.* 31...	55	165
2101	*Bristol.* B on breast no marks by bust; *mm.* 33, 33/55, 28/55, 55, 55/-, 28	135	400
2102	*York.* Є on breast no marks by bust; *mm.* lis...	125	375
2103	**Halfgroat,** *London.* As 2096; *mm.* 12-31	45	135
2104	*Bristol.* B on breast; *mm.* 33/12...	200	600
2105	*Canterbury* (Royal mint). As 2103; *mm.* 33, 11, 11/31, 31	40	120

2106

2106	— C on breast; *mm.* rose...	30	100
2107	— — R. C in centre; *mm.* rose	30	100
2108	— — R. Rose in centre; *mm.* rose...	30	100
2109	*York.* No. Є on breast; *mm.* lis	95	250
2110	**Penny,** *London.* No marks by bust; *mm.* 12-31	35	110
2111	*Bristol.* Similar; *mm.* rose	150	475
2112	*Canterbury* (Royal). Similar; *mm.* 33, 11	45	135
2113	— C on breast; *mm.* rose	70	200
2114	*Durham,* Bp. Booth (1471-6). No marks by neck; *mm.* 12, 44.................	25	95

2115   2116

2115	— — D in centre of *rev.;* B and trefoil by neck; *mm.* 44, 33, 56	25	95
2116	— — — two lis at neck; *mm.* rose...	30	100
2117	— — — crosses over crown, and on breast; *mm.* rose	30	100

		F	*VF*
		£	£
2118	— — — crosses over crown, V under CIVI; *mm.* rose, pansy	30	100
2119	— — — B to l. of crown, V on breast and under CIVI	25	95
2120	— — — As last but crosses at shoulders	25	95
2121	— Sede Vacante (1476). R. D in centre; *mm.* rose	30	100
2122	— Bp. Dudley (1476-83). V to r. of neck; as last	30	95

2123   2125   2134

2123	— — D and V by neck; as last, but *mm.* 31	25	90

Nos. 2117-2123 are from locally-made dies.

2124	*York,* Archb. Neville (1471-2). Quatrefoils by neck. R. Quatrefoil; *mm.* 12 (over lis)	40	125
2125	— — Similar, but G and key by neck; *mm.* 12 (over lis)	25	85
2126	— Neville suspended (1472-5). As last, but no quatrefoil in centre of *rev.*	35	110
2126A	— — no marks by bust, similar; *mm.* annulet	40	125
2127	— — No marks by neck, quatrefoil on *rev.; mm.* 55, cross in circle, 33 .	25	80
2128	— — Similar but Є and rose by neck; *mm.* rose	25	80
2129	— Archb. Neville restored (1475-6). As last, but G and rose	30	95
2130	— — Similar, but G and key by bust	25	80
2131	— Sede Vacante (1476). As 2127, but rose on breast; *mm.* rose	30	95
2132	— Archb. Lawrence Booth (1476-80). B and key by bust, quatrefoil on *rev.; mm.* 33, 31	25	80
2133	— Sede Vacante (1480). Similar, but no quatrefoil on rev.; *mm.* rose	30	95
2134	— Archb. Rotherham (1480-3). T and slanting key by neck, quatrefoil on *rev.; mm.* 33	25	85
2135	— — — Similar, but star on breast	40	100
2136	— — — Star on breast and to r. of crown	45	125
2137	**Halfpenny,** *London.* No marks by neck; *mm.* 12 31	25	85
2138	— Pellets at neck; *mm.* pierced cross	35	100
2139	*Canterbury* (Royal). C on breast and in centre of *rev.; mm.* rose	65	170
2140	— C on breast only; *mm.* rose	60	160
2141	— Without C either side; *mm.* 11	60	160
2142	*Durham,* Bp. Booth. No marks by neck. R. DЄR Ā M, D in centre; *mm.* rose	125	350
2142A	— — Lis either side of neck. R. D or no mark in centre	135	375
2142B	— — B to l. of crown, crosses at shoulders. R. D. in centre; *mm.* rose	135	375
2143	— — — Bp. Dudley V to l. of neck; as last	125	350

Full flan coins are very difficult to find in the small denominations.

On 12th February, 1483, the prolific cinquefoil coinage of Edward IV came to an end and an indenture between the king and the new master of the mint, Bartholomew Reed, saw the introduction of the sun and rose mintmark.

Edward IV died on 9th April, 1483, but the sun and rose coinage continued, essentially unaltered, through the short reign of Edward V and into the reign of Richard III, ending with the indenture of 20th July, 1483, with Robert Brackenbury, who had been Richard's ducal treasurer, and the introduction of the boar's head mintmark.

New dies prepared after the accession of Richard III on 26th June, 1483, bear his name but coins of the sun and rose coinage struck under Edward IV and Edward V can only be distinguished by arranging the dies in sequence. This is possible for the angels (Schneider Sylloge, SCBI 47, p.41) but has not yet been achieved for the silver coinage.

Mintmark: Halved sun and rose.

	F	*VF*
	£	£
2144 **Angel.** Type As 2091, reading EDWARD DEI GRA (Edward IV).........	1500	4750
2144A— Similar but reading EDWARD DI GRA (Edward V)..........................	5250	16500

2145

| 2145 **Half-angel.** As 2093 (probably Edward IV)... | 2250 | 6500 |

2146	2146A	
2146 **Groat.** *London,* pellet below bust, reading EDWARD or EDVARD	750	2500
2146A— — No pellet below, reading EDWARD or EDWRD...........................	725	2350
2147 **Penny.** *London* As 2110	900	3250
2148 **Halfpenny.** *London* As 2137	175	525

Richard's ruthless seizure of the crown left a core of bitter opposition which coalesced around Henry Tudor, earl of Richmond who had found asylum in Brittany. At Bosworth on 22 August, 1485, Richard was killed on the battlefield and the War of the Roses ended.

Richard's coinage follows the pattern of previous reigns. The portrait on the silver denominations remains stylised, though increasingly distinctive. It can be divided into three types according to mintmark. Type 1, the first sun and rose coinage, lasted 24 days to 20th July 1483. Type 2, the boar's head coinage, was issued until about June 1484. Type 3, the second sun and rose coinage, was struck until the end of the reign (Schneider Sylloge, SCBI 47, pp. 41-2).

It is evident that coin dies were stored in a 'loose-box' system which led to extensive muling between types. As an interim measure, after the Indenture of 20th July, 1483, at least eleven existing sun and rose obverse dies, both gold and silver, were overpunched with the boar's head mark. The seven overpunched groat dies included four Edward IV/V dies, then still in use, and three dies of Richard III type 1.

Mintmarks

| SR1 | BH1 | BH2 | SR2 | SR3 | 105 | 33 |

Halved sun and rose, 1, 2 and 3.
Boar's head, 1 (62) 2 (63).
Lis (105, *Durham*)
Rose only (33).

GOLD

	F	VF
	£	£

2149 **Angel.** 1. Reading RICARD. R. R and rose by mast; *mm.* sun and rose 1 .... 1650 5250

2150

2150 — 2a. Reading EDWARD. R. E and rose or R and rose by mast; *mm.* boar's head 1 over sun and rose 1/sun and rose 1 .... 4750 12500

2151 — 2b. Reading RICARD. R. R and rose by mast; mm. boar's head 1 over sun and rose 1/sun and rose 1, boar's head 1, boar's head 2 (often muled) 1500 4500

2152

2153

	F	VF
	£	£
2152 — 3. Reading RICARD or RICAD; *mm.* sun and rose 2	1450	4250
2153 **Half-angel.** 2b. R. R and rose by mast; *mm.* boar's head 1	3250	9000

SILVER

SR1

2154

2155

2154 **Groat.** *London.* Reading RICARD 1. *mm.* sun and rose 1	475	1300
2155 — 2a. Reading EDWARD; *mm.* boar's head 1 over sun and rose 1/sun and rose 1	1250	3000

BH2/1

SR2

2156

2158

2156 — 2b. Reading RICARD; *mm.* boar's head 1 over sun and rose 1/sun and rose 1, boar's head 1, boar's head 2 (often muled)	525	1350
2157 — 3. *mm.* sun and rose 2, sun and rose 3	450	1250
2158 — — Pellet below bust, *mm.* sun and rose 2, sun and rose 3	475	1300
2159 *York.* 3. *mm.* sun and rose 2/-	875	2500
2160 **Halfgroat.** *London.* 2a. Reading EDWARD; *mm.* boar's head 1 over sun and rose 1/- (the *mm.* is indistinct)	1350	4250

2160

2161

2161 — 2b. Reading RICARD; *mm.* boar's head 2/-	975	3250

	F	VF
	£	£
2162 — 3. *mm.* sun and rose 2, sun and rose 2/-	575	1500
2163 — — Pellet below bust; *mm.* sun and rose 2	675	1650

2164

2164 **Penny.** *London.* 2a. Reading EDWARD; *mm.* boar's head 1 over sun and rose 1/-	1000	3500
2165 — 2b. Reading RICARD; *mm.* boar's head 1/-	950	3000

2166

2166 *York.* Archb. Rotherham. T and upright key at neck. R. Quatrefoil in centre; *mm.* boar's head 1/-	200	675
2167 — — *mm.* rose/-	175	625
2168 — No marks at neck; *mm.* sun and rose 2/-	200	675

2169   2171

2169 *Durham.* Bp. Sherwood. S on breast. R. D in centre; *mm.* lis/-	150	525
2170 **Halfpenny.** *London.* 2b. No marks by neck; *mm.* boar's head 1/-	150	575
2171 — 3. *mm.* sun and rose 2/-	135	425
2171A **Farthing.** *London.* 3. *mm.* sun and rose 2/-	750	2250

HENRY VII, 1485-1509

For the first four years of his reign Henry's coins differ only in name and mintmark from those of his predecessors, but in 1489 radical changes were made in the coinage. Though the pound sterling had been a denomination of account for centuries, a pound coin had never been minted. Now a magnificent gold pound was issued, and, from the design of the king enthroned in majesty, was called a 'Sovereign'. A small simplified version of the Sovereign portrait was at the same time introduced on the silver pence. The reverse of the gold 'Sovereign' had the royal arms set in the centre of a Tudor rose. A few years later the angel was restyled and St. Michael, who is depicted about to thrust Satan into the Pit with a cross-topped lance, is no longer a feathered figure but is clad in armour of Renaissance style. A gold ryal of ten shillings was also minted again for a brief period.

The other major innovation was the introduction of the shilling in the opening years of the 16th century. It is remarkable for the very fine profile portrait of the king which replaces the representational image of a monarch that had served on the coinage for the past couple of centuries. This new portrait was also used on groats and halfgroats but not on the smaller denominations.

Mintmarks

| 39 | 41 | 40 | 42 | 33 | 11 | 7a | 123 |

| 105 | 76b | 31 | 78 | 30 | 91 | 43 | 57 |

| 85 | 94 | 118 | 21 | 33 | 53 |

1485-7	Halved sun and rose (39)	
	Lis upon sun and rose (41)	
	Lis upon half rose (40)	
	Lis-rose dimidiated (42)	
	Rose (33, *York*)	
1487	Lis (105)	
	Cross fitchée (11)	
1487-8	Rose (33)	
	Plain cross (7a, *Durham*)	
1488-9	No marks	
1489-93	Cinquefoil (31)	
	Crozier (76b, *Durham*)	
1492	Cross fitchée (11, gold only)	
1493-5	Escallop (78)	
	Dragon (118, gold only)	
	Lis (105, *Canterbury and York*	
	Tun (123, *Canterbury*)	

1495-8	Pansy (30)
	Tun (123, *Canterbury*)
	Lis (105, York)
1498-9	Crowned leopard's head (91)
	Lis issuant from rose (43)
	Tun (123, *Canterbury*)
1499-1502	Anchor (57)
1502-4	Greyhound's head (85)
	Lis (105, profile issue only)
	Martlet (94, *York*)
1504-5	Cross-crosslet (21)
1504-9	Martlet (94, (*York, Canterbury*)
	Rose (33, *York* and *Canterbury*)
1505-9	Pheon (53)

GOLD

	F £	VF £

2172 **Sovereign** (20s; wt. 240 gr.). Group I. Large figure of king sitting on
backless throne. R. Large shield crowned on large Tudor rose. *mm.* 31 .. 23500 90000

2173 — Group II. Somewhat similar but throne has narrow back, lis in
background. R. Large Tudor rose bearing small shield. *mm.* -/11 .... 18500 65000

2174

2174 — III. King on high-backed very ornamental throne, with greyhound
and dragon on side pillars. R. Shield on Tudor rose; *mm.* dragon 13500 37500

2175 — IV. Similar but throne with high canopy breaking legend and broad seat,
mm. 105/118, (also with no *obv.* i.c. *mm.* 105/118, very rare).................. 12500 35000

2176 — Narrow throne with a portcullis below the king's feet (like Henry VIII);
mm. 105/21, 105/53.............. 9500 30000

2177 **Double-sovereign** and **Treble-sovereign** from same dies as 2176. These
piedforts were probably intended as presentation pieces *mm.* 105/21, 105/53 35000 125000

2178

2178 **Ryal** (10s.). As illustration: *mm.* -/11 .... 12500 37500

2179 **Angel** (6s. 8d). I. Angel of old type with one foot on dragon. R. PER
CRVCEM. etc., *mm.* 39, 40, (also muled both ways)............................ 950 2750

2179A— With Irish title, and legend over angel head. mm. 33/-...................... 975 2850

2180 — — Name altered from RICARD? and h on *rev.* from R. mm. 41/39,
41/40, 41/-, 39/? 1000 3000

	2181	2183	2187

	F	VF
	£	£
2181 II. As 2179, but *mm.* none. 31/-.	675	1750
2181A II/III mule. *mm.* 31/78, R. PER CRUC or AVTEM TRANS	675	1750
2182 As 2181. R. IhC AVTEM TRANSIENS etc.; *mm.* none, 31/-	725	2000
2183 III. New dies, angel with both feet on dragons; (large straight lettering) *mm.* 78-85 except 91 (many mules exist)	525	1250
2183A— Angel with very small wings. *mm.* escallop	575	1500
2184 — — R. IhC AVTEM TRANSIENS, etc.; *mm.* escallop	625	1650
2185 IV. Small square lettering; *mm.* 85 (also muled with 2183)	525	1200
2186 — Tall thin lettering; *mm.* 21 (also muled with 2185 obv.)	525	1200
2187 V. Large crook-shaped abbreviation after hENRIC; *mm.* 21 and 53 (combinations and mules exist)	475	1100
2188 **Half-angel or angelet.** I. Mm. 39, 41, (old dies RIII altered)	750	2250
2189 III. Angel with both feet on dragon: *mm.* 30, 57/30, 30/85	575	1350
2190 IV. Small square lettering; *mm.* rose *mm.* -/85	575	1350
2191 — *Obv.* as last. R. Tall thin lettering; *mm.* 33/21	550	1300
2192 V. As angel; *mm.* pheon	475	1150

SILVER

Facing bust issues. Including 'Sovereign' type pennies.

		F	VF
2193 **Groat.** I. Open crown; *mm.* 40 (rose on bust), 39-42 and none (combinations)		90	300

	2194	2195

	F	VF
2194 — — crosses or saltires by neck, 41, 40, 105-33 and none (combinations)	95	325
2195 IIa. Large bust with out-turned hair, crown with two plain arches; *mm.* none, 31, 31/-, 31/78	70	200
2196 — — similar but crosses by neck; *mm.* none, -/105	85	250
2197 — — R. Portcullis over long cross; *mm.* -/lis	2250	7500

| | 2198 | 2199 | 2201 |

	F	VF
	£	£

2198 **Groat.** IIIa. Bust as IIa. Crown with two jewelled arches, *mm.* 31 .... | 225 | 675

2198A IIIb. Similar, but new bust with realistic hair *mm.* 78, 30........................ | 60 | 170

2199 IIIc. Bust as IIIb, but crown with one plain and one jewelled arch, *mm.*
30-21 and none.. | 50 | 160

2199A IIId. As last, but plainer letters. mm 57, 85, 33 and none...................... | 65 | 175

2200 IVa. Wide single arch crown; arch is single or double bar with 4 crockets;
mm. 85, 85/33, 21.. | 70 | 200

2201 IVb. — Similar, but arch is double bar with 6 uprights or crockets as jewels;
mm. 85, 21/85, 21.. | 70 | 200

2202 **Halfgroat,** *London.* I. Open crown, tressure unbroken; *mm.* 40/-, 40/39
(R. III mule) .... | 200 | 675

2203 — IIIa. Double arched crown, rosettes on tressure; mm. escallop .... | 135 | 400

2204 — IIIb. Similar, nothing on tressure. R. Lozenge panel in centre; *mm.* lis | 35 | 110

2205 — — Similar, but also with lis on breast; mm. lis.................................. | 40 | 120

2206 — IIIc. Unarched crown with tressure broken. R. Lozenge panel in centre;
mm. lis .... | 35 | 100

2206A— — — Similar but smaller dies and much smaller lettering................. | 35 | 110

| | 2207 | 2211 |

2207 *Canterbury,* Archb. Morton. I. Open crown, crosses by neck. R. M in centre;
mm. tun/- .... | 40 | 120

2208 — — II. Similar, but double-arched crown; no *mm.* .... | 35 | 110

2209 III King and Archb. jointly. As last but without M ; (a) early lettering,
trefoil stops; *mm.* lis, tun and lis/lis .... | 30 | 100

2210 — — (b) ornate lettering, rosette stops; *mm.* tun, lis in combinations ..... | 25 | 95

2211 — — (c) — saltire or no stops; *mm.* 123, 123 & 30/123......................... | 25 | 90

2212 *York,* Royal mint. (a) Double-arched crown, lis on breast (rarely omitted).
R. Lozenge panel in centre; *mm.* lis.. | 40 | 125

2213 — — (b) Similar, but unarched crown, tressure broken, *mm.* lis. .... | 35 | 110

2214   2221   2226

	F £	VF £
2214 — Archb. Savage. (a) Double-arched crown, keys at neck, no tressure; ornate lettering; *mm.* martlet	30	100
2215 — — (b) Similar, but fleured tressure, small square lettering; *mm.* martlet	30	100
2216 — — (c) As last, but tall thin lettering; *mm.* martlet	30	100
2217 — As last but no keys; *mm.* martlet	40	125
2218 **Penny.** Old type. London; *mm.* 40/-	135	450
2219 — — — crosses by bust, mm. small cross (obv.)	175	500
2220 — *Canterbury,* Archb. Morton. Open crown, *mm.* tun/- R. M in centre ..	185	525
2221 — — King and Archb. jointly, arched crown; *mm.* tun, tun/-	60	165
2222 — *Durham,* Bp. Sherwood. S on breast. R. D in centre; *mm.* 7a/-	50	150
2223 — *York,* Archb. Rotherham. With or without cross on breast, *mm.* 33/-, T and cross or key at neck. R. h in centre	35	110
2224 — — — T and trefoil at neck. R. Quatrefoil in centre and two extra pellets; *mm.* 39/-	35	110
2225 'Sovereign' type. *London.* Early lettering, no stops, no pillars to throne; no *mm.*	90	275
2226 — — — single pillar on king's right side, trefoil stops; no *mm.* or 31/-..	40	110
2227 — — Ornate letters, rosette stops, single pillar; *mm.* lis (can be muled with above)	50	135
2228 — — saltire stops or none, two pillars; *mm.* none, -/30	40	110
2229 — — Similar, but small square lettering; no *mm.*	40	110
2230 — — Similar, but lettering as profile groats two double pillars; *mm.* 21, 53, none (sometimes on one side only)	35	100

2231   2233   2235

	F £	VF £
2231 — *Durham,* Bp. Sherwood. Crozier to r. of king, throne with one pillar. R. D and S beside shield	35	100
2232 — — Throne with two pillars, no crozier. R. As last	40	110
2233 — — Bp. Fox. Throne with one pillar. R. Mitre above shield, RD or DR at sides, no *mm.*	30	90
2234 — — Similar, but two pillars	35	95

		F	VF
		£	£

2235 *York,* Archb. Rotherham. Keys below shield; early lettering, trefoil stops, no pillars to throne, no *mm.* 30 90

2236 — — — single pillar 30 85

2237 — — — — ornate lettering, rosette or no stops, ... 30 90

2238 — — — two pillars sometimes with crosses between legs of throne 30 85

2239 **Halfpenny,** *London.* I. Open crown; *mm.* 40, 42 .... 40 120

2240 — — — trefoils at neck; no *mm.*, rose 50 135

2241 — — — crosses at neck; *mm.* rose, cross fitchée 40 120

2242 — II. Double arched crown; *mm.* cinquefoil, none 30 80

2243 — — — saltires at neck; no *mm.* 30 80

2244 — IIIa. Crown with single arch, ornate lettering; no *mm.*, pansy 20 70

2244A — IIIb. Similar but with rosette stops; *mm.* none, rose, lis 30 90

2245   2248

2245 — IIIc. Much smaller portrait; *mm.* pheon, lis, none 20 65

2246 *Canterbury,* Archb. Morton. I. Open crown, crosses by neck; R. M in centre 65 200

2247 — — II. Similar, but arched crown, saltires by bust; *mm.* profile eye (82) 65 175

2247A — — — no marks at neck 50 150

2248 — III. King and Archb. Arched crown; *mm.* lis, none 45 110

2249   2250

2249 *York,* Archb. Savage. Arched crown, key below bust to l or r. *mm.* martlet 50 125

2250 **Farthing,** *London.* hENRIC DI GRA REX (A), arched crown 150 575

*No.s 2239-49 have *mm.* on *obv.* only.

Profile issue

2251 Testoon (ls.). Type as groat. hENRIC (VS); *mm.* lis 7000 16500

2252 — hENRIC VII; *mm.* lis 7500 17500

2253

2253 — hENRIC SEPTIM; *mm.* lis 8500 20000

2254   2258

		F £	VF £
2254	**Groat,** *Tentative issue* (contemporary with full-face groats). Double band to crown, hᴇɴʀɪᴄ VII; *mm.* none, 105/-, -/105: 105/85, 105, 85, 21	150	500
2255	— — — tressure on *obv.; mm.* cross-crosslet...	2500	6500
2256	— — hᴇɴʀɪᴄ (VS); *mm.* 105, -/105, 105/ 85, none..............................	325	1000
2257	— — hᴇɴʀɪᴄ Sᴇᴘᴛɪᴍ; *mm.* -/105...	2500	6500
2258	*Regular issue.* Triple band to crown; *mm.* 21, 53 (both *mm.*s may occur on *obv.* or *rev.* or both)	95	350
2259	**Halfgroat,** *London.* As last; *mm.* 105, 53/105, 105/53, 53......................	75	250
2260	— — no numeral after King's name, no *mm.,* -/lis..................................	275	800

2261   2262

2261	*Canterbury,* King and Archb. As London, but *mm.* 94, 33, 94/33............	65	200
2262	*York,* Archb. Bainbridge. As London, but two keys below shield; *mm.* 94, 33, 33/94..	65	200
2262A	— Similar but no keys; *mm.* rose..	75	225

2263

2263	— — XB beside shield; *mm.* rose/martlet	225	650
2263A	— — Similar but two keys below shield *mm.* rose(?)/martlet..................	250	675

Henry VIII is held in ill-regard by numismatists as being the author of the debasement of England's gold and silver coinage; but there were also other important numismatic innovations during his reign. For the first sixteen years the coinage closely followed the pattern of the previous issues, even to the extent of retaining the portrait of Henry VII on the larger silver coins.

In 1526, in an effort to prevent the drain of gold to continental Europe, the value of English gold was increased by 10%, the sovereign to 22s. 0d. and the angel to 7s. 4d., and a new coin valued at 4s. 6d.—the Crown of the Rose—was introduced as a competitor to the French *écu au soleil*. The new crown was not a success and within a few months it was replaced by the Crown of the Double Rose valued at 5s but made of gold of only 22 carat fineness, the first time gold had been minted below the standard 23c. At the same time the sovereign was again revalued to 22s. 6d. and the angel to 7s. 6d., with a new coin, the George Noble, valued at 6s. 8d. (one-third pound).

The royal cyphers on some of the gold crowns and half-crowns combine the initial of Henry with those of his queens: Katherine of Aragon, Anne Boleyn and Jane Seymour. The architect of this coinage reform was the chancellor, Cardinal Thomas Wolsey, who besides his other changes had minted at York a groat bearing his initials and cardinal's hat in addition to the other denominations normally authorized for the ecclesiastical mints.

When open debasement of the coinage began in 1544 to help finance Henry's wars, the right to coin of the archbishops of Canterbury and York and of the bishop of Durham was not confirmed. Instead, a second royal mint was opened in the Tower as in subsequent years were six others, at Southwark, York, Canterbury, Bristol, Dublin and Durham House in the Strand. Gold, which fell to 23c. in 1544, 22c. in 1545, and 20c. in 1546 was much less debased than silver which declined to 9oz 2dwt. in 1544, 6oz 2dwt. in 1545 and 4oz 2dwt. in 1546. At this last standard the blanched silver surface of the coins soon wore away to reveal the copper alloy beneath which earned for Henry the nickname 'Old Coppernose'.

Mintmarks

53	69	70	108	33	94	73	11
105	22	23	30	78	15	24	110
52	72a	44	8	65a	114	121	90
36	106	56	S	E	116	135	

1509-26	Pheon (53)		1509-14	Martlet (94, *York*)
	Castle (69)		1509-23	Radiant star (22, *Durham & York*)
	Castle with H (70, gold)		1513-18	Crowned T (135, Tournai)
	Portcullis crowned (108)		1514-26	Star (23, *York & Durham*)
	Rose (33, *Canterbury*)			Pansy (30, *York*)
	Martlet (94, *Canterbury*)			Escallop (78, *York*)
	Pomegranate (73, but broader, *Cant.*)			Voided cross (15, *York*)
	Cross fitchée (11, *Cant.*)		1523-26	Spur rowel (24, *Durham*)
	Lis (105, *Canterbury, Durham*)			
1526-44	Rose (33)		1526-32	Cross patonce (8, *Cant.*)
	Lis (105)			T (114, *Canterbury*)

	Sunburst 110)		Uncertain mark (121,
	Arrow (52)		*Canterbury*)
	Pheon (53)	1529-44	Radiant star (22, *Durham*)
	Lis (106)	1530-44	Key (90, *York*)
	Star (23, *Durham*)	1533-44	Catherine wheel (36,
1526-9	Crescent (72a, *Durham*)		*Canterbury*)
	Trefoil (44 variety,	1544-7	Lis (105 and 106)
	Durham)		Pellet in annulet (56)
	Flower of eight petals and		S (Southwark)
	circle centre (*Durham*)		Є or E (Southwark)
1526-30	Cross (7a, sometimes	1546-7	WS monogram (116, *Bristol*)
	slightly voided, *York*)		
	Acorn (65a, *York*)		

GOLD

First coinage, 1509-26

		F	VF
		£	£

2264 **Sovereign** (20s.). Similar to last sov. of Hen. VII; *mm.* 108 .... 6250 17500

2264A **Ryal** (10s.) King in ship holding sword and shield. R. Similar to 1950,
mm.-/108 .... *Extremely rare*

2265 **Angel** (6s. 8d.). As Hen. VIII, but hЄnRIC? VIII DI GRA RЄX, etc.; *mm.*
53, 69, 70, 70/69, 108, R. May omit h and rose, or rose only; *mm.* 69, 108 .... 550 1250

2266 **Half-angel.** Similar (sometimes without VIII), *mm.* 69, 70, 108/33, 108 .... 425 975

2265

Second coinage, 1526-44

2267

2267 **Sovereign** (22s. 6d.). As 2264, R. single or double tressure *mm.* 110, 105,
105/52.. 5750 15000

2268 **Angel** (7s. 6d.). As 2265, hЄnRIC VIII D(I) G(RA) R(ЄX) etc,; *mm.*
110, 105... 725 2000

2269 **Half-angel.** Similar; *mm.* lis 750 2250

2270   2272

	F £	VF £
2270 **George-noble** (6s. 8d.). As illustration; *mm.* rose	5250	15000
2270A— Similar, but more modern ship with three masts, without initials hR. R.		
St. George brandishing sword behind head.	6250	18500
2271 **Half-George-noble.** Similar to 2270 *mm* rose, lis	6000	16500
2272 **Crown of the rose** (4s. 6d., 23 c. 3 ¹/₂ gr.). As illustration; *mm.* rose,		
two legend varieties	4500	12500
2273 **Crown of the double-rose** (5s., 22 c). Double-rose crowned, hK (Henry and		
Katherine of Aragon) both crowned in field. R. Shield crowned; *mm.* rose	475	1000
2274 — hK both sides; *mm.* rose/lis, lis, arrow	475	1000
2275* — hK/hA or hA/hK; *mm.* arrow	800	2250
2276* — hR/hK or hI/hR; *mm.* arrow	700	1750
2277 — hA (Anne Boleyn); *mm.* arrow	850	2500
2278 — hA/hR; *mm.* arrow	800	2250

2279   2285

2279 — hI (Jane Seymour); *mm.* arrow	525	1250
2280* — hK/hI; *mm.* arrow	750	2000
2281 — hR/hI; *mm.* arrow	725	1850
2282 — hR (Rex); *mm.* arrow	500	1100
2283 — — *mm.* pheon	725	1850
2284 **Halfcrown.** Similar but king's name henric 8 on *rev.*, no initials; *mm.* rose	825	2500
2285 — hK uncrowned on *obv.*; *mm.* rose	425	950
2286 — hK uncrowned both sides; *mm.* rose/lis, lis, arrow	450	1000
2287 — hI uncrowned both sides; *mm.* arrow	550	1350
2288 — hR uncrowned both sides; hIB RЄX; *mm.* pheon	575	1500

*The hK initials may on later coins refer to Katherine Howard (Henry's fifth wife).

Third coinage, 1544-7

2291

		F £	VF £
2289	**Sovereign,** I (20s., Wt. 200 gr., 23 c.). As illustration but king with larger face and larger design; *mm*. lis	7500	26500
2290	II (20s., wt. 200 or 192 grs., 23, 22 or 20 ct.). *Tower.* As illustration; *mm*. lis, pellet in annulet/lis	3000	8750
2291	— *Southwark.* Similar; *mm*. S, Є/S	2850	8500
2292	— — Similar but Є below shield; *mm*. S/Є	3250	9000
2293	— *Bristol.* As London but *mm*. WS/-	4250	12500

2294

		F £	VF £
2294	**Half-sovereign** (wt. 100 or 96 gr.), *Tower.* As illus.; *mm*. lis, pellet in annulet	575	1500
2295	— Similar, but with annulet on inner circle (either or both sides)	600	1600
2296	*Southwark. Mm.* S	600	1600
2297	— Є below shield; *mm*. S, Є, S/Є, Є/S, (known without sceptre; *mm*. S)	575	1500
2298	*Bristol.* Lombardic lettering; *mm*. WS, WS/-	975	3000
2299	**Angel** (8s., 23 c). Annulet by angel's head and on ship, hЄnRIC' 8; *mm*. lis	475	1050
2300	— Similar, but annulet one side only or none	500	1100
2301	**Half-angel.** Annulet on ship; *mm*. lis	475	1050
2302	— No annulet on ship; *mm*. lis	525	1250

2303   2304

		F £	VF £
2303	— Three annulets on ship; *mm*. lis	575	1350
2304	**Quarter-angel** Angel wears armour; *mm*. lis	450	1000
2304A	— Angel wears tunic; *mm*. lis	475	1050

		F £	VF £
2305	**Crown,** *London.* Similar to 2283, but hЄnRIC' 8 ; Lombardic lettering; mm . 56	525	1200
2306	— without RVTILAnS; *mm.* 56	550	1250
2307	— — — with annulet on inner circle	575	1350
2307A	— King's name omitted. DEI GRA both sides, *mm.* 56	675	1750
2308	— *Southwark.* As 2306; *mm.* S, Є, E/S, Є/-, E/Є	600	1450
2309	*Bristol.* hЄnRIC VIII. ROSA etc. R. D G, etc.; *mm.* /WS	475	1100
2310	— Similar but hЄnRIC(VS) 8 R. DЄI) G(RA); *mm.* -/WS, WS	500	1150
2311	**Halfcrown,** *London.* Similar to 2288; *mm.* 56, 56/-	375	875
2312	— — with annulet on inner circle *mm.* 56	400	900
2313	*Southwark.* As 2311; *mm.* S	450	1000
2314	— *O.* hЄnRIC 8 ROSA SINЄ SPIn. R. DЄI GRA, etc.; *mm.* Є	475	1050
2315	*Bristol. O.* RVTILAnS, etc. R. hЄnRIC 8; *mm.* WS/-	575	1350

For other gold coins in Henry's name see page 221-2.

SILVER

First coinage, 1509-26

2316   2327

2316	**Groat.** Portrait of Hen. VII. *London mm.* 53, 69, 108, 108 over 135...	95	325
2317	— *Tournai; mm.* crowned T. R. CIVITAS TORnACЄn*	450	1350
2318	**Halfgroat.** Portrait of Hen. VII. London; *mm.* 108, 108/-	100	350
2319	— *Canterbury,* Archb. Warham. POSVI *rev.; mm.* rose	110	375
2320	— — — WA above shield; *mm.* martlet	85	250
2321	— — — WA beside shield; *mm.* cross fitchee	85	250
2322	— — CIVITAS CAnTOR *rev.,* similar; *mm.* 73, 105, 11/105	65	200
2323	— *York,* POSVI *rev.,* Archb. Bainbridge (1508-14). Keys below shield; *mm.* martlet	60	175
2324	— — — XB beside shield no keys; *mm.* martlet	65	185
2325	— — — Archb. Wolsey (1514-30). Keys and cardinal's hat below shield; *mm.* 94, 22	150	450
2326	— — CIVITAS ЄBORACI *rev.* Similar; *mm.* 22, 23, 30, 78, 15, 15/78	55	165
2327	— — As last with TW beside shield; *mm.* voided cross	90	275
2327A	— *Tournai.* As 2317	575	1750

*Other non-portrait groats and half-groats exist of this mint, captured during an invasion of France in 1513. (Restored to France in 1518.)

		2332		2335		2336

		F	VF
		£	£
2328	**Penny,** 'Sovereign' type, *London; mm.* 69, 108 /-	50	125
2329	— *Canterbury.* WA above shield; *mm.* martlet...................................	85	250
2330	— — — WA beside shield; *mm.* 73/-...	65	175
2331	— *Durham,* Bp. Ruthall (1509-23). TD above shield; *mm.* lis.............	35	90
2332	— — — TD beside shield; *mm.* lis, radiant star................................	35	90
2333	— — Bp. Wolsey (1523-9). DW beside shield, cardinal's hat below; *mm.* spur rowel..	125	375
2334	**Halfpenny.** Facing bust, hЄnRIC DI GRA RЄX (AGL). *London; mm.* 69, 108/-	20	70
2335	— *Canterbury.* WA beside bust; *mm.* 73/-, 11	55	160
2335A	— *York.* Key below bust, *mm.* star, escallop.................................	70	200
2336	**Farthing.** *mm.* 108/-, hЄnRIC DI GRA RЄX, portcullis. R. CIVITAS LOnDON, rose in centre of long cross...........................	200	575

Second coinage, 1526-44

	2337		2337D		2337E	

2337	**Groat.** His own young portrait. *London;* Laker bust A, large renaissance-style bust, crown arch breaking inner circle. Roman/Roman lettering, roses in cross-ends; *mm.* rose	375	1250
2337A	— — Roman/Lombardic lettering, saltires in cross-ends; *mm.* rose	200	675
2337B	— — Lombardic/Lombardic lettering, roses in cross-ends; *mm.* rose	250	850
2337C	— — Lombardic/Lombardic lettering, saltires in cross-ends; *mm.* rose	150	475
2337D	— Laker bust B, smaller face with pointed nose, crown arch does not break inner circle. Lombardic lettering; *mm.* rose	85	300
2337E	— Laker bust D, larger squarer face with roman nose, fluffy hair, crown arch does not break inner circle. Lombardic lettering; *mm.* 33, 105, 110, 52, 53 (sometimes muled)...	75	275
2338	— with Irish title HIB; reads hЄnRIC 8; *mm.* 53, 105, 53/105, 105/53,	250	700
2339	— *York,* Archb. Wolsey. TW beside shield, cardinal's hat below; *mm.* voided cross, acorn, muled (both ways)	85	300
2340	— — — omits TW; *mm.* voided cross	275	850

2342   2343   2348

		F	VF
		£	£
2341	**Halfgroat.** *London;* type as groats, Lombardic lettering both sides. mm. rose to arrow or none (sometimes muled)	50	145
2341A	— — Mainly Roman letters on obv. or on both sides, *mm.* rose	125	400
2342	As 2341 with Irish title HIB; *mm.* pheon	325	975
2343	— *Canterbury*, Archb. Warham (—1532). R. CIVITAS CANTOR, WA beside shield; *mm.* 121, 121/-, 121/33, 8, 8/T, T	45	125
2344	— — — nothing by shield; *mm.* 121/-	50	150
2345	— — Archb. Cranmer (1533—). TC beside shield; *mm.* 36, 36/-	45	135
2346	— *York,* Archb. Wolsey (—1530). R. CIVITAS EBORACI, TW beside shield, hat below; *mm.* 15/-, 15	50	150
2347	— — Sede Vacante (1530/1). No marks; *mm.* key	60	170
2348	— — Archb. Lee (1531-44). EL or LE beside shield; *mm.* key	45	125
2349	**Penny.** 'Sovereign' type h . D . G . ROSA SINE SPINA, *London; mm.* rose to arrow (*obv.* only), *mm.* lis both sides	35	110

2350   2359   2362

2350	— *Canterbury.* WA beside shield; *mm.* 121/-, 8/-, T/-	65	200
2351	— — TC beside shield; *mm.* 36/-	175	575
2352	— *Durham,* Bp. Wolsey (—1529). TW beside shield, hat below; *mm.* 23, 23/44, 23/-, 72a/-, 44, 44/-, 72a/44 (muled with 2333 *obv.*, *mm.* 24/44)	35	100
2353	— — Sede Vacante (1529-30). No marks; *mm.* 23/-, 22/-	40	120
2354	— — Bp. Tunstall (1530—). CD beside shield; *mm.* 23, 23/-, 22/-, 22	35	100
2355	— *York.* EL beside shield; *mm.* key/-	150	525
2356	**Halfpenny.** Facing bust, h D G ROSA SIE SPIA. *London;* sometimes annulet in centre of rev. *mm.* rose to arrow, arrow/-	25	85
2357	— *Canterbury.* WA beside bust; *mm.* 121/-, 8/-, T/-	65	175
2358	— — TC beside bust; *mm.* 36/-	30	90
2359	— *York.* TW beside bust; *mm.* acorn/-	60	165
2359A	— — —; key below bust	85	225
2360	— — Sede Vacante. Key below bust; *mm.* 15/-	60	150
2361	— — EL or LE beside bust; *mm.* key/-	35	100
2362	**Farthing.** *O.* RVTILANS ROSA, portcullis; *mm.* 33/-, 105/-, 110/-. R. DEO GRACIAS, long cross with pellet in each angle	250	650
2363	— — *mm.* arrow/- R. DEO GRACIAS, rose on long cross	325	800
2363A	— *Canterbury. O.* Similar. R. Similar. *mm.* 36/-	525	1500

2364   2368

	F £	VF £

Third coinage, 1544-7 (Silver progressively debased. 9oz (2dwt), 6oz (2dwt) 4oz (2dwt)).

2364	**Testoon.** *Tower.* hЄNRIC'. VIII, etc. R. Crowned rose between crowned h and R.POSVI, etc.; *mm.* lis, lis and 56, lis/two lis	900	4250
2365	— hЄNRIC 8, *mm.* 105 and 56, 105/56, 105 and 56/56, 56	600	2250
2366	— — annulet on inner circle of rev. or both sides; *mm.* pellet in annulet	625	2350
2367	— *Southwark.* As 2365. R. CIVITAS LONDon; *mm.* S, Є, S/Є, Є/S	675	2500
2368	— *Bristol. mm.*-/WS monogram. (Tower or local dies.)	700	2750

2384   Bust 1   Bust 2   Bust 3

2369	**Groat.** *Tower.* As ill. above, busts 1, 2, 3; *mm.* lis/-, lis	75	300
2369A	Bust 1, R. As second coinage; i.e. saltires in forks; *mm.* lis	85	350
2370	Bust 2 or 3 annulet on inner circle, both sides or rev. only	85	325
2371	*Southwark.* As 2367, busts 1, 2, 3, 4; no *mm.* or lis/-; S or S and Є or Є in forks	80	325
2372	*Bristol.* Mm.-/WS monogram, Bristol bust and Tower bust 2 or 3	85	325
2373	*Canterbury.* Busts 1, 2, (2 var.); no *mm,* or lis/–	80	325
2374	*York.* Busts 1 var., 2, 3, no *mm.*	80	325
2375	**Halfgroat.** *Tower.* As 2365, bust 1; *mm.* lis, none	65	225
2376	*Southwark.* As 2367, bust 1; no *mm.*; S or Є and S in forks	100	325
2377	*Bristol.* Mm.-/WS monogram	70	250
2378	*Canterbury.* Bust 1; no *mm.*	45	165
2379	*York.* Bust 1; no *mm.*	50	185
2380	**Penny.** *Tower.* Facing bust; no *mm.* or lis/-	35	110
2381	*Southwark.* Facing bust; *mm.* S/-, Є/-, -/Є	75	250
2382	*Bristol.* Facing bust; no *mm.* (Tower dies or local but truncated at neck)	45	135
2383	*Canterbury.* Facing bust; no *mm.*	35	110
2384	*York.* Facing bust; no *mm.*	35	110
2385	**Halfpenny.** *Tower.* Facing bust; pellet in annulet in *rev.* centre, no *mm.* or lis/-	60	175
2386	*Bristol.* Facing bust; no *mm.*	65	200
2387	*Canterbury.* Facing bust; no *mm.*, (some read H 8)	40	125
2388	*York.* Facing bust; no *mm.*	35	110
2388A	**Farthing** *obv.* Rose. R. Cross and pellets	500	1500

These coins were struck during the reign of Edward VI but bear the name and portrait of Henry VIII, except in the case of the half-sovereigns which bear the youthful head of Edward.

Mintmarks

56	105	52	K	F	116
66	115	33	122	t	94

GOLD

		F	VF
		£	£
2389	**Sovereign** (20 c), *London*. As no. 2290, but Roman lettering; *mm.* lis	4500	12000
2390	— *Bristol*. Similar but *mm.* WS..	4750	12500

2391

2391A

2391	**Half-sovereign.** As 2294, but with youthful portrait with sceptre. *Tower*; *mm.* 52, 105, 94 (various combinations)...	575	1500
2391A	— Similar but no sceptre; *mm.* 52, 52/56	600	1600
2392	— — — K below shield; *mm.*-/K, none,. E/-	600	1600
2393	— — — grapple below shield; *mm.* 122, none, 122/-, -/122................	625	1650
2394	— *Southwark*. Mm. E, E/-, -/E, Є /E. Usually Є or E (sometimes retrograde) below shield (sceptre omitted; *mm.* -/E)....................................	575	1500
2394A	— — — R. As 2296; *mm.*-/S...	625	1650

2395

		F	VF
		£	£
2395	**Crown.** Similar to 2305. *London; mm.* 52, 52/-, -/K, 122, 94, ...	525	1350
2396	— Similar but transposed legends without numeral; *mm.* -/arrow	575	1450
2396A	— As 2395, but omitting RVTILANS; *mm.* arrow	550	1400
2396B	Similar, but RVTILANS both sides; *mm.* arrow	575	1450
2397	— *Southwark.* Similar to 2396; *mm.* E	625	1650
2398	— — King's name on *obv.; mm.* E/-, -/E	600	1500
2399	**Halfcrown.** Similar to 2311. *London; mm.* 52, K/-, 122/-, 94, -/52.....	525	1250
2399A	As last but E over h on *rev., mm.* 56/52..	675	1750
2399B	As 2399 but RVTILANS etc. on both sides, *mm.* arrow	625	1500
2400	— *Southwark. mm.* E, E/-, -/E	500	1200

SILVER

AR (4oz .333)

2401	**Testoon.** *Tower.* As 2365 with lozenge stops one side; -/56, 56..........	1350	6000

Bust 4   Bust 5   Bust 6

Some of the Bristol testoons, groats and halfgroats with WS monogram were struck after the death of Henry VIII but cannot easily be distinguished from those struck during his reign.

....

2403	**Groat.** *Tower.* Busts 4, 5, 6 (and, rarely, 2). ℞. POSVI, etc.; *mm.* 105-94 and none (frequently muled)..	75	300
2404	— *Southwark.* Busts 4, 5, 6. ℞. CIVITAS LONDON; no *mm.* -/E; lis/-, -/lis, K/E; roses or crescents or S and Є in forks, or rarely annulets ...	70	275
2405	— *Durham House.* Bust 6. ℞. REDDE CVIQVE QVOD SVVM EST; *mm.* bow..	135	475
2406	— *Bristol. mm.* WS on *rev.* Bristol bust B, Tower bust 2 and 3............	85	325
2407	— — *mm.* TC on *rev.* Similar, Bristol bust B	90	350
2408	— *Canterbury.* Busts 5, 6; no *mm.* or rose/-......................................	70	275
2409	— *York.* Busts 4, 5, 6; no *mm.* or lis/-, -/lis	70	275

		F	VF
		£	£
2410	**Halfgroat.** Bust 1. *Tower.* POSVI, etc.; *mm.* 52, 52/-, 52/K , -/K, 52/122, 122, -/122	65	225

2411

2411	— *Southwark.* CIVITAS LONDON; *mm.* E, -/E, none, 52/E, K/E......	55	185
2412	— *Durham House.* R. REDD, etc.; *mm.* bow, -/bow...............	325	975
2413	— *Bristol. Mm.* WS on *rev.*	65	225
2414	— — *mm.* TC on *rev.*	70	250
2415	— *Canterbury.* No *mm.* or t/-, -/t, ...	45	140
2416	— *York.* No *mm.*, bust 1 and three quarter facing	50	175

2418   2422   2427

2417	**Penny.** *Tower.* CIVITAS LONDON. Facing bust; *mm.* 52/-, -/52, -/K, 122/-, -/122, none..	35	110
2418	— — three-quarter bust; no *mm.*	35	120
2419	— *Southwark.* As 2417; *mm.* E, -/E...................................	40	130
2420	— *Durham House.* As groat but shorter legend; *mm.* -/bow	350	875
2421	— *Bristol.* Facing busts, as 2382 but showing more body, no *mm.*	60	185
2422	— *Canterbury.* Similar to 2417	35	110
2423	— — three-quarters facing bust; no *mm.*..................................	35	120
2424	— *York.* Facing bust; no *mm.*	35	110
2425	— — three-quarters facing bust; no *mm.*..................................	40	125
2426	**Halfpenny.** *Tower.* 52?, none..	30	110
2427	— *Canterbury.* No *mm.*, sometimes reads H8.....................................	30	110
2428	— *York.* No *mm.*	25	95

Coinage in his own name

The 4 oz. 2.5dwt coins of Henry VIII and those issued under Edward in 1547 and 1548 caused much disquiet, yet at the same time government was prevented by continuing financial necessity from abandoning debasement. A stratagem was devised which entailed increasing the fineness of silver coins, thereby making them appear sound, while at the same time reducing their weight in proportion so that in practice they contained no more silver than hitherto. The first issue, ordered on 24 January 1549, at 8 oz.2 dwt. fine produced a shilling which, at 60 gr., was so light that it was rapidly discredited and had to be replaced in April by another at 6 oz. 2 dwt. Weighing 80 gr., these later shillings proved acceptable.

Between April and August 1551 the issue of silver coins was the worst ever – 3 oz. 2dwt. fine at 72s per lb. before retrenchment came in August, first by a 50% devaluation of base silver coin and then by the issue of a fine standard at 11oz. 1dwt. 'out of the fire'. This was the equivalent of 11oz.3dwt. commixture, and means that since sterling was only 11oz. 2dwt., this issue, which contained four new denominations – the crown, halfcrown, sixpence and threepence – was in effect the finest ever issued under the Tudors.

Some base 'pence' were struck in parallel with the fine silver, but at the devalued rate, they and the corresponding 'halfpence' were used as halfpence and farthings respectively.

The first dates on English coinage appear in this reign, first as Roman numerals and then on the fine issue crowns and halfcrowns of 1551-3, in Arabic numerals.

Mintmarks

| 66 | 52 | 35 | 115 | E | 53 | 122 |

| t | T | 111 | Y | 126 | 94 | 91A |

| 92 | 105 | y | 97 | 123 | 78 | 26 |

1547-8	Arrow (52)				
	E (Southwark)				
1548-50	Bow (66, *Durham House*)		1550	Martlet (94)
1549	Arrow (52)		1550	Leopard's head (91A)
	Grapple (122)		1550-1	Lion (92)
	Rose (35, *Canterbury*)			Lis (105, *Southwark*)
	TC monogram (115, *Bristol*)			Rose (33)
	Pheon (53)		1551	Y or y (117, *Southwark*)
	t or T (*Canterbury*)			Ostrich's head (97, gold only)
1549-50	Swan (111)		1551-3	Tun (123)
	Roman Y (*Southwark*)			Escallop (78)
1549-50	6 (126 gold only)		1552-3	Pierced mullet (26, *York*)

GOLD

First period, Apr. 1547-Jan. 1549

2429   2431

	F £	VF £
2429 **Half-sovereign** (20 c). As 2391, but reading EDWARD 6. Tower; *mm.* arrow	1650	5000
2430 — *Southwark* (Sometimes with E or Є below shield); *mm.* E	1450	4250
2431 **Crown.** RVTILANS, etc., crowned rose between ER both crowned. R. EDWARD 6, etc., crowned shield between ER both crowned; *mm.* arrow, E over arrow/-	2250	7000
2431A — *Obv.* as last. R. As 2305, *mm.* 52/56	1650	5000
2432 **Halfcrown.** Similar to 2431, but initials not crowned; *mm.* arrow	1600	4750

Second period, Jan. 1549-Apr. 1550

2433

2433 **Sovereign** (22 ct). As illustration; *mm.* arrow, –/arrow, Y,	3500	9500
2434 **Half-sovereign.** Uncrowned bust. *London.* TIMOR etc., MDXLIX on *obv. mm.* arrow	3000	8500

2435

2435 — — SCVTVM, etc., as illustration; *mm.* arrow, **6**, Y	1200	3250

	F £	*VF* £
2436 — *Durham House*. Uncrowned, 1/2 length bust with MDXLVIII at end of *obv*. legend; *mm*. bow; SCVTVM etc.	4500	12500
2437 — Normal, uncrowned bust. LVCERNA, etc., on *obv*.; *mm*. bow	4250	11500

2438   2441

2438 — Crowned bust. *London*. EDWARD VI, etc. ℞. SCVTVM, etc.; *mm*. 52, 122, 111/52, 111, Y, 94	1100	3000
2439 — *Durham House*. Crowned, half-length bust; *mm*. bow	4500	12500
2440 — — King's name on *obv*. and *rev*.; *mm*. bow (mule of 2439/37)	4750	13500
2441 **Crown.** Uncrowned bust, as 2435; *mm*. 6, Y, 52/-, Y/-	1250	3500
2442 — Crowned bust, as 2438; *mm*. 52, 122, 111, Y (usually *obv*. only)	1200	3250
2443 **Halfcrown.** Uncrowned bust; ℞. As 2441, *mm*. arrow, Y, Y/-, 52/-	1250	3500
2444 — Crowned bust, as illus. above; *mm*. 52, 52/111, 111, 122, Y, Y/-	1100	3000
2445 — Similar, but king's name on *rev*., *mm*. 52, 122	1200	3250

Third period, 1550-3

2446 **'Fine' sovereign** (30s.). King on throne; *mm*. 97, 123	16500	42500
2447 **Double sovereign.** From the same dies, *mm*. 97	35000	125000

2444   2448

2448 **Angel** (10s.). As illustration; *mm*. 97, 123	5750	15000
2449 **Half-angel.** Similar, *mm*. 97	7500	22500

2450

2450 **Sovereign.** (=20s.). Half-length figure of king r., crowned and holding sword and orb. ℞. Crowned shield with supporters; *mm*. y, tun	2500	6750

2451

	F	VF
	£	£
2451 **Half-sovereign**. As illustration above; *mm*. y, tun	1100	3000
2452 **Crown**. Similar, but *rev*. SCVTVM etc., *mm*. y, tun	1350	3500
2453 **Halfcrown**. Similar, *mm*. tun, y	1450	3750

Small denominations often occur creased or straightened.

SILVER

First period, Apr. 1547-Jan. 1549

2454

2454 **Groat**. Crowned bust r. *Tower*. R. Shield over cross, POSVI, etc.; *mm*. arrow	675	2000
2455 — As last, but EDOARD 6, *mm*. arrow	800	2250
2456 *Southwark*. *Obv*. as 2454. R. CIVITAS LONDON; *mm*.-/E or none, sometimes S in forks	675	2000
2457 **Halfgroat**. *Tower*. *Obv*. as 2454; *mm*. arrow	450	1000
2458 *Southwark*. As 2456; *mm*. arrow, E on reverse only	425	950

2459   2460

2459 *Canterbury*. Similar. No *mm*., reads EDOARD or EDWARD (rare)	275	800
2460 **Penny**. *Tower*. As halfgroat, but E.D.G. etc. R. CIVITAS LONDON; *mm*. arrow	275	950
2461 *Southwark*. As last, but *mm*. -/E.	325	1000
2462 *Bristol*. Similar, but reads ED6DG or E6DG no *mm*.	250	850
2463 **Halfpenny**. *Tower*. O. As 2460, *mm*. E (?). R. Cross and pellets	275	875
2464 *Bristol*. Similar, no *mm*. but reads E6DG or EDG	300	900

Second period, Jan. 1549-Apr. 1550
At all mints except Bristol, the earliest shillings of 1549 were issued at only 60 grains but of 8 oz.
2 dwt standard. This weight and size were soon increased to 80 grains, (S.2466 onwards), but the
fineness was reduced to 6 oz. 2 dwt so the silver content remained the same. Dies, mm G were
prepared for a coinage of 80gr shillings at York, but were not used. Coins from the *mm* are found
suitably overmarked, from other mints, S.2466-8. The shilling bust types are set out in *J. Bispham
'The Base Silver Shillings of Edward VI; BNJ 1985.*

| Bust 1   2465A   Bust 2 |

		F	VF
60 gr; 8oz. 2 dwt.		£	£
2465	**Shilling.** *Tower.* Broad bust with large crown. *Obv.* TIMOR etc. MDXLIX. Ŗ. Small, oval garnished shield dividing ER. EDWARD VI etc., *mm.* 52, no *mm,* Bust 1; *mm,* –/52, Bust 2	225	800
2465A	*Southwark.* As last, Bust 1, *mm.* Y, EY/Y	200	750
2465B	*Canterbury.* As last, Bust 1, *mm.* -/rose	275	1000
2465C	*Durham House.* Bust with elaborate tunic and collar TIMOR etc. MDXLIX. Ŗ. Oval shield, very heavily garnished in different style. EDWARD VI etc., *mm.* bow (2469)	250	900

| Bust 3   Bust 4   Bust 5 |

80 gr; 6oz. 2 dwt.			
2466	*Tower.* Tall, narrow bust with small crown. *Obv.* EDWARD VI etc. MDXLIX or MDL. Ŗ. As 2465 but TIMOR etc., Busts 3, 4 and 5, *mm.* 52-91a (frequently muled)	110	475
2466A	— *Obv.* as last, MDXLIX. Ŗ. Heavily garnished shield, Durham House style, Bust 3 *mm.* grapple	325	1250
2466B	*Southwark.* As 2466, Busts 3, 4 and 5 *mm.* Y, Y/swan	110	450
2466C	— — — Bust 3; Ŗ. as 2466A. *mm.* Y	325	1250
2467	*Bristol. Obv.* similar to 2466, Bust 3 or local die Ŗ. Shield with heavy curved garniture or as 2466, *mm.* TC, or rose over G	625	2500

2466C   2468

| | F | VF |
| | £ | £ |

2468   *Canterbury.* As 2466, Bust 3 and 4 *mm.* T, T/t, t/T, t .... | 150 | 625 |

2465C   2472

2470	*Durham House.* Bust as 2465C. INIMICOS etc., no date. R. EDWARD etc.	125	700
2472	— Bust similar to 2466. EDWARD VI etc. R. INIMICOS etc.	115	525
2472A	— As last but legends transposed	200	900
2472B	*Tower.* Elegant bust with extremely thin neck. Bust 6, R. As 2466, *mm.* martlet	165	750
2472C	*Southwark.* As last, Bust 6, *mm.* Y	135	600

For coins of Edward VI countermarked, see p. 240

Third period, 1550-3

Very base issue (1551) 3oz. 2 dwt.

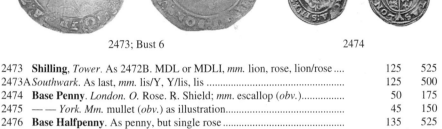

2473; Bust 6   2474

2473	**Shilling,** *Tower.* As 2472B. MDL or MDLI, *mm.* lion, rose, lion/rose	125	525
2473A	*Southwark.* As last, *mm.* lis/Y, Y/lis, lis	125	500
2474	**Base Penny.** *London. O.* Rose. R. Shield; *mm.* escallop (*obv.*)...............	50	175
2475	— — *York. Mm.* mullet (*obv.*) as illustration...	45	150
2476	**Base Halfpenny.** As penny, but single rose	135	525

* The base penny and halfpenny were used as halfpenny and farthing respectively.

Fine silver issue, (1551-3) 11oz. 3 dwt.

2478

		F £	VF £
2478	**Crown**. King on horseback with date below horse. ℞. Shield on cross; *mm*. y. 1551; tun, 1551-3 (1553, wire line inner circle may be missing) .	675	1850

2479

2479	**Halfcrown**. Walking horse with plume; *mm*. y, 1551	575	1350
2480	Galloping horse without plume; *mm*. tun, 1551-3	625	1450
2481	Large walking horse without plume; *mm*. tun, 1553................................	975	3000

2482   2483

2482	**Shilling**. Facing bust, rose l., value XII r. *mm*. y, tun (several bust varieties)	90	375
2483	**Sixpence**. *London*. Similar, as illustration; *mm*. y/-, -/y, y, tun (bust varieties)..	110	475
2484	*York*. As last, but CIVITAS ЄBORACI; *mm*. mullet	145	600

2485   2486

		F	VF
		£	£
2485	**Threepence**. *London*. As sixpence, but III; *mm*. tun	150	625
2486	*York*. As 2484, but III by bust	275	1000

2487   2487A

2487	**Penny**. 'Sovereign' type; *mm*. tun	850	3250
2487A	**Farthing.** *O*. Portcullis, R Cross and Pellets	750	2500

Mary brought English coins back to the sterling standard and struck all her gold coins at the traditional fineness of 0.995. The mintmarks usually appear at the end of the first or second word of the legends.

Pomegranate ♟   Halved rose and castle ♟

GOLD

2488

| | F | VF |
| | £ | £ |

2488   **'Fine' Sovereign** (30s.). Queen enthroned. R. Shield on rose, MDLIII, MDLIIII and undated, *mm.* pomegranate, half-rose (or mule) 2750   7500

2489   **Ryal** (15s.). As illus, MDLIII. R. As 1950 but A DNO etc. *mm.* pomegranate/- 10000   35000

2489   2490

2490   **Angel** (10s.). Class I, annulet stops; *mm.* pomegranate. 1250   3000

2490A— Class II, pellet stops, *mm.* pomegranate (often muled with class I reverse) 1350   3250

2490B — Class III, pellet stops, large Roman letters, *mm.* half-rose and castle.. 1450   3500

2491   **Half-angel.** Similar; *mm.* pomegranate, pomegranate/- 2500   7000

SILVER

2492

		F £	VF £
2492	**Groat**. Crowned bust l. R. VERITAS, etc.; *mm*. pomegranate, pome-granate/-	110	350
2493	**Halfgroat**. Similar	675	2000
2494	**Penny**. Similar, but M. D. G. ROSA, etc.	525	1850

2495

2495	— As last. R. CIVITAS LONDON; no *mm*.	525	1850
2495A	— Base penny. Similar to 2474 but M.D.G. etc.	*All late 19th cent. fabrications*	

The groats and smaller silver coins of this period have Mary's portrait only, but the shillings and sixpences show the bust of the queen's husband, Philip of Spain.

Mintmarks

Lis (105   Half-rose and castle

GOLD

2496

	F £	VF £
2496 **Angel**. As illustration; wire line inner circles, calm sea, *mm.* lis...........	2750	6750
2496A — — New-style, large wings, wire line i.c.	2850	7000
2496B — — As above but beaded i.c.	3000	7500
2497 **Half-angel**. Similar to 2496	4750	13500

SILVER

2498   2500

2498 **Shilling**. Busts face-to-face, full titles, undated, no *mm.*	300	1150
2499 — — — also without mark of value..	325	1250
2500 — — 1554..	300	1200
2501 — English titles only 1554, 1555..	325	1250
2501A— — undated	375	1350
2502 — — without mark of value, 1554, 1555 (rare)...................................	350	1350
2503 — — date below bust, 1554, 1555...	1350	3500
2504 — — As last, but without ANG., 1555...	1500	4000

2505

		F £	*VF* £

2505 **Sixpence**. Similar. Full titles, 1554 (and undated?)................................ 300 1250

2506

2506 — English titles only, 1555 (no *mm.*, rare), 1557 (*mm.* lis, rounder garnishing) 325 1300
2506A— As last but heavy beaded i.c. on obv. 1555. (Irish 4d. obv. mule).... 325 1350
2507 — — date below bust, 1554, 1557 (very rare)...................................... 575 1650

2508

2508 **Groat**. Crowned bust of Mary 1. R. POSVIMVS etc. (several legend vars.);
   mm. lis 125 400
2509 **Halfgroat**. Similar, but POSVIM, *mm.* lis.. 350 950

2510

2510 **Penny**. Similar to 2495, but P. Z. M. etc.; *mm.* lis.................................. 425 1250
2510A **Base penny**. Similar to 2495A, but P. Z. M . etc.; *mm.* halved rose and
   castle or castle/–, (used as a halfpenny) 65 200

Elizabeth's coinage is particularly interesting on account of the large number of different denominations issued. 'Crown' gold coins were again issued as well as the 'fine' gold denominations. In 1559 the base shillings of Edward VI's second and third coinages were called in and countermarked for recirculation at reduced values. Smaller debased coins were also devalued but not countermarked. The old debased groat became a three halfpence and other coins in proportion. The normal silver coinage was initially struck at 0.916 fineness as in the previous reign but between 1560 and 1577 and after 1582 the old sterling standard of 0.925 was restored. Between 1578 and 1582 the standard was slightly reduced and the weights were reduced by 1/32nd in 1601. Gold was similarly reduced slightly in quality 1578-82, and there was a slight weight reduction in 1601.

To help alleviate the shortage of small change, and to avoid the expense of minting an impossibly small silver farthing, a threefarthing piece was introduced to provide change if a penny was tendered for a farthing purchase. The sixpence, threepence, threehalfpence and threefarthings were marked with a rose behind the queen's head to distinguish them from the shilling, groat, half-groat and penny.

Coins of exceedingly fine workmanship were produced in a screw press introduced by Eloye Mestrelle, a French moneyer, in 1561. With parts of the machinery powered by a horse-drawn mill, the coins produced came to be known as 'mill money'. Despite the superior quality of the coins produced, the machinery was slow and inefficient compared to striking by hand. Mestrelle's dismissal was engineered in 1572 and six years later he was hanged for counterfeiting.

Mintmarks

1ST ISSUE	2ND ISSUE				3RD ISSUE		
106	21	94	23	53	33	107	92

	4TH ISSUE		74	71	77	65b	27
7	14	113			5TH ISSUE		

6TH ISSUE		60	54	79	72b	86
1	2	123	124	90	57	0

First Issue			Lis (105, milled)		1584-6	Escallop (79)
1558-60	Lis (106)	1569-71	Castle (71)		1587-9	Crescent (72b)
Second Issue		1572-3	Ermine (77)		1590-2	Hand (86)
1560-1	Cross crosslet (21)	1573-4	Acorn (65b)		1591-5	Tun (123)
	Martlet (94)	1573-8	Eglantine (27)		1594-6	Woolpack (124)
Third Issue		Fourth Issue			1595-8	Key (90)
1560-6	Star (23, milled)	1578-9	Greek cross (7)		1597-1600	Anchor (57)
1561-5	Pheon (53)	1580-1	Latin cross (14)		1600	**0**
1565	Rose (33)	1582	Sword (113)		Sixth Issue	
1566	Portcullis (107)	Fifth Issue			1601-2	**1**
1566-7	Lion (92)	1582-3	Bell (60)		1602	**2**
1567-70	Coronet (74)	1582-4	A (54)			

N.B. *The dates for* mms *sometimes overlap. This is a result of using up old dies, onto which the new mark was punched.*

GOLD

Hammered Coinage
First to Third issues, 1559-78. ('Fine' gold of 0.994. 'Crown' gold of 0 .916 fineness. Sovereigns of 240 gr.). Mintmarks; lis to eglantine.

		F £	VF £
2511	**'Fine' Sovereign** (30 s.) Queen enthroned, tressure broken by throne, reads Z not ET, no chains to portcullis. R. Arms on rose; *mm.* lis. ....,	5500	13500

2512

2512	—— Similar but ET, chains on portcullis; *mm.* crosslet	3500	9500
2513	**Angel.** St. Michael. R. Ship. Wire line inner circles; *mm.* lis.	900	2500
2513A	— Similar, but beaded i.c. on *obv.*, *mm.* lis	850	2250
2514	— — Similar, but beaded inner circles; ship to r.; *mm.* 106, 21, 74, 27,..	725	1750
2515	— — — Similar, but ship to l.; *mm.* 77-27	750	1800
2516	**Half Angel.** As 2513, wire line inner circles; *mm.* lis	1250	3500
2516A	— As last, but beaded i.c.s, legend ends. Z.HIB	925	2500
2517	— As 2514, beaded inner circles; *mm.* 106, 21, 74, 77-27	650	1500
2518	**Quarter Angel.** Similar; *mm.* 74, 77-27	575	1375

2513   2520A

2519	**Half Pound** (10 s.) Young crowned bust l. R. Arms. Wire line inner circles; *mm.* lis...	2000	6750
2520	— Similar, but beaded inner circles; *mm.* 21, 33-107...............................	950	2500
2520A	— — Smaller bust; *mm.* lion	1000	3250
2520B	— — Broad bust, ear visible; *mm.* 92, 74, 71	975	2500
2521	**Crown.** As 2519; *mm.* lis	1750	5250
2522	— Similar to 2520; *mm.* 21, 33-107..	750	2000
2522A	— Similar to 2520B; *mm.* 74, 71, 92	825	2250
2523	**Half Crown.** As 2519; *mm.* lis	1500	4500
2524	— Similar to 2520; *mm.* 21, 33-107 (2 busts)	725	1750
2524A	— Similar to 2520B; *mm.* 107-71..	750	1850

		F	*VF*
		£	£

Fourth Issue, 1578-82 (`Fine' gold only of 0.992). *Mms* Greek cross,
Latin cross and sword.

2525	**Angel**. As 2514; *mm*. 7, 14, 113	725	1750
2526	**Half Angel**. As 2517; *mm*. 7, 14, 113......................................	700	1600
2527	— Similar, but without E and rose above ship; *mm*. latin cross	750	1850
2528	**Quarter Angel**. As last; *mm*. 7, 14, 113...................................	625	1450

Fifth Issue, 1583-1600 (`Fine' gold of 0.995, `crown' gold of 0.916; pound of 174.5 grs. wt.).
Mintmarks: bell to **O**.

2529

| 2529 | **Sovereign** (30 s:). As 2512, but tressure not normally broken by back of throne; *mm*. 54-123 .... | 3000 | 8250 |

2530

| 2530 | **Ryal** (15 s.). Queen in ship. ℞. Similar to 1950; *mm*. 54-86 (*rev*. only) .. | 7000 | 20000 |

2531

2531	**Angel**. As 2514; *mm*. 60-123, 90-**O**	750	1850
2532	**Half Angel**. As 2517; *mm*. 60-86, 90-57...................................	725	1500
2533	**Quarter Angel**. As 2518; *mm*. 60-123, 90-57/–	600	1350

	F	VF
	£	£

2534   Pound (20 s.). Old bust l., with elaborate dress and profusion of hair; *mm.*,
lion and tun/tun, 123-**O**   1400   3750

2535

2535   **Half Pound**. Similar; *mm.* tun   1350   3250
2535A — Similar but smaller bust with less hair; *mm.* 123-**O**   1250   3000

2536

2536   **Crown**. Similar to 2534; *mm.* 123-90. **O**   975   2750
2537   **Half Crown**. Similar; *mm.* -/123, 123-0, **O**   725   1750

Sixth Issue, 1601-3 ('Fine' gold of 0.994, 'crown' gold of 0.916; Pound of 172 gr.). Mintmarks:
1 and **2**

2538   **Angel**. As 2531; *mm.* **1, 2**   850   2250
2539   **Pound**. As 2534; *mm.* **1, 2**   1500   4250
2540   **Half Pound**. As 2535A; *mm.* **1, 2**   1650   4500
2541   **Crown**. As 2536; *mm.* **1, 2**   1450   3750
2542   **Half Crown**. As 2537; *mm.* **1, 2**   1350   3500

Milled Coinage, 1561-70

2543

2543   **Half Pound**. Crowned bust l.; *mm.* star, lis   1650   4750
2544   **Crown**. Similar; *mm.* star, lis   1350   4000
2545   **Half Crown**. Similar; *mm.* star, lis   1750   5250

For further details on both AV and AR milled coinage, *see* D. G. Borden '*An introduction to the
milled coinage of Elizabeth I*'. BNJ 1983

SILVER

Hammered Coinage

Countermarked Edward VI base shillings (1559)

2546   2547

	Fair £	F £
2546 **Fourpence-halfpenny**. Edward VI 2nd period 6oz and 8oz shillings .... cmkd on obv. with a portcullis; *mm*. 66, –/33, 52, t, 111, Y and 122	850	2250
2547 **Twopence-farthing**. Edward VI 3rd period 3 oz. shillings .... countermarked on obverse with a seated greyhound; *mm*. 92. 105, 35 and 87	975	3000
N.B. *Occasionally the wrong countermark was used*		

First Issue, 1559-60 (.916 fine, shillings of 96 grs.)

2548   2551

	F £	VF £
2548 **Shilling**. Without rose or date. ELIZABET(H), wire line inner circles, pearls on bodice, busts 1A, and 1B; *mm*. lis..	375	1500
2549 — Similar, ELIZABETH, wire line and beaded inner circles, no pearls on bodice, busts 1D, 2A and 2B; *mm*. lis	135	575
2550 **Groat**. Without rose or date, wire line or no inner circles (two busts); *mm*. lis	125	525

1A	1D	1D	2A	2B

2551 — Similar, wire line and beaded inner circles, circles *mm*. lis	65	240
2551A— — Small bust and shield (from halfgroat punction)· *mm*. lis	80	325

	F	VF
	£	£
2552 **Halfgroat**. Without rose or date, wire line inner circles; *mm*. lis	110	475
2553 **Penny**. Without rose or date, wire line inner circles; *mm*. lis	150	625
2554 — Similar but dated 1558 on *obv*.; *mm*. lis	325	1200

Second Issue, 1560-1 (0.925 fineness, shilling of 96 gr.)

2555	2559	2560

2555 **Shilling**. Without rose or date, beaded inner circles. ET instead of Z busts 3A, 3B, 3C and 3J; *mm*. 21, 94	110	375
2555A— large bust with pearls on bodice as 2548; *mm*. 21, bust 1A, 94, bust 1B	135	575
2556 **Groat**. Without rose or date, bust as 2551; *mm*. 21, 94	55	175
2557 **Halfgroat**. Without rose or date; *mm*. 21, 94......................................	35	125
2558 **Penny**. Without rose or date (three bust varieties); *mm*. 21, 94............	25	75

3A	3B	3C	3J

Third Issue, 1561-77 (Same fineness and weight as last)

2559 **Sixpence**. With rose and date, large flan (27 *mm*. or more), large bust with hair swept back, 1561; *mm*. pheon...	125	475
2560 — Similar, small bust, 1561; *mm*. pheon...	60	225

		F £	*VF* £
2561	— Smaller flan (26.5 *mm.*). Small regular bust, 1561-6; *mm.* 53-107......	55	175

2561	2561B	2562	2563

		F	*VF*
2561B	— Similar, very large bust, with rose, 1563-5; *mm.* pheon	95	375
2562	— Intermediate bust, ear shows, 1566-74; *mm.* 92-65b (also 1567 *mm.* 71/74)	55	175
2562A	— Similar, without date; *mm.* lion, coronet, ermine.................................	275	850
2563	— Larger bust, 1573-7; *mm.* 77-27..	50	160
2564	**Threepence**. With rose and date 1561, large flan (20.5 *mm.*); *mm.* pheon	40	135
2565	— smaller flan (19 *mm.*). Regular bust, 1561-7; *mm.* 53-92	35	120
2566	— taller bust, ear shows, 1566-77; *mm.* 92-27, 27/-, 27/65b..................	35	120
2566A	— Similar, without rose, 1568; *mm.* coronet	175	525

	2567	2571

		F	*VF*
2567	**Halfgroat**. Without rose or date; *mm.* 107-71	45	150
2568	**Threehalfpence**. With rose and date 1561, large flan (17 *mm.*) *mm.* pheon	35	125
2569	— — Smaller flan (16 *mm.*); 1561-2, 1564-78; *mm.* 53-27......................	30	110
2570	**Penny**. Without rose or date; *mm.* 33-71, 65b, 27, 33/107, 92/107, 74/107	25	80
2571	**Threefarthings**. With rose and date 1561-2, 1564, 1567, 1568, 1572-7; *mm.* 53, 74, 77-27..	55	175

Fourth Issue, 1578-82 (0.921 fineness, "shilling" of 95.6 gr.)

	2572	2573

		F	*VF*
2572	**Sixpence**. As 2563, 1578-82; *mm.* 7-113, 14/113, 14/7	45	150
2573	**Threepence**. As 2566, 1578-82; *mm.* 7-113...	35	110
2574	**Threehalfpence**. As 2569, 1578-9, 1581-2; *mm.* 7-113..........................	30	110
2575	**Penny**. As 2570; *mm.* 7-113, 7/14, 14/7	25	80
2576	**Threefarthings**. As 2571, 1578-9, 1581-2; *mm.* 7-113............................	60	185

Fifth Issue, 1582-1600 (0.925 fineness, shilling of 96 gr.)

	F	VF
	£	£

2577   **Shilling**. Without rose or date, ELIZAB; ear concealed, busts 3B and 6A *mm.*
      60-72b, ear shows. bust 6B *mm.* 79-**0** (mules occur) .... | 90 | 300

2578   **Sixpence**. As 2572, ELIZABETH, 1582, 1583 *mm.* bell .... | 55 | 175

2578A— Similar, ELIZAB, 1582-1600; *mm.* 60-**0**, also 1583 *mm.* 79/54.......... | 50 | 165

2579   **Halfgroat**. Without rose or date, two pellets behind bust. R. CIVITAS
      LONDON; *mm.* 60-**0** (*mm.* bell sometimes without pellets) .... | 25 | 70

2580   **Penny**. Without rose or date. R. CIVITAS LONDON; *mm.* 60-57, 90/-,
      57/-, **0**/- .... | 20 | 70

2581   **Halfpenny**. Portcullis. R. Cross and pellets; *mm.* none, 54-**0** .... | 20 | 70

6A   6B

Sixth Issue, 1601-2 (0.925 fineness, shilling of 92.9 gr.)

2582   2583

	F	VF
2582 **Crown**. As illustration, *mm.* **1**	1200	2850
2582A – Similar, *mm.* **2**	1650	4750
2583 **Halfcrown**. As illustration, *mm.* **1**	800	1850
2583A – Similar, *mm.* **2**	1850	6500
2584 **Shilling**. As 2577; bust 6B *mm.* **1, 2**	95	300
2585 **Sixpence**. As 2578A, 1601-2; *mm.* **1, 2**	55	175
2586 **Halfgroat**. As 2579, *mm.* **1, 2, 2/-**	25	75
2587 **Penny**. As 2580, *mm.* **1, 2, 2/-**	25	75
2588 **Halfpenny**. As 2581, *mm.* **1, 2**	25·	80

F	*VF*
£	£

Milled coinage

		F £	*VF* £
2589	**Shilling**. Without rose or date; *mm*. star. Plain dress, large size (over 31 *mm*.)	475	1500
2590	— decorated dress, large size..	325	900
2591	— — intermediate size (30-31 *mm*.)...	225	675
2592	— — small size (under 30 *mm*.)	200	575

	2593	2594		2595	

2593	**Sixpence**. Small bust, large rose. R. Cross fourchee, 1561 *mm*. star........	95	325
2594	Tall narrow bust with plain dress, large rose, 1561-2; *mm*. star	90	325
2595	— similar, but decorated dress, 1562..	95	350

	2597		2598	

2596	Large broad bust, elaborately decorated dress, small rose, 1562; *mm*. star	85	300
2597	— — cross pattée on *rev*., 1562, 64 *mm*. star	90	300
2598	— similar, pellet border, 1563-4...	95	325
2598A	Bust with low ruff, raised rim, 1564, 1566 (both overdates)....................	110	400

	2599	2600		2601	

2599	Small bust, 1567-8, R. As 2593; *mm*. lis...	85	275
2600	Large crude bust breaking legend; 1570, *mm*. lis; 1571/0, *mm*. castle		
	(over lis)	225	750
2601	**Groat**. As illustration..	120	425
2602	**Threepence**. With rose, small bust with plain dress, 1561	125	450
2603	Tall narrow decorated bust with medium rose, 1562...............................	95	300
2604	Broad bust with very small rose, 1562..	100	325
2605	Cross pattee on *rev*., 1563, 1564/3..	175	600

2606

2606	**Halfgroat**. As groat	135	475

	F	*VF*
	£	£

2607 **Threefarthings**. E . D . G . ROSA, etc., with rose. R. CIVITAS LONDON, shield with 1563 above 1250 4500

Portcullis money

Trade coins of 8, 4, 2, and 1 Testerns were coined at the Tower Mint in 1600/1 for the first voyage of the incorporated 'Company of Merchants of London Trading into the East Indies'. The coins bear the royal arms on the obverse and a portcullis on the reverse and have the *mm*. **O**. They were struck to the weights of the equivalent Spanish silver 8, 4, 2 and 1 reales.

2607A

2607A Eight testerns 1850 5000

2607B

2607B Four testerns 1000 2650

2607C   2607D

2607C Two testerns.. 850 2250
2607D One testern... 650 1650

THE HOUSE OF STUART, THE COMMONWEALTH, AND THE HOUSE OF ORANGE, 1603-1714

JAMES I, 1603-25

With the accession of James VI of Scotland to the English throne, the royal titles and coat of arms are altered on the coinage; on the latter the Scottish rampant lion and the Irish harp now appear in the second and third quarters. In 1604 the weight of the gold pound was reduced and the new coin became known as the 'Unite'. Fine gold of 0·979 and crown gold of 0·916 fineness were both issued, and a gold four-shilling piece was struck 1604-19. In 1612 all the gold coins had their values raised by 10%; but in 1619 the Unite was replaced by a new, lighter 20s. piece, the 'Laurel', and a lighter rose-ryal, spur-ryal and angel were minted.

In 1613 the king granted Lord Harington a licence to coin farthings of copper as a result of repeated public demands for a low value coinage; this was later taken over by the Duke of Lennox. Towards the end of the reign coins made from silver sent to the mint from the Welsh mines had the Prince of Wales's plumes inserted over the royal arms.

Mintmarks

125	105	33	79	84	74	90
60	25	71	45	32	123	132
72b	7a	16	24	125	105	46

First coinage
1603-4   Thistle (125)
1604-5   Lis (105)

Second coinage
1604-5   Lis (105)
1605-6   Rose (33)
1606-7   Escallop (79)
1607   Grapes (84)
1607-9   Coronet (74)

1609-10   Key (90)
1610-11   Bell (60)
1611-12   Mullet (25)
1612-13   Tower (71)
1613   Trefoil (45)
1613-15   Cinquefoil (32)
1615-16   Tun (123)
1616-17   Book on lectern (132)
1617-18   Crescent (72b, gold)
1618-19   Plain cross (7a)

1619   Saltire cross (16, gold)

Third coinage
1619-20   Spur rowel (24)
1620-1   Rose (33)
1621-3   Thistle (125)
1623-4   Lis (105)
1624   Trefoil (46)

GOLD

First coinage, 1603-4 (Obverse legend reads D' . G' . ANG : SCO : etc.)

		F £	VF £
2608	**Sovereign** (20s.). King crowned r., half-length, first bust with plain armour. ℞. EXVRGAT, etc.; *mm*. thistle...	1100	3750
2609	— second bust with decorated armour; *mm*. thistle, lis...........................	1200	4000

2610   2612

2610	**Half-sovereign**. Crowned bust r. ℞. EXVRGAT, etc.; *mm*. thistle..........	1650	5500
2611	**Crown**. Similar. ℞. TVEATVR, etc.; *mm*. 125, 105/125.........................	1350	3500
2612	**Halfcrown**. Similar; *mm*. thistle, lis...	575	1350

N.B. *The Quarter-Angel of this coinage is considered to be a pattern (possibly a later strike), although coin weights are known.*

Second coinage, 1604-19 (Obverse legend reads D' G' MAG : BRIT : etc.)

2613   2614

2613	**Rose-ryal** (30s., 33s. from 1612). King enthroned. ℞. Shield on rose; *mm*. 33-90, 25-132..	1650	4250
2614	**Spur ryal** (15s., 16s. 6d. from 1612). King in ship; *mm*. 33, 79, 74, 25-32, 132	2750	8500
2615	**Angel** (10s., 11s. from 1612). Old type but larger shield; *mm*. 33-74, 60-16	725	1850
2616	—— pierced for use as touch-piece..	450	950
2617	**Half-angel** (5s., 5s. 6d. from 1612). Similar; *mm*. 71-132, 7a, 16	1500	4500

		F	VF
		£	£

2618 **Unite** (20s., 22s. from 1612). Half-length second bust r. ℞. FACIAM
etc.; *mm.* lis or rose 475 1100
2619 — fourth bust; *mm.* rose to cinquefoil 425 950

2620

2622   2624

2620 — fifth bust; *mm.* cinquefoil to saltire 400 900
2621 **Double-crown.** Third bust r. ℞. HENRICVS, etc.; *mm.* lis or rose 325 775
2622 Fourth bust; *mm.* rose to bell 300 750
2623 Fifth bust; *mm.* key, mullet to saltire 275 700
2624 **Britain crown.** First bust r.; *mm.* lis to coronet 200 500
2625 Third bust; *mm.* key to cinquefoil.................................... 200 500
2626 Fifth bust; *mm.* cinquefoil to saltire........................... 185 450

2627

2627 **Thistle crown** (4s.). As illus.; *mm.* lis to plain cross 200 525
2628 — IR on only one side or absent both sides; *mm.* 79, 74, 71-123 .... 210 550
2629 **Halfcrown.** I' D' G' ROSA SINE SPINA. First bust; *mm.* lis to key 185 400
2630 Third bust; *mm.* key to trefoil, trefoil/tower 185 400
2631 Fifth bust; *mm.* cinquefoil to plain cross.................................... 175 375

Third coinage, 1619-25
2632 **Rose-ryal** (30s.; 196.5 grs.). King enthroned. ℞. XXX above shield; lis,
lion and rose emblems around; *mm.* 24, 125, 105 .... 1850 5250
2633 Similar but plain back to throne; *mm.* trefoil... 1900 5500

2634   2635

		F	VF
		£	£
2634	**Spur-ryal** (15s.). As illus. R. Somewhat like 2614, but lis are also crowned. *mm*. 24-125, 46	2500	8250
2635	**Angel** (10s.) of new type; *mm*. 24-46	975	3000
2636	— pierced for use as touch-piece	525	1350
2637	**Laurel** (20s.; 140.5 gr.). First (large) laur, bust l.; *mm*. 24, 24/-	575	1350
2638	Second, medium, square headed bust, `SS' tie ends; *mm*. 24, 33	525	1100
2638A	Third, small rounded head, ties wider apart; *mm*. 33, 125	475	1000

2638B

		F	VF
2638B	Fourth head, very small ties; *mm*. 105, 46	400	850
2638C	Fourth head variety, tie ends form a bracket to value; *mm*. lis	425	950
2639	Fifth, small rather crude bust; *mm*. trefoil	1350	4250

2640   2641A

		F	VF
2640	**Half-laurel**. First bust; *mm*. spur rowel	425	1000
2641	— As 2638A; *mm*. rose	425	1000
2641A	— As 2638B; *mm*. 33-46, 105/-	350	725
2642	**Quarter-laurel**. Bust with two loose tie ends; *mm*. 24-105	185	450
2642A	Bust as 2638C; *mm*. 105, 46, 105/46	185	450

2642B

	F	VF
	£	£

2642B As last but beaded, i.c. on *rev.* or both sides; *mm.* 105, 46....................... 200   475
Rev. mm. on ¹/₂ and ¹/₄ laurels normally follows REGNA.

SILVER

2643

First coinage, 1603-4

2643	**Crown**. King on horseback. R. EXVRGAT, etc., shield; *mm.* thistle, lis	950	2850
2644	**Halfcrown**. Similar..	1100	3500

2645   2646

2645	**Shilling**. First bust, square-cut beard. R. EXVRGAT, etc.; *mm.* thistle ...	90	425
2646	— Second bust, beard appears to merge with collar; *mm.* thistle, lis	75	225
2647	**Sixpence**. First bust; 1603; *mm.* thistle...	75	300

	2649		2650		2651		

		F	VF
		£	£
2648	Second bust; 1603-4; *mm.* thistle, lis	40	175
2649	**Halfgroat**. First bust, II behind head; *mm.* thistle, lis	25	75
2650	**Penny**. First bust I behind head; *mm.* thistle..	45	185
2650A	— Second bust; *mm.* thistle, lis...	15	55
2651	**Halfpenny**. As illustration; *mm.* thistle, lis	15	50

Second coinage, 1604-19

2652	**Crown**. King on horseback. R. QVAE DEVS, etc. *rev.* stops; *mm.* 105-84	800	2500

2653

2653	**Halfcrown**. Similar; *mm.* 105-79	1250	3500
2654	**Shilling**. Third bust, beard cut square and stands out (*cf.* illus. 2657); *mm.* lis, rose	70	225
2655	— Fourth bust, armour plainer (*cf.* 2658); *mm.* 33-74, 90 over 74, or 60 over 74...	70	250

2656

2656	— Fifth bust, similar, but hair longer; usually higher double-arched crown; *mm.* 74-7a, single-arched crown; *mm.* 74 *rare*...	75	275

2657   2658

	F	VF
	£	£
2657 **Sixpence**. Third bust; 1604-6; *mm*. lis, rose, escallop	40	160
2658 — Fourth bust; 1605-16; *mm*. rose to book, 90/60, 25/60	50	185
2658A— Fifth bust, 1618; *mm*. plain cross	675	2000
2659 **Halfgroat**. As illus. but larger crown on *obv*.; *mm*. lis to coronet	15	45

2660   2663

2660 —— Similar, but smaller crown on *obv*.; *mm*. coronet to plain cross	15	45
2660A As before, but TVEATVR legend both sides; *mm*. plain cross over book	30	100
2661 **Penny**. As halfgroat but no crowns; *mm*. 105-32,7a and none, -/84, 32/-	15	45
2662 — As before but TVEATVR legend both sides; *mm*. mullet	25	85
2663 **Halfpenny**. As illus.; *mm*. 105- 25, 32; all *mms* on *rev*. only	15	40

Third coinage, 1619-25

| 2664 **Crown**. As 2652, with plain or grass ground line, colon stops on *obv*., no stops on *rev*.; *mm*. 33-46 | 675 | 1650 |

2665

| 2665 —— plume over shield; *mm*. 125-46 | 850 | 2250 |

2666

	F £	VF £

2666 **Halfcrown**. As 2664 with plain or grass ground line; all have bird-
headed harp; *mm.* 33-46 .... 250 750
2666A— — Similar but no ground line; *mm.* rose 525 1500

2667   2669

2667 — — Plume over shield; groundline *mm.* 125-46 .... 325 1050
2668 **Shilling**. Sixth (large) bust, hair longer and very curly; *mm.* 24-46 .... 90 325
2669 — — plume over shield; *mm.* 125-46 .... 185 650

2670   2672

2670 **Sixpence**. Sixth bust; 1621-4; *mm.* 33-46; 1621/0, *mm.* rose 55 185
2671 **Halfgroat**. As 2660 but no stops on *rev.*; *mm.* 24-46 and none, 105 and 46,
46/- *mm.* 24 with *rev.* stops known 15 45
2671A Similar but no inner circles; *mm.* lis, trefoil over lis 20 60
2672 **Penny**. As illus.; *mm.* 24, 105, two pellets, none, trefoil, ... 15 40
2672A— Similar but without inner circles on one or both sides; *mm.* lis, two
pellets 15 45
2673 **Halfpenny**. As 2663, but no *mm.* 15 35

COPPER

For further details see C. Wilson Peck, *English Copper, Tin and Bronze Coins in the British Museum, 1558-1958.*

2674   2675   2676

		F	VF
		£	£
2674	**Farthing**. 'Harington', small size. 1a, (originally tinned surface). Mintmark on or below cushion of crown. *mm:* A, B, C, D, F, S, Ermine, Millrind, Pellet, :<	50	100
2675	— — 1b, (occasionally tinned surface). Mintmark replaces central jewel on circlet of crown. *mm:* Trefoil, Crescent, Mullet or crown unmodified	35	70
2676	— 2, normal size, mintmark on reverse only; *mm.* Cinquefoil, Cross saltire, Lis, Martlet, Mullet, Trefoil	20	40
2677	'Lennox'. 3a; mintmark on reverse only; *mm.* Bell, Tower	25	50

2678   2679   2680

2678	— 3b; *mm.* mintmark both sides; *mm:* Flower, Fusil	8	20
2679	— — 3c; mintmark on obverse only; *mm.* Annulet, Bell, Coronet, Crescent, Cross flory fitchée, Cross patée fourchée, Dagger, Eagle's head, Fusil, Grapes, Key, Lion passant, Mascle, Quatrefoil, Rose (double), Star, Star (pierced), Thistlehead, Trefoil, Triangle, Triangle (pellet below), Tun, Woolpack	8	20
2680	— — 3d; las 3c but with larger crowns; *mm:* A, Dagger, Fusil, Lion rampant, Lis (three), Mascle, Stirrip, Trefoil, Triangle, Tun	8	20
2681	— 4; oval flan, legend starts at bottom left; *mm:* Cross patée. Originally issued for use in Ireland.	60	120

2681

Numismatically, this reign is one of the most interesting. Some outstanding machine-made coins were produced by Nicholas Briot, a French die-sinker, but they could not be struck at sufficient speed to supplant hand-hammering methods, and the weights often had to be adjusted by blank filing. In 1637 a branch mint was set up at Aberystwyth to coin silver extracted from the Welsh mines and dies supplied from Tower Mint. After the king's final breach with Parliament the parliamentary government continued to issue coins at London with Charles's name and portrait until the king's trial and execution. The coinage of copper farthings continued to be manufactured privately under licences held first by the Duchess of Richmond, then by Lord Maltravers and later by various other persons. The licence was finally revoked by Parliament in 1644.

During the Civil War coins were struck at a number of towns to supply coinage for those areas of the country under Royalist control. Many of these coins have an abbreviated form of the 'Declaration' made at Wellington, Shropshire, Sept., 1642, in which Charles promised to uphold the Protestant Religion, the Laws of England and the Liberty of Parliament. Amongst the more spectacular pieces are the gold triple unites and the silver pounds and half-pounds struck at Shrewsbury and Oxford, and the emergency coins, some made from odd-shaped pieces of silver plate during the sieges of Newark, Scarborough, Carlisle and Pontefract.

Mintmarks

| 105 | 10 | 96 | 71 | 57 | 88 | 101 | 35 |

| 87 | 107 | 60 | 75 | 123 | 57 | 119a | 23 |

| 119b | 98 | 112 | 81 | 120 | 109 |

Tower Mint under Charles I		**Tower Mint under Parliament**
1625	Lis (105)	1633-4	Portcullis (107)	1643-4	P in brackets (98)
1625-6	Cross Calvary (10)	1634-5	Bell (60)	1644-5	R in brackets (112)
1626-7	Negro's head (96)	1635-6	Crown (75)	1645	Eye (81)
1627-8	Castle (71)	1636-8	Tun (123)	1645-6	Sun (120)
1628-9	Anchor (57)	1638-9	Anchor (57)	1646-8	Sceptre (109)
1629-30	Heart (88)	1639-40	Triangle (119a)		
1630-1	Plume (101)	1640-1	Star (23)		
1631-2	Rose (35)	1641-3	Triangle in circle		
1632-3	Harp (87)		(119b)		

Mint mark no. 57 maybe upright, inverted, or horizontal to left or right.

| 59 | B | 58 *var* | 58 |

Briot's Mint

1631-2	Flower and B (59)	1638-9	Anchor (57)
1632	**B**		Anchor and B (58)
			(B upright or on side)
			Anchor and mullet (58v)

61	104	35	92	103	6	65b	71

89	91 *var*	131	84	94 *var*	64	93	34

102	67	127	128	129	25	83	100

134	71	A	B	75

Provincial Mints

1638-42	Book (61, *Aberystwyth*)
1642	Plume (104, *Shrewsbury*)
	Pellets or pellet (*Shrewsbury*)
1642-3	Rose (35, *Truro*)
	Bugle (134, *Truro*)
1642-4	Lion (92, *York*)
1642-6	Plume (103, *Oxford*)
	Pellet or pellets (*Oxford*)
	Lis (105, *Oxford*)
1643	Cross pattee (6, *Bristol*)
	Acorn (65b, *Bristol*)
	Castle (71, *Worcester* or *Shrewsbury*)
	Helmet (89, *Worcester* and *Shrewsbury*)
1643-4	Leopard's head (91 var. *Worcester*)
	Two lions (131, *Worcester*)
	Lis (105, *Worcs.* or *Shrews.*)
	Bunch of grapes (84, *Worcs.* or *Shrews.*)
	Bird (94 var., *Worcs.* or *Shrews.*)

1643-4	Boar's head (64 *Worcs.* or *Shrews.*)
	Lion rampant (93, *Worcs.* or *Shrews.*)
	Rosette (34, *Worcs.* or *Shrews.*)
1643-5	Plume (102, *Bristol*)
	Br. (67, *Bristol*)
	Pellets (*Bristol*)
	Rose (35, *Exeter*)
	Rosette (34, *Oxford*)
1643-6	Floriated cross (127, *Oxford*)
1644	Cross pattee (6, *Oxford*)
	Lozenge (128, *Oxford*)
	Billet (129, *Oxford*)
	Mullet (25, *Oxford*)
1644-5	Gerb (83, *Chester*)
	Pear (100, *Worcester*)
	Lis (105, *Hereford?*)
	Castle (71, *Exeter*)
1645-6	Plume (102, *Ashby, Bridgnorth*)
1645	A (*Ashby*)
1646	B (*Bridgnorth*)
1648-9	Crown (75, *Aberystwyth Furnace*)

GOLD

Tower mint, under the King (1625-42), and under Parliament (1642-9)

Tower Gold

For bust varieties on Tower Mint Gold see H. Schneider BNJ 1955-61

Numbers in brackets following each entry refer to numbers employed in previous editions of this catalogue

		F £	VF £
2682	**Angel**. St. Michael slaying dragon, no mark of value. R. Three masted ship, royal arms on mainsail; mm. lis, cross calvary	1850	6000
2682A	— — — pierced for use as touch-piece (2683)	750	2250
2683	— X in field to right of St. Michael; m.m. negro's head, castle, anchor, heart, castle and negro's head/castle, anchor and castle/anchor (2684)	1450	5000
2683A	— — — pierced for use as touch-piece (2685)	575	1500
2684	— X in field to left of St. Michael; mm. negro's head, heart, rose, harp, portcullis, bell, crown, tun, anchor, triangle, star, triangle-in-circle (2686)	1450	4500

2684A

2684A	— — — pierced for use as touch-piece (2687)	575	1350
2685	**Unite**. Group A, first bust, in coronation robes, bust 1, high double-arched crown. R. Square-topped shield, plain or elaborate garnishing; mm. lis (2688, 2688A)	525	1250
2686	— — bust 1a, flatter single-arched crown; mm. lis, cross calvary (2689, 2689A)	550	1350

2687

2687	Group B, second bust, in ruff, armour and mantle. R. Square-topped shield; m.m. cross calvary, negro's head, castle, anchor, heart (2690)	475	1100
2688	— — more elongated bust, usually dividing legend, mm. anchor, heart, plume (2690A)	475	1100
2689	— — — anchor below bust; mm. (2691)..	1250	3000
2689A	Group B/C mule. R. Oval shield with CR at sides; mm. plume (2691A)..	725	1750
2690	Group C, third bust, shorter with heavier armour. R. Oval shield with CR at sides; mm. plume, rose (2692)	525	1250
2691	Group D, fourth bust, with falling lace collar, bust 4, large bust with jewelled crown.R. Oval shield with CR at sides; mm. harp, portcullis (2693)	475	1100
2692	— — bust 5, smaller bust, unjewelled crown; mm. portcullis, bell, crown, tun, anchor, triangle, star (2693A)	450	1100
2693	— — — (under Parliament); mm. (P), (P)/- (2710)	725	1850

	F £	VF £
2694 Group F, sixth 'Briot's' bust, with stellate lace collar. R. Oval shield with CR at sides, mm. triangle, star, triangle-in-circle (2694)........................	525	1250
2695 — — (under Parliament); mm. (P), (R) (2711)	725	1850

2696

2696 Group G, (under Parliament), seventh bust, smaller collar; mm. eye, sun, sceptre (2712)...	750	2000

2697	2698	2699

	F £	VF £
2697 **Double-crown**. Group A, first bust, in coronation robes, bust 1, high double-arched crown, both arches jewelled. R. Square-topped shield; mm. lis (2696)	600	1500
2698 — — bust 1a, flatter crown, outer arch only jewelled; m.m. lis, cross calvary (2696A)	425	950
2699 Group B, second bust, in ruff, armour and mantle, bust 2. R. Square-topped shield; mm. cross calvary, negro's head, castle, anchor (2697)................	325	800
2700 — — busts 3-4, more elongated bust, usually dividing legend; mm. anchor, heart, plume (2697A)	325	800
2701 Group C, third bust, bust 5. R. Oval shield with CR at sides; mm. plume, rose (2698)..	375	850
2702 Group D, fourth bust, with falling lace collar, bust 6, large bust with jewelled crown. R. Oval shield with CR at sides; mm. harp, crown (2699)	350	850
2703 — — bust 7, smaller head, inner or both arches of crown unjewelled; mm. harp, portcullis, bell, crown, tun (2699A-C)	325	800
2703A— — — Group Da, (under Parliament), re-cut Group D bust punches; m.m. eye (2713)	750	2000
2704 Group E, fifth bust, 'Aberystwyth' bust, bust 8, double-arched crown. R. Oval shield with CR at sides; m.m. anchor (2700)..	575	1500
2705 — — bust 9, smaller 'Aberystwyth' bust, single-arched crown; m.m. anchor, triangle (2700A)..	475	1250
2705A— — — Group Ea, (under Parliament), re-cut bust 9; m.m. sun, sceptre (2714)	575	1500
2706 Group F, sixth 'Briot's' bust, with stellate lace collar, bust 10. R. Oval shield with CR at sides; mm. triangle, star, triangle-in-circle (2701)..................	400	950
2707 — — (under Parliament); mm. (P), (R) (2715)	525	1350
2708 Group H, (under Parliament), bust 11, dumpy crude bust, single flat-arched crown; mm. sun (2716)	825	2500

2709   2715

		F £	VF £
2709	**Crown**. Group A, first bust, in coronation robes, bust 1 var, tall narrow bust, double-arched crown. R. Square-topped shield; mm. lis (2703)..............	200	475
2710	— bust 1, broader, less angular bust; m.m. lis, cross calvary (2703A).....	225	575
2711	Group B, second bust, in ruff, armour and mantle, bust 2. R. Square-topped shield; mm. cross calvary, negro's head, castle (2704)............................	200	450
2712	— — bust 3, narrower; more elongated bust; m.m. anchor, heart, plume (2704A)	185	400
2713	— — — anchor below bust; mm. anchor (2704B)....................................	625	1500
2713A	Group B/C mule. R. Oval shield with CR at sides; mm. plume, rose (2705)	225	525
2714	Group C, third bust, bust 4. R. Oval shield with CR at sides; mm. plume (2706)	375	900
2715	Group D, fourth bust, with falling lace collar, busts 5, 7. R. Oval shield with CR at sides; m.m. harp, -/harp, portcullis, portcullis/bell, bell, crown, tun, anchor, triangle, star/triangle, star, triangle-in-circle (2707)	185	425
2716	— — (under Parliament), bust 5, jewelled crown; m.m. (P), (R), eye, sun (2717)...	250	625
2716A	— — (under Parliament), bust 6, unjewelled crown; m.m. eye, sun, sceptre (2717A)...	250	650
2717	Group E, fifth bust, small 'Aberystwyth' bust, bust 8. R. Oval shield with CR at sides; mm. anchor (2708)...	475	1350
2721C	— Group F, sixth 'Briot's' bust, bust 9, only known as Briot/hammered mule (see 2721C below)	1000	3000

Nicholas Briot's coinage, 1631-2

| 2718 | **Angel**. Type somewhat as Tower but smaller and neater; mm. -/B .... | 2750 | 7500 |

2721

2719	**Unite**. As illustration. R. FLORENT etc.; mm. flower and B/B...............	2250	6000
2720	**Double-crown**. Similar but X. R. CVLTORES, etc. mm. flower and B/B	1500	4000
2720A	Similar but King's crown unjewelled: mm. flower and B/B, B	1500	4000
2721	**Crown**. Similar; mm. B..	2250	6750

Briot's Hammered issue, 1638-9

		F £	VF £

2695

		F £	VF £
2721A	**Unite**. Briot's (sixth) bust, large lace collar. R. FLORENT etc., Briot's square-topped shield dividing crowned C R; *mm.* anchor	2750	9000
2721B	**Double-crown**. Briot's bust, similar. R. CVLTORES etc., square-topped shield dividing crowned C R; *mm.* anchor	1750	5250
2721C	**Crown**. Briot's bust, similar. R. CVLTORES etc., oval shield dividing crowned C R (a Briot hammered issue/Tower mule); *mm.* anchor...........	1000	3000

Provincial issues, 1638-49

Chester mint, 1644

2722	**Unite**. As Tower. Somewhat like a crude Tower sixth bust. R. Crowned, oval shield, crowned CR, *mm.* plume	12500	40000

Shrewsbury mint, 1642 (See also 2749)

2723	**Triple unite**, 1642. Half-length figure l holding sword and olive-branch; *mm.*: R. EXVRGAT, etc., around RELIG PROT, etc., in two wavy lines. III and three plumes above, date below	25000	85000

Oxford mint, 1642-6

2724	**Triple unite**. As last, but *mm.* plume, tall narrow bust, 1642	6250	15000
2725	Similar, but 'Declaration' on continuous scroll, 1642-3	6750	16500
2725A	Large bust of fine style. King holds short olive branch; *mm.* small lis.....	22500	70000
2726	As last, but taller bust, with scarf behind shoulder, 1643, *mm.* plume	6500	16000

2727

2727	Similar, but without scarf, longer olive branch, 1643..............................	6250	15000
2728	Similar, but OXON below 1643, rosette stops.....................................	8500	25000
2729	Smaller size, olive branch varies, bust size varies, 1644 OXON..............	6500	16000
2730	— Obv. as 2729, 1644 / OX..	6750	17500
2731	**Unite**. Tall thin bust. R. 'Declaration' in two wavy lines, 1642; *no mm.*...	1350	3500
2732	— R. 'Declaration' in three lines on continuous scroll, 1642-3	1450	3750
2733	Tall, well-proportioned bust. R. Similar, 1643, no *mm.*	1600	4500
2734	Shorter bust, king's elbow not visible. R. Similar, 1643; *mm.* plume/-....	1250	3250
2735	Similar but longer olive branch curving to l. 1644 / OX; *mm.* plume	1350	3500

2735A

		F	VF
		£	£
2735A	Similar, but dumpy bust breaking lower i.c., small flan	1500	4000
2736	Tall bust to edge of coin. R. Similar, 1643	2500	7250
2737	As 2734. R. 'Declaration' in three straight lines, 1644 / OX	2500	7000
2738	Similar to 2734, but smaller size; small bust, low olive branch. 1645	1750	5250
2739	— R. Single plume above 'Declaration', 1645-6 / OX; *mm.* plume, rosette, none	1500	4500
2740	**Half-unite**. 'Declaration' in three straight lines, 1642	1500	4950
2741	'Declaration' on scroll; *mm.* plume; 1642-3	1500	4250

2742

2742	Bust to bottom of coin, 1643; Oxford plumes	1100	2750
2743	— 1644 / OX. Three Shrewsbury plumes (neater work)	1650	4500
	Bristol mint, 1643-5		
2744	**Unite**. Somewhat as 2734; Two busts known. *mm.* Br. or Br/ plumelet.; 1645...	9500	30000
2745	**Half-unite**. Similar 1645	7000	26500
	Truro mint, 1642–3		
2745A	**Half-Unite**. Crowned bust l. (similar to Tower 4th bust). R. CVLT, etc., crowned shield	7500	27500
	Exeter mint, 1643–5		
2746	**Unite**. *obv.* sim. to early Oxford bust. R. FLORENT, etc., crowned oval shield between crowned CR, *mm.* rose	13500	42500
2747	— R. CVLTORES, etc., similar but no CR	12500	40000
	Worcester mint, 1643-4		
2748	**Unite**. Crude bust R. FLORENT, etc., double annulet stops, crowned oval shield, lion's paws on either side of garniture, no *mm.*.............................	12000	37500
	Salopia (Shrewsbury) mint, 1644		
2749	**Unite**. *Obv.* bust in armour. R. Cr. shield, crowned CR. *mm.* lis/-	12000	37500

Colchester besieged, 1648

2750	**Ten Shillings** Gateway of castle between CR; below OBS COL 16 S/X 48. Uniface – now considered a later concoction		

Pontefract besieged, 1648-9. After the death of Charles I, in the name of Charles II

	F	VF
	£	£

2751 **Unite**. DVM : SPIRO : SPERO around CR crowned. CAROLVS :
SECVИDVS : 16 48, castle, OBS on l., PC above.................................. 35000 125000

2752 **Unite**. CAROL : II, etc., around HANC : DEVS, etc. R. POST : MORTEM,
etc.,around castle. *Octagonal*... 32500 120000

SILVER
Tower mint, under the King (1625-42), and under Parliament (1642-9)

2753 **Crown**. Group I, first horseman, type 1a, king on horseback left, horse
caparisoned with plume on head and crupper. R. Square-topped shield over
long cross fourchee; mm. lis, cross calvary 650 1650

2754 — — 1b. R. Plume above shield, no cross fourchee; mm. lis, cross
calvary, castle.. 950 2500

2755 Group II, second horseman, type 2a, smaller horse, plume on head only,
cross on housing. R. Oval shield over cross fourchee, CR above; mm. harp 575 1350

2756 — — 2b1. R. Plume between CR above shield, no cross fourchee; mm.
plume, rose... 675 1750

2757 — — 2b2. R. Plume between CR, cross fourchee; mm. harp 725 1850

2758

2758 Group III, third horseman, type 3a, horse without caparisons, sword upright.
R. Oval shield without CR; mm. bell, crown, tun, anchor, triangle, star.. 575 1350

2759 — — 3b. R. Plume above shield; mm. portcullis, crown, tun 675 1650

2760 'Briot's' horseman with groundline, lozenge stops on obverse; mm. triangle
in circle... 3000 8500

2761 Group IV, (under Parliament), fourth horseman, type 4, foreshortened horse
R. Oval shield; mm. (P), (R), eye, sun (2838).. 650 1650

2762 Group V, (under Parliament), fifth horseman, type 5, tall spirited horse;
mm. sun (2839) 750 2000

2763

2763 **Halfcrown**. Group I, first horseman, type 1a1, horse caparisoned with plume
on head and crupper, rose on housings, ground-line. R. Square-topped shield
over long cross fourchee; mm. lis (2761)... 285 1000

	F £	VF £
2764 — — 1a2. No rose on housings, no ground-line; mm. lis, cross calvary (2762)	210	575
2765 — — — ground-line; mm. lis (2762A)	375	1250
2766 — — 1a3. No rose on housings, no ground-line. R. No long cross, heavy or light garnishing to shield; mm. cross calvary*, negro's head, castle (2763-2763B)	185	525
2767 — — — 1b. R. Plume above shield, heavy or light garnishing; mm. lis, cross calvary, negro's head, castle, anchor (2765, 2765A)	600	1500
2768 Group II, second horseman, type 2/1b, plume on horse's head only, rose on housings. R. Plume over shield; mm. heart, plume (2766)	1250	2750
2769 — — 2a. Smaller horse, cross on housings. R. Oval shield with CR above (CR divided by rose (very rare), lis over rose (rare), or lis); mm. plume, rose, plume/rose (2767)	95	300
2770 — — — 2b. R. Plume between CR above shield; mm. plume, rose (2768)	175	625
2771 — — 2c. R. Oval draped shield with CR at sides; mm. harp, portcullis, portcullis/harp (2769)	75	225
2772 — — — 2d. R. Plume above shield; mm. harp (2770)	1250	3000

2775   2779

	F	VF
2773 Group III, third horseman, type 3a1, no caparisons on horse, scarf flying from king's waist. R. Oval garnished shield; mm. bell, bell/crown, crown, tun (2771)	65	185
2774 — — — 3b. R. Plume above shield; mm. portcullis, bell, crown, tun (2772)	150	475
2775 — — 3a2. King wears cloak flying from shoulder. R. Oval garnished shield; mm. tun, anchor, triangle, star, triangle-in-circle (2773)	65	185
2776 — — — — rough ground under horse; mm. triangle, star (2774)	65	185
2777 — — horseman of finer style, short busy tail, cloak like arrowhead behind shoulder, no ground below; mm. triangle, star (2773 var.)	100	325
2778 — — 3a3, (under Parliament), no ground, cruder workmanship; mm. (P), (R), eye, sun (2840)	45	150
2779 Group IV, fourth horseman, type 4, foreshortened horse. R. Oval garnished shield; mm. star, triangle in circle (2775)	55	145

2781   2782

2779A — — (under Parliament); mm. (P) (2841)	175	650
2780 Group V, (under Parliament), fifth horseman, type 5, tall spirited horse. R. Oval garnished shield; mm. sun, sceptre (2842)	65	185

Light weight half crowns (204 grains) exist of No. 2766, mm. cross calvary

	F	VF
	£	£

2781 **Shilling**. Group A, first bust, type 1, in coronation robes, bust 1, high double-arched crown, both arches jewelled. R. Square-topped shield over cross fourchee (Sharp A1/1); mm. lis (2776).................................... | 115 | 425

2782 — — bust 2, larger crown, outer arch only jewelled (Sharp A2/1-2); mm. lis*, cross calvary* (2776A, 2777) .... | 100 | 375

2783 — — — 1b1. R. Plume above shield, no cross fourchee (Sharp A2/3); mm. lis, cross calvary (2778) .... | 525 | 1750

2784 Group B, second bust, type 1a, in ruff, armour and mantle. R. Square-topped shield over cross fourchee (Sharp B1-5/1); mm. cross calvary*, negro's head, castle (2779, 2780) .... | 95 | 350

2785 — — 1b2. R. Plume above shield, no cross fourchee (Sharp B1-5/2); mm. cross calvary*, negro's head, castle, anchor, heart, plume (2781, 2781A) | 150 | 575

2786 — — 1b3. R. Plume above shield, cross fourchee (Sharp B2/3); mm. negro's head (2782) .... | 1500 | 4000

2787 Group C, third bust, type 2a, with more visible armour. R. Oval garnished shield with CR above (Sharp C1/1, C2/1-3); mm. plume, rose (2783)..... | 70 | 250

2788 — — 2b. R. Plume above shield (Sharp C1/4, C2/4-6, C3/5); mm. plume, rose (2784) .... | 150 | 575

2789 Group D, fourth bust, type 3.1, with falling lace collar, inner circles. R. Garnished oval shield with CR at sides (Sharp D1-6/1); mm. harp, portcullis (2785) .... | 50 | 240

2790 — — — 3.2. R. Plume above shield (Sharp D1- 3/2); mm. harp (2786) 750 | 2500 |

2791   2799

2791 — — 3a, no inner circles. R. Round garnished shield, no CR (Sharp E1/1-2, E2/1-2; E3/2); mm. bell, crown, tun (2787)... | 35 | 165

2792 — — — rare bust varieties, no inner circles: (a) large crude bust (Sharp E4/2); mm. tun; (b) neat 'Aberystwyth' bust (Sharp E5/2); mm. tun (2787 var.) | 75 | 300

2793 — — 3b. R. Plume above shield (Sharp E1-2/3); mm. bell, crown, tun (2788) | 95 | 350

2794 Group E, fifth "Aberystwyth' bust, type 4.2, double-arched crown, small or large XII. R. Square-topped shield over cross moline (Sharp F1/1); mm. tun, anchor (2791) .... | 65 | 250

2795 — — 4.1, larger bust, single-arched crown, small or large XII (Sharp F2/1); mm. tun, anchor (2789)... | 80 | 325

2796 — — 4.3, smaller bust, single-arched crown, large XII (Sharp F3/1-2); mm. tun, anchor, triangle (2792).. | 40 | 160

2797 — — 4.1var., larger bust with rounded shoulder, large XII (Sharp F5/1-2); mm. anchor, triangle (2790)... | 45 | 185

2798 — — rare bust varieties : (a) small 'Aberystwyth' bust, double-arched crown (Sharp F4/1); mm. anchor (to right); (b) small 'Briot's' bust, with stellate lace collar, single-arched crown (Sharp F6/1-2); mm. triangle; (c) small 'Aberystwyth' bust, single-arched crown (Sharp F7/2); mm. triangle-in-circle (2790 var.).. | 115 | 425

		F	VF
		£	£

2799 Group F, sixth large 'Briot's' bust, type 4.4, with stellate lace collar, double-arched crown. R. Square-topped shield over cross moline (Sharp G 1/1-2); mm. triangle, star, triangle-in-circle (2793) .... | | 35 | 135

2800 — — — (under Parliament) (Sharp G1-2/2); mm. (P), (R), eye, sun (2843) | | 40 | 150

2801 — — 4.4 var., (under Parliament), small thin bust, 'nick' below truncation (Sharp G3/2); mm. sun (2843A) .... | | 250 | 675

2802   2803

2802 Group G, (under Parliament), seventh bust, type 4.5, tall coarse narrow bust. R. Square-topped shield over cross moline (Sharp H1/1); mm. sun, sceptre (2844) .... | | 60 | 225

2803 — — 4.6, shorter slim better proportioned bust (Sharp H2/2); mm. sceptre (2845) .... | | 65 | 250

2804

2804 — — — short broad bust (Sharp H3/2); mm. sceptre (2845A) .... | | 75 | 300

Light weight shillings (81.75 grains) exist of No. 2782, mm. lis, cross calvary over lis; No. 2784, mm. cross calvary; and No. 2785 mm. cross calvary See Sharp BNJ 1977 for bust varieties.

2805 **Sixpence**. Group A, first bust, in coronation robes, type 1, small bust, double-arched crown. R. Square-topped shield over cross fourchee, date above; 1625, mm. lis (2794) .... | | 75 | 300

2806 — — broader bust, larger crown; 1625, mm. lis, cross calvary*; 1626, mm. cross calvary* (2794, 2794A) .... | | 95 | 375

2807 Group B, second bust (several varieties), type 1a1, in ruff, armour and mantle. R. Square-topped shield over cross fourchee, date above; 1625, mm. cross calvary; 1626, mm. cross calvary*, negro's head; 1627, mm. negro's head, castle; 1628, mm. castle, anchor; 1629, mm. anchor, heart (2795, 2795A) | | 85 | 350

2808 — — 1a2. R. No cross fourchee; 1630, mm. heart, plume (2796) .... | | 200 | 675

2809　　　　　　　2811　　　　　　2814

	F £	VF £
2809 Group C, third bust, type 2a. R. Oval garnished shield with CR above; mm. plume, rose (2797)	55	250
2810 — — 2b. R. Plume above shield; mm. plume, rose, plume/rose (2798)	85	375
2811 Group D, fourth bust, type 3, with falling lace collar, inner circles, (medium, large and small bust). R. Oval garnished shield with CR at sides; mm. harp, portcullis (2799)	45	160
2812 — — — omits C R by shield; mm. portcullis (2799A)	125	450
2813 — — 3a, no inner circles (type 3/3a mules exist); mm. bell, crown, tun (2800)	35	145
2814 Group E, fifth 'Aberystwyth' bust, type 4.1, double-arched crown, small or large VI. R. Square-topped shield over cross moline; mm. tun, anchor (2801, 2802)	60	225
2815 — — — R. Lyre cross-ends; mm. tun (2801A)	85	350
2816 — — 4.2, single-arched crown; mm. tun, anchor, triangle (2803, 2804)	35	150
2817 Group F, sixth 'Briot's' bust, type 4.3, with stellate lace collar. R. Square-topped shield over cross moline; mm. triangle, star, triangle-in-circle (2805)	40	175
2818 — — (under Parliament); mm. (P), (R) (2846)	65	250

2819　　　　　2820

2819 Group G, (under Parliament), late 'Aberystwyth' bust with riveted shoulder, type 4.4. R. Square-topped shield over cross moline; mm. (P), (R), eye, sun, sceptre (2847)	55	225
2820 — — 4.5, squat bust of crude style; mm. eye, sun (over eye) (2848)	95	350
2821 — — 4.5 var., small 3a type bust, double-arched crown, inner circle both sides; mm. sun (over eye) (2848A)	250	750

* Light weight sixpences (40.85 grains) exist of No. 2806, 1625, mm. cross calvary, 1626, mm. cross calvary; and No. 2807, 1626, mm. cross calvary

2822　　　　　　2824　　　　　　　2832

2822 **Halfgroat**. Group A, without bust, crowned rose each side, type 1, inner circles on one or both sides;mm. lis, lis/-, cross calvary, castle, none (2806)	25	85

| | | *F* | *VF* |
| | | £ | £ |

2823 — — 1a, without inner circles; mm. negro's head, castle, anchor, heart, plume (2807)........................... 25 85

2824 Group B, second bust, type 2a, in ruff and mantle. R. Oval shield; mm. plume, rose (2808) 25 90

2825 — — 2b. R. plume above shield; mm. plume, plume/-, rose (2809)....... 30 125

2826 Group C, third bust, more armour, crown breaks inner circle; mm. plume, rose (2809A) 25 90

2827 R. Plume above shield; mm. plume (2809B)............................... 35 135

2828 Group D, fourth bust, type 3.1, no inner circles. R. Oval shield dividing C R; mm. harp, portcullis crown (2810) 20 55

2829 — — — — 3.2-4, inner circle on one or both sides; mm. harp, portcullis, ../harp (2811-13) 20 50

2830 — — — 3.5-6. R. Oval shield, no C R, no inner circle or obv. only; mm. harp, portcullis (2814-15).......................... 25 65

2831 — — 3a1. R. Rounder shield, no inner circles; mm. bell, crown, tun, anchor, triangle (2816).................................. 20 50

2832 — — 3a2-3, inner circles on obverse or both sides; mm. anchor, triangle, star, triangle-in-anchor (2817-18)........................ 25 65

2833 — — — (under Parliament), type 3a3, inner circles both sides; mm. (P)/triangle-in-circle, (P), (R), eye, sun, sceptre (2849) 20 65

2834 Group E, fifth 'Aberystwyth' bust, types 3a4-5, no inner circles or on reverse only; mm. anchor (2819-20) 40 100

2835 — — 3a6, very small bust (from penny puncheon), no inner circles; mm. anchor (2821) 50 125

2836 Group G, (under Parliament), seventh bust, type 3a7, older bust with pointed beard; mm. eye, sun, sceptre (2850) 20 65

2837   2843   2844

2837 **Penny**. Group A, without bust, rose each side, type 1, inner circles; mm. lis, negro's head, one or two pellets (2822) 20 45

2838 — — 1a, no inner circles; mm. lis, anchor, one or two pellets (2823).... 20 45

2839 — — 1b, inner circle on reverse; mm. negro's head/two pellets (2824). 40 100

2840 Group B, second bust, type 2, in ruff and mantle. R. Oval shield, inner circles; mm. plume, plume/rose, rose (2825)................. 30 80

2841 — — 2.1, no inner circles; mm. plume, rose (2826) 30 80

2842 Group C, third bust, type 2a1, more armour visible, no inner circles; mm. plume, plume/rose, rose (2827) 20 65

2843 — — 2a2-4, inner circles on obverse, both sides or reverse; mm. plume, rose (2828-30)................................ 25 65

2844 Group D, fourth bust, type 3.1, with falling lace collar. R. CR by shield, no inner circles; mm. harp, one or two pellets (2831) 20 40

2845 — — — 3.2, no C R by shield, no inner circles; mm. harp, portcullis, pellets, none (2832)........................... 20 40

2846 — — — — 3.3-4, inner circles on obverse or reverse; mm. harp, two pellets (2833-34).................................. 20 45

2847 — — 3a1, shield almost round with scroll garniture, no inner circles; mm.
      bell, triangle, one to four pellets, none (2835)   15   45
2848 — — 3a1 var., inner circle on one or both sides; mm. triangle/two pellets
      (2835A)   20   55
2849 Group E, fifth 'Aberystwyth' bust, type 3a3, inner circle on obverse or none;
      mm. triangle, anchor, one or two pellets, none (2836)   20   50
2850 Group G, (under Parliament), seventh bust, type 3a2, older bust, inner circle
      on obverse only; mm. one or two pellets (2851)......................................   20   75

2851

2851 **Halfpenny**. Rose each side, no legend or mm (2837)   15   40

Nicholas Briot's coinage, 1631-9
  First milled issue, 1631-2
2852 **Crown**. King on horseback. R. Crowned shield between CR crowned;
      mm. flower and B / B   725   1750

2853

2853 **Halfcrown**. Similar...   400   1250
2854 **Shilling**. Briot's early bust with falling lace collar. R. Square-topped shield
      over long cross fourchee; R. Legend starts at top or bottom (extr. rare)
      mm. flower and B/B, B...   275   750

2855

2855 **Sixpence**. Similar, but VI behind bust; *mm*. flower and B/B, flower and B/-   135   400

Carlisle

Scarborough

York

Pontefract

Chester

Newark

Ashby de la Zouch

Shrewsbury

Aberystwyth
(Dovey Furnace)
1648-9

Bridgnorth

Aberystwyth
(1638-42)

Hartlebury Castle

Worcester

Hereford

Oxford

Tower of
London

(Parliament)

Bristol

Exeter

Truro

2856   2856A

		F	VF
		£	£
2856	**Halfgroat**. Briot's bust, B below, II behind. R. IVSTITIA, etc., square-topped shield over long cross fourchee	50	135
2856A	Pattern halfgroat. Uncrowned bust in ruff r. R. crowned, interlocked Cs. (North 2687). (Included because of its relatively regular appearance.)....	50	135
2857	**Penny**. Similar, but I behind bust, B below bust; position of legend may vary	55	150

Second milled issue, 1638-9

2859

2858	**Halfcrown**. As 2853, but *mm.* anchor and B	300	850
2859	**Shilling**. Briot's late bust, the falling lace collar is plain with broad lace border, no scarf. R. As 2854 but cross only to inner circle; *mm.* anchor and B, anchor or muled	165	450
2860	**Sixpence**. Similar, but VI; *mm.* anchor, anchor and mullet/anchor	65	185

The two last often exhibit flan reduction marks.

Briot's hammered issue, 1638-9

2861	**Halfcrown**. King on Briot's style horse with ground line. R. Square-topped shield; *mm.* anchor, triangle over anchor. Also muled with Tower *rev.*...	725	2000
2862	**Shilling**. Briot's first hammered issue, Sim. to 2859; R. Square-topped shield over short cross fleury, contraction stops on *obv.*, pellet stops *rev. mm.* anchor	625	1750
2862A	— Briot's second hammered issue. As 2862 but lozenge stops both sides. *mm.* anchor, triangle over anchor or triangle	325	950
2862B	Tower, Group E, obv. type 4.1 var. (S.2797) above R. as Briot's 1st or 2nd hammered issue; mm. Δ over anchor.	225	850
2862C	Tower, Group F, obv. type 4.4 (S.2799 above) R. as Briot's 2nd hammered issue; mm Δ/Δ over anchor.	225	750

Provincial and Civil War issues, 1638-49
York mint, 1643-4. *Mm.* lion

2863	**Halfcrown**. 1. Ground-line below horse. R. Square-topped shield between CR	575	1650
2864	— 2. — R. Oval shield as Tower 3a, groundline grass or dotted	475	1350
2865	— 3. No ground-line. R. Similar	450	1250
2866	*— 4. As last, but EBOR below horse with head held low. Base metal, often very base	75	225
2867	— 5. Tall horse, mane in front of chest, EBOR below. R. Crowned square-topped shield between CR, floral spray in legend	325	900

These pieces are contemporary forgeries (Besly, the York mint of Charles I, BNJ 54, 1984)

2868

		F £	VF £
2868	— 6. As last, but shield is oval, garnished (*rev.* detail variations)	275	750
2869	— 7. Similar, but horse's tail shows between legs. R. Shield as last, but with lion's skin garniture, no CR or floral spray	250	725

2870

2870	**Shilling**. 1. Bust in scalloped lace collar similar to 3¹. R. EBOR above square-topped shield over cross fleury	225	650
2871	— 2. Similar, but bust in plain armour, mantle; coarse work	250	700
2872	— 3. *Obv.* as above illustration. — R. EBOR below oval shield	250	700
2873	— 4. — Similar, but crowned oval shield (*obv.* finer style)	200	575
2874	— 5. — As last, but lion's skin garniture	200	575
2875	**Sixpence**. *Obv.* Sim. to 2870. Crowned oval shield	250	750

2876   2877

2876	— — Crowned CR at sides..	225	625
2877	**Threepence**. As type 1 shilling, but III behind bust. R. As 2870.............	55	150

Aberystwyth mint, 1638/9-42. *Mm.* book.
Plume 1=with coronet and band. Plume 2=with coronet only

2878	**Halfcrown**. Horseman similar to 2773, but plume 2 behind. R. Oval garnished shield with large plume above. *Obv.* plume 2, *rev.* plume 1....	650	2500
2879	— Similar to 2774, plume 1 behind King, ground below horse. *Obv.* squat plume 1, *rev.* plume 1..	750	2750

	F	VF
	£	£

2880 As 2773 but more spirited horse, no ground. FRAN ET HIB, plume 2/1   650   2500

2881

2881 **Shilling**. Bust with large square lace collar, plume 2 before, small XII. R.
As before. No inner circles 375 1250
2882 — inner circle on *rev.* 350 1000
2883 As 2881, but large plume 1 or 2, large XII, inner circles, large or 350 1000
small shield

2884

2884 As last, but small narrow head, square lace collar, large or square plume   425   1350
2885 Small Briot style face, small crown, plume 2, large shield 500 1650
2885A **Sixpence**. *Obv.* as Tower bust 3a, plume before. R. as 2889; inner circles
both sides, *mm.* book (*obv.* only) 375 1000

2886

2886 Somewhat as 2881, but double-arched crown, small VI; no inner circles   300   825
2887 Similar to 2886, but single arched crown, plume 2, inner circle *obv.* Large VI   325   850
2888 Similar, but with inner circles both sides... 325 850
2889 — — *Rev.* with small squat-shaped plume above, sometimes no *rev. mm.* 300 825
2890 Bust as the first Oxford sixpence; with crown cutting inner circle........... 425 1250

	F	VF
	£	£

2891 **Groat**. Large bust, lace collar, no armour on shoulder. Crown breaks or touches inner circle. R. Shield, plume 1 or 2 55   165

2892 — Similar, armour on shoulder, shorter collar. R. Similar...................... 60   175

2893 — Smaller, neater bust well within circle. R. Similar 55   165

2894 **Threepence**. Small bust, plume 2 before. R. Shield, plume 1 or 2 above, *obv.* legend variations.............. 40   130

2895 — Similar, but crown cuts i.c. squat pl. on *obv.*, R. Pl. 2, *obv.* legend variations.. 45   140

2900 **Halfgroat**. Bust as Tower type 3. R. Large plume. No inner circles, *mm.* pellet/book,book.. 45   140

2900A   2905   2907

2900A Bust as 2886. R. As last, no inner circle 50   150

2901 Bust with round lace collar; single arch crown, inner circles, colon stops 45   135

2902 After Briot's bust, square lace collar: inner circles................................ 45   135

2903 **Penny**. As 2901; CARO; no inner circles.. 65   200

2904 As 2901; CARO; inner circles 55   175

2905 As last but reads CAROLVS; inner circles.. 70   225

2906 *Obv.* similar to 2890, tall narrow bust, crown touches inner circle 75   235

2907 **Halfpenny**. No legend. O. Rose. R. Plume 150   525

Aberystwyth-Furnace mint, 1648/9. *Mm.* crown

2908 **Halfcrown**. King on horseback. R. Sim. to 2878 1650   4500

2909 **Shilling**. Aberystwyth type, but *mm.* crown 1750   5250

2910 **Sixpence**. Similar... 950   2500

2911   2913

2911 **Groat**. Similar.. 225   525

2912 **Threepence**. Similar... 175   475

2913 **Halfgroat**. Similar. R. Large plume 275   725

2914 **Penny**. Similar 675   1750

Uncertain mint (? Hereford) 1644-5

2915   2930/1

	F	VF
	£	£
2915 **Halfcrown**. As illustration, dated 1645 or undated	2000	6000
2915A— Scarf with long sash ends. CH (Chirk castle?) below horse. R. Oval shield 1644	2250	6500
2915B — R. Crowned oval shield, lion paws	2000	6000

Shrewsbury mint, 1642. Plume without band used as *mm.* or in field.

2917 **Pound**. King on horseback, plume behind, from the puncheon of Tower grp. 3 crowns. R. Declaration between two straight lines, XX and three Shrewsbury plumes above, 1642 below; *mm.* pellets, pellets/-	1850	4500
2918 Similar, but Shrewsbury horse walking over pile of arms; no *mm.*, pellets	1650	4000
2919 As last, but cannon amongst arms and only single plume and XX above Declaration, no *mm.*	2000	4750
2920 **Half-pound**. As 2917, but X; *mm.* pellets	1250	2850
2921 Similar, but only two plumes on *rev.*; *mm.*, pellets....................................	1650	4000
2922 Shrewsbury horseman with ground-line, three plumes on *rev.*; *mm.*, none, pellets/-	1200	2750
2923 — with cannon and arms or arms below horse; *mm.* pellets/-	1200	2750
2924 — no cannon in arms, no plume in *obv.* field; *mm.* plume/pellets, plume/-	900	1850
2925 **Crown**. Aberystwyth horseman from the puncheon of a Tower halfcrown no ground line	6750	25000

2926

2926 Shrewsbury horseman with ground-line; *mm.* -/pellets, pellets/-, none....	850	2350
2927 **Halfcrown**. *O.* From Aberystwyth die; (S2880); *mm.* book. R. Single plume above Declaration, 1642	1000	3500
2928 Sim. to Aberystwyth die, fat plume behind. R. Three plumes above Declaration; *mm.* pellets, pellets/-	575	1500

		F	VF
		£	£
2929	Shrewsbury horseman, no ground line. R. As 2927, single plume, no *mm.*	625	1750
2929A	— — R. As 2933..................	525	1400
2930	— R. 2: plume; 6, above Declaration......................................	900	3250
2931	— with ground-line. R. Similar	900	3250
2932	— — R. As 2927, single plume......................	625	1750
2933	— — R. Three plumes above Declaration; *mm.* none or pellets	475	1350
2933A	— — R. Aberystwyth die, plume over shield; *mm.* /book..........	1000	3500
2934	As 2933 but no plume behind king; *mm.* plume/pellets..........................	450	1300
2935	**Shilling**. *O.* From Aberystwyth die; S2885 *mm.* book. R. Declaration type	850	2250
2936	*O.* From Shrewsbury die. R. Similar......................................	950	2500

Oxford mint, 1642-6. *Mm.* usually plume with band, except on the smaller denominations when it is lis or pellets. There were so many dies used at this mint that we can give only a selection of the more easily identifiable varieties.

For many years Oxford Halfcrowns and Shillings have been catalogued according to Morrieson obverse die varieties. In many cases, these are very small and difficult to identify. We have, therefore, simplified the obverse classification and used the available space to expand the listing of the more interesting reverse varieties.

2937

2937	**Pound**. Large horseman over arms, no exergual line, fine workmanship. R. Three Shrewsbury plumes and XX above Declaration, 1642 below; *mm.* plume/pellets	2750	7000
2938	— Similar, but three Oxford plumes, 1643; *mm.* as last..........................	2500	6500
2939	Shrewsbury horseman trampling on arms, exergual line. R. As last, 1642	2250	4500
2940	— — cannon amongst arms, 1642-3; *mm.* similar	2000	4250
2941	— as last but exergue is chequered, 1642; *mm.* similar..........................	2250	5250
2942	Briot's horseman, 1643; *mm.* similar......................................	3000	7500
2943	*O.* As 2937. R. Declaration in cartouche, single large plume above, 1644 OX below	4750	12500
2944	**Half-pound**. Shrewsbury horseman over arms, Oxford plume behind. R. Shrewsbury die, 1642; mm. plume/-	975	2500
2945	— R. Three Oxford plumes above, 1642; mm. plume/-	950	2200
2945A	— — 1643; *mm.* plume/-	925	2250

		F	VF
		£	£
2946	**Crown.** Shrewsbury die with groundline. R. Three Oxford plumes,		
	1642; no mm.	900	2250
2946A	— — 1643; no *mm.*	900	2250
2947	Oxford horseman, grass below. R. Three Oxford plumes, 1643; *mm.*		
	plume/-	1250	3750

2948

2948	Rawlins' crown. King riding over a view of the city. R. Floral scrolls		
	above and below Declaration, date in script, 1644 OXON; *mm.*		
	floriated cross/- *(Electrotypes and copies of this coin are common)*	12500	37500
2949	**Halfcrown.** *O.* Shrewsbury die with groundline, plume behind. R.		
	Oxford die, declaration in two lines, three Oxford plumes above,		
	1642 below; no *mm.*	525	1500
2950	— no plume behind. R. as last, 1642; *mm.* plume/-	450	1250
2951	Shrewsbury horseman with groundline, Oxford plume behind. R.		
	Shrewsbury die, 1642; *mm.* plume/-	400	1050
2952	— R. Three Oxford plumes, 1642; *mm.* plume/-	250	675
2953	— — without groundline, 1642; *mm.* plume/-	250	675

2954

2954	Oxford horseman without groundline, 1643; *mm.* plume/-.......................	225	650
2954A	— — R. Shrewsbury die, 1642; *mm.* plume/- or no *mm.*...........................	400	1050
2955	— with groundline. R. Three Oxford plumes, 1643; *mm.* plume/-	225	650
2956	Briot horseman, grassy, rocky or uneven ground. R. Three Oxford plumes,		
	1643; *mm.* plume/-, plume & rosette/-	250	700
2957	— — 1643 OX; *mm.* plume/rosette, rosette	275	725
2958	— — 1644 OX; *mm.* plume/-	275	725
2958A	— — lozenges by OX, 1644 OX; *mm.* plume/-	300	750

	F	VF
	£	£
2959 — — 1645 OX; *mm.* plume/-, plume/rosette	250	700
2959A— — pellets by date, 1645 OX; *mm.* plume/-	350	900
2960 — — 1646 OX; *mm.* plume/-	275	750
2961 — — pellets or annulets by plumes and date, 1646 OX; *mm.* plume/- ...	325	800
2962 — R. Large central plume and two Oxford plumes, 1643; *mm.* plume/- .	300	750
2963 — — 1643 OX; *mm.* plume/-, rosette/-, plume & rosette/rosette, plume & rosette/-	275	725
2964 — — rosettes by OX, 1643 OX; *mm.* rosette/-, plume & rosette/-	325	825

2965   2965A

2965 — — plain, pellets or lozenges by plumes and/or OX, 1644 OX; *mm.* plume/- plume/rosette, rosette	250	675
2965A— — date in script, 1644 OX; *mm.* plume/-	275	725
2966 — — rosettes by plumes and date, 1644 OX; *mm.* plume & rosette/rosette	350	900
2967 — — small plumes by date, 1644 OX; *mm.* plume & rosette/-, rosette ..	450	1250
2968 — R. Large central plume and two small Shrewsbury plumes, lozenges in field, date in script, 1644 OX; *mm.* plume/rosette	450	1250
2969 — — small plumes by date, pellets by OX, 1644 OX; *mm.* plume/-	475	1350
2970 **Shilling.** O. Shrewsbury die. R. Declaration in three lines, three Oxford plumes above, 1642; *mm.* plume/-	675	2000
2971 Oxford bust (small). R. Three Oxford plumes, 1642; *mm.* Oxford plume/-,	275	750
2972 Oxford bust (small or large). R. Three Oxford plumes, 1643; *mm.* Oxford plume/-, Oxford plume/rosette	250	750
2972A— — pellets by date, 1644; *mm.* plume/-	275	800
2972B — — 1644 OX; *mm.* plume/rosette	275	800
2973 — R. Oxford and two Shrewsbury plumes, lozenges by date, 1644 OX; *mm.* plume/-	350	950

2974

2974 — R. Three Shrewsbury plumes, 1643; *mm.* plume/-	300	850

2975

	F £	VF £
2975 Fine Oxford bust. R. Three Oxford plumes, lozenges in field, 1644 OX; *mm.* Shrewsbury plume/-	300	900
2975A— — large date in script, 1644 OX; *mm.* plume/-	325	950
2976 — 1645 OX; *mm.* plume/-	875	2500
2976A— R. Oxford and two Shrewsbury plumes, 1644 OX; *mm.* plume/-	350	975
2977 — R. Three Shrewsbury plumes, 1644 OX; *mm.* plume/-	300	900
2978 — — annulets or pellets at date, 1646; *mm.* plume/floriated cross, plume/-	300	900
2979 Rawlins' die. Fine bust with R. on truncation. R. Three Oxford plumes, rosettes or lozenges by plumes, lozenges by date, 1644 OX; *mm.* Shrewsbury plume/rosette, Shrewsbury plume/-	475	1350
2979A— — pellets by date, no OX, 1644; *mm.* plume/-	500	1350
2979B — R. Oxford and two Shrewsbury plumes, 1644 OX; *mm.* plume/-	575	1500

2980

2980 **Sixpence.** O. Aberystwyth die R. Three Oxford plumes, 1642; *mm.* book/-	275	875
2980A— — 1643; *mm.* book/-	250	750
2981 — R. Three Shrewsbury plumes, 1643; *mm.* book/-...................................	250	675
2982 — R. Shrewsbury plume and two lis, 1644 OX (groat rev. die); *mm.* book/-	575	1350
2983 **Groat.** O. Aberystwyth die. R. Shrewsbury plume and two lis, 1644 OX; *mm.* book/-	175	525
2984 — R. Three Shrewsbury plumes, 1644 OX; mm. book/-	200	625

2985

| 2985 Oxford bust within inner circle. R. As 2983, 1644 OX; mm. floriated cross/- | 145 | 400 |

		F £	*VF* £
2985A—	R. Three Shrewsbury plumes, 1644 OX; *mm.* floriated cross/-	200	600
2985B—	R. Single plume, 2 scrolls and OX monogram over Decl, 1645; *mm.* floriated cross/-	225	650
2986	Large bust to top of coin. R. As 2983, 1644 OX; *mm.* lis/-	250	725
2987	Large bust to bottom of coin. R. As 2983, 1644 OX; no *mm.*	225	650
2988	— R. Single plume, 2 scrolls and OX monogram over Decl, 1645; no *mm.*	150	450
2989	Rawlins' die, no inner circle, R on shoulder. R. As 2983, 1644 OX; no *mm.*	225	675
2990	— R. Single plume, Declaration in cartouche, 1645; no *mm.*	200	575

2990

2991	— — 1646/5; no mm.	200	575
2992	**Threepence.** *O.* Aberystwyth die. R. Three lis over Declaration, 1644 OX; *mm.* book/-...................................	140	425
2993	Rawlins; die, R below shoulder. R. Aberystwyth die, oval shield; *mm.* lis/book..	140	425
2994	— R. Three lis over Declaration, 1644; *mm.* lis/-	110	275

2995   3000

2995	Crown breaks inner circle, no R. R. Three lis, 1646/4; *mm.* lis/-..............	110	275
2996	**Halfgroat.** Small bust, beaded or wireline inner circle. R. Large plume in field; *mm.* mullet/lis, lis, -/lis	110	275
2997	— R. Three lis over Delcration, 1644 OX; *mm.* lis................................	125	300
2998	**Penny.** *O.* Aberystwyth die, CARO. R. Small plume in field; *mm.* book/-	135	400
2999	Aberystwyth die, CAROLVS; R. Large plume; *mm.* book/-	150	425
3000	Rawlins' die, CARO. R. Small plume; *mm.* lis/mullet, lis/-	250	750
3001	Broad bust, CAROL. R. Small plume; *mm.* lis......................................	250	750
3002	— R. Three lis over Declaration, 1644; *mm.* lis	675	1750

Bristol mint, 1643-5. *Mm.* usually plume or Br., except on small denominations

3003	**Halfcrown.** *O.* Oxford die with or without ground-line. R. Declaration, three Bristol plumes above, 1643 below, *mm.* plume/- or plume/cross....	475	1350
3004	— Obv. as above. R as above, but *mm.* Br. 1643	525	1500
3005	King wears unusual flat crown, *obv. mm.* acorn? between four pellets. R. As 3003, 1643	425	1100
3006	— Obv. as above. R as 3004, *mm.* Br., 1643-4......................................	400	950
3007	Shrewsbury plume behind king. R. As last..	325	800
3008	— Obv. as above. R as 3004 but Br below date instead of as *mm* . 1644.	350	850

3009

		F	VF
		£	£
3009	— Obv. as 3007 but Br below horse. ℞ as above but 1644-5..................	325	800
3010	— Obv. as above. ℞ as 3004, *mm.* Br. and Br. below date, 1644-5.........	375	900
3011	**Shilling**. *O.* Oxford die. ℞. Declaration, 1643, 3 crude plumes above, no *mm.*	350	1050

3012   3014

3012	— — ℞ Similar, but *mm.* Br., 1643-4, less crude plumes........................	325	950
3013	—Obv. Coarse bust. ℞. As 3011, no *mm.*	375	1200
3014	— — Coarse bust, ℞. as 3012, *mm.* Br, but 1644	325	950

3015   3017

3015	Obv. Bust of good style, plumelet before face. ℞. As 3012 *mm.* Br. but 1644-5	275	750
3016	— — ℞.as 3012, 1644, but Br below date instead of *mm.*	300	850
3016A	— — ℞ as 3012, 1644 but plume and plumelet either side	275	750
3017	—Obv. Taller bust with high crown, no plumelets before, *mm.* Br. on its side. ℞ As 3016 Br.below 1644-5	325	950
3018	—Obv. As 3017 but no *mm.* ℞ as above but *mm.* Br., no Br. below 1644-5	350	1000
3018A	— — ℞ as above but plume and plumelets, 1645....................................	375	1200
3019	**Sixpence**. Small bust, nothing before. ℞. Declaration surrounded by CHRISTO etc., 1643; *mm.* ./Br..	425	1250

3020

	F £	VF £
3020 Fine style bust. Plumelet before face, 1644; *mm.* ./Br. (on its side)	275	625
3021 **Groat**. Bust l. R. Declaration, 1644...	200	525
3022 — Plumelet before face, 1644...	175	475
3023 — Br. below date, 1644	175	475
3023A— Similar, but larger bust and more spread plume before. Mm. pellet/Br; nothing below 1644..	185	500

| 3024 | 3026 | 3027 |

3024 **Threepence**. *O*. As 2992. Aberystwyth die; *mm.* book. R. Declaration, 1644	165	450
3025 Bristol die, plume before face, no *mm.*, 1644	225	625
3026 **Halfgroat**. Br. in place of date below Declaration	250	675
3027 **Penny**. Similar bust, I behind. R. Large plume with bands.....................	325	850

This penny may belong to the late declaration issue. It has the same reverse plume punch as 3044.

Late 'Declaration' issues, 1645-6

After Bristol surrendered on 11 September 1645, many of the Royalist garrison returned unsearched to Oxford and the Bristol moneyers appear to have continued work, using altered Bristol dies and others of similar type bearing the marks A, B and plume. Ashby de la Zouch was reinforced from Oxford in September 1645 and, following its fall on 28 February 1645/6, Royalist forces marched to Bridgnorth-on-Severn, holding out until 26 April 1646. Mr Boon has suggested (cf. SCBI 33, p. xli) that Ashby and Bridgnorth are plausible mint sites and the most likely candidates for the A and B marked issues, if these do indeed represent fixed mint locations.

Ashby de la Zouch mint (?), 1645

3028

3028 **Halfcrown**. Horseman of Bristol type, A below. R. Altered Bristol die. A (over Br) below date, 1645; *mm.* plume/A (over Br)	2000	6500

		F	*VF*
		£	£
3029	- - R. A below date (new die), 1645; *mm.* plume/A	2000	6500
3030	- - R. Nothing below date 1645; *mm.* plume/A..........................	1750	5250
3031	**Shilling.** Crowned bust left. R. Declaration type, A below date, 1645; mm. plume/A	750	2250

3032

3032	- plumelet before face, 1645; *mm.* plume/A	825	2500
3033	**Sixpence.** Bust of Bristol style, plumelet before face. R. Declaration type, 1645; *mm.* A (on its side)/-	750	1850
3034	**Groat.** Similar, plumelet before face, 1645; *mm.* A (on its side)/-	675	1650
3035	**Threepence.** Similar, plumelet before face. R. Single plumelet above Declaration, 1645; no *mm.*	475	1100

Bridgnorth-on-Severn mint (?), 1646

3036	Halfcrown. Horseman of Bristol type, A below (same die as 3028-30). R. Scroll above Declaration, B below, 1646; *mm.* plume/A	1850	6000
3036A	- - R. Nothing below date, 1646; *mm.* plume/-	1500	4250
3037	- plumelet (over A) below horse (same die as 3028-30 recut). R. Nothing below date, 1646; *mm.* plume, plume/-	875	2500

3038

3038	- - plumelet below date, 1646; *mm.* plume	875	2500
3039	**Shilling.** Crowned bust left, plumelet before face (same die as 3032). R. Scroll above Declaration, 1646; *mm.* plume/plumelet	375	1100
3039A	- Bristol obverse die, nothing before face. R. Scroll above Declaration, 1646; *mm.* Br/-	475	1250
3040	- - plume before face (altered die of 3039A), 1646; *mm.* plumelet (over Br)/-	425	1200

3041

	F £	VF £

3041 **Sixpence.** Crowned bust left, plume before face. R. Scroll above Declaration, 1646; *mm.* B/- ... 250 575

3042 **Groat.** Similar, plumelet before face, 1646; *mm.* plumelet, plumelet/- ... 200 475

3043 **Threepence.** Similar, plumelet before face. R. Single plume above Declaration, 1646; *mm.* plumelet/- ... 175 425

3044 **Halfgroat.** Crowned bust left, II behind. R. Large plume with bands dividing date, 1646; no *mm.* ... 425 1000

Truro mint, 1642-3. *Mm.* rose except where stated

3045 **Crown.** King on horseback, head in profile, sash flies out in two ends. R. CHRISTO, etc., round garnished shield ... 275 750

3046 **Halfcrown.** King on walking horse, groundline below, R. Oblong shield, CR above, *mm.* bugle/– ... 950 2750

3047 Galloping horse, king holds baton. R. Oblong shield, CR at sides ... 1750 6000

3048   3052

3048 Walking horse, king holds sword. R. Similar ... 850 2350

3049 — R. Similar, but CR above ... 850 2350

3050 Galloping horse, king holds sword. R. Similar, but CR at sides ... 1100 3250

3051 — R. Similar, but CR above ... 1200 3500

3052 Trotting horse. R. Similar, but CR at sides ... 675 1750

3053 **Shilling.** Small bust of good style. R. Oblong shield ... 2250 6500

Exeter mint, 1643-6. Undated or dated 1644-5 *Mm.* rose except where stated

3054 **Half-pound.** King on horseback, face towards viewer, sash in large bow. R. CHRISTO, etc., round garnished shield. Struck from crown dies of 3055 on a thick flan ... 2500 8500

3055 **Crown.** King on horseback, sash in large bow. R. Round garnished shield ... 350 850

F	*VF*
£	£

3056 — Shield garnished with twelve even scrolls 375 975
3057 As 3055, ℞ Date divided by *mm.* 16 rose 44 .... 400 1000
3058 — ℞ Date to l. of *mm.* 1644 .... 325 825
3059 — *mm*: rose/EX, 1645 .... 400 1000
3060 King's sash flies out in two ends; *mm.* castle/rose, 1645 .... 525 1350
3061 — *mm.* castle/EX, 1645 .... 325 850
3062 — *mm.* castle, 1645 .... 300 800
3063 **Halfcrown.** King on horseback, sash tied in bow. ℞. Oblong shield
CR at sides 650 1750
3064 — ℞. Round shield with eight even scrolls 275 725

3065   3067

3065 — ℞. Round shield with five short and two long scrolls 250 625
3066 — ℞. Oval shield with angular garnish of triple lines 750 2000

3071

3067 Briot's horseman with lumpy ground. ℞. As 3064 .... 450 1100
3068 — ℞. As 3065 .... 375 900
3069 — ℞. As 3066 .... 750 2000
3070 — ℞. As 3065, date to l. of *mm.* 1644 .... 475 1200
3071 King on spirited horse galloping over arms. ℞. Oval garnished
shield, 1642 in cartouche below 3250 9000
3072 — ℞. As 3070, date to l. of *mm.* 1644-5 .... 3250 10500
3073 — ℞. *mm.* castle, 1645 .... 3500 12000
3074 Short portly king, leaning backwards on ill-proportioned horse,
1644, 16 rose 44 .... 675 1850
3075 Horse with twisted tail, sash flies out in two ends ℞. As 3064 .... 475 1200

3076

	F £	VF £

3076— R. As 3070, date divided by *mm.* 16 rose 44, or date to 1. of *mm.*
1644-5 .... | 450 | 1100 |
3077 — R. *mm.* castle, 1645 .... | 525 | 1250 |
3078 — R. *mm.* EX, 1645 .... | 575 | 1350 |
3079 — R. Declaration type; *mm.* EX. 1644-5 .... | 1750 | 4500 |
3080 — R. Similar, EX also below declaration, 1644 .... | 1600 | 4250 |
3081 **Shilling.** Large Oxford style bust. R. Round shield with eight even
scrolls .... | 850 | 2500 |
3082 — R. Oval shield with CR at sides .... | 850 | 2500 |
3083 Normal bust with lank hair. R. As 3081 .... | 675 | 1650 |
3083A— R. As 3082 .... | 725 | 1850 |
3084 — R. Round shield with six scrolls .... | 475 | 1000 |

3085   3087A

3085 — R. Similar, date 1644, 45 to left of rose *mm.* 16 rose 44 (rare),
1644 to right of rose (very rare) .... | 350 | 900 |
3086 — R. Declaration type, 1645 .... | 900 | 2750 |
3087 **Sixpence.** Similar to 3085, large bust and letters 1644 rose ..... | 275 | 675 |
3087A— Smaller bust and letters from punches used on 3088, small or large
VI, 16 rose 44 .... | 275 | 725 |
3088 **Groat.** Somewhat similar but 1644 at beginning of *obv.* legend.......... | 110 | 285 |

3089   3091   3092

3089 **Threepence.** Similar. R. Square shield, 1644 above .... | 110 | 275 |
3090 **Halfgroat.** Similar, but II. R. Oval shield, 1644 .... | 200 | 575 |
3091 — R. Large rose, 1644 .... | 225 | 600 |
3092 **Penny.** As last but I behind head .... | 275 | 900 |

	F	VF
	£	£

Worcester mint 1643-4

3093 **Halfcrown**. King on horseback l., W below; *mm.* two lions. R. Declaration
type 1644 altered from 1643 Bristol die; *mm.* pellets 1350 3500
3094 — R. Square-topped shield; *mm.* helmet, castle 750 2000
3095 — R. Oval shield; *mm.* helmet.. 850 2250

3096

3096 Similar but grass indicated; *mm.* castle. R. Square-topped shield; *mm.*
helmet or pellets. 675 1850
3097 — R. Oval draped shield, lis or lions in legend..................................... 725 2000
3098 — R. Oval shield CR at sides, roses in legend 725 2000
3099 — R. FLORENT etc., oval garnished shield with lion's paws each side . 825 2250
3100 Tall king, no W or *mm.* R. Oval shield, lis, roses, lions or stars in legend 650 1850
3101 — R. Square-topped shield; *mm.* helmet 700 2000
3102 — R. FLORENT, etc., oval shield; no *mm.* 825 2250
3103 Briot type horse, sword slopes forward, ground-line. R. Oval shield, roses
in legend; *mm.* 91v, 105, none (combinations).. 700 2000
3104 — Similar, but CR at sides, 91v/- 800 2250
3105 Dumpy, portly king, crude horse. R. As 3100; *mm.* 91v, 105, none......... 825 2250

3106

3106 Thin king and horse. R. Oval shield, stars in legend; *mm.* 91v, none...... 650 1850

Worcester or Salopia (Shrewsbury) 1643-4

3107 **Shilling**. Bust of king l., adequately rendered. R. Square-topped shield;
mm. castle.. 875 2750
3108 — R. CR above shield; *mm.* helmet and lion... 875 2750
3109 — R. Oval shield; *mm.* lion, pear... 825 2500

	F £	VF £
3110 — Bust a somewhat crude copy of last (two varieties); *mm*. bird, lis. R. Square-topped shield with lion's paws above and at sides; *mm*. boar's head, helmet	950	3000

3111

3111 — — CR above...	900	3000
3112 — R. Oval shield, lis in legend; *mm*. lis	800	2500
3113 — R. Round shield; *mm*. lis, 3 lis	750	2250
3114 Bust r.; *mm*. pear/-, pear/lis. R. draped oval shield with or without CR. (Halfcrown reverse dies)	1750	5250
3115 **Sixpence**. As 3110; *mm*. castle, castle/boar's hd	750	2250

3116   3117

3116 **Groat**. As 3112; *mm*. lis/helmet, rose/helmet...........................	525	1200
3117 **Threepence**. Similar; *mm*. lis	275	650
3118 **Halfgroat**. Similar; *mm*. lis (*O*.) various (*R*.)	475	1000

Salopia (Shrewsbury) mint, 1644

3119 **Halfcrown**. King on horseback l. SA below; *mm*. lis. R. (*mm*. lis, helmet, lion rampant, none). Cr. oval shield; CHRISTO etc. *mm*. helmet	2500	8500
3120 — R. FLORENT, etc., crowned oval shield, no *mm*.	2500	8500
3121 — SA erased or replaced by large pellet or cannon ball; *mm*. lis in legend, helmet. R. As 3119...	1350	4250
3122 Tall horse and king, nothing below; *mm*. lis. R. Large round shield with crude garniture; *mm*. helmet..	825	2250
3123 — R. Uncrowned square-topped shield with lion's paw above and at sides; *mm*. helmet...	850	2500
3124 — R. Small crowned oval shield; *mm*. various.......................	800	2000

3125

		F	VF
		£	£
3125	— R. As 3120..	825	2250
3126	Finer work with little or no mane before horse. R. Cr. round or oval shield	850	2500
3127	Grass beneath horse. R. Similar; *mm.* lis or rose	950	3250
3128	Ground below horse. R. As 3120...	1000	3500

Hartlebury Castle (Worcs.) mint, 1646

3129

| 3129 | **Halfcrown**. *O. Mm*. pear. R. HC (Hartlebury Castle) in garniture below shield; *mm.* three pears... | 1250 | 3250 |

Chester mint, 1644

3130

| 3130 | **Halfcrown**. As illus. R. Oval shield; *mm.* three gerbs and sword .... | 850 | 2250 |
| 3131 | — Similar, but without plume or CHST; R. Cr. oval shield with lion skin; *mm.* prostrate gerb; -/cinquefoil, ⁻/⁑ .... | 800 | 2250 |

F	*VF*
£	£

3132 — R. Crowned square-topped shield with CR at sides both crowned *rev.*;
   mm. cinquefoil (these dies were later crudely recut) 1000   3250

3133 As 3130, but without plume or CHST. R. Declaration type, 1644 *rev.*; *mm.*
   plume.. 950   2750

3133A **Shilling**. Bust l. R. Oval garnished shield; *mm.* ∴ (obv. only) 875   3000

3133B — R. Square-topped shield; *mm.* as last 900   3000

3133C — R . Shield over long cross 900   3000

3134 **Threepence**. R. Square-topped shield; *mm.*-/ prostrate gerb.................... 875   2650

Welsh Marches mint? 1644

3135

3135 **Halfcrown**. Crude horseman, l. R. Declaration of Bristol style divided by a
   dotted line, 3 plumes above, 1644 below 750   1850

Carlisle besieged, 1644-5

3136 **Three shillings**. Large crown above C R between rosettes III. S below. *rev.*
   OBS . CARL / . 1645, rosette below... 5250   12500

3137   3139

3137 Similar but :- OBS :/-: CARL :./.1645, rosette above and below 5000   12000

3138 **Shilling**. Large crown above C R between trefoil of pellets, XII below.
   rev. as 3137 3500   8500

3139 R. Legend and date in two lines.. 3750   9500

   Note. *(3136-39) Round or Octagonal pieces exist.*

Newark besieged, several times 1645-6, surrendered May 1646

3140   3144

	F	VF
	£	£
3140 **Halfcrown**. Large crown between CR ; below, XXX. *rev.* OBS / NEWARK / 1645	750	1750
3140A— Similar 1646	625	1500
3141 **Shilling**. Similar but crude flat shaped crown, NEWARKE, 1645	575	1350
3142 Similar but normal arched crown, 1645	525	1100
3143 — NEWARK, 1645 or 1646	525	1050
3144 **Ninepence**. As halfcrown but IX, 1645 or 1646	450	1000
3145 — NEWARKE, 1645	475	1050

3146

3146 **Sixpence**. As halfcrown but VI, 1646	550	1350

Pontefract besieged, June 1648-March 1648-9

3147 **Two shillings** (lozenge shaped). DVM : SPIRO : SPERO around CR crowned. R. Castle surrounded by OBS, PC, sword and 1648	4500	13500

3148

		F	VF
		£	£
3148	**Shilling** (lozenge shaped, octagonal or round). Similar	1250	3250

3149   3150

3149	— Similar but XII on r. dividing PC	1000	2750

After the death of Charles I (30 Jan. 1648/9), in the name of Charles II

3150	**Shilling** (octagonal). *O.* As last. Ɍ. CAROLVS : SECVИDVS : 1648, castle gateway with flag dividing PC, OBS on l., cannon protrudes on r..........	1100	3000
3151	CAROL : II : etc., around HANC : DE / VS : DEDIT 1648. Ɍ. POST : MORTEM : PATRIS : PRO : FILIO around gateway etc. as last............	1350	3500

Scarborough besieged, July 1644-July 1645

3156	3165	3169

VF

Type I. Large Castle with gateway to left, SC and value Vs below

3152	**Crown.** (various weights)..	35000

Type II. Small Castle with gateway, no SC, value punched on flan

3153	**Five shillings and eightpence.**	22500
3154	**Crown.** Similar..	30000
3155	**Three shillings.** Similar	16500
3156	**Two shillings and tenpence.** Similar.............................	13500
3157	**Two shillings and sevenpence.** Similar..........................	13500
3158	**Halfcrown.** Similar..	22500
3159	**Two shillings and fourpence.** Similar............................	13500
3161	**One shilling and ninepence.** *Struck from a different punch, possibly of later manufacture....................*	
3162	**One shilling and sixpence.** Similar to 3159	12000
3163	**One shilling and fourpence.** Similar............................	12000
3164	**One shilling and threepence.** Similar..........................	12000
3165	**Shilling.** Similar..	17500
3166	**Sixpence.** Similar...	13500
3167	**Groat.** Similar	12500

Type III. Castle gateway with two turrets, value punched below

3168	**Two shillings and twopence**	9000
3169	**Two shillings.** Castle punched twice..............................	9000
3170	**One shilling and sixpence.** Similar to 3168	8500
3171	**One shilling and fourpence.** Similar............................	8500
3172	**One shilling and threepence.** Similar..........................	8500
3173	**One shilling and twopence.** Similar..............................	7500
3174	**One shilling and one penny.** Similar	7500
3175	**Shilling.** Similar..	10000
3176	**Elevenpence.** Similar	7250
3177	**Tenpence.** Similar	7250
3178	**Ninepence.** Similar...	7250
3178A	**Eightpence.** Similar..	6500
3179	**Sevenpence.** Similar..	6500
3180	**Sixpence.** Similar..	9000

COPPER

For further details see C. Wilson Peck, *English Copper, Tin and Bronze Coins in the British Museum, 1558-1958.*

3181   3183

		F	*VF*
		£	£
3181	**Royal farthing**. 'Richmond' 1a, colon stops, CARO over IACO; *mm.* on *obv.* only; *mm:* Coronet, Crescent with mullet, Dagger, Mascle..	12	24
3182	—— 1b. CARA; (Contemporary forgeries manufactured from official punches. Usually F for E in REX) *mm.* on *obv.* only; *mm:* Annulet, Coronet, Cross patée fourchée, Dagger, Fusil, Key, Mascle, Trefoil, Tun	100	200
3183	—— 1c. CARO; *mm.* on *obv.* only; *mm:* A, A with pellet, Annulet, Annulet with pellet within, Bell, Book, Cinquefoil, Crescent (large and small), Cross (pellets in angles), Cross calvary, Cross patée, Cross patée fitchée, Cross patonce, Cross patonce in saltire, Cross saltire, Dagger, Ermine, Estoile, Estoile (pierced), Eye, Fish hook, Fleece, Fusil, Fusils (two), Gauntlet, Grapes, Halberd, Harp, Heart, Horseshoe, Leaf, Lion passant, Lis (large), Lis (demi), Lis (three), Martlet, Mascle with pellet within, Nautilus, Rose (single), Shield, Spearhead, Tower, Trefoil, Woolpack, Woolpack over annulet..	8	20

3184   3185

3184	—— 1d, apostrophe stops, eagle-headed harp, *mm.* on *obv.* only; *mm:* Crescent (large), Lion rampant, Rose (double), Trefoil............................	10	20
3185	— 1e. Beaded harp, *mm* Rose (double) on *obv.* only................................	8	20
3186	— 1f. Scroll-fronted harp, 5 jewels on circlet *mm* Rose (double) on *obv.* only..	12	35
3187	— 1g. Scroll-fronted harp, 7 jewels on circlet *mm* Rose (double) on *obv.* only..	6	18

3187A

	F £	VF £
3187A— 1g on uncut square flan	150	300
— Longer strips of two to nine farthings also exist	*Extremely Rare*	

3188   3192

3188	Transitional issue 2, double-arched crowns *mm* on *obv*. only; *mm:* Harp, Quatrefoil	18	45
3189	'Maltravers' 3a; inner circles *mm*. on *obv*. only; *mm:* Bell, Rose (double) Woolpack	18	45
3190	— 3b. *mm*. both sides; *mm:* Bell, Cross patée, Lis (large), Lis (small), Martlet, Rose (double), Woolpack	8	20
3191	— 3c. Different *mm*. on each side; *mm:* Bell/Cross patée fitchée, Cross patée fitchée/Bell, Harp/Bell, Harp/Billet, Harp/Woolpack, Lis/Portcullis Martlet/Bell, Woolpack/Portcullis, Woolpack/Rose (double).	8	20
3192	'Richmond' oval. 4a. CARO over IACO; legend starts at bottom left, *mm:* Cross patéee on both sides.	45	90
3193	— 4a, *mm*. Cross patée on *obv*. only	45	90

3194   3200

3194	— 4b. CARO, colon stops; *mm*. Lis (demi) on *obv*. only	30	60
3195	— — *mm*. on *rev*. only; *mm:* Martlet, Millrind	30	60
3196	— — *mm*. on both sides; *mm:* Crescent/Crescent, Scroll/Scroll, 9/9, Lis (demi)/Scroll	30	60
3197	— 4c. apostrophe stops; *mm*. Rose (double) on *obv*. only	30	60
3198	— — *mm*. Rose (double) both sides	45	90
3199	— — *mm*. Rose (double) on *obv*.; Scroll on *rev*.	30	60
3200	'Maltravers' oval. 5, no inner circles, legend starts bottom left, *mm*. Lis (large) on both sides	75	150

3192 to 3200, the oval farthings, were originally issued for use in Ireland

		F	VF
		£	£
3201	**Rose farthing**. 1a. Double-arched crowns; sceptres within inner circle, BRIT; *mm.* on *obv.* or *rev.* or both; *mm:* Lis, Cross pattée......................	12	25
3202	— 1b. similar but sceptres just cross inner circle, BRIT; *mm.* Lis on *obv.* or both sides or not present.	10	20
3203	— 1c. similar but sceptres almost to outer circle, BRIT; *mm.*s as 3201 ...	12	25

3204   3207

3204	— 1d. similar but BRI; *mm.* on *obv.* or *rev.* or both sides or different each side; *mm:* Lis, Mullet, Cross pattée	10	20
3205	Transitional mules of 1d or (rarely) 1c and 2, double and single arched crowns; *mm.* as 3204; *mm:* Lis, Mullet, Crescent.....................................	6	18
3206	— 2. Single-arched crowns; *mm.* as 3204..	4	12
3207	— 3. Sceptres below crown; *mm.* Mullet on both sides............................	30	50

The coins struck during the Commonwealth have inscriptions in English instead of Latin which was considered to savour too much of popery. St. George's cross and the Irish harp take the place of the royal arms. The silver halfpenny was issued for the last time. Coins with *mm.* anchor were struck during the protectorship of Richard Cromwell.

Mintmarks

1649-57 Sun ☼   1658-60 Anchor ⚓

GOLD

	3208			3209	
	F £	VF £		F £	VF £
3208 Unite. As illustration; *mm.* sun,					
1649	1250	3000	1654	1100	2750
1650	1200	2850	1655	1750	4750
1651	1000	2650	1656	1450	3750
1652	1200	2850	1657	1250	3000
1653	1000	2650			
3209 Similar, *mm.* anchor,					
1658	2500	6750	1660	2350	6000
3210 Double-crown. Similar; but X; *mm.* sun,					
1649	900	2000	1654	825	1850
1650	725	1650	1655	1350	3250
1651	675	1450	1656	1100	2500
1652	900	2000	1657	1450	3500
1653	675	1450			
3211 Similar, *mm.* anchor, 1660				1850	5000

3212

3212 Crown. Similar, but V; *mm.* sun,					
1649	700	1650	1654	675	1500
1650	650	1350	1655	925	2650
1651	675	1450	1656	900	2500
1652	650	1350	1657	900	2500
1653	650	1350			

| | F | VF | | F | VF |
| | £ | £ | | £ | £ |

3213 Similar *mm.* anchor,

    1658 1650   4500   1660 1850   5250

SILVER

3215

3214 **Crown.** Same type; *mm.* sun,

    1649 1850   5250   1653 650   1450

    1651 1250   3250   1654 750   1750

    1652 700   1600   1656 675   1500

3215 **Halfcrown.** Similar; *mm.* sun,

    1649 425   1250   1654 275   725

    1651 275   725   1655 750   2500

    1652 275   750   1656 225   525

    1653 225   525   1657 1350   3250

3216 Similar, *mm.* anchor

    1658 850   2000   1660 850   2000

    1659 2250   6000

3217 **Shilling.** Similar; *mm.* sun,

    1649 185   500   1654 145   350

    1651 135   350   1655 250   750

    1652 140   350   1656 145   350

    1653 135   325   1657 400   1000

3218

3218 Similar, *mm.* anchor

    1658 450   1200   1660 450   1200

    1659 1750   5000

	F £	VF £		F £	VF £
3219 **Sixpence.** Similar; *mm.* sun,					
1649	125	375	1654	110	325
1651	110	325	1655	275	850
1652	110	325	1656	110	325
1653	100	300	1657	300	900
3220 Similar; *mm.* anchor,					
1658	400	1000	1660	400	1000
1659	850	2250			

3221   3222

		F £	VF £
3221 **Halfgroat.**		25	75
3222 **Penny.** Similar, but I above shields		20	60

3223

		F £	VF £
3223 **Halfpenny.**		20	50

Oliver Cromwell, 'the Great Emancipator' was born on 25th April 1599 in Huntingdon. He married Elizabeth Bourchier in August 1620 and had nine children seven of whom survived infancy. The Protectorate was established on 16th December 1653, with work on the production of portrait coins authorised in 1655. Although often referred to as patterns, there is in fact nothing to suggest that the portrait coins of Oliver Cromwell were not intended for circulation. Authorised in 1656, the first full production came in 1657 and was followed by a second more plentiful one before Cromwell's death on 3rd September 1658. All coins were machine made, struck from dies by Thomas Simon in the presses of the Frenchman, Pierre Blondeau. Later, some of Simon's puncheons were sold in the Low Countries and an imitation Crown was made there. Other Dutch dies were prepared and some found their way back to the Mint, where in 1738 it was decided to strike a set of Cromwell's coins. Shillings and Sixpences were struck from the Dutch dies, and Crowns from new dies prepared by John Tanner. Thomas Simon who was born in 1618, later died in the Great Plague of 1665. Oliver was succeeded as Lord Protector by his son Richard of whom no coins were struck.

GOLD

	F	VF	EF
	£	£	£

3224 **Fifty shillings**. Laur. head l. R. Crowned Shield of the Protectorate,
die axis ↑↓ 1656. .... 6000 16000 35000
Inscribed edge PROTECTOR · LITERIS · LITERÆ · NUMMIS · CORONA · ET · SALUS

3225
1656 gold Broad

3225 **Broad.** of Twenty Shillings. Laur. head l. R. Crowned Shield of the
Protectorate, but grained edge die axis ↑↓ 1656. .... 4000 6500 12500

SILVER

3226
1658 Crown 8 over 7 - Die flawed drapery

3226	**Crown.** Dr. bust l. R. Crowned shield, 1658/7. Inscribed edge ↑↓	1750	3000	4750
3226A	**Crown.** Dutch copy, similar with AИG legend 1658	1950	3750	7500
3226B	**Crown.** Tanner's copy (struck 1738) dated 1658	1850	3500	7000

	F £	VF £	EF £

3227   **Halfcrown.** Dr. bust l. R. Crowned shield 1656 HI type legend die axis ↑↓   2000   3500   6000

3227A
1658 Halfcrown with HIB obverse legend

3227A Halfcrown. Similar,1658 HIB type legend die axis ↑↓   950   1750   3000

3228
1658 Shilling

3228   **Shilling.** Dr. bust l. R. Crowned shield, grained edge, 1658 die axis ↑↓   500   1000   1950
3229   **Sixpence.** Similar 1658 die axis ↑↓ ....   *Extremely rare*

COPPER

3230
Copper portrait Farthing

3230   **Farthing.** Dr. bust l. R. CHARITIE AND CHANGE, shield ↑↓ .   3000   6500   —
There are also other reverse types for this coin.

For the first two years after the Restoration the same denominations, apart from the silver crown, were struck as were issued during the Commonwealth although the threepence and fourpence were soon added. Then, early in 1663, the ancient hand hammering process was finally superceded by the machinery of Blondeau.

For the emergency issues struck in the name of Charles II in 1648/9, see the siege pieces of Pontefract listed under Charles I, nos. 3150-1.

Hammered coinage, 1660-2

Mintmark: Crown.

3301   3302

GOLD

		F	VF
First issue. Without mark of value; *mm.* crown on *obv.* only		£	£
3301	**Unite** (20s.). Type as illustration	1350	4500
3302	**Double-crown**. As illustration	875	2650
3303	**Crown**. Similar	825	2500

3303   3304

Second issue. With mark of value; *mm.* crown on *obv.* only			
3304	**Unite**. Type as illustration	1200	2850
3305	**Double-crown**. As illustration	800	2250
3306	**Crown**. Similar	825	2500

SILVER

3307

		F	*VF*
		£	£

First issue. Without inner circles or mark of value; *mm.* crown on *obv.* only

3307 **Halfcrown.** Crowned bust, as 3308 900   3000

3308   3309

		F	*VF*
3308	**Shilling.** Similar	325	1100
3309	**Sixpence.** Similar	275	850
3310	**Twopence.** Similar	35	100
3311	**Penny.** Similar	35	95
3312	As last, but without mintmark	45	125

3313   3322

Second issue. Without inner circles, but with mark of value; *mm.* crown on *obv.* only

		F	*VF*
3313	**Halfcrown.** Crowned bust	950	3250
3314	**Shilling.** Similar	425	1250
3315	**Sixpence.** Similar	875	3000
3316	**Twopence.** Similar, but mm. on obv. only	75	275

3310 3317 3326

	F £	VF £
3317 Similar, but mm. both sides (machine made)	20	60
3318 Bust to edge of coin, legend starts at bottom l. (machine made, single arch crown)	20	50
3319 **Penny.** As 3317	25	70
3320 As 3318 (single arch crown)	20	50

3321

Third issue. With inner circles and mark of value; *mm.* crown on both sides

3321 **Halfcrown.** Crowned bust to i.c. (and rarely to edge of coin)	175	600
3322 **Shilling.** Similar, rarely *mm.* crown on *obv.* only	145	425
3323 **Sixpence.** Similar	125	350
3324 **Fourpence.** Similar	25	70
3325 **Threepence.** Similar	25	60
3326 **Twopence.** Similar	20	45
3327 **Penny.** Similar	20	45

Grading of Early and Later Milled Coinage

Milled coinage refers to coins that are struck by dies worked in a mechanical coining press. The early period is defined from the time of the successful installation of Peter Blondeau's hand powered machinery at the mint, initiated to strike the first portrait coins of Oliver Cromwell in 1656. The early period continuing until the advent of Matthew Boulton's steam powered presses from 1790. The coinage of this early period is therefore cruder in it's execution than the latter. When pricing coins of the early peiod, we only attribute grades as high as extremely fine, and as high as uncirculated for the latter period. Most coins that occur of the early period in superior grades than those stated will command considerably higher prices, due to their rarity. We suggest the following definitions for grades of preservation:

Milled Coinage Conditions

Proof   A very carefully struck coin from specially prepared dies, to give a superior definition to the design, with mirror-like fields. Occurs occasionally in the Early Milled Coinage, more frequently in the latter period. Some issues struck to a matt finish for Edward VII.

FDC   *Fleur-de-coin.* Absolutely flawless, untouched, without wear, scratches, marks or hairlines. Generally applied to proofs.

UNC   *Uncirculated.* A coin in as new condition as issued by the Mint, retaining full lustre or brilliance but, owing to modern mass-production methods of manufacture and storage, not necessarily perfect.

EF   *Extremely Fine.* A coin that exhibits very little sign of circulation, with only minimal marks or faint wear, which are only evident upon very close scrutiny.

VF   *Very Fine.* A coin that exhibits some wear on the raised surfaces of the design, but really has only had limited circulation.

F   *Fine.* A coin that exhibits considerable wear to the raised surfaces of the design, either through circulation, or damage perhaps due to faulty striking

Fair   *Fair.* A coin that exhibits wear, with the main features still distinguishable, and the legends, date and inscriptions still readable.

Poor   *Poor.* A coin that exhibits considerable wear, certainly with milled coinage of no value to a collector unless it is an extremely rare date or variety.

Examples of Condition Grading

Early Milled

Gold N Silver R Copper $Æ$

Extremely Fine

Gold A̸   Silver Æ   Copper Æ

Very Fine

Fine

*George III
fifth bust Guinea*

*James II
Second bust Crown*

*George II
old head Halfpenny*

Later Milled

Gold A̸   Silver Æ   Copper Æ

Uncirculated

Later Milled *continued*

Gold Aʋ   Silver Æ   Copper Æ

Extremely Fine

Very Fine

Fine

Victoria
Jubilee head Half-Sovereign

George IV
laureate bust Crown

Victoria
Young head Farthing

Charles II was born at St James Palace on 29th May 1630. He spent a long exile in France and returned after the fall of the Protectorate in 1660. The Restoration commenced and he married Catherine of Braganza, but he bore no legitimate successor. Charles II died on 6th February 1685.

Early in 1663, the ancient hand hammering process was finally superceded by the machinery of Blondeau. John and Joseph Roettier, two brothers, engraved the dies with a safeguard against clipping, the larger coins were made with the edge inscribed DECVS ET TVTAMEN and the regnal year. The medium-sized coins were given a grained edge.

The new gold coins were current for 100s., 40s., 20s. and 10s., and they came to be called 'Guineas' as the gold from which some of them were made was imported from Guinea by the Africa Company (whose badge was the Elephant and Castle). It was not until some years later that the Guinea increased in value to 21s. and more. The Africa Co. badge is also found on some silver and so is the plume symbol indicating silver from the Welsh mines. The four smallest silver denominations, though known today as 'Maundy Money', were actually issued for general circulation: at this period the silver penny was probably the only coin distributed at the Royal Maundy ceremonies. Though never part of the original agreement, smaller coins were eventually also struck by machinery.

A good regal copper coinage was issued for the first time in 1672, but later in the reign, farthings were struck in tin (with a copper plug) in order to help the Cornish tin industry.

Engravers and designers: John Roettier (1631-1700), Thomas Simon (1618-1665)

GOLD

3328
1669 First bust type Five-Guineas

Milled coinage

	F £	VF £	EF £		F £	VF £	EF £
3328 Five Guineas. First laur. bust r., pointed trun., regnal year on edge in words, die axis ↑↓							
(e.g. 1669=VICESIMO PRIMO), R. Crowned cruciform shields, sceptres in angles							
1668 VICESIMO	1250	3750	8000	1671 – TERTIO	1600	4250	9150
1668 V. PRIMO	3000	7500	—	1672 – QVARTO	1500	4500	9000
1669 – PRIMO	1250	3750	8000	1673 – QVINTO	1250	3750	8000
1670 – SECVNDO	1150	3350	7750	1674 – SEXTO	1850	4750	9750
1670 – Similar proof *FDC*	*Extremely rare*						

3328A Five Guineas. First bust. Similar hair of different style. Shorter ties

	F	VF	EF		F	VF	EF
1675 V. SEPTIMO	1600	4250	9150	1677 – NONO	1250	3750	8000
1676 – SEPTIMO	1750	5000	9500	1678/7 – TRICESIMO	1250	3750	8000
1676 – OCTAVO	1500	4500	9000				

3329 Five Guineas. First bust with elephant below, similar die axis ↑↓

	F	VF	EF		F	VF	EF
1668 VICESIMO	1000	3000	7000	1675 V. SEPTIMO	1650	4500	9250
1669 – PRIMO	1850	4750	9750	1677/5 – NONO		*Extremely rare*	

3330
1677 Five-Guineas with elephant and castle provenance mark

	F	VF	EF			F	VF	EF
	£	£	£			£	£	£

3330 Five Guineas. First bust with elephant and castle below, similar die axis ↑↓

1675 – SEPTIMO	*Extremely rare*		1677 – NONO	1500	4000	9000
1676 – OCTAVO	1250	3750	8000	1678/7 – TRICESIMO	1500	4000	9000

3331 Five Guineas. Second laur. bust r., rounded trun. similar die axis ↑↓

1678/7 TRICESIMO	1400	3750	8500	1682 T. QVARTO	1150	3500	8000
1679 – PRIMO	1200	3650	8000	1683 – QVINTO	1100	3350	7750
1680 – SECVNDO	1200	3750	8000	1683/2—QVINTO	1500	4000	8750
1681 – TERTIO	1250	3750	8000	1684 – SEXTO	1200	3250	7750

3332 Five Guineas. Second laur. bust r., with elephant and castle below, similar die axis ↑↓

1680 T. SECVNDO	*Extremely rare*		1683 T. QVINTO	2000	5000	10000
1681 – TERTIO	2000	5000	10000	1684 – SEXTO	1250	3500	8000
1682 – QVARTO	1250	3750	8000				

3333   3334
1664 First bust type Two Guineas   1664 Two Guineas with elephant only belov

3333 Two Guineas. First laur. bust r., pointed trun. ℞. Crowned cruciform shields, sceptres in angles, die axis ↑↓

1664	1000	2500	5000	1669		*Extremely rare*	
1665		*Extremely rare*		1671	950	3800	7000
				1673		*Extremely rare*	

3334 Two Guineas. First bust with elephant below, similar die axis ↑↓

1664	800	2250	5000

3335 Two Guineas. Second laur. bust r., rounded trun, similar die axis ↑↓

1675	1100	3850	6500	1680	1050	3250	6500
1676	1050	3250	6250	1681	850	2750	5750
1677	1100	3650	6500	1682	1100	3650	6500
1678/7	850	2750	5500	1683	950	3000	6000
1679	1100	3650	6500	1684	1150	3800	6750

Overstruck dates are listed only if commoner than the normal date or if no normal date is known.

3335	3339
1679 Two Guineas - second bust	1663 Guinea first bust, elephant below

	F	VF	EF		F	VF	EF
	£	£	£		£	£	£

3336 Two Guineas. Second bust with elephant and castle below, similar die axis ↑↓

1676	1050	3250	6500	1682	1050	3500	7000
1677		*Extremely rare*		1683	950	3000	6250
1678	850	2750	6000	1684	1150	3750	7250

3337 Two Guineas. Second bust with elephant only below, die axis ↑↓ 1678 ..   *Extremely rare*

3337 ABroad of 20s. Laur. and dr. bust r. R. Crowned shield of arms (approx. 3400 issued),
  die axis ↑↓ 1662 ..1000   2250   4000

3338 Guinea. First laur. bust r., R. Crowned cruciform shields, die axis
  ↑↓ 1663 800   2750   6250

3339 Guinea. First bust with elephant below, similar die axis ↑↓ 1663 750   2500   5750

3340 Guinea. Second laur. bust r.,similar die axis ↑↓ 1664 675   2250   5250

3341
1664 Guinea second bust elephant below

3341 Guinea. Second bust with elephant below, similar die axis ↑↓1664..4000   10000   —

3342 Guinea. Third laur. bust r. similar die axis ↑↓

1664	500	2000	5000	1669	550	2750	5750
1665	525	2250	5250	1670	525	2750	5750
1666	550	2750	5750	1671	550	2750	5250
1667	525	2250	5250	1672	550	2750	5250
1668	550	2750	5750	1673	600	2800	5500

3342	3344	3345
1664 Guinea - third bust	Fourth bust	Fourth bust -
		elephant and castle below

3343 Guinea. Third laur. bust r., with elephant below, similar die axis ↑↓

1664	600	2500	5500	1668	*Extremely rare*
1665	700	3000	6000		

	F £	*VF* £	*EF* £		*F* £	*VF* £	*EF* £

3344 Guinea. Fourth laur. bust r., rounded trun. similar die axis ↑↓

1672	450	2000	4350	1678	375	1350	3600
1673	450	2000	4350	1679	380	1250	3350
1674	450	2000	4250	1679 ' O' over' o' on it's side	*Extremely rare*		
1675	450	2000	4350	1680	350	1250	3350
1675 CRAOLVS error	*Extremely rare*			1681	450	2000	4350
1676	375	1350	3600	1682	400	1650	3950
1677	375	1350	3600	1682 rev.@90° axis	750	2750	5600
1675 CRAOLⱯS error	*Extremely rare*			1683	375	1350	3600
1677 GRATIR error	*Extremely rare*			1684	400	1650	3950

3345 Guinea. Fourth laur. bust r., with elephant and castle below, similar die axis ↑↓

1674	*Extremely rare*			1680	600	2250	5100
1675	500	2000	4850	1681	485	1900	4850
1676	425	1650	4150	1682	475	1850	4600
1677	450	1850	4600	1683	600	2500	5600
1678	500	2000	4850	1684	485	1900	4600
1679	475	1850	4350				

3346 Guinea. — — with elephant below bust, similar die axis ↑↓

1677/5	*Extremely rare*	1678	*Extremely rare*

3347
1669 Half-Guinea, first bust

3348
1682 Half-Guinea, second bust

3347 Half-Guinea. First laur. bust r., pointed trun.R. Crowned cruciform shields, sceptres in angles die axis ↑↓

1669	350	1100	3450	1671	375	1150	3700
1670	300	950	3100	1672	375	1150	3700

3348 Half-Guinea. Second laur. bust r., rounded trun. similar die axis ↑↓

1672	325	1000	3100	1678/7	375	1150	3950
1673	425	1350	3700	1679	350	1100	3450
1674	475	1450	3950	1680	425	1350	3950
1675	500	1500	4350	1681	425	1350	3950
1676	300	950	2850	1682	425	1350	3950
1676/4	375	1150	3700	1683	325	1000	3100
1677	350	1100	3450	1684	300	980	2850
1678	350	1100	3450				

3349 Half-Guinea. Second bust with elephant and castle below, similar die axis ↑↓

1676	600	2250	—	1681	*Extremely rare*		
1677	475	1450	3950	1682	475	1450	3950
1678/7	375	1150	3700	1683	*Extremely rare*		
1680	*Extremely rare*			1684	350	1100	3400

SILVER

3350
1662 Crown, first type, rose below bust

	F £	VF £	EF £		F £	VF £	EF £

3350 Crown. First dr. bust r., rose below, R. Crowned cruciform shields, interlinked C's in angles
edge undated, die axis ↑↓ 1662...120   825   3650

3350A Crown. — — — Similar, die axis ↑↑ 1662.......................................275   1400   —

3350B Crown. — — II of legend at 12 o'clock, similar die axis ↑↓ 1662 ....   *Extremely rare*

3351 Crown.— — edge dated,similar die axis ↑↓ 1662..............................140   950   4000

3351A Crown.— — edge dated struck en medaille, similar die axis ↑↑ 1662....200   1250   —

3351B Crown.— striped cloak struck en medaille, similar die axis ↑↑ 1662...275   1400   —

3351C Crown.— striped cloak to drapery, 1662 similar die axis ↑↓ 275   1400   4950

3352 Crown.— no rose, edge dated, similar die axis ↑↓ 1662.................150   1000   4150

3353 Crown.— — edge not dated, similar die axis ↑↓ 1662.....................140   950   4150

3353A Crown. — — — die axis ↑↓ 1662 275   1450   —

3354 Crown.— — legend re-arranged shields altered, 1663, similar regnal year on edge in
Roman figures ANNO REGNI XV die axis ↑↓...................................150   1000   4150
1663 no stops on reverse 600   —   —

3355 Crown. Second dr. bust r., regnal year on edge in Roman figures (e.g. 1664 = XVI), die axis ↑↓
1664 edge XVI........ 110   675   3400   1665 XVII.................725   2000   —
1664 Proof *FDC* £20000   1666 XVIII ....110.........750   3650
1665 XVI ....   *Extremely rare*   1666 XVIII RE·X ....   *Extremely rare*
1665/4 XVII..............725   2000   —   1667 XVIII 2400   —   —

3356 – RE•X variety

3356
Elephant provenance mark

3356 Crown. Second bust elephant below, similar, die axis ↑↓
1666 XVIII 325   1400   —   1666 XVIII RE·X 450   1650   —

3357
1669 Crown - second bust

	F £	VF £	EF £		F £	VF £	EF £

3357   Crown. Second bust, similar Regnal year on edge in words (e.g. 1667= DECIMO NONO)
die axis ↑↓

1667 D. NONO 100	600	3150	1669/8 V· PRIMO..........350	1250	—
1667 — AN.· REG.· ..100	675	3450	1670 V. SECVNDO 125	725	3800
1668 VICESIMO 90	550	3000	1670/69 V. SECVND......150	825	4150
1668 — error edge	*Extremely rare*		1671 V· TERTIO 100	725	3800
1668/7 VICESIMO 100	600	3150	1671 — T/R in ET 950	2650	—
1668/5 VICESIMO	*Extremely rare*		1671 — ET over FR 1200	3450	—
1669 V· PRIMO 325	1100	—			

3358
Third bust Crown

3359
Fourth bust Crown

3358   Crown. Third dr. bust r. R.Similar die axis ↑↓

1671 V. TERTIO 95	600	3450	1675 — EGNI error........900	—	—
1671 V. QVARTO..........	*Extremely rare*		1676 V. OCTAVO 95	600	3450
1672 V. QVARTO 95	600	3450	1676 OCCTAVO............100	775	3800
1673 V. QVARTO	*Extremely rare*		1677 V. NONO 120	775	3800
1673 V. QVINTO 95	600	3450	1677/6 V. NONO 140	1000	—
1673 B/R in BR..........200	1200	—	1678/7 TRICESIMO 140	1000	—
1673/2 V. QVINTO ..150	825	4000	1679 T. PRIMO.............100	675	3450
1674 V. SEXTO	*Extremely rare*		1680/79 T. SECVNDO 120	725	3800
1675/3 V. SEPTIMO..725	2650	—	1680 T. SECVNDO 125	775	4400
1675 — 1150	4400	—			

3359   Crown. Fourth dr. bust r. R.Similar die axis ↑↓

1679 T. PRIMO............95	600	3150	1682/1 T. QVARTO 95	600	3450
1679 HIBR·EX 150	1000	—	1682 T. QVARTO..........650	2250	5400
1680 T. SECVNDO ..100	600	3450	1682/1 QVRRTO error 450	1500	—
1680/79 T. SECVNDO 140	900	—	1683 T. QVINTO 500	1800	—
1681 T. TERTIO 100	600	3450	1684 T. SEXTO.............400	1250	—

3360   Crown.— elephant and castle below bust, die axis ↑↓ 1681 T. TERTIO 2850   5500   —

3361 - First bust Halfcrown   3362 - Second bust Halfcrown

	F	VF	EF		F	VF	EF
	£	£	£		£	£	£

3361 **Halfcrown.** First dr. bust r. R. Crowned cruciform shields, interlinked C's in angles, regnal year on edge in Roman figures die axis ↑↓

	F	VF	EF
1663 XV	95	600	3150
1663 XV V/S in CAROLVS	200	950	—
1663 XV A/T in GRATIA	200	950	—
1663 XV no stops on obverse	175	900	—
1663 XV different die axis to usual	275	1000	—

3362 **Halfcrown.** Second dr. bust r., similar die axis ↑↓ 1664 XVI ... 200 | 1100 | 3900

3363 **Halfcrown.** Third dr. bust r., similar die axis ↑↓ 1666/4 XVIII ... 1050 | 3650 | —

3364 **Halfcrown.** Third bust elephant below, die axis ↑↓ 1666 XVIII ... 900 | 2150 | —

3364
Third bust, elephant below Halfcrown

3365
1670 Halfcrown, third bust

3365 **Halfcrown.** Third dr. bust r. regnal date on edge in words (eg. 1667=DECIMO NONO) ↑↓

1667/4 D. NONO	*Extremely rare*		1669 — R/I in PRIMO ...	*Extremely rare*	
1668/4 VICESIMO	225	1000	—	1670 V. SECVNDO	85	500	3150
1668/4 CAROLVS	350	1350	—	1670 – MRG for MAG	350	1400	—
1669/4 V. PRIMO	225	950	—	1670 V/S CAROLVS	300	1200	—
1669 V. PRIMO	450	1500	—	1670 E/R in ET	350	1350	—

3366
1671 Halfcrown third bust variety

3367
Fourth bust Halfcrown

3366 **Halfcrown.** Third bust variety r. R. Similar die axis ↑↓

1671 V. TERTIO	80	500	2400	1672 V. TERTIO	*Extremely rare*	
1671 A/R in MAG	175	1000	—	1672 V. QVARTO	80	500	2400
1671/0 V. TERTIO	100	600	3500			

	F £	VF £	EF £		F £	VF £	EF £
3367 Halfcrown. Fourth dr. bust r. R. Similar die axis ↑↓							
1672 V. QVARTO 120	500	3150		1679 T. PRIMO................80	400	2400	
1673 V. QVINTO 80	400	2400		1679 — GRATTA error.	*Extremely rare*		
1673 —A/R in FRA........	*Extremely rare*			1679 — REGЯI error.....	*Extremely rare*		
1673 — B/R in BR	*Extremely rare*			1679 — DECNS error......225	850	—	
1673 — FR/M in FRA....	*Extremely rare*			1679 — DNCVS error 400	—	—	
1674 V. SEXTO 125	450	3150		1679 — PRICESIMO 250	900	—	
1674/3 V. SEXTO......325	—	—		1679 — inverted A's for			
1675 V. SEPTIMO 90	450	2900		V's on edge............400	—	—	
1675 — Retrograde 1 100	500	3150		1680 T. SECVNDO........150	800	—	
1676 V. OCTAVO 75	350	2100		1680 T. SECVNꟴO error	*Extremely rare*		
1676 R/T in BR..............	*Extremely rare*			1681 T. TERTIO 90	450	2900	
1676 — Retrograde 1 ..85	400	2400		1681/0 —.....................275	—	—	
1677 F/H in FRA............	*Extremely rare*			1682 T. QVARTO..........100	500	3150	
1676 F/H in FRA............	*Extremely rare*			1682/79 T. QVARTO.....	*Extremely rare*		
1677 V. NONO 80	400	2650		1683 T. QVINTO 80	400	2400	
1678 TRICESIMO 200	800	—		1684/3 T. SEXTO 200	850	—	

3369 - Plume in centre   3370 - Elephant and Castle below bust

3368 Halfcrown. Fourth bust plume below, R. Similar die axis ↑↓

1673 V. QVINTO 2250	—	—	1683 T. QVINTO	*Extremely rare*

3369 Halfcrown.— plume below bust and in centre of *rev.*, die axis ↑↓ 1673 V. QVINTO *Extremely rare*
3370 Halfcrown.— elephant and castle below bust, die axis ↑↓ 1681 T. TERTIO ..2000 6000 23000

SHILLINGS

First bust   First bust variety   Second bust   Third bust

First bust   First bust var.   First bust and   Second bust
                                            first bust variety   single top leaf

3371 - First bust   3371 – Transposed Irish and Scottish shields

	F	VF	EF		F	VF	EF
	£	£	£		£	£	£

3371 Shilling. First dr. bust r.R. Crowned cruciform shields interlinked C's in angles edge milled,

1663 die axis ↑↑ (en medaille)	125	550	1850
1663 die axis ↑↓ as usual	85	350	950
1663 GARTIA error, die axis ↑↓	1100	—	—
1663 Transposed shields of Scotland and Ireland, die axis ↑↓	150	825	2100
1663 A over G in FRA, die axis ↑↓	1000	—	—

3372   3374
1663 Shilling - first bust variety   1666 'Guinea' head shilling

3372 Shilling. First bust variety r. similar die axis ↑↓

1663	80	350	900	1668	450	1600	—
1666	....	*Extremely rare*		1669/6	....	*Extremely rare*	

3373 Shilling. First bust variety r. elephant below bust, die axis ↑↓ 1666 ..400   1400   3600
3374 Shilling. Guinea head, elephant below bust, die axis ↑↓ 1666..........1750   4100   —

3375 - Second bust shilling   3376 - Plume both sides shilling of 1676

3375 Shilling. Second dr. bust r. similar die axis ↑↓

1666	1650	5100	—	1676	75	450	1100
1668	60	350	900	1676 higher bust	....	*Extremely rare*	
1668/7	75	450	1150	1676/5	85	475	1200
1669	....	*Extremely rare*		1677	75	450	1100
1670	90	500	1300	1678	90	500	1300
1671	110	550	1500	1678/7	90	500	1300
1672	75	450	1150	1679	75	450	1100
1673	110	725	1500	1679/7	90	500	1300
1673/2	160	725	1750	1680	....	*Extremely rare*	
1674	135	600	1600	1681	110	550	1500
1674/3	110	550	1400	1681/0	110	550	1500
1675	160	725	1750	1682/1	550	1500	—
1675/4	160	725	1750	1683	....	*Extremely rare*	

	F £	VF £	EF £		F £	VF £	EF £

3376 Shilling. Second Bust — plume below bust and in centre of *rev.* similar die axis ↑↓

1671	200	725	2350	1676	225	775	2600
1673	225	775	2600	1679	250	950	2850
1674	200	725	2350	1680	325	1100	3100
1675	225	775	2600	1680/79	325	1100	3100

3377
1674 Shilling - plume on reverse only

3378
1679 Shilling - plume on obverse only

3377 Shilling. — Plume *rev.* only, similar die axis ↑↓ 1674 ....300 1400 3400

3378 Shilling. — Plume *obv.* only similar die axis ↑↓

1677	500	1900	3950	1679	400	1650	3700

3379 Shilling. — elephant and castle below bust, die axis ↑↓ 1681/0 ....2350 — —

3380
Third bust Shilling

3381
1683 Shilling - fourth bust

3380 Shilling. Third dr. (large) bust r. similar die axis ↑↓

1674	250	1050	3100	1675/3	200	775	2600
1675	200	775	2600				

3381 Shilling. Fourth dr. (large) bust r., older features, similar die axis ↑↓

1683	150	600	1750	1684	125	500	1500

3382
1676 Sixpence

3382 Sixpence. Dr. bust r. R. Crowned cruciform shields, interlinked C's in angles die axis ↑↓

1674	50	300	850	1679	65	350	950
1675	50	300	850	1680	90	400	1100
1675/4	65	375	1000	1681	50	275	750
1676	90	400	1100	1682	90	400	1100
1676/5	90	400	1100	1682/1	65	350	900
1677	50	300	850	1683	50	300	850
1678/7	65	350	900	1684	75	350	900

3383 - Undated Fourpence

	F	VF	EF		F	VF	EF
	£	£	£		£	£	£

3383 Fourpence. Undated. Crowned dr. bust l. to edge of coin, value
behind. R. Shield, die axis ↑↓ 15 45 120

3384 - 1678 Fourpence   3386 - 1678 Threepence

3384 Fourpence. Dated. Dr. bust r. R. Crowned four interlinked Cs quartered emblems die axis ↑↓

1670 12	35	110	1678................................10	25	85
1671 10	30	100	1678/6 10	30	100
1672/1 10	25	90	1678/7 10	30	100
1673 10	25	90	1679................................10	25	85
1674 10	25	90	1680................................10	25	85
1674/4 sideways 12	35	175	1681................................10	25	85
1674 7 over 6 10	30	100	1681 B/R in HIB 12	35	175
1675 10	25	90	1681/0 10	30	100
1675/4 10	30	100	1682................................10	25	85
1676 10	25	90	1682/1 10	30	100
1676 7 over 6 10	30	100	1683................................10	25	85
1676/5 10	30	100	1684................................10	30	100
1677 10	25	85	1684/3 10	25	85

3385 Threepence. Undated. As 3383, die axis ↑↓ 10 30 100

3386 Threepence. Dated. Dr. bust r. R. Crowned three interlinked C's, die axis ↑↓

1670 6	25	85	1678................................6	20	75
1671 6	20	75	1678 on 4d flan 6	20	90
1671 GRɅTIA 10	35	175	1679................................6	20	75
1671 GRɅTIA 8	25	115	1679 O/A in CAROLVS 10	35	175
1672/1 6	20	75	1680................................6	20	75
1673 6	20	75	1681................................6	20	75
1674 6	20	75	1681/0 7	25	85
1675 6	25	85	1682................................6	20	75
1676 6	20	75	1682/1 7	25	85
1676/5 7	25	85	1683................................6	20	75
1676 ERA for FRA.....10	35	175	1684................................6	20	75
1677 6	25	85	1684/3 7	25	85

3387 Twopence. Undated. As 3383 (double arch crown) die axis ↑↓ 6 25 75

3388 - 1678 Twopence   3390 - 1678 Penny

	F	VF	EF		F	VF	EF
	£	£	£		£	£	£

3388 Twopence. Dated. Dr. bust r. R. Crowned pair of linked C's, die axis ↑↓

	F	VF	EF		F	VF	EF
1668 die axis ↑↑	8	25	85	1678/6	8	25	85
1670	6	20	75	1679	6	20	75
1671	6	20	75	1679 HIB over FRA	10	35	175
1672/1	6	20	75	1680	6	20	75
1672/1 GRATIA	10	35	145	1680/79	8	25	85
1673	8	25	85	1681	6	20	75
1674	6	20	75	1682/1	8	25	85
1675	6	20	75	1682/1 ERA for FRA	10	35	175
1676	6	20	75	1683	6	20	75
1677	8	25	85	1683/2	8	25	85
1678	6	25	75	1684	8	25	85

3389 Penny. Undated. As 3383 (double arch crown) die axis ↑↓ .....6 | 30 | 110

3390 Penny. Dated. Dr. bust r. R. Crowned C die axis ↑↓

	F	VF	EF		F	VF	EF
1670	8	25	100	1678 ƆRATIA error	10	35	175
1671	8	25	100	1678	9	30	120
1672/1	8	25	100	1679	9	30	120
1673	8	25	100	1680	8	25	100
1674	8	25	100	1680 on 2d flan		*Extremely rare*	
1674 ƆRATIA error	10	35	175	1681	10	35	145
1675	8	25	100	1682	9	30	110
1675 ƆRATIA error	10	35	175	1682/1	10	35	145
1676	9	30	120	1682 ERA for FRA	10	35	175
1676 ƆRATIA error	10	35	175	1683/1	8	25	100
1677	8	25	100	1684	9	30	120
1677 ƆRATIA error	10	35	175	1684/3	10	35	145

3391 Maundy Set. Undated. The four coins ....85 | 350 | 700

3392 Maundy Set. Dated. The four denominations. Uniform dates

	F	VF	EF		F	VF	EF
1670	70	250	600	1678	70	300	700
1671	60	200	600	1679	65	225	650
1672	70	225	650	1680	60	200	625
1673	60	200	600	1681	70	300	700
1674	60	200	600	1682	65	225	650
1675	65	225	650	1683	60	200	600
1676	65	225	650	1684	65	225	650
1677	65	225	650				

COPPER AND TIN

3393 - 1675 Halfpenny

	F £	VF £	EF £		F £	VF £	EF £

3393 Copper **Halfpenny** Cuir. bust l. R. Britannia seated l. date in ex., die axis ↑↓

1672 50	300	1100	1673 no stops on obv......	*Extremely rare*		
1672 CRAOLVS error....	*Extremely rare*		1673 no rev. stop 85	500	—
1673 40	275	1000	1675 45	275	1050
1673 CRAOLVS error....	*Extremely rare*		1675 no stops on obv..75	450	—
			1675/3 175	600	—

3394 - 1675 Farthing   3395 - Tin Farthing

3394 Copper **Farthing.** Cuir. bust l. R. Britannia sealed l. date in ex., die axis ↑↓

1672 40	225	700	1673 BRITINNIA error..	*Extremely rare*	
1672 Rev.			1673 no stops on obv......	*Extremely rare*	
loose drapery 50	275	900	1673 no rev. stop	*Extremely rare*	
1672 no stops on obv. .60	300	1000	1674 50	250	750
1672 RO/OL on obv. ..75	450	—	1675 40	225	700
1672 die axis ↑↑ 60	300	1000	1675 no stop after CAROLVS	*Extremely rare*	
1673 40	225	700	1679 50	250	750
1673 CAROLA error ..75	450	—	1679 no rev. stop 60	300	1000
1673 O/sideways O.........	*Extremely rare*				

	Fair £	F £	VF £	EF £

Prices for tin coinage based on corrosion free examples, and in the top grades with some lustre

3395 Tin **Farthing.** Somewhat similar, but with copper plug, edge inscribed NUMMORVM
FAMVLVS, and date on edge only die axis ↑↓

| 1684 | various varieties of edge ....50 | 225 | 750 | 3000 |
| 1685 | .... | | *Extremely rare* | |

James II, brother of Charles II, was born on 14th October 1633, he married Anne Hyde with whom he produced 8 children. He lost control of his reign when the loyalist Tories moved against him over his many Catholic appointments. Parliament invited his protestant daughter Mary with husband William of Orange to be joint rulers. James II abdicated and died in exile in France.

During this reign the dies continued to be engraved by John Roettier (1631-1700), the only major difference in the silver coinage being the ommission of the interlinked C's in the angles of the shields on the reverses. The only provenance marked silver coin of this reign is the extremely rare plume on reverse 1685 Shilling. The elephant and castle provenance mark continues to appear on some of the gold coins of this reign. Tin halfpence and farthings provided the only base metal coinage during this short reign. All genuine tin coins of this period have a copper plug.

GOLD

	F	VF	EF		F	VF	EF
	£	£	£		£	£	£

3396 Five Guineas. First laur. bust l., R. Crowned cruciform shields sceptres misplaced in angles smaller crowns date on edge in words (e.g. 1686 = SECVNDO)
die axis ↑↓ 1686 SECVNDO...1500   6000   13500

3397 Five Guineas. First laur bust l. R. similar bust sceptres normal. die axis ↑↓
1687 TERTIO..........1250   5000   11000   1688 QVARTO 1350   5500   12000

3397A
1687 Five Guineas, second bust

3397A Five Guineas. Second laur. bust l. R. similar die axis ↑↓
1687 TERTIO..........1250   4500   9750   1688 QVARTO 1350   4750   10500

3398
1687 Five Guineas, first bust, elephant and castle below

	F £	VF £	EF £		F £	VF £	EF £

3398 Five Guineas. First laur. bust l. Elephant and castle below R. Similar die axis ↑↓

1687 TERTIO	1500	5250	11500	1688 QVARTO	1600	5750	12500

3399
1688 Two Guineas 8 over 7

3399 Two Guineas. Laur. bust l. R. Crowned cruciform shields, sceptres in angles, edge milled, die axis ↑↓

1687	950	3000	5750	1688/7	1200	3750	7000

3400 Guinea. First laur. bust l. R. Crowned cruciform shields, sceptres in angles, edge milled, die axis ↑↓

1685	400	1850	4650	1686	450	2000	4900

3401 Guinea. First bust elephant and castle below R. similar die axis ↑↓

1685	500	2250	5150	1686	....	*Extremely rare*	

3402
1688 Guinea, second bust

3402 Guinea. Second laur. bust l. R. similar die axis ↑↓

1686	325	1650	3900	1687/6	400	1850	4400
1687	325	1650	3900	1688	350	1750	4400

3403
1686 Guinea, second bust, elephant and castle below

3404
1688 Half-Guinea

	F	VF	EF			F	VF	EF
	£	£	£			£	£	£

3403　Guinea. Second bust elephant and castle below R. similar die axis ↑↓
1686 ....525　　2500　　5650　　　1688 ....375　　2000　　5150
1687 ....375　　1750　　4650

3404　Half-Guinea. Laur. bust l. R. Crowned cruciform shields sceptres in angles, edge milled
die axis ↑↓
1686 ....300　　1100　　3400　　　1687 ....400　　1400　　3900
1686 OBV/BVS ....　*Extremely rare*　　　1688 ....350　　1500　　4150

3405　Half-Guinea. Laur bust with elephant and castle below, R. similar die axis ↑↓
1686 ....700　　3650　　　—

SILVER

3406
1686 Crown, first bust, no stops on obverse

3406　Crown. First dr. bust, l. regnal year on edge in words (e.g. 1686 = SECVNDO) die axis ↑↓
1686 SECVNDO...250　　1000　　4650
1686 — No stops on obverse ....400　　1350　　—

3407
1687 Crown, second bust

3407　Crown. Second dr. bust l. R. Crowned cruciform shields edge inscribed in raised letters
die axis ↑↓
1687 TERTIO ....150　　675　　2400　　　1688/7 QVARTO .....175　　825　　3400
1688 QVARTO.........150　　775　　3150

1st bust   2nd bust

3408
1685 Halfcrown, first bust

	F	VF	EF			F	VF	EF
	£	£	£			£	£	£

3408 Halfcrown. First laur and dr. bust, l. regnal year on edge in words
(e.g. 1685 = PRIMO) die axis ↑↓

1685 PRIMO	125	600	2150		1686 TERTIO	150	675	2400
1686 SECVNDO	125	600	2150		1687 TERTIO	125	600	2150
1686/5 —	275	1100	—		1687/6 —	150	675	2400
1686 TERTIO Vover S or B					1687 — 6 over 8		*Extremely rare*	
in JACOBVS	300	1100	—		1687 A/R in GRATIA		*Extremely rare*	

3409 Halfcrown. Second laur and dr. bust l. R. Crowned cruciform shields
edge inscribed in raised letters die axis ↑↓

1687 TERTIO	180	675	2400		1688 QVARTO	125	600	2150

3410
1687 Shilling

3410 Shilling. Laur and Dr. bust l. R. Crowned cruciform shields die axis ↑↓

1685	100	400	1200		1686 G/A in MAG	125	500	1350
1685 no stops on rev.	175	725	2100		1687	150	550	1450
1686	125	500	1350		1687/6	100	400	1200
1686/5	125	500	1350		1687 G/A in MAG	175	600	1850
1686 V/S in JACOBVS	125	500	1350		1688	125	500	1350
					1688/7	150	550	1450

3411 Shilling. Similar, plume in centre of *rev.,* die axis ↑↓ 1685 ......Fair £5500

3412   3413
1686 Sixpence, early shields, indented tops   1688 Sixpence, later shields

3412 Sixpence. Laur and dr. bust l. R. Early type crowned cruciform shields die axis ↑↓

1686	90	400	950		1687/6	100	475	1050
1687	100	450	1050					

3413 Sixpence. Similar R. Late type shields die axis ↑↓

1687	90	400	950		1687 Later/early shields	100	475	1050
1687/6	90	450	1050		1688	90	450	1050

3414 - 1686 Fourpence   3415 - 1687 Threepence

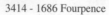

	F	VF	EF		F	VF	EF
	£	£	£		£	£	£

3414 Fourpence. Laur. head l. R. IIII Crowned die axis ↑↓

1686	10	30	110	1688	8	30	110
1686 Date over crown.	10	30	110	1688 1 over 8	20	55	175
1687/6	8	25	100	1688/7	8	30	110
1687 8 over 7	10	30	110				

3415 Threepence. Laur. head l. R. III Crowned die axis ↑↓

1685	8	30	100	1687	10	35	110
1685 Groat flan	30	80	175	1687/6	8	30	100
1686	8	30	100	1688	8	30	100
1686 4d obv. die	10	35	120	1688/7	10	35	110

3416 Twopence. Laur. head l. R. II Crowned die axis ↑↓

1686	10	25	100	1687 ERA for FRA	20	45	150
1686 IΛCOBVS	15	35	120	1688	10	30	110
1687	10	25	100	1688/7	10	30	110

3416 - 1686 Twopence   3417 - 1688 Penny

3417 Penny. Laur. head l. R. I Crowned die axis ↑↓

1685	10	30	110	1687/8	15	35	120
1686	10	30	110	1688	10	30	110
1687	10	30	110	1688/7	10	30	110
1687/6	10	30	110				

3418 Maundy Set. As last four. Uniform dates

1686	75	325	700	1688	75	325	700
1687	75	325	700				

TIN

3419 Tin Halfpenny

	Fair	F	VF	EF
	£	£	£	£

Prices for tin coinage based on corrosion free examples, and in the top grades with some lustre

3419 Halfpenny. Laur. and dr. bust r. R. Britannia seated l. date on edge die axis ↑↓

1685 various varieties of edge	75	200	650	3250
1686	95	225	700	3750
1687	75	200	650	3250

3420
Cuirassed bust Tin Farthing

3420 Farthing. Laur. and Cuir. bust r. R. Britannia seated l. date on edge die axis ↑↓

1684			*Extremely rare*	
1685 various varieties of edge	60	175	550	2250
1686 two varieties of edge	75	200	600	2750
1687			*Extremely rare*	

3421
Draped bust Tin Farthing

3421 Farthing. Dr. bust r.; date on edge, 1687 various varieties of edge ↑↓

	90	225	750	3250

Mary Stuart was born on 30 April 1662, and married William of Orange as part of Charles II's foreign policy. She eventually became William's loyal servant but bore him no children. The Bill and the Claim of Rights were both passed in 1689 and forbade the Royal and Prerogative rights of Monarchs. Mary died from smallpox on 28 December 1694.

Due to the poor state of the silver coinage, much of it worn hammered coin, the Guinea, which was valued at 21s. 6d. at the beginning of the reign, circulated for as much as 30s. by 1694. The elephant and elephant and castle provenance marks continue on some gold coin. The tin Halfpennies and Farthings were replaced by copper coins in 1694. The rampant Lion of Nassau is now placed as an inescutcheon on the centre of the royal arms. The WM monogram appears in the angles of the silver coins of this reign.

Engravers and designers: George Bower (d.1689), Henry Harris (d.1704), John Roettier (1631-1700), James Roettier (1663-1698), Norbert Roettier (b.1665)

3422
1691 Five Guineas

	F	VF	EF		F	VF	EF
	£	£	£		£	£	£

3422 Five Guineas. Conjoined busts r. regnal year on edge in words (e.g. 1691 = TERTIO) ↑↓

	F	VF	EF		F	VF	EF
1691 TERTIO	1100	3250	9000	1693 QVINTO	1250	3750	9500
1692 QVARTO	1250	3750	9500	1694/2 SEXTO	1350	4000	10500
1692 QVINTO	3000	7500	—	1694 SEXTO	1500	4500	11000

3423
Elephant and castle below busts

3424
1694 Two Guineas 4 over 3

3423 Five Guineas. Conjoined busts, elephant and castle below, R. Crowned shield of arms die axis ↑↓

	F	VF	EF		F	VF	EF
1691 TERTIO	1350	4000	10000	1694/2 SEXTO	1350	4250	11500
1692 QVARTO	1350	4000	11000	1694 SEXTO	1500	4500	12000
1693 QVINTO	1500	4500	12000				

3424 Two Guineas. Conjoined busts r. R. Crowned shield of arms, Lion of Nassau at centre die axis ↑↓

	F	VF	EF		F	VF	EF
1693	800	2500	5500	1694/3	800	2500	5500

3425 Two Guineas. Conjoined busts, elephant and castle below, R. similar die axis ↑↓

	F	VF	EF		F	VF	EF
1691		*Extremely rare*		1694/3	900	2750	5750
1693	900	2750	5750				

3426
1689 Guinea

3427
1689 Elephant and castle below busts

	F £	VF £	EF £		F £	VF £	EF £

3426 Guinea. Conjoined busts r. R. Crowned shield of arms Lion of Nassau at centre die axis ↑↓

1689	350	2000	4900	1692	375	2250	5400
1690	375	2500	5650	1693	375	2500	5650
1690 GVLIFLMVS		*Extremely rare*		1694	350	2000	5150
1691	375	2000	5150	1694/3	375	2250	5400

3427 Guinea. Conjoined busts elephant and castle below R. Similar die axis ↑↓

1689	375	2000	5150	1692	375	2250	4900
1690	450	2250	5650	1693		*Extremely rare*	
1691	375	2250	5400	1694	375	2250	5400
				1694/3	400	2250	5400

3428 Guinea. Conjoined busts elephant only below, R. Similar die axis ↑↓

1692	450	2250	5650	1693		*Extremely rare*	

Overstruck dates are listed only if commoner than the normal date or if no normal date is known.

3429
1689 Half-Guinea, first busts, first shield

3430
1690 Half-Guinea, second busts, second shield

3429 Half-Guinea. First busts r. R. First Crowned shield of arms die axis ↑↓

1689	425	1850	4150

3430 Half-Guinea. Second busts r. R. Second Crowned shield of arms die axis ↑↓

1690	325	2000	4650	1693		*Extremely rare*	
1691	350	1850	4150	1693/2		*Extremely rare*	
1692	375	1600	3650	1694	325	1600	3650

3431 Half-Guinea. Second busts elephant and castle below, R. Second shield of arms die axis ↑↓

1691	325	1600	3650	1692	350	1750	4150

3432 Half-Guinea. Second busts elephant only below, R. Second shield of arms die axis ↑↓

1692		*Extremely rare*	

SILVER

3433
1691 Crown

3433 Crown. Conjoined busts r. regnal year on edge in words (e.g. 1691 = TERTIO) die axis ↑↓

1691 TERTIO	275	1000	4150	1692 QVARTO	275	1000	4150
1691 I/E in legend	500	1500	—	1692/ℓ QVARTO	425	1750	—
1691 TERTTIO		*Extremely rare*		1692/ℓ QVINTO	275	1000	4150

Caul frosted → ← Caul not frosted

Pearls → ← No Pearls

Interior frosted ↗ ↘ Interior not frosted

3434
1689 Halfcrown - first reverse

3435
1689 Halfcrown - second reverse

	F £	VF £	EF £		F £	VF £	EF £

3434 Halfcrown. First busts, r. R. First crowned shield, 1689 PRIMO R. Crown with caul and interior frosted, with pearls edge inscribed die axis ↑↓ ....75　350　1500

1689— 2nd L/M in GVLIELMVS ....95　425　1650

1689 — 1st V/A in GVLIELMVS, only caul frosted ....90　400　1600

1689 — — interior also frosted, no pearls ....90　400　1600

1689 Caul only frosted, pearls..80　350　1500

1689 — no pearls...90　400　1600

1689 No frosting, pearls . ...95　425　1650

1689 No stops on obverse ....110　450　1750

1689 FRA for FR..125　650　2300

3435 Halfcrown. First busts r. R. Second crowned shield die axis ↑↓

1689 PRIMO R. Caul ..90 375 1500 and interior frosted with pearls				1689 Caul only frosted, no pearls 90	375	1500

1689 PRIMO R. Caul ..90　375　1500　　　1689 Caul only frosted,
and interior frosted with pearls　　　　　　　no pearls ....90　375　1500

1689 — — no pearls ...100　400　1600　　1689 no frosting, pearls ......85　350　1500

1689 — — — ЕT for ET error *Extremely rare*　　1689 no frosting, no

1689 GVLI Е LMVS ......　　　　　　　　　pearls.......................85　350　1500

　　error ....200　600　—　　1690 SECVNDO — ......100　425　1750

1689 Caul only　　　　　　　　　　　1690 — GRETIA error ....200　800　2750

　frosted pearls ......85　350　1500　　1690 TERTIO ....125　550　2000

1689 interior frosted,

　no pearls ....90　375　1500

3436
1691 Halfcrown, second busts, third reverse

	F	VF	EF		F	VF	EF
	£	£	£		£	£	£

3436   Halfcrown. Second busts r. R. Crowned cruciform shields, WM monogram in angles
die axis ↑↓

	F	VF	EF		F	VF	EF
1691 TERTIO..............90	475	1700		1692 H/B in HI	*Extremely rare*		
1692 QVARTO 90	475	1700		1693 QVINTO............90	400	1500	
1692 R/G in REGINA.....	*Extremely rare*			1693 3/inverted 3......100	475	1700	
1692 QVINTO..........200	925	—		1693 inverted 3.........200	700	2350	

3437	3438
1692 Shilling-inverted 1	1693 Sixpence

3437   Shilling. Conjoined busts r. R. Crowned cruciform shields, WM monogram in angles die axis ↑↓

1692 110	600	1500	1693 9/0....................150	650	1500
1692 inverted 1..........150	700	1750	1693 100	550	1300
1692 RE/ET on R.	*extremely rare*				

3438   Sixpence. Conjoined busts r. R. Crowned cruciform shields, WM monogram in angles die axis ↑↓

1693 100	450	950	1694 110	500	1150
1693 inverted 3 125	550	1250			

3439	3440
1690 Groat, first busts	1692 Groat, second busts

3439   Fourpence. First busts, r. no tie to wreath. R. Crowned 4 die axis ↑↓

1689 GV below bust.....8	25	100	1690 10	30	110
1689 G below bust 8	25	100	1690 6 over 5..............10	35	120
1689 stop befor G........10	30	110	1691 12	35	130
1689 berries in wreath .10	30	110	1691/0........................11	30	115
1689 GVLEELMVS....55	175	–	1694 12	35	130

	F	VF	EF		F	VF	EF
	£	£	£		£	£	£

3440 Fourpence. Second busts r. tie to wreath. R. Crowned 4 die axis ↑↓

	F	VF	EF		F	VF	EF
1692 11	40	115		1693/2 12	40	130
1692/1 12	40	130		1694...............................12	40	130
1692 MAR•IA	*Extremely rare*			1694 small lettering......12	40	130
1693 12	40	130				

3441 Threepence. First busts, r. no tie to wreath. R. Crowned 3 die axis ↑↓

	F	VF	EF		F	VF	EF
1689 7	25	90		1690 6 over 5..................8	30	100
1689 No stops on rev. ..10	35	110		1690 Large lettering 8	30	100
1689 LMV over MVS ..10	35	110		1690 9 over 6..................8	30	100
1689 Hyphen stops on rev. 8	30	100		1691................................30	90	235
1690 8	30	100				

3442 Threepence. Second busts, r. tie to wreath R. Crowned 3 die axis ↑↓

	F	VF	EF		F	VF	EF
1691 10	35	120		1693 GV below bust 9	30	110
1692 G below bust 10	35	120		1694 G below bust 9	30	110
1692 GV below bust......10	35	120		1694 — MΛRIΛ error...10	45	175
1692 GVL below bust ..10	35	120		1694 GV below bust 9	30	110
1693 G below bust 9	30	110		1694 GVL below bust....9	30	110
1693/2 G below bust 9	30	110				

3443 Twopence. Conjoined busts r. R. Crowned 2 die axis ↑↓

	F	VF	EF		F	VF	EF
1689 8	25	100		1694/3 10	35	120
1691 8	25	100		1694/3 no stop after DG 10	35	120
1692 9	30	110		1694 MARLA error 25	55	285
1693 9	30	110		1694 HI for HIB 10	35	120
1693/2 10	35	120		1694 GVLI below bust..10	35	120
1693 GV below bust......10	35	120		1694 GVL below bust..10	35	120
1694 10	35	120				

3444 - 1689 Penny   3445 - Legend intruded

3444 Penny. Legend continuous over busts, R. Crowned 1 die axis ↑↓

	F	VF	EF		F	VF	EF
1689 150	350	650		1689 MΛRIΛ 175	350	700
1689 GVIELMVS error 250	450	900				

3445 Penny. Legend broken by busts, R. Crowned 1 die axis ↑↓

	F	VF	EF		F	VF	EF
1690 14	45	165		1694 date spread 12	40	145
1691/0 12	40	145		1694 no stops on obv. ..15	45	165
1692 14	45	165		1694 HI for HIB 20	55	210
1692/1 15	45	175		1694 — 9/6 15	45	165
1693 12	40	145				

3446 - Maundy Set

3446 Maundy Set. The four denominations. Uniform dates

	F	VF	EF		F	VF	EF
1689 250	600	1100		1693............................150	300	850
1691 95	225	750		1694..............................95	225	750
1692 150	300	850				

TIN AND COPPER

3447
Tin Halfpenny first busts

	Fair	F	VF	EF
	£	£	£	£

Prices for tin coinage based on corrosion free examples, and in the top grades with some lustre

3447 Tin **Halfpenny.** Small dr. busts r.; date on edge ↑↓ 1689....850 1650 — —

— — — obv. with star stops 1689 .... *Extremely rare*

3448
Tin Halfpenny cuirasssed busts

3448 Tin **Halfpenny.** — Large cuir. busts r.; R. Britannia seated L. date only on edge, die axis ↑↓

1690 various edge varieties...75 175 650 2750

3449 Tin **Halfpenny.** Similar date in ex. and on edge die axis ↑↓

1691 various edge varieties...60 150 600 2250

1691 in ex. 1692 on edge .... *Extremely rare*

1692 ....60 150 600 2250

3450 Tin **Farthing.** Small dr. busts r. R. Britannia seated l. die axis ↑↓

1689 ....250 650 2000 —

1689, in ex. 1690 on edge.. *Extremely rare*

3451
1690 Tin Farthing

3451 Tin **Farthing.** Large cuir. busts r. R. Britannia seated l. die axis ↑↓

1690, in ex. 1689 on edge.. *Extremely rare*

1690 various edge varieties...50 150 550 2250

1691 various edge varieties...50 150 550 2250

1692 ....65 175 600 2500

3452
1694 Halfpenny

	F £	VF £	EF £
3452 Copper **Halfpenny,** Conjoined busts r. R. Britannia die axis ↑↓			
1694	60	250	900
1694 GVLIEMVS error	225	600	–
1694 MVRIA error	275	650	–
1694 MΛRIΛ error	175	550	–
1694 BRITΛNNI/Λ	200	575	–
1694 no rev. stop	175	550	–
1694 GVLEELMVS	250	625	–

3453
1694 Farthing

	F £	VF £	EF £
3453 Copper **Farthing**, Conjoined busts r. R. Britannia die axis ↑↓			
1694	60	250	825
1694 MΛRIΛ error	200	500	–
1694 no stop after MΛRIΛ	150	375	–
1694 — BRITΛNNIΛ	175	400	–
1694 no stop on rev.	150	375	–
1694 no stop on obv.	150	375	–
1694 GVLIELMS, BRITΛNNIΛ errors	275	550	–
1694 BRITΛNNIΛ	200	450	–
1694 Broad heavier flan 25.5mm	250	500	–

William of Orange was born on 4th November 1650. He married Mary Stuart under Charles II's foreign policy and was invited to England by Parliament, where he proceeded to supress the Jacobite rebellion. The Bank of England was founded during this reign, and William ruled alone and without issue after Mary's death until his own demise on 8th March 1702 following a serious fall from his horse.

In 1696 a great re-coinage was undertaken to replace the hammered silver that made up most of the coinage in circulation, much of it being clipped and badly worn. Branch mints were set up at Bristol, Chester, Exeter, Norwich and York to help with the re-coinage. For a short time before they were finally demonetized, unclipped hammered coins were allowed to circulate freely provided they were officially pierced in the centre. Silver coins with roses between the coats of arms were made from silver obtained from the West of England mines. The elephant and castle provenance mark continues on some guineas and half-guineas.

Engravers and designers: Samuel Bull (d.c.1720), John Croker (1670-1740), Henry Harris (d.1704), John Roettier (1663-1698).

GOLD

3454	3455
1699 Five Guineas, first bust	Elephant and castle below first bust

	F	VF	EF		F	VF	EF
	£	£	£		£	£	£

3454 Five Guineas. First laur. bust r. regnal year on edge in words (e.g. 1699 = UNDECIMO) ↑↓
1699 UNDECIMO ..1350   5000   10500   1700 DVODECIMO 1450   5500   12000
3455 Five Guineas. First bust elephant and castle below, 1699 UNDECIMO 1500   5250   12500

3456	3457
1701 Five Guineas 'fine work'	'Fine work' Two Guineas

3456 Five Guineas. Second laur. bust r. ('fine work'), R. Crowned cruciform shields Plain or ornamental sceptres DECIMO TERTIO die axis ↑↓ 1701 1250   4750   10000
3457 Two Guineas. ('fine work'), Laur. bust r. similar die axis ↑↓ 1701 1250   3750   5750

3458
1695 Guinea, first bust

| | F | VF | EF | | F | VF | EF |
| | £ | £ | £ | | £ | £ | £ |

3458 Guinea. First laur. bust r. R. Crowned cruciform shields, sceptres in angles die axis ↑↓

1695 250   1750   4150   1697 300   1850   4900

1696 300   2000   5400

3459 Guinea. First bust elephant and castle below R. Similar die axis ↑↓

1695 325   1850   4650   1696 ....   *Extremely rare*

3460   3463   3463
Second bust   1701 Guinea, plain sceptres   Ornamental sceptres

3460 Guinea. Second laur. bust r. R. Similar with human-headed harp in Irish arms. die axis ↑↓

1697 275   1850   4900   1699 300   2000   5650

1698 250   1500   3650   1700 250   1500   3650

3461 Guinea. Second bust elephant and castle below. R. Similar die axis ↑↓

1697 1000   3900   —   1699 .... *Extremely rare*

1698 350   1850   4650   1700 1000   3900   —

3462 Guinea. Second laur. bust. r. R. Similar with Human headed harp. Large lettering and

large date, die axis ↑↓ 1698 250   1750   3900

3463 Guinea. — R. Narrow crowns, plain or ornamented sceptres, axis ↑↓ 1701 250   1750   3900

3464 Guinea. Second bust elephant and castle below, die axis ↑↓ 1701 .... *Extremely rare*

3465 Guinea. Third laur. bust r. ('fine work'), R. Similar die axis ↑↓1701........400   2250   5400

3466   3468
1695 Half-Guinea, early harp   Later harp

3466 Half-Guinea. Laur. bust r. R. With early harp, die axis ↑↓ 1695 225   750   2850

3467 Half-Guinea. Laur. bust elephant and castle below. R. With early harp, die axis ↑↓

1695 325   1250   3350   1696 250   950   3150

3468 Half-Guinea. Laur. bust r. R. Crowned cruciform shields, sceptres in angles with late harp, die axis ↑↓

1697 300   1400   3850   1700 200   650   2600

1698 200   650   2600   1701 200   650   2600

1699 ....   *Extremely rare*

3469 Half-Guinea. Laur. bust elephant and castle below, die axis ↑↓ 1698 275   950   3350

SILVER

3470
1695 Crown - first bust - round collar

	F	VF	EF		F	VF	EF
	£	£	£		£	£	£

3470 Crown. First dr. bust, r. R.First harp, regnal year on edge in words (e.g. 1696 = OCTAVO) ↑↓

	F	VF	EF		F	VF	EF
1695 SEPTIMO............70	300	1400		1696 G/D IN GRA....400	850	—
1695 OCTAVO............75	350	1550		1696 — no stops.......425	950	—
1695 OCTAⱯO error 150	700	—		1696/5.......................425	950	—
1695 TVTA·EN error	*Extremely rare*			1696 GEI for DEI 450	1050	—
1695 plain edge proof *FDC* £6750						
1696 OCTAVO............60	275	1300		1696 — no stops.......475	1100	—
1696 No stops on				1696 plain edge proof *FDC* £6750		
obverse 300	850	—				

3471
1696 Crown, second bust - hair across breast

3471 Crown. Second dr. bust r. R. Second harp (hair across breast), 1696 (two varieties) die axis ↑↓
OCTAVO .... *Each unique*

3472
Third bust, straight breastplate

3472 Crown. Third dr. bust, r. R. First harp, die axis ↑↓ 1696 OCTAVO 70   300   1400
1696 TRICESIMO .... *Extremely rare*
1696 plain edge proof.. *FDC* £7500

	F	VF	EF
	£	£	£

3473 Crown. Similar, R. Second harp, die axis ↑↓ 1697 NONO......................850   3000 13500

3474

1700 Crown, third bust variety

3474 Crown. Third bust variety r. R. Third harp, ↑↓ 1700 DVODECIMO 75   350   1400

1700 DECIMO. TERTIO 90   450   1650

1700 ANN · error on edge...600   —   —

1700 ECIMO error on edge...*Extremely rare*

3475 Halfcrown. First bust r. R. Small shields, 1696 die axis ↑↓ OCTAVO.....55   275   950

— — 1696 DECᗄS error 150   750   —

3476 Halfcrown. B (*Bristol*) below First bust, die axis ↑↓ 1696 OCTAVO 60   300   1100

— 1696 B Similar proof *FDC* £11000

3477 3478

Chester Mint Exeter Mint

3477 Halfcrown. C (*Chester*) below first bust, die axis ↑↓ 1696 OCTAVO....125   500   1400

3478 Halfcrown. E (*Exeter*) below first bust, die axis ↑↓ 1696 OCTAVO 250   650   1900

3479 Halfcrown. N (*Norwich*) below first bust, die axis ↑↓ 1696 OCTAVO 85   350   1100

3480 Halfcrown. y (*York*) below first bust, die axis ↑↓ 1696 OCTAVO 125   500   1400

3480 3481

1696 Halfcrown - York Mint 1696 Halfcrown, large sheild
reverse with early harp

3481 Halfcrown. First bust r. R. Large shield, early harp,

die axis ↑↓ 1696 OCTAVO...60   300   1000

1696 Proof plain edge...*Extremely rare*

	F	*VF*	*EF*		*F*	*VF*	*EF*
	£	*£*	*£*		*£*	*£*	*£*

3482 **Halfcrown.** — B *(Bristol)* below bust, die axis ↑↓ 1696 OCTAVO......60 325 1000

3483 **Halfcrown.** — C *(Chester)* below bust, die axis ↑↓ 1696 OCTAVO.......70 375 1100

3484 **Halfcrown.** — E *(Exeter)* below bust, die axis ↑↓ 1696 OCTAVO........80 475 1200

3485 **Halfcrown.** — N *(Norwich)* below bust, die axis ↑↓ 1696 OCTAVO....175 750 1800

3486 **Halfcrown.** — y *(York)* below bust, die axis ↑↓ 1696 OCTAVO.........75 375 1100

— — die axis ↑↓ 1696 y *(York)*, Scots Arms at date............................... *Extremely rare*

— die axis ↑↓ y over E 1696.. *Extremely rare*

3487
Large shields, ordinary harp

3488
Bristol Mint

3487 **Halfcrown.** First bust r. R. Large shields, ordinary harp die axis ↑↓

1696 OCTAVO 150	625	1550	1697 G/A in MAG..........	*Extremely rare*
1697 NONO...............50	275	950	1697/6 — 120	475 1400
1697 — GRR for GRA ....*Fair* £1150			1697 Proof plain edge *FDC*	*Extremely rare*

3488 **Halfcrown.** — B *(Bristol)* below first bust, die axis ↑↓ 1697 NONO ..55 300 1000

1697 proof on thick flan *FDC* .... *Extremely rare*

1697 — no stops on reverse...70 375 1150

3489
1696 Chester Mint Halfcrown, large shields

3489 **Halfcrown.** — C *(Chester)* below first bust, similar die axis ↑↓

1696 OCTAVO ....120 625 1600 1697 NONO...............60 350 900

3490
1697 Exeter Mint Halfcrown, large shields

	F £	VF £	EF £		F £	VF £	EF £

3490 Halfcrown. — E (*Exeter*) below first bust, similar die axis ↑↓

1696 OCTAVO	125	550	1550	1697 NONO	50	300	950
1696 NONO		*Extremely rare*		1697 — TⱯTAMEN error	*Extremely rare*		
1697 OCTAVO		*Extremely rare*		1697 E over C or B under bust	*Extremely rare*		

3491
1697 Norwich Mint Halfcrown, large shields

3491 Halfcrown. — N (*Norwich*) below first bust, similar die axis ↑↓

1696 OCTAVO	150	625	1900	1697 NONO	60	350	1050
1697 OCTAVO		*Extremely rare*		1697 — Scots Arms at date		*Fair* £1150	

3492 Halfcrown. — — y (*York*) below first bust, similar die axis ↑↓

1697 NONO	50	325	950	1697 OCTAVO		*Extremely rare*	

3493 Halfcrown. Second dr. bust r. (hair across breast), die axis ↑↓ 1696 OCTAVO   *Unique*

3494
1700 Halfcrown, modified large shields

	F	VF	EF		F	VF	EF
	£	£	£		£	£	£

3494 Halfcrown. First dr. bust ℞. Modified large shields die axis ↑↓

1698 OCTAVO .... *Extremely rare*	1699 — Lion of
1698 DECIMO 50 300 900	Nassau inverted ......650 1500 —
1698/7 — .... *Extremely rare*	1700 DVODECIMO........50 275 900
1698 UNDECIMO ....*Extremely rare*	1700 D. TERTIO 60 350 1000
1699 UNDECIMO 80 375 1150	1700 — DEC∀S error ...100 425 1150
1699 — Inverted A's for	1701 D. TERTIO 60 350 1000
V's on edge...........225 800 —	1701 — no stops
1699 — Scots Arms at date*Extremely rare*	on reverse.........................95 425 1150

3495
1701 Halfcrown, elephant and castle below bust

3495 Halfcrown. – elephant and castle below bust, die axis ↑↓ 1701 D. TERTIO *Fair* 1550

3496
1701 Halfcrown, plumes on reverse

3496 Halfcrown. – ℞. Plumes in angles, die axis ↑↓ 1701 D. TERTIO 150   625   1650

SHILLINGS

First bust   Third bust   Third bust variety

3497
First bust

3497
GVLELMVS error

3498
Bristol Mint

3500
Exeter Mint

	F	VF	EF		F	VF	EF
	£	£	£		£	£	£

3497 Shilling. First dr. bust r. R. Crowned cruciform shields edge milled die axis ↑↓

	F	VF	EF		F	VF	EF
1695 40	175	650	1697................................30	150	500
1696 30	150	500	1697 E/A in DEI	*Extremely rare*	
1696 no stops on reverse 70	200	800	1697 GRI for GRA error	*Extremely rare*	
1696 MAB for MAG error	*Extremely rare*		1697 Arms of Scot/Ireland		
1696 GVLIEMVS error ..	*Extremely rare*		transposed....................	*Extremely rare*	
1696 GVLIELMⱯS error	*Extremely rare*		1697 Irish Arms at date	*Extremely rare*	
1696 GⱯLIELMVS error	*Extremely rare*		1697 no stops on reverse 70	200	800
1696 GVLELMVS:..........	*Extremely rare*		1697 GVLELMVS error	*Extremely rare*	
1696 2nd L over M	*Extremely rare*		1697 GVLIELMⱯS error	*Extremely rare*	
1696-1669 error........1050	—	—	1697 L/M in legend..............	*Extremely rare*	

3498 Shilling. Similar B (*Bristol*) below bust die axis ↑↓

1696 50	175	700	1697................................45	175	650

3499
1696 Chester Mint Shilling

3499 Shilling. Similar C (*Chester*) below bust die axis ↑↓

1696 45	175	600	1696 thick flan proof *FDC* ..	*Extremely rare*	
1696 R/V in GRA	*Extremely rare*		1697................................45	175	600

3500 Shilling. Similar E (*Exeter*) below bust die axis ↑↓

1696 45	175	600	1697................................45	175	600
1697 E over N	*Extremely rare*				

3501 Shilling. Similar N (*Norwich*) below bust die axis ↑↓

1696 45	175	600	1697................................45	175	600
1697 no stops on obv.	*Extremely rare*				

	F	*VF*	*EF*		*F*	*VF*	*EF*
	£	£	£		£	£	£

3502 Shilling. Similar y *(York)* below bust die axis ↑↓
1696 45   175   600   1697 Arms of Scot/Ireland
1697 45   175   600   transposed.................... *Extremely rare*
1697 Arms of France/Ireland
transposed...................... *Extremely rare*
3503 Shilling. Similar Y *(York)* below bust die axis ↑↓
1696 90   225   825   1697 70   200   625
1697 Y over ⅄................. *Extremely rare*

3504   3503
Second bust   York Mint – Y

3504 Shilling. Second dr. bust r. (hair across breast), similar die axis ↑↓ 1696   *Unique*

3505   3507   3511
Third bust   Chester Mint   Third bust var.

3505 Shilling. Third dr. bust r., similar die axis ↑↓ 1697 35   150   475
3506 Shilling. Similar B *(Bristol)* below bust, die axis ↑↓ 1697 70   200   675
3507 Shilling. Similar C *(Chester)* below bust die axis ↑↓
1696 185   475   1150   1697 no stops on reverse 85   225   825
1697 45   175   575   1697 Arms of Scotland
1697 FR.A error..........85   225   825   at date .... *Extremely rare*
3508 Shilling. Similar E *(Exeter)* below bust, die axis ↑↓
1696 .... *Extremely rare*   1697 70   200   675
3509 Shilling. Similar N *(Norwich)* below bust, die axis ↑↓ 1697 70   200   675
3510 Shilling. Similar y *(York)* below bust die axis ↑↓
1696 .... *Extremely rare*   1697 70   200   675
3511 Shilling. Third bust variety r. similar die axis ↑↓
1697 GⱯLIELMVS error   *Extremely rare*   1697 GVLIELMⱯS error .... *Extremely rare*
1697 30   150   475   1698 45   175   600
                                                          1698 plain edge proof *FDC* £3000
3512 Shilling. Similar B *(Bristol)* below bust, die axis ↑↓ 1697 70   200   675
3513 Shilling. Similar C *(Chester)* below bust, die axis ↑↓ 1697 165   425   1100
3514 Shilling. Similar R. Plumes in angles, die axis ↑↓ 1698 215   525   1250

Third bust	Fourth bust	Fifth bust

3515
Fourth bust

3516
Fifth bust

	F £	VF £	EF £		F £	VF £	EF £

3515 Shilling Fourth dr. bust ('flaming hair') r. similar die axis ↑↓

1698 85	375	1100		1699 85	375	1100
1698 No stops on reverse	*Extremely rare*			1699 plain edge proof *FDC* £3500		
1698 plain edge proof *FDC* £4000						

3516 Shilling. Fifth dr. bust (hair high) r. similar die axis ↑↓

1699 80	250	725		1700 Tall O's no stops		
1700 45	150	450		on reverse...........70	175	525
1700 Circular small				1701 80	200	625
O's in date...................55	175	500		1701 DEI/GRA...............	*Extremely rare*	
1700 no stop after DEI....	*Extremely rare*					

3517
1699 Shilling, plumes on reverse

3517 Shilling. Similar R. Plumes in angles die axis ↑↓

1699 100	375	1000		1701 100	375	1000

3518
1699 Shilling, roses on reverse

3520
First bust Sixpence

3518 Shilling. Similar R. Roses in angles, die axis ↑↓ 1699.......................140 450 1100

3519 Shilling. Similar plume below bust, die axis ↑↓ 1700.......................1600 3250 —

SIXPENCES

First bust	Third bust	Early harp. large crown.	Later harp, small crown.

| | F £ | VF £ | EF £ | | F £ | VF £ | EF £ |

3520 Sixpence. First dr. bust r. R. Crowned cruciform shields, edge milled early harp die axis ↑↓

1695 45	140	525	1696..Scots Arms at date		*Extremely rare*	
1696 25	95	325	1696/5 50	140	525
1696 Heavy flan..............	*Extremely rare*		1696 no stops on		
1696 French Arms at date	*Extremely rare*		obverse...............40	120	475
1696 GVLIELMⱯS	*Extremely rare*		1696 DFI for DEI	*Extremely rare*	

3521 Sixpence. Similar B *(Bristol)* below bust, die axis ↑↓ 1696.................30 | 95 | 375
  — — 1696 B over E.. *Extremely rare*
3522 Sixpence. Similar C *(Chester)* below bust, die axis ↑↓ 1696 ....35 | 110 | 475
3523 Sixpence. Similar E *(Exeter)* below bust, die axis ↑↓ 1696 ....45 | 120 | 525
3524 Sixpence. Similar N *(Norwich)* below bust, die axis ↑↓ 1696..............55 | 140 | 475

3525
1696 York Mint Sixpence, early harp, first bust

3525 Sixpence. Similar y *(York)* below bust, die axis ↑↓ 1696......................25 | 95 | 375
3526 Sixpence. Similar Y *(York)* below bust, die axis ↑↓ 1696....................45 | 145 | 525
  — — — 1696 no stops on obverse ....80 | 350 | —
3527 Sixpence. Similar R. Later harp, large crowns, die axis ↑↓ 1696..........80 | 245 | 575
  — — — 1696 no stops on obverse ....110 | 295 | 625
3528 Sixpence. — — — B *(Bristol)* below bust, similar die axis ↑↓

1696 80	250	575	1697 45	140	525
1696 no stops on					
obv. 85	275	600			

3529 Sixpence. — — — C *(Chester)* below bust, similar die axis ↑↓ 1697..75 | 245 | 575
3530 Sixpence. — — — E *(Exeter)* below bust, similar die axis ↑↓ 1697 ....40 | 145 | 525
3531 Sixpence. — — — R. small crowns, similar die axis ↑↓

1696 80	250	575	1697 Arms of France/Ireland		
1697 25	95	375	transposed..............	*Extremely rare*	
1697 GVLIELMⱯS.....80	250	575			

3532
Bristol Mint Sixpence, small crowns

	F £	VF £	EF £		F £	VF £	EF £
3532 Sixpence. — — — B *(Bristol)* below bust, similar die axis ↑↓							
1696 80		250	575	1697 35		95	400
1696 no stops on O. 90		275	600	1697 B over E.............45		145	425
3533 Sixpence. — — — C *(Chester)* below bust, similar die axis ↑↓							
1696 110		300	675	1697 Irish shield at date..		*Extremely rare*	
1697 35		95	400	1697 Plain edge 135		325	725
3534 Sixpence. — — — E *(Exeter)* below bust, similar die axis ↑↓							
1697 40		100	425	1697 E over B................		*Extremely rare*	
3535 Sixpence. — — — N *(Norwich)* below bust, similar die axis ↑↓							
1696 80		250	575	1697 35		95	400
1696 GVLIEMVS...........		*Extremely rare*					

3536
York Mint Sixpence

	F £	VF £	EF £				
3536 Sixpence. — — — y *(York)* below bust, similar die axis ↑↓							
1697 50		150	525	1697 Irish shield at date..		*Extremely rare*	

3537   3540
Second bust Sixpence   Chester Mint Sixpence, third bust

	F £	VF £	EF £		F £	VF £	EF £
3537 Sixpence. Second dr. bust r. R. Similar die axis ↑↓							
1696 225		600	1500	1696 GVLELMVS ...275		700	1500
1697 GVLIELMⱯS........		*Extremely rare*		1697 100		325	1050
1697 G/I in GRA		*Extremely rare*		1697 GR/DE in GRA......		*Extremely rare*	
1697 GVLIEMVS...........		*Extremely rare*					
3537A Sixpence. Third dr. bust, r. early harp, large crowns. E *(Exeter)* below bust, 1696					*Extremely rare*		
3537B Sixpence. — — — Y *(York)* below bust, similar die axis ↑↓ 1696					*Extremely rare*		

3538
1699 Sixpence, third bust, later harp, large crowns

	F £	VF £	EF £		F £	VF £	EF £

3538 Sixpence. Third dr. bust, r., R. Later harp, large crowns, similar die axis ↑↓

1697 GVLIEIMVS	55	225	550
1697	25	95	350	1699	80	250	575
1697 GⱯLIELMVS	..110	275	625	1700	35	95	400
1698	35	95	400	1701	40	100	425

3539 Sixpence.— — B *(Bristol)* below bust, similar die axis ↑↓

| 1697 | ....50 | 150 | 525 | 1697 IRA for FRA.......... | *Extremely rare* |

3540 Sixpence.— — C *(Chester)* below bust, similar die axis ↑↓ 1697........80 250 575
3541 Sixpence.— — E *(Exeter)* below bust, similar die axis ↑↓ 1697..........80 250 575
3542 Sixpence. Third dr. bust, r. R. Small crowns, similar die axis ↑↓

| 1697 | ....30 | 120 | 450 | 1697 G/D for GRA .... | *Extremely rare* |
| 1697 D/F in DEI .... | *Extremely rare* |

3543 Sixpence.— — C *(Chester)* below bust, similar die axis ↑↓ 1697........80 250 575
3544 Sixpence.— — E *(Exeter)* below bust, similar die axis ↑↓ 1697..........40 120 475

3545   3547
1699 York Mint Sixpence - Y provenance mark   1699 Sixpence, roses on reverse

3545 Sixpence.— — Y *(York)* below bust, similar die axis ↑↓ 1697 ....80 250 575
3546 Sixpence.— — R. Plumes in angles, similar die axis ↑↓

| 1698 | ....40 | 100 | 425 | 1699 | ....40 | 100 | 425 |

3547 Sixpence.— R. Roses in angles, similar die axis ↑↓

| 1699 | ....80 | 250 | 575 | 1699 GⱯLIELMVS .... | *Extremely rare* |

3548   3549
1700 Sixpence, plume below bust   1698 Groat or Fourpence

3548 Sixpence.— plume below bust, R. Similar die axis ↑↓ 1700 ....1250 — —
3549 Fourpence. Laur. and dr. bust r. R. 4 Crowned die axis ↑↓

1697		*Unique*		1700	11	30	120
1698	14	35	150	1701	14	35	150
1699	11	30	120	1702	10	30	110

3550 - 1695 Threepence 3551 - 1695 Twopence

	F £	VF £	EF £		F £	VF £	EF £

3550 Threepence. Laur. and dr. bust r. R. 3 Crowned die axis ↑↓

1698	11	30	110	1701 GBA for GRA	15	40	150
1699	12	35	120	1701 small lettering	11	30	110
1700	11	30	110	1701 large lettering	12	35	110

3551 Twopence. Laur. and dr. bust r. R. Crown to edge of coin, large figure 2 die axis ↑↓

1698	15	45	120

3551A Twopence. Laur. and dr. bust r. R Crown within inner circle of legend, smaller figure 2, die axis ↑↓

1698	10	35	110	1700	9	30	100
1699	9	30	100	1701	9	30	100

3552 Penny. Laur. and dr. bust r. R. 1 Crowned die axis ↑↓

1698	10	30	100	1699	10	30	110
1698 IRA for FRA error	12	40	120	1700	10	30	110
1698 HI.BREX error	12	40	120	1701	10	30	110

3553 - 1701 Maundy Set

3553 Maundy Set. The four denominations. Uniform dates

1698	75	250	700	1700	90	275	750
1699	90	275	750	1701	75	250	700

COPPER

3554 - 1696 Halfpenny

3554 Halfpenny. First issue. Laur. and cuir. bust r. R. Britannia with r. hand raised die axis ↑↓

1695	35	150	800	1697	25	150	750
1695 BRITΛNNIΛ error	200	—	—	1697 all stops omitted	250	—	—
1695 no stop on rev.	65	275	—	1697 I/E in TERTIVS	250	—	—
1695 no stops on obv.	65	275	—	1697 GVLILMVS, no rev. stop *Extremely rare*			
1696	25	150	750	1697 no stop			
1696 GVLIEMVS, no rev. stop *Extremely rare*				after TERTIVS	50	275	—
1696 TERTVS error	275	—	—	1698	35	175	850

	F £	VF £	EF £		F £	VF £	EF £

3555 Halfpenny. Second issue. Laur. and cuir. bust r. R. Britannia Date in legend die axis ↑↓

	F	VF	EF		F	VF	EF
1698 Stop after date 30	150	800		1699 BRITANNIA error.......250	—	—
1699 no stop after date 25	140	750		1699 GVLIEMVS error 250	—	—
				1699 BRITAN IA error 250	—	—

3556 Halfpenny. Third issue. Laur. and cuir. bust r. R. Britannia with r. hand on knee die axis ↑↓

	F	VF	EF		F	VF	EF
1699 25	140	750		1700 BRITANNIA error 35	150	800
1699 stop after date 250				1700 — no stop after ,......50	200	850
1699 BRITANNIA error ...95	350	—		1700 BRIVANNIA error.....Extremely rare		
1699 GVILELMVS error 275	—	—		1700 GVLIELMS............95	325	—
1699 TERTVS error 275	—	—		1700 GVLIEEMVS 50	200	850
1699 — no rev. stop 250	—	—		1700 TER TIVS...............40	175	800
1699 no stops on obv.......95	350	—		1700 I/V in TERTIVS 225	—	—
1699 no stop after				1701 30	140	750
GVLIELMVS..........95	325	—		1701 BRITANNIA 50	200	850
1700 25	140	750		1701 — no stops on obv. 275	—	—
1700 no stops on obv.......95	325	—		1701 — inverted A's		
1700 no stop after				for V's.....................60	225	900
GVLIELMVS 95	325	—				

3557
1695 Farthing date in exergue

3558
1699 Farthing date in legend

3557 Farthing. First issue Laur. and cuir. bust r. R. Britannia l. die axis ↑↓

	F	VF	EF		F	VF	EF
1695 35	200	750		1698 200	575	—
1695 GVLIELMV error 275	—	—		1698 B/G on rev. 275	—	—
1696 30	175	700		1699 35	200	725
1697 25	150	700		1699 GVLILEMVS•......125	300	—
1697 GVLIELMS error 275	—	—		1700 25	125	675
1697 TERTIV error 250	—	—		1700 RRITANNIA 275	—	—

3558 Farthing. Second issue. Laur. and cuir. bust r. R. Britannia date at end of legend die axis ↑↓

	F	VF	EF		F	VF	EF
1698 Stop after date.........40	225	850		1699 — No stop before or after Extremely rare		
1699 no stop after date 45	250	900		1699 BRITANNIA.........250	—	—
1699 no stop after				1699 BRITANNIA 250	—	—
GVLIELMVS.........Extremely rare						

Anne, the second daughter of James II, was born on 6th February 1665 and as a protestant succeeded to the throne on William III's death. Anne married Prince George of Denmark and produced 17 children, sadly none surviving to succeed to the throne. Anne died on 1st August 1714.

The Act of Union of 1707, which effected the unification of the ancient kingdoms of England and Scotland into a single realm, resulted in a change in the royal arms—on the Post-Union coinage the English lions and Scottish lion are emblazoned per pale on the top and bottom shields. After the Union the rose in the centre of the reverse of the gold coins is replaced by the Garter star.

Following a successful Anglo-Dutch expedition against Spain, bullion seized in Vigo Bay was sent to be minted into coin, and the coins made from this metal had the word VIGO placed below the Queen's bust. The elephant and castle provenance mark continues on some guineas in the Post-Union period.

Engravers and designers: Samuel Bull (d.c1720), Joseph Cave (d.c1760), James Clerk, John Croker (1670-1741), Godfrey Kneller (1646-1723)

GOLD

3560
1705 Pre-Union Five Guineas

Before Union with Scotland. The shields on the reverse are Pre-Union type.

	F £	VF £	EF £		F £	VF £	EF £
3560	**Five Guineas.** Dr. bust l, regnal year on edge in words (e.g. 1705 = QVARTO) die axis ↑↓						
1705 QVARTO	1500	4500	12000	1706 QVINTO	1250	4000	11000
3561	**Five Guineas.** Similar VIGO below bust, die axis ↑↓ 1703 (Three varieties)						
SECVNDO					17500	50000	125000

3562	3563
1706 Pre-Union Guinea	1703 VIGO Guinea

3562 Guinea. Dr. bust l. R. Crowned cruciform shields sceptres in angles die axis ↑↓

1702	400	1750	4100	1706	600	2250	4850
1702 proof *FDC*		*Extremely rare*		1707	550	2000	4600
1705	625	2500	5100				

3565   3564
1703 VIGO Half Guinea   1702 Pre-Union Half-Guinea

	F	VF	EF		F	VF	EF
	£	£	£		£	£	£

3563 **Guinea.** Similar with VIGO below bust, die axis ↑↓ 1703 ....5000 12500 27500

3564 **Half-Guinea.** Dr bust l. R. Crowned cruciform shields sceptres in angles die axis ↑↓
1702 525   1950   4750   1705..............................500   1750   4500

3565 **Half-Guinea.** Similar with VIGO below bust, 1703 ....4000 10000 20000

3566
1706 Post-Union Five Guineas

After Union with Scotland. The shields on the reverse are changed to Post-Union type die axis ↑↓

3566 **Five Guineas.** Dr. bust l., regnal year on edge in words 1706 QVINTO 1750   3750   10000

3567   3568
1709 - Narrow shields   1713 - Broad shields

3567 **Five Guineas.** Similar R. Narrower shields, tall narrow crowns, larger rev. lettering, die axis ↑↓
1709 OCTAVO 1500   4000   11000

3568 **Five Guineas.** New bust l. R. Broader shields edge inscribed die axis ↑↓
1711 DECIMO 1500   3750   10000   1714/3 D. TERTIO 1500   4500   12000
1713 DVODECIMO 1500 4250   11500   1714 D. TERTIO..........1650   4750   12500

3569
1713 Two Guineas

	F	VF	EF		F	VF	EF
	£	£	£		£	£	£

3569 Two Guineas. Dr. bust l.R. Crowned cruciform shields sceptres in angles edge milled die axis ↑↓

| 1709 | 675 | 2250 | 5000 | 1713 | 650 | 2000 | 4500 |
| 1711 | 650 | 2000 | 4500 | 1714/3 | 750 | 2500 | 5500 |

3570 Guinea. First dr. bust l. R. Crowned cruciform shields sceptres in angles edge milled die axis ↑↓

| 1707 | 350 | 1250 | 3100 | 1708 | | | *Extremely rare* |

3571
1707 Guinea, first bust, elephant and castle below

3574
1713 Guinea, third bust

3571 Guinea. First dr. bust l. elephant and castle below, R. Similar die axis ↑↓

| 1707 | 550 | 1650 | 4350 | 1708 | | | *Extremely rare* |

3572 Guinea. Second dr. bust l. R. Similar die axis ↑↓

| 1707 | | *Extremely rare* | | 1709 | 350 | 1100 | 3100 |
| 1708 | 300 | 1250 | 3100 | | | | |

3573 Guinea. Second bust elephant and castle below R. Similar die axis ↑↓

| 1708 | 550 | 1750 | 2350 | 1709 | 500 | 1850 | 4100 |

3574 Guinea. Third dr. bust l. R. Similar die axis ↑↓

1710	325	900	2600	1713	300	750	1600
1711	350	1000	2600	1714	300	750	1600
1712	350	1000	2600	1714 GRATIA	600	1250	3100
1713/1	500	1000	2600				

3575
1713 Half-Guinea

3575 Half-Guinea. Dr. bust l. R. Crowned cruciform shields, sceptres in angles, edge milled die axis ↑↓

1707	325	950	2600	1711	300	900	2350
1708	350	1000	2850	1712	275	850	2100
1709	325	950	2600	1713	250	750	1950
1710	250	750	1950	1714	275	850	2100

SILVER

3576
1703 VIGO Crown

	F	VF	EF		F	VF	EF
	£	£	£		£	£	£

Before Union with Scotland. The shields on the reverse are Pre-Union type.

3576 Crown. VIGO below dr. bust, l., regnal year on edge in words (e.g. 1703 = TERTIO) die axis↑↓
1703 TERTIO 325   1200   3900

3577	3578
1705 Crown, plumes on reverse	1707 Pre-Union crown, roses and plumes

3577 Crown. Dr bust l. R. Plumes in angles, die axis ↑↓ 1705 QVINTO ...500   1750   4900
3578 Crown. R. Similar Crowned cruciform shields Roses and plumes in angles die axis ↑↓
    1706 QVINTO 150   650   2100   1707 SEXTO 175   700   2400

3579
1703 Halfcrown, plain below bust

3579 Halfcrown . Dr. bust l. R. Similar Regnal year on edge in words die axis ↑↓
    1703 TERTIO...650   2500   9500

3580
1703 VIGO Halfcrown

3581
1705 Halfcrown, plumes on reverse

	F	VF	EF		F	VF	EF
	£	£	£		£	£	£

3580 Halfcrown. Similar VIGO below bust, die axis ↑↓ 1703 TERTIO 120   375   1250

3581 Halfcrown. Dr. bust l. R. Plumes in angles, similar die axis ↑↓
  1704 TERTIO............140   625   1900   1705 QVINTO..........120   500   1500

3582
1707 Halfcrown, Pre-Union, roses and plumes

3583
1702 Shilling

3582 Halfcrown. Dr. bust l. R. Roses and plumes in angles, similar die axis ↑↓
  1706 QVINTO 95   375   1150   1707 SEXTO 85   325   1050

First bust   Second bust

3583 Shilling. First dr. bust l. R. Similar die axis ↑↓ 1702..............................75   325   700

3584
1702 Shilling, plumes on reverse

3584 Shilling. Similar R. Plumes in angles, die axis ↑↓ 1702 85   350   750

3585 Shilling. First dr. bust VIGO below , die axis ↑↓
  1702 80   300   700   1702 :ANNA .... *Extremely rare*

3586
1703 VIGO Shilling

3587
1705 'Plain' Shilling

	F	VF	EF		F	VF	EF
	£	£	£		£	£	£

3586 **Shilling.** Second dr. bust, l. VIGO below R. Similar, die axis ↑↓ 1703 ....65 | 225 | 600

3587 **Shilling.** Similar R. Crowned cruciform shields, angles plain, die axis ↑↓
1704 550   1500   —   1705 90   375   775

3588 **Shilling.** Second dr. bust l. R. Plumes in angles die axis ↑↓
1704 90   400   875   1705 75   300   700

3589 **Shilling.** Second dr. bust l. R. Roses and plumes in angles die axis ↑↓
1705 70   250   650   1707 70   275   675

3590 **Sixpence.** Dr. bust l. VIGO below dr. bust, l. die axis ↑↓ 1703.................40   150   375

3591 **Sixpence.** Dr bust l., R. Angles plain, die axis ↑↓ 1705 70   200   600

3592 **Sixpence.** Similar R. Early shields, plumes in angles, die axis ↑↓ 1705 50   175   475

3593
1705 Plumes Sixpence

Early Shield

Late Shield

3593 **Sixpence.** Similar R. Late shields, plumes in angles, die axis ↑↓1705 60   175   550

3594 **Sixpence.** Similar R. Crowned cruciform shields Roses and plumes in angles die axis ↑↓
1705 60   160   525   1707 45   150   425

3595 **Fourpence.** First dr. bust l. small face, curls at back of head point downwards.
R Small crown above the figure 4 die axis ↑↓
1703 10   30   90   1704 8   25   80

3595
1709 Groat or fourpence, first bust

3595C
1710 Groat or Fourpence, second bust

3595A Fourpence. Second dr. bust l. larger face, curls at back of head point upwards die axis ↑↓
1705 10   30   90   1709 8   25   75
1706 8   25   75   1710 8   25   75
1708 8   25   75

3595B –Fourpence. Similar R Large crown with pearls on arch, larger serifs on the figure 4 die axis ↑↓
1710 8   25   75   1713 8   25   80

3595C Fourpence. Second dr. bust l., but with re-engraved hair R. Crowned 4 die axis ↑↓
1710 8   25   75   1713 8   25   80

3596 **Threepence.** First dr. bust l., broader, tie riband pointing outwards. R. Crowned 3 die axis ↑↓
1703 7 above crown 12   35   100   1703 7 not above crown......12   35   100

	F	VF	EF		F	VF	EF
	£	£	£		£	£	£

3596A Threepence. Second dr. bust l., taller and narrow, tie riband pointing inwards die axis ↑↓

1704	10	30	90	1706	8	25	75
1705	10	30	90				

3596B
1707 Threepence, third bust

3596B Threepence. Third larger more finely engraved dr. bust l. R. Crowned 3, die axis ↑↓

1707	8	25	75	1710	8	25	75
1708	8	25	85	1713	8	25	75
1708/7	8	25	75	1713 mule with 4d obv.			
1709	8	25	75	die	12	35	130

3597 Twopence. First dr. bust l., as fourpence, R. Crown to edge of coin, small figure 2 die axis ↑↓

1703	12	30	90	1705	8	25	65
1704	8	25	65	1706	10	25	75
1704 No stops on obv.	12	30	90	1707	10	25	75

3597A Twopence. Second dr. bust l., as fourpence, R Crown within inner circle of legend, large figure 2 die axis ↑↓

1708	8	25	65	1710	8	25	65
1709	10	30	75	1713	8	25	65

3598 Penny. Dr. bust l. R. Crowned 1 die axis ↑↓

1703	12	30	100	1709	10	30	85
1705	10	30	85	1710	14	35	110
1706	10	30	85	1713/0	12	30	100
1708	14	35	110				

3599
1713 Maundy Set

	F	VF	EF		F	VF	EF
	£	£	£		£	£	£

3599 Maundy Set. The four denominations. Uniform dates

1703	75	175	700	1709	75	175	600
1705	75	175	700	1710	80	200	700
1706	65	150	575	1713	70	175	625
1708	80	200	700				

After Union with Scotland

The shields on the reverse are changed to the Post-Union types. The Edinburgh coins have been included here as they are now coins of Great Britain.

3600
1708E Edinburgh Mint Crown

	F	*VF*	*EF*		*F*	*VF*	*EF*
	£	£	£		£	£	£

3600   Crown. Second dr. bust, l. E (Edinburgh) below, R. Crowned
cruciform shields regnal year on edge in words, die axis ↑↓
(e.g. 1708 = SEPTIMO)

1707 SEXTO 100	500	1150	1708/7 SEPTIMO..........150	600	1500
1708 SEPTIMO 120	550	1300	1708/7 M/E on edge 175	700	1800

3601
1708 Crown, second bust, plain reverse

3601   Crown. Second dr. bust l. R. Crowned cruciform shields, angles plain die axis ↑↓

1707 SEPTIMO 120	550	1300	1708 SEPTIMO 200	900	—

3602   Crown. Similar R. Plumes in angles, die axis ↑↓

1708 SEPTIMO 150	600	1500	1708 — BR for BRI ....*Extremely rare*

3603
1713 Crown, third bust, roses and plumes

3603   Crown. Third dr. bust. l. R. Roses and plumes, 1713 DVODECIMO 120   600   1400

3604

1708 Halfcrown, Post-Union

	F	VF	EF		F	VF	EF
	£	£	£		£	£	£

3604   Halfcrown. Dr. bust R. Plain, regnal year on edge in words (e.g. 1709 = OCTAVO), die axis ↑↓

1707 SEPTIMO	60	300	950	1709 OCTAVO	60	300	950
1707 no stops on reverse	125	500	—	1708 SEPTIMO	70	375	1050
1713 DVODECIMO	70	350	1050				

3605   Halfcrown. Dr. bust E below R. Crowned cruciform shields die axis ↑↓

1707 SEXTO	40	200	750	1708 SEPTIMO	70	375	1050
1707 SEPTIMO	*Extremely rare*			1709 OCTAVO	325	1050	—

3606

1708 Halfcrown, plumes on reverse

3609

1707 Edinburgh Mint Shilling

3606   Halfcrown. Similar R. Plumes in angles, die axis ↑↓ 1708 SEPTIMO 80   400   1250

3607

1714 Halfcrown, roses and plumes

3607   Halfcrown. Similar R. Roses and plumes in angles die axis ↑↓

1710 NONO	70	350	1050	1714 D. TERTIO	60	300	950
1712 UNDECIMO	60	250	850	1714/3 D. TERTIO	100	475	1300
1713 DVODECIMO	70	350	1050				

3608
1707 Edinburgh Mint Shilling, second bust

3609
1708 E* Shilling

	F £	VF £	EF £		F £	VF £	EF £
3608 Shilling. Second dr. bust, l. E *(Edinburgh)* below, R. Crowned cruciform shields die axis ↑↓							
1707 45	250	600	1707 Plain edge proof *FDC* £3500			
1707 no stops on reverse *Extremely rare*			1708 100	375	825		
3609 Shilling. Similar E* *(Edinburgh)* below bust die axis ↑↓							
1707 100	375	825	1708/7	*Extremely rare*		
1708 60	275	650	1708 no rays to garter star	*Extremely rare*		
3609A Shilling. Similar E* *(Edinburgh)* local dies die axis ↑↓							
1707 225	700	—	1708 225	650	—		

Third bust   Fourth bust

3610
1707 Shilling, third bust

3611
1708 shilling, plumes on reverse

	F £	VF £	EF £		F £	VF £	EF £
3610 Shilling Third dr. bust. l. R. Crowned cruciform shields, angles Plain, die axis ↑↓							
1707 35	175	500	1709 25	120	375		
1708 25	120	375	1711 200	575	1250		
3611 Shilling. Third dr. bust. l. R. Plumes in angles die axis ↑↓							
1707 45	225	600	1708 35	175	475		
3612 Shilling. Third dr. bust. E below R. angles plain die axis ↑↓							
1707 35	125	500	1708/7 125	400	925		
1708 100	350	825					
3613 Shilling. Second dr. bust l. R. Roses and plumes, die axis ↑↓ 1708 ...125	400	925					

3614
1708 Shilling, roses and plumes

	F £	VF £	EF £		F £	VF £	EF £
3614 Shilling. Third dr. bust l. R. Crowned cruciform shields Roses and plumes die axis ↑↓							
1708 100	375	825	1710 35	175	500		

3615
Edinburgh bust – E* Shilling

3620
Edinburgh Mint Sixpence

3623
1707 Sixpence, plumes on reverse

	F £	VF £	EF £		F £	VF £	EF £
3615 Shilling. 'Edinburgh' bust, E* below, R. Crowned cruciform shields die axis ↑↓							
1707		*Extremely rare*		1709	100	350	825
1708 100		300	700				
3616 Shilling. — E below, R. Similar die axis ↑↓ 1709 275					1000	—	
3617 Shilling. Fourth dr. bust. l. R. Roses and plumes die axis ↑↓							
1710 50		225	550	1713/2 50	225	550	
1710 plain edge proof *FDC*		*Extremely rare*		1714 35	175	500	
1712 35		175	500	1714/3	*Extremely rare*		
3618 Shilling. Similar, R. angles plain, die axis ↑↓							
1711 20		90	250	1711 plain edge proof *FDC*	*Extremely rare*		
3619 Sixpence. Normal dr. bust. l. R. angles plain die axis ↑↓							
1707 30		95	300	1711 30	75	225	
1707 BR. FRA error........		*Extremely rare*		1711 Large Lis............25	70	200	
1708 35		125	350				
3620 Sixpence. Normal dr. bust E *(Edinburgh)* below R. Similar die axis ↑↓							
1707 35		125	350	1708/7 60	200	475	
1707 Proof FDC £3000				1708 45	150	375	
3621 Sixpence. Normal dr. bust E* *(Edinburgh)* below, R. Similar die axis ↑↓							
1708 45		150	400	1708/7 55	200	450	
3622 Sixpence. 'Edinburgh' bust, l. E* below, R. Similar die axis ↑↓ 1708 ..45					150	375	
3623 Sixpence. Normal dr. bust. l. R. Plumes in angles die axis ↑↓							
1707 35		125	325	1708 45	150	375	
3624 Sixpence. Similar R. Roses and plumes in angles, die axis ↑↓ 1710....45					150	375	

COPPER

3625
1714 Farthing

3625 Farthing. Dr. bust l. R. Britannia 1714 pattern only, die axis ↑↓ 275   475   900

GEORGE I, 1714-27

George I was born on 28th May 1660 son of Ernest, Elector of Hanover and Sophia grandaughter of James I, and inherited the English Throne on a technicality, Parliament considered him a better alternative than James Edward Stuart – Anne's half-brother. He was however, thoroughly German, did not want to learn English and spent over half his reign in Germany. He brought two mistresses with him to England while his wife ironically languished in a German prison on a charge of adultery. His reign created a government that could run independently of the King. The office of Prime Minister was created in 1721. He also kept England out of war for his entire reign, and he died on 11 June 1727.

The coins of the first of the Hanoverian kings have the arms of the Duchy of Brunswick and Luneberg on one of the four shields, the object in the centre of the shield being the Crown of Charlemagne. The King's German titles also appear, in abbreviated form, and name him 'Duke of Brunswick and Luneberg. Arch-treasurer of the Holy Roman Empire, and Elector', and on the Guinea of 1714, 'Prince Elector'. A Quarter-Guinea was struck for the first time in 1718, but it was of an inconvenient size, and the issue was discontinued. The elephant and castle provenance mark continues on some guineas and half-guineas, but today are rarely seen.

Silver coined from bullion supplied to the mint by the South Sea Company in 1723 shows the Company's initials S.S.C.; similarly Welsh Copper Company bullion has the letters W.C.C. below the King's bust; and plumes and an interlinked CC in the reverse angles. Roses and plumes together on the reverse indicate silver supplied by the Company for Smelting Pit Coale and Sea Coale.

Engravers and Designers: Samuel Bull (d.c.1720), John Croker (1670-1741), John Rudulf Ochs Snr, (1673-c.1748), Norbert Roettier (b.1665)

Prime Minister: Sir Robert Walpole (1676 – 1745) –Whig, 1721-42

GOLD

3626
1717 Five Guineas

	F	VF	EF		F	VF	EF
	£	£	£		£	£	£

3626 Five Guineas. Laur. head r. regnal year on edge in words (e.g. 1717 = TERTIO) die axis ↑↓

	F	VF	EF		F	VF	EF
1716 SECVNDO.....1750	4500	10500		1720 SEXTO..........2500	7000	18000
1717 TERTIO..........2000	6000	15000		1726 D. TERTIO....1850	5000	12000
1717 Cl edge error...2250	6500	16000				

3627
1717 Two Guineas

	F £	VF £	EF £		F £	VF £	EF £

3627 **Two Guineas.** Laur. head r. R. Crowned cruciform shields, sceptres in angles, edge milled, die axis ↑↓

1717	650	1850	4500	1720/17	750	1950	4750
1720	600	1800	4500	1726	550	1600	4000

3628
1714 'Prince Elector' Guinea

3630
Third bust

3631
Fourth bust

3628 **Guinea.** First laur. head r. R. Legend ends ET PR . EL (Prince Elector), die axis ↑↓

1714	1000	2750	5150

3629 **Guinea.** Second laur. head, r. tie with two ends, R. Crowned cruciform shields, sceptres in angles normal legend ↑↓ 1715 ...... 350 1500 3650

3630 **Guinea.** Third laur. head, r. no hair below truncation R. Similar die axis ↑↓

1715	325	1300	3350	1716	350	1450	3650

3631 **Guinea.** Fourth laur. head, r. tie with loop at one end R. Similar die axis ↑↓

1716	325	1350	3350	1720	375	1600	3900
1717	375	1600	3900	1721	325	1350	3400
1718		*Extremely rare*		1722	300	1250	3150
1718/7		*Extremely rare*		1722/0	400	1650	4150
1719	325	1350	3400	1723	325	1350	3400
1719/6		*Extremely rare*					

3632 **Guinea.** Fourth Laur. head, elephant and castle below R. Similar die axis ↑↓

1721	*Extremely rare*	1722	*Extremely rare*

3633
1724 Guinea, fifth bust

3635
1724 Half Guinea, first bust

3633 **Guinea.** Fifth (older) laur. head, r. tie with two ends R. Similar die axis ↑↓

1723	300	1250	3150	1726	250	1100	2800
1724	400	1750	4150	1727	375	1600	3900
1725	375	1600	3900				

3634 **Guinea.** Fifth laur. head, elephant and castle below, die axis ↑↓ 1726 ...... 1250 3750 8950

	F	VF	EF		F	VF	EF
	£	£	£		£	£	£

3635 Half-Guinea. First laur. head r. R. Crowned cruciform shields, sceptres in angles die axis ↑↓

1715	350	800	2150	1721		*Extremely rare*	
1717	275	650	1650	1722	250	600	1550
1718	200	525	1350	1722/0	300	850	1750
1718/7	250	600	1550	1723	750	—	—
1719	275	650	1650	1724	325	700	1900
1720	275	650	1650				

3636 Half-Guinea. First laur. head elephant and castle below, die axis ↑↓ 1721   *Extremely rare*

3637
Half-Guinea, second bust

3638
1718 Quarter Guinea

3637 Half-Guinea. Second (older) laur. head r. R. Crowned cruciform shields, sceptres in angles die axis ↑↓

1725	200	400	1000	1727	250	600	1550
1726	250	500	1400				

3638 Quarter-Guinea. Laur. head R. Similar die axis ↑↓ 1718 120   250   475

SILVER

3639A
1726 Crown - small roses and plumes

3639 Crown. Laur and dr. bust r. R. Roses and plumes in angles, regnal year on edge in words (e.g. 1716 = SECVNDO) die axis ↑↓

1716 SECVNDO	225	750	3000	1720/18 SEXTO	250	850	3300
1718/6 QUINTO	250	800	3300				

3639A Crown. Similar R. small roses and plumes in angles

1720 SEXTO	300	1000	4400	1726 D. TERTIO	300	900	4200

3640 Crown. Similar R. SSC (South Sea Company) in angles, die axis ↑↓

1723 DECIMO 250   800   2900

3641
1715 Pattern Halfcrown

3641 Halfcrown. Laur and dr. bust r. R. Angles plain (pattern only), die axis ↑↓ 1715 *FDC* £4500

3642
1720 Halfcrown, roses and plumes

3643
1723 SSC Halfcrown

	F £	VF £	EF £		F £	VF £	EF £

3642 Halfcrown. — R. Roses and plumes in angles, regnal year on edge in words (e.g. 1717 = TIRTIO)

1715 SECVNDO	125	575	1800	1717 TIRTIO	150	625	1900
1715 Edge wording out of order	250	750	2000	1720/17 SEXTO	125	575	1800
1715 Plain edge		*Extremely rare*		1720 SEXTO	300	1100	2800

3643 Halfcrown. Similar R. SSC in angles, die axis ↑↓ 1723 DECIMO 120   625   1800

3644
1726 Halfcrown small roses and plumes

3644 Halfcrown. — R. Small roses and plumes, die axis ↑↓ 1726 D. TERTIO ..2250   5500   10500

3645
1716 Shilling, roses and plumes

3646
1721 Shilling, plain reverse

3645 Shilling. First laur. and dr. bust. r. R. Roses and plumes in angles, die axis ↑↓

1715	45	225	700	1721	50	275	800
1716	85	375	1050	1721/0	45	200	700
1717	45	200	700	1721/19	45	250	800
1718	40	175	625	1721/18 plumes and roses error		*Extremely rare*	
1719	75	325	950	1722	45	200	700
1720	45	200	700	1723	45	200	700
1720/18	110	425	1250				

3646 Shilling. First laur. and dr. bust r. R. angles plain (i.e. no marks either side) die axis ↑↓

1720	35	150	575	1721	100	400	1200
1720 large O	40	175	625				

3647
1723 SSC Shilling, first bust

3649
1727 Shilling, second bust

	F	VF	EF		F	VF	EF
	£	£	£		£	£	£

3647 Shilling. First laur. and dr. bust r. ℝ. SSC in angles, die axis ↑↓

1723	30	95	400	1723 C/SS in 3rd			
1723 French Arms at				quarter	45	120	450
date	90	275	925				

3648 Shilling. Second dr. bust, r. bow to tie. ℝ. Similar, die axis ↑↓ 1723 ...50 125 400

3649 Shilling. Similar ℝ. Roses and plumes in angles die axis ↑↓

1723	65	250	650	1726	575	1350	—
1724	65	250	650	1727	625	1500	—
1725	65	250	650	1727 no stops on rev.	600	1450	—
1725 no stops on obv.	95	350	825				

3650
1723 WCC Shilling

3651
1720/17 Sixpence

	F	VF	EF		F	VF	EF
	£	£	£		£	£	£

3650 Shilling. Second laur. and dr. bust r. W.C.C. (Welsh Copper Company) below bust die axis ↑↓

1723	325	900	2650	1725	375	1000	2900
1724	325	900	2650	1726	325	900	2650

3651 Sixpence. Laur. and dr. bust r. ℝ. Roses and plumes in angles, die axis ↑↓

1717	65	225	550	1720/17		65	225	550
1717 Plain edge	*Extremely rare*							

3652
1723 SSC Sixpence

3653
1726 Sixpence, small roses and plumes

3652 Sixpence. Laur. and dr. bust r. ℝ. SSC in angles, die axis ↑↓

1723	25	110	300	1723 larger lettering	30	115	325

3653 Sixpence. Similar ℝ. Small roses and plumes, die axis ↑↓ 1726 ....45 185 550

3654   3655

	F £	VF £	EF £		F £	VF £	EF £

3654 Fourpence. Laur. and dr. bust r. ℞. Crowned 4, die axis ↑↓

| 1717 | 9 | 30 | 100 | 1723 | 9 | 30 | 100 |
| 1721 | 9 | 30 | 100 | 1727 | 12 | 35 | 110 |

3655 Threepence. Laur. and dr. bust r. ℞. Crowned 3, die axis ↑↓

| 1717 | 8 | 30 | 90 | 1723 | 9 | 30 | 100 |
| 1721 | 9 | 30 | 100 | 1727 small lettering | 9 | 30 | 100 |

3656 Twopence. Laur. and dr. bust r. ℞. Crowned 2, die axis ↑↓

1717	6	25	60	1726	5	20	55
1721	5	20	55	1727 small lettering	8	25	65
1723	9	30	75				

3657 Penny. Laur. and dr. bust r. ℞. Crowned 1, die axis ↑↓

1716	5	25	55	1723	6	25	60
1718	5	25	55	1725	5	22	55
1720	5	25	55	1726	8	30	65
1720 HIPEX error	10	65	120	1727 BRI·FR	10	45	85

3658

3658 Maundy Set. As last four. Uniform dates

| 1723 | 80 | 200 | 725 | 1727 | 75 | 175 | 650 |

COPPER

3659

3659 Halfpenny. 'Dump' issue obv. legend continuous over bust, plain edge, die axis ↑↓

1717	25	175	550	1718 no stops on obv	150	450	—
1717 no stops on obv	95	475	—	1719	650	—	—
1718	25	175	550	1719 grained edge	900	—	—
1718 R/B on rev	50	200	800				

3660A

	F £	VF £	EF £		F £	VF £	EF £

3660 Halfpenny. Second issue, second obverse, plain left shoulder strap, less hair to the right of tie knot, R. Britannia plain edge, die axis ↑↓

1719 35	150	625	1722.................................30	125	575
1719 grained edge 900	—	—	1722 Ɐ for V on obv. 100	450	—
1720 25	120	550	1723.................................25	120	550
1721 30	125	575	1723 Thin Flan .... *Extremely rare*
1721 stop after date 40	160	625	1723 no stop on rev. 100	475	—
1721/0 40	160	625	1724.................................25	120	550

3660A Halfpenny. Second issue, second obverse, ornate shoulder straps, die axis ↑↓

1719 40	150	675

3661   3662

3661 Farthing. 'Dump' issue, Similar die axis ↑↓ 1717 200   575   950

3662 Farthing. Second issue laur. and cuir. bust r. R. Britannia, date in ex. die axis ↑↓

1719 small letters..........85	425	—	1721.................................25	100	475
1719 no stop on rev. 60	375	—	1721/0 35	140	525
1719 large lettering on obv. 25	125	475	1721 stop after date 35	125	500
			1722.................................30	120	500
1719 — no stops on obv. 70	400	—	1722 obv. large letters 40	175	575
1719 — no stops on rev ..85	425	—	1723 R/≈ in REX 225	—	—
1720 25	125	475	1723.................................30	120	500
1720 obv. large letters ..85	400	—	1724.................................30	120	500
1719 last A/I on rev. 85	400	—			

George II was born on 30 October 1683 and was raised in Hanover, but upon his succession to the throne as George I's only child, he adapted himself to English society. His passions were the military, music and his wife – Caroline of Anspach, though he despised his eldest son Frederick as his own father despised him. George declared war on Spain in 1739 and he was the last King to have personally led his troops at the battle of Dettingen on 17 June 1743. Upon his death on 25 October 1760 the throne passed to his grandson George as Frederick had already died.

Silver was coined only spasmodically by the Mint during this reign; and no copper was struck after 1754. Gold coins made from bullion supplied by the East India Company bear the Company's E.I.C. initials. Some of the treasure seized by Admiral Anson during his circumnavigation of the globe, 1740-4, and by other privateers, was made into coin, which had the word LIMA below the king's bust to celebrate the expedition's successful harassment of the Spanish Colonies in the New World. Hammered gold was finally demonetized in 1733.

Engravers and designers: John Croker (1670-1741), John Rudolf Ochs Snr (1673-1748) and jnr (1704-88), Johann Sigismund Tanner (c.1706-75)

Prime Ministers: Sir Robert Walpole (1676-1745) Whig, 1721-43; Spencer Compton (1673-1743) Whig 1742-3; Henry Pelham (c.1695-1754) Whig 1743-54; William Cavendish (1720-1764) Whig 1756-7; Thomas Pelham-Holles (1693-1768) Whig 1754-6; 1757-62.

GOLD

3663A
1741 Five Guineas - revised shield

	F	VF	EF		F	VF	EF
	£	£	£		£	£	£

3663 Five Guineas. Young laur. head l. R. Crowned shield of arms, die axis ↑↓ regnal year
on edge in words (e.g. 1729 = TERTIO) 1729 TERTIO..............1750 4750 10500
1729 Plain edge proof *FDC* £30000

3663A Five Guineas. Similar R. Revised shield garnish die axis ↑↓

	F	VF	EF		F	VF	EF
1731 QVARTO...........2250	6000	12500		1738 DVODECIMO.....2000	5250	11500
1731 QVARTO proof *FDC* £35000				1741/38 D. QVARTO....1500	4500	10000
1735 NONO.................2250	6000	12500		1741 D. QVARTO.......1350	4000	9500

3664 Five Guineas. Young laur. head, E.I.C. (East India Company) below, die axis ↑↓
1729 TERTIO N's of ANNO inverted 1250 3750 9000

3665
1746 LIMA Five Guineas

	F	VF	EF		F	VF	EF
	£	£	£		£	£	£

3665 Five Guineas. Old laur. head, l. LIMA below, ↑↓1746 D. NONO ..1350   4000   9500
3666 Five Guineas. Old laur. head plain below, R. Crowned shield, edge inscribed die axis ↑↓
1748 V. SECVNDO 1350   4000   9500   1753 V. SEXTO 1500   4500   10000

3667B
Repositioned legend

3667A
1735 Two Guineas - new reverse

3667 Two Guineas. Young laur. head l. R Crowned shield with rounded arches, die axis ↑↓
1733 Proof *FDC* £20,000   1734/3 1650   3500   —
3667A* Two Guineas. – R. Crown with pointed arches, new type of shield garnishing die axis ↑↓
1735 550   1500   3250
3667B* Two Guineas. Repositioned legend on obverse R. Similar
1738 425   850   2000   1739 400   750   1750
* *Beware recent forgeries*

3668
1740 Two Guineas - Intermediate head

3668* Two Guineas. Intermediate laur. head l. R. Crowned shield of arms die axis ↑↓
1739 450   850   2000   1740 425   800   2000
1740/39 550   1100   2250
3669* Two Guineas. Old laur. head l. R. Crowned shield of arms die axis ↑↓ ..
1748 425   1000   3000   1753 575   1400   3750

**Beware recent forgeries*.
Ↄverstruck dates are listed only if commoner than normal date or if no normal date is known.

	F	VF	EF		F	VF	EF
	£	£	£		£	£	£

3670 Guinea. First young laur. head, l. small lettering, die axis ↑↓ 1727 ...825   2250   4900

3671
1727 Guinea - small reverse shield

3674
1738 Guinea - second young head

	F	VF	EF		F	VF	EF
	£	£	£		£	£	£

3671 Guinea. Similar larger lettering, smaller shield, die axis ↑↓
1727 400   1500   3650   1728 550   2000   4400

3672 Guinea. Second (narrower) young laur. head l. die axis ↑↓
1729 Proof *FDC* £7500   1731 425   1650   3900
1730 450   1750   4150   1732 375   1400   3150

3673 Guinea. Second young laur. head, E.I.C. below R. Crowned shield of arms die axis ↑↓
1729 550   2000   4400   1732 425   1650   3900
1731 475   1750   4150

3674 Guinea. Second young laur. head l. larger lettering R. Crowned shield of arms die axis ↑↓
1732 375   1350   2900   1736 375   1400   3150
1733 350   1000   2650   1737 450   1750   4150
1734 375   1400   3150   1738 425   1650   3900
1735 395   1400   3150

3675 Guinea. — — E.I.C. below, die axis ↑↓ 1732 425   1650   3900

3676 Guinea. Intermediate laur. head l. r. Crowned shield of arms die axis ↑↓
1739 350   1000   2650   1741/39 ....   *Extremely rare*
1740 400   1500   3400   1743 ....   *Extremely rare*

3677 Guinea. Similar E.I.C. below, R. Similar die axis ↑↓ 1739 425   1650   3900

3678 Guinea. Similar larger lettering on *obv.*, GEORGIUS die axis ↑↓
1745 400   1250   3400

3678A
1746 Guinea - GEORGIVS legend

3679
LIMA Guinea

3680
Old head Guinea

3678A Guinea. Similar as last but reads GEORGIVS die axis ↑↓
1746 375   1350   2900

3679 Guinea. Intermediate laur. head LIMA below, die axis ↑↓ 1745 900   2250   4900

3680 Guinea. Old laur. head l. R. Crowned shield of arms die axis ↑↓
1747 300   750   1900   1753 325   775   2050
1748 250   575   1500   1755 325   750   1950
1749 325   775   1950   1756 325   750   1950
1750 300   750   1850   1758 275   650   1750
1751 375   800   2100   1759 275   600   1550
1752 275   600   1600   1760 275   600   1600

| | F | VF | EF | | F | VF | EF |
| | £ | £ | £ | | £ | £ | £ |

3681 **Half-Guinea**. Young laur. head. l. R First shield of arms, die axis ↑↓

| 1728 | ....275 | 750 | 2350 | 1729 | ....350 | 950 | 3100 |

1728 Proof *FDC* £6500

3681A
1730 Half-Guinea - modified shield

3681A **Half-Guinea**. Young laur. head l. R. Modified garnished shield die axis ↑↓

1730	600	2000	—	1736	325	525	3000
1731	325	900	2850	1737	....	*Extremely rare*	
1732	350	950	3100	1738	300	775	2500
1734	325	900	2850	1739	350	950	3100

3682 **Half-Guinea**. Young laur. head l. E.I.C. below R. Similar die axis ↑↓

1729	375	1000	3250	1732	....	*Extremely rare*	
1730	650	2000	—	1739	....	*Extremely rare*	
1731	....	*Extremely rare*					

3676
1740 Guinea - Intermediate head

3683A
1746 Half-guinea - GEORGIVS legend

3683 **Half-Guinea**. Intermediate laur. head l. R. Similar die axis ↑↓

| 1740 | ....375 | 1000 | 3350 | 1745 | ....325 | 925 | 2850 |
| 1743 | .... | *Extremely rare* | | | | | |

3683A **Half-Guinea**. Similar, but reads GEORGIVS, die axis ↑↓ 1746........300   800   2600

3684
1745 LIMA Half-Guinea

3685
1760 Half-Guinea, old head

3684 **Half-Guinea**. Intermediate laur. head LIMA below, die axis ↑↓ 1745 ..800   2750   5150

3685 **Half-Guinea**. Old laur. head l. R. Similar die axis ↑↓

1747	225	625	1700	1753	200	600	1550
1748	225	625	1700	1755	200	575	1450
1749	225	625	1700	1756	175	550	1350
1750	200	600	1550	1758	250	650	1850
1751	225	625	1700	1759	150	500	1100
1751/0	350	1100	2350	1759/8	225	750	1850
1752	225	625	1700	1760	175	550	1350

SILVER

3686
1735 Crown, young head

	F £	VF £	EF £		F £	VF £	EF £

3686   Crown. Young laur. and dr. bust. l. R. Crowned cruciform shields Roses and plumes
in angles, regnal year on edge in words (e.g. 1736 = NONO), die axis ↑↓

1732 SEXTO 150	675	1900	1734 No A in ANNO 225	950	2400
1732 Proof, plain edge *FDC* £4950			1735 OCTAVO 150	675	1900
1734 SEPTIMO 175	725	2150	1735 E/B on edge 175	800	2150
			1736 NONO 125	675	1900

3687   Crown. Similar R. Roses in angles die axis ↑↓

1739 DVODECIMO ..150	625	1900	1741 D. QVARTO 125	625	1650

3688
1743 Crown, old head

3688   Crown. Old laur. and dr. bust l. R. Crowned cruciform shields Roses in angles, die axis ↑↓
1743 D. SEPTIMO 125   625   1650
3689   Crown. — LIMA below, die axis ↑↓ 1746 D. NONO 125   625   1650

3690	3691
Plain reverse	1731 Pattern Halfcrown

3690   Crown. Old laur. and dr. bust l. R. angles Plain (i.e. no marks either side) die axis ↑↓
1746 Proof only, VICESIMO *FDC* £3900
1750 V. QVARTO......175   675   1900   1751 V. QVARTO 200   725   2150
3691   Halfcrown. Young dr. bust l. R. angles plain (pattern only), 1731 *FDC* £4500

3692
1736 Halfcrown, roses and plumes

3693
1741 Halfcrown, roses on reverse

	F	VF	EF		F	VF	EF
	£	£	£		£	£	£

3692 Halfcrown. Young laur. and dr. bust l. R. Roses and plumes, regnal year on edge in words
(e.g. 1732 = SEXTO), die axis ↑↓

1731 QVINTO	75	400	1200	1735 OCTAVO	85	450	1300
1732 SEXTO	75	400	1200	1736 NONO	120	500	1350
1734 SEPTIMO	85	450	1300				

3693 Halfcrown. Young laur. and dr. bust l. R. Roses in angles die axis ↑↓

1739 DVODECIMO	60	225	1000	1741 D. QVARTO	70	350	1050
1741 Large *obv.* letters	85	300	1100	1741/39 D. QVARTO	150	500	1300

3694 Halfcrown. Old dr. bust. l. GEORGIVS R. Roses in angles die axis ↑↓

1743 D. SEPTIMO	55	250	950	1745/3 D. NONO	75	300	1000
1745 D. NONO	55	250	950				

3695 Halfcrown. Old laur. and dr. bust LIMA below die axis ↑↓

1745 D. NONO	45	200	675	1745/3	75	300	950

3695A Halfcrown. Old laur. and dr. bust as last but reads GEORGIVS die axis ↑↓

1746 D. NONO	45	200	675	1746/5 D. NONO	60	250	950

3696
1746 Proof Halfcrown

3696 Halfcrown. Old laur. and dr. bust l. R. Plain angles die axis ↑↓
1746 proof only VICESIMO *FDC* £1750

1750 V. QVARTO	85	425	1200	1751 V. QVARTO	100	475	1500

3697
1731 Plumes Shilling

3697 Shilling. Young laur. dr. bust. l. R. Plumes in angles, die axis ↑↓

1727	60	400	1050	1731	75	450	1300

3698   3699
1727 Shilling, young bust, small letters   Young bust Shilling, large letters

	F	VF	EF		F	VF	EF
	£	£	£		£	£	£

3698 Shilling. Young laur. and dr. bust l. R. Roses and plumes in angles, die axis ↑↓

1727	40	200	700	1731	40	200	700
1728	50	225	800	1732	50	225	800
1729	50	225	800				

3699 Shilling. Similar larger lettering. R. Roses and plumes in angles die axis ↑↓

1734	35	175	650	1736/5	55	250	850
1735	35	175	650	1737	35	175	650
1736	35	175	650				

3700   3701
1728 Shilling, plain reverse   1739 Shilling, roses reverse

3700 Shilling. Young laur. and dr. bust l. R. Plain, die axis ↑↓ 1728..........175   475   1100
3701 Shilling. Young laur. and dr. bust l. R. Roses in angles die axis ↑↓

1739	30	150	600	1741	30	150	600
1739/7	....	*Extremely rare*		1741/39	350	950	—
1739 smaller garter star	100	375	1050				

3702   3703A
1747 Shilling, old bust, roses   LIMA Shilling, GEORGIVS legend

3702 Shilling. Old laur. and dr. bust, l. GEORGIUS R. Roses in angles die axis ↑↓

1743	25	100	525	1745/3	60	250	675
1743/1	55	200	725	1747	30	110	525
1745	35	140	575				

3703 Shilling. Old laur. and dr. bust LIMA below die axis ↑↓ 1745............20   100   475
3703A Shilling. Similar as last but reads GEORGIVS die axis ↑↓

1746	95	300	875	1746/5	125	350	925

3704
1746 Proof shilling

	F £	VF £	EF £		F £	VF £	EF £

3704 Shilling. Old laur. and dr. bust R. plain angles die axis ↑↓

1746 Proof only *FDC* £1250				1750 Wide O..............60	200	700
1750 40	175	650		1751 100	300	850
1750/6 60	200	700		1758 20	65	125

3705	3706	3707
1728 Sixpence, young bust	1728 Sixpence, plumes on reverse	1728 Sixpence, roses and plumes

3705 Sixpence. Young laur. and dr. bust. l. R. Angles plain, die axis ↑↓ 1728 ..75   300   650
1728 Proof *FDC* £2750

3706 Sixpence. Similar R. Plumes in angles die axis ↑↓ 1728 50   200   500

3707 Sixpence. Young laur. and dr. bust l. R. Roses and plumes in angles die axis ↑↓

1728 25	140	375	1735 35	200	500
1731 25	140	375	1735/4 40	225	550
1732 25	140	375	1736 30	175	450
1734 35	200	500			

3708	3711
1739 Sixpence, roses	1746 Proof Sixpence

3708 Sixpence. Young laur. and dr. bust l., R. Roses in angles, die axis ↑↓

| 1739 ....25 | 140 | 375 | 1741 ....25 | 140 | 375 |
| 1739 O/R in legend .....65 | 225 | 550 | | | |

3709
1743 Sixpence, old bust, roses

3709 Sixpence. Old laur. and dr. bust. l. R. Roses in angles die axis ↑↓

| 1743 ....20 | 100 | 300 | 1745/3 ....35 | 175 | 425 |
| 1745 ....20 | 100 | 300 | | | |

	F £	VF £	EF £		F £	VF £	EF £

3710 Sixpence. Old laur. and dr. bust LIMA below bust R. angle plain die axis ↑↓

1745		.20	100	225

3710A Sixpence. Similar as last but reads GEORGIVS die axis ↑↓

1746	15	95	200	1746/5	25	140	350

3711 Sixpence. Old laur. and dr. bust l. R. angles plain die axis ↑↓

1746 *proof only FDC £850*

1750	35	175	400	1758	10	40	80
1751	40	225	525	1758 ÐEI error	35	100	195
1757	10	40	80	1758/7	20	60	110

3712 Fourpence. Young laur. and dr. bust l. R. Small dome-shaped crown without pearls on arch, figure 4

1729	8	25	70	1731	8	25	70

3712A Fourpence. Similar R. Double arched crown with pearls, large figure 4, die axis ↑↓

1732	8	25	70	1740	8	25	70
1735	8	25	70	1743	8	25	70
1737	8	25	70	1743/0	15	65	140
1739	8	25	70	1746	6	20	60
				1760	8	25	65

3713 Threepence. Young laur. and dr. bust l. R. Crowned 3, pearls on arch, die axis ↑↓

1729					8	25	65

3713A Threepence. Similar R. Ornate arch die axis ↑↓

1731 Smaller lettering	8	25	65	1731	8	25	65

3713B Threepence. Similar R. Double arched crown with pearls, die axis ↑↓

1732	8	25	65	1743 Large lettering	6	20	60
1732 with stop over head	10	30	75	1743 Small lettering	6	20	60
1735	8	25	5	1743 — stop over head	7	25	65
1737	6	20	60	1746	6	20	60
1739	6	20	60	1746/3	7	25	65
1740	6	20	60	1760	6	20	60

3714 Twopence. Young laur. and dr. bust l. R. Small crown and figure 2, die axis ↑↓

1729	4	20	50	1731	4	20	50

3714A Twopence. Young laur. and dr. bust l. R. Large crown and figure 2 die axis ↑↓

1732	4	20	50	1743/0	5	20	55
1735	4	20	50	1746	4	20	50
1737	4	20	50	1756	4	20	50
1739	5	20	55	1759	4	20	50
1740	8	25	65	1760	4	20	50
1743	4	20	50				

3715 Penny. Young laur. and dr. bust l. head. R. Date over small crown and figure 1, die axis ↑↓

1729	6	25	55	1731	5	20	50

3715A Penny. Young laur. and dr. bust l. R. Large crown dividing date die axis ↑↓

1732	5	20	50	1753/2	6	25	60
1735	6	25	60	1753	4	20	50
1737	6	25	55	1754	4	20	50
1739	5	20	50	1755	4	20	50
1740	5	20	50	1756	4	20	50
1743	5	20	50	1757	4	20	50
1746	5	20	50	1757 GRATIA:	6	30	70
1746/3	6	25	60	1758	4	20	50
1750	4	20	50	1759	4	20	50
1752	4	20	50	1760	6	25	60
1752/0	6	25	60				

3716

	F	VF	EF		F	VF	EF
	£	£	£		£	£	£

3716 Maundy Set. The four denominations. Uniform dates

1729	60	175	475	1739	50	150	425
1731	60	175	475	1740	50	150	425
1732	50	150	425	1743	60	175	475
1735	50	150	425	1746	45	150	425
1737	50	150	425	1760	75	225	475

COPPER

3717

3717 Halfpenny. Young laur. and cuir. bust l. R. Britannia, date in ex. die axis ↑↓

1729	15	85	375	1733	12	75	350
1729 rev. no stop	20	95	400	1734	12	75	350
1730	12	85	350	1734 R/O on obv	20	120	425
1730 GEOGIVS error	20	125	425	1734/3	30	200	—
1730 stop after date	20	95	375	1734 no stops on obv.	30	200	—
1730 no stop after				1735	12	75	350
REX on rev.	25	140	475	1736	15	95	375
1731	12	75	350	1736/0	20	120	425
1731 rev. no stop	20	120	425	1737	15	95	375
1732	12	85	350	1738	10	70	350
1732 rev. no stop	20	120	425	1738 V/S on obv.	20	120	425
				1739	12	75	350

3718 Halfpenny. Old laur. and cuir. bust l., GEORGIUS R. Britannia, date in ex. die axis ↑↓

1740	10	70	300	1743	10	70	300
1742	10	70	300	1744	10	70	300
1742/0	20	110	400	1745	10	70	300

3719

	F £	VF £	EF £		F £	VF £	EF £

3719 Halfpenny. Old laur. and cuir. bust l. GEORGIVS, R. Britannia, date in ex. die axis ↑↓

1746	10	60	300	1751	10	60	300
1747	10	65	325	1752	10	60	300
1748	10	65	325	1753	10	60	300
1749	10	60	300	1754	10	65	325
1750	10	65	325				

3720   3722

3720 Farthing. Young laur. and cuir. bust l. R. Britannia, date in ex. die axis ↑↓

1730	12	65	275	1735 3 over 5	20	110	350
1731	12	65	275	1736	12	65	275
1732	15	70	300	1736 triple tie ribands	30	110	350
1732/1	20	95	325	1737 small date	10	60	250
1733	12	65	275	1737 large date	10	60	250
1734	15	70	300	1739	10	60	250
1734 no stop on obv.	30	110	350	1739/5		*Extremely rare*	
1735	10	60	250				

3721 Farthing. Old laur. and cuir. bust. GEORGIUS R. Britannia, date in ex. die axis ↑↓

1741	15	70	275	1744	10	55	250

3722 Farthing. Similar 55 R. Britannia, date in ex. die axis ↑↓

1746	8	55	200	1750	15	70	250
1746 V over U		*Extremely rare*		1754	5	35	110
1749	15	70	250	1754/0	25	110	300

George III, grandson of George II was born on 4 June 1738. He married Charlotte of Mecklenburg and they had nine sons and six daughters. The French Revolution and the American War of Independence both happened in his long reign, the longest yet of any King. The naval battle of Trafalgar and the Battle of Waterloo also took place during his reign. Later in his reign, he was affected by what seems to be the mental disease porphyria, and the future George IV was appointed as regent. George III died at Windsor Castle on 29 January 1820.

During the second half of the 18th century very little silver or copper was minted. In 1797 Matthew Boulton's 'cartwheels', the first copper Pennies and Twopences, demonstrated the improvement gleaned from the application of steam power to the coining press.

During the Napoleonic Wars bank notes came into general use when the issue of Guineas was stopped between 1799 and 1813, but gold 7s. pieces, Third-Guineas; were minted to relieve the shortage of smaller money. As an emergency measure Spanish 'Dollars' were put into circulation for a short period after being countermarked, and in 1804 Spanish Eight Reales were overstruck and issued as Bank of England Dollars.

The transition to a 'token' silver coinage began in 1811 when the Bank of England had 3s. and 1s. 6d. tokens made for general circulation. Private issues of token money in the years 1788-95 and 1811-15 helped to alleviate the shortage of regal coinage. A change over to a gold standard and a regular 'token' silver coinage came in 1816 when the Mint, which was moved from its old quarters in the Tower of London to a new site on Tower Hill, began a complete re-coinage. The Guinea was replaced by a 20s. Sovereign, and silver coins were made which had an intrinsic value lower than their face value. The St. George design used on the Sovereign and Crown was the work of Benedetto Pistrucci.

Engravers and Designers:– Conrad Heinrich Kuchler (c.1740-1810), Nathaniel Marchant (1739-1816), John Rudulf Ochs Jnr. (1704-88), Lewis Pingo (1743-1830), Thomas Pingo (d.1776) Benedetto Pistrucci (1784-1855), Johann Sigismond Tanner (c.1706-75), Thomas Wyon (1792-1817), William Wyon (1795-1851), Richard Yeo (d.1779).

Prime Ministers:– Duke of Newcastle, (1693-1768) Whig, 1757-62; Earl of Bute, (1713-1792) Tory 1762-3; George Grenville, (1712-1770), Whig 1763-5; William Pitt 'The Elder', Earl of Chatham (1708-1778), Whig 1766-8; Duke of Gratton, (1735-1811), Whig 1767-70; Lord North, (1732-1790), Tory 1770-82; Marquis of Rockingham, (1730-1782), Whig 1765-6, 1782; Earl of Shelbourne, (1737-1805), Whig 1782-3; Henry Addington, (1757-1844) Tory, 1801-4; William Pitt 'The Younger' (1759-1806), Tory 1783-1801, 1804-6; Lord Grenville, (1759-1854), Whig, 1806-7; Duke of Portland, (1738-1809) Tory 1783, 1807-9; Spencer Perceval, (1762-1812) Tory 1809-12; Earl of Liverpool, (1770-1828) Tory 1812-27 .

GOLD

Early Coinages

3723
1770 Pattern Five Guineas

3723 Five Guineas. Pattern only, young long haired bust r. R. crowned shield of
arms, die axis ↑↑ (en medaille)
1770 *FDC* £90,000   1773 *FDC* £80,000

3723A Five Guineas. Pattern only, young bust right, hair extends under bust similar
1777 *FDC* £70,000

3724
1768 Pattern Two Guineas

3724A
1777 Pattern Two Guineas

3724   Two Guineas. Pattern only, young long haired bust r. R. crowned shield of arms, die axis ↑↑
(en medaille)
1768 *FDC* £22,500   1773 *FDC* £20,000
3724A Two Guineas. Pattern only, young bust right, hair extends under bust similar
1777 *FDC* £16,500
There are six different bust varieties for 3723 and 3724, for further details see Rasmussen & Wilson

3725
1761 Guinea first head, two leaf wreath

	F	VF	EF		F	VF	EF
	£	£	£		£	£	£

3725   Guinea. First laur. head r., 1761 (varieties with two or three leaves at top
of wreath). R. Crowned shield of arms die axis ↑↓ 950   2750   5000

3726
1763 Guinea second head

3726   Guinea. Second laur. head r. R. Crowned shield of arms die axis ↑↓
1763 900   2250   5000   1764 850   2000   4750

3727	3728	3729
Guinea, third head	Guinea, fourth head	1794 Guinea, fifth head, 'spade' type

	F	VF	EF		F	VF	EF
	£	£	£		£	£	£

3727 Guinea. Third laur. head r. R. Crowned shield of arms die axis ↑↓

	F	VF	EF		F	VF	EF
1765	200	425	950	1770	300	525	1100
1766	200	400	925	1771	250	450	975
1767	350	600	1350	1772	225	425	950
1768	225	425	975	1773	175	375	900
1769	275	475	1000	1773 7 over 1	300	850	—

3728 Guinea. Fourth laur. head r. Crowned shield of arms die axis ↑↓

	F	VF	EF		F	VF	EF
1774	150	350	700	1781	185	425	850
1774 Proof *FDC* £4000				1782	165	375	725
1775	125	325	675	1783	200	450	950
1776	150	350	700	1784	175	400	800
1777	175	400	800	1785	125	325	675
1778	200	450	950	1786	165	375	725
1779	175	400	800				

3729 Guinea. Fifth laur. head r. R. 'Spade'-shaped shield, die axis ↑↑

	F	VF	EF		F	VF	EF
1787	125	300	650	1794	140	325	675
1787 Proof *FDC* £2750				1795	150	350	700
1788	140	325	675	1796	180	400	850
1789	150	350	700	1797	180	400	850
1790	150	350	700	1798*	120	275	600
1791	125	300	650	1798/7	200	450	950
1792	150	350	700	1799	175	375	900
1793	140	325	675	*Beware counterfeits*			

3730	3731
1813 Guinea "Military type"	1763 Half-Guinea, first head

3730 Guinea. Sixth laur. head. r. R. Shield in Garter, known as the Military guinea, die axis ↑↑

		F	VF	EF
1813		500	1250	2250

3731 Half-Guinea. First laur. head r. R. Crowned shield of arms die axis ↑↓

	F	VF	EF		F	VF	EF
1762	425	1250	3000	1763	550	1650	3750

3732
1764 Half-Guinea, second head

3733
1775 Half-Guinea, third head

	F	VF	EF		F	VF	EF
	£	£	£		£	£	£

3732 Half-Guinea. Second laur. head r. R. Crowned shield of arms die axis ↑↓

1764	140	375	850	1772		*Extremely rare*	
1765	450	950	—	1773	225	575	1250
1766	150	425	1000	1774	275	625	1550
1768	175	475	1000	1775	325	750	1900
1769	175	475	1050				

3734
1785 Half-Guinea, fourth head

3735
1787 Proof Half-Guinea, fifth head

3733 Half-Guinea Third laur. head (less fine style) r. R. Crowned shield of arms die axis ↑↓

1774		*Extremely rare*		1775	775	1850	4000

3734 Half-Guinea Fourth laur. head r. R. Crowned shield of arms die axis ↑↓

1775	110	275	550	1781	165	400	750
1775 Proof *FDC* £3750				1783	425	1250	—
1776	140	325	625	1784	150	375	700
1777	125	300	600	1785	140	325	625
1778	150	375	700	1786	110	275	550
1779	150	375	700				

3735 Half-Guinea Fifth laur. head. r. R. 'Spade' shaped shield, date below, die axis ↑↑

1787	95	200	425	1794	145	350	600
1787 Proof *FDC* £2000				1795	150	375	675
1788	110	250	500	1796	120	275	525
1789	150	375	675	1797	110	250	500
1790	140	325	575	1798	125	300	550
1791	140	325	575	1798/7	200	350	675
1792	500	1550	—	1800	250	675	—
1793	110	250	500				

3736
1801 Half-Guinea, sixth head

3736 Half-Guinea Sixth laur. head. r. R. Shield in Garter, date below die axis ↑↑

1801	70	140	325	1803	75	165	350
1802	75	165	350				

| | 3737 | | | | 3738 | | 3739 |
| 1813 Half-Guinea, seventh head | | | 1798 Third-Guinea, first type | | | 1803 Third-Guinea, second reverse |

	F	VF	FF		F	VF	EF
	£	£	£		£	£	£

3737 Half-Guinea Seventh laur. head. r. with short hair. R. Shield in garter, date below die axis ↑↑

1804	70	140	325	1809	90	165	400
1805		*Extremely rare*		1810	90	165	400
1806	120	225	500	1811	150	350	750
1808	100	180	425	1813	100	250	525

3738 Third-Guinea. First laur. head r. R. Crown, date in legend, die axis ↑↑

1797	60	120	325	1799	65	150	350
1798	60	120	325	1800	60	120	325

3739 Third-Guinea. First laur. head r. R. Similar but date below crown, die axis ↑↑

1801	60	120	325	1803	60	120	325
1802	60	120	325				

| | 3740 | | | 3741 |
| 1804 Third Guinea, second head | | | 1762 Quarter-Guinea |

3740 Third-Guinea. Second laur. head r. with short hair, R. Similar, die axis ↑↑

1804	65	110	300	1810	65	110	300
1806	70	125	325	1811	200	450	1000
1808	70	125	325	1813	125	300	700
1809	70	125	325				

3741 Quarter-Guinea. Laur. head r. R. Crowned shield die axis ↑↓ 1762 85   250   400

For gold of the 'new coinage', 1817-20, see page 389.

SILVER

| | 3742 | | 3746 |
| 1763 Northumberland shilling | | 1787 Proof Shilling |

3742 Shilling. Young laur. and dr. bust, r. known as the 'Northumberland' shilling, die axis ↑↓

1763 300   600   1250

3743 Shilling. Older laur. and dr. bust, R. No semée of hearts in Hanoverian shield, die axis ↑↑

1787 20   40   100

1787 Proof *FDC* ....   *Extremely rare*

1787 plain edge proof *FDC*...   *Extremely rare*

3744 Shilling. — No stop over head, die axis ↑↑ 1787.................................30   60   150

3745 Shilling. — No stops at date, die axis ↑↑ 1787 35   80   200

3745A Shilling. — No stops on *obv.*, die axis ↑↑ 1787 250   675   1500

3746 Shilling. — R. With semée of hearts, die axis ↑↑ 1787 20   40   100

1787 1/1 retrograde...40   110   300

1787 plain edge proof *FDC* ....   *Extremely rare*

Hanoverian Arms

No semée of hearts   With semée of hearts   3747 - 1798 Shilling

	F £	VF £	EF £		F £	VF £	EF £

3747 **Shilling** No stop over head, 1798: known as the 'Dorrien and Magens' shilling *UNC* £12500

3748 **Sixpence.** Laur. and dr. bust r. R. Without semée of hearts, die axis ↑↑

     1787 10   35   85   1787 Proof *FDC* ....*Extremely rare*

3749 **Sixpence.** Similar R. With semée of hearts, die axis ↑↑ 1787 10   35   85

3749   3750

1787 Sixpence, with hearts

3750 **Fourpence.** Young laur. and dr. bust r. R. Crowned 4, die axis ↑↓

1763 4	15	40	1772/0 5	20	45
1763 Proof *FDC of highest rarity*			1776 4	18	40
1765 200	450	850	1780 4	18	40
1766 5	20	45	1784 5	20	45
1770 5	20	45	1786 6	25	50
1772 5	20	45			

3751   3753   3755

3751 **Fourpence.** Older laur. and dr. bust. R. Thin 4 ('Wire Money'), die axis ↑↑

     1792 10   35   75

3752 **Fourpence.** Older laur. and dr. bust r. R. Normal Crowned 4, die axis ↑↑

     1795 5   18   45   1800 5   18   45

3753 **Threepence.** Young laur. dr. bust r. R. Crowned 3, die axis ↑↓

1762 3	12	35	1772 small III 4	18	40
1763 3	12	35	1772 very large III 4	18	40
1763 Proof *FDC of highest rarity*			1780 4	18	40
1765 150	325	750	1784 5	20	45
1766 5	20	45	1786 4	18	40
1770 5	20	45			

3754 **Threepence.** Older laur. dr. bust. r. R. Thin 3 ('Wire Money'), die axis ↑↑

     1792 10   35   75

3755 **Threepence.** Older laur. and dr. bust r. R. Normal Crowned 3, die axis ↑↑

     1795 5   18   45   1800 5   18   45

	F £	VF £	EF £

3756 Twopence. Young laur. and dr. bust r. ℞. Crowned 2, die axis ↑↓

1763 6	25	45	1776.............................4	18	40
1763 Proof *FDC of highest rarity*			1780.............................4	18	40
1765 100	275	650	1784.............................4	18	40
1766 4	18	40	1786.............................3	15	40
1772 4	18	40	1786 large obv. lettering .3	15	40
1772 second 7/6 5	20	45			

3756

3757 Twopence Older laur. and dr. bust. r. ℞. Thin 2 ('Wire Money'), die axis ↑↑

1792 10	30	75

3758 Twopence Older laur. and dr. bust r. ℞. Normal Crowned 2, die axis ↑↑

1795 3	15	40	1800.............................3	15	40

3759 Penny. Young laur. and dr. bust r. ℞. Crowned 1, die axis ↑↓

1763 5	20	45	1779 4	18	40
1763 Proof *FDC of highest rarity*			1780.............................5	20	45
1766 4	18	40	1781.............................3	12	35
1770 3	12	35	1784.............................3	12	35
1772 4	18	40	1786.............................3	12	35
1776 4	18	40			

3760 Penny. Older laur. and dr. bust. r. ℞. Thin 1 ('Wire Money'), die axis ↑↑

1792 8	30	65

3761 Penny. Older laur. and dr. bust r. ℞. Normal Crowned 1, die axis ↑↑

1795 3	12	40	1800.............................3	12	40

3762 Maundy Set. Young laur. and dr. bust. r. Uniform dates

1763 50	150	375	1780 50	150	375
1763 Proof set *FDC*	*Extremely rare*		1784 50	150	375
1766 50	150	375	1786 50	150	375
1772 50	150	375			

3763 Maundy Set. — Older laur. and dr. bust. r. ℞. Thin numerals ('Wire Money'),

1792 125	275	600

3764 Maundy Set. Older laur. and dr. bust r. ℞. Normal numerals. Uniform dates

1795 40	140	325	1800 35	125	300

Emergency Issue, die axis ↑↑

3765A
Portrait type Dollar with oval countermark

3765 Dollar. Pillar type (current for 4s 9d). Spanish American 8 Reales,

oval countermark with head of George III.

Mexico City Mint — m 450	900	2000
Bolivia, Potosi Mint – PTS monogram 800	2000	—
Peru, Lima Mint – LIMÆ monogram 750	1650	—

	F £	VF £	EF £
3765A Dollar. Portrait type, oval countermark.			
Mexico City Mint — m̥	.95	325	600
Bolivia, Potosi Mint — PTS monogram	.200	575	—
Chile, Santiago Mint — s̥	.600	1600	—
Guatemala Mint — NG	.450	1350	—
Spain, Madrid Mint	.275	725	1850
Spain, Seville Mint	.225	600	1600
Peru, Lima Mint — LIMÆ monogram	.125	400	800
3765B Dollar. — Oval countermark on French Ecu		*Extremely rare*	
3765C Dollar. — Oval countermark on USA Dollar		*Of highest rarity*	

3766   3767
Portrait Dollar with octagonal countermark   Half-Dollar with oval countermark

	F	VF	EF
3766 Dollar octagonal countermarks with head of George III			
Mexico City Mint — m̥	.200	550	975
Bolivia, Potosi Mint — PTS monogram	.700	—	—
Guatamala Mint — NG	.875	1850	—
Peru, Lima Mint — LIME monogram	.325	625	1600
Spain, Madrid Mint	.500	1050	—
Spain, Seville Mint	.550	1300	—
3766A Dollar. — Octagonal countermark on French Ecu		*Of highest rarity*	
3766B Dollar. — Octagonal countermark on USA Dollar		*Extremely rare*	
3767 Half-Dollar. With similar oval countermark. Mints of Potosi,			
Santiago, Madrid & Seville ....*from*	125	325	650
3767A Half Dollar. With Octagonal countermark. Similar .....*from*	350	750	—

Bank of England Issue

3768
Top leaf top left side of E in DEI

	F £	VF £	EF £

3768 Dollar. (current for 5s.). laur. and dr. bust of king. r. ℞.
Britannia seated l., several varieties occur, die axis ↑↑

1804 O. Top leaf to left side of E, R. Upright K to left of shield 110	300	575
1804 ——no stops in CHK on truncation 135	350	625
1804 O. Top leaf to centre of E R. Similar.......................................110	300	575
1804 ——no stop after REX 120	325	600
1804 —R. K inverted to left of shield 160	400	675
1804 —R. K inverted and incuse...160	400	675
1804 O. Top leaf to right side of E, R. normal K 120	325	600
1804 —R. K inverted to left of shield 160	400	675

1804 Proof striking of all varieties above *FDC from* £1000

These dollars were re-struck from Spanish-American 8-Reales until at least 1811. Dollars that show dates and Mint marks of original coin are worth rather more.

3769
1811 Three Shillings, first bust

3770
Three Shillings, second head

	F £	VF £	EF £		F £	VF £	EF £

3769 Three Shillings. Dr and laur. bust in armour r. ℞. BANK / TOKEN /
3 SHILL. / date (in oak wreath), die axis ↑↑

1811 15	60	175	1812 Proof *FDC* £600			
1811 Proof *FDC* £500			1812 Proof in gold *FDC*.	*Extremely rare*		
1812 15	70	200	1812 Proof in platinum *FDC* *Extremely rare*			

3770 Three Shillings. — Laureate head r. Top leaf between I/G ℞. As before but wreath of oak
and olive, die axis ↑↑

1812 15	60	175	1815 15	70	200
1813 15	70	200	1816 175	600	1350
1814 15	70	200			

3771   3772
1811 Eighteenpence, first bust   Eighteenpence, second head

	F	VF	EF			F	VF	EF
	£	£	£			£	£	£

3771 Eighteenpence. Dr. and laur. bust r. in armour ℞ BANK/TOKEN/Is. 6D./date (in oak wreath) ↑↑

1811 10   35   125   1812 10   35   140

1811 Proof *FDC* £450

3772 Eighteenpence. Laureate head r. die axis ↑↑

1812 10   35   125   1813 Platinum proof *FDC* £12500

1812 Proof *FDC* £400   1814 10   40   150

1812 Platinum proof *FDC* £12500   1815 10   40   150

1812 Proof R. Small letters *FDC* £2000   1816 10   40   150

1813 10   40   150

3773   3773A
1812 Pattern Ninepence, 9D type   1812 Pattern Ninepence, PENCE type

3773 Ninepence. Similar, Laur. head 1812, R. 9D type (pattern only) die axis ↑↑ *FDC* £1100

3773A Ninepence. — — 1812, R. 9 pence type (pattern only) die axis ↑↑ FDC.   *Extremely rare*

COPPER

First Issue — Tower Mint, London

3774

3775
REV.C, leaves point between A and N

	F	VF	EF		F	VF	EF
	£	£	£		£	£	£

3774 Halfpenny. Laur. and Cuir. bust r. R. Britannia l. date in ex., die axis ↑↓

	F	VF	EF		F	VF	EF
1770 12	50	250	spear blade 10	45	250
1770 Proof die axis ↑↑ *FDC* £1200			1772 no incuse		
1770 Proof in silver *FDC*	*Extremely rare*		hair coil 10	45	225
1770 no stop on rev. 20	65	275	1772 — no stop on rev. ..20	65	250
1771 10	45	250	1773 10	45	225
1771 no stop on rev. 20	65	275	1773 no stop after		
1771 ball below			REX 18	60	250
spear blade 10	45	250	1773 no stop on rev.......20	65	250
1772 incuse hair coil			1774 different obv.		
on rev. 10	45	250	profile 18	75	275
1772 GEORIVS error 35	90	325	1775 — 10	55	250

3775 Farthing. Laur. and cuir. bust r. R. Britannia l. date in ex., die axis ↑↓

	F	VF	EF		F	VF	EF
1771 REV A. leaf to r. ..20	65	250	1773 no stop after REX ..25	75	250
1771 REV B. leaf to N ..20	65	250	1774 12	45	175
1771 REV C. 20	65	250	1775 12	45	175
1771 1st 7/1 30	200	—	1775 struck en		
1773 10	40	175	medaille ↑↑ 25	75	250
1773 no stop on rev. 15	50	200	1775 GEORGIVS 40	225	—

Second Issue—Soho Mint. Birmingham 'Cartwheel' coinage, die axis ↑↓

3776

3776 Twopence. Legends incuse on raised rim, 1797 35   175   375

   1797 Copper proof *FDC* £800   1797 Gold proof *FDC* £15000
   1797 Bronzed proof *FDC* £750   1797 Gilt copper *FDC* £1250
   1797 Silver proof *FDC* £4000

3777

	VF	EF	UNC		F	VF	EF	UNC
	£	£	£		£	£	£	£

3777 Penny. 1797. Similar, 10 leaves in wreath on obv. ....10 | 55 | 275 | 1000
    1797 11 leaves in wreath on obv. ....15 | 75 | 325 | 1250
    1797 Gilt copper proof *FDC* £950
    1797 Copper proof *FDC* £650
    1797 Bronzed proof *FDC* £600
    1797 Silver proof *FDC* £3250
    1797 Gold proof *FDC* £12500

Halfpence and Farthings of this issue are patterns.

Third Issue—Soho Mint, Birmingham, die axis ↑↓

3778   3779

3778 Halfpenny. Laur. and dr. bust r., R. Britannia l. date below

1799 Ship on rev. with				1799 Ship with			
5 incuse gunports 10	60	150		plain hull	15	75	180
1799 Ship with 6				1799 — raised line			
relief gunports.............12	65	160		on hull................	15	75	180
1799 Ship with 9 relief				1799 Copper proof *FDC* £325			
gunports 15	75	180		1799 Bronzed proof *FDC* £275			
				1799 Gilt copper proof *FDC* £450			

3779 Farthing. Laur. and dr. bust r. date below R. Britannia l.

1799 Obv. with 3 berries				1799 Obv. with 4 berries			
in wreath 8	50	125		in wreath	8	50	125
1799 Copper *FDC* £250				1799 Gold proof *FDC* £7500			
1799 Bronzed proof *FDC* £225				1799 Silver proof *FDC* £2750			
1799 Copper gilt proof *FDC* £375							

Fourth Issue—Soho Mint, Birmingham, die axis ↑↓

3780

	VF	EF	UNC		VF	EF	UNC
	£	£	£		£	£	£

3780 Penny. Shorter haired, laur. and dr. bust r. date below. R. Britannia l. date below

	VF	EF	UNC		VF	EF	UNC
1806 incuse hair curl ....10 by tie knot	10	60	275	1807 10	10	70	300
1806 no incuse hair curl ..15	15	75	300	1807 Copper proof *FDC* £425			
1806 Copper proof *FDC* £325				1807 Bronzed proof *FDC* £400			
1806 Bronzed proof *FDC* £325				1807 Gilt copper proof *FDC* £600			
1806 Gilt copper proof *FDC* £500				1807 Silver proof *FDC* £3500			
1806 Silver proof *FDC* £3500				1807 Gold proof *FDC*		*Extremely rare*	
				1807 Platinum proof *FDC*		*Extremely rare*	
				1808 Proof *FDC*		*Unique*	

3781

3782

3781 Halfpenny. Shorter haired laur. and dr. bust r. date below, R. Britannia l.

	VF	EF	UNC		VF	EF	UNC
1806 rev. no berries..........6	6	35	150	1807 8	8	40	165
1806 rev. 3 berries..........10	10	60	175	1807 Copper proof *FDC* £300			
1806 Copper proof *FDC* £275				1807 Bronzed proof *FDC* £275			
1806 Bronzed proof *FDC* £250				1807 Gilt copper *FDC* £400			
1806 Gilt proof *FDC* £375				1807 Silver proof *FDC* £2500			
1806 Silver proof *FDC* £2750				1807 Gold proof *FDC*		*Extremely rare*	

3782 Farthing. Shorter haired laur. and dr. bust r. date below, R. Britannia l.

	VF	EF	UNC		VF	EF	UNC
1806 K. on tr. 6	6	70	125	1807 8	8	45	150
1806 incuse dot on tr......35	35	100	300	1807 Copper proof *FDC* £275			
1806 Copper proof *FDC* £250				1807 Bronzed proof *FDC* £250			
1806 Bronzed proof *FDC* £225				1807 Gilt copper proof *FDC* £400			
1806 Gilt copper proof *FDC* £375				1807 Silver proof *FDC* £3000			
1806 Silver proof *FDC* £2500				1807 Gold proof *FDC*		*Extremely rare*	
1806 Gold proof *FDC*		*Extremely rare*					

Last or new coinage, 1816-20

The year 1816 is a landmark in the history of our coinage. For some years at the beginning of the 19th century Mint production was virtually confined to small gold denominations, regular full production being resumed only after the Mint had been moved from the Tower of London to a new site on Tower Hill. Steam powered minting machinery made by Boulton and Watt replaced the old hand-operated presses and these produced coins which were technically much superior to the older milled coins.

In 1816 for the first time British silver coins were produced with an intrinsic value substantially below their face value, the first official token coinage. The old Guinea was replaced by a Sovereign of twenty shillings in 1817, the standard of 22 carat (0.916) fineness still being retained.

Mint Master or Engraver's
and/or designer's initials: WWP (William Wellesley Pole)
B.P. (Benedetto Pistrucci 1784-1855)

GOLD

3783

3783 Five Pounds. 1820 LX (Pattern only) laur. head r. date below R. St George and dragon, edge inscribed die axis ↑↓ *FDC* £70000
1820 Similar plain edge proof *FDC* £85000

3784

3784 Two Pounds. 1820 LX (Pattern only) laur. head r. date below R. St George and dragon, edge inscribed die axis ↑↓ *FDC* £17500
1820 Similar plain edge proof *FDC Extremely rare*

3785					3785A			
F	VF	EF	UNC		F	VF	EF	UNC
£	£	£	£		£	£	£	£

3785 Sovereign. laur. head r. coarse hair, legend type A (Descending colon after BRITANNIAR, no space between REX and F:D:). R. St. George and dragon, die axis ↑↓

| 1817 | 250 | 400 | 1000 | 1600 | 1818 | 300 | 600 | 1350 | 2000 |

1817 Proof *FDC* £6750   1819 .... *Extremely rare*

3785ASovereign. Similar legend type B (Ascending colon after BRITANNIAR, space between REX and F:D:) ↑↓

| 1818 | 300 | 600 | 1350 | 2000 | 1818 Proof *FDC* £8500 |

	F	VF	EF	UNC		F	VF	EF	UNC
	£	£	£	£		£	£	£	£

3785B Sovereign. laur head r. hair with tighter curls, legend type A. (as above) R. Similar die axis ↑↓
1818 .... *Extremely rare*

3785C
Large date, open 2 variety

3785C
Closed 2 variety

3785C Sovereign. Similar legend type B. (as above) die axis ↑↓

1818 .... *Extremely rare*
1820 Roman I.............. *Extremely rare*
1820 Small O, closed
    2 thin date 325   650 1200 1850
1820 Proof *FDC* £7000
1820 Slender date Proof *FDC* £9000

1820 large date open
    2 close to 8 ...275 450 1050 1650
1820 short date 2
    nearly closed ..325 600 1200 —
1820 closed 2 ....350 700 1750 —
1820 spread 18 and 20
    short date .... *Extremely rare*

3786
1817 Half-Sovereign

3786 Half-Sovereign. laur head r. date below R. Crowned shield, edge milled die axis ↑↓

1817 ....85 175 300 500
1817 Proof *FDC* £3750
1818/7 ....275 550 1400 —

1818 Proof *FDC* £4500
1818 ....95 200 350 575
1820 ....95 200 350 575

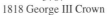

3787
1818 George III Crown

3787 Crown. Laur. head r. R. Pistrucci's St. George and dragon within Garter edge inscribed, die axis ↑↓

		F	VF	EF	UNC
1818, edge LVIII	....	.25	60	325	750
1818	LVIII error edge inscription...*Extremely rare*				
1818	LVIII Proof *FDC* ....*Extremely rare*				
1818	LIX...	.25	60	325	750
1818	LIX TUT ∧MEN error	.50	200	—	—
1819	LIX...	.20	50	300	700
1819	LIX no stops on edge	.45	100	475	1100
1819	LIX R. Thicker ruled garter	.75	225	575	—
1819/8	LIX...	.50	175	575	—
1819	LX	.30	70	350	800
1819	LX no stop after TUTAMEN...	.50	175	525	—
1820	LX	.25	60	325	750
1820	LX R.S/T in SOIT..	.75	225	395	—
1820/19	LX	.75	225	575	—

3788

1816 Halfcrown, large bust

	F	VF	EF	UNC		F	VF	EF	UNC
	£	£	£	£		£	£	£	£

3788 Halfcrown. Large laur. bust or 'bull' head r. date below R. Crowned garter and shield die axis ↑↑

1816	20	65	250	400	1817 E/R in DEI			*Extremely rare*	
1816 Proof *FDC* £2000					1817 S/I in PENSE			*Extremely rare*	
1816 Plain proof *FDC* £2000					1817 Proof *FDC* £2000				
1817	20	65	250	400	1817 Plain edge proof *FDC* £2250				
1817 D/T in DEI	45	175	575	—					

3789

1817 Halfcrown, small head

	F	VF	EF	UNC		F	VF	EF	UNC
	£	£	£	£		£	£	£	£

3789 Halfcrown. Small laur. head r. date below, R. Crowned garter and shield die axis ↑↑

1817	20	60	200	425	1818 Proof *FDC* £2500				
1817 Proof *FDC* £2000					1819 Proof *FDC* £2250				
1817 Plain edge proof *FDC* £2000					1819	20	60	275	450
1817 Reversed s's in garter			*Extremely rare*		1819/8			*Extremely rare*	
1818 Reversed s's in garter			*Extremely rare*		1820	30	85	325	550
1818	25	70	275	500	1820 Proof *FDC* £2500				
					1820 Plain edge proof *FDC* £2000				

3790

1817 Shilling

3790 Shilling. laur head r. date below R. Crowned Shield in Garter edge milled, die axis ↑↑

1816	10	15	45	95	1818	20	40	180	300
1816 Proof *FDC* £500					1818 High 8	30	75	175	375
1816 Plain edge proof *FDC* £500					1819/8	20	40	100	250
1816 Proof in gold *FDC*			*Extremely rare*		1819	10	20	55	135
1817	10	18	50	100	1820	10	20	55	135
1817 RRITT flaw	15	25	100	—					
1817 Proof plain edge *FDC* £400					1820 I/S in HONI	40	80	225	475
1817 GEOE error	100	225	500	—	1820 Proof *FDC* £450				

3791
1819 Sixpence

	F	VF	EF	UNC		F	VF	EF	UNC
	£	£	£	£		£	£	£	£

3791 Sixpence. laur head r. date below R. Crowned Shield in Garter edge milled, die axis ↑↑

	F	VF	EF	UNC		F	VF	EF	UNC
1816 6	12	35	75		1819/8 12	25	50	95
1816 Proof plain edge *FDC* £500					1819 10	20	45	85
1816 Proof in gold *FDC*		*Extremely rare*			1819 small 8 10	20	45	85
1817 8	15	40	80		1820 10	20	45	85
1817 Proof plain edge *FDC* £500					1820 inverted 1 75	275	450	—
1817 Proof milled edge *FDC* £950					1820 I/S in HONI 75	275	425	—
1818 10	20	45	85		1820 obv. no colons ..100	375	550	—
1818 Proof milled edge *FDC* £900					1820 Proof *FDC* £900			

3792

3792 Maundy Set. (4d., 3d., 2d. and 1d.) laur. head, date below die axis ↑↑

1817	60	150	375	1820		60	150	375
1818	60	150	375					

3793 — Fourpence. 1817, 1818, 1820 ....*from*		15	45
3794 — Threepence. 1817, 1818, 1820 ....*from*		15	45
3795 Twopence. 1817, 1818, 1820 ....*from*		10	35
3796 — Penny. 1817, 1818, 1820 ....*from*		10	30

George IV, eldest son of George III, was born on 12 August 1762 and was almost a complete opposite to his father. He was very extravagant and lived in the height of luxury. He especially influenced fashion of the time which became known as the 'Regency' style. He had numerous mistresses, and had an arranged marriage with Caroline of Brunswick. She later moved to Italy with their only daughter, but returned to claim her place as Queen upon George's accession. George banned her from ever being crowned, and he died without ever conceiving a son on 26 June 1830, when his younger brother William ascended the throne.

The Mint resumed the coinage of copper farthings in 1821, and pennies and halfpennies in 1825. A gold Two Pound piece was first issued for general circulation in 1823. A full cased proof set of the new bare head coinage was issued in limited quantities in 1826.

Engraver's and/or designer's initials on the coins:
    B. P. (Benedetto Pistrucci)   W. W. P. (William Wellesley Pole) – Master of the Mint
    J. B. M. (Jean Baptiste Merlen)

Engravers and Designers:– Francis Legett Chantrey (1781-1842) Jean Baptiste Merlen (1769-c.1850) Benedetto Pistrucci (1784-1855) William Wyon (1795-1851)
Prime Ministers:– Earl of Liverpool, (1770-1828) Tory, 1812-27; George Canning, (1770-1827) Tory, 1827; Viscount Goderich, (1782-1859), Tory 1827-8; Duke of Wellington, (1769-1852), Tory, 1828-30.

GOLD

3797

3797 Five Pounds. 1826 Bare head l. date below R. Crowned shield and mantle, inscribed edge,
    die axis ↑↓   Proof *FDC* £11500
    1826 Piedfort proof *FDC*..*Extremely rare*

3798

	VF	EF	UNC
	£	£	£

3798 Two Pounds. 1823 Proof *FDC* £4750
    1823 Proof no JBM below truncation *FDC* ....   *Extremely rare*
    1823 Large bare head. l. R. St. George, inscribed edge ↑↓ 700 1350 2250
3799 Two Pounds. Bare head l. date below R. Crowned shield and mantle inscribed edge
    die axis ↑↓
    1824 Proof *FDC*   *Extremely rare*   1826. Piedfort proof *FDC*   *Extremely rare*
    1825 Proof plain edge *FDC* £6500   1826. Proof *FDC* £4500

3800	3801
1822 Sovereign, first type	1826 Sovereign, second type

	F	VF	EF	UNC		F	VF	EF	UNC
	£	£	£	£		£	£	£	£

3800 Sovereign. Laur. head. l. R. St. George and dragon date in ex., die axis ↑↓

1821	250	400	1000	1600	1823	400	1350	3750	—
1821 Proof *FDC* £3750					1824	300	450	1150	1750
1822*	275	425	1100	1700	1825	350	1100	3000	—

*Beware counterfeits.

3801 Sovereign. Bare head. date below l. R. Crowned shield, die axis ↑↓

1825	225	400	850	1350	1827*	250	450	900	1500
1825 Proof *FDC* £3750					1828	2000	4000	10000	—
1825 Plain edge proof *FDC* £3750					1829	275	475	1000	1600
1826	225	400	850	1350	1830	275	475	1000	1600
1826 Proof *FDC* £2750									

*Beware counterfeits

3802	3803
1821 Proof Half-Sovereign	1825 Half-Sovereign, second reverse

3802 Half-Sovereign. Laur. head. l. R. Ornately garnished Crowned shield. die axis ↑↓

1821	400	1000	2000	3250
1821 Proof *FDC* £3750				

3803 Half-Sovereign. Laur. head l. R. Plain Crowned shield die axis ↑↓

1823	80	200	425	700	1825	70	150	375	600
1824	75	175	400	650					

3804	3804A
1825 Half Sovereign, bare head	Extra tuft of hair to left of ear

3804 Half-Sovereign. Bare head. date below l. R. Crowned garnished shield die axis ↑↓

1826	80	150	350	650	1827	80	150	375	650
1826 Proof *FDC* £1300					1828	80	150	375	700

3804A Half-Sovereign. Similar with extra tuft of hair to l. ear, much heavier border, die axis ↑↓

1826	70	120	325	600	1827	70	120	325	600
1826 Proof *FDC* £1250					1828	75	140	350	650

SILVER

3805
1821 Laureate bust Crown

	F	VF	EF	UNC		F	VF	EF	UNC
	£	£	£	£		£	£	£	£

3805 Crown. Laur. head. l. R. St. George, date in exergue, B.P. to upper right, WWP under lance, die axis ↑↓

1821, edge	SECUNDO	30	185	1000	2250
1821	SECUNDO WWP inverted under lance		*Extremely rare*		
1821	SECUNDO Proof *FDC* £3000				
1821	SECUNDO Proof in copper *FDC* £3250				
1821	TERTIO Proof *FDC* £4000				
1822	SECUNDO	45	250	1150	2500
1822	TERTIO	30	185	1000	2250

3806
1826 Proof Crown, bare head

3806 Crown. Bare head. l. R. Shield with crest inscribed edge, die axis ↑↓

1825 Proof *FDC* £6500　　　　　　　　1826 Proof *FDC* £4250

3807　　　　　　　　　　　　　　　　　3807
1820 Halfcrown, lightly garnished shield　　　Heavier garnishing

3807 Halfcrown. Laur. head. l. R. Crowned Garnished shield, die axis ↑↓

1820	20	50	275	475
1820 Proof *FDC* £1000				
1820 Plain edge proof *FDC* £1500				
1821	20	50	275	475

1821 Heavier shield garnishing

	25	60	325	525
1823 —	650	1750	5000	—

3808
1823 Halfcrown, second reverse

3809
1826 Halfcrown, bare head, third reverse

	F	VF	EF	UNC		F	VF	EF	UNC
	£	£	£	£		£	£	£	£

3808 Halfcrown. Laur. head l. R. Crowned Shield in garter and collar die axis ↑↓

1823	20	50	250	475	1824	25	65	300	600
1823 Proof *FDC* £2500					1824 Proof *FDC* £2750				

3809 Halfcrown. Bare head. date below l. R. Crowned Shield with crest die axis ↑↓

1824		*Extremely rare*			1826	20	45	175	450
1824 Proof *FDC* £3000					1826 Proof *FDC* £875				
1825	25	55	150	475	1828	30	90	325	650
1825 Proof *FDC* £1000					1829	25	80	275	600
1825 Plain edge proof *FDC* £1500									

3810 - First reverse   3811 - Second reverse   3812 - Third reverse

3810 Shilling. Laur. head. l. R. Crowned garnished shield, die axis ↑↓

1821						10	40	165	400
1821 Proof *FDC* £850									

3811 Shilling. Laur. head l. R. Crowned shield in Garter die axis ↑↓

1823	25	65	275	650	1825	18	50	200	450
1823 Proof *FDC* £2250					1825 Proof *FDC* £2250				
1824	10	40	165	400	1825/3			*Extremely rare*	
1824 Proof *FDC* £2250									

3812 Shilling. Bare head l. date below R. Lion on crown die axis ↑↓

1825	10	40	140	350	1826/2			*Extremely rare*	
1825 Roman I		*Extremely rare*			1827	20	65	325	650
1825 Proof *FDC* £750					1829	15	50	225	550
1826	8	30	125	300	1829 Proof *FDC* £2250				
1826 Proof *FDC* £425									

3813 - First reverse   3814 - Second reverse   3815 -Third reverse

3813 Sixpence. Laur. head. l. R. Crowned Garnished shield, die axis ↑↓

1821	10	25	95	300	1821 BBITANNIAR	50	225	700	—
1821 Proof *FDC* £550									

3814 Sixpence. Laur. head l. R. Crowned Shield in Garter die axis ↑↓

1824	10	25	95	300	1825 Proof *FDC* £1000				
1824 Proof *FDC* £1000					1826	20	65	250	600
1825	10	25	95	300	1826 Proof *FDC* £1350				

3815 Sixpence. Bare head. l. with or without tuft of hair to l. of ear date below R. Lion on crown die axis ↑↓

1826	10	25	95	300	1828	10	30	150	375
1826 Proof *FDC* £325					1829	10	25	95	325
1827	18	55	250	600	1829 Proof *FDC* £1100				

3816

	EF £	FDC £		EF £	FDC £
3816 Maundy Set. (4d., 3d., 2d. and 1d.) laur head l. die axis ↑↓					
1822	130	295	1827	110	250
1822 Proof set *FDC*	*Extremely rare*		1828	110	250
1823	110	250	1828 Proof set *FDC*	*Extremely rare*	
1824	130	295	1829	110	250
1825	110	250	1830	110	250
1826	110	250			

	EF	FDC
3817 Maundy Fourpence. 1822-30 ....*from*	15	35
3818 — Threepence. small head, 1822..	30	55
3819 — Threepence. normal head, 1823-30 ....*from*	14	30
3820 — Twopence. 1822-30...*from*	12	25
3821 — Penny. 1822-30 ....*from*	10	20

COPPER

First Issue, 1821-6

3822   3824

	F £	VF £	EF £	UNC £		F £	VF £	EF £	UNC £
3822 Farthing. Laur. and dr. bust l. R. Britannia r. date in ex. die axis ↑↓									
1821 2		10	60	120	1823 — I for 1 in date ..25	85	275	—	
1822 leaf ribs incuse 2		10	55	100	1825 — 2	10	60	110	
1822—inv. A's legend .25		95	275	—	1825 — D/U in DEI 20	75	250	—	
1822 leaf ribs raised........2		10	55	110	1825 leaf ribs raised 4	15	65	130	
1822 Proof *FDC* £650					1825 gold proof *FDC*	*Extremely rare*			
1822 Proof die axis ↑↑ *FDC* £800					1826 — 5	15	70	150	
1823— 3		12	65	120	1826 R/E in GRATIA....20	75	250	—	

3823

Second issue, 1825-30

	F £	VF £	EF £	UNC £		F £	VF £	EF £	UNC £

3823 Penny. Laur. head. l. R. Britannia, with shield bearing saltire of arms die axis ↑↑

1825 12	40	200	475	1826-Proof *FDC*...450
1825 Proof *FDC*£1150				1826 thick line on
1826 plain saltire				saltire 15 60 225 525
on rev. 10	40	175	475	1826-Proof *FDC*.£400
1826-Proof *FDC*.£400				1827 plain saltire ..150 500 1850 —
1826 thin line on				
saltire 10	40	200	475	

3824 Halfpenny. die axis ↑↑ Laur. head. l. R. Britannia, with shield bearing saltire of arms

1825 12	45	175	375	1826 rev. raised line
1826 rev. two incuse				on saltire 10 30 125 275
lines on saltire ..8	20	100	225	1827 rev. two incuse lines
1826 Proof *FDC*..£300				on saltire.........10 25 110 250

3825

3825 Farthing. die axis ↑↑ Laur. head. l. R. Britannia, with shield bearing saltire of arms

1826 2	10	55	110	1828 2	10	60	120
1826 Proof *FDC* £225				1829 3	15	75	185
1826 Roman I 20	60	250	–	1830 2	10	60	120
1827 3	10	65	135				

3826   3827

3826 Half-Farthing. (for use in Ceylon). Laur. head. l. date below R.Britannia die axis ↑↑

1828 rev. helmet intrudes				1830 — ....25 75 250 —
legend 10	25	110	300	1830 rev. helmet intrudes
1828 rev. helmet to base				legend 10 25 110 300
of legend.........10	25	100	250	

3827 Third-Farthing. (for use in Malta). Laur. head. l. date below R.Britannia die axis ↑↑

1827   15   65   175

1827 Proof *FDC* £400

Copper coins graded in this catalogue as UNC have full mint lustre.

PS1 Proof Set, new issue, 1826. Five pounds to Farthing (11 coins) *FDC* £22000

PS1A — — Similar, including Maundy Set (15 coins) *FDC* £23000

William IV was born on 21 August 1765, and ascended the throne on his elder brother's death. From c.1791-1811 while Duke of Clarence, he was cohabiting with the actress Dorothea Jordan (1762-1816) who bore him ten illegitimate children. After the death of George IV's daughter, William was forced into a legitimate marriage with Adelaide of Saxe-Coburg and Meinigen. She bore him two daughters who both died in childhood. His reign was most notable for the introduction of the Reform bill and abolition of slavery. William was the last King of Hanover, and died on 20 June 1837 when the throne passed to his niece Victoria.

In order to prevent confusion between the Sixpence and Half-Sovereign the size of the latter was reduced in 1834, although the weight remained the same. The smaller gold piece was not acceptable to the public and in the following year it was made to the normal size. In 1836 the silver Groat was again issued for general circulation: it is the only British silver coin which has a seated Britannia as the type and was revised upon the suggestion of Mr Joseph Hume thus rendering the nickname "Joey". Crowns were not struck during this reign for general circulation; but proofs or patterns of this denomination were made and are greatly sought after. Silver Threepences and Three-Halfpence were minted for use in the Colonies.

Engraver's and/or designer's initials on the coins:
W. W. (William Wyon)
Engravers and Designers:– Francis Legett Chantry (1781-1842) Jean Baptiste Merlen (1769-c.1850) William Wyon (1795-1851).
Prime Ministers:– Earl Grey, (1764-1845), Whig, 1830-34; William Lamb, Viscount Melbourne (1779-1848) Whig, 1834, 1835-41; Sir Robert Peel, (1788-1850), Tory, 1834-5.

GOLD

3828
1831 Proof Two Pounds

3828   Two Pounds. bare head r. R. crowned shield and mantle, date below, edge plain. die axis ↑↓
1831 (proof only). .... *FDC* £5500

				3829A 1831 Sovereign, no stops on trun. first bust				3829B Second bust with broad ear top			
	F £	VF £	EF £	UNC £			F £	VF £	EF £	UNC £

3829   Sovereign. First bust. r. top of ear narrow and rounded, nose to 2nd N of BRITANNIAR, fine obv. beading. R. Crowned shield. Die axis ↑↓
1831 275   450   1200   1850   1832 250   425   1100   1750
1832 Proof *FDC* £5500

3829A Sovereign. Similar, WW without stops die axis ↑↓
1831 650   1250   2750   4250

3829B Sovereign. Second bust. r. top of ear broad and flat, nose to 2nd I in BRITANNIAR, coarser obv. beading. ↑↓
1830 plain edge proof *FDC* £6500   1835 275   425   1200   1700
1831 ....   *Extremely rare*   1836 275   425   1150   1600
1831 Proof plain edge *FDC* £2750   1836 N of ANNO struck in shield *Extremely rare*
1832 * 250   400   1100   1500   1837 300   450   1200   1700
1833 275   425   1150   1650   1837 Tailed 8 350   650   1350   —

Beware of counterfeits

	3830					3831		
	1831 Proof Half-sovereign					Large size Half-Sovereign		
F	VF	EF	UNC		F	VF	EF	UNC
£	£	£	£		£	£	£	£

3830 Half-Sovereign. Small size, bare head r.R. Crowned shield and mantle. die axis ↑↓
1831 Proof plain edge *FDC* £2000   1834 125   250   700   1150
1831 Proof milled edge *FDC* £4000

3831 Half-Sovereign. Large size, bare head r.R. Crowned shield and mantle.die axis ↑↓
1835 125   250   600   950   1837 125   275   650   1000
1836 150   300   675   1000

3832 Half-Sovereign. *Obv*. struck from Sixpence. die in error, 1836......1100   2250   4000   —

SILVER

3832	3833
Half-Sovereign - Sixpence obverse die

3833 Crown. R. Shield on mantle, 1831 Proof only W.W. on trun. struck ↑↓ ....*FDC* £10000
1831 Proof struck in gold *FDC* £85000
1831 Bare head r. W. WYON on trun. struck ↑↑ en medaille (medal die axis) *FDC* £12500
1831 Bare head r. similar die axis ↑↓ *FDC* £13000
1834 Bare head r. W.W. on trun. struck die axis ↑↓ ....*FDC* £17500
3834 Halfcrown. Bare head.WW in script on trun. R. Shield on mantle, die axis ↑↓

WW script

| 3834 | WW block |

1831 Plain edge proof *FDC* £950	1835 ....30 100 375 775
1831 Milled edge proof *FDC* £1750	1836/5 ....40 100 475 925
1834 ....20 60 250 525	1836 ....20 60 250 525
1834 Plain edge proof *FDC* £2850	1836 Proof *FDC* £2100
1834 Milled edge proof *FDC* £1350	1837 ....35 125 425 875

3834A Halfcrown. Bare head r. block WW on trun. R. Similar. die axis ↑↓
1831 Proof *FDC* £875
1834 40   150   525   1000

3835   3836

	F	VF	EF	UNC		F	VF	EF	UNC
	£	£	£	£		£	£	£	£

3835 Shilling. Bare head r. ℞. Value in wreath, date below. die axis ↑↓

1831 Proof *FDC* £550				1835 Proof *FDC* £1750			
1831 Milled edge proof *FDC* £2150				1836 20	40	200	425
1834 15	35	175	400	1836 Proof *FDC* £2500			
1834 Proof *FDC* £1250				1837 28	60	250	575
1835 20	40	200	425	1837 Proof *FDC* £1750			

3836 Sixpence. Bare head r. ℞. Value in wreath, date below. die axis ↑↓

1831 10	20	125	275	1835 10	20	125	275
— Proof *FDC* die axis ↑↓ or ↑↑ £275				1835 Proof *FDC* Extremely rare			
1831 Proof milled edge *FDC* £600				1836 18	40	200	375
1834 10	20	125	275	1836 Proof *FDC* Extremely rare			
1834 large date 20	30	150	325	1837 15	35	200	375
1834 Proof *FDC* £850				1837 Proof *FDC* Extremely rare			

3837   3839

3837 Groat. Bare head r. ℞. Britannia seated, date in ex. die axis ↑↑

1836 5	15	60	120	1837 10	20	70	125
1836 Proof *FDC* £650				1837 Proof *FDC* £800			
1836 Plain edge proof *FDC* £550				1837 Plain edge proof *FDC* £800			
1836 Proof in gold *FDC* £7500							

3838 Threepence (for use in the West Indies). As Maundy threepence but with a dull surface, ↑↓

1834 4	12	75	175	1836 4	12	75	175
1835 4	10	65	150	1837 10	20	90	200

3839 Three-Halfpence (for Colonial use). Bare head r. ℞. Value, Crowned in wreath, die axis ↑↓

1834 5	10	40	80	1836 6	15	45	95
1835/4 6	15	45	95	1837 15	35	110	290
1835 10	25	70	185	1837 Proof *FDC* £750			

3840

	EF	FDC			EF	FDC
	£	£			£	£

3840 Maundy Set (4d., 3d., 2d. and 1d.). Bare head r. Die axis ↑↓

1831	130	325	1834	100	275
— Proof *FDC* £425			1835	100	275
1831 Proof struck in gold *FDC* £12500			1836	130	325
1832	110	300	1837	130	325
1833	100	275			

3841	— **Fourpence**, 1831-7 ....*from*	12	30
3842	— **Threepence**, 1831-7 ....*from*	20	40
3843	— **Twopence**, 1831-7 ....*from*	10	25
3844	— **Penny**, 1831-7 ....*from*	10	20

COPPER

3845

	F	VF	EF	UNC		F	VF	EF	UNC
	£	£	£	£		£	£	£	£

3845 Penny. Bare head r. No initials on trun. date below. R. Britannia r. die axis ↑↑

1831		18	50	275	700	1834	20	60	325	750
1831 Proof *FDC* ↑↓ £450						1837	45	110	475	1200
1831 Proof *FDC* ↑↑ £500										

3846 Penny. Bare head r. date below. incuse initials on trun. R. Britannia r. die axis ↑↑

| 1831 W.W on trun | *Extremely rare* | 1831 .W.W on trun.30 | 85 | 350 | 750 |

3847 Halfpenny. Bare head r. date below. R. Britannia r. die axis ↑↑

1831		12	25	100	275	1834	12	25	110	275
1831 Proof *FDC* ↑↓ £300						1837	10	20	95	250
1831 Proof *FDC* ↑↑ £400										

3847   3848

3848 Farthing. Bare head r. date below. R. Britannia r. die axis ↑↑

1831 rev. incuse line				1835 die axis ↑↓	5	20	95	185
on saltire	2	10	60	120	1835 die axis ↑↑	2	10	60	120
1831 Proof *FDC* ↑↓ £275					1835 rev. incuse line				
1831 Proof *FDC* ↑↑ £325					on saltire	2	10	60	120
1834 incuse saltire	2	10	60	120	1836 rev. raised line				
1834 rev. raised line					on saltire	2	10	60	120
on saltire	2	10	60	120	1837 —	2	10	60	120

3849 Half-Farthing (for use in Ceylon). Bare head r. date below. R. Britannia r. die axis ↑↑

| 1837 | 50 | 160 | 325 | — |

3849   3850

3850 Third-Farthing (for use in Malta). Bare head r. date below. R. Britannia r. die axis ↑↑

| 1835 | 5 | 15 | 80 | 225 |

1835 Proof *FDC* £450

Copper coins graded in this catalogue as UNC have full mint lustre

PS2 Proof set. Coronation, 1831. Two pounds to farthing (14 coins). *FDC* £20000

VICTORIA, 1837-1901

Victoria was born on 24 May 1819, and enjoyed the longest reign of any Monarch so far. She marrried the German, Prince Albert with whom she enjoyed 17 years of Marriage. Upon Albert's death she became the 'Widow of Windsor' descending into a 25 year period of mourning. She skillfully avoided conflict with other European powers, and produced connections with many Royal houses all over Europe. The Great Exhibition of 1851 was a sign of the power of the largest Empire in the world. Victoria died on 22 January 1901 at the age of 81.

In 1849, as a first step towards decimalization, a silver Florin (¹/₁₀ th pound) was introduced, but the coins of 1849 omitted the usual *Dei Gratia* and these so-called 'Godless' Florins were replaced in 1851 by the 'Gothic' issue. The Halfcrown was temporarily discontinued but was minted again from 1874 onwards. Between 1863 and 1880 reverse dies of the gold and silver coins were numbered in the course of Mint experiments into the wear of dies. The exception was the Florin where the die number is on the obverse below the bust.

The gold and silver coins were redesigned for the Queen's Golden Jubilee in 1887. The Double-Florin which was then issued was abandoned after only four years; the Jubilee Sixpence of 1887, known as the 'withdrawn' type, was changed to avoid confusion with the Half-Sovereign. Gold and silver were again redesigned in 1893 with an older portrait of the Queen, but the 'old head' was not used on the bronze coinage until 1895. The heavy copper Penny had been replaced by the lighter bronze 'bun' Penny in 1860. In 1874-6 and 1881-2 some of the bronze was made by Heaton in Birmingham, and these have a letter H below the date. From 1897 Farthings were issued with a dark surface.

Early Sovereigns had a shield-type reverse, but Pistrucci's St. George design was used again from 1871. In order to increase the output of gold coinage, branches of the Royal Mint were set up in Australia at Sydney and Melbourne and, later, at Perth for coining gold of imperial type.

Engraver's and/or designer's initials on the coins:

W. W. (William Wyon 1795-1851)   T. B. (Thomas Brock 1847-1922)
L. C. W. (Leonard Charles Wyon 1826-91)   B. P. (Benedetto Pistrucci, 1784-1855)
J. E. B. (Joseph Edgar Boehm 1834-90)

Engravers and Designers: George William De Saulle, (1862-1903) William Dyce (1806-64), Jean Baptiste Merlen (1769-c.1850) Edward Poynter (1836-1919)

Prime Ministers: Viscount Melbourne, (1779-1848), Whig, 1835-41; Sir Robert Peel, (1788-1850), Tory, 1841-6; Earl of Aberdeen, (1784-1860), Tory 1852-5, Viscount Palmerston, (1784-1865), Liberal, 1855-8 1859-65; Lord John Russell, (1792-1878), Whig, 1846-52 1865-6; Earl of Derby, (1799-1869), Conservative, 1852, 1858-9 1866-8; Benjamin Disraeli, Earl of Beaconsfield (1804-1881), Conservative, 1868, 1874-80; William Ewart Gladstone (1809-1898) Liberal, 1868-74, 1880-85, 1886, 1892-94 ; Earl of Salisbury, (1830-1903), Conservative, 1885-6. 1886-92, 1895-1902; Earl of Rosebery, (1847-1929), Liberal, 1894-5.

Young Head Coinage, 1838-87

GOLD

3851
1839 Five Pounds - DIRIGE reverse

3851 Five Pounds. 1839. Young filleted bust l. plain rear fillet R. 'Una and the lion' (proof only)
DIRIGIT legend, inscribed edge, die axis ↑↑   *FDC* £28,500
– 1839 Similar – DIRIGIT legend, struck on thick flan   *FDC* £36,500
– 1839 Similar – DIRIGIT legend, plain edge die axis ↑↑   *FDC* £27,500
– 1839 –13 leaves to rear fillet, R. DIRIGE legend–proof   *FDC* £26,000
– 1839 Similar – DIRIGE legend edge letters off-centre   *FDC* £28,500
– 1839 Similar – DIRIGE legend edge plain proof   *FDC* £28,500
– 1839 –9 leaves to rear fillet, DIRIGE legend   *FDC* £23,500
– 1839 Similar – DIRIGE legend edge plain   *FDC* £31,500
– 1839 Similar – DIRIGE legend edge letters off-centre   *FDC* £28,500
– 1839 Similar – DIRIGIT legend edge plain proof   *FDC* £31,500

3852
Sovereign - first young head

	F £	VF £	EF £	UNC £		F £	VF £	EF £	UNC £

3852 Sovereign. First (small) young head. l. date below. R. First shield. London mint, die axis ↑↓

	F £	VF £	EF £	UNC £		F £	VF £	EF £	UNC £
1838 225	650	1500	3000		1844 large 44 90	125	300	500
1838 Proof *FDC*......*Extremely rare*					1844 small 44......150	250	600	1250
1838Plain edge proof *FDC* £5000					1844 4/ ᵷ ....*Extremely rare*			
1839 300	725	1750	3250		1845 4/ꞧ...................*Extremely rare*			
1839 die axis ↑↓ Proof *FDC* £3500					1845 90	125	300	500
1839 die axis ↑↑ Proof *FDC* £3750					1845 Roman I 500	1000	—	—
1839Milled edge proof *FDC* £7500					1846 90	125	300	500
1841 1250	2750	6000	—		1846 4/ᵷ ....*Extremely rare*			
1842 90	125	300	500		1846 Roman I 500	1000	—	—
1842Open 2.........500	—	—	—		1847 90	125	300	500
1843 90	125	300	500		1847 Roman I ....*Extremely rare*			
1843/2 175	275	750	1650		1848 375	800	2750	—

3852A	3852B	3852C
Leaves differently arranged	Narrow shield	Second large head

3852A Sovereign. Similar R similar but leaves of the wreath arranged differently with tops of leaves closer to crown.

1838 2500	4750	—	—

3852B Sovereign. Similar narrower shield. Considerably modified floral emblems, different leaf arrangement ↑↓

1843 2750	5250	—	—

3852C Sovereign. Second (large) head. l. W W still in relief. date below R. Shield with repositioned legend die axis ↑↓

	F	VF	EF	UNC		F	VF	EF	UNC
1848 ....BV	95	250	450		1852 Roman I 500	1000	1500	—
1849 ....BV	95	250	450		1852 ....BV	90	225	400
1849 Roman I 400	800	1550	—		1853 ....BV	90	225	400
1850 ....BV	110	275	500		1854 135	275	750	—
1850 Roman I 500	1000	—	—		1855 120	200	375	—
1851 ....BV	90	225	400		1872 ....BV	90	175	375

3852D	3852E	
WW Incuse	Extra line in ribbon - Ansell	3852F/3853A
		827 on truncation

3852D Sovereign. Similar — WW incuse on trun. die axis ↑↓

1853 95	175	400	—		1860 ꓱICTORIA ....*Extremely rare*			
— Proof *FDC* £7000					1860 DEI GRꓥ ....*Extremely rare*			
1854 ....BV	90	200	400		1860 ....BV	90	200	400
1855 ....BV	90	200	400		1860 large 0 90	125	300	650
1856 ....BV	90	200	400		1861 ....BV	90	200	400
1857 ....BV	90	200	400		1861 Roman I 200	425	950	—
1858 ....BV	90	250	425		1862 wide date ......BV	90	200	400
1858 8/7 ....*Extremely rare*					1862 R/ ꓤ in VICTORIA ....*Extremely rare*			
1859 ....BV	90	200	400		1862 F/ V in DEF narrow date ......*Extremely rare*			
1860 O over C in obverse leg. ..*Extremely rare*					1863 ....BV	90	200	400
1860 Roman I 500	1000	—	—		1863 Roman I (1/1) 250	600	—	—

	F	VF	EF	UNC		F	VF	EF	UNC
	£	£	£	£		£	£	£	£

3852E Sovereign. Similar — As 3852D 'Ansell' ribbon. Additional raised line on the lower part of the ribbon ↑↓

1859 ....300 950 3500 —

3852F Sovereign. Similar — As 3852D with die number 8⅞7 on trun. die axis ↑↓

1863 ....2500 4500 — —

3853   3853B

Die number location   WW in relief on truncation

3853 Sovereign. Similar As 3852D R. die number in space below wreath, above floral emblem, die axis ↑↓

1863	...........BV	90	200	350	1866/5 DIE 17 only ...85	175	350	750
1864	...........BV	85	175	325	1868 ....BV	90	200	350
1865	...........BV	90	200	375	1869 ....BV	85	175	325
1866	...........BV	85	175	325	1870 ....BV	100	225	400

3853A Sovereign. Similar — As 3853 with die number 827 on trun. R. die number is always no. 22 die axis ↑↓

1863 ....2250 4000 — —

3853B Sovereign. Similar — WW in relief on trun. R. die number below wreath, above floral emblem die axis ↑↓

1870	...........BV	90	200	375	1873 ....BV	90	200	350
1871	...........BV	80	150	325	1874...........1000	2250	4750	—
1872	...........BV	80	150	325				

Melbourne Mint mark   Sydney Mint mark

3854   3855

3854 Sovereign Second (large) head. l. WW in relief date below R. M below wreath for Melbourne Mint, Australia ↑↓

1872 M	...........BV	75	135	700	1883 M	85	200	500	1500
1872/1 M	125	250	750	2000	1884 M	...........BV	75	110	500
1874 M	...........BV	75	165	1000	1885 M	...........BV	75	110	500
1880 M	300	600	1600	3600	1886 M	600	2000	3000	5600
1881 M	...........BV	85	180	1250	1887 M	325	600	2000	3750
1882 M	...........BV	75	135	600					

3855 Sovereign. Similar — As 3854 R. with S below wreath for Sydney Mint, Australia die axis ↑↓

1871 S	...........BV	75	110	600	1880 S .... VICTORIA	*Extremely rare*		
1872 S	...........BV	75	135	900	1881 S	...........BV	75	135	750
1873 S	...........BV	75	130	750	1882 S	...........BV	75	110	550
1875 S	...........BV	75	135	750	1883 S	...........BV	75	110	550
1877 S	...........BV	75	110	500	1884 S	...........BV	75	100	500
1878 S	...........BV	75	110	500	1885 S	...........BV	75	100	500
1879 S	...........BV	75	110	500	1886 S	...........BV	75	100	500
1880 S	...........BV	75	120	750	1887 S	...........BV	75	165	825

3855A Sovereign. Second (large) head WW incuse on trun. date below R. with S below wreath for Sydney Mint die axis ↑↓

1871 S 75 95 140 650

3856A   3856C

Horse with long tail   Horse with short tail

Small BP in exergue   No BP in exergue

	F	VF	EF	UNC		F	VF	EF	UNC
	£	£	£	£		£	£	£	£

3856 Sovereign. First young head. l. WW buried in narrow trun. ℞. St. George.
London mint. Horse with short tail. Large BP and date in ex. die axis ↑↓

| 1871 | .... | BV | 85 | 125 | 300 |

1871 Proof milled edge*FDC* £9500

1871 Plain edge proof *FDC* £5000

3856A Sovereign. — — As 3856 ℞. Horse with long tail. Small BP and date in ex.die axis ↑↓

1871	....	BV	75	100	250	1876	....	BV	75	100	250
1871 Proof *FDC* plain edge £6500					1878	....	BV	75	100	250
1872	....	BV	75	110	275	1879	....	125	300	1250	—
1873	....	BV	75	100	250	1880	....	BV	75	100	250
1874	....	BV	75	110	275						

3856B Sovereign. — — As 3856 ℞. Horse with short tail, small BP and date in ex.die axis ↑↓

| 1880 | .... | BV | 75 | 100 | 250 | 1884 | .... | BV | 75 | 100 | 250 |
| 1880 8/7 | .... | 60 | 95 | 140 | 300 | 1885 | .... | BV | 75 | 125 | 275 |

3856C Sovereign. — — As 3856 ℞. Horse with short tail, date but no BP in ex.die axis ↑↓

| 1880 Second 8/7 | .... | BV | 95 | 140 | 300 |

3856D Sovereign. Second head. l. WW complete, on broad trun. ℞.
    Horse with long tail, small BP and date in ex.die axis ↑↓

| 1880 8/7 | .... | 60 | 95 | 140 | 300 |
| 1880 | .... | BV | 75 | 100 | 250 |

3856E Sovereign. — — As 3856D ℞. Horse with short tail. Date but no BP in ex. die axis ↑↓

| 1880 | .... | BV | 75 | 100 | 250 |

3856F Sovereign. — — As 3856E ℞. Horse with short tail, small BP and date in ex. die axis ↑↓

| 1880 | .... | 65 | 95 | 140 | 300 | 1885 | .... | BV | 75 | 110 | 275 |
| 1884 | .... | BV | 75 | 110 | 275 | | | | | | |

3857   3857A

Melbourne Mint   Horse with short tail

WW buried in truncation   No BP in exergue

3857 Sovereign. — — First head. l. WW buried in trun. M below head for Melbourne Mint,
    Australia. ℞. Horse with long tail, small BP and date in ex. die axis ↑↓

1872 M	....	110	185	625	2500	1877 M	....	BV	75	135	550
1873 M	....	BV	80	165	900	1878 M	....	BV	75	135	550
1874 M	....	BV	80	165	900	1879 M	....	BV	70	100	550
1875 M	....	BV	75	135	650	1880 M	....	BV	75	110	550
1876 M	....	BV	75	130	550	1881 M	....	BV	75	110	550

3857A Sovereign. — — As 3857 ℞. horse with short tail, date but no BP in ex die axis ↑↓

| 1881 M | .... | BV | 70 | 110 | 550 | 1884 M | .... | 65 | 100 | 250 | — |
| 1882 M | .... | BV | 75 | 110 | 525 | | | | | | |

	F £	VF £	EF £	UNC £		F £	VF £	EF £	UNC £

3857B Sovereign. First head l. WW buried in trun. M below head for Melbourne Mint, Australia ℞.
Horse with short tail, small BP and date in ex. die axis ↑↓

1879 M	*Extremely rare*				1883 M	BV	65	100	500
1880 M	*Extremely rare*				1884 M	BV	65	100	425
1882 M	BV	75	110	550	1885 M	BV	65	100	450

3857C Sovereign. —— Second head. l. WW complete on broad truncation. ℞. Horse with short tail, small BP in ex.

1882 M	BV	75	110	550	1885 M	BV	65	100	450
1883 M	BV	65	100	500	1886 M	BV	65	100	425
1884 M	BV	65	100	425	1887 M	BV	75	110	550

3858 Sovereign First head. l. WW buried in narrow trun. S below head for Sydney Mint, Australia,
℞. Horse with short tail, large BP and date in ex. die axis ↑↓

1871 S						70	135	500	1600

3858A Sovereign. —— As 3858 ℞. Horse with long tail, small BP and date in ex. die axis ↑↓

1871 S	BV	100	400	1250	1875 S	BV	85	165	900
1872 S	BV	85	165	900	1876 S	BV	85	165	750
1873 S	BV	90	180	1150	1879 S		60	120	750	2150
1874 S	BV	85	165	1250	1880 S	BV	80	125	650

3858B Sovereign. —— As 3858 ℞. Horse with short tail, date but no BP in ex. die axis ↑↓

1880 S	BV	75	125	650	1881 S	BV	70	110	650

3858C	3859	3859A
Sydney Mint WW on broad truncation	Type A1	Type A2

3858C Sovereign. Second head. l. WW complete on broad trun. ℞.
Horse with long tail, small BP and date in ex. die axis ↑↓

1880 S						BV	80	125	650

3858D Sovereign. —— As 3858C ℞. Horse with short tail, date but no BP in ex. die axis ↑↓

1881 S		75	110	650	1882 S	BV	65	100	350

3858E Sovereign. —— As 3858D ℞. Horse with short tail small BP and date in ex. die axis ↑↓

1882 S	BV	65	100	350	1885 S	BV	65	100	500
1883 S	BV	80	140	1000	1886 S	BV	65	100	500
1884 S	BV	65	100	500	1887 S	BV	65	100	550

3859 Half-Sovereign. Type A1. First (smallest) young head. date below l. ℞. First shield, die axis ↑↓

1838	75	125	325	700	1849	45	95	275	500
1839 die axis ↑↓ or ↑↑ Proof only *FDC* £1950					1850	125	300	1000	—
1839 Milled edge proof *FDC* Extremely rare					1851	45	80	225	425
1841	80	125	350	750	1852	65	95	275	525
1842	45	95	275	550	1853	45	80	225	425
1843	70	135	375	650	1853 Proof small date *FDC* £4000				
1844	65	110	325	600	1853 Proof large date *FDC* £6000				
1845	125	375	1250	—	1855	45	80	225	425
1846	65	110	325	600	1856	45	80	225	425
1847	65	110	325	600	1856/5	85	140	325	600
1848 Close date	65	110	325	600	1857	65	95	275	525
1848/7	110	200	450	800	1858	65	95	275	525
1848 Wide date	80	135	375	700					

3859A Half-Sovereign. Type A2, Second (larger) young head. date below. ℞. First shield die axis ↑↓

1858	45	80	225	425	1861	45	80	225	425
1859	45	80	225	425	1862	325	1000	3750	—
1860	45	80	225	425	1863	45	80	225	425

3860	3860C	3860D	3860E	3860F
Die number location	Repositioned legend	Type A3	Type A4	Type A5

F	VF	EF	UNC		F	VF	EF	UNC
£	£	£	£		f	£	£	£

3860 Half-Sovereign. Type A2, second head, date below R. die number below shield, die axis ↑↓

1863	65	95	300	550	1867	45	80	225	400
1864	45	80	225	400	1869	45	80	225	400
1865	45	80	225	400	1870	45	80	225	400
1866	45	80	225	400	1871	45	80	225	400

3860A Half-Sovereign. Second head, date below R. Re-engraved shield legend and rosettes closer to border, coarse boarder teeth both sides, with die number below shield die axis ↑↓

1870	100	250	750	—	1871	100	250	750	—

3860B Half-Sovereign. Second head, date below R. As last but with normal border teeth and no die number below shield die axis ↑↓

1871	200	425	1000	—

3860C Half-Sovereign. Second head, date below obv. with repositioned legend, nose now points to T in VICTORIA. R Similar to last but with die number below shield die axis ↑↓

1871	125	275	800	—	1872	100	225	675	—

3860D Half-Sovereign. Type A3, Third (larger still) young head l, date below. R. As 3860A, with die number below shield die axis ↑↓

1872	45	80	225	400	1875	45	75	225	350
1873	45	80	225	400	1876	45	75	225	350
1874	45	85	225	400	1877	45	75	225	350

3860E Half-Sovereign. Type A4. Fourth young head l. hair ribbon now narrow, date below. R. As last with die number below shield die axis ↑↓

1876	45	75	175	350	1878	45	75	175	350
1877	45	75	175	350	1879	60	100	325	600

3860F Half-Sovereign. Type A5. Fifth young head l. in very low relief, date below. R. As last with die number below shield die axis ↑↓

1880	50	95	325	600

3861	3862
Type A5	Sydney Mint

3861 Half-Sovereign. Fifth head, date below. R. Cross on crown buried in border. Legend and rosettes very close to heavy border, no die number below shield die axis ↑↓

1880	45	85	200	400	1885	45	75	175	300
1883	45	75	175	300	1885/3	80	140	300	650
1884	45	75	175	300					

3862 Half-Sovereign. Type A2, Second (larger) young head l. nose points between T and O. Date below R. First crowned shield cross clear of border with S below shield for Sydney Mint, Australia, die axis ↑↓

1871 S	45	100	600	2150

	F	VF	EF	UNC		F	VF	EF	UNC
	£	£	£	£		£	£	£	£

3862A Half-Sovereign. Similar obv. with repositioned legend, nose now points to T in VICTORIA.
Date below R Re-engraved shield cross touches border, S below shield die axis ↑↓

1872 S 45   100   600   2150

3862B Half-Sovereign. Type A3. Third (larger still) young head l. I of DEI points to rear fillet.
Date below R. As last die axis ↑↓

1875 S 45   100   600   2150

3862C Half-Sovereign. Type A4. Fourth young head l. front hair fillet now narrow. R. As last, die axis ↑↓

1879 S 45   110   525   2150

3862D Half-Sovereign. Type A5. Fifth young head l. in low relief wider tr. no front ear lobe. Date
below R as last. die axis ↑↓

1882 S 140   475   2650   6850   1883 S 55   110   500   3000

3862E Half-Sovereign. Fifth head, date below R. Cross on crown buried in border. Legend and
rosettes very close to heavy border, S below shield die axis ↑↓

1880 S 45   120   650   2650   1883 S 45   110   500   3000
1881 S 45   135   800   2900   1886 S 45   120   800   2400
1882 S 120   475   2650   6850   1887 S 55   120   650   2000

3863
Melbourne Mint

3863 Half-Sovereign. Type A3. Third (larger still) young head l. Date below R. Re-engraved shield
with M below shield for Melbourne Mint, Australia die axis ↑↓

1873 M 45   120   650   2350   1877 M 45   110   580   2150

3863A Half-Sovereign. Type A4, fourth young head l. hair ribbon now narrow. R. As last die axis ↑↓

1877 M 45   110   600   2150   1882 M 45   110   500   1650

3863B Half-Sovereign. Type A5. Fifth young head l. in low relief.Date below R. As last die axis ↑↓

1881 M 70   150   1250   3650   1885 M 140   350   1850   5150
1882 M 45   110   500   1650   1886 M 75   175   1350   3650
1884 M 55   220   1350   3850   1887 M 100   275   1850   5150

Jubilee Coinage, 1887-93, die axis ↑↑

3864
1887 Five Pounds

3864* Five Pounds. Jubilee bust 1. R. St. George date in ex. 1887...........450   675   850   1100
— Proof *FDC* £2750
— Proof no B.P. in exergue £3250

3864A* Five Pounds. Jubilee bust 1. R. St George, S on ground for Sydney Mint, Australia 1887 S
Extremely rare

* *Beware recent forgeries*

3865
1887 Two Pounds

3866B
1887 Proof Sovereign

	EF	UNC		F	VF	EF	UNC
	£	£		£	£	£	£

3865* Two Pounds. Jubilee bust 1. R. St George die axis ↑↑ 1887 200   275   375   500
1887 Proof *FDC* £900
1887 Proof no BP in exergue FDC.. *Extremely rare*
3865A* Two Pounds. R. St George, S on ground for Sydney Mint, Australia ↑↑ 1887S.... *Extremely rare*
3866* Sovereign. Normal JEB (angled J) designer's initials fully on trun. R. St. George. die axis ↑↑
1887.. 75   150   1888   95   175
3866A Sovereign. Similar with tiny JEB (hooked J) designer's initials at base of truncation die axis ↑↑
1887 .... *Extremely rare*
3866B Sovereign. Similar repositioned legend. G: of D:G: now closer to crown. Normal JEB (angled J)
     designer's initials at base of trun. ↑↑
1887 Proof *FDC* £650   1890 .... BV   85   165
1888.. 85   165   1891 ....   *Extremely rare*
1889..BV 85   165
3866C Sovereign. Similar obv. as last. R. Horse with longer tail die axis ↑↑
1891.. 85   165   1892 .... BV   85   165

3867
Melbourne Mint

3869
1887 Half-Sovereign

3867 Sovereign. Similar with small spread JEB (angled J)designer's initials fully on trun. R. M on
     ground for Melbourne Mint, Australia, die axis ↑↑
1887M.. BV   80   165
3867A Sovereign. Similar with normal JEB designer's initials on trun. die axis ↑↑
1887M.. BV   80   165
1888M... *Extremely rare*
1889M... *Extremely rare*
1890M... *Extremely rare*
3867B Sovereign. Similar repositioned legend. G: of D: G: now closer to crown. Normal JEB (angled J)
     initials at base of trun. die axis ↑↑
1887M.................................... 80   165   1889M .... BV   70   125
1888M.................................... 85   175   1890M .... BV   90   165
3867C Sovereign. Similar obv. as last. R. Horse with longer tail die axis ↑↑
1891M.................................... 90   165   1893M .... BV   95   220
1892M.................................... 80   135
3868 Sovereign. Similar with normal JEB (hooked J) initials in arc on trun. R. S on ground for
     Sydney Mint, Australia die axis ↑↑
1887S.. 135   225   1250
1887S Proof .... *Extremely rare*
3868A Sovereign. Similar with small spread JEB designer's initials straight on trun.(hooked J) die
axis ↑↑
1887S.. *Extremely rare*
1888S.. BV   90   165
1889S.. *Extremely rare*

* Beware recent forgeries

	VF	EF	UNC		F	VF	EF	UNC
	£	£	£		£	£	£	£

3868B Sovereign. Similar repositioned legend. G: of D:G: now closer to crown. Normal JEB (angled J) initials on trun. die axis ↑↑

1888S	90	165	1890S	BV	90	165
1889S	70	125				

3868C Sovereign. Similar obv. as last. ℞. Horse with longer tail die axis ↑↑

1891S	90	165	1893S	BV	100	195
1892S	70	125				

3869 Half-Sovereign. Similar obv. normal JEB designer's initials. on trun. ℞. High shield die axis ↑↑

1887	60	95	1890	120	225	—

— Proof *FDC* £350

3869A   3869B - Lower shield

3869C
Plain trun., higher shield

3869A Half-Sovereign. Similar small close JEB intitials. on trun. ℞. High shield die axis ↑↑

1887	120	225	—

3869B Half-Sovereign. Similar normal JEB initials. on trun. ℞. Lower shield, date therefore spread apart, complete cross at top, die axis ↑↑

1890	120	225	—	1892	120	225	—

3869C Half-Sovereign. Similar no JEB initials on trun. ℞. High Shield die axis ↑↑

1887	120	225	—	1891	120	225	—
1890	BV	60	95	1892	120	225	—

3869D Half-Sovereign. Jubilee bust 1. ℞. Lower shield, date therefore spread apart die axis ↑↑

1890	BV	60	95	1892	BV	60	95
1891	BV	75	110	1893	BV	85	120

3870   3870A

3870 Half-Sovereign. Similar small very spread JEB initials on trun. ℞. High shield, M below for Melbourne Mint, Australia, die axis ↑↑

1887M	40	75	225	800

3870A Half-Sovereign. Similar small close JEB initials on trun. ℞. As last die axis ↑↑

1887M	40	75	225	800

3870B Half-Sovereign. Similar normal JEB initials on trun. ℞. Lower shield, date therefore spread part die axis ↑↑

1893M	40	120	450	1650

3871 Half-Sovereign. Similar small very spread JEB initials on trun. (hooked J) ℞. High shield S below for Sydney Mint, Australia ↑↑

1887S	40	75	225	825

3871A Half-Sovereign. Similar small close JEB initials on trun. ℞ As last. die axis ↑↑

1887S	40	75	225	825

	F	VF	EF	UNC
	£	£	£	£

3871B Half-Sovereign. Jubilee bust 1. Normal JEB initials on trun. R. Lower shield, date therefore spread apart, S below for Sydney Mint, Australia die axis ↑↑

1889S 45   125   450   1650

3871C Half-Sovereign. Jubilee bust 1. Normal JEB initials on trun. R. High shield, S below for Sydney Mint, Australia die axis ↑↑

1891S 45   125   450   1650

3871D Half-Sovereign. Jubilee bust 1. No JEB initials on trun. R. As last die axis ↑↑

1891S 45   125   450   1650

Old Head coinage, 1893-1901, die axis ↑↑

3872
1893 Five Pounds

3872* Five Pounds. Old veiled bust 1. R. St. George and dragon, date and BP in ex.

1893 500   850   1350   2000

1893 Proof *FDC* £3500

3873	3874
1893 Two Pounds	1893 Sovereign

	EF	UNC		F	VF	EF	UNC
	£	£		£	£	£	£

3873* Two Pounds. Old veiled bust 1. R. St. George and dragon, date and BP in ex. die axis ↑↑

1893 220   350   500   800

1893 Proof *FDC* £900

3874 Sovereign. Old veiled bust 1. R. St. George, London Mint die axis ↑↑

1893	80	140	1898			75	125
1893 Proof *FDC* £650			1899			75	125
1894		75	125	1900		75	125
1895		75	125	1901		75	125
1896		75	125				

3875 Sovereign. Similar R. St. George. M on ground for Melbourne Mint, Australia die axis ↑↑

1893 M	95	200	1898 M	65	95
1894 M	70	100	1899 M	65	95
1895 M	75	110	1900 M	65	95
1896 M	65	95	1901 M	65	95
1897 M	65	95			

* beware recent forgeries

3876
Perth Mint mark

3877
Sydney Mint mark

	F	VF	EF	UNC		F	VF	EF	UNC
	£	£	£	£		£	£	£	£

3876 Sovereign. Similar — P on ground for Perth Mint, Australia die axis ↑↑

1899 P	.60	125	300	1150	1901 P			.80	150
1900 P			80	150					

3877 Sovereign. Similar — S on ground for Sydney Mint, Australia die axis ↑↑

1893 S			.75	110	1898 S			.80	150
1894 S			.65	95	1899 S			.65	95
1895 S			.75	110	1900 S			.70	100
1896 S			.80	150	1901 S			.70	100
1897 S			.70	100					

3878
1893 Half-Sovereign

3878 Half-Sovereign. Old veiled bust l.R. St. George. Date in ex. London Mint die axis ↑↑

1893		.50	100	1897		50	100
— Proof *FDC* £475				1898		50	100
1894		.50	100	1899		50	100
1895		.50	100	1900		50	100
1896		.50	100	1901		50	100

3879 Half-Sovereign. Similar — M on ground for Melbourne Mint, Australia die axis ↑↑

1893 M			*Extremely rare*		1899 M	.40	100	325	1400
1896 M	.40	100	325	1350	1900 M	.45	110	325	1400

3880 Half-Sovereign. Similar — P on ground for Perth Mint, Australia die axis ↑↑

1899 P		Proof only *unique*		1900 P	.65	135	415	1850

3881 Half-Sovereign. Similar — S on ground for Sydney Mint, Australia die axis ↑↑

1893 S	.40	85	250	1000	1900 S	.40	75	215	1000
1897 S	.40	85	225	1000					

SILVER

Young head coinage, die axis ↑↓

3882
1844 Crown

	F	VF	EF	UNC			F	VF	EF	UNC
	£	£	£	£			£	£	£	£

3882 Crown. Young head. l. Ṛ. Crowned shield, regnal year on edge in Roman figures (eg 1847 = XI)

1839 Proof only *FDC* £4250

	F	VF	EF	UNC
1844 Star stops VIII	30	125	975	2500
1844 Cinquefoil stops VIII	30	125	975	2500
1844 Mistruck edge lettering	75	250	1250	–
1845 Star stops VIII	30	125	975	2500
1845 Cinquefoil stops VIII	30	125	975	2500
1847 XI	40	200	1250	2950

3883
1847 Gothic Crown

3885
Type 'A1' Halfcrown

3883*Crown. 'Gothic' type, bust 1. Ṛ. Crowned cruciform Shields, emblems in angles. inscribed edge, mdcccxlvii=1847 Undecimo on edge die axis ↑↓ 450 800 1350 2500

1847 Septimo on edge of highest rarity.   1847 Proof, Plain edge die axis ↑↑ *FDC* £3500
1847 Proof in gold plain edge *FDC* of highest rarity   1847 Proof in white metal plain edge *FDC* £6000
Beware of recent forgeries.

3884 Crown. Similar mdccliii=1853. Septimo on edge die axis ↑↑ Proof *FDC* £6000
    1853 plain edge proof *FDC* £8000

3885 Halfcrown. Type A^1. Young head l. with one ornate and one plain fillet binding hair. WW in
    relief on trun. Ṛ. Crowned shield of arms, edge milled. Die axis ↑↓

1839.......................150   450 1350 4000   1839 Proof plain edge *FDC* £1350
1839 Milled edge Proof *FDC Extremely rare*

3886 Halfcrown. Type A^2 Similar, but two ornate fillets binding hair.die axis ↑↓
    1839 Proof only *FDC* £2500

3886A Halfcrown. Type A$^{2/3}$ Similar, Two plain fillets, WW relief, die axis ↑↓ plain edge
    1839 Proof *FDC* £3750

3887 Halfcrown. Type A^3. Similar two plain fillets. WW incuse on trun. die axis ↑↓

1839.......................500   1750 4000   —   1839 Milled edge Proof *FDC* £2250
1839 Plain edge Proof *FDC* £3000   1840........................30   100   525 1000

	F	VF	EF	UNC		F	VF	EF	UNC
	£	£	£	£		£	£	£	£

3888 Halfcrown. Type A⁴. Similar but no initials on trun. die axis ↑↓

1841	125	400	1500	2500	1849 large date	30	90	500	1100
1842	25	85	475	950	1849/7		*Extremely rare*		
1843	30	125	600	1250	1849 small date	40	120	600	1200
1844	20	60	400	800	1850	25	80	550	1100
1844 not in edge collar		*Extremely rare*			1850 Proof *FDC Extremely rare*				
1845	20	60	400	800	1853 Proof *FDC* £1750				
1845 5/3		*Extremely rare*			1862 Proof *FDC Extremely rare*				
1846	20	60	400	800	1862 Plain edge Proof *FDC* £3750				
1848/6	60	175	700	1750	1864 Proof *FDC* £4000				
1848/7		*Extremely rare*			1864 Plain edge Proof *FDC* £3750				
1848	25	275	975	2000					

3889
Type A5 Halfcrown

3890
1849 'Godless' Florin

3889 Halfcrown. Similar Type A⁵. As last but design of inferior workmanship ℞. Crowned cruciform shields, die axis ↑↓

1874	15	40	150	400	1881	15	40	150	400
1874 Proof *FDC* £3750					1881 Proof *FDC* £3250				
1875	15	40	150	400	1881 Plain edge proof *FDC* £3750				
1875 Proof *FDC* £3750					1882	15	45	175	425
1876	15	45	175	425	1883	15	40	150	400
1876/5	30	55	315	650	1883 Plain edge proof *FDC* £3750				
1877	15	40	150	400	1884	15	40	150	400
1878	15	40	150	400	1885	15	40	150	400
1878 Proof *FDC* £3250					1885 Proof *FDC* £3000				
1879	15	45	200	450	1886	15	40	150	400
1879 Proof *FDC* £3750					1886 Plain edge proof *FDC* £3750				
1880	15	40	150	400	1887	20	50	175	400
1880 Proof *FDC* £3750					1887 Proof *FDC* £3250				

3890 Florin. 'Godless' type A (i.e. without D.G.), WW behind bust within linear circle, die axis ↑↓

1848 Plain edge (Pattern) *FDC* £950					1849 WW obliterated	35	75	235	425
1848 Milled edge ↑↑ or ↑↓ Proof *FDC* £2250					1849	18	40	150	275

3891 Florin. 'Gothic' type B¹. Reads brit:, WW below bust, date at end of obverse legend in gothic numerals (1851 to 1863) Crowned cruciform Shields, emblems in angles, edge milled. die axis ↑↓

mdcccli		*Extremely rare*			mdccclvii Proof *FDC* £2500				
mdccclii	18	40	150	350	mdccclviii	20	45	150	375
mdccclii Proof *FDC* £2000					mdccclviii Proof *FDC* £2500				
mdccclii, ii/i	20	50	175	425	mdccclix	20	45	150	375
mdcccliii	18	40	150	350	mdccclx	25	50	175	400
mdcccliii Proof *FDC* £1750					mdccclxii	50	150	650	1450
mdcccliv	275	800	3000	—	mdccclxii Plain edge Proof *FDC* £2750				
mdccclv	25	75	200	450	mdccclxiii	100	325	975	2000
mdccclvi	25	75	200	450	mdccclxiii Plain edge Proof *FDC* £2750				
mdccclvii	20	45	150	375					

3891
1853 Florin Type B1

3892
1865 Florin Type B2

	F	VF	EF	UNC		F	VF	EF	UNC
	£	£	£	£		£	£	£	£

3892 Florin. Type B². Similar as last but die number below bust (1864 to 1867) die axis ↑↓

mdccclxiv 20	45	150	400	mdccclxv 40	100	285	525		
mdccclxiv heavy flan 250	500	1000	1850	mdccclxvi 35	75	235	450		
mdccclxiv heavy flan Proof	*FDC* £3000			mdccclxvii 30	70	235	450		

3893 Florin. Type B³. Similar reads britt:, die number below bust (1868 to 1879) die axis

mdccclxvii Proof *FDC* £2750				mdccclxxiii 20	50	175	350		
mdccclxviii 30	85	265	575	mdccclxxiii Proof *FDC* £2600					
mdccclxix 25	75	265	525	mdccclxxiv 25	55	200	425		
mdccclxix Proof *FDC* £2850				mdccclxxiv iv/iii......35	75	265	525		
mdccclxx 20	45	150	375	mdccclxxv 25	50	175	400		
mdccclxx Proof *FDC* £2850				mdccclxxvi 20	45	150	375		
mdccclxxi 20	50	175	400	mdccclxxvii 25	50	175	400		
mdccclxxi Proof *FDC* £2350				mdccclxxix	*Extremely rare*				
mdccclxxii 18	40	125	325						

3894 Florin. Type B⁴. Similar as last but with border of 48 arcs and no WW below bust die axis ↑↓
1877 mdccclxxvii ....   *Extremely rare*

3895 Florin. Type B⁵. Similar but border of 42 arcs (1867, 1877 and 1878) die axis ↑↓

mdccclxvii	*Extremely rare*			mdccclxxviii 20	45	150	350		
mdccclxxvii 25	55	200	475	mdccclxxviii Proof *FDC*	*Extremely rare*				

3896 Florin. Type B⁵/6. Similar as last but no die number below bust (1877, 1879) die axis ↑↓

mdccclxxvii 100	225	475	950	mdccclxxix 100	225	475	950		

3897 Florin. Type B⁶. Similar reads britt:, WW; Border of 48 arcs (1879) die axis ↑↓
mdccclxxix ....20 | 45 | 150 | 375

3898 Florin. Type B⁷. Similar as last but no WW, Border of 38 arcs (1879) die axis ↑↓

mdccclxxix 20	45	150	375
mdccclxxix Proof *FDC*..	*Extremely rare*		

3899 Florin. Type B³/8. Similar as next but younger portrait (1880) die axis ↑↓
mdccclxxx..   *Extremely rare*

3900 Florin. Type B⁸. Similar but border of 34 arcs (1880 to 1887) die axis ↑↓

mdccclxxx 15	40	150	350	mdccclxxxiii Proof *FDC* £2350					
mdccclxxx Proof *FDC*£2350				mdccclxxxiv 18	40	125	300		
mdccclxxxi 18	40	125	350	mdccclxxxv 20	45	150	325		
mdccclxxxi Proof *FDC* £2350				mdccclxxxv Proof *FDC* £2350					
mdccclxxxi/xxri.......30	75	200	450	mdccclxxxvi 15	35	125	325		
mdccclxxxiii 18	40	125	350	mdccclxxxvi Proof *FDC* £2600					

3901 Florin. Type B⁹. Similar but border of 46 arcs die axis ↑↓

1887 mdccclxxxvii 30	60	250	475
mdccclxxxvii Proof *FDC*	*Extremely rare*		

3902 Shilling. Type A¹. First head l., WW on trun.R. crowned mark of value within wreath, date
below, die axis ↑↓

1838........................15	35	165	350	1839 10	30	150	325	
1838 Proof *FDC* £1850				1839 Proof *FDC* £950				

3903 Shilling Type A². Second head, l. WW on trun. (proof only), 1839 die axis ↑↑ *FDC* £500

3904
Type A3 Shilling

	F £	VF £	EF £	UNC £		F £	VF £	EF £	UNC £

3904 Shilling Type A³. Second head, l. no initials on trun. ℞. Similar die axis ↑↓

1839 10	25	135	300	1852 10	20	100	225
1839 Proof plain edge *FDC* £525				1853 10	20	90	225
1839 Proof milled edge *FDC Extremely rare*				1853 Proof *FDC* £475			
1840 15	50	190	350	1854 50	150	600	1600
1840 Proof *FDC* £2500				1854/1 150	575	1750	—
1841 15	50	190	350	1855 10	20	90	225
1842 10	20	115	250	1856 10	20	90	225
1842 Proof *FDC* £2500				1857 10	20	90	225
1843 15	30	165	350	1857 REG F:Ɔ:error 125	350	950	—
1844 10	20	115	250	1858 10	20	90	225
1845 10	20	125	300	1859 10	20	90	225
1846 10	20	115	250	1859 Proof *FDC* £2750			
1848 over 6..............45	100	575	950	1860 15	25	135	300
1849 15	25	125	300	1861 15	25	135	300
1850 120	850	1750	—	1861 D/B in FD		*Extremely rare*	
1850/49.................150	650	1950	—	1862 20	40	190	375
1851 30	85	350	800	1863 25	60	300	650
1851 Proof *FDC* £3000				1863/1 75	200	550	—

3905 Shilling Type A⁴. Similar as last, ℞. Die number above date die axis ↑↑

1864 10	20	90	225	1866 BBITANNIAR..50	175	500	—
1865 10	20	90	225	1867 10	20	100	225
1866 10	20	90	225				

3906 Shilling Type A⁵. Third head, l. ℞. Similar no die number above date die axis ↑↓

1867 Proof £2250	1879	*Extremely rare*
1867 Proof plain edge £2750		

3906A
Type A6 Shilling

Die number location
above date

3906A Shilling Type A⁶. Third head, l. ℞. Similar die number above date die axis ↑↓

1867 45	135	650	—	1874 10	20	90	225
1868 10	25	90	225	1875 10	20	90	225
1869 20	35	125	250	1876 15	30	100	250
1870 20	35	125	250	1877 10	20	90	225
1871 10	20	90	225	1878 10	20	90	225
1871 Plain edge proof *FDC* £2350				1878 Proof *FDC* £2350			
1871 Milled edge proof *FDC* £2150				1879 25	65	250	500
1872 10	20	90	225	1879 Proof *FDC* £1650			
1873 10	20	90	225				

	F	VF	EF	UNC		F	VF	EF	UNC
	£	£	£	£		£	£	£	£

3907 Shilling Type A⁷. Fourth head, l. R. Similar no die number above date die axis ↑↓

	F	VF	EF	UNC		F	VF	EF	UNC
1879............10	20	90	200		1883 plain edge Proof *FDC* £3750			
1879 Proof *FDC* £2350					1884............10	20	80	175
1880............10	20	80	175		1884 Proof *FDC* £2150			
1880 Proof plain edge £2150					1885............10	15	70	150
1880 Proof milled edge £1650					1885 Proof *FDC* £2150			
1881............10	20	80	175		1886............10	15	70	150
1881 Proof plain edge £2750					1886 Proof *FDC* £2150			
1881 Proof milled edge £1850					1887............,,15	30	100	250
1882............,,15	40	125	250		1887 Proof *FDC* £1850			
1883............10	20	80	175					

3907A Shilling. Type A7. Fourth head, R. Similar die number above date die axis ↑↓

1878............	*Extremely rare*				1879............	*Extremely rare*		

3908

Type A1 Sixpence

3908 Sixpence. Type A¹. First head l. R. Crowned mark of value within wreath, date below die axis ↑↓

	F	VF	EF	UNC		F	VF	EF	UNC
1838............8	15	75	200		1852............4	12	75	150
1838 Proof *FDC* £950					1853............6	14	70	125
1839............8	15	75	200		1853 Proof *FDC* £450			
1839 Proof *FDC* £400					1854............50	140	500	1100
1840............8	15	80	225		1855............6	14	70	210
1841............8	18	85	250		1855/3............12	25	85	250
1842............8	15	75	215		1855 Proof *FDC*	*Extremely rare*		
1843............8	15	75	215		1856............7	15	75	215
1844 Small 44............6	14	70	210		1857............7	15	75	215
1844 Large 44............10	25	85	250		1858............7	15	75	215
1845............7	15	75	215		1858 Proof *FDC*	*Extremely rare*		
1846............6	14	70	210		1859............6	14	70	210
1848............30	85	325	775		1859/8............10	20	75	225
1848/6 or 7............40	100	375	825		1860............7	15	75	215
1850............7	15	75	215		1862............30	100	350	775
1850/3............15	30	115	300		1863............18	65	225	650
1851............7	15	75	215		1866............	*Extremely rare*		

3909

Die number location above date

3912

Type 'A5' Sixpence

3909 Sixpence. Type A². First head, R. Similar die number above date die axis ↑↓

	F	VF	EF	UNC		F	VF	EF	UNC
1864............7	15	75	215		1866............7	15	75	215
1865............8	18	85	250					

3910 Sixpence. Type A³. Second head, l. R. Similar die number above date die axis ↑↓

	F £	VF £	EF £	UNC £		F £	VF £	EF £	UNC £
1867	10	18	80	250	1873	5	12	60	210
1867 Proof FDC £1350					1874	5	12	60	210
1868	10	18	80	250	1875	5	12	60	210
1869	10	20	110	300	1876	10	18	85	275
1869 Proof FDC £1600					1877	5	12	60	210
1870	10	20	110	300	1878	5	12	60	210
1870 plain edge Proof FDC £1600					1878 DRITANNIAR	30	80	500	—
1871	7	15	65	215	1878 Proof FDC £1350				
1871 plain edge Proof FDC £1350					1878/7	35	100	450	—
1872	7	15	65	215	1879	10	18	85	275

3911 Sixpence. Type A⁴. Second head, l. R. Similar No die number die axis ↑↓

	F £	VF £	EF £	UNC £		F £	VF £	EF £	UNC £
1871	8	16	75	225	1879 milled edge Proof FDC £1350				
1871 Proof FDC £1250					1879 plain edge Proof FDC £1600				
1877	7	15	65	210	1880	8	16	75	215
1879	7	15	65	210					

3912 Sixpence. Type A⁵. Third head l. R. Similar die axis ↑↓

	F £	VF £	EF £	UNC £		F £	VF £	EF £	UNC £
1880	5	10	50	125	1883 plain edge Proof FDC	*Extremely rare*			
1880 Proof FDC £1500					1884	5	10	45	110
1881	5	10	45	110	1885	5	10	45	110
1881 plain edge Proof FDC	*Extremely rare*				1885 Proof FDC £1350				
1881 milled edge Proof FDC	*Extremely rare*				1886	5	10	45	110
1882	10	30	80	250	1886 Proof FDC £1350				
1883	5	10	45	110	1887	4	8	40	100
1883 Small R legend	15	35	95	275	1887 Proof FDC £850				

3913
1842 Groat

3913 Groat (4d.). Young head l.R. Britannia seated r. date in ex, edge milled, die axis ↑↓

	F £	VF £	EF £	UNC £		F £	VF £	EF £	UNC £
1837 Proof only FDC of highest rarity					1846	4	14	45	120
1838	2	10	40	110	1847/6 (or 8)	25	80	375	—
1838 plain edge Proof FDC £750					1848/6	25	120	375	—
1838/∞	3	20	50	165	1848	3	12	40	110
1839	3	12	40	110	1848/7	10	28	90	250
1839 die axis ↑↑ Proof FDC £300					1849	3	12	40	110
1839 die axis ↑↓ Proof FDC £375					1849/8	5	14	45	120
1840	3	12	40	110	1851	20	70	200	525
1840 small round o	5	18	45	135	1852	35	100	275	625
1841	4	14	50	120	1853	40	120	325	725
1842	4	14	45	120	1853 Proof FDC milled edge £475				
1842 Proof FDC £700					1853 Proof FDC plain edge	*Extremely rare*			
1842/1	5	18	50	165	1854	3	12	35	95
1843	4	14	45	120	1855	3	12	35	95
1843 4 over 5	8	22	55	175	1857 Proof only FDC £1100				
1844	4	14	45	120	1862 Proof only FDC.	*Extremely rare*			
1845	4	14	45	120					

Threepence. R. Crowned 3; as Maundy threepence but with a less prooflike surface

3914
Type A1 Threepence

	F	VF	EF	UNC		F	VF	EF	UNC
	£	£	£	£		£	£	£	£

3914 Threepence. Type A¹. First bust, young head, high relief, ear fully visible. Dei axis ↑↓
R Tie ribbon closer to tooth border, cross on crown further from tooth border, figure 3

	F	VF	EF	UNC		F	VF	EF	UNC
1838*	5	10	60	125	1851	5	10	60	135
1838 BRITANNIAB....	*Extremely rare*				1851 5 over 8	10	30	110	—
1839*	5	18	75	175	1852*	60	175	500	—
1839 Proof (see Maundy)					1853	10	25	85	200
1840*	5	14	70	150	1854	5	10	60	125
1841*	5	18	75	175	1855	5	18	75	175
1842*	5	18	75	175	1856	5	10	55	120
1843*	5	12	60	125	1857	5	18	75	175
1844*	5	18	75	175	1858	5	10	55	120
1845	3	8	45	100	1858 BRITANNIAB ..	*Extremely rare*			
1846	10	20	85	200	1858/6	10	20	110	—
1847*	50	150	350	750	1858/5	8	18	90	—
1848*	40	125	325	700	1859	5	10	55	120
1849	5	18	75	175	1860	5	18	75	175
1850	3	8	50	90	1861	5	10	55	120

*Issued for Colonial use only.

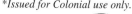

3914A	3914C	3914D
Type A2	Type A4	Type A5

3914A Threepence. Type A². First bust variety, slightly older portrait with aquiline nose ↑↓

	F	VF	EF	UNC		F	VF	EF	UNC
1859	5	10	55	110	1865	5	18	75	150
1860	5	10	55	110	1866	5	10	55	110
1861	5	10	55	110	1867	5	10	55	110
1862	5	10	55	110	1868	5	10	55	110
1863	5	18	75	150	1868 RRITANNIAR ..	*Extremely rare*			
1864	5	10	55	110					

3914B Threepence. Type A³. Second Bust, slightly larger, lower relief, mouth fuller,
nose more pronounced, rounded truncation die axis ↑↓

	F	VF	EF	UNC
1867	5	18	75	150

3914C Threepence. Type A⁴. Obv. as last. R. Tie ribbon further from tooth border, cross on
crown nearer to tooth border die axis ↑↓

	F	VF	EF	UNC		F	VF	EF	UNC
1866	*Extremely rare*				1874	3	8	40	70
1867	5	18	75	150	1875	3	8	40	70
1868	5	18	75	150	1876	3	8	40	70
1869	10	20	85	175	1877	4	10	50	80
1870	4	12	60	100	1878	4	10	50	80
1871	5	14	65	125	1879	4	10	50	80
1872	5	14	65	125	1879 Proof *FDC*	*Extremely rare*			
1873	3	8	40	70	1884	3	6	35	60

	F £	VF £	EF £	UNC £		F £	VF £	EF £	UNC £

3914D Threepence. Type A[5]. Third bust, older features, mouth closed, hair strands leading from 'bun' vary, die axis ↑↓

	F	VF	EF	UNC		F	VF	EF	UNC
1880	4	10	45	75	1885	3	6	30	60
1881	3	6	30	60	1885 Proof *FDC*		*Extremely rare*		
1882	5	10	55	110	1886	3	6	30	60
1883	3	6	30	60	1887	4	10	45	75

3914E Twopence. Young head 1. R̶. Date divided by a crowned 2 within a wreath, die axis ↑↓

	F	VF	EF	UNC		F	VF	EF	UNC
1838	3	7	20	50	1848	5	10	25	60

3915 - Three-Halfpence

3915 Three-Halfpence. (for Colonial use). Young head 1. R. Crowned value and date, die axis ↑↓

	F	VF	EF	UNC		F	VF	EF	UNC
1838	5	12	35	75	1843 Proof *FDC*		*Extremely rare*		
1838 Proof *FDC* £500					1843/34	8	20	80	175
1839	4	10	30	70	1843/34 Proof *FDC*		*Extremely rare*		
1840	8	22	75	150	1860	6	18	60	125
1841	5	14	40	90	1862	6	18	60	125
1842	5	14	40	90	1862 Proof *FDC* £650				
1843	3	6	25	65	1870 Proof only £650				

3916 - 1880 Maundy Set

	EF £	FDC £		EF £	FDC £

3916 Maundy Set. (4d., 3d., 2d. and 1.) Young head 1., die axis ↑↓

	EF	FDC		EF	FDC
1838	85	175	1864	75	135
1838 Proof *FDC* £800			1865	75	135
1838 Proof in gold *FDC* £12500			1866	75	135
1839	95	200	1867	75	135
1839 Proof die axis ↑↑ *FDC* £400			1867 Proof set *FDC* £600		
1840	95	200	1868	75	135
1841	100	235	1869	80	150
1842	95	200	1870	70	125
1843	95	200	1871	70	125
1844	95	200	1871 Proof set *FDC* £600		
1845	85	175	1872	70	125
1846	100	235	1873	70	125
1847	95	200	1874	70	125
1848	95	200	1875	70	125
1849	100	235	1876	70	125
1850	75	150	1877	70	125
1851	75	150	1878	70	125
1852	85	175	1878 Proof set *FDC* £600		
1853	85	175	1879	70	125
1853 Proof *FDC* £500			1880	70	125
1854	85	175	1881	70	125
1855	85	175	1881 Proof set *FDC* £600		
1856	80	150	1882	70	125
1857	80	150	1882 Proof set *FDC* £600		
1858	80	150	1883	70	125
1859	80	150	1884	70	125
1860	75	135	1885	70	125
1861	75	135	1886	70	125
1862	75	135	1887	75	150
1863	75	135			

					from	EF	FDC
3917 — Fourpence, 1838-87					*from*	10	25
3918 — Threepence, 1838-87					*from*	15	40
3919 — Twopence, 1838-87					*from*	8	20
3920 — Penny, 1838-87					*from*	7	15

Maundy Sets in the original dated cases are worth approximately £10, and £5 for undated cases more than the prices quoted.

Jubilee Coinage 1887-93, die axis ↑↑

3921
1887 Crown

	F	VF	EF	UNC		F	VF	EF	UNC
	£	£	£	£		£	£	£	£

3921 Crown. Jubilee bust 1. R. St. George and dragon, date in ex, edge milled, die axis ↑↑

	F	VF	EF	UNC		F	VF	EF	UNC
1887	15	25	65	175	1889	15	30	70	200
1887 Proof *FDC* £450					1890	15	35	95	225
1888 narrow date	15	35	95	225	1891	15	40	110	250
1888 wide date	60	175	475	—	1892	20	45	125	275

3922
1887 Double-Florin - Roman I in date

3922 Double-Florin (4s.). Jubilee bust 1. R. Crowned cruciform shields. Septre in angles. Roman I in date, die axis ↑↑

	F	VF	EF	UNC
1887	12	20	45	100
1887 Proof *FDC* £350				

3923 Double-Florin Jubilee bust 1. R. Similar but Arabic 1 in date, die axis ↑↑

	F	VF	EF	UNC		F	VF	EF	UNC
1887	12	20	45	100	1889	12	20	55	110
1887 Proof *FDC* £250					1889 inverted 1 for I in				
1888	12	20	60	130	VICTORIA	25	60	175	385
1888 inverted 1 for I in					1890	12	20	60	120
VICTORIA	25	60	175	385					

<table>
<tr><td colspan="4">3924</td><td colspan="4">3925</td></tr>
<tr><td colspan="4">1887 Halfcrown</td><td colspan="4">1887 Florin</td></tr>
</table>

	F £	VF £	EF £	UNC £		F £	VF £	EF £	UNC £

3924 Halfcrown. Jubilee bust 1. R. Crowned shield in garter and collar, die axis ↑↑

1887	7	12	25	80	1890	10	20	60	150
1887 Proof *FDC* £125					1891	10	20	60	150
1888	10	15	45	130	1892	10	20	60	150
1889	10	20	60	145					

3925 Florin. Jubilee bust 1. R. Crowned cruciform shields, sceptres in angles, die axis ↑↑

1887	5	10	20	60	1890	10	30	85	265
1887 Proof *FDC* £95					1891	20	55	175	475
1888	6	15	35	85	1892	20	50	140	400
1889	8	20	40	95	1892 Proof *FDC*		*Extremely rare*		

	3926		3927	
	1887 small head Shilling		large Jubilee head	

3926 Shilling. Small Jubilee head. R. Crowned shield in Garter, die axis ↑↑

1887	3	8	14	40	1888/7	5	10	25	75
1887 Proof *FDC* £80					1889	35	90	300	485

3927 Shilling. Large Jubilee head. R. Similar as before, die axis ↑↑

1889	5	9	30	80	1891	5	15	40	90
1889 Proof *FDC* £850					1891 Proof *FDC* £1500				
1890	5	10	35	85	1892	5	15	40	90

	3928			3929			3930		
	1887 'withdrawn type' Sixpence			1889 Sixpence			1888 Groat		

	F £	VF £	EF £	UNC £		F £	VF £	EF £	UNC £

3928 Sixpence. JEB designer's initials below trun. R. Shield in Garter (withdrawn type), die axis ↑↑

1887	2	6	12	40	1887 JEB on trun.	15	45	100	215
1887 R/V in					1887 Proof *FDC* £70				
VICTORIA	10	35	80	185					

3929 Sixpence. R. Jubilee bust l. Crowned, value in wreath, die axis ↑↑

1887	2	6	12	40	1890	4	10	20	65
1887 Proof *FDC* £650					1890 Proof *FDC*		*Extremely rare*	
1888	4	10	20	60	1891	6	15	25	70
1888 Proof *FDC* £1250					1892	8	20	30	100
1889	4	10	20	60	1893	300	700	2350	—

3930 Groat (for use in British Guiana). Jubilee Bust l. R. Britannia seated r. date in axis, die axis ↑↑

1888 Proof *FDC* £775	1888	10	25	50	110

3931 Threepence. As Maundy but less prooflike surface, die axis ↑↑

1887	—	1	5	12	1890	1	3	10	20
1887 Proof *FDC* £35					1891	1	3	10	20
1888	2	5	15	30	1892	2	5	15	30
1889	1	3	10	20	1893	15	40	100	250

3932
1888 Maundy Set

3932 Maundy Set. (4d., 3d., 2d. and 1d.) Jubilee bust l. die axis ↑↑

	EF £	FDC £		EF £	FDC £
1888	75	120	1890	75	120
1888 Proof set *FDC*	*Extremely rare*		1891	75	120
1889	75	120	1892	75	120
3933 — Fourpence, 1888-92	*from*			10	20
3934 — Threepence, 1888-92	*from*			15	25
3935 — Twopence, 1888-92	*from*			8	15
3936 — Penny, 1888-92	*from*			8	15

Maundy Sets in the original dated cases are worth approximately £10 and £5 for undated cases more than the prices quoted.

Old Head Coinage 1893-1901, die axis ↑↑

3937
1893 Old Head Crown

	F	VF	EF	UNC
	£	£	£	£

3937 Crown. Old veiled bust l. R. St. George. date in ex. Regnal date on edge, die axis ↑↑

	F	VF	EF	UNC
1893 edge LVI	15	30	140	375
1893 Proof *FDC* £500				
1893 LVII	25	60	225	500
1894 LVII	15	40	165	450
1894 LVIII	15	40	165	450
1895 LVIII	15	35	140	425
1895 LIX	15	35	140	425
1896 LIX	18	50	190	475
1896 LX	15	35	140	425
1897 LX	15	35	140	425
1897 LXI	15	35	140	425
1898 LXI	25	60	225	500
1898 LXII	15	40	165	450
1899 LXII	15	40	165	450
1899 LXIII	15	40	165	450
1900 LXIII	20	50	225	500
1900 LXIV	20	50	200	450

3938

1893 Halfcrown

	F	VF	EF	UNC			F	VF	EF	UNC
	£	£	£	£			£	£	£	£

3938 Halfcrown. Old veiled bust l. R. Shield in collar, edge milled, die axis ↑↑

	F	VF	EF	UNC			F	VF	EF	UNC
1893	8	15	40	100		1897	8	15	40	100
1893 Proof *FDC* £150						1898	10	16	45	115
1894	10	18	60	140		1899	10	16	45	115
1895	9	16	45	115		1900	10	16	45	115
1896	9	16	45	115		1901	10	16	45	115

3939

Old Head Florin

	F	VF	EF	UNC			F	VF	EF	UNC
	£	£	£	£			£	£	£	£

3939 Florin. Old veiled bust l. R. Three shields within garter, die axis ↑↑

	F	VF	EF	UNC			F	VF	EF	UNC
1893	5	10	40	80		1897	6	12	40	85
1893 Proof *FDC* £110						1898	6	15	45	95
1894	8	16	60	125		1899	6	12	40	85
1895	7	18	50	95		1900	6	12	40	85
1896	6	12	40	85		1901	6	12	40	85

3940 Shilling. Old veiled bust l. R. Three shields within Garter, small rose, die axis ↑↑

1893	4	8	25	65	1894	5	10	30	80
1893 small lettering	6	15	40	80	1895	10	20	50	110
1893 Proof *FDC* £95								

3940   3941

1901 Shilling   1893 Sixpence

3940A Shilling. Old veiled bust l. R. Second reverse, larger rose, die axis ↑↑

1895	4	10	30	75	1899	4	10	30	75
1896	4	10	25	70	1900	4	10	30	75
1897	4	10	25	70	1901	4	10	25	70
1898	4	10	25	70					

3941 Sixpence. Old veiled bust l. R. Value in wreath, die axis ↑↑

1893	3	8	18	50	1897	4	10	20	50
1893 Proof *FDC* £65					1898	4	10	20	50
1894	5	12	25	55	1899	4	10	20	50
1895	4	10	20	50	1900	4	10	20	50
1896	4	10	20	50	1901	4	8	15	45

3942 Threepence. Old veiled bust l. R. Crowned 3. As Maundy but less prooflike surface, die axis ↑↑

1893	1	2	5	15	1897	1	2	6	18
1893 Proof *FDC* £40					1898	1	2	6	18
1894	1	3	7	20	1899	1	2	5	15
1895	1	3	7	20	1900	1	2	5	15
1896	1	2	6	18	1901	1	2	6	18

3943

1899 Maundy Set

	EF £	FDC £		EF £	FDC £
3943 Maundy Set. (4d., 3d., 2d. and 1d.) Old veiled bust l., die axis ↑↑					
1893	60	90	1897	60	90
1893 Proof from 1893 proof set FDC £85			1898	60	90
1894	65	95	1899	70	95
1895	60	90	1900	70	95
1896	60	90	1901	60	90
3944 — Fourpence. 1893-1901			*from*	6	12
3945 — Threepence. 1893-1901			*from*	12	22
3946 — Twopence. 1893-1901			*from*	6	12
3947 — Penny. 1893-1901			*from*	6	18

Maundy Sets in the original dated cases are worth approximately £5 more than the prices quoted.

COPPER AND BRONZE

3948
1843 Penny
Rev. with ornamental trident prongs (OT)

Young Head Copper Coinage, 1838-60, die axis ↑↑

	F	VF	EF	UNC		F	VF	EF	UNC
	£	£	£	£		£	£	£	£

3948 Penny. Young head l. date below R. Britannia seated r.

	F	VF	EF	UNC		F	VF	EF	UNC
1839 Bronzed proof *FDC* £1000					1851 OT DEF: 10	20	110	350
1841 Rev. OT 5	10	75	300		1853 OT DEF—: 5	12	75	175
1841 Proof *FDC* £1250					1853 Proof *FDC* £500			
1841 Silver Proof *FDC* £3500					1853 Plain trident, (PT)			
1841 OT. no colon					DEF:...............10	20	95	325
after REG..........5	10	75	375		1854 PT 5	12	75	185
1843 OT. —.............65	250	1100	2750		1854/3 PT 12	25	110	350
1843 OT REG: 35	125	925	2250		1854 OT DEF—: 8	15	80	210
1844 OT...................10	15	85	225		1855 OT —...............5	12	75	175
1844 Proof *FDC* £1500					1855 PT DEF:...........5	12	75	175
1845 OT...................15	25	135	400		1856 PT DEF:...........65	175	450	1300
1846 OT...................10	20	110	350		1856 Proof *FDC* £1250			
1846 OT colon close					1856 OT DEF—: 25	50	185	1000
to DEF 15	25	120	400		1857 OT DEF—: 8	15	80	210
1847 — — 8	15	85	225		1857 PT DEF:...........5	10	75	175
1847 OT DEF—: 8	15	85	225		1858 OT DEF—: 5	10	75	175
1848/7 OT 5	15	80	200		1858/7 — — 5	10	75	175
1848 OT 5	15	80	200		1858/3 25	75	400	—
1848/6 OT 20	75	400	—		1858 no ww on trun..5	15	85	225
1849 OT 50	125	1200	—		1859 5	10	75	210
1851 OT 10	20	110	400		1859 Proof *FDC* £2000			
					1860/59 200	650	2250	—

The 1860 large copper pieces are not to be confused with the smaller and commoner bronze issue with date on reverse (nos. 3954, 3956 and 3958).

3949

1854 Halfpenny, dots on shield

	F	VF	EF	UNC		F	VF	EF	UNC
	£	£	£	£		£	£	£	£

3949 Halfpenny. Young head l. date below R. Britannia seated r., die axis ↑↑

	F	VF	EF	UNC		F	VF	EF	UNC
1838 5	12	45	130		1853 Rev. incuse dots			
1839 Bronzed proof FDC £300					1852 Rev. normal shield 8	18	55	160
1841 4	10	40	120		1853 dots on shield......3	8	30	105
1841 — Proof FDC £800					1853 — Proof FDC £200			
1841 Silver proof FDC	*Extremely rare*				1853/2 — 15	35	105	285
1843 25	45	115	385		1854 —.......................3	8	30	105
1844 6	15	50	140		1855 —.......................3	8	30	105
1845 50	125	675	—		1856 —.......................5	15	50	140
1846 8	18	55	150		1857 —.......................4	10	40	110
1847 8	18	55	150		1857 Rev. normal			
1848 10	20	60	185		shield 4	10	40	110
1848/7.........................8	18	55	150		1858 —.......................5	10	45	130
1851 5	15	50	140		1858/7 — 5	10	45	130
1851 Rev. incuse dots					1858/6 — 5	10	45	130
on shield 5	15	50	140		1859 —.......................5	10	45	130
1852 Similar 8	18	55	160		1859/8 — 10	20	70	210
					1860 —..................650	2000	4500	—

Overstruck dates are listed only if commoner than normal date, or if no normal date is known.

3950

1847 Farthing

3950 Farthing. Young head l. date below R. Britannia seated r. die axis ↑↑

	F	VF	EF	UNC		F	VF	EF	UNC
1838 WW raised on trun.5	10	40	110		1851 10	20	65	175
1839 4	8	40	95		1851 D/ɔ in DEI 25	50	215	—
1839 Bronzed Proof FDC £275					1852 10	20	65	175
1839 Silver Proof FDC	*Extremely rare*				1853 5	10	45	110
1840 4	8	40	95		1853 WW incuse			
1841 4	8	40	95		on trun 10	30	95	285
1841 Proof FDC	*Extremely rare*				1853 Proof FDC £400			
1842 15	35	115	285		1854 5	10	40	90
1843/2....................10	30	85	235		1855 5	10	50	120
1843 4	8	40	100		1855 WW raised.........8	15	55	130
1843 I for 1 in date ..50	275	—	—		1856 WW incuse 8	20	60	175
1844 45	100	475	—		1856 R/E in			
1845 8	10	45	110		VICTORIA 15	40	150	—
1846 8	15	60	150		1857 5	10	45	110
1847 5	10	45	110		1858 5	10	40	110
1848 5	10	45	110		1859 10	20	65	175
1849 30	60	285	—		1860 825	2000	4500	
1850 5	10	45	110		1864 IWW on truncation	*Extremely rare*		
1850 5/4 10	30	85	260					

*These 1860 large copper pieces are not to be confused with the smaller and commoner bronze
issue with date on reverse (nos. 3954, 3956 and 3958).*

	F	VF	EF	UNC		F	VF	EF	UNC
	£	£	£	£		£	£	£	£

3951 Half-Farthing. Young head l. R. Crowned Value and date, die axis ↑↑

	F	VF	EF	UNC		F	VF	EF	UNC
1839 5	10	40	110		1852 4	10	45	105
1839 Bronzed proof *FDC* £350					1853 5	15	50	145
1842 5	10	40	110		1853 Proof *FDC* £350			
1843	5	30	80		1854 8	25	75	170
1844	3	25	70		1856 8	25	75	170
1844 E/N in REGINA10	20	75	210		1856 Large date 50	110	275	625
1847 4	8	30	95		1868 Proof *FDC* £450			
1851 5/0 10	20	85	195		1868 Cupro nickel Proof *FDC* £600			
1851 5	10	45	105					

3951	3952	3953
1839 Half-Farthing	1844 Third-Farthing	1853 Quarter-Farthing

3952 Third-Farthing (for use in Malta). Young head l. date below R. Britannia seated r. die axis ↑↑

1844 20	35	95	235		1844 RE for REG 30	65	325	725

3953 Quarter-Farthing (for use in Ceylon). Young head l. R. Crowned Value and date, die axis ↑↑

1839 10	18	45	110		1853 10	20	55	130
1851 10	20	50	130		1853 Proof *FDC* £700			
1852 10	18	45	110		1868 Proof *FDC* £500			
1852 Proof *FDC* £500					1868 Cupro-nickel Proof *FDC* £600			

Copper coins graded in this catalogue as UNC have full mint lustre.

Bronze Coinage, 'Bun Head' Issue, 1860-95, die axis ↑↑

When studying an example of the bronze coinage if the minutiae of the variety is not evident due to wear from circulation, then the coin will not be of any individual significance. Proofs exist of most years and are generally extremely rare for all denominations.

3954
1860 Beaded Border Penny

H Mint mark location
3955

Bronze Coinage, "Bun Head" Issue, 1860-95, die axis ↑↑
When studying an example of the bronze coinage, if the minutiae of the variety is not evident due to wear from circulation, then the coin will not be of any individual significance. Proofs exist of most years and are generally extremely rare for all denominations.

3954 The Bronze Penny. The bronze coinage is the most complicated of the milled series from the point of view of the large number of different varieties of obverse and reverse and their combinations. Below are set out good illustrations with explanations of all the varieties. The obverse and reverse types listed below reflect those as listed originally by C W Peck in his British Museum Catalogue of Copper, Tin and Bronze Coinage 1558-1958, and later in "the Bronze Coinage of the United Kingdom" by Michael J Freeman which gives much fuller and detailed explanations of the types. Reference can also be compared to "The British Bronze Penny" by Michael Gooby.

OBVERSES

Obverse 1 (1860) - laureate and draped bust facing left, hair tied in bun, wreath of 15 leaves and 4 berries, L C WYON raised on base of bust, beaded border and thin linear circle.

Obverse 2 (1860-62) - laureate and draped bust facing left, hair tied in bun, wreath of 15 leaves and 4 berries, L C WYON raised lower on base of bust and clear of border, toothed border and thin linear circle both sides,

Obverse 1* (1860) - laureate and draped bust facing left, hair tied in bun, more bulging lowered eye with more rounded forehead, wreath of 15 leaves and 4 berries, which are weaker in part, L C WYON raised on base of bust, beaded border and thin linear circle.

Obverse 3 (1860-61) - laureate and draped bust facing left, hair tied in bun, complete rose to drapery, wreath of 15 leaves and 4 berries, two leaves have incuse outlines, L C WYON raised on base of bust nearly touches border, toothed border and thin linear circle both sides,

Obverse 4 (1860-61) - laureate and draped
bust facing left, hair tied in bun, finer hair
strands at nape of neck, wreath of 15 leaves
and 4 berries, two leaves have incuse outlines,
L C WYON below bust, nearly touches border,
toothed border of shorter teeth, and thin linear
circle both sides,

Obverse 6 (1860-74) - laureate and draped
bust facing left, hair tied in bun, finer hair
strands at nape of neck, wreath of 16 leaves,
leaf veins raised, no signature, toothed border
and thin linear circle both sides,

Obverse 5 (1860-61) - laureate and draped
bust facing left, hair tied in bun, finer hair
strands at nape of neck, wreath of 15 leaves
and 4 berries, leaf veins incuse, two leaves
have incuse outlines, no signature below bust,
toothed border and thin linear circle both
sides,

Obverse 7 (1874) - laureate and draped bust
facing left, hair tied in bun, finer hair strands
at nape of neck, wreath of 17 leaves, leaf veins
raised, 6 berries, no signature, toothed border
and thin linear circle both sides.

Obverse 8 (1874-79) - laureate and draped bust facing left, hair tied in bun, with close thicker ties to ribbons, wreath of 17 leaves, leaf veins raised, 6 berries, no signature, toothed border and thin linear circle both sides,

Obverse 10 (1880-81) - laureate and draped bust facing left, hair tied in bun, with close thicker ties, wreath of 15 leaves, leaf veins raised and recessed, 4 berries, no signature, toothed border and thin linear circle both sides,

Obverse 9 (1879-81) - laureate and draped bust facing left, hair tied in bun, with close thicker ties, wreath of 17 leaves, double leaf veins incuse, 6 berries, no signature, toothed border and thin linear circle both sides,

Obverse 11 (1881-83) - laureate and draped bust facing left, more hooked nose, hair tied in bun, with close thicker ties, nose more hooked, wreath of 15 leaves, leaf veins raised, 4 berries, no signature, toothed border and thin linear circle both sides, weak circle on obverse,

REVERSES

Obverse 12 (1881-94) - laureate and draped bust facing left, hair tied in bun, with close thicker ties, no curls at nape of neck, nose more hooked, wreath of 15 leaves, leaf veins raised, 4 berries, no signature, toothed border, more numerous teeth, and thin linear circle both sides, weak on obverse, larger lettering.

Reverse A (1860) - Britannia seated right on rocks with shield and trident, crosses on shield outlined with double raised lines, L.C.W. incuse below shield, date below in exergue, lighthouse with 4 windows to left, ship sailing to right, beaded border and linear circle.

Obverse 13 (1889) - laureate and draped bust facing left, hair tied in bun, with close thicker ties, no curls at nape of neck, nose more hooked, wreath of 14 leaves, leaf veins raised, no signature, toothed border and thin linear circle both sides, larger lettering.

Reverse B (1860) - Britannia with one incuse hemline, seated right on rocks with shield and trident, crosses on shield outlined with treble incuse lines, L.C.W. incuse below shield, date below in exergue, lighthouse with 4 windows to left, ship sailing to right, beaded border and linear circle.

Reverse C (1860) - Britannia seated right on rocks with shield and trident, crosses on shield outlined with wider spaced thinner double raised lines, thumb touches St. George Cross, L.C.W. incuse below shield, date below in exergue, lighthouse with 4 windows to left, rocks touch linear circle, ship sailing to right, beaded border and linear circle.

Reverse E (1860) - Britannia seated right on rocks with thick rimmed shield and trident, crosses on shield outlined with wider spaced thinner double raised lines, thumb touches St. George Cross, L.C.W. incuse below foot, date below in exergue, lighthouse with sharper masonry to left, rocks touch linear circle, ship sailing to right, toothed border.

Reverse D (1860-61) - Britannia seated right on rocks with shield and trident, crosses on shield outlined with wider spaced thinner double raised lines, thumb touches St. George Cross, L.C.W. incuse below shield, date below in exergue, lighthouse with 4 windows to left, rocks touch linear circle, ship sailing to right, toothed border.

Reverse F (1861) - Britannia seated right on rocks with thick rimmed shield and trident, incuse lines on breastplate, crosses on shield outlined with wider spaced thinner double raised lines, thumb touches St. George Cross, no L.C.W. extra rocks, date below in exergue, lighthouse with rounded top and sharp masonry, three horizontal lines between masonry and top, rocks touch linear circle, ship sailing to right, toothed border.

Reverse G (1861-75) - Britannia seated right on rocks with convex shield and trident, no signature, date below in exergue, bell-topped lighthouse to left, lamp area depicted with five vertical lines, no rocks to left, sea crosses linear circle, ship sailing to right, toothed border.

Reverse I (1874) - Britannia seated right on rocks with convex shield and trident, thick trident shaft, no signature, narrow date below in exergue, thicker lighthouse to left with 4 windows, lamp area of four vertical lines, close date numerals, tiny rock to left, sea touches linear circle, ship sailing to right, toothed border.

Reverse H (1874-75, 1877) - Britannia seated right on rocks, smaller head, thinner neck, with convex shield and trident, no signature, narrow date below in exergue, tall thin lighthouse to left with 6 windows, lamp area of four vertical lines, close date numerals, tiny rock to left, sea touches linear circle, ship sailing to right, toothed border.

Reverse J (1875-81) - larger Britannia seated right on rocks with shield and trident, left leg more visible, wider date below in deeper exergue, lighthouse to left, ship sailing to right, sea does not meet linear circle either side, toothed border.

Reverse K (1876, 1879) - Britannia with larger head seated right on rocks with convex shield and trident, thicker helmet, no signature, narrow date and in exergue, tall thin lighthouse to left, tiny rock to left, sea touches linear circle, ship sailing to right, toothed border.

Reverse M (1881-82) - larger Britannia seated right on rocks with shield and trident, flatter shield heraldically coloured, date and H below in exergue, lighthouse to left with faint masonry, ship sailing to right, sea does not meet linear circle, toothed border.

Reverse L (1880) - Britannia seated right on rocks with shield and trident, extra feather to helmet plume, trident with three rings above hand, date below in exergue, lighthouse with cluster of rocks to left, ship sailing to right, toothed border.

Reverse N (1881-94) - thinner Britannia seated right on rocks with shield and thinner trident, helmet plume ends in a single strand, shield heraldically coloured with different thickness crosses, date in exergue, thinner lighthouse to left, ship sailing to right, sea meets linear circle, toothed border with more teeth.

Reverse O (1882 - proof only) – larger Britannia seated right on rocks withshield and trident, flatter shield heraldically coloured, date and H in exergue, lighthouse to left with faint masonry, ship sailing to right, sea meets linear circle, toothed border with more teeth.

	F	VF	EF	UNC		F	VF	EF	UNC
	£	£	£	£		£	£	£	£

3954 Penny. Laur. bust l. R. Britannia seated r. date in ex. lighthouse l. ship to r., die axis ↑↑

	F	VF	EF	UNC		F	VF	EF	UNC
1860 obv 1, rev A 40	90	230	725	1867 obv 6, rev G 8	25	100	525
1860 obv 1, rev B 10	25	80	475	1868 obv 6, rev G 15	35	150	725
1860 obv 1*, rev A 50	110	360	925	1869 obv 6, rev G 55	200	560	1750
1860 obv 1, rev C 30	60	230	775	1870 obv 6, rev G 8	25	120	475
1860 obv 1*, rev C 8	40	150	575	1871 obv 6, rev G 30	85	360	900
1860 obv 1, rev D 110	375	1000	2100	1871 wide date - rev H	*Extremely rare*		
1860 obv 2, rev A 110	375	1000	2100	1872 obv 6, rev G 5	15	65	300
1860 obv 2, rev D 5	15	50	250	1873 obv 6, rev G 5	15	65	300
1860 — heavy flan	*Extremely rare*			1874 obv 6, rev G 5	15	85	475
1860 N/Z in ONE, 2+D ..	*Extremely rare*			1874 obv 7, rev G 10	35	100	375
1860 obv 3, rev D 5	15	60	250	1874 obv 8, rev G 25	55	150	625
1860 obv 3, rev E 75	165	460	1100	1874 obv 8 rev H.........20	50	120	575
1860 obv 4, rev D 2	10	60	300	1874 obv 6, rev H 30	80	285	625
1860 obv 5, rev D 10	40	145	475	1874 obv 7, rev H 10	35	95	375
1860 obv 6, rev D 30	110	285	700	1875 obv 8, rev G 2	10	60	275
1861 obv 2, rev D 25	80	175	625	1875 obv 8, rev H 3	10	50	150
1861 obv 2, rev F 25	85	315	875	1875 obv 8, rev J............5	15	65	300
1861 obv 2, rev G 30	110	285	700	1877 obv 8, rev J............2	10	60	275
1861 obv 3, rev D 90	275	660	1200	1877 obv 8, rev H	*Extremely rare*		
1861 obv 4, rev D 3	15	65	300	1878 obv 8, rev J............3	15	80	475
1861 — — heavy flan	*Extremely rare*			1879 obv 8, rev J.........10	20	105	525
1861 obv 4, rev F 110	275	700	1750	1879 obv 9, rev J............2	7	50	200
1861 obv 4, rev G 30	110	285	900	1879 obv 9, rev K 30	95	285	700
1861 obv 5, rev D 2	10	60	275	1880 obv 9, rev J............3	15	100	375
1861 obv 5, rev F	*Extremely rare*			1880 obv 9, rev L 3	15	100	375
1861 obv 5, rev G 110	225	560	1450	1881 obv 9, rev J............4	15	80	475
1861 obv 6, rev D 2	10	60	250	1881 obv 10, rev J........30	95	285	700
1861 — — — 6 over 8 ..	*Extremely rare*			1881 obv 11, rev J........25	55	150	625
1861 obv 6, rev F 110	350	850	—	1882* obv 11, rev N	*Extremely rare*		
1861 obv 6, rev G 2	10	60	275	1883 obv 12, rev N 3	10	60	250
1861 — 8 over 6	*Extremely rare*			1883 obv11, rev N.........3	10	60	250
1862 obv 2, rev G	*Extremely rare*			1884 obv 12, rev N 2	8	50	175
1862 obv 6, rev G 2	10	60	250	1885 obv 12, rev N 2	8	50	175
1862 — 8 over 6	*Extremely rare*			1886 obv 12, rev N 2	10	50	200
1862 — Halfpenny numerals	*Extremely rare*			1887 obv 12, rev N 2	8	50	175
1863 obv 6, rev G 2	10	60	250	1888 obv 12, rev N 2	10	50	200
1863 Die number below ..	*Extremely rare*			1889 obv 13, rev N 2	8	45	175
1863 slender 3..................	*Extremely rare*			1889 obv 12, rev N 4	15	80	475
1864 Upper serif..........20	85	360	1100	1890 obv 12, rev N 2	8	45	175
1864 Crosslet 4.............25	95	460	1500	1891 obv 12, rev N 2	7	40	150
1865 obv 6, rev G 8	20	105	475	1892 obv 12, rev N 2	8	45	175
1865/3 obv 6, rev G 40	110	285	1000	1893 obv 12, rev N 2	8	45	175
1866 obv 6, rev G 5	15	70	300	1894 obv 12, rev N 3	15	65	250

* not to be confused with Heaton Mint

3955 Penny. Similar R. Britannia, H Mint mark below date – (struck by Ralph Heaton & Sons, Birmingham)

	F	VF	EF	UNC		F	VF	EF	UNC
1874 H obv 6, rev G 5	20	80	325	1876 H obv 8, rev J 10	30	120	425
1874 H obv 6, rev H 10	30	120	425	1881 H obv 11, rev M 3	15	60	300
1874 H obv 7, rev G 10	30	100	375	1881 H obv 9, rev M	*Extremely rare*		
1874 H obv 7, rev H 5	20	80	325	1882 H obv12,rev M.......10	25	90	475
1874 H obv 7, rev I..........	*Extremely rare*			1882 H obv 12, rev N 2	10	50	200
1875 H obv 8, rev J......35	100	675	—	1882/1 H obv 11, rev M10 25	80	475	
1876 H obv 8, rev K 2	15	60	250				

3956
1860 Halfpenny Beaded border

	F	*VF*	*EF*	*UNC*		*F*	*VF*	*EF*	*UNC*
	£	£	£	£		£	£	£	£

3956 Halfpenny. Laur. bust l. R. Britannia seated r. date in ex. lighthouse l. ship to r., die axis ↑↑

1860 Beaded border 1	5	45	150		1863 large 3 2	6	60	200
1860 no tie to wreath 5	15	75	275		1864.........................2	10	65	250
1860 Toothed border ..2	10	55	200		1865.........................3	15	75	325
1860 round top light house	15	75	275		1865/3....................40	100	285	725
1860 5 berries in					1866.........................2	10	65	250
wreath 4	12	65	250		1867.........................3	15	75	325
1860 — 15 leaves,					1868.........................2	10	70	275
4 berries.............3	10	60	175		1869.........................10	40	200	525
1860 — rounded					1870.........................2	8	60	200
lighthouse 4	12	65	250		1871.......................15	50	235	525
1860 — Double incuse					1872.........................2	7	55	175
leaf veins 5	15	75	275		1873.........................2	10	65	250
1860 — 16 leaves					1873 R. hemline to			
wreath 10	30	110	375		drapery 2	10	65	250
1860 TB/BBmule		*Extremely rare*			1874.........................5	25	120	425
1861 5 berries in					1874 narrow date 15	50	275	—
wreath 10	30	100	325		1874 older features ..5	25	120	425
1861 15 leaves in					1875.........................1	6	55	175
wreath 6	20	75	275		1877.........................1	6	55	175
1861 — R. no hemline					1878.........................3	15	75	325
to drapery..........10	30	100	325		1878 wide date........50	100	285	575
1861 — R. Door on					1879.........................1	5	45	150
lighthouse 5	15	75	275		1880.........................2	7	55	175
1861 4 leaves double					1881.........................2	7	55	175
incuse veins 2	10	55	175		1883.........................1	7	55	175
1861 16 leaves wreath ..5	15	75	275		1883 rose for brooch obv.		*Extremely rare*	
1861 — R. LCW incuse					1884.........................1	4	45	150
on rock..............10	30	100	325		1885.........................1	4	45	150
1861 — R. no hemline					1886.........................1	4	45	150
to drapery...........3	12	65	250		1887.........................1	4	40	125
1861 — R. door on					1888.........................1	4	45	150
lighthouse 1	5	45	150		1889.........................1	4	45	150
1861 HALP error		*Extremely rare*			1889/8 10	20	75	275
1861 6 over 8		*Extremely rare*			1890.........................1	4	40	125
1862 1	4	40	125		1891.........................1	4	40	125
1862 Die letter A B or C to left of					1892.........................1	6	55	175
lighthouse		*Extremely rare*			1893.........................1	4	45	150
1863 small 3 2	6	60	200		1894.........................1	7	55	175

3957 Halfpenny. Similar R. Britannia, H Mint mark below date (struck by Ralph Heaton & Sons, Birmingham)

1874 H 1	5	55	175		1881 H.......................1	5	55	175
1875 H 2	6	60	200		1882 H.......................1	5	55	175
1876 H 1	5	55	175					

3958
1878 Farthing

3960
1884 Third-Farthing

	F	VF	EF	UNC			F	VF	EF	UNC
	£	£	£	£			£	£	£	£

3958 Farthing. Laur bust l. R. Britannia seated r. date in ex. lighthouse l. ship to r. die axis ↑↑

	F	VF	EF	UNC		F	VF	EF	UNC
1860 Beaded border	5	30	100		1875 small date 10	25	95	325	
1860 Toothed border	3	25	85		1875 —older features..8	20	85	275	
1860 — 5 berries	3	28	95		1877 Proof only £3250				
1860 TB/BB mule............	*Extremely rare*				1878	2	20	75	
1861 5 berries	3	28	95		1879 large 9	5	25	95	
1861 4 berries	4	30	100		1879 normal 9	2	20	80	
1862	3	30	95		1880...........................	3	30	100	
1862 large 8	*Extremely rare*				1881	2	20	85	
1863 20	45	175	425		1883 2	10	40	120	
1864 4 no serif	5	35	110		1884	1	15	50	
1864 4 with serif.............	8	40	120		1885	1	15	50	
1865	3	28	95		1886	1	15	50	
1865/2............................	10	35	140		1887	2	25	80	
1866	3	25	85		1888	2	20	75	
1867	4	30	105		1890	2	20	75	
1868	4	30	105		1891	1	15	65	
1869	10	40	140		1892 2	10	40	120	
1872	3	28	95		1893	1	15	65	
1873	2	28	95		1894	2	18	75	
1875 large date 5	10	40	145		1895 10	20	65	170	

Bronze coins graded in this catalogue as UNC have full mint lustre

3959 Farthing. Similar R. Britannia. H Mint mark below date (struck by Ralph Heaton & Sons, Birmingham)

	F	VF	EF	UNC		F	VF	EF	UNC
1874 H older features 5	10	35	110		1876 H large 6 10	30	75	170	
1874 H,◯over G's obv. ..	*Extremely rare*				1876 H normal 6 5	10	40	120	
1875 H younger features..20	50	140	500		1881 H 2	5	25	85	
1875 H older features	2	15	75		1882 H 2	5	25	85	

3960 Third-Farthing (for use in Malta). Laur. head l. R. Crowned date and Value die axis ↑↑

	F	VF	EF	UNC		F	VF	EF	UNC
1866 1	3	18	60		1881 2	4	20	70	
1868 1	3	18	60		1884 1	3	18	60	
1876 2	4	20	70		1885 1	3	18	60	
1878 1	3	18	60						

Old Head Issue, 1885-1901, die axis ↑↑

Proofs exist of most years and are generally extremely rare for all denominations

3961
1897 Penny

	VF	EF	UNC			VF	EF	UNC
	£	£	£			£	£	£

3961 Penny. Old veiled bust l. R. Britannia seated r. date in ex., die axis ↑↑

	VF	EF	UNC			VF	EF	UNC
1895	2	16	60	1898		4	18	65
1896	2	15	55	1899		2	16	60
1897	2	15	55	1900		3	12	45
1897 O'NE flawed	75	250	650	1901		1	10	25

3961 'High Tide'
Horizon is level with folds in robe

3961A 'Low Tide'
Horizon is level with hem line of robe

		VF	EF	UNC
3961A Penny. Similar As last but 'Low tide', 1895		50	200	475
3961B Penny. Similar, higher tide level above two folds of robe, 1897		35	125	350

3962 Halfpenny. Old veiled bust l. R. Britannia seated r. date in ex., die axis ↑↑

	VF	EF	UNC			VF	EF	UNC
1895	2	6	30	1898		2	5	25
1896	2	5	25	1899			5	25
1897	2	5	25	1900			8	30
1897 Higher tide level	5	10	35	1901			2	20

3963 Farthing. Old veiled bust l. R. Britannia seated r. date in ex. Bright finish, die axis ↑↑

	VF	EF	UNC			VF	EF	UNC
1895	2	5	25	1897		2	5	30
1896	2	5	25					

3962
Old Head Halfpenny

3964
Old Head Farthing

3964 Farthing. Similar Dark finish, die axis ↑↑

	VF	EF	UNC			VF	EF	UNC
1897	2	5	20	1899		2	5	20
1897 Higher tide level	5	10	30	1900		3	8	25
1898	2	5	20	1901			2	15

Proof Sets

PS3 Young head, **1839.** 'Una and the Lion' Five Pounds, and Sovereign to Farthing
(15 coins) ....*FDC* £32500

PS4 — **1853.** Sovereign to Half-Farthing, including Gothic type Crown
(16 coins) ....*FDC* £30000

PS5 Jubilee head. Golden Jubilee, **1887.** Five pounds to Threepence (11 coins).*FDC* £6500

PS6 — — **1887.** Crown to Threepence (7 coins)..*FDC* £1350

PS7 Old head, **1893.** Five Pounds to Threepence (10 coins) ....*FDC* £7750

PS8 — — **1893.** Crown to Threepence (6 coins)..*FDC* £1700

THE HOUSE OF SAXE-COBURG-GOTHA, 1901-1910
EDWARD VII, 1901-10

'Edward the Peacemaker' was born on 9 November 1841, and married Princess Alexandra of Denmark. He indulged himself in every decadent luxury, while his wife tried to ignore his extra-marital activities. Edward travelled extensively and was crucial in negotiating alliances with Russia and France. Edward VII died on 6 May 1910.

Five Pound pieces, Two Pound pieces and Crowns were only issued in 1902. A branch of the Royal Mint was opened in Canada at Ottawa and coined Sovereigns of imperial type from 1908.

Unlike the coins in most other proof sets, the proofs issued for the Coronation in 1902 have a matt surface in place of the more usual brilliant finish.

Designer's initials: De S. (G. W. De Saulles 1862-1903)
B. P. (Benedetto Pistrucci, d. 1855)

Engravers and Designers: WHJ Blakemore, George WIlliam De Saulles (1862-1903), Benedetto Pistrucci (1784-1855)

Prime Ministers:– Earl of Salisbury (1830-1903), Conservative 1895-1902, Arthur James Balfour (1848-1930), Conservative 1902-5, Sir Henry Campbell-Bannerman (1836-1908), Liberal 1905-8, Herbert Henry Asquith (1852-1928), Liberal 1908-16

GOLD

Die axis: ↑↑

3966
Matt Proof Five Pounds 1902

	EF	UNC		F	VF	EF	UNC
	£	£		£	£	£	£

3965 Five Pounds. Bare head r. R. St. George and dragon, date in ex.
1902 .... 400 600 750 1000
3966 Five Pounds. Similar Proof. 1902. *Matt surface FDC* £950
3966A Five Pounds. Similar Proof 1902S. S on ground for Sydney Mint, Australia *Extremely rare*

3967 3969
1902 Two Pounds 1902 Sovereign

3967 Two Pounds. Bare head r. R. St George and dragon, date in ex.
1902 .... 175 225 350 470
3968 Two Pounds. Similar Proof. 1902. *Matt surface FDC* £450
3968A Two Pounds. Similar Proof 1902S. S on ground for Sydney Mint, Australia *Extremely rare*
3969 Sovereign. Bare head r. R . St. George and dragon, date in ex. London mint, die axis ↑↑

1902 Matt proof *FDC* £200				1906		BV	80	120
1902	BV	80	120	1907		BV	80	120
1903	BV	80	120	1908		BV	80	120
1904	BV	80	120	1909		BV	80	120
1905	BV	80	120	1910		BV	80	120

3970 Sovereign. Similar R. C on ground for Ottawa Mint, Canada

1908 C (Satin proof only) *FDC* £2750			1910 C	BV	110	200
1909 C	120	225				

	UNC £			UNC £

3971 Sovereign. Similar R. St. George M on ground for Melbourne Mint, Australia, die axis ↑↑

1902 M	100	1907 M	90
1903 M	90	1908 M	90
1904 M	90	1909 M	90
1905 M	90	1910 M	90
1906 M	90		

3972 Sovereign. Similar R. P on ground for Perth Mint, Australia die axis ↑↑

1902 P	100	1907 P	90
1903 P	90	1908 P	90
1904 P	90	1909 P	90
1905 P	90	1910 P	90
1906 P	90		

3973 Sovereign. Similar R. S on ground for Sydney Mint, Australia die axis ↑↑

1902 S	100	1906 S	90
1902 S Proof	*Extremely rare*	1907 S	90
1903 S	90	1908 S	90
1904 S	110	1909 S	90
1905 S	90	1910 S	90

3974A
1902 Half-Sovereign, no BP in exergue

	F £	VF £	EF £	UNC £		F £	VF £	EF £	UNC £

3974 A Half-Sovereign. Bare head r. R. St. George. London Mint no BP in exergue, die axis ↑↑

1902 Matt proof *FDC* £120					1903	BV		40	65
1902	BV	50	75		1904	BV		40	65

3974 B Half-Sovereign. R. Similar with BP in exergue

1904	BV		40	65	1909	BV		40	65
1905	BV		40	65	1910	BV		40	65
1906	BV		40	65					
1907	BV		40	65					
1908	BV		40	65					

3975 Half-Sovereign. Similar R. M on ground for Melbourne Mint, Australia, die axis ↑↑

1906 M	50	100	350	1300	1908 M	BV		75	375
1907 M	BV	40	75	375	1909 M	50		75	425

3976 A Half-Sovereign. — P on ground for Perth Mint, Australia R. no BP in exergue, die axis ↑↑

1904 P	65	165	580	1250

3976 B Half-Sovereign. Similar R. P on ground for Perth Mint, Australia R. with BP in exergue, die axis ↑↑

1904 P	65	165	580	1250	1909 P	60	150	415	1250
1908 P	65	165	500	1575					

3977 A Half-Sovereign. Similar R. S on ground for Sydney Mint, Australia R. No BP in exergue, die axis ↑↑

1902 S	50	95	325	1903 S	40	100	425
1902 S Proof	*Extremely rare*						

3977 B Half-Sovereign. — S on ground for Sydney Mint, Australia R. with BP in exergue, die axis ↑↑

1906 S	40	75	300	1910 S	40	60	150
1908 S	40	60	150				

SILVER

3978
1902 Crown

	F	VF	EF	UNC
	£	£	£	£

3978 Crown. Bare head r. R. St. George and dragon date in ex. die axis ↑↑

1902 45   75   125   200

3979 Crown. Similar Matt proof *FDC* £185

3980
1904 Halfcrown

	F	VF	EF	UNC
	£	£	£	£

3980 Halfcrown. Bare head r. R. Crowned Shield in Garter, die axis ↑↑

1902 15	35	60	100	1906 20	45	200	600
1902 Matt proof *FDC* £125				1907 20	45	200	600
1903 65	250	625	1350	1908 25	50	325	800
1904 50	200	475	1100	1909 20	45	275	700
1905* 195	475	1100	2950	1910 15	35	175	500

3981 Florin. Bare head r. R. Britannia standing on ship's bow die axis ↑↑

1902 8	20	50	85	1906 10	25	100	325
1902 Matt proof *FDC* £75				1907 10	30	110	350
1903 10	25	100	325	1908 15	40	185	475
1904 12	30	110	350	1909 15	40	160	425
1905 50	125	425	875	1910 10	20	85	275

*Beware of recent forgeries.

	3981			3982				3983		
	1903 Florin			1902 Shilling				1902 Sixpence		

F	VF	EF	UNC		F	VF	EF	UNC
£	£	£	£		£	£	£	£

3982 Shilling. Bare head r. R. Lion rampant on crown die axis ↑↑

	F	VF	EF	UNC		F	VF	EF	UNC
1902	5	15	50	75	1906	5	10	50	150
1902 Matt proof *FDC* £70					1907	5	10	55	175
1903	8	20	90	275	1908	10	20	90	300
1904	8	15	80	225	1909	10	20	90	300
1905	50	150	525	1200	1910	3	10	45	125

3983 Sixpence. Bare head r. R. Value in wreath die axis ↑↑

	F	VF	EF	UNC		F	VF	EF	UNC
1902	5	10	30	50	1906	4	10	30	80
1902 Matt proof *FDC* £60					1907	5	10	35	85
1903	4	10	30	80	1908	5	12	40	90
1904	6	15	45	105	1909	4	10	35	85
1905	5	12	35	90	1910	3	5	25	55

3984 Threepence. As Maundy but dull finish die axis ↑↑

	F	VF	EF	UNC		F	VF	EF	UNC
1902	4		8	15	1906	2	7	25	45
1902 Matt proof *FDC* £18					1907	1	7	25	45
1903	1	7	25	45	1908	1	2	10	25
1904	3	7	35	70	1909	1	7	25	45
1905	2	7	25	65	1910		1	10	30

3985
1902 Maundy Set

	EF	FDC		EF	FDC
	£	£		£	£

3985 Maundy Set (4d., 3d., 2d. and 1d.) Bare head r. die axis ↑↑

	EF	FDC		EF	FDC
1902	55	75	1906	55	70
1902 Matt proof *FDC* £70			1907	55	70
1903	55	70	1908	55	70
1904	55	70	1909	65	100
1905	55	70	1910	65	100

	EF	FDC
	£	£
3986 — Fourpence. 1902-10 ....*from*	6	12
3987 — Threepence. 1902-10 ....*from*	6	15
3988 — Twopence. 1902-10 ....*from*	6	10
3989 — Penny. 1902-10...*from*	7	12

Maundy sets in the original dated cases are worth approximately £5 more than the prices quoted.

BRONZE

3990A
1902 Penny - 'Low Tide'

3990 'High Tide'				3990A 'Low Tide'			
VF	EF	UNC		F	VF	EF	UNC
£	£	£		£	£	£	£

1902 1	8	45	1906 3	15	65
1903 Normal 3 2	12	55	1907 4	20	75
1903 Open 3 35	175	—	1908 3	15	65
1904 5	35	120	1909 4	20	75
1905 4	30	90	1910 2	12	55

3990A Penny. Similar R. As last but 'Low tide', 1902 5   20   90   185

3991
1903 Halfpenny

	VF	EF	UNC		F	VF	EF	UNC
	£	£	£		£	£	£	£

3991 Halfpenny. Bare head r. R. Britannia seated r. date in ex. die axis ↑↑

1902	1	5	25	1908	1	8	30	
1903	2	10	35	1909	2	10	40	
1904	2	10	40	1910	2	10	35	
1905	2	10	40					
1906	2	10	35					
1907	1	8	30					

3991A Halfpenny. Similar R. As last but 'Low tide', 1902 10   30   70   150

3992
1907 Farthing

3993
1902 Third-Farthing

3992 Farthing. Bare head r. R. Britannia seated r. date in ex. Dark finish die axis ↑↑

1902	—	5	20	1907	1	5	20
1903	1	5	20	1908	1	5	20
1904	2	8	25	1909	1	5	20
1905	1	5	20	1910	2	8	25
1906	1	5	20				

3993 Third-Farthing (for use in Malta) Bare head r. R. Crowned date and value die axis ↑↑.

1902   10   35

No proofs of the bronze coins were issued in 1902

Proof Sets
PS9   Coronation, **1902.** Five Pounds to Maundy Penny, matt surface, (13 coins) *FDC*   £2000
PS10 — 1902. Sovereign to Maundy Penny, matt surface, (11 coins) ....*FDC*   £825

THE HOUSE OF WINDSOR, 1910-
GEORGE V, 1910-36

George V, the second son of Edward VII, was born on 3 June 1865 and married Mary of Teck who bore him five sons and a daughter. He was King through World War I and visited the front on several occassions. He suffered a fall breaking his pelvis on one of these visits, an injury that would pain him for the rest of his life. He watched the Empire divide; Ireland, Canada, Australia, New Zealand and India all went through changes. He died on 20th January 1936 only months after his Silver Jubilee.

Paper money issued by the Treasury during the First World War replaced gold for internal use after 1915 but the branch mints in Australia and South Africa (the main Commonwealth gold producing countries) continued striking Sovereigns until 1930-2. Owing to the steep rise in the price of silver in 1919/20 the issue of standard (.925) silver was discontinued and coins of .500 silver were minted.

In 1912, 1918 and 1919 some Pennies were made under contract by private mints in Birmingham. In 1918, as Half-Sovereigns were no longer being minted, Farthings were again issued with the ordinary bright bronze finish. Crown pieces had not been issued for general circulation but they were struck in small numbers about Christmas time for people to give as presents in the years 1927-36, and in 1935 a special commemorative Crown was issued in celebration of the Silver Jubilee.

As George V died on 20 January, it is likely that all coins dated 1936 were struck during the reign of Edward VIII.

Engravers and Designers:– George Kuger Gray (1880-1943), Bertram MacKennal (1863-1931), Benedetto Pistrucci (1784-1855) Percy Metcalfe (1895-1970)

Prime Ministers:– Herbert Henry Asquith (1852-1928), Liberal 1908-16, David Lloyd George, (1863-1945) Liberal 1916-22, Andrew Bonor Law (1858-1923), Conservative, 1922-3, Stanley Baldwin, (1867-1947) Conservative, 1923, 1924-1, 1935-7, James Ramsey MacDonald, (1866-1937) Labour 1924-7, 1929-35

Designer's initials:

B. M. (Bertram Mackennal) P. M. (Percy Metcalfe)
K. G. (G. Kruger Gray) B. P. (Benedetto Pistrucci; d. 1855)

Die axis: ↑↑

GOLD

3994
1911 Proof Five Pounds
FDC
£

3994 Five Pounds.* Bare head l. R. St. George and dragon, date in ex., 1911 (Proof only) 1650
3995 Two Pounds.* Bare head l. R. St. George and dragon, date in ex., 1911 (Proof only) 675

3996

	VF £	EF £	UNC £		VF £	EF £	UNC £
3996 Sovereign. Bare head l. R. St. George and dragon. London Mint die axis: ↑↑							
1911 ....BV		80	120	1914 ....BV		80	120
1911 Proof *FDC* £375				1915 ....BV		80	120
1911 Matt Proof *FDC of highest rarity*				1916 ....BV		85	135
1912 ....BV		80	120	1917* 2000		4750	—
1913 ....BV		80	120	1925 ....BV		80	110

*Forgeries exist of these and of most other dates and mints.

	F	VF	EF	UNC		F	VF	EF	UNC
	£	£	£	£		£	£	£	£

3997 Sovereign. Bare head l. R. St George, C on ground for the Ottawa Mint, Canada die axis: ↑↑

1911 C	BV	95	140	1917 C	BV	95	140
1913 C	100	500	—	1918 C	BV	95	140
1914 C	140	325	—	1919 C	BV	95	140
1916 C*	3250	7500	—				

* Beware of recent forgeries

3997	3998	4004
Canada Mint mark	India Mint mark	South Africa Mint mark

3998 Sovereign. Similar R. I on ground for Bombay Mint, India 1918 95

3999 Sovereign. Similar R. M on ground for Melbourne Mint, Australia die axis: ↑↑

1911 M	85	1920 M	750	1750	2250	3150
1912 M	85	1921 M	2000	3500	5500	6850
1913 M	85	1922 M	1500	2750	4250	6000
1914 M	85	1923 M				85
1915 M	85	1924 M				85
1916 M	85	1925 M				85
1917 M	85	1926 M				85
1918 M	85	1928 M	500	850	500	2000
1919 M	70	100				

4000 Sovereign. Similar small bare head l. die axis: ↑↑

1929 M	500	900	1400	1850	1931 M	110	200	250	375
1930 M		95	120	165					

4000	4001
1931 M Sovereign, small head	Perth Mint Sovereign

4001 Sovereign. Similar R. P on ground for Perth Mint, Australia die axis: ↑↑

1911 P	85	1920 P				85
1912 P	85	1921 P				85
1913 P	85	1922 P				85
1914 P	85	1923 P				85
1915 P	85	1924 P	65	90	115	150
1916 P	85	1925 P	100	150	200	275
1917 P	85	1926 P	500	1000	1400	1750
1918 P	85	1927 P	85	200	300	450
1919 P	85	1928 P	65	100	150	165

	VF	EF	UNC		F	VF	EF	UNC
	£	£	£		£	£	£	£

4002 Sovereign. Similar — small bare head l. die axis: ↑↑

1929 P	85	1931 P	85
1930 P	85		

4003 Sovereign. Similar R. S on ground for Sydney Mint, Australia die axis: ↑↑

1911 S	85	1919 S				85
1912 S	85	1920 S				*Extremely rare*
1913 S	85	1921 S 400	650	1000	1500
1914 S	85	1922 S 3100	5000	7300	9150
1915 S	85	1923 S 2500	4000	6500	7650
1916 S	85	1924 S 325	575	850	1250
1917 S	85	1925 S			85
1918 S	85	1926 S 4100	7750	11500	13000

4004 Sovereign. Similar R. SA on ground for Pretoria Mint, South Africa die axis: ↑↑

1923 SA 900	1750	3500	1926 SA	85
1923 SA Proof *FDC* £475			1927 SA	85
1924 SA 1500	3000	—	1928 SA	85
1925 SA	85			

4005 Sovereign. Similar — small head die axis: ↑↑

1929 SA	85	1931 SA	85
1930 SA	85	1932 SA	95

4002	4003	4006
Small head	1921 Sydney Sovereign	1914 Half-sovereign

4006 Half-Sovereign. Bare head l. R. St. George and dragon date in ex. London Mint die axis: ↑↑

1911 ....BV	35	60	1913	35	60
1911 Proof *FDC* £225			1914	35	60
1911 Matt Proof *FDC of highest rarity*			1915	35	60
1912 ....BV	35	60			

4007 Half-Sovereign. Similar R. M on ground for Melbourne Mint, Australia die axis: ↑↑

1915 M ....BV	45	80

4008 Half-Sovereign. Similar R. P on ground for Perth Mint, Australia die axis: ↑↑

1911 P 55	100	125	1918 P 125	250	500	825
1915 P 55	85	750				

4009 Half-Sovereign. Similar R. S on ground for Sydney Mint, Australia die axis: ↑↑

1911 S 45	60	80	1915 S ....BV	45	60
1912 S 40	50	70	1916 S ....BV	45	60
1914 S ....BV	45	65			

4010 Half-Sovereign. Similar R. SA on ground for Pretoria Mint, South Africa die axis: ↑↑

1923 SA Proof *FDC* £275			1926 SA ....BV	35	55
1925 SA ....BV	35	55			

SILVER

First Coinage. Sterling silver (.925 fine)

4011
1918 Halfcrown

	F	VF	EF	UNC			F	VF	EF	UNC
	£	£	£	£			£	£	£	£

4011 Halfcrown. Bare head l. ℞. Crowned shield in Garter die axis: ↑↑

	F	VF	EF	UNC		F	VF	EF	UNC
1911.........................5	18	40	100	1915.........................4	10	25	70
1911 Proof *FDC* £90				1916.........................4	10	25	70
1912.........................6	25	55	115	1917.........................5	15	40	80
1913.........................8	30	65	130	1918.........................4	10	25	70
1914.........................4	10	25	70	1919.........................5	15	40	80

4012
1911 Florin

4012 Florin. Bare head l. ℞. Crowned Cruciform shields sceptres in angles die axis: ↑↑

	F	VF	EF	UNC		F	VF	EF	UNC
1911.........................5	10	35	85	1916.........................4	10	25	65
1911 Proof *FDC* £80				1917.........................6	12	30	75
1912.........................5	15	45	90	1918.........................4	10	25	65
1913.........................8	25	65	130	1919.........................6	12	30	75
1914.........................4	10	25	65				
1915.........................6	20	40	90				

4013 Shilling. Bare head l. ℞. Lion rampant on crown, within circle die axis: ↑↑

	F	VF	EF	UNC		F	VF	EF	UNC
1911.........................2	8	20	45	1915.......................	4	20	45
1911 Proof *FDC* £60				1916.......................	4	20	45
1912.........................4	12	30	65	1917.......................	5	25	50
1913.........................8	15	45	85	1918.......................	4	20	45
1914.........................3	10	25	50	1919.........................4	10	30	60

4013
1919 Shilling

4014
1913 Sixpence

	F £	VF £	EF £	UNC £		F £	VF £	EF £	UNC £

4014 Sixpence. Bare head l. ℞. Lion rampant on crown, within circle die axis: ↑↑

1911	2	8	15	35	1916	2	8	15	35
1911 Proof *FDC* £45					1917	5	15	30	65
1912	4	10	25	50	1918	2	8	15	35
1913	5	12	30	55	1919	4	10	20	45
1914	2	8	15	35	1920	4	10	25	50
1915	2	8	15	35					

4015 Threepence. As Maundy but dull finish die axis: ↑↑

1911	1	5	15	1916	1	3	10
1911 Proof *FDC* £35				1917	1	3	10
1912	1	5	15	1918	1	3	10
1913	1	5	15	1919	1	3	10
1914	1	5	15	1920	1	5	15
1915	1	5	15				

4016
1911 Maundy Set

	EF £	FDC £		EF £	FDC £

4016 Maundy Set (4d., 3d., 2d. and 1d.) die axis: ↑↑

1911	55	85	1916	55	85
1911 Proof *FDC* £80			1917	55	85
1912	55	85	1918	55	85
1913	55	85	1919	55	85
1914	55	85	1920	55	85
1915	55	85			

4017 — Fourpence. 1911-20	*from*	8	15
4018 — Threepence. 1911-20	*from*	10	18
4019 — Twopence. 1911-20	*from*	7	12
4020 — Penny. 1911-20	*from*	8	15

Second Coinage. Debased silver (.500 fine). Types as before.

	F	VF	EF	UNC		F	VF	EF	UNC
	£	£	£	£		£	£	£	£

4021 Halfcrown. Deeply engraved. Bare head l. R. Crowned shield in garter die axis: ↑↑

	F	VF	EF	UNC		F	VF	EF	UNC
1920......................4	8	25	70						

4021A — recut shallow portrait

	F	VF	EF	UNC		F	VF	EF	UNC
1920......................6	12	40	90		1924 Specimen Finish...........*Extremely rare*				
1921......................5	10	30	80		1925...................20	50	175	325	
1922......................4	8	25	70		1926......................5	10	35	85	
1923......................3	5	15	45		1926 No colon				
1924......................5	10	35	80		after OMN ,,,,10	25	85	175	

4022 Florin. Deeply engraved. Bare head l. R. Crowned cruciform shields, sceptres in angles die axis: ↑↑

	F	VF	EF	UNC
1920......................3	8	30	85

4022A — recut shallow portrait

	F	VF	EF	UNC		F	VF	EF	UNC
1920......................5	12	40	95		1924......................4	10	40	80	
1921......................3	8	30	65		1924 Specimen Finish...........*Extremely rare*				
1922......................3	6	25	55		1925...................25	45	125	225	
1922 Proof in gold *FDC of highest rarity*					1926......................3	10	40	80	
1923......................2	5	20	50						

4023 Shilling. Deeply engraved. Bare head l. R. Lion rampant on crown within circle die axis: ↑↑

	F	VF	EF	UNC		F	VF	EF	UNC
1920......................3	6	25	50		1921 nose to S 8	20	45	90	

4023A — recut shallow portrait

	F	VF	EF	UNC		F	VF	EF	UNC
1921 nose to SV ...5	15	40	100		1924......................3	8	30	55	
1922......................3	6	25	50		1925......................5	10	45	85	
1923......................2	5	20	45		1926......................3	6	20	50	

4024 Sixpence. Bare head l. R. Lion rampant on crown within circle die axis: ↑↑

	F	VF	EF	UNC		F	VF	EF	UNC
1920......................2	4	12	30		1924......................2	4	12	30	
1921......................2	4	12	30		1924 Specimen Finish ....*Extremely rare*				
1922......................2	5	15	35		1924 Proof in gold *FDC of highest rarity*				
1923......................3	6	20	45		1925......................2	4	15	35	

4025
1926 Sixpence

4026
George V Threepence

4025 Sixpence. Similar new beading and broader rim die axis: ↑↑

	F	VF	EF	UNC		F	VF	EF	UNC
1925......................2	4	12	30		1926......................2	4	15	30	

4026 Threepence. Bare head l. R. Crowned 3 die axis: ↑↑

	F	VF	EF	UNC		F	VF	EF	UNC
1920......................	1	3	15		1924 Proof in gold *FDC of highest rarity*				
1921......................	1	3	15		1925...................—	2	14	25	
1922......................	1	10	20		1926......................1	3	15	30	
1924 Specimen Finish ....*Extremely rare*									

	EF	FDC		EF	FDC
	£	£		£	£

4027 Maundy Set. (4d., 3d., 2d. and 1d.) die axis: ↑↑

	EF	FDC		EF	FDC
1921	55	85	1925	55	85
1922	55	85	1926	55	85
1923	55	85	1927	55	85
1924	55	85			

		EF	FDC
4028 — Fourpence. 1921-7 ....*from*		10	15
4029 — Threepence. 1921-7 ....*from*		10	18
4030 — Twopence. 1921-7 ....*from*		7	12
4031 — Penny. 1921-7 ....*from*		8	15

2nd coinage
BM more central on tr.

3rd coinage
Modified Effigy
BM to right of tr.

Third Coinage. As before but modified effigy, with details of head more clearly defined. The BM on truncation is nearer to the back of the neck and without stops; beading is more pronounced.

	F	VF	EF	UNC		F	VF	EF	UNC
	£	£	£	£		£	£	£	£

4032 Halfcrown. Modified effigy l. R. Crowned Shield in Garter die axis: ↑↑

| 1926 | .....5 | 10 | 35 | 65 | 1927 Proof in gold *FDC of highest rarity* |
| 1927 | .....4 | 7 | 25 | 45 |

4033 Shilling. Modified effigy l. R. Lion rampant on crown, within circle die axis: ↑↑

| 1926 | .....2 | 4 | 18 | 35 | 1927 | .....2 | 6 | 25 | 45 |

4034 Sixpence. Modified effigy l. R. Lion rampant on crown, within circle die axis: ↑↑

| 1926 | ..... | 3 | 10 | 25 | 1927 | .....2 | 4 | 15 | 30 |

4035 Threepence. Modified effigy l. R. Crowned 3 die axis: ↑↑

| 1926 | .... | | | | | 1 | 8 | 30 |

Fourth Coinage. New types, 1927-36

4036
1932 'Wreath' Crown

4036 Crown. Modified Bare head l. R. Crown and date in wreath die axis: ↑↑

1927 –15,030 struck Proof only *FDC* £200				1931 –4056 struck....45	120	250	400
1927 Matt Proof *FDC of highest rarity*				1932 –2395 struck....95	165	325	525
1928 –9034 struck....45	110	200	350	1933 –7132 struck....45	110	200	375
1929 –4994 struck....45	110	200	350	1934 –932 struck....300	675	1300	2350
1930 -4847 struck.....45	110	200	350	1936 –2473 struck....75	135	300	475

| | 4037 | | | | | 4038 | | |
| | 1930 Halfcrown | | | | | 1928 Florin | | |

| F | VF | EF | UNC | | F | VF | EF | UNC |
| £ | £ | £ | £ | | £ | £ | £ | £ |

4037 Halfcrown. Modified bare head l. R. Shield die axis: ↑↑

1927 Proof only *FDC* £60				1932..................4	8	15	40
1927 Matt Proof *FDC of highest rarity*				1933..................2	5	10	25
1928..................2	5	10	25	1934..................4	10	25	55
1929..................2	5	10	25	1935..................	5	10	25
1930..................10	25	100	275	1936..................	3	8	20
1931..................2	5	10	30				

4038 Florin. Modified bare head l. R. Cruciform shields, sceptre in each angle die axis: ↑↑

1927 Proof only *FDC* £50				1931..................2	5	10	30
1927 Matt Proof *FDC* of highest rarity				1932..................20	50	125	300
1928..................	3	10	25	1933..................	3	10	30
1929..................	3	10	25	1935..................	3	10	25
1930..................2	5	10	30	1936..................	2	10	25

| | 4039 | | | | 4040 | | |
| | 1928 Shilling | | | | 1928 Sixpence | | |

4039 Shilling. Modified bare head l. R. Lion rampant on crown, no inner circles die axis: ↑↑

1927..................2	4	15	35	1931..................2	4	10	25
1927 Proof *FDC* £40				1932..................2	4	10	25
1927 Matt Proof *FDC Extremely rare*				1933..................	3	10	25
1928..................	3	10	25	1934..................2	5	16	35
1929..................	3	10	25	1935..................	3	10	25
1930..................3	6	20	45	1936..................	3	8	25

4040 Sixpence. Modified bare head l. R. Three oak sprigs with six acorns die axis: ↑↑

1927 Proof only *FDC* £25				1929..................	2	4	20
1927 Matt Proof *FDC Extremely rare*				1930..................	2	4	20
1928..................	2	5	20				

4041 Sixpence. Similar closer milling die axis: ↑↑

1931..................2	3	8	25	1934..................2	3	10	25
1932..................2	4	14	30	1935..................	2	6	18
1933..................2	3	8	22	1936..................	2	5	16

4042
1934 Threepence

4043
George V Maundy Set

	F	VF	EF	UNC		F	VF	EF	UNC
	£	£	£	£		£	£	£	£

4042 Threepence. Modified Bare head l. R. Three oak sprigs with three acorns die axis: ↑↑

	F	VF	EF	UNC		F	VF	EF	UNC
1927 Proof only *FDC* £45					1932			1	10
1927 Matt Proof *FDC of highest rarity*					1933			1	10
1928	1	3	14	40	1934			1	10
1930	1	3	14	40	1935			1	10
1931			1	10	1936			1	10

	EF	FDC		EF	FDC
	£	£		£	£

4043 Maundy Set. As earlier sets die axis: ↑↑

	EF	FDC		EF	FDC
1928	55	85	1933	55	85
1929	55	85	1934	55	85
1930	55	85	1935	55	85
1931	55	85	1936	55	85
1932	55	85			

The 1936 Maundy was distributed by King Edward VIII

		EF	FDC
4044 — Fourpence. 1928-36	*from*	10	15
4045 — Threepence. 1928-36	*from*	10	15
4046 — Twopence. 1928-36	*from*	10	15
4047 — Penny. 1928-36	*from*	12	18

Silver Jubilee Commemorative issue, die axis: ↑↑

4048
1935 'Jubilee' Crown

	VF	EF	UNC
	£	£	£
4048 Crown. 1935. R. St. George, incuse lettering on edge –714,769 struck	10	15	30
1935 — error edge		*Extremely rare*	
4049 Crown. Similar Specimen striking issued in box			55

4050 Crown. Similar raised lettering on edge 2,500 struck.Proof (.925 Æ) *FDC* £325
— error edge inscription Proof *FDC* £1500
— Proof in gold –28 struck £17500

GEORGE V
BRONZE

H Mint mark location – 4052

4052
1912 H Penny

KN Mint mark location – 4053

	F £	VF £	EF £	UNC £		F £	VF £	EF £	UNC £

4051 Penny. Bare head l. R. Britannia seated right die axis: ↑↑

	F	VF	EF	UNC		F	VF	EF	UNC
1911	2	10	40		1919	3	15	45
1912	3	15	45		1920	3	15	45
1913	4	18	50		1921	3	15	45
1914	3	15	45		1922	5	25	55
1915	3	15	45		1922 Rev. of 1927			*Extremely rare*	
1916	3	15	45		1922 Specimen finish			*Extremely rare*	
1917	3	15	45		1924 Specimen finish			*Extremely rare*	
1918	3	15	45		1926	6	30	65

4052 Penny. Bare head l. R. Britannia, H (Heaton Mint, Birmingham, Ltd.) to l. of date die axis: ↑↑

	F	VF	EF	UNC		F	VF	EF	UNC
1912 H	10	85	225		1919 H	15	220	500
1918 H	20	200	450					

4053 Penny. Bare head l. R. Britannia KN (King's Norton Metal Co.) to l. of date die axis: ↑↑

	F	VF	EF	UNC		F	VF	EF	UNC
1918 KN	3	30	275	725	1919 KN	3	35	325	800

4054 Penny. Modified effigy l. R. Britannia Seated r. shorter index finger date in ex. die axis: ↑↑

	F	VF	EF	UNC		F	VF	EF	UNC
1926	20	125	750	1550	1927	2	10	35	

4055 Penny. Small bare head l. R. Britannia Seated r. date in ex. die axis: ↑↑

	F	VF	EF	UNC		F	VF	EF	UNC
1928	2	10	35		1933			*Extremely rare*	
1929	2	10	35		1934	4	20	50	
1930	3	15	40		1935	1	8	35	
1931	3	15	40		1936	0.50	6	30	
1932	5	25	55						

4056 Halfpenny. Bare head l. R. Britannia Seated r. date in ex. die axis: ↑↑

	F	VF	EF	UNC		F	VF	EF	UNC
1911		5	30		1919		6	35	
1912		6	35		1920		6	35	
1913		6	35		1921		6	35	
1914		6	35		1922		8	40	
1915		6	35		1923		6	35	
1916		6	35		1924		6	35	
1917		6	35		1924 Specimen finish		*Extremely rare*		
1918		6	35		1925		6	35	

4057 Halfpenny. Modified effigy l. R. Britannia Seated r. date in ex. die axis: ↑↑

	F	VF	EF	UNC		F	VF	EF	UNC
1925		8	40		1927		6	35	
1926		6	35						

4056
1923 Halfpenny

4058
Small head

	EF £	UNC £		EF £	UNC £

4058 Halfpenny. Small bare head l. R. Britannia Seated r. date in ex. die axis: ↑↑

	EF	UNC		EF	UNC
1928	5	25	1933	5	25
1929	5	25	1934	8	30
1930	5	25	1935	5	25
1931	5	25	1936	4	20
1932	5	25			

4059
1917 Farthing

4062
1913 Third-Farthing

4059 Farthing. Bare head l. R. Britannia Seated r. date in ex. Dark finish die axis: ↑↑

	EF	UNC		EF	UNC
1911	3	12	1915	4	15
1912	2	10	1916	2	10
1913	2	10	1917	1	10
1914	2	10	1918	9	25

4060 Farthing. Similar Bright finish, die axis: ↑↑ 1918-25 .... 1　　10
4061 Farthing. Modified effigy l. R. Britannia Seated r. date in ex. die axis: ↑↑

	EF	UNC		EF	UNC
1926	1	5	1932	1	5
1927	1	5	1933	1	5
1928	1	5	1934	2	8
1929	1	5	1935	2	5
1930	1	5	1936	1	5
1931	1	5			

4062 Third-Farthing (for use in Malta). Bare head l. R. Crowned date and Value die axis: ↑↑
1913 .... 12　　30

Proof Sets

PS11	Coronation, **1911.** Five pounds to Maundy Penny (12 coins)	*FDC*	£3250
PS12	— **1911.** Sovereign to Maundy Penny (10 coins)	*FDC*	£1150
PS13	— **1911.** Half crown to Maundy Penny (8 coins)	*FDC*	£500
PS14	New type, **1927.** Wreath type Crown to Threepence (6 coins)	*FDC*	£375

Succeeded his father on 20 January 1936. Abdicated 10 December.

Edward VIII was born 23 June 1894, and was very popular as Prince of Wales. He ruled only for a short time before announcing his intended marriage to the American divorcee Wallis Simpson; a potential religious and political scandal. Edward was not a traditionalist, as evidenced on the proposed coinage, where he insisted against all advice on having his effigy face the same way as his father's, instead of opposite. He abdicated in favour of his brother, and became Edward, Duke of Windsor, marrying Mrs Simpson in France, where they lived in exile. He governed the Bahamas from 1940-45 and died on 28 May 1972.

No coins of Edward VIII were issued for currency within the United Kingdom bearing his name and portrait. The Mint had commenced work on a new coinage prior to the Abdication, and various patterns were made. No Proof Sets were issued for sale and only a small number of sets were struck.

Coins bearing Edward's name, but not his portrait, were issued for the colonial territories of British East Africa, British West Africa, Fiji and New Guinea. The projected U.K. coins were to include a Shilling of essentially `Scottish' type and a nickel brass Threepence with twelve sides which might supplement and possibly supersede the inconveniently small silver Threepence.

Engravers and Designers:– George Kruger Gray (1880-1943), Thomas Humphrey Paget (1893-1974), Benedicto Pistucci (1784-1855) Frances Madge Kitchener, Percy Metcalfe (1895-1970), H Wilson Parker (1896-1980)

Designer's initials: H. P. (T. Humphrey Paget)   B.P. (Benedetto Pistrucci, d. 1855)
                            K. G. (G. Kruger Gray)   M. K. (Madge Kitchener)
                            W. P. (H. Wilson Parker)

Prime Minister:– Stanley Baldwin (1867-1947), Conservative 1935-7
Die axis ↑↑

4063
Edward VIII Proof Five Pounds

4063 Proof Set
Gold, Five Pounds, Two Pounds and Sovereign, 1937...   *not issued*

Silver Crown, Halfcrown, Florin, Scottish shilling, sixpence and threepence, 1937   *not issued*

Sovereign, Bare head l. R. St George and dragon date in ex............................ *Extremely rare*
Crown, Bare head l. R. Crowned Shield of arms and supporters..................... *Extremely rare*
Halfcrown, Bare head l. R. Quartered Standard of arms................................. *Extremely rare*
Florin, Bare head l. R. Crowned rose and emblems... *Extremely rare*
Shilling, Bare head l. R. Lion seated facing on crown .... *Extremely rare*
Sixpence, Bare head l. R. Six interlinked rings .... *Extremely rare*
Threepence, Bare head l. R. three interlinked rings... *Extremely rare*

4064A Nickel brass. **Threepence**, 1937 Bare head l. R. Thrift plant below   35000
        Bronze. **Penny. Halfpenny and Farthing**, 1937 ....   *not issued*

Pattern

Edward VIII Brass Threepence

4064B Nickel brass dodecagonal **Threepence**, 1937. Bare head l. R. Thrift plant of more
        naturalistic style than the modified proof coin. A small number of these
        coins were produced for experimental purposes and a few did get into .
        circulation   32000

George VI was born on 14 December 1895 and never expected to be King. He suffered ill-health through much of his life and had a stammer. He married Elizabeth Bowes Lyon and together they became very popular especially through the ravages of World War II, when Buckingham Palace was bombed. The war took its toll on George, and ever a heavy smoker he succumbed to lung cancer on 6th February 1952. Elizabeth, known after his death as 'Queen Elizabeth the Queen Mother', lived on to the age of 101 dying on 30 March 2002.

Though they were at first issued concurrently, the twelve-sided nickel-brass Threepence superseded the small silver Threepence in 1942. Those dated 1943-4 were not issued for circulation in the U.K. In addition to the usual English 'lion' Shilling, a Shilling of Scottish type was issued concurrently. This depicts the Scottish lion and crown flanked by the shield of St. Andrew and a thistle. In 1947, as silver was needed to repay the bullion lent by the U.S.A. during the war, silver coins were replaced by coins of the same type and weight made of cupro-nickel. In 1949, after India had attained independence, the title IND:IMP (*Indiae Imperator)* was dropped from the coinage. Commemorative Crown pieces were issued for the Coronation and the 1951 Festival of Britain.

Engravers and Designers:– Frances Madge Kitchener, George Kruger Gray (1880-1943), Percy Metcalfe (1895-1970) Thomas Humphrey Paget (1893-1974), H Wilson Parker (1896-1980), Benedetto Pistrucci (1784-1855)

Designer's initials: K. G. (G. Kruger Gray)   B. P. (Benedetto Pistrucci, d. 1855)
                     H. P. (T. Humphrey Paget)   W. P. (Wilson Parker)

Prime Ministers:– Stanley Baldwin, (1867-1947) Conservative, 1935-37, Arthur Neville Chamberlain, (1869-1940) National 1937-40, Sir Winston Leonard Spencer Churchill,(1874-1965) National 1940-45. 1951-55 Conservative, Clement Richard Attlee, (1883-1967) Labour 1945-51

Die axis ↑↑

GOLD

4074
1937 Proof Five Pounds

4076
1937 Proof Sovereign

FDC
£

4074 Five Pounds. Bare head l. Ŗ. St. George, 1937. Proof plain edge only (5001 struck)..   700
4074-4077 Proof Struck to Matt finish *FDC of highest rarity*
4075 Two Pounds. Similar, 1937. Proof plain edge only (5001 struck)...............................   400
4076 Sovereign. Similar, 1937. Proof plain edge only (5001 struck)   1150
4077 Half-Sovereign. Similar, 1937. Proof plain edge only (5001 struck)   325

SILVER

First coinage. Silver, .500 fine, with title IND:IMP

4078
1937 Crown

	VF £	EF £	UNC £
4078 Crown. Coronation commemorative, 1937. ℞. Arms and supporters	10	20	30

4079 Crown. Similar 1937 Proof *FDC* £45
       Similar 1937 Frosted 'VIP' Proof £400
       — 1937 Matt Proof *FDC of highest rarity*

4080
1937 Halfcrown

4081
1937 Florin

4080 Halfcrown. Bare head l. ℞. Shield die axis: ↑↑

	EF £	UNC £		EF £	UNC £
1937	4	15	1941	5	15
1937 Proof *FDC* £20			1942	3	10
1937 Matt Proof *FDC of highest rarity*			1943	5	15
1938	8	30	1944	3	10
1939	5	15	1945	3	10
1940	5	15	1946	3	10

4081 Florin. Bare head l. ℞. Crowned rose, etc. die axis: ↑↑

	EF £	UNC £		EF £	UNC £
1937	3	10	1941	4	12
1937 Proof *FDC* £15			1942	3	10
1937 Matt Proof *FDC of highest rarity*			1943	3	10
1938	8	25	1944	3	10
1939	4	12	1945	3	10
1940	4	12	1946	3	10

4082
1945 'English' Shilling

4083
1937 'Scottish' Shilling

4082 Shilling. 'English' reverse. Bare head l. ℞. Lion rampant on large crown die axis: ↑↑

	EF £	UNC £		EF £	UNC £
1937	2	8	1941	3	12
1937 Proof *FDC* £15			1942	2	10
1937 Matt Proof *FDC of highest rarity*			1943	2	10
1938	8	25	1944	2	10
1939	3	12	1945	1	8
1940	3	12	1946	1	8

	EF £	UNC £		VF £	EF £	UNC £

4083 Shilling. 'Scottish' reverse. Bare head l. R. Lion seated facing on crown die axis: ↑↑

	EF £	UNC £		VF £	EF £	UNC £
1937	1	8	1941		3	12
1937 Proof *FDC* £15			1942		2	10
1937 Matt Proof *FDC of highest rarity*			1943		2	10
1938	8	25	1944		2	10
1939	3	12	1945		1	8
1940	3	12	1946		1	8

4084
1937 Sixpence

4085
1937 Threepence

4084 Sixpence. Bare head l. R. GRI crowned die axis: ↑↑

	EF £	UNC £		VF £	EF £	UNC £
1937	1	8	1941		2	10
1937 Proof *FDC* £10			1942		1	8
1937 Matt Proof *FDC of highest rarity*			1943		1	8
1938	6	15	1944		1	8
1939	2	10	1945		1	8
1940	2	10	1946		1	8

4085 Threepence. Bare head l. R. Shield on rose die axis: ↑↑

	EF £	UNC £		VF £	EF £	UNC £
1937	1	8	1941		6	20
1937 Proof *FDC* £12			1942*	5	15	50
1937 Matt Proof *FDC of highest rarity*			1943*	5	20	65
1938	1	8	1944*	10	30	95
1939	6	15	1945*		*Extremely rare*	
1940	3	12	** issued for Colonial use only*			

4086
1937 Maundy Set

	FDC £		FDC £

4086 Maundy Set. Silver, .500 fine. Uniform dates die axis: ↑↑

	FDC £		FDC £
1937	65	1941	85
1937 Proof *FDC* £70		1942	85
1937 Matt Proof *FDC of highest rarity*		1943	85
1938	85	1944	85
1939	85	1945	85
1940	85	1946	85

	FDC		*FDC*
	£		£
4087 — **Fourpence.** 1937-46 ....*from*	12		
4088 — **Threepence.** 1937-46 ....*from*	12		
4089 — **Twopence.** 1937-46 ....*from*	12		
4090 — **Penny.** 1937-46 ....*from*	18		

Second coinage. Silver, .925 fine, with title IND:IMP (Maundy only)
4091 Maundy Set (4d., 3d., 2d. and 1d.). Uniform dates die axis: ↑↑

1947	85	1948	85

4092 — **Fourpence,** 1947-8	12
4093 — **Threepence,** 1947-8	12
4094 — **Twopence,** 1947-8	12
4095 — **Penny,** 1947-8	18

Third coinage. Silver, .925 fine, but omitting IND:IMP. (Maundy only)
4096 Maundy Set (4d., 3d., 2d. and 1d.). Uniform dates die axis: ↑↑

1949	85	1951	85
1950	85	1952	85
1951 Matt Proof *FDC Extremely rare*		1952 Proof in copper *FDC Extremely rare*	

The 1952 Maundy was distributed by Queen Elizabeth II.

4097 — **Fourpence,** 1949-52 ....*from*	12
4098 — **Threepence,** 1949-52 ....*from*	12
4099 — **Twopence,** 1949-52 ....*from*	12
4100 — **Penny,** 1949-52 ....*from*	18

CUPRO-NICKEL

Second coinage. Types as first (silver) coinage, IND:IMP.

	EF	*UNC*		*EF*	*UNC*
	£	£		£	£
4101 Halfcrown. Bare head l. R. Shield die axis: ↑↑					
1947	1	8	1948	1	8
4102 Florin. Bare head l. R. Crowned rose die axis: ↑↑					
1947	1	8	1948	1	8
4103 Shilling. 'English' reverse. Bare head l. die axis: ↑↑					
1947	1	8	1948		6
4104 Shilling. 'Scottish' reverse. Bare head l. die axis: ↑↑					
1947	1	8	1948		6
4105 Sixpence. Bare head l. R. GRI crowned die axis: ↑↑					
1947		6	1948		5

Third coinage. Types as before but title IND:IMP. omitted

4106
1951 Halfcrown

	EF £	UNC £		VF £	EF £	UNC £

4106 Halfcrown. Bare head l. R. Shield die axis: ↑↑

	EF £	UNC £		VF £	EF £	UNC £
1949	3	10	1951..............	1	8	20
1950	5	15	1951 Proof *FDC* £25			
1950 Proof *FDC* £20			1951 Matt Proof *FDC of highest rarity*			
1950 Matt Proof *FDC of highest rarity*			1952		*Extremely rare*	

4107 Florin. Bare head l. R. Crowned rose die axis: ↑↑

1949	4	12	1951		6	18
1950	5	12	1951 Proof *FDC* £25			
1950 Proof *FDC* £15			1951 Matt Proof *FDC of highest rarity*			
1950 Matt Proof *FDC of highest rarity*						

4108 Shilling. 'English' reverse. Bare head l. die axis: ↑↑

1949	4	12	1951		6	18
1950	5	15	1951 Proof *FDC* £15			
1950 Proof *FDC* £15			1951 Matt Proof *FDC Extremely rare*			

4109 Shilling. 'Scottish' reverse. Bare head l. die axis: ↑↑

1949	5	15	1951		6	18
1950	5	15	1951 Proof *FDC* £15			
1950 Proof *FDC* £15			1951 Matt Proof *FDC Extremely rare*			
1950 Matt Proof *FDC Extremely rare*						

4110
1952 Sixpence

4110 Sixpence. Bare head l. R. Crowned cypher die axis: ↑↑

1949	1	8	1951		5	15
1950	1	8	1951 Proof *FDC* £12			
1950 Proof *FDC* £10			1951 Matt Proof *FDC Extremely rare*			
1950 Matt Proof *FDC Extremely rare*			1952 5	20	60	

Festival of Britain issue die axis: ↑↑

4111
Festival of Britain Crown

	EF	UNC
	£	£

4111 Crown. Bare head l. R. St. George and dragon, date in ex, 1951. *Proof-like*   10   20
     Similar — 1951 Frosted 'VIP' Proof £350
     Similar — 1951 Matt Proof *FDC of highest rarity*
     Similar — 1951 Plain edge Proof *FDC* £1000

NICKEL BRASS

First issue, with title IND:IMP.

4112   4113
1937 Brass Threepence   Second issue obverse

	VF	EF	UNC		VF	EF	UNC
	£	£	£		£	£	£

4112 Threepence (dodecagonal). Bare head l. R. Thrift plant die axis: ↑↑

	VF	EF	UNC		VF	EF	UNC
1937		2	10	1942		3	10
1937 Proof *FDC* £15				1943		3	10
1937 Matt Proof *FDC of highest rarity*				1944		3	10
1938		6	20	1945		5	15
1939		10	40	1946	15	75	325
1940		6	20	1948		8	45
1941		3	10				

Second issue, omitting IND:IMP.
4113 Threepence. Bare head l. R. Similar die axis: ↑↑

	VF	EF	UNC		VF	EF	UNC
1949	15	65	300	1951		20	75
1950	15		50	1951 Proof *FDC* £40			
1950 Proof *FDC* £35				1951 Matt Proof *FDC of highest rarity*			
1950 Matt Proof *FDC of highest rarity*				1952		5	15

BRONZE

First issue, with title IND:IMP.

4114
1937 Penny

	EF £	UNC £		EF £	UNC £

4114 Penny. Bare head l. R. Britannia Seated r. date in ex die axis: ↑↑

1937		6	1944 —		6	18
1937 Proof *FDC* £15			1945 —		5	15
1938	1	8	1946 —		5	15
1939	4	12	1947 —			6
1940	10	40	1948 —			6
1940 Double exergue line	4	12	1946 ONE' die flaw		35	—

4115
1937 Halfpenny

4116
1937 Farthing

4115 Halfpenny. Bare head l. R. Ship sailing l. date below die axis: ↑↑

1937		6	1943			6
1937 Proof *FDC* £10			1944			6
1938	1	8	1945	1		8
1939	2	10	1946	2		10
1940	3	12	1947	1		8
1941		6	1948			6
1942		6				

4116 Farthing. Bare head l. R. Wren l. date above die axis: ↑↑

1937	4	1943		4
1937 Proof *FDC* £10		1944		4
1938	6	1945		4
1939	4	1946		4
1940	4	1947		4
1941	4	1948		4
1942	4			

Second issue, without IND.IMP. Types as before

	VF £	EF £	UNC £		VF £	EF £	UNC £

4117 Penny. Bare head l. R. Britannia Seated r. date in ex. die axis: ↑↑

1949...			6	1951 10		35	60
1950........................6		18	40	1951 Proof *FDC* £40			
1950 Proof *FDC* £25				1952 Proof only			*Unique*

4118
Second issue Halfpenny

4119
Second issue Farthing

4118 Halfpenny. Bare head l. R. Ship Sailing l. date below die axis: ↑↑

1949	4	12	1951		5	20
1950	3	10	1951 Proof *FDC* £12			
1950 Proof *FDC* £10			1952		1	8

4119 Farthing. Bare head l. R. Wren l. date above die axis: ↑↑

1949..	5	1951..		6
1950..	5	1951 Proof *FDC* £18		
1950 Proof *FDC* £10		1952..		5

The coins dated 1952 were issued during the reign of Elizabeth II.

Proof Sets

PS15 Coronation, **1937.** Five pounds to Half-sovereign (4 coins).........................*FDC*		£2650
PS16 — 1937. Crown to Farthing, including Maundy Set (15 coins) ....*FDC*		£300
PS17 Mid-Century, **1950.** Halfcrown to Farthing (9 coins)....................................*FDC*		£100
PS18 Festival of Britain, **1951.** Crown to Farthing (10 coins)..............................*FDC*		£125

Elizabeth II was born on 21 April 1926. Our current Monarch has lived a long and glorious reign celebrating her Golden Jubilee in 2002. She married Philip a distant cousin in 1947 and has four children, Charles, Anne, Andrew and Edward. Significantly she is the first Monarch to pay taxes and her coinage has been an interesting one with the change to decimal coinage and the numerous bust changes since 1953.

The earliest coins of this reign have the title BRITT:OMN, but in 1954 this was omitted from the Queen's titles owing to the changing status of so many Commonwealth territories. The minting of 'English' and 'Scottish' shillings was continued. A Coronation commemorative crown was issued in 1953, another crown was struck on the occasion of the 1960 British Exhibition in New York and a third was issued in honour of Sir Winston Churchill in 1965. A very small number of proof gold coins were struck in 1953 for the national museum collections, but between 1957 and 1968 gold sovereigns were minted again in quantity for sale in the international bullion market and to counteract the activities of counterfeiters.

Owing to inflation the farthing had now become practically valueless; production of these coins ceased after 1956 and the coins were demonetized at the end of 1960. In 1965 it was decided to change to a decimal system of coinage in the year 1971. As part of the transition to decimal coinage the halfpenny was demonetized in August 1969 and the halfcrown in January 1970. (See also introduction to Decimal Coinage.

Prime Ministers:-
Winston Churchill, Conservative, 1951-55
Sir Anthony Eden, Conservative, 1955-57
Harold Macmillan, Conservative, 1957-63
Sir Alec Douglas-Home, Conservative, 1963-64
Harold Wilson, Labour, 1964-70
Edward Heath, Conservative, 1970-74
Harold Wilson, Labour, 1974-76
James Callaghan, Labour, 1976-79
Margaret Thatcher, Conservative, 1979-90
John Major, Conservative, 1990-97
Tony Blair, Labour, 1997-

Designer's initials:
A. V. (Avril Vaughan)
B. P. (Benedetto Pistrucci, 1784-1855)
B. R. (Bruce Rushin)
C. T. (Cecil Thomas)
D. C. (David Cornell)
E. F. (Edgar Fuller)
G. L. (Gilbert Ledward)
I. R. B. (Ian Rank-Broadley)
J. B. (James Butler)
J. M. (Jeffrey Matthews)
J. M. M. (John Mills)
M. B. (Matthew Bonaccorsi)
M. G. (Mary Gillick)
M. M. D. (Mary Milner Dickens)
M. N. (Michael Noakes)
M. R. (Michael Rizzello)
N. S. (Norman Sillman)
P. N. (Philip Nathan)
R. D. (Ron Dutton)
R. D. M. (Raphael David Maklouf)
R. E. (Robert Elderton)
r. e. (Robert Evans)
R. L. (Robert Lowe)
T. N. (Timothy Noad)
W. G. (William Gardner)
W. P. (Wilson Parker 1896-1980)

Other designers whose initials do not appear on the coins:
Christopher Ironside (1913-
Arnold Machin (1911-99)
David Wynne
Professor Richard Guyatt
Eric Sewell
Oscar Nemon
Leslie Durbin
Derek Gorringe
Bernard Sindall
Tom Phillips
Edwina Ellis
David Gentleman

PRE-DECIMAL ISSUES
Die axis ↑↑
GOLD

First coinage, with title BRITT.OMN, 1953. *Proof only* .... *of the highest rarity*
4120 Five Pounds. Young laur. head r. R. St. George .... *None issued for collectors*
4121 Two Pounds. Young laur. head r. R. St. George .... *None issued for collectors*
4122 Sovereign. Young laur. head r. R. St. George .... *None issued for collectors*
4123 Half-Sovereign. Young laur. head r. R. St. George .... *None issued for collectors*

Second issue, BRITT.OMN omitted

4125
1958 Sovereign

	EF	UNC
	£	£
4124 Sovereign. Young laur head r. R. St. George, fine graining on edge		
1957...BV		85
1957 Proof *FDC* £4500		

	UNC		UNC
	£		£
4125 Sovereign. Similar, but coarser graining on edge			
1958....................................... 75		1963 Proof *FDC* £5750	
1958 Proof *FDC* £4500		1964	75
1959....................................... 85		1965	75
1959 Proof *FDC* £4500		1966	75
1962....................................... 85		1967	75
1963....................................... 85		1968	75

SILVER

The Queen's Maundy are now the only coins struck regularly in silver.
The location of the Maundy ceremony is given for each year.

First issue, with title BRITT:OMN:	FDC
	£
4126 Maundy Set (4d., 3d., 2d. and 1d.), 1953. *St Paul's Cathedral*	475
1953 Proof struck in gold *FDC of highest rarity*	
1953 Proof struck in nickel bronze *FDC Extremely rare*	
1953 Matt Proof *FDC Extremely rare*	
4127 — Fourpence. 1953	100
4128 — Threepence. 1953	100
4129 — Twopence. 1953	100
4130 — Penny. 1953	200

Second issue, with BRITT:OMN: omitted

4131
1962 Maundy Set

	FDC			FDC
	£			£
4131 Maundy Set (4d., 3d., 2d. and 1d.). Uniform dates				
1954 *Westminster*............................... 90			1956 *Westminster*	90
1955 *Southwark*................................... 90			1957 *St. Albans*.....................................	90

	FDC		FDC
	£		£
1958 *Westminster*	90	1965 Canterbury	90
1959 *Windsor*	90	1966 Westminster	90
1960 *Westminster*	90	1967 Durham	90
1961 *Rochester*	90	1968 Westminster	90
1962 *Westminster*	90	1969 Selby	90
1963 *Chelmsford*	90	1970 Westminster	90
1964 Westminster	90		

4132 — Fourpence. 1954-70	*from*	12
4133 — Threepence. 1954-70	*from*	12
4134 — Twopence. 1954-70	*from*	12
4135 — Penny. 1954-70	*from*	18

CUPRO-NICKEL

First issue, 1953, with title BRITT.OMN.

4136
1953 Coronation Crown

	EF	UNC	PROOF FDC
	£	£	£
4136 Crown. Queen on horseback. ℞. Crown in centre of emblematical cross, shield of Arms in each angle, 1953	6	10	40
Similar 1953 Frosted 'VIP' proof £400			
Similar 1953 Matt Proof *FDC of highest rarity*			

4137   4138
1953 Halfcrown   1953 Florin

	EF	UNC
4137 Halfcrown. with title BRITT:OMN: Young laur. head r. ℞. Arms, 1953	5	15
4138 Florin. Young laur. head r. ℞. Double rose, 1953	4	10

4139
1953 'English' Shilling

4140
'Scottish' reverse

4141
1953 Sixpence

4139 Shilling. 'English' reverse. Young laur. head r. R. Three lions, 1953 .... 2 8
4140 Shilling. '—' 'Scottish' reverse. Young laur. head r. R. Lion rampant in shield, 1953 2 8
4141 Sixpence. Young laur. head r. R. Interlaced rose, thistle, shamrock and leek, 1953 1 6
4142 Sixpence. Set of 9 uncirculated cu-ni, ni-br and Æ coins (2/6 to 1/4d.)
    in Royal Mint plastic envelope 30

Second issue, similar types but omitting BRITT.OMN.

4143
1960 Crown

4144
1965 Churchill Crown

	EF £	UNC £
4143 Crown, 1960. Young laur. head r. R. As 4136...	5	10
— — Similar, from polished dies (New York Exhibition issue).........................	10	30
— — 'VIP' *Proof,* frosted design *FDC* £400		
4144 Crown, Churchill commemorative, 1965. As illustration. R. Bust of Sir Winston Churchill r.		2
— — Similar, "Satin-Finish". VIP *Specimen*..		850

4145 Halfcrown. Young laur. head r. R. As 4137

	EF £	UNC £		EF £	UNC £		EF £	UNC £
1954	3	20	1960		6	1965		4
1955		8	1961		4	1966		
1956		10	1961 Polished die ..		10	1967		
1957		5	1962		4	1970 Proof *FDC* £5		
1958	3	20	1963		4			
1959	5	30	1964		6			

4146
1955 Florin

	EF £	UNC £		UNC £
4146 Florin. Young laur. head r. R. As 4138				
1954	5	40	1962	4
1955		6	1963	4
1956		6	1964	4
1957	5	40	1965	4
1958	4	20	1966	2
1959	5	35	1967	2
1960		5	1970 Proof *FDC* £5	
1961		5		

4147 Shilling. 'English' reverse. Young laur. head r. R. As 4139

1954		5	1961	2
1955		5	1962	1
1956		10	1963	1
1957		4	1964	1
1958	2	15	1965	1
1959		4	1966	1
1960		4	1970 Proof *FDC* £3	

4148 Shilling. 'Scottish' reverse. Young laur. head r. R. As 4140

1954		5	1961	6
1955		6	1962	4
1956		10	1963	1
1957	2	15	1964	1
1958		3	1965	1
1959	2	15	1966	1
1960		4	1970 Proof *FDC* £2	

4149 Sixpence. Young laur. head r. R. As 4141

1954	6	1962	1.50
1955	4	1963	1.50
1956	4	1964	1.50
1957	3	1965	1
1958	3	1966	1
1959	2	1967	1
1960	3	1970 Proof *FDC* £3	
1961	2		

ELIZABETH II

NICKEL BRASS

First issue, with title BRITT.OMN.

4152
1953 Brass Threepence

4153
Second issue

4152 Threepence (dodecagonal). Young laur. head r. ℞. Crowned portcullis, 1953 5
— Proof *FDC* £10

Second issue (omitting BRIT.OMN)
4153 Threepence Similar type

1954	6	1962	1
1955	8	1963	1
1956	8	1964	1
1957	5	1965	1
1958	8	1966	0.50
1959	5	1967	0.50
1960	5	1970 Proof *FDC* £3	
1961	2		

BRONZE

First issue, with title BRITT.OMN.

4154
1953 Penny

4155
1953 Halfpenny

	VF	EF	UNC	Proof FDC
	£	£	£	£
4154 Penny. Young laur. head r. ℞. Britannia (only issued with Royal Mint set in plastic envelope), 1953 Beaded border	1	5	15	20
1953 Toothed border			*Extremely rare*	
4155 Halfpenny. Young laur. head r. ℞. Ship, 1953			4	10
4156 Farthing. Young laur. head r. ℞. Wren, 1953			3	8

Second issue, omitting BRITT.OMN.

	UNC		UNC
	£		£
4157 Penny. Young laur. head r. ℞. Britannia (1954-60 *not issued*)			
1954	*Unique*	1965	0.50
1961	2	1966	0.50
1962	1	1967	0.25
1963	1	1970 Proof *FDC* £4	
1964	0.50		

4158 Halfpenny. Young laur. head r. R. Ship (1961 *not issued*)

1954	4	1960	1
1954 larger border teeth	5	1962	1
1955	3	1963	1
1956	3	1964	1
1957	3	1965	1
1957 calm sea	30	1966	0.50
1958	2	1967	0.50
1959	1	1970 Proof *FDC* £3	

4156
1953 Farthing

4159
Second issue

		EF £	UNC £
4159 Farthing. Young laur. head r. R. Wren			
1954	4		
1955 Rev. with thin rim	4		
1956 Rev. with thin rim		3	6

Proof Sets

PS19 Coronation, **1953.** Crown to Farthing (10 coins)	*FDC*	100
PS20 'Last Sterling', **1970.** Halfcrown to Halfpenny plus medallion	*FDC*	20

PRE-DECIMAL PROOF SETS

All prices quoted assume coins are in their original case. Issued by the Royal Mint in official case from 1887 onwards, but earlier sets were issued privately by the engraver. All pieces have a superior finish to that of the current coins.

		No. of coins	FDC £
PS1	**George IV, 1826.** New issue, Five Pounds to Farthing	(11)	21500
PS1A	— — Similar to above, including Maundy Set	(15)	22500
PS2	**William IV, 1831.** Coronation, Two Pounds to Farthing	(14)	20000
PS3	**Victoria, 1839.** Young head. "Una and the Lion" Five Pounds and Sovereign to Farthing	(15)	32500
PS4	— **1853.** Sovereign to Half-Farthing, including Gothic type Crown	(16)	30000
PS5	— **1887.** Jubilee bust for Golden Jubilee, Five Pounds to Threepence	(11)	6500
PS6	— **1887.** Silver Crown to Threepence	(7)	1350
PS7	— **1893.** Old bust, Five Pounds to Threepence	(10)	7500
PS8	— **1893.** Silver Crown to Threepence	(6)	1700
PS9	**Edward VII, 1902.** Coronation, Five Pounds to Maundy Penny. Matt finish to surfaces	(13)	2000
PS10	— **1902.** Sovereign to Maundy Penny. Matt finish	(11)	850
PS11	**George V, 1911.** Coronation, Five Pounds to Maundy Penny	(12)	3250
PS12	— **1911.** Sovereign to Maundy Penny	(10)	1150
PS13	— **1911.** Silver Halfcrown to Maundy Penny	(8)	500
PS14	— **1927.** New Coinage. Wreath type Crown to Threepence	(6)	375
PS15	**George VI, 1937.** Coronation. Five Pounds to Half-Sovereign	(4)	2650
PS16	— **1937.** Coronation. Crown to Farthing, including Maundy Set	(15)	300
PS17	— **1950.** Mid-Century, Halfcrown to Farthing	(9)	100
PS18	— **1951.** Festival of Britain, Crown to Farthing	(10)	125
PS19	**Elizabeth II, 1953.** Coronation. Crown to Farthing	(10)	100
PS20	— **1970.** "Last Sterling" set. Halfcrown to Halfpenny plus medallion	(8)	20

A decision to adopt decimal currency was announced in March 1966 following the recommendation of the Halsbury Committee of Enquiry which had been appointed in 1961. The date for the introduction of the new system was 15 February 1971 and it was evident that the Royal Mint facilities which had been located on Tower Hill for more than 150 years would be unable to strike the significant quantities of coins required on that site. The Government therefore decided to build a new mint at Llantrisant in South Wales.

The new system provided for three smaller bronze coins and very large numbers were struck and stock piled for D-Day but the five and ten new pence denominations with the same specifications as the former shilling and florin were introduced in 1968. A further change was the introduction of a 50 new pence coin to replace the ten shilling banknote.

In 1982 and 1983 two more new coins were introduced; the 20 pence which helped to reduce demand for five and ten pence pieces, and the first circulating non-precious metal £1 coin which replaced the bank note of the same value.

Increasing raw material costs, and inflation also play a part in the development of a modern coinage system and a smaller 50 pence was introduced in the autumn of 1997. The bimetallic circulating £2 was also introduced.

For the collector, many of these changes have been accompanied by special issues often in limited editions struck in precious metal. New designs, particularly on the £1 coins, have added interest to the coins that circulate, and may hopefully stimulate new collectors.

In the period since decimalisation there has been a marked increase in the issue of commemorative coins. The crown size pieces, which by virtue of their size allow much scope for interesting designs seem to be reserved for the commemoration of Royal events or anniversaries, and other denominations such as the £2 and the 50 pence have honoured other interesting themes.

The major change in the coinage in 1998 was the new, and fourth, portrait of H. M. The Queen. Designed by Ian Rank-Broadley, a whole new series has started which will stimulate interest among collectors everywhere.

GOLD

       4201   4204

4201   Five pounds. As illustration
      1980 Proof *FDC** £500   1982 Proof *FDC** £450
      1981 Proof *FDC* (Issued: 5,400)** £500   1984 Proof *FDC* (Issued: 905) £500
4202   As 4201 but, 'U' in a circle to left of date
      1984 (Issued: 15,104) *Unc* £425
4203   Two pounds
      1980 Proof *FDC** £250   1983 Proof *FDC* (Issued: 12,500)** £225
      1982 Proof *FDC** £250

* *Coins marked thus were originally issued in Royal Mint Sets.*
** *Numbers include coins sold in sets.*

4204 Sovereign. As illustration

1974	Unc £75	— Proof *FDC* (Issued: 81,200) £85
1976	Unc £75	1981	Unc £80
1976 VIP Proof *FDC* .... *Extremely rare*		— Proof *FDC* (Issued: 32,960) £100
1978	Unc £75	1982	Unc £80
1979	Unc £75	— Proof *FDC* (Issued: 20,000) £100
— Proof *FDC* (Issued: 50,000) £100		1983 Proof *FDC* (Issued: 21,250)** £125
1980	Unc £80	1984 Proof *FDC* (Issued: 12,880) £125

4205 Half-sovereign

1980 Proof *FDC* (Issued: 76.700) £60		1983 Proof *FDC* (Issued: 19,710)** £80
1982	Unc £50	1984 Proof *FDC* (Issued: 12,410) £80
— Proof *FDC* (Issued: 19,090) £60			

SILVER

	FDC		*FDC*
	£		£

4211 Maundy Set (4p, 3p, 2p and 1p). Uniform dates. Types as 4131

1971 *Tewkesbury Abbey*	85	1990 *Newcastle Cathedral*	85
1972 *York Minster*	85	1991 *Westminster Abbey*	85
1973 *Westminster Abbey*	85	1992 *Chester Cathedral*	85
1974 *Salisbury Cathedral*	85	1993 *Wells Cathedral*	85
1975 *Peterborough Cathedral*	85	1994 *Truro Cathedral*	85
1976 *Hereford Cathedral*	85	1995 *Coventry Cathedral*	100
1977 *Westminster Abbey*	85	1996 *Norwich Cathedral*	100
1978 *Carlisle Cathedral*	85	1997 *Bradford Cathedral*	100
1979 *Winchester Cathedral*	85	1998 *Portsmouth Cathedral*	100
1980 *Worcester Cathedral*	85	1999 *Bristol Cathedral*	10
1981 *Westminster Abbey*	85	2000 *Lincoln Cathedral*	100
1982 *St. David's Cathedral*	85	2001 *Westminster Abbey*	95
1983 *Exeter Cathedral*	85	2002 *Canterbury Cathedral*	125
1984 *Southwell Minster*	85	2002 *Proof in gold from set*	
1985 *Ripon Cathedral*	85	*(see PCGS1)*	1000
1986 *Chichester Cathedral*	85	2003 *Gloucester Cathedral*	120
1987 *Ely Cathedral*	85	2004 *Liverpool Cathedral*	120
1988 *Lichfield Cathedral*	85	2005 *Wakefield Cathedral*	120
1989 *Birmingham Cathedral*	85		

4212	**— fourpence,** 1971-96	*from*	13
4213	**— threepence,** 1971-96	*from*	13
4214	**— twopence,** 1971-96	*from*	13
4215	**— penny,** 1971-96	*from*	15

The place of distribution is shown after each date.

*Coins marked thus were originally issued in Royal Mint sets
** numbers include coins sold in sets

NICKEL-BRASS

4221   4222

	UNC £
4221 One pound (Royal Arms design). Edge DECUS ET TUTAMEN	
1983..	5
— Specimen in presentation folder (issued: 484,900)...............................	5
— Proof *FDC** £5 — Proof piedfort in silver *FDC* (Issued: 10,000) £125	
— Proof in silver *FDC* (Issued: 50,000) £35	
4222 One pound (Scottish design). Edge NEMO ME IMPUNE LACESSIT	
1984..	5
— Specimen in presentation folder (Issued: 27,960)...................................	5
— Proof *FDC** £5 — Proof piedfort in silver *FDC* (Issued: 15,000) £55	
— Proof in silver *FDC* (Issued: 44,855) £21	

CUPRO-NICKEL

4223   4224

	UNC £		UNC £		UNC £
4223 Fifty new pence (seven-sided). ℞. Britannia r.					
1969	2	1976..........................	2	1979...........................	2
1970	4	— Proof *FDC** £2		— Proof *FDC** £3	
1971 Proof *FDC** £4		1977..........................	2	1980...........................	2
1972 Proof *FDC** £5		— Proof *FDC** £2		— Proof *FDC** £2	
1974 Proof *FDC** £3		1978..........................	2	1981...........................	2
1975 Proof *FDC** £3		— Proof *FDC** £3		— Proof *FDC** £2	

4224 Accession to European Economic Community. ℞. Clasped hands, 1973..................... 1.50
—Proof *FDC*** £3

4224A—Design as 4224 above, but struck in very small numbers in silver on thicker blank. Sometimes referred to as a piedfort but not twice the weight of the regular cupro-nickel currency issue. The pieces were presented to EEC Finance Ministers, and possibly senior officials on the occasion of the United Kingdom joining the European Economic Community.. 2000

* *Coins marked thus were originally issued in Royal Mint sets as shown on page 492.*
** *Issued as an individual proof coin and in the year set shown on page 492.*

4225

4225 Fifty (50) pence. 'New' omitted. As illustration

1982 2   1983 2   1984* 3
— Proof *FDC** £2   — Proof *FDC** £2   — Proof *FDC** £2

4226

4226 Twenty-five pence. Silver Wedding Commemorative, 1972 2
— Proof *FDC** (in 1972 Set, See PS22) £4
— Silver proof in case *FDC* (Issued: 100,000) £30

4227

| | UNC |
| | £ |

4227 Twenty-five pence Silver Jubilee Commemorative, 1977 .... 1.50
— Specimen in presentation folder 2
— Proof *FDC** (in 1977 Set, See PS27) £4
— Silver proof in case *FDC* (Issued: 377,000) £22

* Coins marked thus were originally issued in Royal Mint sets

4228

4228 **Twenty-Five pence** Queen Mother 80th Birthday Commemorative, 1980   2
— Specimen in presentation folder..   3
— Silver proof in case *FDC* (issued: 83,672) £40

4229

4229 **Twenty-five pence.** Royal Wedding Commemorative, 1981   2
— Specimen in presentation folder..   3
— Silver proof in case *FDC* (Issued: 218,142) £30

4230

	UNC £		UNC £		UNC £
4230 **Twenty (20) pence.** R crowned rose					
1982	0.40	1983.........................	0.40	1984.........................	0.40
— Proof *FDC** £2		— Proof *FDC** £1		— Proof *FDC** £1	
— Proof piedfort					
in silver *FDC* (Issued: 10,000) £50					

* *Coins marked thus were originally issued in Royal Mint sets*

4231	4232

4231 Ten new pence. R. Lion passant guardant.

1968	0.30	1974	0.40	1978 Proof *FDC** £4	
1969	0.30	— Proof *FDC** £1		1979	0.50
1970	0.30	1975	0.50	— Proof *FDC** £2	
1971	0.40	— Proof *FDC** £1		1980	0.75
— Proof *FDC** £2		1976	0.50	— Proof *FDC** £1	
1972 Proof *FDC** £3		— Proof *FDC** £1		1981	0.75
1973	0.40	1977	0.50	— Proof *FDC** £1	
— Proof *FDC** £2		— Proof *FDC** £2			

4232 Ten (10) pence. As illustration

1982*	3	1983*	3	1984*	2
— Proof *FDC** £1		— Proof *FDC** £2		— Proof *FDC** £1	

4233	4234

4233 Five new pence. R. Crowned thistle

1968	0.20	1974 Proof *FDC** £2		— Proof *FDC** £1	
1969	0.30	1975	0.20	1979	0.20
1970	0.30	— Proof *FDC** £1		— Proof *FDC** £1	
1971	0.20	1976 Proof *FDC** £2		1980	0.20
— Proof *FDC** £2		1977	0.20	— Proof *FDC** £1	
1972 Proof *FDC** £2		— Proof *FDC** £1		1981 Proof *FDC** £1	
1973 Proof *FDC** £2		1978	0.20		

4234 Five (5) pence. As illustration

1982*	2	1983*	2	1984*	2
— Proof *FDC** £2		— Proof *FDC** £2		— Proof *FDC** £1	

* Coins marked thus were originally issued in Royal Mint sets.

BRONZE

4235   4236

	UNC £		UNC £		UNC £

4235 Two new pence. R. Plumes

1971	0.10	1976	0.20	— Proof *FDC** £1	
— Proof *FDC** £1		— Proof *FDC** £1		1980	0.15
1972 Proof *FDC** £2		1977	0.10	— Proof *FDC** £1	
1973 Proof *FDC** £2		— Proof *FDC** £1		1981	0.15
1974 Proof *FDC** £2		1978	0.30	— Proof *FDC** £1	
1975	0.20	— Proof *FDC** £1			
— Proof *FDC** £1		1979	0.15		

4236 Two (2) pence. As illustration

1982*	1	1983*	1	£250 .... 1984*	1
— Proof *FDC** £1		— Proof *FDC** £1		— Proof *FDC** £1	

4236A — Error reverse. The word "new" was dropped from the reverse of the currency issues in 1982 but a number of 2 pence coins were struck in 1983 with the incorrect die, similar to coins listed as 4235. Reports suggest that the error coins, or "Mules" were contained in Royal Mint uncirculated sets issued in 1983 400

4237   4238   4239   4240

4237 One new penny. R. Crowned portcullis

1971	0.10	1975	0.20	— Proof *FDC** £1	
— Proof *FDC** £1		— Proof *FDC** £1		1979	0.10
1972 Proof *FDC**£2		1976	0.20	— Proof *FDC** £1	
1973	0.20	— Proof *FDC** £1		1980	0.10
— Proof *FDC** £1		1977	0.10	— Proof *FDC** £1	
1974	0.20	— Proof *FDC** £1		1981	0.20
— Proof *FDC** £1		1978	0.20	— Proof *FDC** £1	

4238 One (1) penny. As illustration

1982	0.10	1983	0.20	1984*	1
— Proof *FDC** £1		— *FDC** £1		— Proof *FDC** £1	

4239 Half new penny. R. Crown

1971	0.10	1975	0.25	— Proof *FDC** £1	
— Proof *FDC** £1		— Proof *FDC** £1..		1979	0.10
1972 Proof *FDC** £2		1976	0.20	— Proof *FDC** £1	
1973	0.20	— Proof *FDC** £1..		1980	0.10
— Proof *FDC** £1		1977	0.10	— Proof *FDC** £1	
1974	0.20	— Proof *FDC** £1..		1981	0.20
— Proof *FDC** £1		1978	0.10	— Proof *FDC** £1	

4240 Half (1/2) penny. As illustration

1982	0.10	1983	0.25	1984*	2.00
— Proof *FDC** £1		— Proof *FDC** £1..		— Proof *FDC** £2	

* Coins marked thus were originally issued in Royal Mint sets.

The new effigy was designed by Raphael David Maklouf, FRSA. It is the third portrait of the Queen to be used on UK coinage, the previous change of portrait being in 1968 with the introduction of decimal coins. The designer's initials R.D.M. appear on the truncation. There is no portrait change on the Maundy coins (see 4211-4215).

GOLD

4251   4253

4251 **Five pounds.** R. St. George
1985 Proof *FDC* (Issued: 281) £500
1990 Proof *FDC** £525   1993 Proof *FDC** £550   1996 Proof *FDC** £550
1991 Proof *FDC** £525   1994 Proof *FDC** £550   1997 Proof *FDC** £550
1992 Proof *FDC** £550   1995 Proof *FDC** £550

4252 **Five pounds** R. St George, 'U' in a circle to left of date.

	UNC		*UNC*
1985 (Issued: 13,626)...............	£425	1993 (Issued: 906)	£450
1986 (Issued: 7,723)................	£425	1994 (Issued: 1,000)	£500
1990 (Issued: 1,226)................	£450	1995 (Issued: 1,000)	£500
1991 (Issued: 976)...................	£450	1996 (Issued: 901)	£500
1992 (Issued: 797)...................	£450	1997 (Issued: 802)	£500

4253 **Five pounds** Uncouped portrait of Queen Elizabeth II. As illustration. R. St. George, 'U' in a circle to left of date.
1987 (Issued: 5,694)............... £450   1988 (Issued: 3,315) £450

4254 **Five pounds** 500th Anniversary of Sovereign. As illustration 4277
1989 (Issued: 2,937)............... £600   — — Proof *FDC** £650

4261 **Two pounds.** R. St. George
1985 Proof *FDC** £250   1991 Proof *FDC* (Issued: 620) £250
1987 Proof *FDC* (Issued: 1,801) £225   1992 Proof *FDC* (Issued: 476) £250
1988 Proof *FDC* (Issued: 1,551) £225   1993 Proof *FDC* (Issued: 414) £250
1990 Proof *FDC* (Issued: 716)   £250   1996 Proof *FDC*   £250

4263 **Two pounds** 500th Anniversary of Sovereign. As illustration 4277
1989 Proof *FDC* (Issued: 2,000) £300

The 1986 £2, 1994 £2 and two types of 1995 £2 commemorative coins in gold previously listed as 4262, 4264, 4265 & 4266 respectively are now shown in the section commencing 4311 with their respective types in other metals.

4271 **Sovereign.** R. St. George
1985 Proof *FDC* (Issued: 11,393) £175   1992 Proof *FDC* (Issued: 4,772) £250
1986 Proof *FDC* (Issued: 5,079) £175   1993 Proof *FDC* (Issued: 4,349) £250
1987 Proof *FDC* (Issued: 9,979) £175   1994 Proof *FDC* (Issued: 4,998) £250
1988 Proof *FDC* (Issued: 7,670) £175   1995 Proof *FDC* (Issued: 7,500) £250
1990 Proof *FDC* (Issued: 4,767) £200   1996 Proof *FDC* (Issued: 7,500) £250
1991 Proof *FDC* (Issued: 4,713) £200   1997 Proof *FDC* (Issued: 7,500) £250

* Coins marked thus were originally issued in Royal Mint sets. Where numbers of coins issued or the Edition limit is quoted, these refer to individual coins. Additional coins were included in sets which are listed in the appropriate section.

4272 Sovereign. 500th Anniversary of Sovereign. As illustration 4277
1989 Proof *FDC* (Issued: 10,535) £500

4277

4276 Half-sovereign. R. St. George

1985 Proof *FDC* (Issued: 9,951) £100	1992 Proof *FDC* (Issued: 3,783) £120
1986 Proof *FDC* (Issued: 4,575) £100	1993 Proof *FDC* (Issued: 2,910) £120
1987 Proof *FDC* (Issued: 8,187) £100	1994 Proof *FDC* (Issued: 5,000) £120
1988 Proof *FDC* (Issued: 7,074) £100	1995 Proof *FDC* (Issued: 4,900) £120
1990 Proof *FDC* (Issued: 4,231) £100	1996 Proof *FDC* (Issued: 5,730) £120
1991 Proof *FDC* (Issued: 3,588) £100	1997 Proof *FDC* (Issued: 7,500) £120

4277 Half-sovereign 500th Anniversary of Sovereign. As illustration 4277
1989 Proof *FDC* (Issued: 8,888) £175

4281

UNC   *UNC*

4281 Britannia. One hundred pounds. (1oz of fine gold) R. Britannia standing.

1987	£275	— Proof *FDC* (Issued: 626) £350	
— Proof *FDC* (Issued: 2,486) £350		1989	£275
1988	£275	— Proof *FDC* (Issued: 338) £350	

4282 Britannia. One hundred pounds. (1oz of fine gold alloyed with silver) R. Britannia standing.

1990	£300	— Proof *FDC** £450	
— Proof *FDC* (Issued: 262) £350		1994	£300
1991	£300	— Proof *FDC** £450	
— Proof *FDC* (Issued: 143) £400		1995	£300
1992	£300	— Proof *FDC** £500	
— Proof *FDC** £450		1996	£300
1993	£300	— Proof *FDC** £500	

Where numbers of coins are quoted, these refer to individual coins. Additional coins were included in sets which are listed in the appropriate section.

* Coins marked thus were originally issued in Royal Mint sets.

4283

4283 **Britannia. One Hundred pounds.** (1 oz of fine gold, alloyed with silver) R. Standing figure of Britannia in horse drawn chariot. 10th Anniversary of Britannia issue

1997... £400   1997 Proof *FDC* (Issued: 164) £600

4286

4286 **Britannia. Fifty pounds.** (1/2oz of fine gold). R. Britannia standing.

1987...	£150	— Proof *FDC** £160	
— Proof *FDC* (Issued: 2,485) £160		1989	£150
1988...	£150	— Proof *FDC** £175	

4287 **Britannia. Fifty pounds.** (1/2oz of fine gold, alloyed with Silver)
R. Britannia standing.

1990...	£175	— Proof *FDC** £250	
— Proof *FDC** £200		1994	£175
1991...	£175	— Proof *FDC** £250	
— Proof *FDC** £200		1995	£175
1992...	**	— Proof *FDC** £250	
— Proof *FDC** £250		1996	£175
1993...	£175	— Proof *FDC** £250	

4288

4288 **Britannia. Fifty pounds.** (1/2 oz fine gold, alloyed with silver) R. Standing figure of Britannia in horse drawn chariot 10th Anniversary of Britannia issue
1997 Proof *FDC** £300

* *Coins marked thus were originally issued in Royal Mint sets*

** *Issues of bullion quality coins of these years were modest and should command a premium*

4291   4296

4291 Britannia. Twenty five pounds. (1/4oz of fine gold). R. Britannia standing.
1987.. £80   — Proof *FDC** £85
— Proof *FDC* (Issued: 3,500) £85   1989 .... £80
1988.. £80   — Proof *FDC** £100

4292 Britannia. Twenty five pounds. (1/4oz of fine gold alloyed with silver).
R. Britannia standing.
1990.. £100   — Proof *FDC** £135
— Proof *FDC** £120   1994 .... £80
1991.. £100   — Proof *FDC** £135
— Proof *FDC** £135   1995 .... £80
1992.. £100   — Proof *FDC** £135
— Proof *FDC** £135   1996 .... £80
1993.. ***   — Proof *FDC** £135

4293

4293 Britannia. Twenty five pounds. (1/4 oz fine gold, alloyed with silver) R. Standing figure of
Britannia in horse drawn chariot. 10th Anniversary of Britannia issue
1997 Proof *FDC* (Issued: 923) £180

4296 Britannia. Ten pounds. (1/10oz of fine gold). R. Britannia standing.
1987.. £40   — Proof *FDC* (Issued: 2,694) £50
— Proof *FDC* (Issued: 3,500) £50   1989 .... £40
1988.. £40   — Proof *FDC* (Issued: 1,609) £55

4297 Britannia. Ten pounds. (1/10oz of fine gold alloyed with silver). R. Britannia standing.
1990.. £50   — Proof *FDC* (Issued: 997)   £75
— Proof *FDC* (Issued: 1,571) £65   1994 .... **
1991.. £50   — Proof *FDC* (Issued: 994)   £75
— Proof *FDC* (Issued: 954)   £65   1995 .... £50
1992.. *   — Proof *FDC* (Issued: 1,500) £65
— Proof *FDC* (Issued: 1,000) £65   1996 .... £50
1993.. £50   — Proof *FDC* (Issued: 2,379) £65

* Coins marked thus were originally issued in Royal Mint sets.
** Issues of bullion quality coins of these years were modest and coins should command a premium
*** Extremely small numbers issued.

4298

4298 Britannia. Ten pounds. (1/10 oz fine gold, alloyed with silver) R. Standing figure of
Britannia in horse drawn chariot. 10th Anniversary of Britannia issue
1997 Proof *FDC* (Issued: 1,821) £80

SILVER

4300

4300 Britannia. Two pounds. (1 oz fine silver) R. Standing figure of Britannia in horse drawn
chariot. 10th Anniversary of Britannia issue
1997 Proof *FDC* (Issued: 4,173) £50

4300A

4300A Britannia. One pound. (1/2 oz of fine silver) R. Standing figure of Britannia in horse drawn
chariot. 10th Anniversary of Britannia issue
1997 Proof *FDC** £25

* Coins marked thus were originally issued in Royal Mint Sets.

4300B

4300B Britannia. Fifty pence. (1/4 oz of fine silver) ℞. Standing figure of Britannia in horse drawn
chariot. 10th Anniversary of Britannnia issue
1997 Proof *FDC** £20

4300C

4300C Britannia. Twenty pence. (1/4 oz of fine silver) ℞. Standing figure of Britannia in horse
drawn chariot. 10th Anniversary of Britannia issue
1997 Proof *FDC* (Issued: 8,686) £15

CUPRO-NICKEL

4301

	UNC
	£
4301 Five pounds (crown). Queen Mother 90th birthday commemorative. 1990	8
— Specimen in presentation folder (Issued: 45,250)	10
— Proof in silver *FDC* (Issued: 56,102) £50	
— Proof in gold FDC (Issued: 2,500) £650	

* Coins marked thus were originally issued in Royal Mint Sets.

4302

4302 **Five pounds (crown).** 40th Anniversary of the Coronation. 1993............................... 7
— Specimen in presentation folder.. 9
— Proof *FDC* (in 1993 set, see PS51)* £9
— Proof in silver *FDC* (Issued: 58,877) £35
— Proof in gold *FDC* (Issued: 2,500) £600

4303

4303 **Five pounds (crown).** 70th Birthday of Queen Elizabeth II. Ŗ. The Queen's personal flag, the Royal Standard, the Union Flag, two pennants bearing the dates '1926' and '1996' all against a backdrop of Windsor Castle. Edge: VIVAT REGINA ELIZABETHA.
1996.. 7
— Specimen in presentation folder (issued: 73,311)... 9
— Proof *FDC* (in 1996 set, See PS57) * £12
— Proof in silver *FDC* (Issued: 39,336) £45
— Proof in gold *FDC* (Issued: 2,127) £600

* *Coins marked thus were originally issued in Royal Mint Sets.*

4304

4304 **Five pounds (crown).** Golden Wedding of Queen Elizabeth II and Prince Philip. Conjoint
portraits of The Queen and Prince Philip. ℞. Royal Arms and Arms of Prince Philip
surmounted by St. Edward's crown which divides the dates 1947 and 1997 20 November, and
an anchor below with the denomination.

1997.. 7
— Specimen in presentation folder.. 9
— Proof *FDC* (in 1997 set, See PS59)* £12
— Proof in silver *FDC* (Issued: 33,689) £45
— Proof in gold *FDC* (Issued: 2,574) £600

NICKEL-BRASS

4311

	UNC		*UNC*
	£		£

4311 **Two pounds.** ℞. St. Andrew's cross surmounted by a thistle of Scotland. Edge XIII
COMMONWEALTH GAMES SCOTLAND 1986... 5
— Specimen in presentation folder   5   — Proof in silver *FDC* (Issued: 59,779) £35
— .500 silver (Issued: 58,881)   12   — Proof in gold *FDC* (Issued: 3,277) £225
— Proof *FDC** £6

* Coins marked thus were originally issued in Royal Mint Sets.

4312   4313

4312 **Two pounds** 300th Anniversary of Bill of Rights. R Cypher of William and Mary, House of Commons mace and St. Edward's crown.

1989....................................... 4 — Proof in silver *FDC* (Issued: 25,000) £30
— Specimen in presentation folder 5 — Proof piedfort in silver *FDC** £60
— Proof *FDC** £6

4313 **Two pounds** 300th Anniversary of Claim of Right (Scotland). R. As 4312, but with crown of Scotland.

1989....................................... 8 — Proof in silver *FDC* (Issued: 24,852) £30
— Specimen in presentation folder 10 — Proof piedfort in silver *FDC** £60
— Proof *FDC** £10

4314

4314 **Two pounds** 300th Anniversary of the Bank of England. R: Bank's original Corporate Seal, with Crown & Cyphers of William III & Mary II. Edge SIC VOS NON VOBIS.

1994....................................... 5 — Proof piedfort in silver *FDC* (Issued: 9,569) £60
— Specimen in presentation folder 5 — Proof in gold *FDC* (Issued: 1,000) £450
— Proof *FDC** £6................... — gold error. Obverse as 4251 (Included in
— Proof in silver *FDC* (Issued: 27, 957) £30   above) £1200

* *Coins marked thus were originally issued in Royal Mint sets.*

4315

UNC
£

4315 **Two pounds** 50th Anniversary of the End of World War II. ℞: A Dove of Peace.
Edge 1945 IN PEACE GOODWILL 1995
1995.. 5
— Specimen in presentation folder 5
— Proof *FDC* *£6................... — Proof piedfort in silver *FDC* (Edition: 10,000) £60
— Proof in silver *FDC* (Issued: 35,751) £30 — Proof in gold *FDC* (Issued: 2,500) £350

4316

4316 **Two pounds** 50th Anniversary of the Establishment of the United Nations. ℞: 50th
Anniversary symbol and an array of flags. Edge NATIONS UNITED FOR PEACE
1945-1995.
1995.. 5
— Specimen in presentation folder... 5
— Proof in silver *FDC* (Edition: 175,000) £30   — Proof in gold *FDC* (Edition: 17,500) £35C
— Proof piedfort in silver *FDC* (Edition: 10,000) £60

4317

4317 **Two pounds** European Football Championships. ℞: A stylised representation of a football.
Edge: TENTH EUROPEAN CHAMPIONSHIP.
1996.. 5
— Specimen in presentation folder... 5
— Proof *FDC** £6.................. — Proof piedfort in silver *FDC* (Issued: 7,634) £65
— Proof in silver *FDC* (Issued: 25,163) £35 — Proof in gold *FDC* (Issued: 2,098) £350

* Coins marked thus were originally issued in Royal Mint Sets.

4318

	UNC		*UNC*
	£		£

4318 Two pounds Bimetallic currency issue. ℞. Four concentric circles representing the Iron Age, 18th century industrial development, silicon chip, and Internet. Edge: STANDING ON THE SHOULDERS OF GIANTS

1997... 4

— Specimen in presentation folder.. 6

— Proof *FDC** £6

— Proof in silver FDC (Issued: 29,910) £29

— Proof piedfort in silver *FDC* (Issued: 10,000) £60

— Proof in gold *FDC* (Issued: 2,482) £325

4331   4332

4331 One pound (Welsh design). Edge PLEIDIOL WYF I'M GWLAD

1985.. 4

— Specimen in presentation folder (Issued: 24,850)... 4

— Proof *FDC** £5

— Proof in silver *FDC* (Issued: 50,000) £21

— Proof piedfort in silver *FDC* (Issued: 15,000) £60

1990.. 5

— Proof *FDC** £6

— Proof in silver *FDC* (Issued: 23,277) £24

4332 One pound (Northern Irish design). Edge DECUS ET TUTAMEN

1986.. 5

— Specimen in presentatioon folder (Issued: 19,908).. 5

— Proof *FDC** £4

— Proof in silver *FDC* (Issued: 37, 958) £26

— Proof piedfort in silver *FDC* (Issued: 15,000) £60

1991.. 5

— Proof *FDC** £6

— Proof in silver *FDC* (Issued: 22,922) £24

* *Coins marked thus were originally issued in Royal Mint sets.*

4333   4334

4333 One pound (English design). Edge DECUS ET TUTAMEN
1987.. 4
— Specimen in presentation folder (Issued: 72,607)...................................... 4
— Proof *FDC** £6
— Proof in silver *FDC* (Issued: 50,000) £26
— Proof piedfort in silver *FDC* (Issued: 15,000) £60
1992.. 5
— Proof *FDC** £6
— Proof in silver *FDC* (Issued: 13,065) £30

4334 One pound (Royal Shield). Edge DECUS ET TUTAMEN
1988.. 5
— Specimen in presentation folder (Issued: 29,550).................................... 5
— Proof *FDC** £6
— Proof in silver *FDC* (Issued: 50,000) £35
— Proof piedfort in silver *FDC* (Issued: 10,000) £60

4335 One pound (Scottish design). Edge NEMO ME IMPUNE LACESSIT (Illus. as 4222)
1989.......................................   5   — Proof in silver *FDC* (Issued: 22,275) £21
— Proof *FDC** £6   — Proof piedfort in silver *FDC* (Issued: 10,000) £60

4336 One pound (Royal Arms design). Edge DECUS ET TUTAMEN (Illus. as 4221)
1993.......................................   5   — Proof in silver *FDC* (Issued: 16,526) £30
— Proof *FDC** £6   — Proof piedfort in silver *FDC* (Issued: 12,500) £60

4337   4338   4339   4340

4337 One pound (Scottish design). Ɍ: Lion rampant within a double tressure. Edge NEMO ME
IMPUNE LACESSIT
1994.......................................   4   — Proof in silver *FDC* (Issued: 25,000) £30
— Specimen in presentation folder   5   — Proof piedfort in silver *FDC* (Issued: 11,722) £60
— Proof *FDC** £6

4338 One pound (Welsh design). Ɍ. Heraldic dragon Edge PLEIDIOL WYF I'M GWLAD
1995.......................................   4
— Specimen in presentation folder (Issued: 23,728) £5
— Proof *FDC** £5
— Proof in silver *FDC* (Issued: 27,445) £26
— Proof in piedfort in silver *FDC* (Issued: 8,458) £60

* *Coins marked thus were originally issued in Royal Mint sets.*

4339 **One pound** (Northern Irish design). R. A Celtic cross incorporating a pimpernel at its centre.
Edge DECUS ET TUTAMEN

1996.. 4 — Proof in silver *FDC* (Issued: 25,000) £26
— Specimen in presentation folder 6 — Proof piedfort in silver *FDC* (Issued: 10,000) £50
— Proof *FDC** £6

4340 **One pound** (English design) R. Three lions. Edge: DECUS ET TUTAMEN.

1997.. 4
— Specimen in presentation folder (Issued 56,996) £5
— Proof *FDC** £5
— Proof in silver *FDC* (Issued: 20,137) £26
— Proof piedfort in silver *FDC* (Issued: 10,000) £50

CUPRO-NICKEL

4351

4351 **Fifty pence.** R. Britannia r. (4341)

1985	5	— Proof *FDC** £3....		1995*........................		3
— Proof *FDC** £3		1990*........................	4	— Proof *FDC** £4		
1986*...............	3	— Proof *FDC** £5....		1996*........................		3
— Proof *FDC** £3		1991*........................	4	— Proof *FDC** £4		
1987*...............	3	— Proof *FDC** £5....		— Proof in silver *FDC** £15		
— Proof *FDC** £3		1992*........................	4	1997........................		3
1988*...............	3	— Proof *FDC** £5....		— Proof *FDC** £4		
— Proof *FDC** £4		1993*........................	4	— Proof in silver *FDC** £24		
1989*...............	4	— Proof *FDC** £4				

4352

4352 **Fifty pence** Presidency of the Council of European Community Ministers and completion of
the Single Market. R. Conference table top and twelve stars

1992-1993 .... 7 — Proof piedfort in silver *FDC* (Issued: 10,993) £45
— Proof *FDC** £10................ — Proof in gold *FDC* (Issued: 1,864) £400
— Proof in silver *FDC** (Issued: 26,890) £24

4352A— Specimen in presentation folder with 1992 date 4351 10

* *Coins marked thus were originally issued in Royal Mint sets.*

4353

4353 Fifty pence 50th Anniversary of the Normandy Landings on D-Day. R: Allied Invasion Force.

1994... 2

— Specimen in presentation folder 3

— Proof *FDC** £5

— Proof in silver *FDC* (Issued: 40,000) £30

— Proof piedfort in silver *FDC* (Issued: 10,000) £50

— Proof in gold *FDC* (Issued: 1,877) £425

4354 Fifty pence R. Britannia: diam 27.3mm

1997... 1

— Proof *FDC** £4

— Proof in silver *FDC* (Issued: 1,632) £27

— Proof piedfort in silver *FDC* (Issued: 7,192) £46

4361

4361 Twenty pence. R. Crowned double rose

1985		— Proof *FDC** £3.....	1994...........................
— Proof *FDC** £2		1990...........................	— Proof *FDC** £3
1986*	1	— Proof *FDC** £3.....	1995...........................
— Proof *FDC** £2		1991...........................	— Proof *FDC** £3
1987		— Proof *FDC** £3.....	1996...........................
— Proof *FDC** £2		1992...........................	— Proof *FDC** £3
1988		— Proof *FDC** £3.....	— Proof in silver *FDC** £15
— Proof *FDC** £3		1993...........................	1997...........................
1989		— Proof *FDC** £3.....	— Proof *FDC** £3

4366

	UNC		*UNC*		*UNC*
	£		£		£

4366 Ten pence. R. Lion passant guardant

1985*	3	1988*........................	3	1991*........................	4
— Proof *FDC* * £2		— Proof *FDC** £3....		— Proof *FDC** £3	
1986*	2	1989*........................	4	1992*........................	3
— Proof *FDC** £2		— Proof *FDC** £3.....		— Proof *FDC** £4	
1987*	3	1990*........................	4	— Proof in silver *FDC** £14	
— Proof *FDC** £3		— Proof *FDC** £3			

* *Coins marked thus were originally issued in Royal Mint sets.*

4367

4367 **Ten pence** R Lion passant guardant: diam. 24.5mm

1992..	1995......................
— Proof *FDC** £3..................	— Proof *FDC** £2
— Proof in silver *FDC** £14..	1996......................
— Proof piedfort in silver *FDC** (Issued: 14,167) £40	— Proof *FDC** £2
1993*......................................	— Proof in silver *FDC** £15
— Proof *FDC** £2..................	1997......................
1994*......................................	— Proof *FDC** £2
— Proof *FDC** £2..................	

4371

4371 **Five pence.** R. Crowned thistle

1985*...............	1	— Proof *FDC** £2....	1990*......................... 2
— Proof *FDC** £1		1988...........................	— Proof *FDC** £3
1986*...............	1	— Proof *FDC** £2....	— Proof in silver *FDC** £12
— Proof *FDC** £1		1989...........................	
1987..................		— Proof *FDC** £2	

4372

4372 **Five pence.** R. Crowned thistle: diam 18mm

1990..................	1992	— Proof *FDC** £2
— Proof *FDC** £2	— Proof *FDC** £2....	1996...........................
— Proof in silver *FDC** £12	1993*.........................	— Proof *FDC** £2
— Proof piedfort in silver	— Proof *FDC** £2....	— Proof in silver *FDC** £15
FDC (Issued: 20,000) £25	1994...........................	1997...........................
1991	— Proof *FDC** £2....	— Proof *FDC** £2
— Proof *FDC** £2	1995...........................	

* *Coins marked thus were originally issued in Royal Mint sets.*

BRONZE

4376   4381

4376 Two pence. R. Plumes

1985	1988	1991 ....
— Proof *FDC** £1	— Proof *FDC** £1....	— Proof *FDC** £1
1986	1989	1992* ....
— Proof *FDC** £1	— Proof *FDC** £1....	— Proof *FDC** £1
1987	1990	
— Proof *FDC** £1	— Proof *FDC** £1	

4381 One penny. R. Portcullis with chains

1985	1988	1991 ....
— Proof *FDC** £1	— Proof *FDC** £1....	— Proof *FDC** £1
1986	1989	1992* ....
— Proof *FDC** £1	— Proof *FDC** £1....	— Proof *FDC** £1
1987	1990	
— Proof *FDC** £1	— Proof *FDC** £1	

COPPER PLATED STEEL

4386 Two pence R. Plumes

1992	— Proof *FDC** £1....	— Proof *FDC** £1
1993	1995	— Proof in silver *FDC** £15
— Proof *FDC** £1	— Proof *FDC** £1....	1997 ....
1994	1996	— Proof *FDC** £1

4391 One penny R. Portcullis with chains

1992	— Proof *FDC** £1....	— Proof *FDC** £1
1993	1995	— Proof in silver *FDC** £15
— Proof *FDC** £1	— Proof *FDC** £1....	1997 ....
1994	1996	— Proof *FDC** £1

* Coins marked thus were originally issued in Royal Mint sets.

GOLD

4400

4400 Five pounds. ℞. St.George
1998 Proof *FDC** £650 1999 Proof *FDC** £650 2004 Proof *FDC** £650
2000 Bullion type £350 2001 Proof *FDC** £650 — Unc £500
— Proof *FDC** £650 2003 Proof *FDC** £650
— Unc (Issued: 762) £500

4401   4402

4401 Five pounds. ℞. Shield, as illustration
2002 Proof *FDC** £600   Unc (Issued: 1,370) £535

4402 Five pounds. ℞. St.George
2005 Proof *FDC*⁺ £650

4410 Five pounds. ℞. St. George, 'U' in a circle to left of date
1998 (Issued: 825) £500   2000 (Issued: 994) £500
1999 (Issued: 970) £500   2001 (Issued: 1,000) £500

4420 Two pounds. ℞. St. George
1998 Proof *FDC** £300   2003 Proof *FDC** £300
2000 Proof *FDC** £300   2004 Proof *FDC** £300

4421 Two pounds. ℞. Shield
2002 Proof *FDC** £300

4422 Two pounds. ℞. St.George
2005 Proof *FDC** £300

4430 Sovereign. ℞. St.George
1998 Proof *FDC* (Issued: 10,000) £200   2003 Bullion type......................£80
1999 Proof *FDC* (Issued: 10,000) £200   — Proof *FDC* (Issued: 12,166) £130
2000 Bullion type (Issued: 139,961) £85   2004 Bullion type......................£80
— Proof *FDC* (Issued: 9,909) £150   — Proof *FDC* (Edition:15,000) £130
2001 Bullion type £85
— Proof *FDC* (Issued: 8,915) £150

4431 Sovereign. R. Shield
        2002 (issued: 80,499 ....   £85
        - Proof *FDC* (Issued: 12,500) £220

4432 Sovereign. R. St.George
        2005 Bullion type.........£85
        - Proof FDC (Edition 12,500) £140

4440 Half sovereign. R. St.George
        1998 Proof FDC (Issued: 6,147) £120
        1999 Proof FDC (Issued: 7,500) £150
        2000 Bullion type (Issued: 157,101) £50
        - Proof FDC (Issued: 7,458) £80
        2001 Bullion type £50
        - Proof FDC (Issued: 4,596) £80

        2003 Bullion type......................£43
        -   Proof FDC (Issued: 4,622)   £75
        2004 Bullion type......................£43
        -   Proof FDC (Edition:10,000)   £78

4441 Half Sovereign. R. Shield
        2002 (issued: 62,540)........£55
        - Proof *FDC* (Issued: 10,000) £120

4442 Half sovereign. R. St.George
        2005 Bullion type.........£45
        - Proof FDC (Edition 7,500) £80

4450

4450 Britannia. One Hundred pounds. (1oz fine gold alloyed with silver) R. Standing figure of Britannia
        1998 Proof *FDC** £500   2000 Proof *FDC** £500
        1999 ....£300   2002 Proof *FDC* * £500
        1999 Proof *FDC** £500   2004 Proof *FDC** £500
        2000 ....£300

4451

4451 Britannia. One Hundred pounds. (1oz fine gold alloyed with silver) R. Helmeted figure of
Britannia holding a trident and a shield with a lion in the background
        2001 ....£350   2001 Proof *FDC** £500

* Coins marked thus were originally issued in Royal Mint sets.

4452

4452 Britannia. One Hundred pounds. (1oz fine gold alloyed with silver) R. Helmeted figure of Britannia with stylised waves

2003 ....£350   2003 Proof *FDC** £500

4453

4453 Britannia. One Hundred pounds. (1oz fine gold alloyed with silver) R. Seated figure of Britannia facing left

2005 Proof *FDC* * £500

4460

4460 Britannia. Fifty pounds. (1/2 oz fine gold alloyed with silver) R. Standing figure of Britannia

1998 Proof *FDC** £275   2000 Proof *FDC** £275
1999......................£160   2002 Proof *FDC* * £275
1999 Proof *FDC** £275   2004 Proof *FDC* * £275
2000......................£160

4461 Britannia. Fifty pounds. (1/2 oz fine gold alloyed with silver) R. Helmeted figure of Britannia holding a trident and a shield with a lion in the background (see 4451)

2001 ....£220   2001 Proof *FDC** £275

4462 Britannia. Fifty pounds. (1/2 oz fine gold alloyed with silver) R. Helmeted figure of Britannia with stylised waves (see 4452)

2003 Proof *FDC** £250

4463 Britannia. Fifty pounds. (1/2 oz fine gold alloyed with silver) R. Seated figure of Britannia facing left

2005 Proof *FDC* * £275

* Coins marked thus were originally issued in Royal Mint sets.

4470

4470 **Britannia. Twenty five pounds.** (1/4 oz fine gold alloyed with silver) ℞. Standing figure of Britannia

1998 Proof *FDC* (Issued: 560) £125
1999 ....£100
1999 Proof *FDC* (Issued: 1,000) £125
2000 ....£100

2000 Proof *FDC* (Issued: 500) £125
2002 Proof *FDC* (Issued: 750) £125
2004 Proof *FDC* (Edition: 750) £120

4471 **Britannia. Twenty five pounds.** (1/4 oz fine gold alloyed with silver) ℞. Helmeted figure of Britannia holding a trident and a shield with a lion in the background (see 4451)

2001................................£100   2001 Proof *FDC* (Issued: 500) £125

4472 **Britannia. Twenty five pounds.** (1/4 oz fine gold alloyed with silver) ℞. Helmeted figure of Britannia with stylised waves (see 4452)

2003 Proof *FDC* (Issued: 604) £115

4473 **Britannia. Twenty five pounds.** (1/4 oz fine gold alloyed with silver) ℞. Seated figure of Britannia facing left

2005 Proof *FDC* (Issued: 750) £135

4480 **Britannia. Ten pounds.** (1/10 oz fine gold alloyed with silver) ℞. Standing figure of Britannia

1998 Proof *FDC* (Issued: 392) £60
1999 ....£50
1999 Proof *FDC* (Issued: 1,058) £60
2000 ....£50

2000 Proof *FDC* (Issued: 659) £60
2002 ....£50
2002 Proof *FDC* (Issued: 1,500) £125
2004 Proof *FDC* (Edition: 1,500) £70

4481 **Britannia. Ten pounds.** (1/10 oz fine gold alloyed with silver) ℞. Helmeted figure of Britannia holding a trident and a shield with a lion in the background (see 4451)

2001................................£50   2001 Proof *FDC* (Issued: 1,557) £65

4482 **Britannia. Ten pounds.** (1/10 oz fine gold alloyed with silver) ℞. Helmeted figure of Britannia with stylised waves (see 4452)

2003 ....£50   2003 Proof *FDC* (Issued: 1,351) £65

4483 **Britannia. Ten pounds.** (1/10 oz fine gold alloyed with silver) ℞. Seated figure of Britannia facing left

2005 Proof *FDC* (Edition: 1,500) £75

SILVER

4500

4500 **Britannia. Two pounds.** (1 oz of fine silver) ℞. Standing figure of Britannia

1998 (Issued: 88,909) £15
- Proof *FDC* (Issued: 2,168) £50
2000 (Issued: 81,301) £15

2002 (Issued: 36,543) £15
2004 (Edition: 100,000) £14
- Proof *FDC* (Edition: 5,000) £40

4501 **Britannia. Two pounds.** (1 oz of fine silver) R. Standing figure of Britannia in
horse drawn chariot (Illus. as 4300)
1999 (Issued: 69,394) £12

4502 **Britannia. Two pounds.** (1 oz of fine silver) R. Helmeted figure of Britannia holding a
trident and a shield with a lion in the background (see 4451)
2001 (Issued: 44,816) £13   — Proof *FDC* (Issued: 3,047) £45

4503

4503 **Britannia. Two pounds.** (1oz fine silver) R. Helmeted figure of Britannia with stylised waves
2003 (Issued: 73,271) £13   — Proof *FDC* (Issued: 1,833) £37

4504

4504 **Britannia. Two pounds.** (1 oz of fine silver) R. Seated figure of Britannia facing left
2005 (Edition: 100,000) £14
Proof *FDC* (Edition: 2,500) £43

4510

4510 **Britannia. One pound.** (1/2 oz of fine silver) R. Standing figure of Britannia
1998 — Proof *FDC** £25

* Coins marked thus were originally issued in Royal Mint sets.

4511 Britannia. One pound. (1/2 oz of fine silver) R. Helmeted figure of Britannia holding a trident and a shield with a lion in the background (see 4451)
2001 — Proof *FDC** £25

4512 Britannia. One pound. (1/2 oz fine silver) R. Helmeted figure of Britannia with stylised wave (see 4503)
2003 — Proof *FDC** £25

4513 Britannia. One pound. (1/2 oz of fine silver) R. Seated figure of Britannia facing left
2005 – Proof *FDC**

4514 Britannia. Fifty pence. (1/4 oz of fine silver) R. Seated figure of Britannia facing left
2005 – Proof *FDC**

4515 Britannia. Twenty pence. (1/10 oz of fine silver) R. Seated figure of Britannia facing left
2005 – Proof *FDC**

4520

4520 Britannia. Fifty pence. (1/4 oz of fine silver) R. Standing figure of Britannia
1998 — Proof *FDC** £20

4521 Britannia. Fifty pence. (1/4 oz of fine silver) R. Helmeted figure of Britannia holding a trident and a shield with a lion in the background (see 4451)
2001 — Proof *FDC** £20

4522 Britannia. Fifty pence. (1/4 oz fine silver) R. Helmeted figure of Britannia with stylised wave (see 4503)
2003 — Proof *FDC** £20

4530

4530 Britannia. Twenty pence. (1/10 oz of fine silver) R. Standing figure of Britannia
1998 — Proof *FDC* (Issued: 2,724) £15

4531 Britannia. Twenty pence. (1/10 oz of fine silver) R. Helmeted figure of Britannia holding a trident and a shield with a lion in the background (see 4451)
2001 — Proof *FDC* (Edition: 10,000) £18

4532 Britannia. Twenty pence. (1/10 oz fine silver) R. Helmeted figure of Britannia with stylised wave (see 4503)
2003 — Proof *FDC* (Issued: 1,003) £18

* *Coins marked thus were originally issued in Royal Mint sets.*

CUPRO-NICKEL

4550

4550 Five pounds (crown). Prince of Wales 50th Birthday. ℞. Portrait of The Prince of Wales with the inscriptions 'The Prince's Trust' and 'Helping young people to succeed' on a ribbon at the base of the portrait with the denomination 'Five Pounds' and the dates 1948 and 1998. 1998.. £7
— Specimen in presentation folder £10
— Proof *FDC* (in 1998 set, see PS 61)* £12
— Proof in silver *FDC* (Issued: 13,379) £60
— Proof in gold *FDC* (Issued: 773) £650

4551

4551 Five pounds (crown). Diana, Princess of Wales Memorial. ℞. Portrait of Diana, Princess of Wales with the inscription 'In memory of Diana, Princess of Wales' with the denomination 'Five Pounds' and the dates 1961 and 1997
1999.. £7
— Specimen in presentation folder £10
— Proof *FDC* (in 1999 set, see PS63)* £12
— Proof in silver *FDC* (Issued: 49,545) £45
— Proof in gold *FDC* (Issued: 7,500) £650

* Coins marked thus were originally issued in Royal Mint sets.

4552   4552A

4552 Five pounds (crown). Millennium commemorative. R. In the centre, on a patterned circle, a
representation of the British Isles with a pair of clock hands emanating from Greenwich, set
at 12 o'clock with the inscription 'Anno Domini' with the denomination 'Five Pounds' and
the dates 1999 and 2000

1999...   £7

— Specimen in presentation folder £10
— Proof in silver *FDC* (Issued: 49,057) £30
— Proof in gold *FDC* (Issued: 2,500) £600

2000...   £7

— Specimen in presentation folder £10
— Proof *FDC* (in 2000 set, see PS65)* £12
— Proof in gold *FDC* (Issued: 1,487) £600

4552A — Specimen in presentation folder with Dome mint mark £15

(See illustration above - the mintmark is located within the shaded area at 3 o'clock).

4552B —Proof in silver *FDC* (Issued: 14,255) £45

(The reverse design is the same as the 1999 issue but with the British Isles coloured with 22
carat gold)

4553

4553 Five pounds (crown). Queen Mother commemorative. R Portrait of the Queen Mother
with Inscription "Queen Elizabeth the Queen Mother" and cheering crowds in 19th
Century and modern day dress with the Queen Mother's signature below and the
denomination 'Five Pounds' and the dates 1900 and 2000.

2000..   £7

— Specimen in presentation folder £10
— Proof in silver *FDC* (Issued: 31,316) £35
— Proof piedfort in silver *FDC* (Issued: 14,850) £40
— Proof in gold *FDC* (Issued: 3,000) £650

* Coins marked thus were originally issued in Royal Mint sets.

4554

4554 **Five pounds** (crown) Victorian anniversary. R. A classic portrait of the young Queen Victoria based on the Penny Black postage stamp with a V representing Victoria, and taking the form of railway lines and in the background the iron framework of the Crystal Palace, and the denomination "Five Pounds" and the dates 1901 and 2001.

2001.. £7
— Specimen in presentation folder £10
— Proof *FDC* (in 2001 set, see PS68)* £10
— Proof in silver *FDC* (Issued: 19,216) £40
— Proof in gold *FDC* (Issued: 2,098) £600

4554A — Proof in silver *FDC* with "reverse frosting" giving matt appearance.
(Issued: 596 – issued with sovereigns of 1901 and 2001)* £100

4554B — Proof in gold *FDC* with "reverse frosting" giving matt appearance.
(Issued: 733 – issued with four different type sovereigns of Victoria, - Young Head with shield, and St.George reverse, Jubilee Head and Old Head.)* £750

4555

4555 **Five pounds.** (crown) Golden Jubilee commemorative 2002. O. New portrait of The Queen with the denomination "Five pounds". R. Equestrian portrait of the The Queen with the inscription "Elizabeth II DEI GRA REGINA FID DEF" around the circumference and "AMOR POPULI PRAESIDIUM REG" within, and the date 2002 below separated by the central element of the Royal Arms

2002.. £5
— Specimen in presentation folder £10
— Proof *FDC* (in 2002 set, see PS 72)* £10
— Proof in silver *FDC* (Issued: 54,012) £35
— Proof in gold *FDC* (Issued: 3,272) £650

* *Coins marked thus were originally issued in Royal Mint sets.*

4556

4556 Five pounds, (crown) Queen Mother memorial 2002. R. Three quarter portrait of the Queen
Mother within a wreath with the inscription "QUEEN ELIZABETH THE QUEEN
MOTHER" and the dates 1900 and 2002, with an edge inscription "STRENGTH, DIGNITY
AND LAUGHTER"
2002...£5
— Specimen in presentation folder £15
— Proof in silver *FDC* (Issued: 16,117) £45
— Proof in gold *FDC* (Issued: 2,086) £575

4557

4557 Five pounds. (crown) Coronation commemorative 2003. O. Profile portrait of The Queen in
linear form facing right with the inscription "Elizabeth II DEI GRA REGINA F D ". R. In
the centre the inscription "GOD SAVE THE QUEEN" surrounded by the inscription
"CORONATION JUBILEE" the denomination "FIVE POUNDS" and the date 2003.
2003.. £5
— Specimen in presentation folder £10
— Proof *FDC* (in 2003 set, see PS 78)* £10
— Proof in silver *FDC* (Issued: 27,350) £35
— Proof in gold *FDC* (Issued: 1,860) £575

* Coins marked thus were originally issued in Royal Mint sets.

4558

4558 Five pounds. (crown) Centenary of Entende Cordiale 2004. R. In the centre the head
and shoulders of Britannia and her French counterpart Marianne with the inscription
"Entende Cordiale" separated by the dates "1904" and "2004"
2004 ....£5
— Specimen in presentation folder £10
— Proof *FDC* (Edition: 50,000) £14
— Proof in silver *FDC* (Edition: 15,000) £35
— Proof Piedfort in silver *FDC* (Issued: 2,500) £150
— Proof in gold *FDC* (Edition: 1,500) £575
— Proof Piedfort in platinum *FDC* (Edition: 501) £2,995

4559

4559 Five pounds. (crown) Two hundredth anniversary of the Battle of Trafalgar 2005. R. In
the centre the Royal Navy ships Victory and Temeraine as viewed from the French fleet
the dates "1805" and "2005" and "Trafalgar" with the edge inscription "England expects
that every man will do his duty"
2005...£5
— Specimen in presentation folder £10
— Proof *FDC* (in 2005 set, see PS84)*
— Proof in silver *FDC* (Edition: 30,000) £35
— Proof piedfort in silver *FDC* (see PSS21)*
— Proof in gold *FDC* (Edition: 1,805) £555

* Coins marked thus were originally issued in Royal Mint sets.

4560

4560 Five pounds. (crown) Two hundredth anniversary of the death of Nelson 2005. R. In the
centre a portrait of Nelson with the dates "1805" and "2005" and "Horatio Nelson" with
the edge inscription "England expects that every man will do his duty"
2005..£5
— Specimen in presentation folder £10
— Proof *FDC* (in 2005 set, see PS84)*
— Proof in silver *FDC* (Edition: 30,000) £35
— Proof piedfort in silver *FDC* (see PSS21)*
— Proof in gold *FDC* (Edition: 1,805) £555

NICKEL-BRASS

4570

4570 Two pounds. Bimetallic currency issue. R. Four concentric circles, representing the Iron
Age, 18th century industrial development, silicon chip and Internet. Edge: STANDING OF
THE SHOULDERS OF GIANTS
1998.. £4
— Proof *FDC** £6
— Proof in silver *FDC* (Issued: 19,978) £29
— Proof piedfort in silver *FDC* (Issued: 7,646) £50
1999.. £4
2000   2001
— Proof *FDC** £6   — Proof *FDC** £6
— Proof in silver *FDC** £30
2002
— Proof *FDC* (in 2002 set, see PS72)* £6
— Proof in gold *FDC* (in 2002 set, see PGJS1)* £300

* Coins marked thus were originally issued in Royal Mint sets.

4571

4571 **Two pounds.** Rugby World Cup. ℞. In the centre a rugby ball and goal posts surrounded by a styalised stadium with the denomination 'Two Pounds' and the date 1999

1999... £4
— Specimen in presentation folder £6
— Proof *FDC* (in 1999 set, see PS63)* £6
— Proof in silver *FDC* (Issued: 9,665) £35
— Proof piedfort in silver *FDC* (Issued: 10,000) £150
— Proof in gold *FDC* (Issued: 311) £350

4572

4572 **Two pounds.** Marconi commemorative. ℞. Decorative radio waves emanating from a spark of electricity linking the zeros of the date to represent the generation of the signal that crossed the Atlantic with the date 2001 and the denomination "Two Pounds". Edge: WIRELESS BRIDGES THE ATLANTIC... MARCONI 1901

2001
— Specimen in presentation folder £7
— Proof *FDC* (in 2001 set, see PS68)* £10
— Proof in silver *FDC* (Issued: 11,488) £29
— Proof piedfort in silver *FDC* (Issued: 6,759) £35
— Proof in gold *FDC* (Issued: 1,658) £325
4572A— Proof in silver *FDC*, with reverse frosting. (Issued: 14,803 in a 2-coin set with a Canadian $5 Marconi silver proof) £29

---

* *Coins marked thus were originally issued in Royal Mint sets.*

4573   4574

4573 Two pounds. Commonwealth Games commemorative. England. ℞. A moving figure of an athlete holding a banner, the top of which being divided into lines to symbolise lanes of a running track or swimming pool with a cameo of the English flag and the inscription "XVII Commonwealth Games 2002" and the denomination "£2". Edge inscription SPIRIT OF FRIENDSHIP. MANCHESTER 2002.

2002...

— Specimen (in Presentation set, see US24)*£6

— Proof *FDC* (in set, see PS76)* £8

— Proof in Silver *FDC* (in set, see PSS12)* £35

— Proof in gold *FDC* (in set, see PCGS1)* £350

4573A As above but with colour added to the flag and parts of the banner, Proof Piedfort in Silver *FDC* (in set, see PSS13)* £60

4574 Two pounds. Commonwealth Games commemorative. ℞. Northern Ireland. As above but with a cameo of the Northern Ireland flag. Edge inscription SPIRIT OF FRIENDSHIP. MANCHESTER 2002.

2002...

— Specimen (in Presentation set, see US24)* £6

— Proof *FDC* (in set, see PS76)* £8

— Proof in Silver *FDC* (in set, see PSS12)* £35

— Proof in gold *FDC* (in set, see PCGS1)* £350

4574A As above but with colour added to the flag and parts of the banner, Proof Piedfort in Silver *FDC* (in set, see PSS13)* £60

4575   4576

4575 Two pounds. Commonwealth Games commemorative. ℞. Scotland. As above but with a cameo of the Scottish flag. Edge inscription SPIRIT OF FRIENDSHIP. MANCHESTER 2002.

2002...

— Specimen (in Presentation set, see US24)* £6

— Proof *FDC* (in set, see PS76)* £8

— Proof in Silver *FDC* (in set, see PSS12)* £35

— Proof in gold *FDC* (in set, see PCGS1)* £350

4575A As above but with colour added to the flag and parts of the banner, Proof Piedfort in Silver *FDC* (in set, see PSS13)* £60

* Coins marked thus were originally issued in Royal Mint sets.

4576 Two pounds. Commonwealth Games commemorative. ℞. Wales. As above but with a cameo
of the Welsh flag. Edge inscription SPIRIT OF FRIENDSHIP. MANCHESTER 2002.
2002...
— Specimen (in Presentation set, see US24)* £6
— Proof *FDC* (in set, see PS76)* £8
— Proof in Silver *FDC* (in set, see PSS12)* £35
— Proof in gold *FDC* (in set, see PCGS1)* £350
4576A As above but with colour added to the flag and parts of the banner, Proof Piedfort in Silver
FDC (in set, see PSS13)* £60

4577

4577 Two pounds. Discovery of the structure of DNA. England. ℞. In the centre the spiraling
double helix structure of DNA with the inscription "DNA DOUBLE HELIX" and the dates
1953 and 2003 separated by the denomination "TWO POUNDS". Edge:
DEOXYRIBONUCLEIC ACID
2003...
— Specimen in presentation folder £7
— Proof *FDC* (in set, see PS78)*
— Proof in Silver *FDC* (Issued: 9,974) £30
— Proof piedfort in silver *FDC* (Issued: 8,632) £50
— Proof in gold *FDC* (Issued: 1,434) £325

4578

4578 Two pounds. ℞.In the centre a depiction of Trevithick's Locomotive Penydarren and the
denomination "Two Pounds" surrounded by a cog representing the Industrial Revolution and
the inscription "R.Trevithick 1804 Invention Industry Progress 2004" Patterned Edge.
2004 ....
— Specimen in presentation folder £7
— Brilliant uncirculated in silver (Edition: 50,000) £15
— Proof *FDC* (in 2004 set, see PS81)*
— Proof in Silver *FDC* (Edition: 25,000) £30
— Proof piedfort in silver *FDC* (Edition: 10,000) £50
— Proof in gold *FDC* (5,000) £350

* Coins marked thus were originally issued in Royal Mint sets.

4579

4579 Two pounds. 400th Anniversary of the Gunpowder Plot. R. In the centre in a circular
arrangement the symbols of state the mace, crosier and sword the denomination "Two
Pounds" and the dates "1605 and 2005" with the edge inscription "Remember remember
the fifth of November".
2005.....................................
— Specimen in presentation folder £7
— Proof *FDC* (in 2005 set, see PS84)*
— Proof in Silver *FDC* (Edition: 10,000) £30
— Proof piedfort in silver *FDC* (Edition: 5,000) £50
— Proof in gold *FDC* (1,500) £325

4580

4580 Two pounds. 60th Anniversary of the end of World War II. R. In the centre a depiction
of the front of St.Paul's Cathedral in full floodlights with the denomination "Two
Pounds" and the dates "1945 and 2005" with the edge inscription "In Victory
magnanimity in peace goodwill".
2005.....................................
— Specimen in presentation folder with medal £10
— Proof *FDC* (in 2005 set, see PS84)*
— Proof in Silver *FDC* (Edition: 25,000) £30
— Proof piedfort in silver *FDC* (Edition: 5,000) £50
— Proof in gold *FDC* (3,500) £325

4590

4590 One pound (Royal Arms design). Edge: DECUS ET TUTAMEN (Illus. as 4221)
1998*... £10
— Proof *FDC** £6
— Proof in silver *FDC* (Issued: 13,863) £30
— Proof piedfort in silver *FDC* (Issued: 7,894) £45
2003 ....
— Proof *FDC* (in 2003 set, see PS78)*
— Proof in silver *FDC* (Issued: 14,235) £30
— Proof piedfort in silver *FDC* (Issued: 9,508) £49

4591 **One pound.** (Scottish lion design). Edge: NEMO ME IMPUNE LACESSIT (Illus as 4337)
1999..
— Specimen in presentation folder £4
— Proof *FDC* (in 1999 set, see PS63)* £6
— Proof in silver *FDC* (Issued: 16,328) £30
— Proof piedfort in silver *FDC* (Issued: 9,975) £45
4591A— Proof in silver *FDC*, with reverse frosting, (Issued: 1,994)* £40
4592 **One pound.** (Welsh design). Edge: PLEIDIOL WYF I'M GWLAD (Illus. as 4338)
2000..
— Proof *FDC* (in 2000 set, see PS65)* £6
— Proof in silver *FDC* (Issued: 15,913) £30
— Proof piedfort in silver *FDC* (Issued: 9,994) £47
4592A— Proof in silver *FDC*, with reverse frosting, (Issued: 1,994)* £50
4593 **One pound.** (Northern Irish design). Edge: DECUS ET TUTAMEN (Illus. as 4339)
2001 ....
— Proof *FDC** £6
— Proof in silver *FDC* (Issued: 11,697) £30
— Proof piedfort in silver *FDC* (Issued: 8,464) £35
4593A— Proof in silver *FDC*, with reverse frosting, (Issued: 1,540)* £55
4594 **One pound.** (English design) Edge: DECUS ET TUTAMEN (Illus. as 4340)
2002
— Proof *FDC* (in 2002 set, see PS72)* £6
— Proof in silver *FDC* (Issued: 17,693) £30
— Proof piedfort in silver *FDC* (Issued: 6,559) £49
— Proof in gold *FDC* (in 2002 set, see PGJS1)* £300
4594A— Proof in silver *FDC*, with reverse frosting, (Issued: 1,540)* £55

4595   4595A

4595 **One pound.** Scotland R. In the centre a depiction of the Forth Rail Bridge and the
denomination "One Pound" and a border representing a railway track. Patterned Edge.
2004 ....
— Specimen in presentation folder £5
— Proof *FDC* (in 2004 set, see PS81)* £6
— Proof in silver *FDC* (Edition: 25,000) £27
— Proof piedfort in silver *FDC* (Edition: 10,000) £49
— Proof in gold *FDC* (Edition; 5,000) £345
4595A **One pound pattern.** Scotland. Design as 4595 above but dated 2003 with plain edge and
hallmark
— Proof in silver *FDC* *
— Proof in gold *FDC* *

* Coins marked thus were originally issued in Royal Mint sets.

4595B   4596

4595B One pound pattern. Scotland. R. Unicorn with the word "Pattern" below with plain edge and hallmark
— Proof in silver *FDC* *
— Proof in gold *FDC* *

4596 One pound. Wales. R. Menai Straits Bridge and the denomination "One pound"
— Specimen in presentation folder £6
— Proof *FDC* (in 2004 set, see PS84)* £6
— Proof in silver *FDC* (Edition: 15,000) £28
— Proof piedfort in silver *FDC* (Edition: 7,500) £50
— Proof in gold *FDC* (Edition: 1,500) £345

4596A   4596B

4596A One pound pattern. Wales. R. Menai Straits Bridge but dated 2003 with plain edge and hallmark
— Proof in silver *FDC* *
— Proof in gold *FDC* *

4596B One pound pattern. Wales. R Dragon and the word "Pattern" below with plain edge and hallmark
— Proof in silver *FDC* *
— Proof in gold *FDC* *

4597A   4597B

4597A One pound pattern. Northern Ireland. R.MacNeill's Egyptian Arch with plain edge and hallmark
4597A   4598A
— Proof in silver *FDC* *
— Proof in gold *FDC* *

4597B One pound pattern. Northern Ireland. R Stag and the word "Pattern" below with plain edge and hallmark
— Proof in silver *FDC* *
— Proof in gold *FDC* *

* Coins marked thus were originally issued in Royal Mint sets.

4598A 4598B

4598A One pound pattern. England. R. Millennium Bridge with plain edge and hallmark
— Proof in silver *FDC* *
— Proof in gold *FDC* *
4598B One pound pattern. England. R. Lion with the word "Pattern" below with plain edge
and hallmark
— Proof in silver *FDC* *
— Proof in gold *FDC* *

CUPRO-NICKEL

4610 Fifty pence. R. Britannia. (Illus. as 4351)
1998
— Proof *FDC* (in 1998 set, see PS61)* £3
1999
— Proof *FDC* (in 1999 set, see PS63)* £3
2000
— Proof *FDC* (in 2000 set, see PS65)* £3
— Proof in silver *FDC** £25
2001
— Proof *FDC* (in 2001 set, see PS68)* £3

2002
— Proof *FDC* (in 2002 set, see PS72)* £3
— Proof in gold *FDC* (see PGJS1)* £250
2003
— Proof *FDC* (in 2003 set, see PS78) * £3
2004
— Proof *FDC* (in 2004 set, see PS81) * £3
2005
— Proof *FDC* (in 2005 set, see PS84) * £3

4611

4611 Fifty pence. R. Celebratory pattern of twelve stars reflecting the European flag with the dates
1973 and 1998 commemorating the 25th Anniversary of the United Kingdom's membership
of the European Union and Presidency of the Council of Ministers.
1998.. £2
— Proof *FDC** £5
— Proof in silver *FDC* (Issued: 8,859) £30
— Proof piedfort in silver *FDC* (Issued: 8,440) £50
— Proof in gold *FDC* (Issued: 1,177) £250

* Coins marked thus were originally issued in Royal Mint sets.

4612   4613

4612 **Fifty pence.** R. A pair of hands set against a pattern of radiating lines with the words Fiftieth
Anniversary and the value 50 pence with the initials NHS.
1998.. £2
— Specimen in presentation folder £3
— Proof in silver *FDC* (Issued: 9,032) £30
— Proof piedfort in silver *FDC* (Issued: 5,117) £50
— Proof in gold *FDC* (Issued: 651) £350

4613 **Fifty pence.** Library commemorative. R. The turning pages of a book above the pediment of
a classical library building which contains the inscription 'Public Libraries' and the
denomination'50 pence' and the dates 1850 and 2000
2000.. £2
— Specimen in presentation folder £5
— Proof *FDC** £5
— Proof in silver *FDC* (Issued: 7,634) £25
— Proof piedfort in silver *FDC* (Issued: 5,721) £35
— Proof in gold *FDC* (Issued: 710) £300

4614

4614 **Fifty pence**. Anniversary of the Suffragette Movement commemorative. R. A standing figure
of a   woman holding a banner bearing the initials WSPU with railings in the background and
a poster with the words "GIVE WOMEN THE VOTE" the denomination "50 pence" and the
dates 1903 and 2003
2003 ....
— Specimen in presentation folder £5
— Proof *FDC* (in 2003 set, see PS78)* £5
— Proof in silver *FDC* (Issued: 6,503) £25
— Proof piedfort in silver *FDC* (Issued 5,372) £47
— Proof in gold *FDC* (Issued: 939) £300

* *Coins marked thus were originally issued in Royal Mint sets.*

4615

4615 Fifty pence. 50th anniversary of the first sub four-minute mile. ℞. The lower half of a
running athlete with a stop clock showing the time and the denomination "50 pence"
2004 ....
— Specimen in presentation folder £5
— Proof *FDC* (in 2004 set, see PS81)* £5
— Proof in silver *FDC* (Edition: 15,000) £26
— Proof piedfort in silver *FDC* (Edition: 7,500) £47
— Proof in gold *FDC* (Edition: 1,250) £300

4616

4616 Fifty pence. 250th anniversary of the publication of Samuel Johnson's Dictionary of the
English language. ℞. An interpretation of the words "Fifty" and "Pence" as they
appeared in Johnson's dictionary together with denomination "50" and "Johnson's
Dictionary 1755"
2005
— Proof *FDC* (in 2005 set, see PS84)* £5
— Proof in silver *FDC* (Edition: 7,500) £27
— Proof piedfort in silver *FDC* (Edition: 5,000) £47
— Proof in gold *FDC* (Edition: 1,000) £265

4630 Twenty pence. ℞. Crowned double rose. (Illus. as 4230)

1998	1999	2000
— Proof *FDC** £3	— Proof *FDC** £3	— Proof *FDC** £3
		— Proof in silver *FDC**
2001	2002	
— Proof *FDC** £3	— Proof *FDC** £3	
	— Proof in gold *FDC* (in 2002 set, see PGJS1)* £200	
2003	2004	
— Proof *FDC** £3	— Proof *FDC** £3	

4650 Ten pence. ℞. Lion passant guardant. (Illus. as 4232)

1998*	1999*	2000
— Proof *FDC** £3	— Proof *FDC** £3	— Proof *FDC** £3
		— Proof in silver *FDC**
2001	2002	
— Proof *FDC** £3	— Proof *FDC** £3	
	— Proof in gold *FDC* (in 2002 set, see PGJS1)* £150	
2003	2004	
— Proof *FDC** £3	— Proof *FDC** £3	

* *Coins marked thus were originally issued in Royal Mint sets*

4670 Five pence. R. Crowned thistle. (Illus. as 4234)

1998	1999	2000
— Proof *FDC** £3	— Proof *FDC** £3	— Proof *FDC** £3
		— - Proof in silver *FDC**
2001	2002	
— Proof *FDC** £3	— Proof *FDC**£3	
	— Proof in gold *FDC* (in 2002 set, see PGJS1)* £100	
2003	2004	
— Proof *FDC** £3	— Proof *FDC** £3	

COPPER PLATED STEEL

4690 Two pence. R. Plumes. (Illus. as 4376)

1998	1999	2000
— Proof *FDC** £3	— Proof *FDC** £3	— Proof *FDC** £3
		— Proof in silver *FDC**
2001	2002	
— Proof *FDC** £3	— Proof *FDC** £3	
	— Proof in gold *FDC* (in 2002 set, see PGJS1)* £150	
2003	2004	
— Proof *FDC** £3	— Proof *FDC** £3	

BRONZE

4700 Two pence. R. Plumes. (Illus. as 4376)
1998

COPPER PLATED STEEL

4710 One pence. R. Portcullis with chains. (Illus. as 4381)

1998	1999	2000
— Proof *FDC** £3	— Proof *FDC** £3	— Proof *FDC** £3
		— Proof in silver *FDC**
2001	2002	
— Proof *FDC** £3	— Proof *FDC** £3	
	— Proof in gold *FDC* (in 2002 set, see PGJS1)* £100	
2003	2004	
— Proof *FDC** £3	— Proof *FDC** £3	

* Coins marked thus were originally issued in Royal Mint sets

The practice of issuing annual sets of coins was started by the Royal Mint in 1970 when a set of the £SD coins was issued as a souvenir prior to Decimalisation. There are now regular issues of brilliant uncirculated coin sets as well as proofs in base metal, and issues in gold and silver. In order to simplify the numbering system, and to allow for the continuation of the various issues in the future, the Prefix letters have been changed. The base metal proof sets will continue the series of numbers from the 1970 set, PS20. For ease of reference, where collectors have the 2001 Edition of the Catalogue, the previous numbers are shown in brackets.

In addition to the annual sets of uncirculated and proofs coins sold by the Royal Mint to collectors and dealers, the Mint has produced specially packaged sets and single coins for companies. No details are made available of these issues and therefore no attempt has been made to include them in the listings below. The Mint also sells "Christening" and "Wedding" sets in distinctive packaging but the numbers circulating in the market are relatively modest and of limited appeal after the year of issue.

Uncirculated Sets

US01–**1982** (PS21)	Uncirculated (specimen) set in Royal Mint folder, 50p to ¹/₂p, new reverse type, including 20 pence (Issued: 205,000)	(7)	9
US02–**1983** (PS22)	'U.K.' £1 (4221) to ¹/₂p (Issued: 637,100)	(8)	15
US03–**1984** (PS23)	'Scottish' £1 (4222) to ¹/₂p (Issued: 158,820)	(8)	13
US04–**1985** (PS24)	'Welsh' £1 (4331) to 1p, new portrait of The Queen (Issued: 102,015).	(7)	13
US05–**1986** (PS25)	Commonwealth Games £2 (4311) plus 'Northern Irish' £1 (4332) to 1p, ((Issued: 167,224)	(8)	14
US06–**1987** (PS26)	'English' £1 (4333) to 1p, (Issued: 172,425)	(7)	12
US07–**1988** (PS27)	'Arms' £1 (4334) to 1p, (Issued: 134,067)	(7)	15
US08–**1989** (PS28)	'Scottish' £1 (4335) to 1p, (Issued: 77,569)	(7)	22
US09–**1989** (PS29)	Bill of Rights and Claim of Right £2s (4312 and 4313) in Royal Mint folder (Issued: not known)	(2)	15
US10–**1990** (PS30)	'Welsh' £1 (4331) to 1p plus new 5p, (Issued: 102,606)	(8)	20
US11–**1991** (PS31)	'Northern Irish' £1 (4332) to 1p, (Issued: 74,975)	(7)	20
US12–**1992** (PS32)	'English' £1 (4333), 'European Community' 50p (4352) and Britannia 50p, 20p to 1p plus new 10p (Issued: 78,421)	(9)	20
US13–**1993** (PS33)	'UK' £1 (4336), 'European Community' 50p to 1p ((Issued: 56,945)...	(8)	25
US14–**1994** (PS34)	'Bank' £2 (4314), 'Scottish' £1 (4337) and 'D-Day' 50p (4353) to 1p, (Issued: 177,971)	(8)	15
US15–**1995** (PS35)	'Peace' £2 (4315) and 'Welsh' £1 (4338) to 1p (Issued: 105, 647)	(8)	15
US16–**1996** (PS36)	'Football' £2 (4317) and 'Northern Irish' £1 (4339) to 1p (Issued: 86,501)	(8)	15
US17–**1997** (PS37)	'Bimetallic' £2 (4318), 'English' £1 (4340) to 1p plus new 50p (Issued: 109,557)	(9)	15
US18–**1998** (PS38)	'Bimetallic' £2 (4570), 'UK' £1 (4590) and 'EU' 50 pence (4611) to 1 pence (Issued: 96,192)	(9)	20
US19–**1998** (PS39)	'EU' and Britannia 50 pence (4611 and 4610) in Royal Mint folder.	(2)	6
US20–**1999** (PS40)	'Bimetallic' £2 (4571), 'Scottish' £1 (4591) to 1p (Issued: 136,696) .	(8)	15
US21–**2000** (PS41)	'Bimetallic' £2 (4570), 'Welsh' £1 (4592) to 1p plus 'Library' 50 pence (Issued: 117,750)	(9)	15
US22–**2001**	'Bimetallic' £2 (4570), 'Bimetallic' £2 (4572), 'Irish' £1 (4594) to 1p (Issued: 57,741)	(9)	14
US23–**2002**	'Bimetallic' £2 (4570), 'English' £1 (4594) to 1p (Issued: 60,539).	(8)	14
US24–**2002**	'Bimetallic' £2 (4573, 4574, 4575 and 4576) Commonwealth Games (Issued: 47,895)	(4)	15
US25–**2003**	"Bimetallic" "DNA" £2 (4577), "Bimetallic" £2 (4570), "UK" £1 (4590), "Suffragette" 50 pence (4614) and "Britannia" 50 pence (4610) to 1p.	(10)	14
US26 – **2004**	"Bimetallic" "Penydarren engine" £2 (4578), "Bimetallic" £2 (4570),		

	"Forth Rail Bridge" £1 (4595),"Sub four-minute mile" 50 pence (4615)		
	and "Britannia"50pence(4610) to1p ....(10)		14
US27 – **2004**	"Bimetallic" "Penydarren engine" £2 (4578), "Forth Rail Bridge" £1		
	(4595),"Sub four-minute mile" 50 pence (4615).............................. (3)		9
US28 – **2005**	"Bimetallic" "Gunpowder Plot" £2 (4579), "Bimetallic" £2		
	(4570), "Menai Straits Bridge" £1 (4596), "Samuel Johnson's		
	Dictionary" 50 pence (4616) and "Britannia" 50 pence (4610)		
	to 1p.. (10)		15
US29 – **2005**	"Bimetallic" "Gunpowder Plot" £2 (4579), "Menai Straits		
	Bridge" £1 (4596), "Samuel Johnson's Dictionary" 50 pence		
	(4616) .... (3)		10
US30 – **2005**	"Trafalgar" £5, struck in c/n (4559) and "Nelson" £5 struck		
	in c/n (4560) .... (2)		19

Proof Sets

PS21–**1971** (PS47)	Decimal coinage set, 50 new pence ('Britannia' to $1/2$ new pence,		
	plus medallion in sealed plastic case with card wrapper		
	(Issued: 350,000) .... (6)		15
PS22–**1972** (PS48)	Proof 'Silver Wedding' Crown struck in c/n (4226) plus 50p to		
	$1/2$p (Issued: 150,000)... (7)		20
PS23–**1973** (PS49)	'EEC' 50p (4224) plus 10p to $1/2$p, (Issued: 100,000) .... (6)		15
PS24–**1974** (PS50)	Britannia 50p to $1/2$p, as 1971 (Issued: 100,000) .... (6)		12
PS25–**1975** (PS51)	50p to $1/2$p (as 1974), (Issued: 100,000)... (6)		12
PS26–**1976** (PS52)	50p to $1/2$p, as 1975, (Issued: 100,000) .... (6)		12
PS27–**1977** (PS53)	Proof 'Silver Jubilee' Crown struck in c/n (4227) plus 50p to		
	$1/2$p, (Issued: 193,000).. (7)		12
PS28–**1978** (PS54)	50p to $1/2$p, as 1976, (Issued: 86,100) .... (6)		12
PS29–**1979** (PS55)	50p to $1/2$p, as 1978, (Issued: 81,000) .... (6)		12
PS30–**1980** (PS56)	50p to $1/2$p, as 1979, (Issued: 143,000) .... (6)		15
PS31–**1981** (PS57)	50p to $1/2$p, as 1980, (Issued: 100,300) .... (6)		15
PS32–**1982** (PS58)	50p to $1/2$p including 20 pence (Issued: 106,800) .... (7)		12
PS33–**1983** (PS59)	'U.K.' £1 (4221) to $1/2$p in new packaging (Issued: 107,800) .... (8)		17
PS34–**1984** (PS60)	'Scottish' £1 (4222) to $1/2$p, (Issued: 106,520) .... (8)		16
PS35–**1985** (PS61)	'Welsh' £1 (4331) to 1p, (Issued: 102,015)...................................... (7)		16
PS36–**1985** (PS62)	As last but packed in deluxe red leather case (Included above)....... (7)		20
PS37–**1986** (PS63)	Commonwealth games £2 (4311) plus 'Northern Irish' £1 (4332)		
	to 1p, (Issued: 104,597).. (8)		20
PS38–**1986** (PS64)	As last but packed in deluxe red leather case (Included above)....... (8)		23
PS39–**1987** (PS65)	'English' £1 (4333) to 1p, (Issued: 88,659)....................................... (7)		20
PS40–**1987** (PS66)	As last but packed in deluxe leather case (Included above)............. (7)		24
PS41–**1988** (PS67)	'Arms' £1 (4334) to 1p, (Issued: 79,314)... (7)		25
PS42–**1988** (PS68)	As last but packed in deluxe leather case (Included above)............. (7)		29
PS43–**1989** (PS69)	Bill of Rights and Claim of Right £2s (4312 and 4313), 'Scottish'		
	£1 (4335) to 1p, (Issued: 85,704)... (9)		30
PS44–**1989** (PS70)	As last but packed in red leather case, (Included above)................... (9)		35
PS45–**1990** (PS71)	'Welsh' £1 (4331) to 1p plus new 5p, (Issued: 79,052) .... (8)		27
PS46–**1990** (PS72)	As last but packed in red leather case (Included above)................... (8)		32
PS47–**1991** (PS73)	'Northern Irish' £1 (4332) to 1p, (Issued: 55,144) .... (7)		27
PS48–**1991** (PS74)	As last but packed in red leather case (Included above)................... (7)		33
PS49–**1992** (PS75)	'English' £1 (4333), 'European community' 50p (4352) and		
	Britannia 50p, 20p to 1p plus new 10p, (Issued: 44,337)................ (9)		28
PS50–**1992** (PS76)	As last but packed in red leather case (Issued: 17,989)................... (9)		33
PS51–**1993** (PS77)	'Coronation Anniversary' £5 struck in c/n (4302), 'U.K.' £1		
	(4336), 50p to 1p, (Issued: 43,509) .... (8)		30
PS52–**1993** (PS78)	As last but packed in red leather case (Issued: 22,571)................... (8)		35
PS53–**1994** (PS79)	'Bank' £2 (4314), 'Scottish' £1 (4337), 'D-Day' 50p (4353) to		

	1p, (Issued: 44,643)	(8)	30
PS54–**1994** (PS80)	As last but packed in red leather case (Issued: 22,078)	(8)	35
PS55–**1995** (PS81)	'Peace' £2 (4315), 'Welsh' £1 (4338) to 1p, (Issued: 42,842)	(8)	32
PS56–**1995** (PS82)	As last but packed in red leather case (Issued: 17,797)	(8)	35
PS57–**1996** (PS83)	Proof '70th Birthday' £5 struck in c/n (4303), 'Football' £2 (4317), 'Northern Irish' £1 (4339) to 1p, (Issued: 46,295)	(9)	32
PS58–**1996** (PS84)	As last but packed in red leather case (Issued: 21,286)	(9)	37
PS59–**1997** (PS85)	Proof 'Golden Wedding' £5 struck in c/n (4304), 'Bimetallic' £2 (4318), 'English' £1 (4340) to 1p plus new 50p (Issued: 48,761)	(10)	33
PS60–**1997** (PS86)	As last but packed in red leather case (Issued: 31,987)	(10)	40
PS61–**1998** (PS87)	Proof £5 'Prince of Wales 50th Birthday', struck in c/n (4550), 'Bimetallic' £2 (4570), 'UK'. £1 (4590), 'EU' 50 pence (4611) to 1 pence. (Issued: 36,907)	(10)	33
PS62–**1998** (PS88)	As last, but packed in red leather case. (Issued: 26,763)	(10)	40
PS63–**1999** (PS89)	Proof £5 'Diana, Princess of Wales', struck in c/n (4551), 'Bimetallic' 'Rugby' £2 (4571), 'Scottish' £1 (4591) to 1p. (Issued: 40,317)	(9)	34
PS64–**1999** (PS90)	As last, but packed in red leather case. (Issued: 39,827)	(9)	40
PS65–**2000** (PS91)	Proof £5 'Millennium', struck in c/n (4552), 'Bimetallic' £2 (4570), 'Welsh' £1 (4592), 'Library' 50 pence (4613) and 'Britannia' 50 pence (4610) to 1p Standard Set, (Issued: 41,379)	(10)	£30
PS66–**2000** (PS92)	As last, but Deluxe set (Issued: 21,573 above)	(10)	£40
PS67–**2000** (PS93)	As last, but Executive set (Issued: 9,517)	(10)	£70
PS68–**2001**	Proof £5 'Victoria', struck in c/n (4554), 'Bimetallic' £2 (4570), 'Bimetallic' £2 (4572), 'Irish' £1 (4593) to 1p. Standard Set. (Issued: 28,244)	(10)	34
PS69–**2001**	As last, but Gift Set (Issued: 1,351)	(10)	43
PS70–**2001**	As last, but packed in red leather case (Isssued: 16,022)	(10)	48
PS71–**2001**	As last, but Executive Set (Issued: 3,755)	(10)	60
PS72–**2002**	Proof £5 'Golden Jubilee', struck in c/n (4555), 'Bimetallic' £2 (4570), 'English' £1 (4594) to 1p. Standard set. (Issued: 30,884)	(9)	32
PS73–**2002**	As last, but Gift Set (Issued:1,544)	(9)	40
PS74–**2002**	As last, but packed in red leather case (Issued: 23,342)	(9)	46
PS75–**2002**	As last, but Executive Set (Issued: 5,000)	(9)	70
PS76–**2002**	'Bimetallic' £2 (4573, 4574, 4575 and 4576) Commonwealth Games.. (Issued: 3,358)	(4)	25
PS77–**2002**	As last, but Display Set (Issued: 673)	(4)	33
PS78–**2003**	Proof £5 "Coronation", struck in c/n (4557), "Bimetallic" "DNA" £2 (4577), "Bimetallic" £2 (4570), "UK" £1 (4590), "Suffragette" 50 pence (4614)and "Britannia" 50 pence (4610) to 1p. Standard set. (Issued: 23,305)	(11)	34
PS79–**2003**	As last, but packed in red leather case (Issued: 14,947)	(11)	47
PS80–**2003**	As last, but Executive Set (Issued: 5,000)	(11)	70
PS81–**2004**	"Bimetallic" "Penydarren engine" £2 (4578), "Bimetallic" £2 (4570), "Forth Rail Bridge" £1 (4595), "Sub four-minute mile" 50 pence (4615) and "Britannia" 50 pence (4610) to 1p. Standard set. (Edition: 75,000)	(10)	30
PS82–**2004**	As last, but packed in red leather case (Edition: 15,000)	(10)	40
PS83– **2004**	As last, but Executive Set (Edition: 10,000)	(10)	65
PS84– **2005**	Proof £5 "Trafalgar", struck in c/n (4559), Proof £5 "Nelson", struck in c/n (4560) "Bimetallic" "Gunpowder Plot" £2 (4579), "Bimetallic" £2 (4570), "Menai Straits Bridge" £1 (4596),"Samuel Johnson's Dictionary" 50 pence (4616) and "Britannia"50 pence (4610) to 1p (Edition: 30,000)	(12)	38

| PS85– **2005** | As last, but packed in red leather case (Edition:15,000) | (12) | 49 |
| PS86– **2005** | As last, but Executive Set (Edition: 5,000) | (12) | 75 |

Silver Sets

PSS01–**1989** (PS96)	Bill of Rights and Claim of Right £2s (4312 and 4313), Silver piedfort proofs (Issued: 10,000)	(2)	85
PSS02–**1989** (PS97)	As last but Silver proofs (Issue figure not known)	(2)	60
PSS03–**1990** (PS98)	2 x 5p Silver proofs (4371 and 4372), (Issued: 35,000)	(2)	30
PSS04–**1992** (PS99)	2 x 10p Silver proofs (4366 and 4367), (Not known)	(2)	34
PSS05–**1996** (PS100)	25th Anniversary of Decimal Currency (4339, 4351, 4361, 4367, 4372, 4386, 4391) in Silver proof (Edition: 15,000)	(7)	100
PSS06–**1997** (PS101)	2 x 50p silver proofs (4351 and 4354) (Issued: 10,304)	(2)	65
PSS07–**1997** (PS102)	Britannia proofs, £2 – 20 pence (4300, 4300A, 4300B, 4300C) (Issued: 11,832)	(4)	105
PSS08–**1998** (PS103)	Britannia proofs, £2 – 20 pence (4500, 4510, 4520, 4530) (Issued: 3,044)	(4)	120
PSS09–**1998** (PS104)	'EU' and 'NHS' Silver proofs (4611 and 4612)	(2)	50
PSS10–**2000** (PS105)	'Millennium' £5, 'Bimetallic' £2, 'Welsh' £1, 50p to 1p, and Maundy coins, 4p-1p in silver proof (4552, 4570, 4592, 4610, 4630, 4650, 4670, 4212-4215) (Issued: 13,180)	(13)	245
PSS11–**2001**	Britannia proofs, £2–20 pence (4502, 4511, 4521, 4531) (Issued: 4,596)	(4)	90
PSS12–**2002**	Commonwealth Games 'Bimetallic' £2 (4573, 4574, 4575 and 4576) in silver (Issued: 2,553)	(4)	140
PSS13–**2002**	As above with the addition of colour and piedfort in silver. (4573A, 4574A, 4575A and 4576A) (Issued: 3,497)	(4)	240
PSS14–**2003**	Britannia proofs, £2 – 20 pence (4503, 4512, 4522, 4532) (Issued: 3,623)	(4)	90
PSS15–**MD**	Britannia £2 set of four different designs, 1999 - 2003 (4500, 4501, 4502, 4503)(Edition: 5,000)	(4)	50
PSS16–**MD**	£5"Golden Jubilee"(4555) and £5 "Coronation" (4557) silver proofs	(2)	69
PSS17–**2003**	£5 "Coronation"(4557), £2 "Britannia"(4503), £2 "DNA"(4577), £1 "UK"(4590) and 50 pence "Suffragette(4614)silver proofs (Edition:)	(5)	140
PSS18–**2004**	£5 "Entende Cordial" (4558), £2 "Britannia" (4500), £2 "Penydarren" (4578) £1 "Forth Rail Bridge" (4595) and 50 pence "Sub four-minute mile" (4615) silver proofs (Edition:)	(5)	145
PSS19–**2004**	"Bimetallic" "Penydarren engine" £2 (4578), "Forth Rail Bridge" £1 (4595),"Sub four-minute mile" 50 pence (4615) Silver piedfort proofs	(3)	145
PSS20 – **2005**	"Bimetallic" Gunpowder Plot" £2 (4579), Bimetallic" "World War II" £2 (4580), "Menai Straits Bridge" £1 (4596), "Samuel Johnson's Dictionary" 50 pence Silver piedfort proofs	(4)	190
PSS21– **2005**	£5 "Trafalgar" (4559) and £5 "Nelson" (4560) silver piedfort proofs, (Edition: 3,000)	(2)	135

Gold Sovereign Proof Sets

PGS01–**1980** (PS111)	Gold £5 to half-sovereign (4201, 4203-4205) (Issued: 10,000)	(4)	850
PGS02–**1981** (PS112)	U.K. Proof coin Commemorative collection. (Consists of £5, sovereign, 'Royal Wedding' Crown (4229) in silver, plus base metal proofs 50p to 1/2p), (Not known)	(9)	650
PGS03–**1982** (PS113)	Gold £5 to half-sovereign (Issued: 2,500)	(4)	900
PGS04–**1983** (PS114)	Gold £2, sovereign and half-sovereign, (Not known)	(3)	375
PGS05–**1984** (PS115)	Gold £5, sovereign and half-sovereign, (Issued: 7,095)	(3)	675
PGS06–**1985** (PS116)	Gold £5 to half-sovereign (4251, 4261, 4271, 4276) (Issued: 5,849)	(4)	900
PGS07–**1986** (PS117)	Gold Commonwealth games £2, (4311) sovereign and half-sovereign (Issued: 12,500)	(3)	425
PGS08–**1987** (PS118)	Gold £2 (4261), sovereign and half-sovereign (Issued: 12,500)	(3)	425

PGS09–**1988** (PS119) Gold £2 to half-sovereign (Issued: 11,192) .... (3) 425
PGS10–**1989** (PS120) Sovereign Anniversary Gold £5 to half-sovereign (4254, 4263,
4272, 4277), (Issued: 5,000) .... (4) 1500
PGS11–**1989** (PS121) Gold £2 to half-sovereign (Issued: 7,936) .... (3) 800
PGS12–**1990** (PS122) Gold £5 to half-sovereign (as 1985 issue), (Issued: 1,721) .... (4) 900
PGS13–**1990** (PS123) Gold £2 to half-sovereign (as 1988 issue), (Issued: 1,937) .... (3) 500
PGS14–**1991** (PS124) Gold £5 to half-sovereign (Issued: 1,336) .... (4) 900
PGS15–**1991** (PS125) Gold £2 to half-sovereign (Issued: 1,152) .... (3) 500
PGS16–**1992** (PS126) Gold £5 to half-sovereign (Issued: 1,165) .... (4) 900
PGS17–**1992** (PS127) Gold £2 to half-sovereign (Issued: 967) .... (3) 500
PGS18–**1993** (PS128) Gold £5 to half-sovereign with silver Pistrucci medal in case
(Issued: 1,078) .... (5) 1100
PGS19–**1993** (PS129) Gold £2 to half-sovereign (Issued: 663) .... (3) 500
PGS20–**1994** (PS130) Gold £5, £2 (as 4314), sovereign and half-sovereign (Issued: 918)..... (4) 1000
PGS21–**1994** (PS131) Gold £2, (as 4314), sovereign and half-sovereign (Issued: 1,249)... (3) 550
PGS22–**1995** (PS132) Gold £5, £2 (as 4315), sovereign and half-sovereign (Issued: 718). (4) 950
PGS23–**1995** (PS133) Gold £2 (as 4315), sovereign and half-sovereign (Issued: 1,112).... (3) 550
PGS24–**1996** (PS134) Gold £5 to half-sovereign (as 1992 issue) (Issued: 742) .... (4) 950
PGS25–**1996** (PS135) Gold £2 to half-sovereign (as 1992 issue) (Issued: 868) .... (3) 500
PGS26–**1997** (PS136) Gold £5, £2 (as 4318), sovereign and half-sovereign
(Issued: 860) .... (4) 950
PGS27–**1997** (PS137) Gold £2 (as 4318) to half-sovereign (Issued: 817) .... (3) 550
PGS28–**1998** (PS138) Gold £5 to half sovereign (4400, 4420, 4430, 4440) (Issued: 789)........ (4) 1000
PGS29–**1998** (PS139) Gold £2 to half sovereign (4420, 4430, 4440) (Issued: 560)............ (3) 550
PGS30–**1999** (PS140) Gold £5, £2 (as 4571), sovereign and half sovereign (Issued: 991) ...... (4) 1000
PGS31–**1999** (PS141) Gold £2 (as 4571), sovereign and half sovereign (Issued: 912)........ (3) 550
PGS32–**2000** (PS142) Gold £5 to half-sovereign (as 1998 issue) (Issued: 1,000) .... (4) 1000
PGS33–**2000** (PS143) Gold £2 to half-sovereign (as 1998 issue) (Issued: 1,250) .... (3) 550
PGS34–**2001**   Gold £5, £2 (as 4572), sovereign and half sovereign (Issued: 1,000)... (4) 1000
PGS35–**2001**   Gold £2 (as 4572), sovereign and half sovereign (Issued: 891) .... (3) 450
PGS36–**2002**   Gold £5 to half sovereign (4401, 4421, 4431, 4441) (Issued: 3,000) . (4) 1100
PGS37–**2002**   Gold £2 to half sovereign (4421, 4431, 4441) (Issued: 3,947)......... (3) 450
PGS38–**2003**   Gold £5 to half sovereign (as 1998 issue) (Issued: 2,250) .... (4) 1050
PGS39–**2003**   Gold £2 (as 4577) sovereign and half sovereign (Issued: 1,717) ..... (3) 425
PGS40–**2004**   Gold £5 to half sovereign (as 1998 issue) (Edition: 2,250)............. (4) 1050
PGS41–**2004**   Gold £2 (as 4578) sovereign and half sovereign (Edition: 2,500).... (3) 425
PGS42–**2005**   Gold £5 to half sovereign (4402, 4422, 4432, 4442
(Edition: 2,500) .... (4) 995
PGS43–**2005**   Gold £2 to half sovereign (4422, 4432, 4442) (Edition: 2,500.... (3) 450

Britannia Series

PBS01–**1987** (PS147) Britannia Gold Proofs £100, £50, £25, £10 (4281, 4286, 4291,
4296), (Issued: 10,000) .... (4) 750
PBS02–**1987** (PS148) Britannia Gold Proofs £25, £10 (4291 and 4296) (Issued: 11,100) . (2) 125
PBS03–**1988** (PS149) Britannia Proofs £100–£10 (as 1987 issue) (Issued: 3,505)............. (4) 750
PBS04–**1988** (PS150) Britannia Proofs £25, £10 (as 1987 issue) (Issued: 894)............... (2) 125
PBS05–**1989** (PS151) Britannia Proofs £100 – £10 (as 1987) (Issued: 2,268).................. (4) 700
PBS06–**1989** (PS152) Britannia Proofs £25, £10 (as 1987 issue) (Issued: 451)................. (2) 150
PBS07–**1990** (PS153) Britannia Proofs, £100-£10, gold with the addition of silver alloy
(4282, 4287, 4292, 4297) (Issued: 527)........................... (4) 850
PBS08–**1991** (PS154) Britannia Proofs, as PS153 (Issued: 509) .... (4) 850
PBS09–**1992** (PS155) Britannia Proofs, as PS153 (Issued: 500) .... (4) 900
PBS10–**1993** (PS156) Britannia Proofs, as PS153 (Issued: 462) .... (4) 950
PBS11–**1994** (PS157) Britannia Proofs, as PS153 ((Issued: 435) .... (4) 950
PBS12–**1995** (PS158) Britannia Proofs, as PS153 (Issued: 500) .... (4) 950
PBS13–**1996** (PS159) Britannia Proofs, as PS153 (Issued: 483) .... (4) 950
PBS14–**1997** (PS160) Britannia proofs £100, £50, £25, £10 (4283, 4288, 4293, 4298)

	(Issued: 892)	(4)	1100
PBS15–**1998** (PS161)	Britannia proofs £100, £50, £25, £10 (4450, 4460, 4470, 4480) (Issued: 750)	(4)	950
PBS16–**1999** (PS162)	Britannia Proofs, as PS161 (Issued: 740)	(4)	950
PBS17–**2000** (PS163)	Britannia Proofs, as PS161 (Issued: 750)	(4)	950
PBS18–**2001**	Britannia Proofs £100, £50, £25, £10 (4451, 4461, 4471, 4481) (Issued: 1,000)	(4)	950
PBS19–**2002**	Britannia Proofs, as PBS17 (Issued: 945)	(4)	950
PBS20–**2003**	Britannia Proofs £100, £50, £25, £10 (4452, 4462, 4472, 4482) (Issued: 1,250)	(4)	950
PBS21–**2003**	Britannia Proofs £50, £25, £10 (4462, 4472, 4482) (Issued: 816)	(3)	400
PBS22–MD	Britannia £100 set of four different designs, 1987, 1997, 2001, 2003 (4281,4283,4451,4452) (Edition: 2,500)	(4)	1,350
PBS23–**2004**	Britannia Proofs, as PBS15 (Edition: 1,250)	(4)	950
PBS24–**2004**	Britannia Proofs, £50, £25, £10 (4460,4470, 4480) (Edition: 1,500)	(3)	450
PBS25–**2005**	Britannia Proofs, £100, £50, £25, £10 (4453, 4463, 4473, 4483) (Edition: 1,500)	(4)	935
PBS26–**2005**	Britannia Proofs, £50, £25, £10 (4463, 4473, 4483) (Edition: 500)	(3)	430

Gold Coin Proof Sets

PCGS1–**2002**	Commonwealth Games 'Bimetallic' £2 (4573, 4574, 4575 and 4576) in gold (Issued: 315)	(4)	1400
PGJS1–**2002**	'Golden Jubilee' £5, 'Bimetallic' £2, 'English' £1, 50p to 1p and Maundy coins, 4p-1p in gold proof (4555, 4570, 4594, 4610, 4630, 4650, 4670, 4212-4215) (Issued: 2,002)	(13)	3000

Pattern Proof sets

PPS1–**2003**	Silver proof set of £1 designs with plain edge and hallmark (4595A, 4596A, 4597A, 4598A) (Edition: 7,500)	(4)	98
PPS2–**2003**	Gold proof set of £1 designs with plain edge and hallmark (4595A, 4596A, 4597A, 4598A) (Edition: 3,000)	(4)	1000
PPS3–**2004**	Silver proof set of £1 designs with plain edge and hallmark (4595B, 4596B, 4597B, 4598B) (Edition: 5,000)	(4)	98
PPS4–**2004**	Gold proof set of £1 designs with plain edge and hallmark (4595B, 4596B, 4597B, 4598B) (Edition: 2,250)	(4)	1125

A SELECT NUMISMATIC BIBLIOGRAPHY

Listed below is a selection of general books on British numismatics and other works that the specialist collector will need to consult.

General Books:
BROOKE, G. C. *English Coins.* 3rd ed., 1966.
CHALLIS, C. E. (ed.) *A New History of the Royal Mint.* 1992
GRUEBER, H. A. *Handbook of the Coins of Great Britain and Ireland.* Revised 1970
KENYON, R. Ll. *Gold Coins of England.* 1884
NORTH, J. J. *English Hammered Coinage,* Vol. I, c. 650-1272. 1994; Vol. II, 1272-1662. 1991
SUTHERLAND, C. H. V. *English Coinage, 600-1900.* 1972

Specialist Works:
ALLEN, D. *The Origins of Coinage in Britain: A Reappraisal.* Reprint 1978
ALLEN, D. F. *The Coins of the Coritani.* (SCBI no. 3) 1963
ALLEN, D. F. *English Coins in the British Museum: The Cross-and-Crosslets ('Tealby') type of Henry II.* 1951
ARCHIBALD, M. M. and BLUNT, C. E. *British Museum. Anglo-Saxon Coins. Athelstan to the reform of Edgar. 924-c 973.* 1986
ASKEW, G. *The Coinage of Roman Britain.* (1951) Reprinted 1980.
BESLY, E. M. *Coins and Medals of the English Civil War.* 1990
BLACKBURN, M. A. S. *Anglo-Saxon Monetary History.* 1986
BLUNT, C. E. and WHITTON, C. A. *The Coinages of Edward IV and of Henry VI (Restored).*
BLUNT, C. E., STEWART, B.H.I.H. and LYON, C.S.S. *Coinage in Tenth-Century England. From Edward the Elder to Edgar's Reform.* 1989
BRAND, J.D. *The English Coinage 1180-1247: Money, Mints and Exchanges* 1994
BROOKE, G. C. *English Coins in the British Museum: The Norman Kings.* 1916
BROWN, I. D. and DOLLEY, M. *Bibliography of Coin Hoards of Great Britain and Ireland 1500-1967.* 1971
CARSON, R. A. G. *Mints, Dies and Currency. Essays in Memory of Albert Baldwin.* 1971
DE JERSEY, P. *Coinage in Iron Age Armorica.* 1994
DOLLEY, R. H. M. (ed.). *Anglo-Saxon Coins; studies presented to Sir Frank Stenton.* 1964
GRIERSON, P. and BLACKBURN, M. A. S. *Medieval European Coinage, vol. 1, The Early Middle Ages.* 1986
HOBBS, R. *British Iron Age Coins in the British Museum.* 1996
KEARY, C. and GREUBER, H. *English Coins in the British Museum: Anglo-Saxon Series.* 1887, reprinted, 1970, 2 volumes.
LAKER, A. J. *The portrait Groats of Henry VIII.* 1978
LAWRENCE, L. A. *The Coinage of Edward III from 1351.*
LINECAR, H. W. A. *The Crown Pieces of Great Britain and the British Commonwealth.* 1962
—— *English Proof and Pattern Crown-Size Pieces.* 1968

MACK, R. P. *The R. P. Mack Collection, Ancient British, Anglo-Saxon and Norman Coins.* (SCBI no. 20) 1973

MANVILLE, H. E. *Encyclopedia of British Numismatics. Numismatic Guide to British and Irish Periodicals 1731-1991.* 1993

MANVILLE, H. E. and ROBERTSON, T. J. *An Annotated Bibliography of British Numismatic Auction Catalogues from 1710 to the Present.* 1986

MARSH, M. A. *The Gold Half Sovereign.* 2nd Edition, revised 2004

MARSH, M. A. *The Gold Sovereign.* 2nd Edition 1999

MASS, J. P. *The J. P. Mass collection of English Short Cross Coins 1180-1247. (SCBI 56). 2001*

NORTH, J. J. *Edwardian English Silver Coins 1279-1351. (SCBI 39)* 1989

NORTH, J. J. and PRESTON-MORLEY, P. J. *The John G. Brooker Collection: Coins of Charles I. (SCBI 33)* 1984

PECK, C. W. *English Copper, Tin and Bronze Coins in the British Museum, 1558-1958.* 1970

RAYNER, P.A. *The English Silver Coinage from 1649.* 5th ed. 1992

REECE, R. *Coinage in Roman Britain,* 1987.

ROBINSON, Dr. B. *The Royal Maundy.* 1992

RUDING, REV. R. *Annals of the Coinage of Great Britain.* 3rd Edition 1840

SEAR, D. R. *Roman Coins and their Values. 4th Edition* (1999) Reprinted 2000

SEAR, DAVID R. *The History and Coinage of the Roman Imperators 49-27 BC.* 1998

THOMPSON, J. D. A. *Inventory of British Coin Hoards, A.D. 600-1500.* 1956

VAN ARSDELL, R. *Celtic Coinage of Britain.* 1989.

VAN ARSDELL, R. D. *The Coinage of the Dobunni.* 1994

WHITTON, C. A. *The Heavy Coinage of Henry VI.*

WOODHEAD, P. *English Gold Coins 1257-1603. The Herbert Schneider Collection, vol. 1 (SCBI 47)* 1996

— — *English Gold Coins 1603-20th Century. The Herbert Schneider Collection, vol. 2 (SCBI 57) 2002*

WREN, C. R. *The Short-cross coinage 1180-1247. Henry II to Henry III. An illustrated Guide to Identification.* 1992

— — *The Voided Long-Cross Coinage 1247-1279. Henry III and Edward I.* 1993

— — *The English Long-Cross Pennies 1279-1489. Edward I-Henry VII.* 1995

For further references to British hammered coinage see *Sylloge of Coins of the British Isles,* a serial publication now comprising 54 volumes cataloguing collections in private hands and institutions. For full list of the 54 volumes published to date in this series, please contact Spink at the address below.

Other authoritative papers are published in the *Numismatic Chronicle, British Numismatic Journal and Spink's Numismatic Circular.* A complete book list is available from Spink & Son Ltd., 69 Southampton Row, Bloomsbury, London WC1B 4ET. Tel: 020 7563 4046 Fax: 020 7563 4068.

LATIN OR FOREIGN LEGENDS ON ENGLISH COINS

A DOMINO FACTUM EST ISTUD ET EST MIRABILE IN OCULIS NOSTRIS. (This is the Lord's doing and it is marvellous in our eyes: *Psalm 118.23.*) First used on 'fine' sovereign of Mary.

AMOR POPULI PRAESIDIUM REGIS. (The love of the people is the King's protection.) Reverse legend on angels of Charles I.

ANNO REGNI PRIMO, etc. (In the first year of the reign, etc.) Used around the edge of many of the larger milled denominations.

CHRISTO AUSPICE REGNO. (I reign under the auspice of Christ.) Used extensively in the reign of Charles I.

CIVIUM INDUSTRIA FLORET CIVITAS. (By the industry of its people the State flourishes.) On the 1951 Festival Crown of George VI.

CULTORES SUI DEUS PROTEGIT. (God protects His worshippers.) On gold double crowns and crowns of Charles I.

DECUS ET TUTAMEN. (An ornament and a safeguard: Virgil, *Aenid,* v.262.) This inscription on the edge of all early large milled silver was suggested by Evelyn, he having seen it on the vignette in Cardinal Richelieu's Greek Testament, and of course refers to the device as a means to prevent clipping. This legend also appears on the edge of U.K. and Northern Ireland one pound coins.

DIEU ET MON DROIT. (God and my right.) On halfcrowns of George IV and later monarchs

DIRIGE DEUS GRESSUS MEOS. (May the Lord direct my steps.) On the 'Una' Five pounds of Queen Victoria.

DOMINE NE IN FURORE TUO ARGUAS ME. (O Lord, rebuke me not in Thine anger: *Psalm 6, 1.*). First used on the half-florin of Edward III and then on all half-nobles.

DomiNus Deus Omnipotens REX. (Lord God, Almighty King.) Viking coins.

DUM SPIRO SPERO. (Whilst I live, I hope.) On the coins struck at Pontefract Castle during the Civil War after Charles I had been imprisoned.

EXALTABITUR IN GLORIA. (He shall be exalted in glory.) On all quarter-nobles.

EXURGAT DEUS ET DISSIPENTUR INIMICI EIUS. (Let God arise and let His enemies be scattered: *Psalm* 68, 1.) On the Scottish ducat and early English coins of James I (VI) and was chosen by the King himself. Also on Charles I, civil war, and Declaration coins,

FACIAM EOS IN GENTEM UNAM. (I will make them one nation: *Ezekiel, 37, 22.)* On unites and laurels of James I.

FLORENT CONCORDIA REGNA. (Through concord kingdoms flourish.) On gold unite of Charles I and broad of Charles II.

HANC DEUS DEDIT. (God has given this, i.e. the crown .) On siege-pieces of Pontefract struck in the name of Charles II.

HAS NISI PERITURUS MIHI ADIMAT NEMO. (Let no one remove these [letters] from me under penalty of death.) On the edge of crowns and half-crowns of Cromwell.

HENRICUS ROSAS REGNA JACOBUS. (Henry united the roses, James the kingdoms.) On English and Scottish gold coins of James I (VI).

HONI SOIT QUI MAL Y PENSE. (Evil to him who evil thinks.) The Motto of the Order of the Garter, first used on the Hereford (?) halfcrowns of Charles I. It also occurs on the Garter Star in the centre of the reverse of the silver coins of Charles II, but being so small it is usually illegible; it is more prominent on the coinage of George III.

ICH DIEN. (I serve.) Aberystwyth Furnace 2d, and Decimal 2p. The motto of The Prince of Wales.

INIMICOS EJUS INDUAM CONFUSIONE. (As for his enemies I shall clothe them with shame: *Psalm* 132, 18.) On shillings of Edward VI struck at Durham House, Strand.

JESUS AUTEM TRANSIENS PER MEDIUM ILLORUM IBAT. (But Jesus, passing through the midst of them, went His way: *Luke iv. 30.*) The usual reverse legend on English nobles, ryals and hammered sovereigns before James I; also on the very rare Scottish noble of David II of Scotland and the unique Anglo-Gallic noble of Edward the Black Prince.

JUSTITIA THRONUM FIRMAT. (Justice strengthens the throne.) On Charles I half-groats and pennies and Scottish twenty-penny pieces.

LUCERNA PEDIBUS MEIS VERBUM EST. (Thy word is a lamp unto my feet: *Psalm 119, 105.*) Obverse legend on a rare half-sovereign of Edward VI struck at Durham House, Strand.

MIRABILIA FECIT. (He made marvellously.) On the Viking coins of (?) York.

NEMO ME IMPUNE LACESSIT. (No-one provokes me with impunity.) On the 1984 Scottish one pound. Motto of The Order of the Thistle.

NUMMORUM FAMULUS. (The servant of the coinage.) The legend on the edge of the English tin coinage at the end of the seventeenth century.

O CRUX AVE SPES UNICA. (Hail! O Cross, our only hope.) On the reverse of all half-angels.

PAX MISSA PER ORBEM. (Peace sent throughout the world.) The reverse legend of a pattern farthing of Anne.

PAX QUÆRITUR BELLO. (Peace is sought by war.) The reverse legend of the Cromwell broad.

PER CRUCEM TUAM SALVA NOS CHRISTE REDEMPTOR. (By Thy cross, save us, O Christ, our Redeemer.) The normal reverse of English angels.

PLEIDIOL WYF I'M GWLAD. (True am I to my country.) Used on the 1985 Welsh one pound. Taken from the Welsh National Anthem.

POST MORTEM PATRIS PRO FILIO. (After the death of the father for the son.) On siege-pieces struck at Pontefract in 1648 (old style) after the execution of Charles I.

POSUI DEUM ADJUTOREM MEUM. (I have made God my Helper: *comp. Psalm* 54, 4.) Used on many English and Irish silver coins from Edward III until 1603. Altered to POSUIMUS and NOSTRUM on the coins of Philip and Mary.

PROTECTOR LITERIS LITERÆ NUMMIS CORONA ET SALUS. (A protection to the letters [on the face of the coin], the letters [on the edge] are a garland and a safeguard to the coinage.) On the edge of the rare fifty-shilling piece of Cromwell.

QUÆ DEUS CONJUNXIT NEMO SEPARET. (What God hath joined together let no man put asunder: *Matthew 19, 6.*) On the larger silver English and Scottish coins of James I after he succeeded to the English throne.

REDDE CUIQUE QUOD SUUM EST. (Render to each that which is his own.) On a Henry VIII type groat of Edward VI struck by Sir Martin Bowes at Durham House, Strand.

RELIGIO PROTESTANTIVM LEGES ANGLIÆ LIBERTAS PARLIAMENTI. (The religion of the Protestants, the laws of England, the liberty of the Parliament.) This is known as the 'Declaration' and refers to Charles I's declaration to the Privy Council at Wellington, 19 September, 1642; it is found on many of his coins struck at the provincial mints during the Civil War. Usually abbreviated to REL:PROT:LEG: ANG:LIB:PAR: ROSA SINE SPINA. (A rose without a thorn.) Found on some gold and small coins of Henry VIII and later reigns.

RUTILANS ROSA SINE SPINA. (A dazzling rose without a thorn.) As last but on small gold only.

SCUTUM FIDEI PROTEGET EUM or EAM. (The shield of faith shall protect him, or her.) On much of the gold of Edward VI and Elizabeth.

SIC VOS NON VOBIS (Thus we labour but not for ourselves). 1994 £2 Bank of England.

TALI DICATA SIGNO MENS FLUCTUARI NEQUIT. (Consecrated by such a sign the mind cannot waver: from a hymn by Prudentius written in the fourth century, entitled 'Hymnus ante Somnum'.) Only on the gold 'George noble' of Henry VIII.

TIMOR DOMINI FONS VITÆ. (The fear of the Lord is a fountain of life: *Proverbs, 14, 27.)* On many shillings of Edward VI.

TVAETVR VNITA DEVS. (May God guard these united, i.e. kingdoms.) On many English Scottish and Irish coins of James I.

VERITAS TEMPORIS FILIA. (Truth, the daughter of Time.) On English and Irish coins of Mary Tudor.

Some Royal Titles:

REX ANGL*orum*—King of the English.

REX SAXONIORVM OCCIDENTALIVM —King of the West Saxons.

DEI GRA*tia* REX *ANGLiae ET FRANCiae DomiNus HYBerniae ET AQVITaniae*—By the Grace of God, King of England and France, Lord of Ireland and Aquitaine.

D*ei GRAtia Magnae Britanniae, FRanciae ET Hiberniae REX Fidei Defensor BRunsviciensis ET Luneburgen-sis Dux, Sacri Romani Imperii Archi-THesaurarius ET ELector*=By the Grace of God, King of Great Britain, France and Ireland, Defender of the Faith, Duke of Brunswick and Luneburg, High Treasurer and Elector of the Holy Roman Empire.

BRITANNIARUM REX —King of the Britains (i.e. Britain and British territories overseas).

BRITT:OMN:REX:FID:DEF:IND:IMP: —King of all the Britains, Defender of the Faith, Emperor of India.

VIVAT REGINA ELIZABETHA — Long live Queen Elizabeth. On the 1996 £5 Queen's 70th birthday £5 crown.

APPENDIX III

NUMISMATIC CLUBS AND SOCIETIES

Coin News, The Searcher and *Treasure Hunting,* are the major monthly magazines covering numismatics. Spink's *Numismatic Circular* is long established, its first issue appeared in December 1892, and is now published 6 times a year. Many local clubs and societies are affiliated to the British Association of Numismatic Societies, (B.A.N.S) which holds an annual Congress. Details of your nearest numismatic club can be obtained from the Hon. Secretary, Philip Mernick, British Association of Numismatic Societies, c/o General Services, 42 Campbell Road, London E3 4DT email: bans@mernicks.com.

The two principal learned societies are the Royal Numismatic Society, c/o Department of Coins and Medals, the British Museum, Great Russell Street, Bloomsbury, London WC1B 3DG, and the British Numismatic Society, c/o The Secretary, C.R.S. Farthing, c/o Warburg Institute, Woburn Square, London WC1H 0AH Tel: 01329 284 661. Both these societies publish an annual journal.

APPENDIX IV

MINTMARKS AND OTHER SYMBOLS ON ENGLISH COINS

A Mintmark (*mm.*), is a term borrowed from Roman and Greek numismatics where it showed the place of mintage; it was generally used on English coins to show where the legend began (a religious age preferred a cross for the purpose). Later, this mark, since the dating of coins was not usual, had a periodic significance, changing from time to time. Hence it was of a secret or 'privy' nature; other privy marks on a coin might be the code-mark of a particular workshop or workman. Thus a privy mark (including the *mintmark.*) might show when a coin was made, or who made it. In the use of precious metals this knowledge was necessary to guard against fraud and counterfeiting.

Mintmarks are sometimes termed 'initial marks' as they are normally placed at the commencement of the inscription. Some of the symbols chosen were personal badges of the ruling monarch, such as the rose and sun of York, or the boar's head of Richard III, the dragon of Henry Tudor or the thistle of James I; others are heraldic symbols or may allude to the mint master responsible for the coinage, e.g. the *mm.* bow used on the Durham House coins struck under John Bowes and the WS mark of William Sharrington of Bristol.

A table of mintmarks is given on the next page. Where mintmarks appear in the catalogue they are sometimes referred to only by the reference number, in order to save space, i.e. *mm. 28* (=mintmark Sun), *mm.28/74 (=mm.* Sun on obverse, *mm.* Coronet on reverse), *mm. 28/- (=mm.* Sun on obverse only).

MINTMARKS AND OTHER SYMBOLS

1	Edward III, Cross 1 (Class B+C).	45	Slipped Trefoil, James I (1).	91A	Crowned Leopard's Head with collar (Edw. VI).
2	Edward III, broken Cross 1 (Class D).	46	Slipped Trefoil, James I (2).	92	Lion.
		47	Quatrefoil.	93	Lion rampant.
3	Edward III, Cross 2 (Class E)	48	Saltire.	94	Martlet.
4	Edward III, Cross 3 (Class G)	49	Pinecone.	95	Mascle.
5	Cross Potent (Edw. III Treaty)	50	Leaf (-mascle, Hen. VI).	96	Negro's Head.
		51	Leaf (-trefoil, Hen. VI).	97	Ostrich's Head.
6	Cross Pattee (Edw. III Post Treaty Rich. III).	52	Arrow.	98	P in brackets.
		53	Pheon.	99	Pall.
7	(a) Plain of Greek Cross.	54	A.	100	Pear.
	(b) Cross Moline.	55	Annulet.	101	Plume.
8	Cross Patonce.	56	Annulet-with-pellet.	102	Plume. Aberystwyth and Bristol.
9	Cross Fleuree.	57	Anchor.	103	Plume. Oxford.
10	Cross Calvary (Cross on steps).	58	Anchor & B.	104	Plume. Shrewsbury.
		59	Flower & B.	105	Lis.
11	Long Cross Fitchee.	60	Bell.	106	Lis.
12	Short Cross Fitchee.	61	Book.	107	Portcullis.
13	Restoration Cross (Hen. VI).	62	Boar's Head (early Richard III).	108	Portcullis, Crowned.
14	Latin Cross.			109	Sceptre.
15	Voided Cross (Henry VI).	63	Boar's Head (later Richard III).	110	Sunburst.
16	Saltire Cross.			111	Swan.
17	Cross and 4 pellets.	64	Boar's Head, Charles I.	112	R in brackets.
18	Pierced Cross.	65	Acorn (a) Hen. VIII	113	Sword.
19	Pierced Cross & pellet.		(b) Elizabeth.	114	T (Henry VIII).
20	Pierced Cross & central pellet.	66	Bow.	115	TC monogram.
		67	Br. (Bristol, Chas. I).	116	WS monogram.
21	Cross Crosslet.	68	Cardinal's Hat.	117	y or Y.
22	Curved Star (rayant).	69	Castle (Henry VIII).	118	Dragon (Henry VII).
23	Star.	70	Castle with H.	119	(a) Triangle
24	Spur Rowel.	71	Castle (Chas. I).		(b) Triangle in Circle.
25	Mullet.	72	Crescent (a) Henry VIII	120	Sun (Parliament).
26	Pierced Mullet.		(b) Elizabeth.	121	Uncertain mark.
27	Eglantine.	73	Pomegranate. (Mary; Henry VIII's is broader).	122	Grapple.
28	Sun (Edw. IV).			123	Tun.
29	Mullet (Henry V).	74	Coronet.	124	Woolpack.
30	Pansy.	75	Crown.	125	Thistle.
31	Heraldic Cinquefoil (Edw. IV).	76	Crozier (a) Edw. III	126	Figure 6 (Edw. VI).
			(b) Hen. VIII.	127	Floriated cross.
32	Heraldic Cinquefoil (James I).	77	Ermine.	128	Lozenge.
		78	Escallop (Hen. VII).	129	Billet.
33	Rose (Edw. IV).	79	Escallop (James I).	130	Plume. Bridgnorth or late declaration
34	Rosette (Edw. IV).	80	Eye (in legend Edw. IV).		
35	Rose (Chas. I).	81	Eye (Parliament).	131	Two lions.
36	Catherine Wheel.	82	Radiate Eye (Hen. VII).	132	Clasped book.
37	Cross in circle.	83	Gerb.	133	Cross pomee.
38	Halved Sun (6 rays) & Rose.	84	Grapes.	134	Bugle.
39	Halved Sun (4 rays) & Rose.	85	Greyhound's Head.	135	Crowned T (Tournai, Hen VIII)
40	Lis-upon-Half-Rose.	86	Hand.		
41	Lis-upon-Sun & Rose.	87	Harp.	136	An incurved pierced cross
42	Lis-Rose dimidiated.	88	Heart.		
43	Lis-issuant-from-Rose.	89	Helmet.		
44	Trefoil.	90	Key.		
		91	Leopard's Head.		

The reign listed after a mintmark indicates that from which the drawing is taken. A similar mm. may have been used in another reign and will be found in the chronological list at the beginning of each reign.